A Guide to Business Inclusion Programs in Government Contracting

U.S. FEDERAL, STATE, AND LOCAL PROGRAMS AND LAWS

Tisidra Jones

AMERICAN BAR ASSOCIATION

Solo, Small Firm and General Practice Division

Cover design by Mary Anne Kulchawik/ABA Design

Printed in the United States of America.

27 26 25 24 23   5 4 3 2 1

ISBN 978-1-63905-379-7

A catalog record for this book is available from the Library of Congress.

Contents

Thank You

I would like to thank the law students from years ago who assisted in research related to this topic. A thank you to Jessica Johnson for her diligent work in helping to keep me organized and in contacting state agencies to confirm my questions regarding whether the programs and policies I researched were still in place. Thanks to my team at Strong & Starlike Consulting, Inc. for taking on additional work to allow me the space to complete the research for this book: much appreciation Lenora, Gerardo, and Mirtha. Thank you, Dr. Artika Tyner, for being an inspiration to the wide range of students you have taught across your career, myself included. A special thank you to my friends and family who served as a sounding board. Lastly, a very special heartfelt thank you to my husband, Sidiq, for all of your support and encouragement throughout this process. You were such a shining light on the long days researching and writing.

Acknowledgments

Throughout the research and writing for the book, state agencies and organizations were contacted to confirm the status of laws and programs to ensure, as much as possible, that the most current information was included in the book. Following are entities and individuals who took the time to respond to inquiries and were open to being acknowledged.

Alabama
Alabama APEX Accelerators, Lindsey Frey, Program Manager

Arizona
Arizona APEX Accelerators, Kathryn Bynge
Arizona Government Research, Arizona State Legislature, Anna Nguyen, Government Research Analyst

California
Procurement Technical Assistance Center—Northern California (Norcal PTAC)

Colorado
Representative Jennifer Bacon
Representative Naquetta Ricks

Florida
Florida SBDC at Pinellas County Economic Development, Office of Small Business and Supplier Diversity

Georgia
Georgia Tech Procurement Center

Kentucky
Kentucky APEX Accelerators, Nancy Brown

Maryland
Maryland APEX Accelerators

Minnesota
Minnesota Department of Administration Office of Equity in Procurement, Tammy Gaglioti

New Jersey
NJIT APEX Accelerators, Sheryl P. Rose
Small Business Action Center

New York
Office of Supplier Diversity
Empire State Development, New York
Empire State Development, Small Business Liaison and Outreach

Texas
University of Houston APEX Accelerators

Utah
Utah Department of Government Operations, Division of Purchasing and General Services, Angi Kaufus, Purchasing Agent II

Wisconsin
City of Madison Department of Civil Rights

About the Author

Tisidra Jones has been working at the intersection of creativity, policy, and entrepreneurship for more than 15 years. Tisidra has a BA in music, with a minor in the sociology of difference from George Mason University. She acquired her JD from the University of St. Thomas School of Law and is licensed to practice law in New York and Minnesota. Tisidra has had articles and research published pertaining to diversity, access, and advancing economic inclusion. She has been invited to serve as a keynote speaker; panel moderator; TEDx presenter; grant and funding judge and CLE presenter for events focused on entrepreneurship, organizational infrastructure building, business inclusion in government contracting, and equal economic opportunity. Tisidra has also developed training programs for government entity staff pertaining to business inclusion.

Tisidra is passionate about creating systems that allow for more people to thrive. Throughout her career, and in her current role as CEO of Strong & Starlike, Consulting, Inc., Tisidra has worked with government entities, nonprofits, and businesses to design sustainable programs and policies related to economic development, economic opportunity, and business inclusion. She has drafted ordinances for municipalities and state statutes, and she has promulgated federal regulations. She has also worked with artists to engage hundreds of business owners and residents through community engagement to inform program and policy development for entities. Tisidra's work at the intersection of art, law, and entrepreneurship has resulted in multiple awards and honors, including the 2017 International Arts and Culture Citizen Award; 2020 Minnesota Lawyer's Diversity and Inclusion Award; the Lawyers of Color 2020 Hot List; the Minneapolis/St. Paul Business Journal 2021 Women in Business Award; and 2022 Fearless Commerce Honoree. She was also named as the 2020–2021 Law and Public Policy Scholar for the University of St. Thomas' Center on Race, Leadership, and Social Justice.

Introduction

The federal government spent $1.1 trillion dollars alone in FY2022 on "contractual services and supplies."[1] When state and local dollars for contracted services are added, that total only continues to multiply. Navigating government contracting can seem like a daunting process and even more challenging for small and diverse businesses who may not have the capacity to dedicate someone to understanding this process. Across the nation, there are programs and laws focused on including small businesses and diverse businesses in government contracting opportunities that are available. This book is intended as a high-level guide to aid in understanding and navigating business inclusion programs and laws in government contracting at the federal, state, and local levels of government.

Who Should Read This Book

Although this book has a focus on laws and policies, it is not only limited to lawyers and law students working and/or interested in this field. In addition to lawyers and law students, this book may be beneficial to the following:

- Government entities
- Economic and business development organizations
- Business technical assistance organizations
- Business certification organizations
- Chambers of commerce
- Business associations
- Business owners, entrepreneurs, and public art artists

1. *Spending Explorer*, USASpending.gov, https://www.usaspending.gov/explorer/object_class (last visited May 13, 2023).

What Is Meant by "Business Inclusion"

Business inclusion may be used interchangeably with terms like vendor inclusion or supplier diversity. Overall, what is meant by any of these terms in the context of this book is: laws, programs, policies, practices, and initiatives that seek to include in government contracting opportunities or increase access to government contracting opportunities for small and diverse businesses. A small business is further defined in Chapter 1, and what constitutes a diverse business is further defined in each state chapter. Generally, when noting small and diverse businesses throughout the book, it is in reference to the following:

- Small business enterprises
- Minority business enterprises
- Women business enterprises
- Veteran business enterprises
- Service-disabled veteran business enterprises
- Persons with disabilities business enterprises
- Lesbian, gay, bisexual, and transgender business enterprises

For purposes of this book, it focuses on business inclusion programs and relevant procurement laws that exist as a result of a federal regulation, state statute, state administrative rule, and/or a city ordinance.

What Is Covered in the Book

The programs, laws, policies, and procedures addressing business inclusion in all 50 states and the federal government are vast. This book is not intended to cover every single aspect in depth. Rather, the book should be viewed as an introductory overview and high-level guide. Each chapter follows a similar format so if a reader wants to compare programs, laws, and policies, they will know what to expect. The format includes the following:

- *Overview of Business Inclusion Program, Policies, and Practices.* This provides the foundation for race- and gender-neutral and race- and gender-conscious programs under an Equal Protection Clause analysis. This section is similar from state to state. For each of the 50 states, the section concludes with an overview of the state entities that certify businesses for business inclusion programs in that state.
- *Summary of Certification Programs and Requirements.* This section outlines the business inclusion certification programs, certification types available, and eligibility requirements for each.

- *Procurement Laws Intersecting with Business Inclusion.* Business inclusion laws may intersect with a vast number of state agency practices. This section is limited to laws that pertain to bidding preferences, contracting goals, good faith efforts, contract awarding processes with business inclusion requirements or contract terms, prompt payment and payment terms pertaining to business inclusion, and various solicitation laws that are particular to small and diverse businesses.
- *Additional Related Laws, Policies, and Programs.* This section may include laws, programs, and policies related to access to capital, technical assistance, and finding contracting opportunities.
- *Major City Snapshot.* Lastly, for each state that has a major city that has a business inclusion program, information about the certification program and any procurement-related laws are included as a high-level snapshot.

What Is Not Covered in the Book

This book is a high-level guide, which means it cannot cover everything. Following are a few things that are outside the scope of this book or are only briefly touched on:

- Specific private sector certifications (e.g., National Minority Supplier Development Council and Women's Business Enterprise National Council). If a state accepts third-party certifications, the chapter would note that.
- This is not a guide on how to do business with each entity. Rather it is a guide on the certification programs that exist; the eligibility requirements for each under federal, state, and local law and administrative rules; and the laws and policies pertaining to such programs at the intersection of business inclusion and procurement/government contracting.
- Section 3 business certifications.
- Environmental Protection Agency disadvantaged business enterprise programs in each state. This is touched on in the federal chapter.
- Programs and laws pertaining to contracting programs specific to contracting with companies and organizations receiving preference for employing inmates and those employing people who are blind. These programs are referenced in the Federal Acquisition Regulation and exist in the states; however, this information is outside the scope of this book.

- Some states may certify or include nonprofit organizations that provide employment for persons with disabilities. This book, however, is intended to focus on (1) for-profit entities owned by individuals that would qualify for small or diverse and (2) nonprofits only if mentioned as eligible for certification as a small or diverse business as a result of those managing and controlling the nonprofit as being diverse under the state and local laws.

Suggestions on How to Read the Book

This book is written in a manner that it may be read from beginning to end, or someone may find the jurisdictions most relevant to them and only read those chapters. It is recommended that readers at the beginner level of this subject matter read "Chapter 1: Federal Government Business Inclusion" prior to reading any other jurisdiction, as Chapter 1 provides a foundation that is referenced in all subsequent chapters.

Friendly Reminder: Laws and Programs Change Daily

Laws, programs, and policies change every day. Throughout the process of writing this book, state and local agencies, as well as technical assistance providers, were contacted so as to best ensure that what was included in the book was current and active at the time of writing it. With that said, laws, programs, and policies change. In addition, several jurisdictions had bills and disparity studies pending at the time of completion of the book, such that various programs and laws may need updating. Please be sure to visit the program websites and/or contact the jurisdictions if you have additional questions beyond the scope of this book. Links and citations are present in the footnotes in each chapter to help with this.

CHAPTER 1

Federal Government Business Inclusion

Overview of Business Inclusion Program, Policies, and Practices

For all business inclusion programs addressed in this chapter, a business must first be small. Under the Federal Acquisition Regulation (FAR) (48 C.F.R. § 2.101) a business is a "small business concern" if it is "a concern, including its affiliates, that is independently owned and operated, not dominant in its field of operation, and qualified as a small business under the criteria and size standards in 13 CFR part 121."[1] Under 13 C.F.R. part 121, it notes that the Small Business Administration (SBA) size standards determine whether or not a business is small.[2] The SBA sets small business size standards on an industry-by-industry basis.[3] The industry classification system that the SBA uses is the North American Industry Classification System codes (NAICS codes). There are more than 900 six-digit NAICS codes under the following 18 sectors:[4]

- Sector 11 Agriculture, Forestry, Fishing and Hunting
- Sector 21 Mining, Quarrying, and Oil and Gas
- Sector 22 Utilities

1. In addition to 48 C.F.R. § 2.101, 15 U.S.C. § 632(a) also defines "small business concern."
2. 13 C.F.R. § 121.101 (2023).
3. 48 C.F.R. § 19.102 (2023); 13 C.F.R. pt. 121 (2023).
4. *Table of Small Business Size Standards Matched to North American Industry Classification System Codes*, U.S. Small Bus. Admin., https://www.sba.gov/sites/default/files/2022-09/Table%20of%20Size%20Standards_NAICS%202022%20Final%20Rule_Effective%20October%201%2C%202022.pdf (last modified Oct. 1, 2022) (hereinafter *Table of Small Business Size Standards*).

- Sector 23 Construction
- Sector 31–33 Manufacturing
- Sector 42 Wholesale Trade
- Sector 44–45 Retail Trade
- Sector 48–49 Transportation and Warehousing
- Sector 51 Information
- Sector 52 Finance and Insurance
- Sector 53 Real Estate and Rental and Leasing
- Sector 54 Professional, Scientific and Technical Services
- Sector 55 Management of Companies and Enterprises
- Sector 56 Administrative and Support and Waste Management and Remediation Services
- Sector 61 Educational Services
- Sector 62 Health Care and Social Assistance
- Sector 71 Arts, Entertainment, and Recreation
- Sector 72 Accommodation and Food Services
- Sector 81 Other Services

Whether or not a business is "small" may be determined by annual revenue for a business or by the number of employees a business has employed. Under the most recent size standards,[5] small can range from $2 million to $41.5 million in terms of revenue,[6] and from 100 employees to 1,500 employees.[7] The SBA size standards are used as a basis for determining "small" for various business inclusion programs across all 50 states.

Small business inclusion dates back to 1953 with the codification of the Small Business Act of 1953. However, since 1953, small business inclusion has evolved to include additional types of small business concerns. The following timeline provides a high-level overview of the evolution of business inclusion in the public sector.[8]

---

5. The most recent update at this time was completed on October 1, 2022.

6. *Id.* For some of the sector 52 industries the size standard is based on $750 million in assets.

7. *Table of Small Business Size Standards, supra* note 4.

8. *1950s to Now: The History of the Supplier Diversity Business Initiatives*, Detroit Reg'l Chamber of Com., https://www.detroitchamber.com/1950s-to-now-the-history-of-the-supplier-diversity-business-initiatives/ (last modified Aug. 31, 2021) (hereinafter *1950s to Now*). The 'Buy Indian Act' of 1910 provided the authority for "the Department of the Interior's Bureau of Indian Affairs, Bureau of Indian Education, and the offices of the Assistant Secretary-Indian Affairs and the Department of Health and Human Services' Indian Health Service provide contracting preferences to qualified Indian tribes and Native American-owned and -controlled businesses." (ROBERT JAY DILGER ET AL., CONG. RSCH. SERV., R45576, AN OVERVIEW OF SMALL BUSINESS CONTRACTING 24 (2022)). Although this is not a small business program it is relevant to the discussion of business inclusion in America.

- 1953: Small Business Inclusion Act of 1953 passed.[9]
- 1964: Civil Rights Act of 1964 increased opportunities for minority-owned firms.[10]
- 1978: Small Business Act of 1978 incorporated the language of "socially and economically disadvantaged persons" and noted expanding efforts to procure goods and services from such individuals.[11]
- 1980: Under the authority of the Civil Rights Act of 1964, the Department of Transportation (DOT) implemented a minority/women's business enterprise (MBE) program to encourage grant recipient contracting with MBEs.[12]
- 1983: No less than 10 percent of the expenditures under the Surface Transportation Assistance Act of 1982 are to be spent with small business concerns owned and controlled by socially and economically disadvantaged individuals.[13] Because this act applied to federal highway and mass transit programs, the DOT created the Disadvantaged Business Enterprise (DBE) program.[14]
- 1987: The Surface Transportation and Uniform Relocation Assistance Act of 1987 amended and presumed women to be disadvantaged. "Hispanic" was also amended to align with the definition used by the SBA.[15] Amendments were also made to how minority, women, and disadvantaged businesses counted toward contracting goals.[16]
- 1990: The 1990 Clean Air Act Amendments authorized the creation of the Environmental Protection Agency (EPA) DBE program.[17]
- 1992: Final rule amended 49 C.F.R. part 23 to require DBE participation included within airport concessions.[18]

---

9. *1950s to Now*, *supra* note 8.
10. *Id.*
11. 15 U.S.C. § 631 (2022).
12. DILGER ET AL., *supra* note 8, at 21.
13. *DBE Laws, Policy and Guidance*, U.S. Dep't of Transp., https://www.transportation.gov/civil-rights/disadvantaged-business-enterprise/dbe-laws-policy-and-guidance#:~:text=The%20DBE%20program%20is%20intended,reduce%20burdens%20on%20small%20businesses (last visited Oct. 31, 2022) (hereinafter *DBE Laws, Policy and Guidance*); *History of the DOT DBE Program*, U.S. Dep't of Transp., https://www.transportation.gov/civil-rights/disadvantaged-business-enterprise/history-dot-dbe-program (last visited Oct. 31, 2022).
14. DILGER ET AL., *supra* note 8, at 21.
15. *Id.*
16. *Id.*
17. *Id.*
18. *DBE Laws, Policy and Guidance*, *supra* note 13.

- 1997 The HUBZone Empowerment Act was passed and a 3 percent contracting goal with HUBZone businesses across federal spends was set.[19]
- 1999 Veterans Entrepreneurship and Small Business Development Act of 1999 includes spending goals for veteran-owned small businesses and service-disabled small businesses.[20]
- 2000–present Cities and states across the United States have added LGBTQ-owned business certifications and/or accepting certifications from the National LGBT Chamber of Commerce.[21]

As demonstrated in the preceding timeline, small business inclusion programs have evolved over time to extend beyond only small businesses, to include small businesses that are owned by minorities, women, veterans, disabled individuals, and LGBT individuals. As a result, in addition to assessing whether or not a business is small, business inclusion programs also consider whether or not a program will be (1) race and gender conscious or (2) race and gender neutral.

Under the Equal Protection Clause of the Fourteenth Amendment of the U.S. Constitution it states that, "No State shall make or enforce any law which shall abridge the privileges or immunities of citizens of the United States; nor shall any State deprive any person of life, liberty, or property, without due process of law; nor *deny to any person within its jurisdiction the equal protection of the laws*" (emphasis added). As it relates to business inclusion, courts have reviewed programs and laws to determine whether they have violated the Equal Protection Clause. In doing this, the level of judicial review used has depended on whether the program was race and gender conscious or race and gender neutral.

- *Race- and Gender-Conscious Programs*: A race- and gender-conscious program is one that considers the race, ethnicity, and/or gender of a business owner. Such programs may set goals and/or have programs targeting businesses owned by minorities and/or businesses owned by women. Courts apply strict scrutiny when a government actor is creating policies based

19. *1950s to Now*, *supra* note 8.

20. *Id.*; Rules and Regulations, 66 Fed. Reg. 53,492 (Oct. 22, 2001) (to be codified at 48 C.F.R pts. 19, 52, and 53).

21. *Government Contracting as an LGBTBE*, Nat'l LGBT Chamber of Com., https://nglcc.org/lgbtbe-certification/benefits-of-certification/public-sector-inclusion-opportunities/ (last visited Feb. 1, 2023); *Certify with the City*, N.Y.C. Small Bus. Servs., https://www.nyc.gov/site/sbs/businesses/certify-with-the-city.page (last visited Feb. 1, 2023); Dan Avery, *N.Y.C Now Largest U.S. City to Grant LGBTQ Businesses Access to Minority Contracts*, NBC News (Jan. 19, 2021), https://www.nbcnews.com/feature/nbc-out/n-y-c-now-largest-u-s-city-grant-lgbtq-n1254782; Alex Bustillos, *Major Cities Creating LGBT Business Certifications*, Contractor News, (Nov. 1, 2021), https://www.contractornews.com/338/major-cities-creating-lgbt-business-certifications.

on race. Strict scrutiny is the highest level of judicial review that can be applied. It requires the government actor to demonstrate that (1) past discrimination exists such that the entity has a *compelling government interest* in rectifying it and (2) the policies and programs created to do so are *narrowly tailored.* In instances where only a gender-conscious program is being evaluated, some courts have applied intermediate scrutiny instead of strict scrutiny. However, when a program is both race and gender conscious, strict scrutiny has been applied. In determining whether a government actor has adequately demonstrated that the entity had a compelling government interest and that the business inclusion policies and programs created were narrowly tailored, courts across the United States have decided upon this for various programs.[22] Two pivotal Supreme Court cases include *City of Richmond v. J.A. Croson Co.* and *Adarand Constructors, Inc. v. Pena (Adarand I).* In *Croson*, the court held that the City of Richmond's minority business enterprise ("MBE") set-aside program was unconstitutional under the Equal Protection Clause.[23] As it relates to demonstrating a compelling government interest, the Supreme Court stated that, "[t]o show that a plan is justified by a compelling government interest, a municipality that wishes to employ a racial preference cannot rest on broad-brush assumptions of historical discrimination."[24] Furthermore, "[f]indings of societal discrimination will not suffice; the findings must concern 'prior discrimination by the government unit involved.'"[25] In *Adarand I*, the Supreme Court held that strict scrutiny does apply when racial classifications are used in federal programs, under the Equal Protection Clause of the Fifth Amendment.[26] As a result,

22. *See Promoting Opportunity and Equality in America: A Guide to Federal Circuit Authority on Permissible Government Actions to Promote Racial and Gender Equality*, Am. Civ. Liberties Union & the Opportunity Agenda (Dec. 2010), https://www.aclu.org/sites/default/files/field_document/Promoting_Opportunity_and_Equality_in_America.pdf, *citing case including, but not limited to* Harrison & Burrowes Bridge Constructors, Inc. v. Cuomo, 981 F.2d 50 (2d Cir. 1992); Independent Enter., Inc. v. Pittsburgh Water & Sewer Auth., 103 F.3d 1165 (3d Cir. 1997); Contractors Ass'n of E. Pa., Inc. v. City of Phila., 945 F.2d 1260 (3d Cir. 1991); Contractors Ass'n of E. Pa., Inc. v. City of Phila., 6 F.3d 990 (3d Cir. 1993); W.H. Scott Constr. Co., Inc. v. City of Jackson, Mississippi, 199 F.3d 206 (5th Cir. 1999); Associated Gen. Contractors of Ohio, Inc., v. Drabnik, 214 F.3d 730 (6th Cir. 2000); Builders Assoc. of Greater Chi. v. Cnty. of Cook, 256 F.3d 642 (7th Cir. 2001); N. Contracting, Inc. v. Illinois, 473 F.3d 715 (7th Cir. 2007); Sherbrooke Turf, Inc. v. Minn. Dep't of Transp., 345 F.3d 964 (8th Cir. 2003), *cert. denied*, 124 S. Ct. 2158 (2004); W. States Paving Co., Inc. v. Wash. State Dep't of Transp., 407 F.3d 983 (2005).

23. 488 U.S. 469 (1989).

24. City of Richmond v. J.A. Croson Co., 488 U.S. 469 (1989), citing Wygant v. Jackson Bd. of Educ., 476 U.S. 267 (1986).

25. City of Richmond v. J.A. Croson Co., 488 U.S. 469, 274 (1989).

26. Adarand Constructors, Inc. v. Pena, 515 U.S. 200 (1995).

it solidified that whether a race-based classification is used in a local, state, or federal program, strict scrutiny will apply at all levels of government.[27]

- *Race- and Gender-Neutral Program:* Race- and gender-neutral programs are programs that are not only accessible to minority-owned and women-owned businesses, but also to all small businesses. Under the law, the level of judicial review applied to such a policy to determine its constitutionality is rational basis, which is the lowest threshold for a government to satisfy. For a government entity to satisfy rational basis, the policy or program created must be "related to a legitimate government purpose."[28] In some instances where government actors have created a race- and gender-conscious program, courts have determined that race- and gender-neutral methods could be used in programming.[29]

Croson, through outlining different types of data to assess and demonstrate prior discrimination, laid the foundation for what is often included in disparity studies used by entities to demonstrate that a disparity exists in the utilizaiton of minority-owned business enterprises and/or woman-owned business enterprises (MWBEs) in a government entity's contracting spends and the availability of such businesses in the government entity's marketplace, such that there would be a compelling interest in having a race- and gender-conscious program.[30] Disparity studies have become a standard tool used to assist a government entity in withstanding a challenge to its race- and gender-conscious business inclusion programs. Under the law, it has been determined that, "the government has a compelling interest in remedying past discrimination against a racial or ethnic minority. The past discrimination must have been persistent and readily identifiable."[31] A disparity study demonstrates whether a government entity has engaged in past discrimination in its contracting practices.[32] Disparity studies assess (1) a government entity's utilization of minority-owned and women-owned businesses[33] in its contracting practice; (2) the number of

27. *Id.*

28. City of Richmond v. J.A. Croson Co., 488 U.S. 469 (1989).

29. *Id.*

30. *Promoting Opportunity and Equality in America*, *supra* note 22.

31. *Id.*

32. *Promoting Opportunity and Equality in America*, *supra* note 22.

33. Depending on the jurisdiction, and the definitions applied to each category of business engaged in a government unit's business inclusion program, the disparity study may be assessing the utilization of disadvantaged business enterprises (DBEs) rather than or in addition to minority-owned and women-owned businesses (M/WBEs).

minority-owned and women-owned businesses contractors "available" in the entity's marketplace; and (3) whether the government entity is underutilizing minority-owned and women-owned businesses, in comparison to the availability in the marketplace, such that it has a compelling government interest in creating a race- and gender-conscious business inclusion program to remedy any disparity that may exist between their utilization of MWBEs and their respective availability in the marketplace for that entity. Lastly, disparity studies present recommendations that are both race and gender conscious, as well as race and gender neutral. Even with the evidence of past discrimination, the government entity must ensure that its policies and programs are narrowly tailored, and using race- and gender-neutral means often assists with this.

Although the SBA and Small Business Act are frequently cited in the preceding timeline, there are other federal agencies that administer business inclusion programs. Under 15 U.S.C. § 644(k) all federal agencies with procurement powers are required to establish ". . . an office to be known as the 'Office of Small and Disadvantaged Business Utilization.'" The only exception to this is that the SBA is not required to have an Office of Small and Disadvantaged Business Utilization (OSDBU).[34] "The OSDBU's primary responsibility is to ensure that small businesses, SDBs [small disadvantaged businesses], WOSBs [women-owned small businesses], SDVOSBs [service-disabled veteran-owned small businesses], and HUBZone small businesses are treated fairly and that they have an opportunity to compete and be selected for a fair amount of the agency's contract dollars."[35] As it relates to the DOT's DBE program, it is applicable to any recipient of the following types of funds: Federal Highway Administration (FHWA), Federal Aviation Administration (FAA), and Federal Transit Administration (FTA).[36] As a result, any state or local transportation agency receiving these funds must implement a DBE program, certify DBEs, and establish participation goals for DBEs.[37]

A term used in both the SBA contracting programs and the DOT DBE program is "socially and economically disadvantaged individual," which means:

> [A]ny individual who is a citizen (or lawfully admitted permanent resident) of the United States and who has been subjected to racial or ethnic prejudice or cultural bias within American

34. Dilger et al., *supra* note 8, at 10.
35. *Id., citing* 15 U.S.C. § 644(k).
36. 49 C.F.R. § 26.21(a) (2023).
37. *Id.* § 26.3.

> society because of his or her identity as a members of groups and without regard to his or her individual qualities. The social disadvantage must stem from circumstances beyond the individual's control.
>
> (1) Any individual who a recipient finds to be a socially and economically disadvantaged individual on a case-by-case basis. An individual must demonstrate that he or she has held himself or herself out, as a member of a designated group if you require it.
>
> (2) Any individual in the following groups, members of which are rebuttably presumed to be socially and economically disadvantaged:
>
> (i) "Black Americans," which includes persons having origins in any of the Black racial groups of Africa;
>
> (ii) "Hispanic Americans," which includes persons of Mexican, Puerto Rican, Cuban, Dominican, Central or South American, or other Spanish or Portuguese culture or origin, regardless of race;
>
> (iii) "Native Americans," which includes persons who are enrolled members of a federally or State recognized Indian tribe, Alaska Natives, or Native Hawaiians;
>
> (iv) "Asian-Pacific Americans," which includes persons whose origins are from Japan, China, Taiwan, Korea, Burma (Myanmar), Vietnam, Laos, Cambodia (Kampuchea), Thailand, Malaysia, Indonesia, the Philippines, Brunei, Samoa, Guam, the U.S. Trust Territories of the Pacific Islands (Republic of Palau), Republic of the Northern Marianas Islands, Samoa, Macao, Fiji, Tonga, Kirbati, Tuvalu, Nauru, Federated States of Micronesia, or Hong Kong;
>
> (v) "Subcontinent Asian Americans," which includes persons whose origins are from India, Pakistan, Bangladesh, Bhutan, the Maldives Islands, Nepal, or Sri Lanka;
>
> (vi) Women;
>
> (vii) Any additional groups whose members are designated as socially and economically disadvantaged by the SBA, at such time as the SBA designation becomes effective."[38]

To be able to count toward contracting goals or be eligible for specific contracting opportunities, oftentimes a business must be certified as a specific type of business concern. The next section outlines the different types of certification programs for these various business concerns.

38. *Id.* § 26.5.

Summary of Certification Programs and Requirements

Across the United States, there are business inclusion programs that require a rigorous certification process, while others allow businesses to self-certify.[39] The following paragraphs outline the requirement for each SBA contracting program and the DOT DBE program.

- *Small Disadvantaged Business (SDB)*: To meet the eligibility requirements for an SDB business, a firm must be (1) small, under the SBA size standard for its corresponding industry NAICS code, and (2) 51 percent owned and controlled by socially and economically disadvantaged individuals.[40] A firm may register as an SDB business through SAM.gov.[41]
- *8(a) Program*: A business must first be certified through the SBA prior to participation in the 8(a) Program. To be eligible, a business must be (1) a small business according to SBA size standards;[42] (2) owned by a U.S. citizen and such individual(s) is residing in the United States;[43] (3) unconditionally owned and controlled by one or more socially disadvantaged[44] and economically disadvantaged individual;[45] (4) owned by a socially and economically disadvantaged individual(s) whose net worth is less than $850,000 and personal income averaged over the prior three years is less than $400,000;[46] (5)

---

39. Certification processes are those where a business submits documentation that demonstrates that they are, in fact, who they say they are, for example tax returns to demonstrate they are within the small business size standards. For programs with a certification process the governing authority has designated individuals to review documentation provided and approve or deny certification for entities. Sometimes the certification process may be less rigorous and simply require a business to submit a certification that has been provided by a third-party certifying entity. For programs that allow for self-certification, a business notes that they are eligible for a particular program and may not have to submit any supporting documentation to demonstrate this.

40. 13 C.F.R. § 124.1001 (2022).

41. *Small Disadvantaged Business*, U.S. SMALL BUS. ADMIN., https://www.sba.gov/federal-contracting/contracting-assistance-programs/small-disadvantaged-business (last visited Oct. 31, 2022).

42. 13 C.F.R. § 124.102 (2022). Generally, to remain eligible for the program a firm must remain small within the size standards.

43. *Id.* § 124.10.

44. *Id.* § 124.103. There is a rebuttable presumption that the following groups are socially disadvantaged: Black Americans; Hispanic Americans; Native Americans; Asian Pacific Americans; Subcontinent Asian Americans, and groups designated periodically by the SBA. To be socially disadvantaged an individual must have experienced "racial or ethnic prejudice or cultural bias within American society because of their identities as members of groups and without regard to their individual qualities. The social disadvantage must stem from circumstances beyond their control."

45. *Id.* § 124.104. "Economically disadvantaged individuals are socially disadvantaged individuals whose ability to compete in the free enterprise system has been impaired due to diminished capital and credit opportunities as compared to others in the same or similar line of business who are not socially disadvantaged."

46. *Id.*

owned by those "of good character";[47] and (6) able to demonstrate potential for success.[48] An "Alaska Native Corporation; a concern owned by a Native Hawaiian Organization; or a concern owned by a Community Development Corporation" meeting the eligibility requirements may also be certified for the 8(a) Program.[49] A firm denied admission to the program may appeal the denial to the SBA's Office of Hearings and Appeals.[50] A firm may apply for certification through certify .sba.gov/.

- *Women-Owned Small Business (WOSB)*: To be eligible for the WOSB program, a business must (1) be a small business according to SBA size standards; (2) be at least 51 percent owned and controlled by one or more women who are U.S. citizens; and (3) have women manage day-to-day operations who also make long-term decisions.[51] Previously, self-certification was available, but this is no longer the case.[52] There is no formal appeal process for denial of certification. After 90 days, the business may reapply.[53]
- *Economically Disadvantaged Women-Owned Small Business (EDWOSB)*: To be eligible for the EDWOSB program, a business must (1) meet all the requirements of the WOSB Federal Contracting program; (2) be owned and controlled by one or more women, each with a personal net worth less than $850,000; (3) be owned and controlled by one or more women, each with $400,000 or less in adjusted gross income averaged over the previous three years; and (4) have the fair market value of the women owner's assets not exceed $6.5 million (including her primary residence and the value of her business).[54] Previously, self-certification was available, but this is no longer the case.[55] There is no formal appeal process for denial of certification. After 90 days, the business may reapply.[56]

---

47. *Id.* § 124.101.
48. *Id.* § 124.107.
49. *Id.* § 124.102.
50. *Id.* § 124.205.
51. *Id.* § 127.200; *Women-Owned Small Business Federal Contracting Program*, U.S. SMALL BUS. ADMIN., https://www.sba.gov/federal-contracting/contracting-assistance-programs/women-owned -small-business-federal-contracting-program (last visited Nov. 1, 2022).
52. *Id.* In 2020 the ability to self-certify was removed.
53. 13 C.F.R. §§ 127.304–127.305 (2022).
54. 13 C.F.R. §§ 127.200–127.203 (2023).
55. *Women-Owned Small Business Federal Contracting Program*, *supra* note 51; in 2020, the ability to self-certify was removed.
56. 13 C.F.R. §§ 127.304–127.305 (2022).

- *HUBZone Program*: A business must meet the following eligibility requirements to be certified for the HUBZone program: (1) be a small business according to SBA size standards;[57] (2) be at least 51 percent owned and controlled by U.S. citizens, a Community Development Corporation, an agricultural cooperative, an Alaska Native corporation, a Native Hawaiian organization, or an Indian tribe;[58] and (3) have its principal office located in a HUBZone, except for concerns owned in whole or in part by one or more Indian Tribal governments.[59] There is no formal appeal process for denial of certification. After 90 days, the business may reapply.[60]
- *Veteran-Owned Small Businesses (VOSB)*: To be eligible for the VOSB certification a business must be (1) a small business under the SBA size standards for their industry NAICS code[61] and (2) at least 51 percent owned and controlled by a veteran/veterans.[62] A business must also register as a small business at SAM.gov.[63] Effective January 1, 2023, the SBA, instead of the Department of Veteran Affairs, now handles the certification of veteran-owned businesses.[64] Businesses may apply for certification through the Veteran Small Business Certification Portal (VetCert): veterans.certify.sba.gov.
- *Service-Disabled Veteran-Owned Small Businesses (SDVOSB)*: Historically, a business has been able to self-certify as an SDVOSB. However, with the SBA taking over certification pertaining to veterans, this option is transitioning out and will be fully effective (including for those previously self-certified who have a grace period for 2023) January 1, 2024.[65] To be eligible for the SDVOSB certification, a business must be (1) a small business under the SBA size standards for their industry NAICS code and (2) at least "51% owned and controlled by one or more service-disabled veterans or, in the case of a veteran with a

---

57. *Id.* § 126.200(b).
58. *Id.* § 126.200(a).
59. *Id.* § 126.200(d).
60. *Id.* § 126.309.
61. *Id.* § 128.200(a).
62. *Id.*
63. *Veteran Small Business Certification (VetCert)*, U.S. Small Bus. Admin., https://veterans.certify.sba.gov/ (last visited Feb. 1, 2023).
64. *Veteran Contracting Assistance Programs*, U.S. Small Bus. Admin., https://www.sba.gov/federal-contracting/contracting-assistance-programs/veteran-contracting-assistance-programs (last visited Feb. 1, 2023).
65. *Memorandum*, Off. of Veteran Aff., https://www.va.gov/osdbu/docs/memorandum-guidance-for-self-certified-sdvosbs-concerning-transfer-of-verification-function-to-sba-20220923.pdf (last visited Feb. 1, 2023).

disability that is rated by the Secretary of Veterans Affairs as a permanent and total disability who are unable to manage the daily business operations of such concern, the spouse or permanent caregiver of such veteran."[66]

- *Alaska Native Corporation (ANC)*: "For all purposes of Federal law, a Native Corporation shall be considered to be a corporation owned and controlled by Natives and a minority and economically disadvantaged business enterprise if the Settlement Common Stock of the corporation and other stock of the corporation held by holders of Settlement Common Stock and by Natives and descendants of Natives, represents a majority of both the total equity of the corporation and the total voting power of the corporation for the purposes of electing directors."[67] Direct and indirect subsidiaries of an ANC will also be considered as a minority and economically disadvantaged business enterprise if the majority of stock and voting power are held by the ANC.[68]
- *Disadvantaged Business Enterprise (DBE)*: To qualify as a DBE, a business must (1) be for-profit;[69] (2) be a small business concern—with "small" determined by the Small Business Administration (SBA) small business size standard—that does not exceed $30.40 million in gross annual receipts;[70] (3) have at least 51 percent ownership by socially and economically disadvantaged individuals;[71] (4) be controlled by one or more of the socially and economically disadvantaged owners;[72] (5) have socially and economically disadvantaged owners who are U.S. citizens or lawfully admitted permanent residents;[73] and (6) have socially and economically disadvantaged owner(s) with a personal net worth that does not exceed $1.32 million.[74] A firm denied certification may make an administrative appeal for that determination to the DOT.[75]

---

66. 13 C.F.R. § 128.200(b) (2023).
67. 43 U.S.C. § 1626(e)(1).
68. *Id.*
69. 49 C.F.R. § 26.5 (2023).
70. *Id.* § 26.5 (2023); *id.* § 26.65(b); it is worth noting that under 49 C.F.R. § 26.65(b) the DBE size standard may be adjusted annually for inflation such that in subsequent years the size standard may no longer be $30.40 million.
71. *Id.* § 26.67.
72. *Id.* § 26.5.
73. *Id.* § 26.67.
74. *Id.*
75. *Id.* § 26.89.

- *Airport Concessions Disadvantaged Business Enterprise (ACDBE)*: Businesses may also be certified as an Airport Concessions Disadvantaged Business Enterprise (ACDBE) under 49 C.F.R. part 23. To qualify as an ACDBE, a business must (1) be a concession for-profit small business concern;[76] (2) qualify as small—the size standard is that its average gross receipts over the prior three years does not exceed $56.42 million;[77] (3) be 51 percent owned by one or more socially and economically disadvantaged individuals;[78] (4) have one or more of the socially and economically individuals control and manage the daily business operations;[79] and (5) have the socially and economically disadvantaged owner(s)' personal net worth not exceed $1.32 million.[80]
- *Fostering Small Business Participation under 46 C.F.R. § 26.39*: Although it is not a separate certification, 46 C.F.R. § 26.39 requires recipients of DOT funds to include within their DBE programs a race- and gender-neutral means of facilitating competition and participation of small business concerns. This is of note in this section because a number of state DOT programs have used 46 C.F.R. § 26.39 as a vehicle for creating a small business enterprise (SBE) program as a part of their DBE program.

Procurement Laws Intersecting with Business Inclusion

Government contracting for the federal government is guided by the Federal Acquisition Regulation (FAR). The FAR system is created in adherence to 41 U.S.C. §§ 1301–1328.[81] At the intersection of procurement and business inclusion, contract opportunities must be publicized by contracting officers in order to "[a]ssist small business concerns, veteran-owned small business concerns, service-disabled veteran-owned small business concerns, HUBZone small business concerns, small disadvantaged business concerns, and women-owned small business concerns in

76. *Id.* § 23.3.

77. *Id.* § 23.33(a). The size standards for the following are exceptions to this: bank and financial institutions is $1 billion in assets; car rental companies are $75.23 million average annual gross receipts; pay telephones is 1,500 employees; and automobile dealers is 350 employees.

78. *Id.*

79. *Id.*

80. *Id.* § 23.35.

81. 41 U.S.C. § 1326.

obtaining contracts and subcontracts."[82] Related to this, contractors and subcontractors awarded a contract exceeding the simplified acquisition threshold may transmit notice of their contracting opportunities in an effort to increase various business concern participation.[83]

Throughout the FAR there are references to the various business concerns noted in the preceding section. However, regulations pertaining to "Small Business Programs" may be found under 48 C.F.R. part 19. Following are the most relevant aspects of the FAR and 15 U.S.C. § 644 at the intersection of government contracting and business inclusion at the federal level of government.[84] Heads of contracting agencies are responsible for implementing these programs and achieving the program goals.[85]

- *Sole Source*: Contracts may be awarded on a sole source basis to section 8(a) participants, HUBZone small business concerns, SDVOSBs, EDWOSBs, or WOSBs.[86] A sole source contract is "a contract for the purchase of supplies or services that is entered into or proposed to be entered into by an agency after soliciting and negotiating with only one source."[87]
    - *8(a) Participants*: "The SBA may not accept for negotiation a sole-source 8(a) contract that exceeds $25 million unless the requesting agency has completed a justification in accordance with the requirements of 6.303."[88]
    - *HUBZone*: Provided there are no exclusions, a contracting officer must consider a contract award to a HUBZone business on a sole source basis before considering a small business set-aside if (1) the contracting officer does not

82. FAR § 5.002 (2023).

83. *Id.* § 5.206. "(a) The following entities may transmit a notice to the GPE to seek competition for subcontracts, to increase participation by HUBZone small business, small, small disadvantaged, women-owned small business, veteran-owned small business and service-disabled veteran-owned small business concerns, and to meet established subcontracting plan goals: (1) A contractor awarded a contract exceeding the simplified acquisition threshold that is likely to result in the award of any subcontracts. (2) A subcontractor or supplier, at any tier, under a contract exceeding the simplified acquisition threshold, that has a subcontracting opportunity exceeding $15,000. (b) The notices must describe (1) The business opportunity; (2) Any prequalification requirements; and (3) Where to obtain technical data needed to respond to the requirement."

84. There are sections throughout the FAR that speak to agency heads facilitating access to contracting opportunities or considering unnecessary bundling of scopes that may impact small business concerns, small disadvantaged business concerns, women-owned, veteran-owned, HUBZone, and service-disabled veteran-owned small business concerns. The goal of this section is to highlight regulations that have tangible goals, preferences, set asides, and outcomes directly tied to contracts for businesses.

85. FAR § 19.201(b) (2023).

86. *Id.* § 18.115–18.117.

87. *Id.* § 2.101.

88. *Id.* § 19.808-1(a).

reasonably expect that two or more HUBZone businesses will submit offers; (2) the estimated total contract amount will not exceed $7 million for manufacturing contracts or $4.5 million for all other contracts; (3) an 8(a) business is not currently performing the contract; (4) the HUBZone business is a responsible contractor; and (5) the award can be made at a fair and reasonable price.[89]

- *SDVOSB*: Provided there are no exclusions, a contracting officer must consider a contract award to an SDVOSB on a sole-source basis before considering a small business set-aside if (1) the contracting officer does not reasonably expect that two or more SDVOSB businesses will submit offers; (2) the estimated total contract amount will not exceed $7 million for manufacturing contracts or $4.5 million for all other contracts; (3) an 8(a) business is not currently performing the contract; (4) the SDVOSB is a responsible contractor; and (5) the award can be made at a fair and reasonable price.[90]
- *EDWOSB*: Provided there are no exclusions, a contracting officer must consider a contract award to an EDWOSB on a sole-source basis before considering a small business set-aside if (1) the NAICS code assigned to the acquisition is one in which the SBA has determined there is substantial underrepresentation of WOSBs (including EDWOSBs) in federal procurement; (2) the contracting officer does not reasonably expect that two or more EDWOSBs businesses will submit offers; (3) the estimated total contract amount will not exceed $7 million for manufacturing contracts or $4.5 million for all other contracts; (4) an 8(a) business is not currently performing the contract; (5) the EDWOSB is a responsible contractor; and (6) the award can be made at a fair and reasonable price.[91]
- *WOSB*: Provided there are no exclusions, a contracting officer must consider a contract award to a WOSB on a sole-source basis before considering a small business set-aside if (1) the NAICS code assigned to the acquisition is one in which the SBA has determined there is substantial underrepresentation of WOSBs (including EDWOSBs) in federal procurement; (2) the contracting officer does not reasonably expect that

89. *Id.* § 19.1306.
90. *Id.* § 19.1406.
91. *Id.* § 19.1506.

two or more WOSBs businesses will submit offers; (3) the estimated total contract amount will not exceed $7 million for manufacturing contracts or $4.5 million for all other contracts; (4) an 8(a) business is not currently performing the contract; (5) the WOSB is a responsible contractor; and (6) the award can be made at a fair and reasonable price.[92]

- *Set-Asides*: Contracting officers may set aside solicitations for small business concerns, section 8(a) participants, HUBZone small business concerns, SDVOSBs, EDWOSBs, or WOSBs where such businesses would only be competing with other similar businesses (e.g.: WOSB would only be competing with other WOSB businesses).[93] It is worth noting that under FAR § 8.405-5, blank purchase agreements may be set aside for small business concerns. Following are some of the nuances for each program.
  - *Small Business Set-Asides*: "Each acquisition of supplies or services that has an anticipated dollar value above the micro-purchase threshold, but not over the simplified acquisition threshold, shall be set aside for small business unless the contracting officer determines there is not a reasonable expectation of obtaining offers from two or more responsible small business concerns that are competitive in terms of fair market prices, quality, and delivery."[94]
  - *8(a) Participants*: Under the FAR, an acquisition may be limited to competition among 8(a) participants if (1) the contracting officer reasonably expects that two or more 8(a) participants will submit offers and the award would be made at a fair and reasonable price; and (2) "[t]he anticipated total value of the contract, including options, will exceed $7 million for acquisitions assigned" manufacturing NAICS codes and $4.5 million for all other acquisitions.[95]
  - *HUBZone*: Under the FAR, a contracting officer may set aside acquisitions for HUBZone concerns (1) when the acquisition exceeds the micro-purchase threshold and the contracting officer must consider a set-aside for a HUBZone concern prior to considering a sole-source award; (2) when the contracting officer reasonably believes that two or more HUBZone concerns will submit offers and the

92. *Id.*
93. *Id.* §§ 6.203–6.207.
94. *Id.* § 19.502-2(a).
95. *Id.* § 19.805-1(a).

award will be made at a fair and reasonable price; (3) if only one acceptable offer is made by a HUBZone concern, the contracting officer may make the award.[96] If there are no acceptable offers received from a HUBZone concern then the set-aside must be withdrawn.[97]

- *SDVOSB*: Under the FAR, a contracting officer may set aside acquisitions for SDVOSB concerns (1) when the acquisition exceeds the micro-purchase threshold and the contracting officer must consider a set-aside for an SDVOSB concern prior to considering a sole-source award; (2) when the contracting officer reasonably believes that two or more SDVOSB concerns will submit offers and the award will be made at a fair and reasonable price; (3) if only one acceptable offer is made by a SDVOSB concern that contracting officer may make the award.[98] If there are no acceptable offers received from an SDVOSB concern then the set-aside must be withdrawn.[99]
- *EDWOSB*: Under the FAR, a contracting officer may set aside acquisitions for EDWOSB concerns when (1) the acquisition exceeds the micro-purchase threshold; (2) the acquisition is within an NAICS code where the SBA has determined that EDWOSB concerns are underrepresented; (3) the contracting officer reasonably believes that two or more EDWOSB firms will submit offers and the award will be made at a fair and reasonable price; (4) the EDWOSB concern is small under the acquisition-assigned NAICS code and is certified as an EDWOSB or has a pending application; and if (5) only one acceptable offer is made by an EDWOSB concern that contracting officer may make the award.[100] If there are no acceptable offers received from an EDWOSB concern then the set-aside must be withdrawn.[101]
- *WOSB*: Under the FAR, a contracting officer may set aside acquisitions for WOSB concerns when (1) the acquisition exceeds the micro-purchase threshold; (2) the acquisition is for an NAICS code where the SBA has determined that WOSB concerns are substantially underrepresented; (3) the contracting officer reasonably believes that two or more

96. *Id.* § 19.1305.
97. *Id.*
98. *Id.* § 19.1405.
99. *Id.*
100. *Id.* § 19.1505.
101. *Id.*

WOSB firms will submit offers and the award will be made at a fair and reasonable price; (4) the WOSB concern is small under the acquisition-assigned NAICS code and is certified as a WOSB or has a pending application; (5) only one acceptable offer is made by a WOSB concern that contracting officer may make the award.[102] If there are no acceptable offers received from a WOSB concern then the set-aside must be withdrawn.[103]

- *Price Evaluation Preference*
  - *HUBZone*: On acquisitions using full and open competition, a 10 percent price evaluation preference must be used, except in the following instances: (1) when price is not a selection factor; (2) some awards are related to multiple award contracts; (3) "offers from HUBZone small business concerns that have not waived the evaluation preference"; and (4) "otherwise successful offers from small business concerns."[104] If the two highest rated offers are from a large business and a HUBZone business concern, and with the price preference the cost is the same, the award must be made to the HUBZone business concern.[105]
- *Contracting Goals*
  - *Small Business Concerns*: There is a goal of not less than 23 percent of all prime and subcontracting dollars to small business concerns.[106]
  - *Small Business Concerns Owned and Controlled by Socially and Economically Disadvantaged Individuals*: There is a goal to spend 5 percent of all prime and subcontracting dollars with individuals in this category.[107]
  - *HUBZone*: There is a goal to spend 3 percent of all prime and subcontracting dollars with HUBZone businesses.[108]
  - *SDVOSB*: There is a goal to spend 3 percent of all prime and subcontracting dollars with SDVOSBs.[109]

---

102. *Id.*
103. *Id.* § 19.1505.
104. *Id.* § 19.1307.
105. *Id.* § 19.1307(d).
106. 15 U.S.C. § 644(g)(1)(A)(i).
107. *Id.* § 644(g)(1)(A)(iv).
108. *Id.* § 644(g)(1)(A)(iii); *FY 2022 Goaling Guidelines*, U.S. SMALL BUS. ADMIN. https://www.sba.gov/sites/default/files/2022-06/FY22%20Small%20Business%20Goaling%20Guidelines_Final_220623%28R%29.pdf (last modified Mar. 2022); *HUBZone Administration*, U.S. SMALL BUS. ADMIN., https://www.sba.gov/partners/contracting-officials/contracting-program-administration/hubzone-administration (last visited Nov. 1, 2022).
109. *Id.* § 644(g)(1)(A)(ii).

- *WOSB*: There is a goal to spend 5 percent of all prime and subcontracting dollars with WOSBs (this is inclusive of EDWOSBs).[110]

- *Contracting Requirements, Subcontracting Plans, and Good Faith Efforts*: Contractors receiving a contract over the simplified acquisition threshold[111] must agree in their contract that, "small business, veteran-owned small business, service-disabled veteran-owned small business, HUBZone small business, small disadvantaged business, and women-owned small business concerns will have the maximum practicable opportunity to participate in contract performance consistent with its efficient performance."[112] On negotiated acquisitions over $750,000 (more than $1.5 million for construction), if there are subcontracting opportunities, then the "apparently successful offeror" must submit a subcontracting plan that is acceptable.[113] Failure to submit an acceptable subcontracting plan would deem the offeror ineligible for award.[114] Similarly, in instances of sealed bidding, if there are subcontracting opportunities available on contracting opportunities over $750,000 (more than $1.5 million for construction), a subcontracting plan must be submitted by the bidder selected for award within the designated time arranged by the contracting officer.[115] Failure to do so will deem the bidder ineligible for award.[116] "When a contractor fails to make a good faith effort to comply with a subcontracting plan, these objectives are not achieved, and 15 U.S.C. 637(d)(4)(F) directs that liquidated damages shall be paid by the contractor."[117]

The DOT DBE and ACDBE programs are governed by 49 C.F.R. part 26 and part 23, respectively. The bullet points that follow highlight key laws specific to contracting with DBEs and ACDBEs in terms of contracting set-asides and goals.

- *Set-Asides*: Contracts may not be set aside for DBEs on DOT-assisted contracts.[118] The only time a set-aside may be used

110. *Id.* § 644(g)(1)(A)(v).

111. Under FAR § 2.101, the current simplified acquisition threshold is $250,000, unless one of the exceptions apply. In which case, the threshold may be higher or lower.

112. FAR § 19.702 (2023).

113. *Id.*

114. *Id.*

115. *Id.*

116. *Id.*

117. *Id.* 19.705-7(a).

118. 49 C.F.R. § 26.43 (2023).

is if there is no other method available to "redress egregious instances of discrimination."[119]

- *Contracting Goals*
  - *National Goal*: There is a national 10 percent aspirational goal for spends with DBEs.[120]
  - *DOT-Assisted Contract Goals*: Fund recipients must set an overall DBE participation goal for their DOT-assisted contracts.[121] The one exception to this is if the fund recipient received FTA or FAA funds and the total amount reasonably anticipated to award from the funds is $250,000 or less in prime contracts, then an overall DBE goal is not required.[122]
  - *Race-Neutral Means*: For fund recipients required to establish an overall goal, they must "meet the maximum feasible portion" using race-neutral means.[123]
- *Prompt Payment to Subcontractors*: Although under the FAR prompt payment is set at seven days from receipt of payment in terms of payment from contractors to subcontractors,[124] under 49 C.F.R. part 26, contractors on state DOT-funded projects must pay subcontractors within 30 days of receipt of payment from the state DOT agency for satisfactory performance.[125]
- *Payment of Retainage to Subcontractors*: Contractors must pay amounts withheld for retainage to subcontractors within 30 days of their work being satisfactorily completed.[126]
- *Good Faith Efforts*: If a fund recipient acts in good faith, they will not be penalized for failing to meet an overall goal.[127] When a contract has a DBE goal, the contract award must go to the bidder who has met the goal or established good faith efforts to meet the goal.[128] Contract award is conditioned upon meeting the goal or establishing good faith efforts to meet the goal.[129]

119. *Id.*
120. *Id.* § 26.41.
121. *Id.* § 26.45(a)(1).
122. *Id.* § 26.45(a)(2).
123. *Id.* § 26.51(a).
124. FAR § 52.232-27(c)(1) (2023).
125. 49 C.F.R. § 26.29(a) (2023).
126. *Id.* § 26.29(b).
127. *Id.* § 26.47(a).
128. *Id.* § 26.53.
129. *Id.*

Additional Tools and Resources

The SBA website and the DOT website have a variety of resources and tools available to small businesses. Following are a few that go beyond contracting to assistance with learning, growing, and funding.

- SBA
  - SBA Learning Platform: https://www.sba.gov/sba-learning-platform
  - Contracting Assistance Programs—this includes information on APEX Accelerators (formerly the Procurement Technical Assistance Centers [PTAC]), Procurement Center Representatives, and Commercial Market Representatives: https://www.sba.gov/local-assistance/federal-contracting-assistance. Related to this, the following is a link to PTAC offices across the country: https://www.aptac-us.org/find-a-ptac/
  - Small Business Funding Programs: https://www.sba.gov/funding-programs
- DOT
  - Mentor Protégé Program: https://www.transportation.gov/osdbu/procurement-assistance/mentor-protege-pilot-program
  - Bonding Education Program: https://www.transportation.gov/osdbu/financial-assistance/bonding-education/bonding-education-program
  - USDOT's Women & Girls in Transportation Initiative (WITI): https://www.transportation.gov/osdbu/women-and-girls
- SAM.gov
  - To participate in government contracting register here: https://sam.gov/content/home

CHAPTER 2

Alabama

Overview of Business Inclusion Program, Policies, and Practices

Government entities seeking to create business inclusion programs have two primary options in terms of the type of program they may create, in terms of who is eligible for the program: (1) a race- and gender-conscious program or (2) a race- and gender-neutral program. Under the Equal Protection Clause of the Fourteenth Amendment, strict scrutiny is applied by the courts when a government actor is creating policies based on race. Strict scrutiny is the highest level of judicial review that may be applied. It requires the government actor to demonstrate that (1) past discrimination exists such that the entity has a "compelling government interest" in rectifying it, and (2) the policies and programs created to do so are "narrowly tailored."[1] Although intermediate scrutiny is often applied when reviewing programs based on gender, strict scrutiny is applied when reviewing race- and gender-conscious business inclusion programs.[2] Disparity studies have become a standard tool used to assist a government entity in withstanding a challenge to its race- and gender-conscious business inclusion programs. These studies aid in demonstrating whether a government entity has engaged

1. City of Richmond v. J.A. Croson Co., 488 U.S. 469 (1989).

2. Since the 1980s with the Supreme Court decision in *City of Richmond v. J.A. Croson Company*, there have been a number of cases across the county that have assessed race- and gender-conscious business inclusion programs. *See* Adarand Constructors, Inc. v. Pena, 515 U.S. 200 (1995); Virdi v. DeKalb Cnty. Sch. Dist., 135 Fed. App'x 262, 268 (11th Cir. 2005); Sherbrooke Turf, Inc. v. Minn. Dep't of Transp., 345 F.3d 964, 971 (8th Cir. 2003); Mountain West Holding Co., Inc. v. The State of Montana, Montana DOT, et al., 2017 WL 2179120 (9th Cir. May 16, 2017).

in past discrimination in its contracting practices, such that the entity may have a compelling government interest in rectifying it.[3]

Conversely, race- and gender-neutral programs are programs that are not only accessible to minority-owned and women-owned businesses but to all businesses, regardless of race or gender. A small business inclusion program would fall into this category. The level of judicial review applied to such a policy to determine its constitutionality is rational basis, which is the lowest threshold for a government to satisfy. For a government entity to satisfy rational basis, the policy or program created must be "related to a legitimate government purpose."[4] Even when a government entity has a race- and gender-conscious program, oftentimes the program may still require the government actor to seek to meet the goals of their program through race- and gender-neutral means where able, so as to be taking the most narrowly tailored means of accomplishing the program goals.

At the state level of government, the state of Alabama has two main entities managing business inclusion programs: (1) the Alabama Department of Economic and Community Affairs Office of Minority Business Enterprise (OMBE) and (2) the Alabama Department of Transportation (ALDOT).

Summary of Certification Programs and Requirements

OMBE certifies minority-owned businesses and women-owned businesses.[5] Eligibility requirements for both are noted next.

- *Minority-Owned Business Enterprise (MBE) / Women-Owned Business Enterprise (WBE)*: A business must (1) have been in operation for at least one year prior to applying for certification; (2) have a license to operate a business in Alabama; (3) have owners who are legal residents of the United States; (4) be at least 51 percent owned, controlled, and operated on a daily basis by one or more minorities or women; and (5) have qualifying owners that are socially disadvantaged (such as African American, Native American or Alaskan Native, Hispanic-American, Women, Asian-Pacific American, and Asian-Indian

3. *Promoting Opportunity and Equality in America: A Guide to Federal Circuit Authority on Permissible Government Actions to Promote Racial and Gender Equality*, AM. CIV. LIBERTIES UNION & THE OPPORTUNITY AGENDA (Dec. 2010), https://www.aclu.org/sites/default/files/field_document/Promoting_Opportunity_and_Equality_in_America.pdf.

4. 488 U.S. 469 (1989).

5. *Office of Minority Business Enterprise*, ALA. DEP'T OF ECON. & CMTY. AFFS., https://adeca.alabama.gov/ombe/ (last visited Apr. 20, 2023).

American) and economically disadvantaged ("defined as those individuals whose ability to compete in the free enterprise system has been impaired due to diminished capital and credit opportunities").[6]

ALDOT administers the Disadvantaged Business Enterprise (DBE) program and the Airport Concession Disadvantaged Business Enterprise (ACDBE) program.[7] It also has a Small Business Element program that is further addressed later in this chapter.

- *Disadvantaged Business Enterprise (DBE) Program*: Pursuant to 49 C.F.R. part 26, ALDOT administers the state's DBE certification program. As is required under 49 C.F.R. § 26.81, Alabama has a Unified Certification Program (UCP). The UCP makes all DBE certification decisions and provides a "one-stop shop" to DBE applicants.[8] To qualify as a DBE, a business must (1) be for-profit;[9] (2) be a small business concern—with "small" determined by the Small Business Administration (SBA) small business size standards—and does not exceed $30.40 million in gross annual receipts;[10] (3) be at least 51 percent owned by socially and economically disadvantaged individuals—there is a rebuttable presumption that women, Black Americans, Hispanic Americans, Native Americans, Asian-Pacific Americans, Subcontinent Asian Americans, or other minorities are disadvantaged;[11] (4) be controlled by one or more of the socially and economically disadvantaged owners;[12] (5) have the socially and economically disadvantaged owners be U.S. citizens or lawfully admitted permanent residents;[13] and (6) have the personal net worth for any socially and economically disadvantaged owner not exceed $1.32 million.[14] The DBE program is required on contracting opportunities that have received funding from the Federal Highway Administration

6. *Id.*
7. *Disadvantaged Business Enterprise Program (DBE)*, ALA. DEP'T OF TRANSP., https://www.dot.state.al.us/programs/DBE.html (last visited May 4, 2023).
8. 49 C.F.R. § 26.81(b)(2) (2022).
9. *Id.* § 26.5.
10. *Id.* §§ 26.5, 26.65(b). It is worth noting that under 49 C.F.R. § 26.65(b), the DBE size standard may be adjusted annually for inflation such that in subsequent years the size standard may no longer be $30.40 million.
11. *Id.* § 26.67.
12. *Id.* § 26.5.
13. *Id.* § 26.67.
14. *Id.*

(FHWA), Federal Aviation Administration (FAA), or Federal Transit Administration (FTA).[15]

- *Airport Concession Disadvantaged Business Enterprise (ACDBE) Program*: In addition to being certified as a DBE under 49 C.F.R. part 26, businesses may also be certified as an Airport Concession Disadvantaged Business Enterprise (ACDBE) under 49 C.F.R. part 23. To qualify as an ACDBE, a business must (1) be a concession for-profit small business concern;[16] (2) qualify as small by having its prior three-year average gross receipts not exceed the applicable size standard of $56.42 million;[17] (3) be 51 percent owned by one or more socially and economically disadvantaged individuals;[18] (4) have one or more of the socially and economically disadvantaged individuals with control and managing the daily business operations;[19] and (5) have the personal net worth for any socially and economically disadvantaged owner not exceed $1.32 million.[20]

Procurement Laws Intersecting with Business Inclusion

In the state of Alabama there are two key statutes that govern public contracts: (1) title 41, chapter 16, governs state and local public contracts;[21] and (2) public works contracts are governed by title 39.[22] Contracting goals are not set for MBEs and WBEs, however there is a bidding preference.

- *Bidding Preference*: "[I]n the event the lowest bid for an item of personal property or services to be purchased or contracted for is received from a foreign entity, where the county, a municipality, or an instrumentality thereof is the awarding authority, the awarding authority may award the contract to a responsible bidder whose bid is no more than 10 percent greater than the foreign entity if the bidder has a place of business within

---

15. *Id.* § 26.21(a).
16. *Id.* § 23.3.
17. *Id.* § 23.33(a). The size standards for the following are exceptions to this: bank and financial institutions is $1 billion in assets; car rental companies are $75.23 million average annual gross receipts; pay telephones is 1,500 employees; and automobile dealers is 350 employees.
18. *Id.*
19. *Id.*
20. *Id.* § 23.35.
21. Peter D. Lejeune et al., Guide to State Procurement: A 50-State Primer on Purchasing Laws, Processes, and Procedures 713–14 (Melissa Javon Copeland ed., A.B.A. 2d. ed., 2016).
22. *Id.*

the local preference zone or is a responsible bidder from a business within the state that is a woman-owned enterprise, an enterprise of small business, as defined in Section 25-10-3, a minority-owned business enterprise, a veteran-owned business enterprise, or a disadvantaged-owned business enterprise. For the purposes of this subsection, foreign entity means a business entity that does not have a place of business within the state."[23]

- *Prompt Payment to Subcontractors*: "A party who receives a payment from the state in connection with a contract shall pay each of its subcontractors or sub-subcontractors the portion of the state's payment to the extent of that subcontractor's or sub-subcontractor's interest in the state's payment in accordance with the payment terms agreed to by the contractor and the subcontractor, but if payment terms are not agreed to, then within seven days after receipt of payment from the state. The payment shall include interest, if any, that is attributable to work performed by the subcontractor or sub-subcontractor."[24]

Additional Related Laws, Policies, and Programs

- *Advocacy and Technical Assistance*: Within the Alabama Department of Commerce, its Business Development Division[25] has an Office of Small Business Advocacy. The office is there to serve as an advocate "on behalf of small businesses."[26] This takes many forms, including but not limited to the following: (1) participation in legislation; (2) representing the views of small businesses; (3) collaborating with other agencies to share information about programs and resources for small businesses; and (4) evaluating efforts to assist minority small businesses.[27] In addition, the office has a responsibility to "[e]stablish a central reference program and general counseling service to assist small businesses."[28]
- *State Procurement Portal*: Alabama Buys is the state e-Procurement portal: https://alabamabuys.gov/page.aspx/en/usr/login.

23. Ala. Code § 41-16-50 (2021).
24. *Id.* § 41-16-3.
25. *Business Development Division*, Ala. Dep't of Com. (Oct. 25, 2022), https://www.madeinalabama.com/business-development/.
26. Ala. Code § 41-29-223 (2021).
27. *Id.*
28. *Id.*

Contracting opportunities where the ALDOT DBE program applies have several requirements that intersect directly with procurement, contracting, and business inclusion.

- *Fostering Small Business Participation*: Pursuant to 49 C.F.R. § 26.39, ALDOT has engaged in efforts to foster small business participation through its Small Business Element (SBE) program.[29] This program is race and gender neutral.[30] This program is a set-aside for small business prime contracts under $400,000.[31] To qualify for the program, a business must be small, under the size standard under 49 C.F.R. § 26.65, and it must be prequalified with ALDOT.[32]
- *Goals*: Contract opportunities may not use quotas or set-asides for DBEs.[33] The only exception for using a set-aside is in a limited or extreme circumstance, "when no other method could be reasonably expected to redress egregious instances of discrimination."[34] Instead, an overall goal must be set.[35] The goal must be based on evidence of available "ready, willing and able" DBEs in the market.[36] Once the assessment of "ready, willing and able" DBEs is completed, an overall goal may be established as a percentage of the total amount of contracts receiving U.S. DOT funds.[37] Participation goals must be set for all certified DBEs and not divided into subcategories.[38] Race- and gender-neutral means must be used to "meet the maximum feasible portion of your overall goal."[39] ALDOT, as a recipient of U.S. DOT funds, will not be penalized for failing to meet the overall goal set, if it can establish good faith efforts to meet the goal.[40] When there is a DBE goal on a specific contract opportunity, only the bidder meeting the goal, or establishing good faith efforts to meet the goal, may be awarded the contract.[41]

---

29. *Disadvantaged Business Enterprise Program Plan*, Ala. Dep't of Transp. 17 (2021), https://www.dot.state.al.us/programs/pdf/DBE/ProgramPlan.pdf.
30. *Id.*
31. *Id.*
32. *Id.*
33. 49 C.F.R. § 26.43 (2022).
34. *Id.* § 26.43.
35. *Id.* § 26.45(a)(1).
36. *Id.* § 26.45(b).
37. *Id.* § 26.45(e).
38. *Id.* § 26.45(h).
39. *Id.* § 26.51.
40. *Id.* § 26.47.
41. *Id.* § 26.53.

- *Prompt Payment to Subcontractors*: Under 49 C.F.R. part 26, contractors must pay subcontractors within 30 days of receipt of payment from the state DOT for satisfactory performance.[42]
- *Payment of Retainage*: Contractors must pay amounts withheld for retainage to subcontractors within 30 days of their work being completed satisfactorily.[43]

Major City Snapshot: Birmingham

Purchasing for the City of Birmingham, Alabama, is governed by title 3, chapter 3 "Purchasing and Contracting"—short title: "Purchasing Ordinance of the City of Birmingham." Under this ordinance in "Sec. 3-3-17. – Minority- and women-owned business participation in solicitations and contracts" it is required to include "written language in all solicitations for bids or proposals (RFPs) and contracts encouraging minority- and women-owned business participation."

42. 49 C.F.R. § 26.29(a) (2023).
43. *Id.* § 26.29(b).

CHAPTER 3

Alaska

Overview of Business Inclusion Program, Policies, and Practices

Government entities seeking to create business inclusion programs have two primary options in terms of the type of program they may create, in terms of who is eligible for the program: (1) a race- and gender-conscious program or (2) a race- and gender-neutral program. Under the Equal Protection Clause of the Fourteenth Amendment, strict scrutiny is applied by the courts when a government actor is creating policies based on race. Strict scrutiny is the highest level of judicial review that may be applied. It requires the government actor to demonstrate that (1) past discrimination exists such that the entity has a "compelling government interest" in rectifying it, and (2) the policies and programs created to do so are "narrowly tailored."[1] Although intermediate scrutiny is often applied when reviewing programs based on gender, strict scrutiny is applied when reviewing race- and gender-conscious business inclusion programs.[2] Disparity studies have become a standard tool used to assist a government entity in withstanding a challenge to its race- and gender-conscious business inclusion programs. These studies aid in demonstrating whether a government entity has engaged

1. City of Richmond v. J.A. Croson Co., 488 U.S. 469 (1989).

2. Since the 1980s with the Supreme Court decision in *City of Richmond v. J.A. Croson Company*, there have been a number of cases across the county that have assessed race- and gender-conscious business inclusion programs. *See* Adarand Constructors, Inc. v. Pena, 515 U.S. 200 (1995); Virdi v. DeKalb Cnty. Sch. Dist., 135 Fed. App'x 262, 268 (11th Cir. 2005); Sherbrooke Turf, Inc. v. Minn. Dep't of Transp., 345 F.3d 964, 971 (8th Cir. 2003); Mountain West Holding Co., Inc. v. The State of Montana, Montana DOT, et al., 2017 WL 2179120 (9th Cir. May 16, 2017).

in past discrimination in its contracting practices, such that the entity may have a compelling government interest in rectifying it.[3]

Conversely, race- and gender-neutral programs are programs that are not only accessible to minority-owned and women-owned businesses but to all businesses, regardless of race or gender. A small business inclusion program would fall into this category. The level of judicial review applied to such a policy to determine its constitutionality is rational basis, which is the lowest threshold for a government to satisfy. For a government entity to satisfy rational basis the policy or program created must be "related to a legitimate government purpose."[4] Even when a government entity has a race- and gender-conscious program, oftentimes the program may still require the government actor to seek to meet the goals of their program through race- and gender-neutral means where able, so as to be taking the most narrowly tailored means of accomplishing the program goals.

In the state of Alaska, at the state level, there is only one state agency that certifies businesses for business inclusion programs: the Alaska Department of Transportation and Public Facilities (ADOT&PF) manages a Disadvantaged Business Enterprise (DBE) program.[5] Although there are bidder preferences that exist under state statute, at the state level, the Alaska DOT DBE program is the only business inclusion program that consists of a certification program and sets goals for inclusion on applicable contracts.

Summary of Certification Programs and Requirements

ADOT&PF administers the DBE program and Airport Concession Disadvantaged Business Enterprise (ACDBE) program.

- *Disadvantaged Business Enterprise (DBE) Program*: ADOT&PF Civil Rights Office administers the state's DBE certification program in accordance with 49 C.F.R. part 26. As is required under 49 C.F.R. § 26.81, ADOT&PF has a Unified Certification Program (UCP). The UCP makes all DBE certification decisions and provides a "one-stop shop" to DBE applicants.[6] The

3. *Promoting Opportunity and Equality in America: A Guide to Federal Circuit Authority on Permissible Government Actions to Promote Racial and Gender Equality*, Am. Civ. Liberties Union & The Opportunity Agenda (Dec. 2010), https://www.aclu.org/sites/default/files/field_document/Promoting_Opportunity_and_Equality_in_America.pdf.

4. 488 U.S. 469 (1989).

5. *Disadvantaged Business Enterprise (DBE) Program*, Alaska Dep't of Transp. & Pub. Facilities Civ. Rights Off., https://dot.alaska.gov/cvlrts/aucp.shtml (last visited May 4, 2023).

6. 49 C.F.R. § 26.81(b)(2) (2022).

ADOT&PF UCP has more than 20 members who use the UCP for certification of the DBEs they may contract with on opportunities.[7] ADOT&PF serves as the lead agency responsible for the certification of DBEs.[8] To qualify as a DBE, a business must (1) be for-profit;[9] (2) be a small business concern—with "small" determined by the Small Business Administration (SBA) small business size standards—and does not exceed $30.40 million in gross annual receipts;[10] (3) be at least 51 percent owned by socially and economically disadvantaged individuals—there is a rebuttable presumption that women, Black Americans, Hispanic Americans, Native Americans, Asian-Pacific Americans, Subcontinent Asian Americans, or other minorities are disadvantaged;[11] (4) be controlled by one or more of the socially and economically disadvantaged owners;[12] (5) have the socially and economically disadvantaged owners be U.S. citizens or lawfully admitted permanent residents;[13] and (6) have the personal net worth for any socially and economically disadvantaged owner not exceed $1.32 million.[14] The DBE program is required on contracting opportunities that have received funding from the Federal Highway Administration (FHWA), Federal Aviation Administration (FAA), or Federal Transit Administration (FTA).[15]

- *Airport Concession Disadvantaged Business Enterprise (ACDBE) Program*: In addition to being certified as a DBE under 49 C.F.R. part 26, businesses may also be certified as an Airport Concession Disadvantaged Business Enterprise (ACDBE) under 49 C.F.R. part 23. To qualify as an ACDBE, a business must (1) be a concession for-profit small business concern;[16] (2) qualify as small by having its prior three-year average gross receipts

---

7. *Alaska Unified Certification Program (AUCP) Members*, Alaska Dep't of Transp. & Pub. Facilities Civ. Rights Off., https://dot.alaska.gov/cvlrts/aucpmemb.shtml (last visited Jan. 12, 2023).

8. *Disadvantaged Business Enterprise (DBE) Program*, *supra* note 5.

9. 49 C.F.R. § 26.5 (2022).

10. *Id.* §§ 26.5, 26.65(b). It is worth noting that under 49 C.F.R. § 26.65(b), the DBE size standard may be adjusted annually for inflation such that in subsequent years the size standard may no longer be $30.40 million.

11. *Id.* § 26.67.

12. *Id.* § 26.5.

13. *Id.* § 26.67.

14. *Id.*

15. *Id.* § 26.21(a).

16. *Id.* § 23.3.

not exceed the applicable size standard of $56.42 million;[17] (3) be 51 percent owned by one or more socially and economically disadvantaged individuals;[18] (4) have one or more of the socially and economically disadvantaged individuals with control and managing the daily business operations;[19] and (5) have the personal net worth for any socially and economically disadvantaged owner not exceed $1.32 million.[20]

Procurement Laws Intersecting with Business Inclusion

Public contracts in Alaska are governed by title 36. Under title 36, section 36.30.321, it addresses bidder-related preferences. A bid preference provides preference to one bidder (e.g.: Bidder A) over another (e.g.: Bidder B) in instances where Bidder B may be the lowest responsive and responsible bidder or is tied with Bidder A, but Bidder A meets a qualification that would allow the contracting authority to prefer, or choose, Bidder A over Bidder B. Often, bid preferences relate to geography (e.g.: a local bidder preference) or sometimes diverse, disadvantaged, or veteran businesses.[21] Following are two bidding preferences relevant to business inclusion:

- *Persons with Disabilities*: A 10 percent preference is applied to the price of the bid such that if the person with disabilities entity bidding is within 10 percent of the lowest responsive and responsible bidder's price, the preference would be for the person with disabilities bidder.[22] To qualify for this, in addition to the firm being owned by a person/persons with a disability, the bidder must also be an Alaska bidder.[23] A "person with disabilities" is defined under section 36.30.321(k).
- *Veterans*: A 5 percent preference is applied to the price of the bid.[24] To qualify for this, in addition to the firm being owned by a person who is a veteran, the bidder must also be an Alaska

17. *Id.* § 23.33(a). The size standards for the following are exceptions to this: bank and financial institutions is $1 billion in assets; car rental companies are $75.23 million average annual gross receipts; pay telephones is 1,500 employees; and automobile dealers is 350 employees.

18. *Id.*

19. *Id.*

20. *Id.* § 23.35.

21. *Tie Bid Preference*, The Institute for Public Procurement, https://www.nigp.org/dictionary-of-terms?search=Tie+Bid+Preference (last visited Jan. 20, 2023).

22. Alaska Stat. § 36.30.321(d) (2021).

23. *Id.*

24. *Id.* § 36.30.321(f).

bidder.[25] A "veteran" is defined under section 36.30.321(f)(3). This preference is not to exceed $5,000.[26]

Contracting opportunities where the ADOT&PF DBE program applies have several requirements that intersect directly with procurement, contracting, and business inclusion.

- *Fostering Small Business Participation*: Pursuant to 49 C.F.R. § 26.39, ADOT&PF has engaged in efforts to foster small business participation.[27] In 2012, it had its SBE plan approved.[28] Within the plan it notes that an SBE must be certified by the State of Alaska as a DBE or self-certified with the SBA, and that to be considered small it must satisfy the SBA size standards.[29] Efforts to foster SBE inclusion include unbundling contracts and outreach and networking.[30]
- *Goals*: Contract opportunities may not use quotas or set-asides for DBEs.[31] The only exception for using a set-aside is in a limited or extreme circumstance, "when no other method could be reasonably expected to redress egregious instances of discrimination."[32] Instead, an overall goal must be set.[33] The goal must be based on evidence of available "ready, willing and able" DBEs in the market.[34] Once the assessment of "ready, willing and able" DBEs is completed, an overall goal may be established as a percentage of the total amount of contracts receiving U.S. DOT funds.[35] Participation goals must be set for all certified DBEs and not divided into subcategories.[36] Race- and gender-neutral means must be used to "meet the maximum feasible portion of your overall goal."[37] ADOT&PF, as a recipient of U.S. DOT funds, will not be penalized for failing to meet the overall goal set, if it can establish good faith efforts to meet the goal.[38] When there is a DBE goal on a

---

25. *Id.*
26. *Id.*
27. *Fostering Small Business Participation—SBE Plan*, Alaska Dep't of Transp. & Pub. Facilities Civ. Rights Off. 1 (2012), https://dot.alaska.gov/cvlrts/forms/SBE-FHWA-SBE_Plan.pdf.
28. *Id.*
29. *Id.*
30. *Id.*
31. 49 C.F.R. § 26.43 (2022).
32. *Id.* § 26.43.
33. *Id.* § 26.45(a)(1).
34. *Id.* § 26.45(b).
35. *Id.* § 26.45(e).
36. *Id.* § 26.45(h).
37. *Id.* § 26.51.
38. *Id.* § 26.47.

contract opportunity, only the bidder meeting the goal, or establishing good faith efforts to meet the goal, may be awarded the contract.[39]

- *Prompt Payment*: Under 49 C.F.R. part 26, contractors must pay subcontractors within 30 days of receipt of payment from the state DOT for satisfactory performance.[40]
- *Payment of Retainage*: Contractors must pay amounts withheld for retainage to subcontractors within 30 days of their work being satisfactorily completed.[41]

Additional Related Laws, Policies, and Programs

- *Alaska Bidder Preference*: Although not specific to a small, minority, women, veteran, disabled, or LGBT-owned enterprise, the state of Alaska does have a 5 percent bidder preference for Alaska bidders under section 36.30.321(a). This is relevant pertaining to business inclusion in Alaska because, as noted earlier, to qualify for the persons with disabilities as well as the veterans bid preferences each must also be an Alaska bidder. To be considered an Alaska bidder, a bidder must meet the following requirements: (1) bidder must have a valid Alaska business license;[42] (2) the name on the business license must match the name of the firm on the bid submitted;[43] (3) for at least six months prior to the bid date, the bidder must have maintained a place of business within Alaska with an employee or the bidder there;[44] (4) bidder is incorporated or qualified to do business in Alaska (if it is a sole proprietor or a partnership the owners must be residents of Alaska);[45] and (5) if it is a joint venture it must meet the preceding (1)–(4) requirements.[46]
- *Prompt Payment to Subcontractors*: "The prime contractor and a subcontractor on a public construction or public works contract must include in a subcontract between the prime contractor and subcontractor for the public construction or public

39. *Id.* § 26.53.
40. 49 C.F.R. § 26.29(a) (2023).
41. *Id.* § 26.29(b) (2023).
42. *Alaska Administrative Manual—Procurement*, AAM 81, https://doa.alaska.gov/dof/manuals/aam/resource/81.pdf (last visited Jan. 12, 2023).
43. *How to Do Business with the State of Alaska*, Off. of Procurement & Prop. Mgmt. (last revised Feb. 2021), https://oppm.doa.alaska.gov/media/1449/htdbws.pdf.
44. *Id.*
45. *Id.*
46. *Id.*

works a clause that requires the prime contractor to pay . . . the subcontractor for satisfactory performance under the subcontract within eight working days after receiving payment from which the subcontractor is to be paid. . . ."[47]

Major City Snapshot: Juneau

The City and Borough of Juneau, Alaska, is a member of the Unified Certification Program.[48] It has established within its city ordinance provisions to guide implementation and management of its DBE program.[49] Under chapter 53.50, "Purchasing of Supplies and Services of the City Code," the city states that the city manager, or their designee, is authorized to create policies and procedures related to the DBE program.[50] The ordinance further notes that "[s]uch policies and procedures may include . . . [s]etting of disadvantaged business enterprise contracting goals and procedures required by state or federal law. . . ."[51]

47. Alaska Stat. § 36.90.210 (2023).
48. *Alaska Unified Certification Program (AUCP) Members*, *supra* note 7.
49. Juneau, Alaska Code § 53.50.095 (2022).
50. *Id.*
51. *Id.*

CHAPTER 4

Arizona

Overview of Business Inclusion Programs, Policies, and Practices

Government entities seeking to create business inclusion programs have two primary options in terms of the type of program they may create, in terms of who is eligible for the program: (1) a race- and gender-conscious program or (2) a race- and gender-neutral program. Under the Equal Protection Clause of the Fourteenth Amendment, strict scrutiny is applied by the courts when a government actor is creating policies based on race. Strict scrutiny is the highest level of judicial review that may be applied. It requires the government actor to demonstrate that (1) past discrimination exists such that the entity has a "compelling government interest" in rectifying it, and (2) the policies and programs created to do so are "narrowly tailored."[1] Although intermediate scrutiny is often applied when reviewing programs based on gender, strict scrutiny is applied when reviewing race- and gender-conscious business inclusion programs.[2] Disparity studies have become a standard tool used to assist a government entity in withstanding a challenge to its race- and gender-conscious business inclusion programs. These studies aid in demonstrating whether a government entity has engaged

1. City of Richmond v. J.A. Croson Co., 488 U.S. 469 (1989).

2. Since the 1980s with the Supreme Court decision in *City of Richmond v. J.A. Croson Company*, there have been a number of cases across the county that have assessed race- and gender-conscious business inclusion programs. *See* Adarand Constructors, Inc. v. Pena, 515 U.S. 200 (1995); Virdi v. DeKalb Cnty. Sch. Dist., 135 Fed. App'x 262, 268 (11th Cir. 2005); Sherbrooke Turf, Inc. v. Minn. Dep't of Transp., 345 F.3d 964, 971 (8th Cir. 2003); Mountain West Holding Co., Inc. v. The State of Montana, Montana DOT, et al., 2017 WL 2179120 (9th Cir. May 16, 2017).

in past discrimination in its contracting practices, such that the entity may have a compelling government interest in rectifying it.[3]

Conversely, race- and gender-neutral programs are programs that are not only accessible to minority-owned and women-owned businesses but to all businesses, regardless of race or gender. A small business inclusion program would fall into this category. The level of judicial review applied to such a policy to determine its constitutionality is rational basis, which is the lowest threshold for a government to satisfy. For a government entity to satisfy rational basis, the policy or program created must be "related to a legitimate government purpose."[4] Even when a government entity has a race- and gender-conscious program, oftentimes the program may still require the government actor to seek to meet the goals of their program through race- and gender-neutral means where able, so as to be taking the most narrowly tailored means of accomplishing the program goals.

In the state of Arizona, at the state level of government, the only state agency that certifies businesses for business inclusion programs is the Arizona Department of Transportation (ADOT).

Summary of Certification Programs and Requirements

ADOT, as a member of the Unified Certification Program, administers the Disadvantaged Business Enterprise (DBE) program, Airport Concession Disadvantaged Business Enterprise (ACDBE) program, and the Small Business Concern (SBC) Registration.

- *Disadvantaged Business Enterprise (DBE) Program*: As is required under 49 C.F.R. § 26.81, Arizona has a Unified Certification Program (AZUCP). The AZUCP makes all DBE certification decisions and provides a "one-stop shop" to DBE applicants.[5] To qualify as a DBE, a business must (1) be for-profit;[6] (2) be a small business concern—with "small" determined by the Small Business Administration (SBA) small business size standards and does not exceed $30.40 million in gross annual

3. *Promoting Opportunity and Equality in America: A Guide to Federal Circuit Authority on Permissible Government Actions to Promote Racial and Gender Equality*, Am. Civ. Liberties Union & the Opportunity Agenda (Dec. 2010), https://www.aclu.org/sites/default/files/field_document/Promoting_Opportunity_and_Equality_in_America.pdf.

4. 488 U.S. 469 (1989).

5. 49 C.F.R. § 26.81(b)(2) (2022).

6. *Id.* § 26.5.

receipts;[7] (3) be at least 51 percent owned by socially and economically disadvantaged individuals—there is a rebuttable presumption that women, Black Americans, Hispanic Americans, Native Americans, Asian-Pacific Americans, Subcontinent Asian Americans, or other minorities are disadvantaged;[8] (4) be controlled by one or more of the socially and economically disadvantaged owners;[9] (5) have the socially and economically disadvantaged owners be U.S. citizens or lawfully admitted permanent residents;[10] and (6) have the personal net worth for any socially and economically disadvantaged owner not exceed $1.32 million.[11] The DBE program is required on contracting opportunities that have received funding from the Federal Highway Administration (FHWA), Federal Aviation Administration (FAA), or Federal Transit Administration (FTA).[12]

- *Airport Concession Disadvantaged Business Enterprise (ACDBE) Program*: In addition to being certified as a DBE under 49 C.F.R. part 26, businesses may also be certified as an Airport Concession Disadvantaged Business Enterprise (ACDBE) under 49 C.F.R. part 23. To qualify as an ACDBE, a business must (1) be a concession for-profit small business concern;[13] (2) qualify as small by having its prior three-year average gross receipts not exceed the applicable size standard of $56.42 million;[14] (3) be 51 percent owned by one or more socially and economically disadvantaged individuals;[15] (4) have one or more of the socially and economically disadvantaged individuals with control and managing the daily business operations;[16] and (5) have the personal net worth for any socially and economically disadvantaged owner not exceed $1.32 million.[17]

---

7. *Id.* §§ 26.5, 26.65(b). It is worth noting that under 49 C.F.R. § 26.65(b), the DBE size standard may be adjusted annually for inflation such that in subsequent years the size standard may no longer be $30.40 million.
8. *Id.* § 26.67.
9. *Id.* § 26.5.
10. *Id.* § 26.67.
11. *Id.*
12. *Id.* § 26.21(a).
13. *Id.* § 23.3.
14. *Id.* § 23.33(a). The size standards for the following are exceptions to this: bank and financial institutions is $1 billion in assets; car rental companies are $75.23 million average annual gross receipts; pay telephones is 1,500 employees; and automobile dealers is 350 employees.
15. *Id.*
16. *Id.*
17. *Id.* § 23.35.

- *Small Business Concern (SBC) Registration*: AZUCP has implemented a small business element within its DBE program called the Small Business Concern (SBC) Registration, pursuant to 49 C.F.R. § 26.39.[18] This is a registration process rather than a "complex certification process."[19] One way AZUCP seeks to foster small business participation, as required by 49 C.F.R. § 26.39, is that it "will include language in their contracts to encourage the use of SBCs on transportation projects."[20]

Procurement Laws Intersecting with Business Inclusion

Arizona procurement is guided by state statutes under title 41, chapter 23, sections 41-2501 *et seq.* and the Arizona Administrative Code title 2, chapter 7, R2-7-101 *et seq.* The Arizona State Procurement Office manages state procurement. Through a review of both the state statute and the administrative code pertaining to procurement, it appears that there are no specific laws or regulations that intersect with business inclusion in the sense of increasing purchasing with or tracking spends with minority-owned, women-owned, veteran-owed, disabled-owned, and/or LGBT-owned businesses.[21] Although there are provisions under the Arizona Administrative Code that allow for certification of nonprofit organizations serving disabled individuals,[22] as it relates to disabled-owned businesses, there are not any specific laws or regulations for for-profit enterprises that are owned by individuals with a disability. There is, however, a procurement set-aside for small businesses.[23]

- *Small Business Set-Aside*: "Any procurement that does not exceed the aggregate dollar amount of less than one hundred thousand dollars shall be restricted, if practicable, to small businesses as defined in rules adopted by the director. The procurement officer shall rotate the small business solicited to compete for any procurement of less than one hundred thousand dollars. If it is

18. *Small Business Concern (SBC) Registration*, ARIZ. DEP'T OF TRANSP., https://azdot.gov/business/business-engagement-and-compliance/business-registration-and-certification/small-business (last visited May 4, 2023).

19. *Id.*

20. *Id.*

21. A review was conducted (1) of the Arizona Procurement Code; (2) of the Arizona Revised Statutes for business inclusion programs, certifications, and preferences for women-owned businesses, minority-owned businesses, veteran-owned businesses, disability-owned businesses; and (3) by contacting state agencies to confirm programs, laws, and policies.

22. ARIZ. REV. STAT. § 41-2636 (2022).

23. *Id.* § 41-2535(B).

impracticable to restrict a particular procurement to small businesses, the procurement officer shall make a determination setting forth the reasons and place it in the contract file."[24] A small business is defined as "a for-profit or not-for-profit organization, including its affiliates, with fewer than 100 full-time employees or gross annual receipts of less than $4 million for the last complete fiscal year."[25]

- *Reporting on State Contracts*: Although there is no reference to a veteran-owned business certification in state statute, in 2011, a bill was passed that required the Arizona Department of Administration to report on state contracts awarded to veteran-owned businesses, and the state e-Procurement system added the veteran-owned classification.[26] This requirement was established for one year and is no longer required.[27]
- *Prompt Payment to Subcontractors*: "If a subcontractor or material supplier has performed in accordance with the provisions of a construction contract, the contractor shall pay to its subcontractors or material suppliers and each subcontractor shall pay to its subcontractors or material suppliers, within seven days of receipt by the contractor or subcontractor of each progress payment, retention release or final payment, the full amount received for such subcontractor's work and materials supplied based on work completed or materials supplied under the subcontract. . . ."[28]

Contracting opportunities where the DBE program applies have several requirements that intersect directly with procurement, contracting, and business inclusion.

- *Goals*: Contract opportunities may not use quotas or set-asides for DBEs.[29] The only exception for using a set-aside is in a limited or extreme circumstance, "when no other method could be reasonably expected to redress egregious instances of discrimination."[30] Instead, an overall goal must be set.[31] The goal must be based on evidence of available "ready, willing and able" DBEs in the

24. *Id.* § 41-2535(B).
25. Ariz. Admin. Code § R2-7-101(45) (2022).
26. *Veteran-Owned Business Definitions and Requirements*, Ariz. Dep't of Admin., https://spointra.az.gov/sites/default/files/Veteran-Owned%20Business%20Definitions%20and%20Requirements.pdf (last visited Jan. 12, 2023); S.B. 1373, 2011 Leg., 15th Sess. (Ariz. 2011).
27. This was confirmed through a call with the Arizona Legislature Government Research Team.
28. Ariz. Rev. Stat. § 32-1183(B) (2022).
29. 49 C.F.R. § 26.43 (2022).
30. *Id.* § 26.43.
31. *Id.* § 26.45(a)(1).

market.[32] Once the assessment of "ready, willing and able" DBEs is completed, an overall goal may be established as a percentage of the total amount of contracts receiving U.S. DOT funds.[33] Participation goals must be set for all certified DBEs and not divided into subcategories.[34] Race- and gender-neutral means must be used to "meet the maximum feasible portion of your overall goal."[35] ADOT and its fellow AZUCP members, as a recipient of U.S. DOT funds, will not be penalized for failing to meet the overall goal set, if it can establish good faith efforts to meet the goal.[36] When there is a DBE goal on a specific contract opportunity, only the bidder meeting the goal, or establishing good faith efforts to meet the goal, may be awarded the contract.[37]

- *Prompt Payment*: Under 49 C.F.R. part 26, contractors must pay subcontractors within 30 days of receipt of payment from the state DOT for satisfactory performance.[38]
- *Payment of Retainage*: Contractors must pay amounts withheld for retainage to subcontractors within 30 days of their work being satisfactorily completed.[39]

Additional Related Laws, Policies, and Programs

- *Governor's Office on Tribal Relations*: Under Arizona Revised Statutes section 41-2052, the Governor's Office on Tribal Relations may "[w]ork in conjunction with state agencies involved in economic development to design and initiate programs to stimulate economic growth of the American Indian population, including minority-owned and women-owned businesses."
- *Historically Underserved Farmers*: Under Arizona Revised Statutes section, the University of Arizona Cooperative Extension Office is charged with adopting rules that "[p]rovide a preference for food-producing agricultural organizations owned or operated by farmers and ranchers who are located in rural or tribal areas or who are historically underserved." Historically underserved is defined as, "(a) . . . a beginning farmer or rancher, a socially disadvantaged farmer or rancher or a

32. *Id.* § 26.45(b).
33. *Id.* § 26.45(e).
34. *Id.* § 26.45(h).
35. *Id.* § 26.51.
36. *Id.* § 26.47.
37. *Id.* § 26.53.
38. 49 C.F.R. § 26.29(a) (2023).
39. *Id.* § 26.29(b).

veteran farmer or rancher as defined in 7 United States Code section 2279. (b) Includes other limited-resource farmers or ranchers."[40]

- *Arizona Procurement Portal*: To participate in Arizona procurement opportunities, businesses must register on the Arizona Procurement Portal:[41] http://app.az.gov.

Major City Snapshot: Phoenix

The City of Phoenix Equal Opportunity Department manages the certification program, which includes three certifications:[42] Small Business Enterprise (SBE), DBE, and ACDBE. A high-level overview of some of the city's business inclusion efforts follows.

- *Certifications*
  - *Small Business Enterprise (SBE)*: The SBE program is governed by sections 18-100 through 18-304 of the City of Phoenix Code of Ordinance.[43] To qualify as an SBE for the program, a business must be "a small business that is an independent and continuing enterprise for profit; that performs a commercially useful function; is owned and controlled by one or more persons each of whose personal net worth does not exceed limits identified by U.S. DOT regulations, 49 CFR, Parts 23 and 26; and meets the current small business size standard in its primary industry or trade area."[44] The applicable small business size standard is defined by the SBA.[45]
  - *Disadvantaged Business Enterprise (DBE)*: As a member of the AZUCP, the authority for the DBE program and the eligibility requirements are the same as those noted earlier in the "Summary of Certification Programs and Requirements" section.
  - *Airport Concessions Disadvantaged (ACDBE)*: As a member of the AZUCP, the authority for the ACDBE program and the eligibility requirements are the same as those noted earlier

40. Ariz. Rev. Stat. § 3-127 (2022).
41. *How to Do Business with the State of Arizona*, Ariz. Dep't of Admin., https://spo.az.gov/suppliers/how-do-business-state (last visited May 4, 2023).
42. *Business Programs*, City of Phx., https://www.phoenix.gov/eod/programs (last visited Jan. 12, 2023).
43. Phx., Ariz. Code ch. 18 (2022).
44. *Id.* § 18-101.
45. *Id.*

in the "Summary of Certification Programs and Requirements" section.

- *Goals*: The City Manager, or their designee, determines SBE contracting participation goals on projects.[46]
- *Utilization Plans*: When an SBE goal is set on a project, the city manager, or their designee, must approve "the bidder's SBE utilization plan or [grant] the bidder a waiver on the project."[47] If the plan is not approved or a waiver is not granted, then an award cannot be made to that bidder.[48]
- *Penalties:* Failure of a prime contractor to comply with any provisions of the SBE program under the Phoenix Code of Ordinances may result in withholding future payments and/or rejecting future bids until the prime contractor has cured its breach.[49]

For additional information on the City of Phoenix's certification programs please visit https://www.phoenix.gov/eod/programs.

46. *Id.* §§ 18-103, 104.
47. *Id.* § 18-105.
48. *Id.*
49. *Id.* § 18-110.

CHAPTER 5

Arkansas

Overview of Business Inclusion Program, Policies, and Practices

Government entities seeking to create business inclusion programs have two primary options in terms of the type of program they may create, in terms of who is eligible for the program: (1) a race- and gender-conscious program or (2) a race- and gender-neutral program. Under the Equal Protection Clause of the Fourteenth Amendment, strict scrutiny is applied by the courts when a government actor is creating policies based on race. Strict scrutiny is the highest level of judicial review that may be applied. It requires the government actor to demonstrate that (1) past discrimination exists such that the entity has a "compelling government interest" in rectifying it, and (2) the policies and programs created to do so are "narrowly tailored."[1] Although intermediate scrutiny is often applied when reviewing programs based on gender, strict scrutiny is applied when reviewing race- and gender-conscious business inclusion programs.[2] Disparity studies have become a standard tool used to assist a government entity in withstanding a challenge to its race- and gender-conscious business inclusion programs. These studies aid in demonstrating whether a government entity has engaged

1. City of Richmond v. J.A. Croson Co., 488 U.S. 469 (1989).

2. Since the 1980s with the Supreme Court decision in *City of Richmond v. J.A. Croson Company*, there have been a number of cases across the county that have assessed race- and gender-conscious business inclusion programs. *See* Adarand Constructors, Inc. v. Pena, 515 U.S. 200 (1995); Virdi v. DeKalb Cnty. Sch. Dist., 135 Fed. App'x 262, 268 (11th Cir. 2005); Sherbrooke Turf, Inc. v. Minn. Dep't of Transp., 345 F.3d 964, 971 (8th Cir. 2003); Mountain West Holding Co., Inc. v. The State of Montana, Montana DOT, et al., 2017 WL 2179120 (9th Cir. May 16, 2017).

in past discrimination in its contracting practices, such that the entity may have a compelling government interest in rectifying it.[3]

Conversely, race- and gender-neutral programs are programs that are not only accessible to minority-owned and women-owned businesses but to all businesses, regardless of race or gender. A small business inclusion program would fall into this category. The level of judicial review applied to such a policy to determine its constitutionality is rational basis, which is the lowest threshold for a government to satisfy. For a government entity to satisfy rational basis, the policy or program created must be "related to a legitimate government purpose."[4] Even when a government entity has a race- and gender-conscious program, oftentimes the program may still require the government actor to seek to meet the goals of their program through race- and gender-neutral means where able, so as to be taking the most narrowly tailored means of accomplishing the program goals.

In the state of Arkansas, at the state level, there are two main entities that certify businesses for business inclusion programs: (1) the Arkansas Economic Development Commission (AEDC) and (2) the Arkansas Department of Transportation (ARDOT).

Summary of Certification Programs and Requirements

The AEDC Minority and Women-Owned Business Enterprise (MWOBE) Division certifies businesses as Minority-Owned Businesses (MBEs) and Women-Owned Businesses (WBEs).[5]

- *Minority-Owned Business (MBE)*: To be eligible for certification as an MBE a business must (1) be a lawful permanent resident of the state of Arkansas;[6] (2) be 51 percent owned by one or more minorities, which includes African American, Hispanic American, American Indian, Asian American, Pacific Islander American; or a service-disabled veteran as designated by the U.S. Department of Veterans Affairs;[7] (3) be controlled by

3. *Promoting Opportunity and Equality in America: A Guide to Federal Circuit Authority on Permissible Government Actions to Promote Racial and Gender Equality*, Am. Civ. Liberties Union & The Opportunity Agenda (Dec. 2010), https://www.aclu.org/sites/default/files/field_document/Promoting_Opportunity_and_Equality_in_America.pdf.

4. 488 U.S. 469 (1989).

5. Ark. Code Ann. § 15-4-209(a)(8) (2019); *Minority and Women-Owned Business Enterprise (MWBE) Certification*, Ark. Econ. Dev. Comm'n, https://www.arkansasedc.com/community-resources/Minority-and-Women-Owned-Business-Enterprise-Resources/detail/get-certified (last visited Jan. 21, 2023).

6. Ark. Code Ann. § 15-4-303(2) (2020).

7. *Id.* §§ 15-4-303(2), 15-4-306.

a minority;[8] (4) have been in operation for at least two years prior to applying;[9] (5) majority owners are U.S. citizens;[10] (6) have a license to operate in Arkansas;[11] (7) demonstrate proof of income on federal and state tax return for the prior two years;[12] (8) be a for-profit entity;[13] and (9) have annual gross revenues less than $10 million.[14]

- *Women-Owned Business (WBE)*: To qualify for certification as a WBE, a business must meet all of the preceding requirement for an MBE with the exception of (2) and (3) (being a minority is not required for a WBE certification). Instead, a business must be 51 percent owned and controlled by a female.[15]

ARDOT administers the Disadvantaged Business Enterprise (DBE) program, Airport Concession Disadvantaged Business Enterprise (ACDBE) program, and the Small Business Provision (SBP).

- *Disadvantaged Business Enterprise (DBE) Program*: As is required under 49 C.F.R. § 26.81, Arkansas has a Unified Certification Program (UCP). The UCP makes all DBE certification decisions and provides a "one-stop shop" to DBE applicants.[16] To qualify as a DBE a business must (1) be for-profit;[17] (2) be a small business concern—with "small" determined by the Small Business Administration (SBA) small business size standards and does not exceed $30.40 million in gross annual receipts;[18] (3) be at least 51 percent owned by socially and economically disadvantaged individuals—there is a rebuttable presumption that women, Black Americans, Hispanic Americans, Native Americans, Asian-Pacific Americans, Subcontinent Asian Americans, or other minorities are disadvantaged;[19] (4) be controlled by one or more of the socially and economically disadvantaged owners;[20] (5) have the socially and economically disadvantaged owners

8. *Id.* § 15-4-314(b)(1)(B).
9. *Minority and Women-Owned Business Enterprise (MWBE) Certification*, *supra* note 5.
10. *Id.*
11. *Id.*
12. *Id.*
13. *Id.*
14. 168.00.07 Ark. Code R. § 004.
15. Ark. Code Ann. §§ 15-4-303(9), 15-4-314(b)(1)(B).
16. 49 C.F.R. § 26.81(b)(2) (2022).
17. *Id.* § 26.5.
18. *Id.* §§ 26.5, 26.65(b). It is worth noting that under 49 C.F.R. § 26.65(b), the DBE size standard may be adjusted annually for inflation such that in subsequent years the size standard may no longer be $30.40 million.
19. *Id.* § 26.67.
20. *Id.* § 26.5.

be U.S. citizens or lawfully admitted permanent residents;[21] and (6) have the personal net worth for any socially and economically disadvantaged owner not exceed $1.32 million.[22] The DBE program is required on contracting opportunities that have received funding from the Federal Highway Administration (FHWA), Federal Aviation Administration (FAA), or Federal Transit Administration (FTA).[23]

- *Airport Concession Disadvantaged Business Enterprise (ACDBE) Program*: In addition to being certified as a DBE under 49 C.F.R. part 26, businesses may also be certified as an Airport Concession Disadvantaged Business Enterprise (ACDBE) under 49 C.F.R. part 23. To qualify as an ACDBE, a business must (1) be a concession for-profit small business concern;[24] (2) qualify as small by having its prior three-year average gross receipts not exceed the applicable size standard of $56.42 million;[25] (3) be 51 percent owned by one or more socially and economically disadvantaged individuals;[26] (4) have one or more of the socially and economically disadvantaged individuals with control and managing the daily business operations;[27] and (5) have the personal net worth for any socially and economically disadvantaged owner not exceed $1.32 million.[28]
- *Small Business Provision (SBP)*: ARDOT has implemented a small business element within its DBE program called the Small Business Provision (SBP), pursuant to 49 C.F.R. § 26.39.[29] To be eligible for the provision, a business must be small, which is defined as "an independent for profit business, which performs a commercially useful function and has total gross receipts of not more than $28.48 million (over a three-year average) and not more than $1.32 million in personal net worth."[30]

---

21. *Id.* § 26.67.
22. *Id.*
23. *Id.* § 26.21(a).
24. *Id.* § 23.3.
25. *Id.* § 23.33(a). The size standards for the following are exceptions to this: bank and financial institutions is $1 billion in assets; car rental companies are $75.23 million average annual gross receipts; pay telephones is 1,500 employees; and automobile dealers is 350 employees.
26. *Id.*
27. *Id.*
28. *Id.* § 23.35.
29. *Disadvantaged Business Enterprise Program*, Ark. Dep't of Transp. 21 (Feb. 2023), https://www.ardot.gov/wp-content/uploads/DBE-Manual-Final-Feb-2023.pdf.
30. *Id.*

Procurement Laws Intersecting with Business Inclusion

The Arkansas procurement laws are found in title 19, chapter 11, subchapter 2 of the Arkansas Code Annotated.[31] The Department of Transformation and Shared Services Office of State Procurement (OSP) handles state procurement.[32] Following are some laws that pertain to minority-owned, women-owned, and veteran-owned businesses.

- *Small Order Procurement*: A "small procurement" is defined under Arkansas Code Annotated section 19-11-204(13)(A)(i) as, "a procurement not exceeding a purchase price of twenty thousand dollars ($20,000)." This type of purchase does not require competitive bidding.[33] When a vendor is a certified MWBE, the small order purchase threshold is not $20,000, but instead it is $40,000.[34]

The Minority-Owned and Women-Owned Business Economic Development Act (Ark. Code Ann. section 15-4-301-315) governs MWBE inclusion for the state through the AEDC. Under this law, duties, roles, and responsibilities pertaining to MWBE inclusion are noted for various state agencies. Following are specific laws that relate to contracting and goal setting. It is worth noting that under Arkansas Code Annotated section 15-4-309, some contracts may be exempt from the requirements of the Minority-Owned and Women-Owned Business Economic Development Act. Other statutes that intersect with this act are also included here:

- *Inclusion Goals*: Under Arkansas Code Annotated section 15-4-302,[35] inclusion goals for MWBEs are noted. These goals are as follows: (1) 10 percent MBE goal that is broken down into 2 percent toward service-disabled veteran-owned MBEs and 8 percent for all other MBEs, and (2) a 5 percent goal for WBEs.[36] These goals are not intended to be quotas. All state agencies must attempt to ensure participation on "state-funded

31. *State of Arkansas Procurement Manual*, Ark. Dep't of Transformation of Shared Servs. 1 (2021), https://www.transform.ar.gov/wp-content/uploads/2021/04/State-of-Arkansas-Procurement-Manual_1.pdf.
32. *Id.* at v.
33. *Id.* at 3.
34. Ark. Code Ann. § 15-4-315 (2020).
35. *Id.* § 15-4-302(c)(1)(A).
36. *Id.* § 15-4-302(c)(2).

and state-directed public construction programs and in the purchase of goods and services."[37]

- *Accelerated Payments*: Under Arkansas Code Annotated section 15-4-313, state agencies contracting with MWBEs must accelerate payments to MWBEs so as not to create accounts receivables problems.
- *Reporting Requirements*: Under Arkansas Code Annotated section 25-36-104, OSP must track MWBE participation on state contracts of more than $50,000. OSP is required to report on this semiannually to the Governor, the Minority and Women-Owned Business Advisory Council, Legislative Council, and the Legislative Joint Auditing Committee.[38] Each state agency and each state college or university budget report must include a listing of all contracts exceeding $50,000 that were awarded to MWBEs.[39] In addition to this reporting requirement, state agencies must also submit a report to the Minority and Women-Owned Business Advisory Council that includes (1) total procurements for all state contracts, (2) total dollar amount of contracts to MWBEs, and (3) total percentage of state contracts to MWBEs.[40]

Contracting opportunities where the ARDOT DBE program applies have several requirements that intersect directly with procurement, contracting, and business inclusion.

- *Fostering Small Business Participation*: Pursuant to 49 C.F.R. § 26.39, ARDOT has engaged in efforts to foster small business participation.[41] Such efforts include but are not limited to (1) unbundling contracts and (2) race-neutral small business set-asides.[42] There is a goal to spend between $4 million and $6 million dollars with SBP certified businesses.[43]
- *Goals*: Contract opportunities may not use quotas or set-asides for DBEs.[44] The only exception for using a set-aside is in a limited or extreme circumstance, "when no other method could be reasonably expected to redress egregious instances of

37. *Id.* § 15-4-302.
38. *Id.* § 25-36-104.
39. *Id.*
40. *Id.* § 15-4-312.
41. *Disadvantaged Business Enterprise Program, supra* note 29.
42. *Id.*
43. *Id.*
44. 49 C.F.R. § 26.43 (2022).

discrimination."[45] Instead, an overall goal must be set.[46] The goal must be based on evidence of available "ready, willing and able" DBEs in the market.[47] Once the assessment of "ready, willing and able" DBEs is completed, an overall goal may be established as a percentage of the total amount of contracts receiving U.S. Department of Transportation (U.S. DOT) funds.[48] Participation goals must be set for all certified DBEs and not divided into subcategories.[49] Race- and gender-neutral means must be used to "meet the maximum feasible portion of your overall goal."[50] ARDOT, as a recipient of U.S. DOT funds, will not be penalized for failing to meet the overall goal set, if it can establish good faith efforts to meet the goal.[51] When there is a DBE goal on a specific contract opportunity, only the bidder meeting the goal, or establishing good faith efforts to meet the goal, may be awarded the contract.[52]

- *Prompt Payment*: Under 49 C.F.R. part 26, contractors must pay subcontractors within 30 days of receipt of payment from the state DOT for satisfactory performance.[53]
- *Payment of Retainage*: Contractors must pay amounts withheld for retainage to subcontractors within 30 days of their work being completed satisfactorily.[54]

Additional Related Laws, Policies, and Programs

- *In-State Bidding Preferences*: Under Arkansas Code Annotated section 19-11-259, preference is given to a "firm resident in Arkansas" if their bid does not exceed the lowest qualified bid by more than 5 percent in commodity purchases by competitive bidding. A "firm resident in Arkansas" must (1) have an office in Arkansas; (2) have paid taxes in Arkansas for the preceding two years on any property used or intended to be used for the business; and (3) have paid taxes on real or personal property in Arkansas in the preceding two years.[55]

---

45. *Id.* § 26.43.
46. *Id.* § 26.45(a)(1).
47. *Id.* § 26.45(b).
48. *Id.* § 26.45(e).
49. *Id.* § 26.45(h).
50. *Id.* § 26.51.
51. *Id.* § 26.47.
52. *Id.* § 26.53.
53. 49 C.F.R. § 26.29(a) (2023).
54. *Id.* § 26.29(b).
55. Ark. Code Ann. § 19-11-259(a)(2)(B) (2020).

- *Lotteries*: Under Arkansas Code Annotated section 23-115-401, the Office of the Arkansas Lottery must adopt a plan to encourage to the "greatest extent feasible" participation of minority-owned businesses and female-owned businesses as vendors and retailers participating in the lotteries.
- *Technical Assistance and Outreach*: Under Arkansas Code Annotated section 15-4-314, AEDC's program also should have an educational program to assist businesses in getting certified as well as engage in outreach efforts to have the broadest participation of MWBEs.[56]
- *Arkansas Procurement Portal*: Arkansas uses ARBuy as its e-Procurement system. Additional information and contract opportunities may be found here: https://www.arkansas.gov/tss/procurement/bids/index.php

Major City Snapshot: Hot Springs

The City of Hot Springs, under its ordinance 2-6-1.6, states: "The city will attempt to use disadvantaged business enterprises and minority business enterprises when possible." In addition, the Hot Springs Intracity Transit department has a policy statement regarding its DBE program.[57] As a recipient of federal funds from the U.S. DOT, the city must comply with 49 C.F.R. part 26 just like ARDOT, as noted previously in this chapter. To find eligible DBEs, the city will use the ARDOT DBE directory.[58]

56. *Id.* § 15-4-314.

57. *Hot Springs Intracity Transit DBE Program Policy Statement*, City of Hot Springs (2021), https://www.cityhs.net/DocumentCenter/View/5898/DBE-Goals.

58. *Id.* at 4.

CHAPTER 6

California

Overview of Business Inclusion Program, Policies, and Practices

Government entities seeking to create business inclusion programs have two primary options in terms of the type of program they may create, in terms of who is eligible for the program: (1) a race- and gender-conscious program or (2) a race- and gender-neutral program. Under the Equal Protection Clause of the Fourteenth Amendment, strict scrutiny is applied by the courts when a government actor is creating policies based on race. Strict scrutiny is the highest level of judicial review that may be applied. It requires the government actor to demonstrate that (1) past discrimination exists such that the entity has a "compelling government interest" in rectifying it, and (2) the policies and programs created to do so are "narrowly tailored."[1] Although intermediate scrutiny is often applied when reviewing programs based on gender, strict scrutiny is applied when reviewing race- and gender-conscious business inclusion programs.[2] Disparity studies have become a standard tool used to assist a government entity in withstanding a challenge to its race- and gender-conscious business inclusion programs. These studies aid in demonstrating whether a government entity has engaged

1. City of Richmond v. J.A. Croson Co., 488 U.S. 469 (1989).

2. Since the 1980s with the Supreme Court decision in *City of Richmond v. J.A. Croson Company*, there have been a number of cases across the county that have assessed race- and gender-conscious business inclusion programs. *See* Adarand Constructors, Inc. v. Pena, 515 U.S. 200 (1995); Virdi v. DeKalb Cnty. Sch. Dist., 135 Fed. App'x 262, 268 (11th Cir. 2005); Sherbrooke Turf, Inc. v. Minn. Dep't of Transp., 345 F.3d 964, 971 (8th Cir. 2003); Mountain West Holding Co., Inc. v. The State of Montana, Montana DOT, et al., 2017 WL 2179120 (9th Cir. May 16, 2017).

in past discrimination in its contracting practices, such that the entity may have a compelling government interest in rectifying it.[3]

Conversely, race- and gender-neutral programs are programs that are not only accessible to minority-owned and women-owned businesses but to all businesses, regardless of race or gender. A small business inclusion program would fall into this category. The level of judicial review applied to such a policy to determine its constitutionality is rational basis, which is the lowest threshold for a government to satisfy. For a government entity to satisfy rational basis, the policy or program created must be "related to a legitimate government purpose."[4] Even when a government entity has a race- and gender-conscious program, oftentimes the program may still require the government actor to seek to meet the goals of their program through race- and gender-neutral means where able, so as to be taking the most narrowly tailored means of accomplishing the program goals.

In the state of California, at the state level of government, there are three main entities that certify businesses for business inclusion programs: (1) the Department of General Services (DGS), Office of Small Business and Disabled Veteran Business Enterprise Services (OSDS); (2) the California Public Utilities Commission (CPUC) Supplier Diversity Program; and (3) the California Department of Transportation (Caltrans).

Summary of Certification Programs and Requirements

The OSDS certifies the following types of businesses: Small Business for the Purpose of Public Works (SB-PW), Small Business (SB), and Disabled Veteran Business Enterprise (DVBE).[5] The eligibility requirements for each follow:

- *Small Business for the Purpose of Public Works (SB-PW)*: "(1) Be independently owned and operated; (2) Not dominant in field of operation; (3) Principal office located in California; (4) Owners, Officers, Members/Managers, Partners must be domiciled

3. *Promoting Opportunity and Equality in America: A Guide to Federal Circuit Authority on Permissible Government Actions to Promote Racial and Gender Equality*, Am. Civ. Liberties Union & The Opportunity Agenda (Dec. 2010), https://www.aclu.org/sites/default/files/field_document/Promoting_Opportunity_and_Equality_in_America.pdf.

4. 488 U.S. 469 (1989).

5. *Apply for or Re-Apply for Certification as a Small Business and/or Disabled Veteran Business Enterprise*, Dep't of Gen. Servs., Procurement Div., Off. of Small Bus. & Disabled Veteran Bus. Enter. Servs. (OSDS), https://www.dgs.ca.gov/PD/Services/Page-Content/Procurement-Division-Services-List-Folder/Certify-or-Re-apply-as-Small-Business-Disabled-Veteran-Business-Enterprise (last visited Jan. 21, 2023).

in California; (5) Average $37 million or less in gross annual receipts over the last three tax years (including affiliates); and (6) A business with 200 or fewer employees (including affiliates)."[6] This certification is only for public works contracts.

- *Small Business (SB)*: Certification of a small business requires the following: (1) independently owned and operated business; (2) not dominant in its field of operation; (3) the principal office is located in California; (4) the officers are domiciled in California; (5) has 100 or fewer employees (including affiliates); and (6) average annual gross receipts of $16 million dollars (or the amount adjusted during the biennial review informed by the California Consumer Price Index) or less over the previous three years.[7] If the firm is a manufacturer it must have 100 or fewer employees.[8] In addition to small businesses being certified, under the statute microbusinesses are also automatically certified if a firm has, "average annual gross receipts of [five million dollars ($5,000,000)] or less over the previous three years, or is a manufacturer, as defined in subdivision (c), with 25 or fewer employees."[9]
- *Disabled Veteran Business Enterprise (DVBE)*: A disabled veteran is defined as "a veteran of the military, naval, or air service of the United States, including, but not limited to, the Philippine Commonwealth Army, the Regular Scouts, 'Old Scouts,' and the Special Philippine Scouts, 'New Scouts,' who has at least a 10-percent service-connected disability and who is domiciled in the state."[10] To be eligible for DVBE certification, a business must be (1) 51 percent or more owned by a disabled veteran; (2) management and control of daily operations rests with a disabled veteran; and (3) its home office is located in the United States.[11]

The California Public Utilities Commission requires that both community choice aggregators and "electric utilities, gas utilities, water utilities, wireless telecommunications service providers, telephone utilities,

---

6. *Id.*; Cal. Gov't Code § 14837(d)(1)(B) (2018).

7. Cal. Gov't Code § 14837(d)(1)(A) (2018); *Apply for or Re-Apply for Certification as a Small Business and/or Disabled Veteran Business Enterprise*, *supra* note 5.

8. Cal. Gov't Code § 14837(d)(1)(A) (2018); *Apply for or Re-Apply for Certification as a Small Business and/or Disabled Veteran Business Enterprise*, Dep't of Gen. Servs., Procurement Div., Off. of Small Bus. & Disabled Veteran Bus. Enter. Servs. (OSDS), https://www.dgs.ca.gov/PD/Services/Page-Content/Procurement-Division-Services-List-Folder/Certify-or-Re-apply-as-Small-Business-Disabled-Veteran-Business-Enterprise (last visited Jan. 21, 2023).

9. Cal. Gov't Code § 14837(d)(2) (2018).

10. Cal. Mil. & Vet. Code § 999(b)(6) (2019).

11. *Id.* § 999(b)(7)(A).

and electric service providers with gross annual California revenues exceeding $15,000,000 . . ." submit annual plans regarding their efforts to increase procurement from small businesses, local businesses, minority business enterprises, women business enterprises, LGBT business enterprises, persons with disability business enterprises, and disabled veteran business enterprises.[12] The California Public Utilities Commission, through the Supplier Clearinghouse, certifies the following types of businesses for its supplier diversity program.

- *Minority Business Enterprise (MBE)*: "51-percent owned by a minority group or groups; or, in the case of any publicly owned business, at least 51 percent of the stock of which is owned by one or more minority groups, and whose management and daily business operations are controlled by one or more of those individuals. The contracting utility shall presume that minority includes African Americans, Hispanic Americans, Native Americans, and Asian Pacific Americans."[13]
- *Women Business Enterprise (WBE)*: "at least 51-percent owned by a woman or women; or, in the case of any publicly owned business, at least 51 percent of the stock of which is owned by one or more women; and whose management and daily business operations are controlled by one or more of those individuals."[14]
- *LGBT Business Enterprise (LGBTBE)*: "at least 51-percent owned by a lesbian, gay, bisexual, or transgender person or persons; or, in the case of any publicly owned business, at least 51 percent of the stock of which is owned by one or more lesbian, gay, bisexual, or transgender persons; and whose management and daily business operations are controlled by one or more of those individuals."[15]
- *Persons with Disabilities Enterprise (PDBE)*: "at least 51 [percent] owned by a person or persons with a disability or (b) if a publicly owned business, at least 51 [percent] of the stock of which is owned by one or more persons with a disability; and (2) whose management and daily business operations are controlled by one or more of those individuals."[16]

---

12. Rules Governing the Development of Programs to Increase Participation, Gen. Ord. 156 (Apr. 2022), https://docs.cpuc.ca.gov/PublishedDocs/Published/G000/M466/K761/466761945.pdf; Cal. Pub. Util. Code §§ 366.2(m)(1), 366.2(m)(2) (2019).

13. Cal. Pub. Util. Code § 8282(d) (2019).

14. *Id.* § 8282(g).

15. *Id.* § 8282(c).

16. Rules Governing the Development of Programs to Increase Participation, *supra* note 12, at 5.

- *Disabled Veteran Business (DVBE)*: The business is (1) 51 percent owned by one or more disabled veterans; (2) one or more disabled veterans manage and control the daily business operations; and (3) the business's home office is in the United States.[17]

Caltrans administers the Disadvantaged Business Enterprise (DBE) program and Airport Concession Disadvantaged Business Enterprise (ACDBE) program.

- *Disadvantaged Business Enterprise (DBE) Program*: As is required under 49 C.F.R. § 26.81, California has a Unified Certification Program (CAUCP). The CAUCP makes all DBE certification decisions and provides a "one-stop shop" to DBE applicants.[18] To qualify as a DBE, a business must (1) be for-profit;[19] (2) be a small business concern—with "small" determined by the Small Business Administration (SBA) small business size standards—and does not exceed $30.40 million in gross annual receipts;[20] (3) be at least 51 percent owned by socially and economically disadvantaged individuals—there is a rebuttable presumption that women, Black Americans, Hispanic Americans, Native Americans, Asian-Pacific Americans, Subcontinent Asian Americans, or other minorities are disadvantaged;[21] (4) be controlled by one or more of the socially and economically disadvantaged owners;[22] (5) have the socially and economically disadvantaged owners be U.S. citizens or lawfully admitted permanent residents;[23] and (6) not have the personal net worth for any socially and economically disadvantaged owner exceed $1.32 million.[24] The DBE program is required on contracting opportunities that have received funding from the Federal Highway Administration (FHWA), Federal Aviation Administration (FAA), or Federal Transit Administration (FTA).[25]

---

17. *Id.* at 10.
18. 49 C.F.R. § 26.81(b)(2) (2022).
19. *Id.* § 26.5.
20. *Id.* §§ 26.5, 26.65(b). It is worth noting that under 49 C.F.R. § 26.65(b), the DBE size standard may be adjusted annually for inflation such that in subsequent years the size standard may no longer be $30.40 million.
21. *Id.* § 26.67.
22. *Id.* § 26.
23. *Id.* § 26.67.
24. *Id.*
25. *Id.* § 26.21(a).

- *Airport Concession Disadvantaged Business Enterprise (ACDBE) Program*: In addition to being certified as a DBE under 49 C.F.R. part 26, businesses may also be certified as an Airport Concession Disadvantaged Business Enterprise (ACDBE) under 49 C.F.R. part 23. To qualify as an ACDBE, a business must (1) be a concession for-profit small business concern;[26] (2) qualify as small by having its prior three-year average gross receipts not exceed the applicable size standard of $56.42 million;[27] (3) be 51 percent owned by one or more socially and economically disadvantaged individuals;[28] (4) have one or more of the socially and economically disadvantaged individuals with control and managing the daily business operations;[29] and (5) have the personal net worth for any socially and economically disadvantaged owner not exceed $1.32 million.[30]

Procurement Laws Intersecting with Business Inclusion

California's procurement laws may primarily be found in Government Code section 14615.1 and Public Contract Code sections 100–102 and 1100–22355. The State Contracting Manual is also available online as a resource on state contracting.[31] In 1996, the California Civil Rights Initiative (Proposition 209) was passed and banned affirmative action in public contracting.[32] This impacted MWBE programs.[33] Following are some laws that relate to business inclusion more broadly:

- *Small Business (SB) and Microbusiness Preferences*: SBs shall receive a 5 percent bidding preference when the small business or microbusiness is within 5 percent of the lowest responsive and responsible bidder. A non-small business firm may also

26. *Id.* § 23.3.

27. *Id.* § 23.33(a). The size standards for the following are exceptions to this: bank and financial institutions is $1 billion in assets; car rental companies are $75.23 million average annual gross receipts; pay telephones is 1,500 employees; and automobile dealers is 350 employees.

28. *Id.*

29. *Id.*

30. *Id.* § 23.35.

31. *State Contracting Manual—Volume 1*, Dep't of Gen. Servs., Off. of Legal Servs., https://www.dgs.ca.gov/OLS/Resources/Page-Content/Office-of-Legal-Services-Resources-List-Folder/State-Contracting (last visited Jan. 21, 2023).

32. *Promoting Opportunity and Equality in America: A Guide to Federal Circuit Authority on Permissible Government Actions to Promote Racial and Gender Equality*, Am. Civ. Liberties Union & The Opportunity Agenda (Dec. 2010), https://www.aclu.org/sites/default/files/field_document/Promoting_Opportunity_and_Equality_in_America.pdf. [This citation is noted in footnote 3 above)

33. *Id.*

receive this 5 percent preference if they can demonstrate subcontracting participation of 25 percent of the net price to small businesses or microbusinesses.[34] If the solicitation is based on evaluation and scoring, similarly, if the small business or microbusiness is within 5 percent of the highest responsible bidder's highest score, then the preference is for the small business or microbusiness.

- *Disabled Veteran Business Enterprise (DVBE) Preferences*: In the event of a tie on a bid where a small business or microbusiness is the lowest responsible bidder and a disabled veteran business enterprise is tied as the lowest responsible bidder, the contract will be awarded to the disabled veteran business enterprise.[35]
- *Contracting Goals*: Contracting goals are not set-asides or quotas,[36] instead they are considered a "numerically expressed objective that awarding departments and contractors are required to make efforts to achieve."[37] For statewide contracting the goals are (1) 25 percent of the state's annual contract dollars for small businesses and microbusinesses; (2) 3 percent of the state's annual contract dollars for disabled veteran business enterprises;[38] (3) 15 percent of the state's annual contract dollars for minority business enterprises;[39] (4) 5 percent of the state's annual contract dollars for women business enterprises.[40] Goals as they relate to the CPUC Supplier Diversity Program are (1) 15 percent for MBEs; (2) 5 percent for WBEs; (3) 1.5 percent for DVBEs; (4) 1 percent for LGBTBEs; and (5) there is not a set goal yet for persons with disability business enterprises.[41] As it relates to the CPUC Supplier Diversity Program, there is no penalty for failure to meet the goals.[42]
- *Awarding Contracts*: When a DVBE goal has been set by an agency on a solicitation, a bidder must meet the goal to be

34. Cal. Gov't Code § 14838(b)(1) (2023); Cal. Code Regs. tit. 2, § 1896.8.
35. Cal. Gov't Code § 14838(g) (2023); Cal. Code Regs. tit. 2, § 1896.8(f).
36. Rules Governing the Development of Programs to Increase Participation, *supra* note 12, at 6.
37. Cal. Pub. Cont. Code § 10115.1(g) (2019).
38. *Id.* § 10115.13.
39. *Id.*
40. *Id.*
41. Rules Governing the Development of Programs to Increase Participation, *supra* note 12, at 7.
42. *Id.* at 19.

considered a responsive bidder. Failure to do so will deem the bidder nonresponsive.[43]

- *Failure to Meet Goals*: If, after award, a prime contractor agrees to accomplishing a certain DVBE participation goal and fails to do so, then the agency may hold $10,000 from the final payment until the contractor complies with the agreed upon participation goal.[44]
- *Prompt Payment*: State agencies are to pay undisputed, properly submitted invoices within 45 calendar days.[45] Failure to do so will result in a late payment penalty.[46] When the payment is not made to a small business or microbusiness, the penalty is higher.[47]
- *SB/DVBE Option*: The SB/DVBE Option allows for state agencies to go directly to a small business, microbusiness, or disabled veteran business enterprise on solicitations over $5,000 but less than $250,000.[48] The agencies must receive at least two quotes from two certified businesses.[49]

Contracting opportunities where Caltrans' DBE program applies have several requirements that intersect directly with procurement, contracting, and business inclusion.

- *Fostering Small Business Participation*: Pursuant to 49 C.F.R. § 26.39, Caltrans has engaged in efforts to foster small business participation. The 2016 DBE Program Plan states that "Caltrans has incorporated a non-discriminatory element to its DBE Program, in order to facilitate competition on USDOT-assisted public works projects by small business concerns (both DBE and non-DBE small businesses)."[50]
- *Goals*: Contract opportunities may not use quotas or set-asides for DBEs.[51] The only exception for using a set-aside is in a limited or extreme circumstance, "when no other method could be reasonably expected to redress egregious instances

43. State Contracting Manual, Dep't of Gen. Servs., Off. of Legal Servs. 124 (Apr. 2022), https://www.dgs.ca.gov/-/media/Divisions/OLS/Resources/SCM-VI---04-2022-Update/SCM-Vol-1-rev-04112022-final.pdf.

44. Cal. Mil. & Vet. Code § 999.7 (2019).

45. Cal. Gov't Code § 927 (2010).

46. *Id.* § 927.4.

47. *Id.* § 927.6.

48. Cal. Gov't Code § 14838.5 (2019).

49. *Id.*

50. *DBE Program Plan*, Cal. Dep't of Transp. 30 (2016), https://dot.ca.gov/-/media/dot-media/programs/civil-rights/documents/f0004052-caltransdbeprogramplan-a11y.pdf.

51. 49 C.F.R. § 26.43 (2022).

of discrimination."[52] Instead, an overall goal must be set.[53] The goal must be based on evidence of available "ready, willing and able" DBEs in the market.[54] Once the assessment of "ready, willing and able" DBEs is completed, an overall goal may be established as a percentage of the total amount of contracts receiving U.S. Department of Transportation (U.S. DOT) funds.[55] Participation goals must be set for all certified DBEs and not divided into subcategories.[56] Race- and gender-neutral means must be used to "meet the maximum feasible portion of your overall goal."[57] Caltrans, as a recipient of U.S. DOT funds, will not be penalized for failing to meet the overall goal set, if it can establish good faith efforts to meet the goal.[58] When there is a DBE goal on a specific contract opportunity, only the bidder meeting the goal, or establishing good faith efforts to meet the goal, may be awarded the contract.[59]

- *Prompt Payment to Subcontractors*: Under 49 C.F.R. part 26, contractors must pay subcontractors within 30 days of receipt of payment from the state DOT for satisfactory performance.[60]
- *Payment of Retainage*: Contractors must pay amounts withheld for retainage to subcontractors within 30 days of their work being completed satisfactorily completed.[61]

Additional Related Laws, Policies, and Programs

- *Statewide Supplier Diversity Program*: DGS has a Statewide Supplier Diversity Program (SSDP).[62] SSDP engages in a number of strategies to increase utilization of small and diverse businesses in state procurement, as well as outreach activities.[63]
- *Reporting Requirements for Insurance Companies*: "Commencing July 1, 2020, and biennially on July 1 of each even-numbered year thereafter, each admitted insurer, with California

52. *Id.* § 26.43.
53. *Id.* § 26.45(a)(1).
54. *Id.* § 26.45(b).
55. *Id.* § 26.45(e).
56. *Id.* § 26.45(h).
57. *Id.* § 26.51.
58. *Id.* § 26.47.
59. *Id.* § 26.53.
60. 49 C.F.R. § 26.29(a) (2023).
61. *Id.* § 26.29(b).
62. *Statewide Supplier Diversity Program*, Dep't of Gen. Servs., https://www.dgs.ca.gov/PD/About/Page-Content/PD-Branch-Intro-Accordion-List/Statewide-Supplier-Diversity-Program/Statewide-Supplier-Diversity-Program (last visited May 5, 2023).
63. *Id.*

premiums written of seventy-five million dollars ($75,000,000) or more, shall report to the commissioner on its minority, women, LGBT, veteran, and disabled veteran-owned business procurement efforts during the previous two years."[64] In addition, under California Insurance Code section 927.4 an Insurance Diversity Task Force is required to be established by the Insurance Commissioner.

- *Support for Small and Diverse Businesses*: Under Government Code section 12100.61, the Governor's Office of Business and Economic Development seeks to collaborate with various agencies and nonprofit organizations offering technical assistance and support to small and diverse businesses. The California Small Business Development Technical Assistance Expansion Act of 2018 furthers these efforts.
- *California Cannabis Equity Act*: Business and Professions Code section 26246 seeks to "facilitate greater equity in business ownership and employment in the cannabis market"; this includes engaging minority business owners. The Department of Cannabis Control further notes that "cannabis equity efforts support people and communities harmed by cannabis criminalization. These efforts lower barriers to the cannabis industry for those hit hardest by the War on Drugs."[65]
- *California State Contracts Register (CSCR)*: Current contracting opportunities may be found on the state's CSCR website: https://caleprocure.ca.gov/pages/Events-BS3/event-search.aspx

Major City Snapshot: Los Angeles

The City of Los Angeles (city) has a business inclusion and certification program in place. A high-level overview of the city's efforts follows.

- *Certification*: The city certifies the following types of businesses: (1) Minority Business Enterprise (MBE); (2) Women Business Enterprise (WBE); (3) Disadvantaged Business Enterprise (DBE); (4) Airport Concession Disadvantaged Business Enterprise (ACDBE); (5) Small, Local Business Enterprise (SLBE); (6) Small Business Enterprise—City (SBE—City); (7) Small Business Enterprise—Proprietary (SBE—Proprietary);

---

64. CAL. INS. CODE § 927.2 (2022).

65. *Cannabis Equity*, DEP'T OF CANNABIS CONTROL, https://cannabis.ca.gov/resources/equity (last visited Jan. 22, 2023).

(8) Emerging Business Enterprise (EBE); (9) Disabled Veteran Business Enterprise (DVBE); (10) Local Business Enterprise (LBE); and (11) Transitional Job Opportunities Program (TJOP).[66] Under article 23, sections 10.49–10.49.10, the city has authority for the creation and administration of a local business, local small business, and local-state disabled veteran business enterprise program.

- *Contracting Preference*: On contracting opportunities including only city funds, a preference for local businesses exists under article 4, sections 10.25–10.25.10.
  - *Eligibility*: To be eligible for the preferences, a business must be certified as a local business, local small business, and/or a local transitional employer.[67]
  - *Applicability*: The preference may apply on bids as well as proposals.[68]
  - *Contracts Up to $150,000*: For contract opportunities up to $150,000 a 10 percent preference exists for local small businesses and local transitional employers.[69]
  - *Contracts over $150,000*: For contracting opportunities over $150,000 an 8 percent preference to local businesses exists.[70] If a local business is also certified as a local small business and local transitional employer, it will receive an additional 2 percent preference for each additional certification in addition to the 8 percent preference.[71] The maximum amount of preferences is 12 percent, and the total value cannot exceed $1 million.[72]
  - *Subcontracting*: For noncertified contractors that identify subcontractors that are certified as a local business, local small business, and/or local transitional employer, that contractor will receive up to a 5 percent preference.[73]
- *Contract Compliance*: Under city ordinance article 10, section 22.359–22.359.2, contract compliance for the Department of Public Works is noted and requires that the Office of Contract

---

66. *Certification Program Description*, City of L.A., https://bca.lacity.org/certification-program-description (last visited Jan. 20, 2023); *The Contractor's Handbook: A Guide to Doing Business with the City of Los Angeles*, Dep't of Pub. Works, Off. of Fin. 5, https://bca.lacity.org/Uploads/cca/Contractors%20Handbook.pdf (last visited Jan. 20, 2023)
67. Los Angeles Admin. Code § 10.25.2 (2021).
68. *Id.* § 10.25.3.
69. *Id.* § 10.25.4.
70. *Id.* § 10.25.5.
71. *Id.*
72. *Id.* § 10.25.5(d).
73. *Id.* § 10.25.5(c).

compliance "ensure utilization of Disadvantaged, Minority and Women–Owned Business Enterprises as otherwise required in contracts relating to construction, procurement and personal service contracts." This falls under, "Franchises for the Collection, Transportation and Processing of Commercial and Multifamily Solid Waste" and applies to Franchisee.[74]

For more information on the City of Los Angeles business inclusion efforts, please visit the following:

- Certification: https://bca.lacity.org/certification
- Business Inclusion Program: https://bca.lacity.org/BIS%20Program%20and%20Local%20Business%20Preference

74. *Id.* §§ 22.359–22.359.2.

CHAPTER 7

Colorado

Overview of Business Inclusion Program, Policies, and Practices

Government entities seeking to create business inclusion programs have two primary options in terms of the type of program they may create, in terms of who is eligible for the program: (1) a race- and gender-conscious program or (2) a race- and gender-neutral program. Under the Equal Protection Clause of the Fourteenth Amendment, strict scrutiny is applied by the courts when a government actor is creating policies based on race. Strict scrutiny is the highest level of judicial review that may be applied. It requires the government actor to demonstrate that (1) past discrimination exists such that the entity has a "compelling government interest" in rectifying it, and (2) the policies and programs created to do so are "narrowly tailored."[1] Although intermediate scrutiny is often applied when reviewing programs based on gender, strict scrutiny is applied when reviewing race- and gender-conscious business inclusion programs.[2] Disparity studies have become a standard tool used to assist a government entity in withstanding a challenge to its race- and gender-conscious business inclusion programs. These studies aid in demonstrating whether a government entity has engaged

1. City of Richmond v. J.A. Croson Co., 488 U.S. 469 (1989).

2. Since the 1980s with the Supreme Court decision in *City of Richmond v. J.A. Croson Company*, there have been a number of cases across the county that have assessed race- and gender-conscious business inclusion programs. *See* Adarand Constructors, Inc. v. Pena, 515 U.S. 200 (1995); Virdi v. DeKalb Cnty. Sch. Dist., 135 Fed. App'x 262, 268 (11th Cir. 2005); Sherbrooke Turf, Inc. v. Minn. Dep't of Transp., 345 F.3d 964, 971 (8th Cir. 2003); Mountain West Holding Co., Inc. v. The State of Montana, Montana DOT, et al., 2017 WL 2179120 (9th Cir. May 16, 2017).

in past discrimination in its contracting practices, such that the entity may have a compelling government interest in rectifying it.[3]

Conversely, race- and gender-neutral programs are programs that are not only accessible to minority-owned and women-owned businesses but to all businesses, regardless of race or gender. A small business inclusion program would fall into this category. The level of judicial review applied to such a policy to determine its constitutionality is rational basis, which is the lowest threshold for a government to satisfy. For a government entity to satisfy rational basis the policy or program created must be "related to a legitimate government purpose."[4] Even when a government entity has a race- and gender-conscious program, oftentimes the program may still require the government actor to seek to meet the goals of their program through race- and gender-neutral means where able, so as to be taking the most narrowly tailored means of accomplishing the program goals.

At the state level in Colorado, the Colorado Department of Transportation's (CDOT) small business programs, consisting of the Disadvantaged Business Enterprise (DBE) program and Emerging Small Business (ESB) program, are the only business inclusion programs that consist of a certification program and set goals for inclusion on applicable contracts.[5] Certifications for the federal Airport Concession Disadvantaged Business Enterprise Program (ACDBE) are handled by the City and County of Denver, rather than CDOT.[6] Over the last one to two years in the State of Colorado, bills have been passed and studies conducted pertaining to business inclusion for businesses such as historically underutilized businesses, which includes businesses owned by minorities, women, people with disabilities, LGBT individuals, and veterans.[7] These studies included recommendations to create and pilot programs; however, at this time there are no other state agencies that have a state-specific business inclusion program fully implemented focused on the inclusion of small, minority-owned, women-owned,

---

3. *Promoting Opportunity and Equality in America: A Guide to Federal Circuit Authority on Permissible Government Actions to Promote Racial and Gender Equality*, Am. Civ. Liberties Union & The Opportunity Agenda (Dec. 2010), https://www.aclu.org/sites/default/files/field_document/Promoting_Opportunity_and_Equality_in_America.pdf.

4. 488 U.S. 469 (1989).

5. *Small Business Programs: DBE & ESB*, Colo. Dep't of Transp., https://www.codot.gov/business/civilrights/smallbusiness (last visited Feb. 20, 2023).

6. *Colorado Unified Certification Program*, https://coucp.dbesystem.com/ (last visited Feb. 20, 2023).

7. *State of Colorado Disparity Study*, Dep't of Pers. & Admin., Off. of the State Controller, https://osc.colorado.gov/spco/procurement-resources/state-of-colorado-disparity-study (last visited Feb. 20, 2023); *Identifying Barriers to Historically Underutilized Businesses in Local Government Procurement SMART Impact Report*, Colo. Dep't of Local Affairs (2023), https://leg.colorado.gov/sites/default/files/images/2023_hubs_and_lg_procurement_smart_act_final.pdf.

veteran-owned, persons with disabilities-owned, and/or LGBT-owned businesses in government contracting.[8]

Summary of Certification Programs and Requirements

The following bullet points summarize the certification requirements for the business inclusion programs:

- *Disadvantaged Business Enterprise Program (DBE)*: As is required under 49 C.F.R. § 26.81, Colorado has a Unified Certification Program (UCP). CDOT and the City and County of Denver are the certifying agencies for the UCP.[9] The UCP makes all DBE certification decisions and provides a "one-stopshop" to DBE applicants.[10] To qualify as a DBE, a business must (1) be for-profit;[11] (2) be a small business concern—with "small" determined by the Small Business Administration (SBA) small business size standards and does not exceed $30.40 million in gross annual receipts;[12] (3) be at least 51 percent owned by socially and economically disadvantaged individuals—there is a rebuttable presumption that women, Black Americans, Hispanic Americans, Native Americans, Asian-Pacific Americans, Subcontinent Asian Americans, or other minorities are disadvantaged;[13] (4) be controlled by one or more of the socially and economically disadvantaged owners;[14] (5) have the socially and economically disadvantaged owners be U.S. citizens or lawfully admitted permanent residents;[15] and (6) not have the personal net worth for any socially and economically disadvantaged owner exceed $1.32 million.[16] The DBE program is required on contracting opportunities that have received funding from the Federal Highway Administration (FHWA), Federal Aviation Administration (FAA), or Federal Transit Administration (FTA).[17]

---

8. *State of Colorado Disparity Study*, *supra* note 7; S.B. 19-135, 69th Leg., 2019 Reg. Sess. (Colo. 2019); Colo. Rev. Stat. §§ 24-49.5-105, 24-103-1101 to 24-103-1105, 24-103-1001 to 24-103-1004 (2022).

9. *Colorado Unified Certification Program*, *supra* note 6.

10. 49 C.F.R. § 26.81(b)(2) (2022).

11. *Id.* § 26.5.

12. *Id.* §§ 26.5, 26.65(b). It is worth noting that under 49 C.F.R. § 26.65(b), the DBE size standard may be adjusted annually for inflation such that in subsequent years the size standard may no longer be $30.40 million.

13. *Id.* § 26.67.

14. *Id.* § 26.5.

15. *Id.* § 26.67.

16. *Id.*

17. *Id.* § 26.21(a).

- *Airport Concession Disadvantaged Business Enterprise Program (ACDBE)*: In addition to being certified as a DBE under 49 C.F.R. part 26, businesses may also be certified as an ACDBE under 49 C.F.R. part 23 through the Colorado UCP. To qualify as an ACDBE, a business must (1) be a concession for-profit small business concern;[18] (2) qualify as small by having its prior three-year average gross receipts not exceed the applicable size standard of $56.42 million;[19] (3) be 51 percent owned by one or more socially and economically disadvantaged individuals;[20] (4) have one or more of the socially and economically disadvantaged individuals with control and managing the daily business operations;[21] and (5) have the personal net worth for any socially and economically disadvantaged owner not exceed $1.32 million.[22]
- *Emerging Small Business (ESB)*: To be eligible for CDOT's ESB certification program, a business must meet the following criteria: (1) business must be in good standing with the Secretary of State of Colorado; (2) the business must be independent such that it does not depend on any other business relationship; (3) the services performed by the business must be either professional services, practice of research, or construction; and (4) the average annual receipts from the prior three years' tax returns must meet the program size limits at level 1 and level 2, which are as follows: (a) level 1—$1 million for professional services and $3 million for construction and (b) for level 2 are 50 percent of the Small Business Administration size standard for the business's primary NAICS code.[23] If a business surpasses the level 1 and level 2 size standards but still meets the SBA small business size standard for their primary NAICS code, they will be designated as a Small Business Enterprise (SBE).[24] The ESB program is a race- and gender-neutral program.[25]

18. *Id.* § 23.3.
19. *Id.* § 23.33(a). The size standards for the following are exceptions to this: bank and financial institutions is $1 billion in assets; car rental companies are $75.23 million average annual gross receipts; pay telephones is 1,500 employees; and automobile dealers is 350 employees.
20. *Id.*
21. *Id.*
22. *Id.* § 23.35.
23. 2 Colo. Code Regs. 604-1, ch. 3.2 (2022).
24. *Id.*
25. *Id.* at ch. 3.1.

Procurement Laws Intersecting with Business Inclusion

Colorado Procurement Code may be found in title 24, articles 101–112. Under the Procurement Code, there are some procurement preferences that intersect with business inclusion, as noted here:

- *Service-Disabled Veteran-Owned Small Business Preference*: The state has a goal to have 3 percent of state contract dollars awarded to service-disabled veteran-owned small businesses.[26]
- *Reporting Requirements*: Under C.R.S. section 24-103-905, each year, "the executive director shall submit a report regarding the state's progress in satisfying the three percent goal established in this section to the department of military and veterans affairs, the members of the Colorado board of veterans affairs, and to the members of the committees of the house of representatives and the senate that have jurisdiction over state affairs and veterans affairs."
- *Disparity Study*: Under C.R.S. sections 24-103-1001 to 24-103-1004, it addresses the need to conduct a disparity study. A disparity study was conducted in 2020.[27] The recommendations of the study have not yet been fully implemented.[28]

Contracting opportunities where the CDOT DBE program or ESB program applies have several requirements that intersect directly with procurement, contracting, and business inclusion.

- *Fostering Small Business Inclusion*: Pursuant to 49 C.F.R. § 26.39, CDOT has engaged in efforts to foster small business participation.[29] CDOT's ESB program is the program CDOT uses to foster small business participation.[30]
- *Goals*: Contract opportunities may not use quotas or set-asides for DBEs.[31] The only exception for using a set-aside is in a limited or extreme circumstance, "when no other method could be reasonably expected to redress egregious instances of discrimination."[32]

---

26. Colo. Rev. Stat. § 24-103-905 (2022).
27. *State of Colorado Disparity Study*, *supra* note 7.
28. This was confirmed through contacting various state agencies in the state of Colorado.
29. *Disadvantage Business Enterprise Program Manual*, Colo. Dep't of Transp. 4 (2016), https://www.codot.gov/business/civilrights/smallbusiness/assets/dbe-manual/cdot-dbe-program-manual-ch-2-administrative-requirements-2016.pdf.
30. *Id.*
31. 49 C.F.R. § 26.43 (2022).
32. *Id.* § 26.43.

Instead, an overall goal must be set.[33] The goal must be based on evidence of available "ready, willing and able" DBEs in the market.[34] Once the assessment of "ready, willing and able" DBEs is completed an overall goal may be established as a percentage of the total amount of contracts receiving U.S. Department of Transportation (U.S. DOT) funds.[35] Participation goals must be set for all certified DBEs and not divided into subcategories.[36] Race- and gender-neutral means must be used to "meet the maximum feasible portion of your overall goal."[37] CDOT, as a recipient of U.S. DOT funds, will not be penalized for failing to meet the overall goal set, if it can establish good faith efforts to meet the goal.[38] When there is a DBE goal on a specific contract opportunity only the bidder meeting the goal, or establishing good faith efforts to meet the goal, may be awarded the contract.[39]

- *Prompt Payment*: Under 49 C.F.R. part 26, contractors must pay subcontractors within 30 days of receipt of payment from the state DOT for satisfactory performance.[40] Under 2 Colorado Code of Regulations 604-1 section 4.5 and Colorado Revised Statutes section 24-91-103, prime contractors must pay subcontractors within seven calendar days of payment from CDOT and may have additional prompt payment requirements for projects with ESB primes or subcontractors.
- *Payment of Retainage*: Contractors must pay amounts withheld for retainage to subcontractors within 30 days of their work being satisfactorily completed.[41]

Additional Related Laws, Policies, and Programs

- *Identifying Barriers to Historically Underutilized Businesses in Local Government Procurement*: In 2021, House Bill 21-1168, which focused on identifying barriers for historically underutilized businesses (HUBs) in local government procurement, was passed and ultimately codified in Colorado Revised Statutes

33. *Id.* § 26.45(a)(1).
34. *Id.* § 26.45(b).
35. *Id.* § 26.45(e).
36. *Id.* § 26.45(h).
37. *Id.* § 26.51.
38. *Id.* § 26.47.
39. *Id.* § 26.53.
40. 49 C.F.R. § 26.29(a) (2023).
41. *Id.* § 26.29(b).

sections 29-1-1501 through 29-1-1503.[42] A study was conducted by the Department of Local Affairs to identify barriers to entry as well as local government entities' interactions and practices in regards to HUBs.[43]

- *Access to Capital and Technical Assistance*: The Colorado Office of Economic Development and International Trade offers a number of resources pertaining to access to capital and technical assistance for small and diverse businesses through its *Programs and Funding* page located here: https://oedit.colorado.gov/programs-and-funding. In addition, under Colorado Revised Statutes section 43-1-106 (8)(p) it states that the Transportation Commission of Colorado may provide technical assistance to small businesses.
- *Finding Solicitations*: The Colorado Office of the State Controller has a "Solicitations" page that highlights, by purchasing unit, where to find solicitations: https://osc.colorado.gov/spco/solicitations.

Major City Snapshot: City and County of Denver

The City of Denver Office of Small Business Opportunity certifies small and diverse businesses in accordance with the "Denver Revised Municipal Codes (D.R.M.C.), Title I, Chapter 28, Article III and Article VII as well as the Code of Federal Regulations (C.F.R.), Title 49, Part 26, Subpart A, B, D and E."[44]

- *Certifications*: The City and County of Denver certifications available include the following: Small Business Enterprise (SBE); Minority Business Enterprise (MBE); Women Business Enterprise (WBE); Small Business Enterprise Concessionaire (SBEC); Emerging Business Enterprise (EBE); and Disadvantaged Business Enterprise (DBE).[45] The Airport Concessions Disadvantaged Business Enterprise (ACDBE) certifications are processed

42. This was verified through contacting the state of Colorado legislature.

43. *Identifying Barriers to Historically Underutilized Businesses in Local Government Procurement SMART Impact Report*, Colo. Dep't of Local Affs. (2023), https://leg.colorado.gov/sites/default/files/images/2023_hubs_and_lg_procurement_smart_act_final.pdf.

44. *Frequently Asked Questions: About Certification*, Div. of Small Bus. Opportunity (2021), https://www.denvergov.org/files/assets/public/economic-development/documents/dsbo/faqs-about-certification-101221.pdf.

45. *Certification*, Div. of Small Bus. Opportunity, https://www.denvergov.org/Government/Agencies-Departments-Offices/Agencies-Departments-Offices-Directory/Economic-Development-Opportunity/Business-Owners-Entrepreneurs/Do-Business-with-the-City/Certification (last visited Feb. 22, 2023).

by the Denver International Airport (DEN) Commerce Hub.[46] A complete list of certification eligibility requirements may be found in the Division of Small Business Opportunity *Certification Eligibility Criteria Guide*: https://www.denvergov.org/Government/Agencies-Departments-Offices/Agencies-Departments-Offices-Directory/Economic-Development-Opportunity/Business-Owners-Entrepreneurs/Do-Business-with-the-City/Certification.

- *Inclusion Goals*: The director of the Office of Contract Compliance must establish (1) an annual aspirational M/WBE utilization goal[47] and (2) project-specific M/WBE participation goals based on factors including but not limited to availability of such businesses.[48]
- *M/WBE Utilization and Contractor Good Faith Efforts*: On contracts for construction, reconstruction, remodeling, professional design, and construction services bidders must submit documentation highlighting all of the M/WBEs to be utilized to meet the contract participation goals.[49] If a bidder has not achieved the participation goal, then good faith efforts must be submitted.[50] Failure to demonstrate good faith efforts will deem the bidder nonresponsive.[51] The director of the Division of Small Business Opportunity may also set SBE utilization requirements on contracting opportunities.[52] Failure of a bidder or proposer to meet the SBE utilization requirements would deem the bidder or proposer nonresponsive.[53]
- *Prompt Payment to M/WBEs*: City contracts with M/WBEs as subcontractors require that the prime pay the subcontractors within 35 days of receipt of the subcontractor's invoice.[54]
- *Sanctions*: If a contractor violates any provision of article III of title I, chapter 28, then it will be subject to sanctions.[55]
- *Reporting Requirements*: The director of the Office of Contract Compliance must report to the mayor, city council, and other department directors on the city's progress to meet the annual goal no less than twice a year.[56]

---

46. *Id.*
47. Denver Rev. Mun. Code § 28-57 (2022).
48. *Id.* § 28-58.
49. *Id.* §§ 28-57, 28-63.
50. *Id.* §§ 28-60, 28-64.
51. *Id.* §§ 28-60, 28-64.
52. *Id.* § 28-309.
53. *Id.* § 28-213.
54. *Id.* § 28-72.
55. *Id.* § 28-76.
56. *Id.* § 28-78.

- *SBE, SBEC, EBE Only Contract Opportunities*: The director of the Division of Small Business Opportunity may, under article VII, restrict certain contracts for award to SBE, SBEC, and EBE businesses only.[57]

57. *Id.* § 28-207.

CHAPTER 8

Connecticut

Overview of Business Inclusion Program, Policies, and Practices

Government entities seeking to create business inclusion programs have two primary options in terms of the type of program they may create, in terms of who is eligible for the program: (1) a race- and gender-conscious program or (2) a race- and gender-neutral program. Under the Equal Protection Clause of the Fourteenth Amendment, strict scrutiny is applied by the courts when a government actor is creating policies based on race. Strict scrutiny is the highest level of judicial review that may be applied. It requires the government actor to demonstrate that (1) past discrimination exists such that the entity has a "compelling government interest" in rectifying it and (2) the policies and programs created to do so are "narrowly tailored."[1] Although intermediate scrutiny is often applied when reviewing programs based on gender, strict scrutiny is applied when reviewing race- and gender-conscious business inclusion programs.[2] Disparity studies have become a standard tool used to assist a government entity in withstanding a challenge to its race- and gender-conscious business inclusion programs. These studies aid in demonstrating whether a government entity has engaged

1. City of Richmond v. J.A. Croson Co., 488 U.S. 469 (1989).

2. Since the 1980s with the Supreme Court decision in *City of Richmond v. J.A. Croson Company*, there have been a number of cases across the county that have assessed race- and gender-conscious business inclusion programs. *See* Adarand Constructors, Inc. v. Pena, 515 U.S. 200 (1995); Virdi v. DeKalb Cnty. Sch. Dist., 135 Fed. App'x 262, 268 (11th Cir. 2005); Sherbrooke Turf, Inc. v. Minn. Dep't of Transp., 345 F.3d 964, 971 (8th Cir. 2003); Mountain West Holding Co., Inc. v. The State of Montana, Montana DOT, et al., 2017 WL 2179120 (9th Cir. May 16, 2017).

in past discrimination in its contracting practices, such that the entity may have a compelling government interest in rectifying it.[3]

Conversely, race- and gender-neutral programs are programs that are not only accessible to minority-owned and women-owned businesses but to all businesses, regardless of race or gender. A small business inclusion program would fall into this category. The level of judicial review applied to such a policy to determine its constitutionality is rational basis, which is the lowest threshold for a government to satisfy. For a government entity to satisfy rational basis, the policy or program created must be "related to a legitimate government purpose."[4] Even when a government entity has a race- and gender-conscious program, oftentimes the program may still require the government actor to seek to meet the goals of their program through race- and gender-neutral means where able, so as to be taking the most narrowly tailored means of accomplishing the program goals.

In the state of Connecticut, at the state level, there are three state agencies that certify businesses for business inclusion programs: (1) the Department of Administrative Services, (2) Department of Veteran Affairs, and (3) the Connecticut Department of Transportation (CTDOT).

Summary of Certification Programs and Requirements

The Department of Administrative Services Supplier Diversity Program certifies businesses as minority businesses enterprises (MBEs) and small business enterprises (SBEs).[5] Both of these certifications are valid for up to two years prior to needing to renew.[6] Prior to submitting an application for SBE or MBE certification, a business must register with the federal General Services Administration SAM system.[7] The eligibility requirements for both follow:

---

3. *Promoting Opportunity and Equality in America: A Guide to Federal Circuit Authority on Permissible Government Actions to Promote Racial and Gender Equality*, AM. CIV. LIBERTIES UNION & THE OPPORTUNITY AGENDA (Dec. 2010), https://www.aclu.org/sites/default/files/field_document/Promoting_Opportunity_and_Equality_in_America.pdf.

4. 488 U.S. 469 (1989).

5. *SBE/MBE Program Certification Application (Small or Minority Business Enterprise)*, DEP'T OF ADMIN. SERVS., https://portal.ct.gov/DAS/Procurement/Supplier-Diversity/SBE-MBE-Program-Certification-Application-Small-or-Minority-Business-Enterprise (last visited Feb. 18, 2023).

6. CONN. GEN. STAT. § 4a-60g(k) (2022); *FAQs, SBE/MBE Program Certification Application (Small or Minority Business Enterprise)*, https://portal.ct.gov/DAS/Procurement/Supplier-Diversity/SBE-MBE-Program-Certification-Application-Small-or-Minority-Business-Enterprise/FAQ (last visited Feb. 22, 2023).

7. CONN. GEN. STAT. § 4a-60g(k) (2022); *FAQs, SBE/MBE Program Certification Application (Small or Minority Business Enterprise)*, *supra* note 6.

- *Minority Business Enterprise (MBE)*: To satisfy the eligibility criteria to be certified as an MBE, a business (1) must be a small contractor defined as follows: (a) a business that maintains a principal place of business in Connecticut and is registered as a small business in the federal General Services Administration database or (b) an independent nonprofit with a principal place of business in Connecticut whose annual gross receipts do not exceed $20 million in the fiscal year prior to submitting its application;[8] (2) must be 51 percent owned, in terms of assets or capital stock, by one or more minorities—minorities are defined as including individuals who are Black Americans; Hispanic Americans; "Persons having origins in the Iberian Peninsula"; American Indians; "Asian Pacific Americans and Pacific [I]slanders"; women; and individuals with a disability;[9] (3) owner must have authority over the daily affairs of the business and power to direct the management of the business;[10] and (4) owner must "possess managerial and technical competence and experience directly related to the principal business activities of the enterprise."[11] An MBE may also be a nonprofit corporation where 51 percent of those engaged in the following tasks are minorities: (1) authority over the daily affairs of the nonprofit and power to direct the management of the nonprofit and (2) "possess managerial and technical competence and experience directly related to the principal business activities of the enterprise."[12]
- *Small Business Enterprise (SBE)*: Under the Regulations of Connecticut State Agencies (R.C.S.A.) section 4a-60h-1, a small business enterprise is defined the same as a "small contractor" under General Statutes of Connecticut section 4a-60g(1). This means that to satisfy the eligibility requirements for being an SBE an enterprise must (1) maintain a principal place of business in Connecticut and be registered as a small business in the federal General Services Administration database or (2) be an independent nonprofit with a principal place of business in Connecticut whose annual gross receipts do not exceed $20 million in the fiscal year prior to submitting its application.[13]

---

8. Conn. Gen. Stat. § 4a-60g(l) (2022).
9. *Id.* §§ 4a-60g(4)(A), 32-9n(a).
10. *Id.* § 4a-60g(4)(A).
11. *Id.*
12. *Id.* § 4a-60g(4)(B).
13. *Id.* § 4a-60g(l).

The Department of Administrative Services Supplier Diversity Program does not have a specific women-owned business enterprise (WBE) or persons with a disability-owned business enterprise (PDBE) certification, however, through the definition for an MBE, both types of businesses may be certified as an MBE.[14]

The Connecticut Department of Veteran Affairs certifies businesses as CT Veteran-Owned Micro Businesses.[15]

- *CT Veteran-Owned Micro Businesses*: To satisfy the eligibility requirements, a business must (1) have annual gross revenues from the prior fiscal year of $3 million or less and (2) be 51 percent owned by one or more veterans.[16]

CTDOT administers the Disadvantaged Business Enterprise (DBE) program, Airport Concession Disadvantaged Business Enterprise (ACDBE) program, and the Small Business Participation (SBP) program.

- *Disadvantaged Business Enterprise (DBE) Program*: Pursuant to 49 C.F.R. part 26, the CTDOT administers the state's DBE certification program. As is required under 49 C.F.R. § 26.81, Connecticut has a Unified Certification Program (CT UCP). The CT UCP makes all DBE certification decisions and provides a "one-stop shop" to DBE applicants.[17] To qualify as a DBE, a business must (1) be for-profit;[18] (2) be a small business concern, with "small" determined by the Small Business Administration (SBA) small business size standards and does not exceed $30.40 million in gross annual receipts;[19] (3) be at least 51 percent owned by socially and economically disadvantaged individuals—there is a rebuttable presumption that women, Black Americans, Hispanic Americans, Native Americans, Asian-Pacific Americans, Subcontinent Asian Americans, or other minorities are disadvantaged;[20] (4) be controlled by

---

14. *Women-Owned Businesses*, CONN. DEP'T OF ECO. & CMTY. DEV., https://portal.ct.gov/DECD/Content/Business-Development/01_Type_of_Business/Women-Owned-Businesses (last visited Feb. 18, 2023); CONN. GEN. STAT. §§ 4a-60g(4)(A), 832-9n(a).

15. *Apply for CT Veteran-Owned Micro Business Certification*, CONN. DEP'T OF VETERAN AFFS., https://portal.ct.gov/DVA/Pages/Apply-for-CT-Veteran-Owned-Micro-Business-Certification/Eligibility (last visited Feb. 18, 2023).

16. CONN. GEN. STAT. § 4a-59(c) (2022); *Connecticut Veteran-Owned Micro Business Certification Application*, DEP'T OF VETERAN AFFS. (2019), https://portal.ct.gov/-/media/Departments-and-Agencies/DVA/Pages/Micro-Business-application-updated-4302019.pdf.

17. 49 C.F.R. § 26.81(b)(2) (2022).

18. *Id.* § 26.5.

19. *Id.* §§ 26.5, 26.65(b). It is worth noting that under 49 C.F.R. § 26.65(b), the DBE size standard may be adjusted annually for inflation such that in subsequent years the size standard may no longer be $30.40 million.

20. *Id.* § 26.67.

one or more of the socially and economically disadvantaged owners;[21] (5) have the socially and economically disadvantaged owners be U.S. citizens or lawfully admitted permanent residents;[22] and (6) not have the personal net worth for any socially and economically disadvantaged owner exceed $1.32 million.[23] The DBE program is required on contracting opportunities that have received funding from the Federal Highway Administration (FHWA), Federal Aviation Administration (FAA), or Federal Transit Administration (FTA).[24]

- *Airport Concession Disadvantaged Business Enterprise (ACDBE) Program*: In addition to being certified as a DBE under 49 C.F.R. part 26, businesses may also be certified as an Airport Concession Disadvantaged Business Enterprise (ACDBE) under 49 C.F.R. part 23. To qualify as an ACDBE, a business must (1) be a concession for-profit small business concern;[25] (2) qualify as small by having its prior three-year average gross receipts not exceed the applicable size standard of $56.42 million;[26] (3) be 51 percent owned by one or more socially and economically disadvantaged individuals;[27] (4) have one or more of the socially and economically disadvantaged individuals with control and managing the daily business operations;[28] and (5) not have the personal net worth for any socially and economically disadvantaged owner exceed $1.32 million.[29]
- *Small Business Participation (SBP) Program*: CTDOT has implemented a small business element within its DBE program called the Small Business Participation (SBP) program, pursuant to 49 C.F.R. § 26.39.[30] This program is race- and gender-neutral.[31] To be eligible for the program, a business must (1) be a small business under the SBA size standards; (2) for purposes of being considered a DBE for the FHA and FTA, the business must have average annual gross receipts from the

21. *Id.* § 26.5.
22. *Id.* § 26.67.
23. *Id.*
24. *Id.* § 26.21(a).
25. *Id.* § 23.3.
26. *Id.* § 23.33(a). The size standards for the following are exceptions to this: bank and financial institutions is $1 billion in assets; car rental companies are $75.23 million average annual gross receipts; pay telephones is 1,500 employees; and automobile dealers is 350 employees.
27. *Id.*
28. *Id.*
29. *Id.* § 23.35.
30. *DBE Program*, Conn. Dep't of Transp. 16 (2020), https://portal.ct.gov/-/media/DOT/documents/dcontractcompliance/DBE-Program-19Mar2020.pdf.
31. *Id.* at 17.

prior three fiscal years that do not exceed the cap in 49 C.F.R. § 26.65(b); and (3) have a current certification from one of the following: (a) a DBE certification; (b) SBE certification from the Connecticut Department of Administrative Services; or (c) a small business certification from any state or local governmental agency.[32]

Procurement Laws Intersecting with Business Inclusion

Connecticut procurement contracting laws may be found in General Statutes of Connecticut section 4a-58. Many procurement laws that intersect with business inclusion may be found in General Statutes of Connecticut sections 4a-60g, 4a-59(c), and 4a-60(b). Following are some laws that pertain to small businesses, minority-owned businesses, and veteran-owned businesses.

- *Microbusiness Preferences*: A company with gross revenues under $3 million is considered a microbusiness.[33] A contracting agency may provide the microbusiness a 10 percent price preference.[34] If the business is a veteran-owned microbusiness, then the price preference is up to 15 percent.[35]
- *Small Contractor and Minority Business Enterprise Set-Asides and Goals*: State agencies must set aside 25 percent of the total value of all contracts made available by that agency in a fiscal year (or portions of contracts) for set-asides on a competitive bidding basis for award to small contractors.[36] Not less than 25 percent of the total amount set aside for small contractors must be reserved for minority business enterprises.[37] This also applies, at the subcontracting level, to municipalities and quasi-public agencies receiving state financial assistance.[38] The provisions of the statute setting these goals does not apply to state agencies if the total anticipated value of all contracts, or a portion of the contracts, is $10,000 or less.[39] Similarly, municipal public works contracts or quasi-public agency contracts

32. *Id.*
33. CONN. GEN. STAT. § 4a-59(c) (2022).
34. *Id.*
35. *Id.*
36. *Id.* § 4a-60g(b)(2).
37. *Id.*
38. *Id.* §§ 4a-60(b)(3), 4a-60g(b)(4).
39. *Id.* § 4a-60g(h).

where the anticipated value is $50,000 or less are exempt from establishing such goals.[40]

- *Contractor Good Faith Efforts*: Under General Statutes of Connecticut section 4a-60(b), on state and municipal public works contracts as well as quasi-public agency contracts, a contractor must agree and warrant that they will make a good faith effort to subcontract to minority business enterprises and use them as suppliers.
- *Prompt Payment to Subcontractors*: Construction contracts must note that the "contractor pay any amounts due any subcontractor or supplier, whether for labor performed or materials furnished, not later than twenty-five days after the date the contractor receives payment from the owner. . . ."[41]
- *Violations and Penalties*: If a state agency has reason to believe that a contractor or subcontractor has willfully violated the provisions of General Statutes of Connecticut section 4a-60g, "Set-aside programs for small contractors and minority business enterprises," then notice must be provided to the contractor or subcontractor.[42] Such notice will note (1) the alleged violation, (2) a short statement, (3) the maximum civil penalty, and (4) information on the hearing.[43]
- *Reporting Requirements*: Annually, each state agencies setting aside contracts under General Statutes of Connecticut section 4a-60g must create a report that outlines its intended set-aside goals for the year.[44] This report is submitted to "the Commissioner of Administrative Services, the Commission on Human Rights and Opportunities and the [co-]chairpersons and ranking members of the joint standing committees of the General Assembly having cognizance of matters relating to planning and development and government administration."[45] For those state agencies that set aside contracts and submit annual reports, they must also provide status updates on their progress on a quarterly basis.[46]

40. *Id.*
41. *Id.* § 42-158j(a).
42. *Id.* § 4a-60g(j).
43. *Id.*
44. *Id.* § 4a-60g(l).
45. *Id.*
46. *Id.* § 4a-60g(m).

Contracting opportunities where the CTDOT DBE program applies have several requirements that intersect directly with procurement, contracting, and business inclusion.

- *Goals*: Contract opportunities may not use quotas or set-asides for DBEs.[47] The only exception for using a set-aside is in a limited or extreme circumstance, "when no other method could be reasonably expected to redress egregious instances of discrimination."[48] Instead, an overall goal must be set.[49] The goal must be based on evidence of available "ready, willing and able" DBEs in the market.[50] Once the assessment of "ready, willing and able" DBEs is completed, an overall goal may be established as a percentage of the total amount of contracts receiving U.S. Department of Transportation (U.S. DOT) funds.[51] Participation goals must be set for all certified DBEs and not divided into subcategories.[52] Race- and gender-neutral means must be used to "meet the maximum feasible portion of your overall goal."[53] CTDOT, as a recipient of U.S. DOT funds, will not be penalized for failing to meet the overall goal set, if it can establish good faith efforts to meet the goal.[54] When there is a DBE goal on a specific contract opportunity only the bidder meeting the goal, or establishing good faith efforts to meet the goal, may be awarded the contract.[55]
- *Prompt Payment*: Under 49 C.F.R. part 26, contractors must pay subcontractors within 30 days of receipt of payment from the state DOT for satisfactory performance.[56]
- *Payment of Retainage*: Contractors must pay amounts withheld for retainage to subcontractors within 30 days of their work being satisfactorily completed.[57]

47. 49 C.F.R. § 26.43 (2022).
48. *Id.* § 26.43.
49. *Id.* § 26.45(a)(1).
50. *Id.* § 26.45(b).
51. *Id.* § 26.45(e).
52. *Id.* § 26.45(h).
53. *Id.* § 26.51.
54. *Id.* § 26.47.
55. *Id.* § 26.53.
56. 49 C.F.R. § 26.29(a) (2023).
57. *Id.* § 26.29(b).

Additional Related Laws, Policies, and Programs

- *Access to Capital and Technical Assistance*: The Connecticut Small Business Boost Fund is supported by the Connecticut Department of Economic and Community Development.[58] The fund provides loans ranging from $5,000 to $500,000 for small businesses and nonprofits.[59] The Connecticut Department of Economic and Community Development also created a Minority Business Revolving Loan Fund that is administered by a third party, Hartford Economic Development Corporation.[60] This fund provides loans and lines of credit ranging from $10,000 to $100,000.[61]
- *Finding Contract Opportunities*: The Department of Administrative Services has a bid board available online at https://portal.ct.gov/DAS/CTSource/BidBoard where contracting opportunities may be viewed.

Major City Snapshot: Hartford

The City of Hartford has a Supplier Diversity certification program.[62] Following is an overview outlining some key components of the program.

- *Certifications*: The definitions and eligibility requirements for a small contractor and a minority business enterprise, under the city ordinance, has the same definition as noted in the state statute under General Statutes of Connecticut sections 4a-60g and 32-9n, as noted previously in this chapter.[63]
- *Solicitation Requirements*: Solicitations are required to include the following: (1) specific small contractor and MBE percentages under state statute and (2) substantiation of ownership

---

58. *Connecticut Small Business Boost Fund*, Conn. Dep't of Econ. & Cmty. Dev., https://portal.ct.gov/DECD/Content/Business-Development/05_Funding_Opportunities/Connecticut-Small-Business-Boost-Fund (last visited Feb. 22, 2023).
59. *Id.*
60. *Minority Business Funding*, Conn. Dep't of Econ. & Cmty. Dev., https://portal.ct.gov/DECD/Content/Business-Development/05_Funding_Opportunities/Minority-Business-Funding (last visited Feb. 22, 2023).
61. *Id.*
62. *Procurement*, City of Hartford, Conn., https://www.hartfordct.gov/Government/Departments/Finance/Procurement (last visited Feb. 22, 2023).
63. City Of Hartford, Conn., ch. 2, art. VIII, div. 9 § 2-660(A) (2022).

for MBE and WBE firms; and (3) any other necessary requirements including but not limited to things such as good faith efforts.[64]

- *Small Contractor and Minority Business Enterprise Set-Asides*: The set-aside program established under City ordinance chapter 2, section 2-660 "Set-aside programs for Small Contractors and Minority Business Enterprises" mirrors the set-aside established under General Statutes of Connecticut section 4a-60g(b)(2) outlined earlier. The only distinction is that rather than basing the percentage on the total dollar value of all contracts let for the contracting state agency for the year, the city bases it off of the average of the total contract value from the prior three years.[65]
- *City-Based Small Business Preference*: Under the City ordinance there is a 15 percent preference for city-based small businesses.[66] If a city-based small business is within 15 percent of the lowest bid, then the city-based small business may agree to accept the contract award at the amount of the low bid.[67] A city-based small business is defined the same as a small contractor.[68]
- *HUBZone Bid Preference*: A HUBZone business certified with the SBA that is within 10 percent of the lowest bid shall receive a 10 percent bid preference.[69] This preference would allow the HUBZone business to be considered the low bid if its bid was no more than 10 percent higher than the lowest bid.[70]
- *Liquidated Damages*: Failure of a developer to comply with the M/WBE contracting inclusion requirements will result in liquidated damages being calculated.[71]
- *Reporting Requirements*: When submitting the annual budget, the supplier diversity program must provide to the mayor, and subsequently the mayor upon approval to Common Council, a status report on the program's implementation.[72] Agencies must also submit quarterly status reports to the director of the Office of Human Relations.[73]

---

64. *Id.* at ch, 2, art. VIII, div. 9 § 2-660(C).
65. *Id.* at ch. 2, art. VIII, div. 9 § 2-660(B).
66. *Id.* at ch. 2, art. VIII, div. 9 § 2-661.
67. *Id.*
68. *Id.*
69. *Id.*
70. *Id.*
71. *Id.* at ch. 2, art. X, div. 5 § 2-720(b)(2).
72. *Id.* at ch. 2, art. VIII, div. 11 § 2-698.
73. *Id.*

CHAPTER 9

Delaware

Overview of Business Inclusion Program, Policies, and Practices

Government entities seeking to create business inclusion programs have two primary options in terms of the type of program they may create, in terms of who is eligible for the program: (1) a race- and gender-conscious program or (2) a race- and gender-neutral program. Under the Equal Protection Clause of the Fourteenth Amendment, strict scrutiny is applied by the courts when a government actor is creating policies based on race. Strict scrutiny is the highest level of judicial review that may be applied. It requires the government actor to demonstrate that (1) past discrimination exists such that the entity has a "compelling government interest" in rectifying it, and (2) the policies and programs created to do so are "narrowly tailored."[1] Although intermediate scrutiny is often applied when reviewing programs based on gender, strict scrutiny is applied when reviewing race- and gender-conscious business inclusion programs.[2] Disparity studies have become a standard tool used to assist a government entity in withstanding a challenge to its race- and gender-conscious business inclusion programs. These studies aid in demonstrating whether a government entity has engaged

1. City of Richmond v. J.A. Croson Co., 488 U.S. 469 (1989).

2. Since the 1980s with the Supreme Court decision in *City of Richmond v. J.A. Croson Company*, there have been a number of cases across the county that have assessed race- and gender-conscious business inclusion programs. *See* Adarand Constructors, Inc. v. Pena, 515 U.S. 200 (1995); Virdi v. DeKalb Cnty. Sch. Dist., 135 Fed. App'x 262, 268 (11th Cir. 2005); Sherbrooke Turf, Inc. v. Minn. Dep't of Transp., 345 F.3d 964, 971 (8th Cir. 2003); Mountain West Holding Co., Inc. v. The State of Montana, Montana DOT, et al., 2017 WL 2179120 (9th Cir. May 16, 2017).

in past discrimination in its contracting practices, such that the entity may have a compelling government interest in rectifying it.[3]

Conversely, race- and gender-neutral programs are programs that are not only accessible to minority-owned and women-owned businesses but to all businesses, regardless of race or gender. A small business inclusion program would fall into this category. The level of judicial review applied to such a policy to determine its constitutionality is rational basis, which is the lowest threshold for a government to satisfy. For a government entity to satisfy rational basis, the policy or program created must be "related to a legitimate government purpose."[4] Even when a government entity has a race- and gender-conscious program, often times the program may still require the government actor to seek to meet the goals of their program through race- and gender-neutral means where able, so as to be taking the most narrowly tailored means of accomplishing the program goals.

In the state of Delaware, at the state level of government, there are two main entities that certify businesses for business inclusion programs: (1) the Delaware Office of Supplier Diversity and (2) the Delaware Department of Transportation (DelDOT).

Summary of Certification Programs and Requirements

The Delaware Office of Supplier Diversity certifies the following types of businesses:

- *Minority Business Enterprise (MBE)*: To be eligible for the MBE certification, a business must (1) be a for-profit business; (2) be 51 percent owned (or 51 percent of the voting rights), controlled, and actively managed by one or more minorities (minorities include African (Black) Americans, Asian/Asian-Pacific Americans, Hispanic Americans, Native Americans, Subcontinent Asian Americans); (3) have the ownership be "real, substantial and continuing"; (4) have the minority owners qualifying for the 51 percent be U.S. citizens or lawful permanent residents; and (5) have "[t]he [minority] owner(s) . . .

3. *Promoting Opportunity and Equality in America: A Guide to Federal Circuit Authority on Permissible Government Actions to Promote Racial and Gender Equality*, Am. Civ. Liberties Union & The Opportunity Agenda (Dec. 2010), https://www.aclu.org/sites/default/files/field_document/Promoting_Opportunity_and_Equality_in_America.pdf.

4. 488 U.S. 469 (1989).

demonstrate that they possess the experience, expertise and knowledge to operate their particular type(s) of business."[5]

- *Women Business Enterprise (WBE)*: To be eligible for the WBE certification, a business must (1) be a for-profit business; (2) be 51 percent owned (or 51 percent of the voting rights for a corporation), controlled, and actively managed by one or more women; (3) have the ownership be "real, substantial and continuing"; (4) have women owners who make up the 51 percent be U.S. citizens or lawful permanent residents; and (5) have "[t]he [women] owner(s) . . . demonstrate that they possess the experience, expertise and knowledge to operate their particular type(s) of business."[6]
- *Veteran-Owned Business Enterprise (VOBE)*: To be eligible for the VOBE certification, a business must (1) be a for-profit business; (2) be 51 percent owned (or 51 percent of the voting rights for a corporation), controlled, and actively managed by one or more veterans (veteran defined as someone who "who has served in the United States military or has served in the National Guard of the Unites States for six months and has received a discharge other than a dishonorable discharge"); (3) have the ownership be "real, substantial and continuing"; (4) have the veteran owners qualifying for the 51 percent ownership be U.S. citizens or lawful permanent residents; and (5) have "[t]he [veteran] owner(s) . . . demonstrate that they possess the experience, expertise and knowledge to operate their particular type(s) of business."[7]
- *Service-Disabled Veteran-Owned Business Enterprise (SDVOBE)*: To be eligible for the SDVOBE certification, a business must (1) be a for-profit business; (2) be 51 percent owned (or 51 percent of the voting rights for a corporation), controlled, and actively managed by one or more service-disabled veterans (a service-disabled veteran is defined as someone who is a veteran as defined above and "is verified through VetBiz.gov or the Veteran Administration as a Service Disabled Veteran"); (3) have the ownership be "real, substantial and continuing"; (4) have the service disabled veteran owners qualifying for the 51 percent ownership be U.S. citizens or lawful permanent

---

5. *Policy, Eligibility, Application, and Affidavit regarding Certification as Diverse Business (MBE, WBE, VOBE, SDVOBE, IWDBE) and Small Business (SBF) Enterprises*, Del. Off. of Supplier Diversity 3–6 (2017), https://business.delaware.gov/wp-content/uploads/sites/118/2022/12/Diverse_Small-Business_Certification-Application.pdf.
6. *Id.*
7. *Id.*

residents; and (5) have "[t]he [service-disabled veteran] owner(s) . . . demonstrate that they possess the experience, expertise and knowledge to operate their particular type(s) of business."[8]

- *Individual with Disability-Owned Business Enterprise (IWDBE)*: To be eligible for the IWDBE certification, a business must (1) be a for-profit business; (2) be 51 percent owned (or 51 percent of the voting rights for a corporation), controlled, and actively managed by one or more individual(s) with a disability (individual(s) with a disability are defined as someone whose "standing is verified by a certificate or letter from a government office that: certifies an individual as such, or by the Social Security Administration, or a Doctor letter identifying the fact of a disability and the expected duration of same"); (3) have the ownership be "real, substantial and continuing"; (4) have the individual(s) with a disability owners qualifying for the 51 percent ownership be U.S. citizens or lawful permanent residents; and (5) have "[t]he [individual(s) with a disability] owner(s) . . . demonstrate that they possess the experience, expertise and knowledge to operate their particular type(s) of business."[9]
- *Small Business Focus (SBF)*: To be eligible for the SBF certification, a business must (1) be a for-profit business with "useful business function(s)" such that it is not a pass-through for a larger business; (2) have the owners be U.S. citizens or lawful permanent residents; (3) not have the business owned or controlled by one or more businesses larger than the SBF size standards; and (4) meet the SBF size standards for the following SBF certification industries: architecture and engineering services, construction, manufacturing, retail, service, and wholesale.[10]

DelDOT certifies the following types of businesses:

- *Disadvantaged Business Enterprise (DBE)*: Pursuant to 49 C.F.R. part 26, DelDOT administers the state's DBE certification program. As is required under 49 C.F.R. § 26.81, Delaware has a Unified Certification Program, however DelDOT makes all DBE certification decisions and provides a "one-stop shop" to

8. *Id.*
9. *Id.*
10. *Policy, Eligibility, Application, and Affidavit regarding Certification as Diverse Business (MBE, WBE, VOBE, SDVOBE, IWDBE) and Small Business (SBF) Enterprises*, Del. Off. of Supplier Diversity 3–7 (2017), https://business.delaware.gov/wp-content/uploads/sites/118/2022/12/Diverse_Small-Business_Certification-Application.pdf.

DBE applicants.[11] To qualify as a DBE, a business must (1) be for-profit;[12] (2) be a small business concern—with "small" determined by the Small Business Administration (SBA) small business size standards and does not exceed $30.40 million in gross annual receipts;[13] (3) be at least 51 percent owned by socially and economically disadvantaged individuals—there is a rebuttable presumption that women, Black Americans, Hispanic Americans, Native Americans, Asian-Pacific Americans, Subcontinent Asian Americans, or other minorities are disadvantaged;[14] (4) be controlled by one or more of the socially and economically disadvantaged owners;[15] (5) have the socially and economically disadvantaged owners be U.S. citizens or lawfully admitted permanent residents;[16] and (6) have the personal net worth for any socially and economically disadvantaged owner not exceed $1.32 million.[17] The DBE program is required on contracting opportunities that have received funding from the Federal Highway Administration (FHWA), Federal Aviation Administration (FAA), or Federal Transit Administration (FTA).[18]

- *Airport Concession Disadvantaged Business Enterprise (ACDBE)*: In addition to being certified as a DBE under 49 C.F.R. part 26, businesses may also be certified as an Airport Concession Disadvantaged Business Enterprise (ACDBE) under 49 C.F.R. part 23. To qualify as an ACDBE, a business must (1) be a concession for-profit small business concern;[19] (2) qualify as small by having its prior three-year average gross receipts not exceed the applicable size standard of $56.42 million;[20] (3) be 51 percent owned by one or more socially and economically disadvantaged individuals;[21] (4) have one or more of the socially and economically disadvantaged individuals with control and

---

11. 49 C.F.R. § 26.81(b)(2) (2022); *Disadvantaged Business Enterprise Program Plan*, DEL. DEP'T OF TRANSP. 13 (Oct. 2017), https://deldot.gov/Business/dbe/contentFolder/pdfs/dbeProgram.pdf.
12. 49 C.F.R. § 26.5 (2022).
13. *Id.* §§ 26.5, 26.65(b). It is worth noting that under 49 C.F.R. § 26.65(b), the DBE size standard may be adjusted annually for inflation such that in subsequent years the size standard may no longer be $30.40 million.
14. *Id.* § 26.67.
15. *Id.* § 26.5.
16. *Id.* § 26.67.
17. *Id.*
18. *Id.* § 26.21(a).
19. *Id.* § 23.3.
20. *Id.* § 23.33(a). The size standards for the following are exceptions to this: bank and financial institutions is $1 billion in assets; car rental companies are $75.23 million average annual gross receipts; pay telephones is 1,500 employees; and automobile dealers is 350 employees.
21. *Id.*

managing the daily business operations;[22] and (5) have the personal net worth for any socially and economically disadvantaged owner not exceed $1.32 million.[23]

Procurement Laws Intersecting with Business Inclusion

Delaware procurement laws may be found in title 29, chapter 69. Within the Delaware Procurement Statutes no contracting inclusion goals, preferences, or set-asides exist for small and diverse businesses. Following are some policies and orders that pertain to small, minority-owned, women-owned, and service-disabled veteran-owned businesses.

- *Inclusion Goals*: Currently, outside of participation goals set through the DelDOT (see the DBE section that follows), business inclusion statewide aspirational goals and project-specific participation goals for SBEs, MBEs, WBEs, VOBEs, SDVOBEs, and IWDBEs are not set.[24] A 2022 disparity study was conducted in the state of Delaware and did recommend establishing a race- and gender-neutral program with a 20 percent aspirational SBE goal, diverse business aspirational goals, and project-specific goals.[25]
- *Prompt Payment to Small Businesses*: Construction contracts are required to include a payment clause that notes that the contractor must pay the subcontractors and suppliers within 30 days of receiving payment from the owner.[26]
- *Reporting Requirements*: Under Executive Order 49, the Supplier Diversity Council (SDC) was created.[27] Within the Executive Order, there are several reporting requirements not just for the Council but also other state agencies that include the following: (1) the SDC provides an annual report to the governor; (2) Executive Branch Agencies are to designate a supplier diversity liaison who will prepare reports when necessary to the Office of Supplier Diversity (OSD) and the SDC; (3) the

---

22. *Id.*
23. *Id.* § 23.35.
24. *Policy, Eligibility, Application, and Affidavit regarding Certification as Diverse Business (MBE, WBE, VOBE, SDVOBE, IWDBE) and Small Business (SBF) Enterprises*, *supra* note 10, at 10.
25. *State of Delaware 2022 Disparity Study*, MGT Consulting 152–53 (2022), https://mymarketplace.delaware.gov/results-de/documents/disparity-report-2022.pdf.
26. 6 Del. Code § 3506(b) (2023).
27. *Governor's Supplier Diversity Council*, Off. of Supplier Diversity, https://business.delaware.gov/osd/sdc/ (last visited Feb. 25, 2023).

Office of Management and Budget/the director of Government Support Services must provide quarterly reports that break out the state's procurement spending by classification to the director of OSD; (4) each Executive Branch agency must report annually to OSD on their progress to enhance opportunities for diverse businesses; and (5) OSD will provide an annual report on the state's "progress in enhancing opportunities for diverse businesses and businesses eligible for the Program."[28]

Contracting opportunities where the DelDOT DBE program applies have several requirements that intersect directly with procurement, contracting, and business inclusion.

- *Fostering Small Business Inclusion*: Pursuant to 49 C.F.R. § 26.39, DelDOT has engaged in efforts to foster small business participation.[29] Per its 2017 DBE Program Plan, this program is race- and gender-neutral.[30] One such effort to foster small business participation was to set aside opportunities for competition only between small business concerns.[31]
- *Goals*: Contract opportunities may not use quotas or set-asides for DBEs.[32] The only exception for using a set-aside is in a limited or extreme circumstance, "when no other method could be reasonably expected to redress egregious instances of discrimination."[33] Instead, an overall goal must be set.[34] The goal must be based on evidence of available "ready, willing and able" DBEs in the market.[35] Once the assessment of "ready, willing and able" DBEs is completed, an overall goal may be established as a percentage of the total amount of contracts receiving U.S. DOT funds.[36] Participation goals must be set for all certified DBEs and not divided into subcategories.[37] Race- and gender-neutral means must be used to "meet the maximum feasible portion of your overall goal."[38] DelDOT, as a recipient of U.S. DOT funds, will not be penalized for failing

28. *Executive Order 49*, Off. of the Governor (June 2021), https://governor.delaware.gov/executive-orders/eo49/.
29. *Disadvantage Business Enterprise Program Plan*, *supra* note 11, at 26.
30. *Id.*
31. *Id.*
32. 49 C.F.R. § 26.43 (2022).
33. *Id.*
34. *Id.* § 26.45(a)(1).
35. *Id.* § 26.45(b).
36. *Id.* § 26.45(e).
37. *Id.* § 26.45(h).
38. *Id.* § 26.51.

to meet the overall goal set, if it can establish good faith efforts to meet the goal.[39] When there is a DBE goal on a specific contract opportunity, only the bidder meeting the goal, or establishing good faith efforts to meet the goal, may be awarded the contract.[40]

- *Prompt Payment*: Under 49 C.F.R. part 26, contractors must pay subcontractors within 30 days of receipt of payment from the state DOT for satisfactory performance.[41]
- *Payment of Retainage*: Contractors must pay amounts withheld for retainage to subcontractors within 30 days of their work being satisfactorily completed.[42]

Additional Related Laws, Policies, and Programs

- *Access to Capital*: The State of Delaware provides the Encouraging Development, Growth and Expansion (EDGE) grant for qualifying small businesses.[43] The grant is a matching grant and may allow for up to $100,000 for STEM companies and $50,000 for non-STEM companies.
- *Finding Contract Opportunities*: Information about Delaware's procurement portal may be found on the Office of Management and Budget's "MyMarketplace Delaware's Procurement Portal" page: https://mymarketplace.delaware.gov/

Major City Snapshot: Wilmington

The City of Wilmington, through its Small and Minority Business Enterprise Office within the Office of Economic Development, manages a business inclusion program.[44] Authority for the program is found within chapter 35, article IV of the city's code.[45] Following is a snapshot of the program.

- *Certifications*: The city certifies businesses as DBEs. To qualify for the city's DBE program, a business must be "a new, small

39. *Id.* § 26.47.
40. *Id.* § 26.53.
41. 49 C.F.R. § 26.29(a) (2023).
42. *Id.* § 26.29(b).
43. *EDGE Grant*, Div. of Small Bus., https://business.delaware.gov/edge/ (last visited Feb. 25, 2023).
44. *Disadvantaged Business Enterprise Program*, Off. of Econ. Dev., https://www.wilmingtonde.gov/business/minority-business-development-program (last visited Feb. 25, 2023).
45. *Id.*

or local business, whether a sole proprietorship, partnership, corporation or other entity, or any business that is at least 51 percent owned and controlled by one or more socially disadvantaged individuals who, in fact, control the management and daily business operations of that business."[46] In addition, an individual owner's net worth must be under $500,000.[47]

- *Contractor Good Faith Efforts*: Bidders must demonstrate good faith efforts to utilize DBEs when submitting their bids.[48] Failure to do so will be grounds for disqualifying the bid as nonresponsive.[49]
- *Inclusion Goals*: The city sets inclusion goals for DBEs in the following categories: (1) construction contracts have a 20 percent goal; (2) goods and services has a 10 percent goal; and (3) professional services has a 5 percent goal.[50]

---

46. City of Wilmington, Del. ch. 35, art. IV, § 35-132 (2023).
47. *Id.*
48. *Id.* at ch. 35, art. IV, § 35-135.
49. *Id.*
50. *Id.* at ch. 35, art. IV, § 35-134; *Disadvantaged Business Enterprise Program, supra* note 44.

CHAPTER 10

Florida

Overview of Business Inclusion Program, Policies, and Practices

Government entities seeking to create business inclusion programs have two primary options in terms of the type of program they may create, in terms of who is eligible for the program: (1) a race- and gender-conscious program or (2) a race- and gender-neutral program. Under the Equal Protection Clause of the Fourteenth Amendment, strict scrutiny is applied by the courts when a government actor is creating policies based on race. Strict scrutiny is the highest level of judicial review that may be applied. It requires the government actor to demonstrate that (1) past discrimination exists such that the entity has a "compelling government interest" in rectifying it, and (2) the policies and programs created to do so are "narrowly tailored."[1] Although intermediate scrutiny is often applied when reviewing programs based on gender, strict scrutiny is applied when reviewing race- and gender-conscious business inclusion programs.[2] Disparity studies have become a standard tool used to assist a government entity in withstanding a challenge to its race- and gender-conscious business inclusion programs. These studies aid in demonstrating whether a government entity has engaged

1. City of Richmond v. J.A. Croson Co., 488 U.S. 469 (1989).

2. Since the 1980s with the Supreme Court decision in *City of Richmond v. J.A. Croson Company*, there have been a number of cases across the county that have assessed race- and gender-conscious business inclusion programs. *See* Adarand Constructors, Inc. v. Pena, 515 U.S. 200 (1995); Virdi v. DeKalb Cnty. Sch. Dist., 135 Fed. App'x 262, 268 (11th Cir. 2005); Sherbrooke Turf, Inc. v. Minn. Dep't of Transp., 345 F.3d 964, 971 (8th Cir. 2003); Mountain West Holding Co., Inc. v. The State of Montana, Montana DOT, et al., 2017 WL 2179120 (9th Cir. May 16, 2017).

in past discrimination in its contracting practices, such that the entity may have a compelling government interest in rectifying it.[3]

Conversely, race- and gender-neutral programs are programs that are not only accessible to minority-owned and women-owned businesses but to all businesses, regardless of race or gender. A small business inclusion program would fall into this category. The level of judicial review applied to such a policy to determine its constitutionality is rational basis, which is the lowest threshold for a government to satisfy. For a government entity to satisfy rational basis, the policy or program created must be "related to a legitimate government purpose."[4] Even when a government entity has a race- and gender-conscious program, oftentimes the program may still require the government actor to seek to meet the goals of their program through race- and gender-neutral means where able, so as to be taking the most narrowly tailored means of accomplishing the program goals.

In the state of Florida, at the state level, there are two state entities that certify businesses for business inclusion programs: (1) the Florida Department of Management Services Office of Supplier Diversity (OSD) and (2) the Florida Department of Transportation (FDOT).

Summary of Certification Programs and Requirements

OSD certifies businesses as minority-owned businesses enterprises (MBEs), woman-owned business enterprises (WBEs), and veteran-owned business enterprises (VBEs).[5] The eligibility requirements for all are as follows:

- *Minority-Owned Business Enterprise (MBE)*: The business must (1) be based in Florida and registered to do business there; (2) be for-profit; (3) be 51 percent owned and managed by a person or persons who are minorities who are involved in the day-to-day control and financial risk of the business; (4) have owners who are Florida residents; (5) currently be doing business; (6) have a net worth less than $5 million; (7) have 200 or fewer full-time employees; (8) "[h]ave a professional license,

3. *Promoting Opportunity and Equality in America: A Guide to Federal Circuit Authority on Permissible Government Actions to Promote Racial and Gender Equality*, Am. Civ. Liberties Union & The Opportunity Agenda (Dec. 2010), https://www.aclu.org/sites/default/files/field_document/Promoting_Opportunity_and_Equality_in_America.pdf.

4. 488 U.S. 469 (1989).

5. *Get Certified*, Fla. Dep't of Mgmt. Servs. Off. of Supplier Diversity, https://www.dms.myflorida.com/agency_administration/office_of_supplier_diversity_osd/get_certified (last visited Apr. 1, 2023).

if required by the industry, in the name of the . . . minority business owner" and demonstrated expertise in their trade or profession; (9) be performing a "useful business function"; and (10) be registered in MyFloridaMarketPlace.[6]

- *Woman-Owned Business Enterprise (WBE)*: The requirements to be certified as a WBE are the same as those for an MBE except the qualifying owner must be a woman or women.[7]
- *Veteran-Owned Business Enterprise (VBE)*: A business must (1) be independently owned and operated; (2) have a net worth that is $5 million or less; (3) have 200 or fewer employees; (4) be domiciled in Florida; (5) engage in commercial transactions; (6) be 51 percent or more owned by one or more wartime veteran(s) or service-disabled veteran(s); (7) be controlled in terms of day-to-day operations and management by "one or more wartime veterans or service-disabled veterans or, for a service-disabled veteran having a permanent and total disability, by the spouse or permanent caregiver of the veteran"; and (8) be registered in MyFloridaMarketPlace.[8]

The Florida Department of Transportation (FDOT) administers the Disadvantaged Business Enterprise (DBE) program and Airport Concession Disadvantaged Business Enterprise (ACDBE) program.

- *Disadvantaged Business Enterprise (DBE) Program*: Pursuant to 49 C.F.R. part 26 FDOT administers the state's DBE certification program. As is required under 49 C.F.R. § 26.81, Florida has a Unified Certification Program (UCP). The UCP makes all DBE certification decisions and provides a "one-stop shop" to DBE applicants.[9] To qualify as a DBE, a business must (1) be for-profit;[10] (2) be a small business concern—with "small" determined by the Small Business Administration (SBA) small business size standards and does not exceed $30.40 million in gross annual receipts;[11] (3) be at least 51 percent owned by socially and economically disadvantaged individuals—there is a rebuttable presumption that women, Black Americans, Hispanic Americans, Native Americans, Asian-Pacific

6. *Id.*; Fla. Admin. Code Ann. r. 60A-9.005 (1996); Fla. Stat. § 287.0943(2)(e) (2022).
7. *Get Certified*, *supra* note 5.
8. Fla. Stat. § 295.187(3)(c) (2022); *Get Certified*, *supra* note 5.
9. 49 C.F.R. § 26.81(b)(2) (2022).
10. *Id.* § 26.5.
11. *Id.* §§ 26.5, 26.65(b). It is worth noting that under 49 C.F.R. § 26.65(b), the DBE size standard may be adjusted annually for inflation such that in subsequent years the size standard may no longer be $30.40 million.

Americans, Subcontinent Asian Americans, or other minorities are disadvantaged;[12] (4) be controlled by one or more of the socially and economically disadvantaged owners;[13] (5) have the socially and economically disadvantaged owners be U.S. citizens or lawfully admitted permanent residents;[14] and (6) have the personal net worth for any socially and economically disadvantaged owner not exceed $1.32 million.[15] The DBE program is required on contracting opportunities that have received funding from the Federal Highway Administration (FHWA), Federal Aviation Administration (FAA), or Federal Transit Administration (FTA).[16]

- *Airport Concession Disadvantaged Business Enterprise (ACDBE) Program*: In addition to being certified as a DBE under 49 C.F.R. part 26, businesses may also be certified as an Airport Concession Disadvantaged Business Enterprise (ACDBE) under 49 C.F.R. part 23. To qualify as an ACDBE, a business must (1) be a concession for-profit small business concern;[17] (2) qualify as small by having its prior three-year average gross receipts not exceed the applicable size standard of $56.42 million;[18] (3) be 51 percent owned by one or more socially and economically disadvantaged individuals;[19] (4) have one or more of the socially and economically disadvantaged individuals with control and managing the daily business operations;[20] and (5) have the personal net worth for any socially and economically disadvantaged owner not exceed $1.32 million.[21]

Procurement Laws Intersecting with Business Inclusion

In terms of procurement laws and administrative rules that intersect with business inclusion laws and administrative rules, previously

12. *Id.* § 26.67.
13. *Id.* § 26.5.
14. *Id.* § 26.67.
15. *Id.*
16. *Id.* § 26.21(a).
17. *Id.* § 23.3.
18. *Id.* § 23.33(a). The size standards for the following are exceptions to this: bank and financial institutions is $1 billion in assets; car rental companies are $75.23 million average annual gross receipts; pay telephones is 1,500 employees; and automobile dealers is 350 employees.
19. *Id.*
20. *Id.*
21. *Id.* § 23.35.

contracting goals and utilization plan requirements existed.[22] However, over the last 10 to 20 years, a number of such laws and rules have been repealed.[23] As a result, at this time no agency aspirational goals, contracting goals, or set-asides are established for MBEs, WBEs, or VBEs.[24] Despite this, the Office of Supplier Diversity does still engage in certifying businesses, leading a number of outreach events, and tracking agency spends with certified businesses.

- *Monitoring Reporting Requirements*: Under Florida Statutes section 287.09451, the Office of Supplier Diversity "monitor[s] the degree to which agencies procure services, commodities, and construction from minority business enterprises in conjunction with the Department of Financial Services . . ." and "establish[es] a system to record and measure the use of certified minority business enterprises in state contracting."

Contracting opportunities where the FDOT DBE program applies have several requirements that intersect directly with procurement, contracting, and business inclusion.

- *Fostering Small Business Participation*: Pursuant to 49 C.F.R. § 26.39, FDOT has engaged in efforts to foster small business participation.[25] These efforts are race neutral.[26] In 2006, FDOT implemented "a Business Development Initiative (BDI) to cultivate small businesses by providing them opportunities and support to move from subcontracting and sub-consulting to prime contracting and consulting roles."[27] The program may set aside contracts for small businesses.[28] A business must satisfy the following criteria to be eligible for the program: "(1) Meet the small business definition as defined by FDOT. (2) Submit a notarized affidavit on a form provided by FDOT attesting to meeting the definition of a small business. (3) Provide a listing

---

22. Executive Order 99-281 noted that state agencies could no longer use "racial or gender set-asides, preferences, or quotas or artificial, arbitrary goals" in state contracting. This impacted existing statutes and rules related to contracting goals, preferences and set asides. This, in addition to Executive Order 11-01, which sought to remove any "duplicative" administrative rules, contributed to the repeal of a number of administrative rules per state agency pertaining to minority business utilization and goals.

23. *Id.*

24. *Id.*

25. *Disadvantage Business Enterprise Program Plan*, Fla. Dep't of Transp. 20–21 (2019), https://fdotwww.blob.core.windows.net/sitefinity/docs/default-source/equalopporunity/dbeprogram/dbe-program-plan0208008ad2b948889d591795932ab4a6.pdf.

26. *Id.*

27. *Id.*

28. Fla. Stat. § 337.027 (2022).

of contracts on which the firm has performed either as a prime or subcontractor or sub-consultant."[29]

- *Goals*: Contract opportunities may not use quotas or set-asides for DBEs.[30] The only exception for using a set-aside is in a limited or extreme circumstance, "when no other method could be reasonably expected to redress egregious instances of discrimination."[31] Instead, an overall goal must be set.[32] The goal must be based on evidence of available "ready, willing and able" DBEs in the market.[33] Once the assessment of "ready, willing and able" DBEs is completed, an overall goal may be established as a percentage of the total amount of contracts receiving U.S. Department of Transportation (U.S. DOT) funds.[34] Participation goals must be set for all certified DBEs and not divided into subcategories.[35] Race- and gender-neutral means must be used to "meet the maximum feasible portion of your overall goal."[36] FDOT, as a recipient of U.S. DOT funds, will not be penalized for failing to meet the overall goal set, if it can establish good faith efforts to meet the goal.[37] When there is a DBE goal on a specific contract opportunity only the bidder meeting the goal, or establishing good faith efforts to meet the goal, may be awarded the contract.[38]
- *Prompt Payment*: Under 49 C.F.R. part 26, contractors must pay subcontractors within 30 days of receipt of payment from the state DOT for satisfactory performance.[39]
- *Payment of Retainage*: Contractors must pay amounts withheld for retainage to subcontractors within 30 days of their work being satisfactorily completed.[40]

Additional Related Laws, Policies, and Programs

- *Outreach and Technical Assistance*: OSD engages in a number of outreach activities for MBEs, WBEs, and VBEs, such as its

29. *Disadvantage Business Enterprise Program Plan*, *supra* note 25, at 21.
30. 49 C.F.R. § 26.43 (2022).
31. *Id.* § 26.43.
32. *Id.* § 26.45(a)(1).
33. *Id.* § 26.45(b).
34. *Id.* § 26.45(e).
35. *Id.* § 26.45(h).
36. *Id.* § 26.51.
37. *Id.* § 26.47.
38. *Id.* § 26.53.
39. 49 C.F.R. § 26.29(a) (2023).
40. *Id.* § 26.29(b).

Supplier Diversity Exchanges[41] and "[a]ssisting agencies and contractors by providing outreach to minority businesses, by specifying and monitoring technical and managerial competence for minority business enterprises, and by consulting in planning of agency procurement to determine how best to provide opportunities for minority business enterprises."[42]

- *Prompt Payment to Subcontractors*: In terms of timely payment to subcontractors on purchases of construction services, Florida law states: "When a contractor receives payment from a public entity for labor, services, or materials furnished by subcontractors and suppliers hired by the contractor, the contractor shall remit payment due to those subcontractors and suppliers within 10 days after the contractor's receipt of payment. When a subcontractor receives payment from a contractor for labor, services, or materials furnished by subcontractors and suppliers hired by the subcontractor, the subcontractor shall remit payment due to those subcontractors and suppliers within 7 days after the subcontractor's receipt of payment."[43]
- *Finding Contract Opportunities*: The Florida Department of Management Services posts current bid opportunities here: https://www.dms.myflorida.com/agency_administration/office_of_supplier_diversity_osd/vendor_resources2/current_bid_opportunities. In addition, Florida's e-Procurement system, MyFloridaMarketPlace (MFMP), is found here: https://vendor.myfloridamarketplace.com/.

Major City Snapshot: Tallahassee

The City of Tallahassee completed a disparity study in 2019 and adopted a consolidated Minority & Women Small Business Enterprise (MWSBE) policy between the City of Tallahassee, Leon County government, and Blueprint Intergovernmental Agency in 2020.[44]

41. *FY 2020-2021 Office of Supplier Diversity Annual Report*, FLA. DEP'T OF MGMT. SERVS. OFF. OF SUPPLIER DIVERSITY 4, https://www.dms.myflorida.com/content/download/156667/1039427/OfficeofSupplierDiversityAnnualReportFY2020-21.pdf (last visited Apr. 1, 2023).

42. FLA. STAT. § 287.09451 (2022).

43. *Id.* § 255.073(3).

44. *Minority Business Enterprise*, CITY OF TALLAHASSEE, https://www.talgov.com/doingbusiness/mbe (last visited Apr. 1, 2023); *Minority & Women Small Business Enterprise Policy*, OFF. OF ECON. VITALITY 3 (2020), https://oevforbusiness.org/Wp-Content/Uploads/MWSBE-Policy-2020_1.pdf.

- *Certifications*: The program certifies minority business enterprises (MBEs), women business enterprises (WBEs), and small business enterprises (SBEs).[45]
- *Solicitations, Utilization Plans, and Contractor Good Faith Efforts*: When evaluating MWBE participation on projects assigned a goal, responses to solicitations are reviewed to ensure there is a completed MWBE participation plan and/or good faith efforts.[46] Failure to meet the requirements of the solicitation pertaining to the MWBE project-specific goals and including the proper documentation may be deemed nonresponsive.[47]
- *Inclusion Goals*: The MWBE program has aspirational MBE and WBE goals based on the 2019 disparity study market availability and procurement categories.[48] In addition to the aspirational goals, project specific goals are also set.[49]
- *Contracting Set Asides*: Contracts valued at $150,000 or less may be reserved for competition only among certified SBEs.[50]
- *Reporting Requirements*: Prime contractors and consultants have a responsibility to make information available on a monthly basis pertaining to their efforts to advance the MWSBE inclusion.[51] Annually, the MWSBE division compiles a report based on information submitted by prime contractors and consultants.[52]

45. *Id.* at 39.
46. *Id.* at 19.
47. *Id.*
48. *Id.* at 15.
49. *Id.*
50. *Id.* at 26.
51. *Id.* at 38.
52. *Id.*

CHAPTER 11

Georgia

Overview of Business Inclusion Program, Policies, and Practices

Government entities seeking to create business inclusion programs have two primary options in terms of the type of program they may create, in terms of who is eligible for the program: (1) a race- and gender-conscious program or (2) a race- and gender-neutral program. Under the Equal Protection Clause of the Fourteenth Amendment, strict scrutiny is applied by the courts when a government actor is creating policies based on race. Strict scrutiny is the highest level of judicial review that may be applied. It requires the government actor to demonstrate that (1) past discrimination exists such that the entity has a "compelling government interest" in rectifying it, and (2) the policies and programs created to do so are "narrowly tailored."[1] Although intermediate scrutiny is often applied when reviewing programs based on gender, strict scrutiny is applied when reviewing race- and gender-conscious business inclusion programs.[2] Disparity studies have become a standard tool used to assist a government entity in withstanding a challenge to its race- and gender-conscious business inclusion programs. These studies aid in demonstrating whether a government entity has engaged

1. City of Richmond v. J.A. Croson Co., 488 U.S. 469 (1989).

2. Since the 1980s with the Supreme Court decision in *City of Richmond v. J.A. Croson Company*, there have been a number of cases across the county that have assessed race- and gender-conscious business inclusion programs. *See* Adarand Constructors, Inc. v. Pena, 515 U.S. 200 (1995); Virdi v. DeKalb Cnty. Sch. Dist., 135 Fed. App'x 262, 268 (11th Cir. 2005); Sherbrooke Turf, Inc. v. Minn. Dep't of Transp., 345 F.3d 964, 971 (8th Cir. 2003); Mountain West Holding Co., Inc. v. The State of Montana, Montana DOT, et al., 2017 WL 2179120 (9th Cir. May 16, 2017).

in past discrimination in its contracting practices, such that the entity may have a compelling government interest in rectifying it.[3]

Conversely, race- and gender-neutral programs are programs that are not only accessible to minority-owned and women-owned businesses but to all businesses, regardless of race or gender. A small business inclusion program would fall into this category. The level of judicial review applied to such a policy to determine its constitutionality is rational basis, which is the lowest threshold for a government to satisfy. For a government entity to satisfy rational basis, the policy or program created must be "related to a legitimate government purpose."[4] Even when a government entity has a race- and gender-conscious program, oftentimes the program may still require the government actor to seek to meet the goals of their program through race- and gender-neutral means where able, so as to be taking the most narrowly tailored means of accomplishing the program goals.

In the state of Georgia, there is a collaboration between the Georgia Department of Administrative Services (DOAS) and Georgia Department of Transportation (GDOT) regarding certification of businesses.[5] This collaboration allows for, as a first step, a business seeking to be certified as a disadvantaged business enterprise (DBE) to first get certified with GDOT.[6] Then, that business may also be able to be certified as a minority business enterprise with DOAS without having to submit another application.[7]

Summary of Certification Programs and Requirements

In terms of small business and diverse business certifications in the state of Georgia, at the state level, there are the following: (1) a small business election (not a certification); (2) a minority business enterprise (MBE) certification; (3) a DBE certification; (4) an Airport Concession Disadvantaged Business Enterprise (ACDBE) certification; and (5) GDOT's SBE program to foster small business participation under 49 C.F.R. § 26.39. Businesses owned by women may be certified as DBEs and ACDBEs, as noted later in the chapter. The bullet points that

3. *Promoting Opportunity and Equality in America: A Guide to Federal Circuit Authority on Permissible Government Actions to Promote Racial and Gender Equality*, Am. Civ. Liberties Union & The Opportunity Agenda (Dec. 2010), https://www.aclu.org/sites/default/files/field_document/Promoting_Opportunity_and_Equality_in_America.pdf.

4. 488 U.S. 469 (1989).

5. *Minority Business Enterprise Certification*, Dep't of Admin. Servs., https://doas.ga.gov/state-purchasing/supplier-services/minority-business-enterprise-certification (last visited Feb. 15, 2023).

6. *Id.*

7. *Id.*

directly follow outline the eligibility requirements for each. Currently, there is no specific women-owned, veteran-owned, disability-owned, or LGBT-owned business certification in Georgia specific to public sector government certifications, contracting, or state law. However, in a 2022 report by DOAS entitled *Small Business and Supplier Diversity Initiative Report*, DOAS makes recommendations to the governor to expand its small and diverse business certifications to include certifications for the following: small businesses, veteran-owned businesses, and women-owned businesses; however, to date these recommendations have not yet been acted upon.

- *Small Business*: Georgia does not have a small business enterprise (SBE) certification.[8] However, a business may designate themselves as a small business within the DOAS supplier registration located here: https://doas.ga.gov/state-purchasing/team-georgia-marketplace/tgm-resources-for-suppliers. Under Georgia law, a small business is defined as (1) a business that is "independently owned and operated"; (2) "Tier one: has ten or fewer employees or $1 million or less in gross receipts per year"; "Tier two: has 100 or fewer employees or $10 million or less in gross receipts per year"; or "Tier three: has 300 or fewer employees or $30 million or less in gross receipts per year."[9] Small businesses are eligible for various preferences such as those listed in the next section.
- *Georgia Resident Business and Georgia Resident Small Business*: A business that meets the following criteria will be considered a Georgia Resident Business: (1) the business maintains a space regularly in Georgia from which business is physically conducted and has done so for a year prior to bidding on a state contracting opportunity; and (2) for a new business, the business must be domiciled in Georgia and the location from which business is conducted cannot be a mail box, P.O. box, site trailer, or temporary structure.[10] If a business meets the requirements of a small business and a Georgia Resident Business, it qualifies to be considered as a Georgia Resident Small Business.[11]

---

8. *Get Certified*, GA. DEP'T OF ECON. DEV., https://www.georgia.org/small-business/start/certification (last visited Feb. 15, 2023).
9. GA. CODE ANN. § 50-5-121 (2022).
10. *Id.* § 50-5-121.
11. *Georgia Procurement Manual*, DEP'T OF ADMIN. SERVS. 12 (July 2022), https://doas.ga.gov/assets/State%20Purchasing/GPM%20Documents/GPM%20V10%20July%202022.pdf.

- *Minority Business Enterprise (MBE)*: A business that meets the following definition is considered a minority business enterprise: (1) a small business concern; (2) authorized to do business in Georgia; (3) paying Georgia taxes; (4) domiciled in Georgia; (5) 51 percent owned by one or more minorities, or 51 percent of its stocks owned by minorities if publicly traded; (6) one or more minorities controls the management and daily business operations.[12] Minorities, under the Official Code of Georgia, Annotated, section 50-5-131, is defined as "an individual who is a member of a race which comprises less than 50 percent of the total population of the state."[13] A business may become certified as a minority business enterprise by submitting its application and all required documents[14] through the unified certification process that exists between GDOT and DOAS.[15] This process has businesses first submit their application for a DBE certification with GDOT, and through this application, DOAS is able to capture all the information it needs.[16] This process is intended to minimize duplication for applicants.[17] If a business is denied certification, the business may appeal the decision.[18]
- *Disadvantaged Business Enterprise (DBE)*: Pursuant to 49 C.F.R. part 26, the GDOT administers the state's DBE certification program. As is required under 49 C.F.R. § 26.81, Georgia has a Unified Certification Program (GUCP). The GUCP consists of GDOT and the Metropolitan Atlanta Rapid Transit Authority (MARTA).[19] The UCP makes all DBE certification decisions and provides a "one-stop shop" to DBE applicants.[20] To qualify as a DBE, a business must (1) be for-profit;[21] (2) be a small business concern—with "small" determined by the Small Business Administration (SBA) small business size standards and does not exceed $30.40 million in gross annual receipts;[22] (3) be

12. Ga. Code Ann. § 50-5-131 (2022).
13. *Id.*
14. *Id.* § 50-5-132.
15. *Minority Business Enterprise Certification*, *supra* note 5.
16. *Id.*
17. *Id.*
18. *Id.*
19. *Disadvantaged Business Enterprise*, Ga. Dep't of Transp., https://www.dot.ga.gov/GDOT/Pages/DBE.aspx (last visited Feb. 15, 2023).
20. 49 C.F.R. § 26.81(b)(2) (2022).
21. *Id.* § 26.5.
22. *Id.* §§ 26.5, 26.65(b). It is worth noting that under 49 C.F.R. § 26.65(b), the DBE size standard may be adjusted annually for inflation such that in subsequent years the size standard may no longer be $30.40 million.

at least 51 percent owned by socially and economically disadvantaged individuals—there is a rebuttable presumption that women, Black Americans, Hispanic Americans, Native Americans, Asian-Pacific Americans, Subcontinent Asian Americans, or other minorities are disadvantaged;[23] (4) be controlled by one or more of the socially and economically disadvantaged owners;[24] (5) have the socially and economically disadvantaged owners be U.S. citizens or lawfully admitted permanent residents;[25] and (6) have the personal net worth for any socially and economically disadvantaged owner not exceed $1.32 million.[26] The DBE program is required on contracting opportunities that have received funding from the Federal Highway Administration (FHWA), Federal Aviation Administration (FAA), or Federal Transit Administration (FTA).[27]

- *Airport Concession Disadvantaged Business Enterprise (ACDBE)*: In addition to being certified as a DBE under 49 C.F.R. part 26, businesses may also be certified as an Airport Concession Disadvantaged Business Enterprise (ACDBE) under 49 C.F.R. part 23. To qualify as an ACDBE, a business must (1) be a concession for-profit small business concern;[28] (2) qualify as small by having its prior three-year average gross receipts not exceed the applicable size standard of $56.42 million;[29] (3) be 51 percent owned by one or more socially and economically disadvantaged individuals;[30] (4) have one or more of the socially and economically disadvantaged individuals with control and managing the daily business operations;[31] and (5) have the personal net worth for any socially and economically disadvantaged owner not exceed $1.32 million.[32]
- *GDOT Small Business Enterprise (SBE) Program*: Per GDOT's last posted DBE plan, it has implemented a small business enterprise program within its DBE program for SBE certification

23. *Id.* § 26.67.
24. *Id.* § 26.5.
25. *Id.* § 26.67.
26. *Id.*
27. *Id.* § 26.21(a).
28. *Id.* § 23.3.
29. *Id.* § 23.33(a). The size standards for the following are exceptions to this: bank and financial institutions is $1 billion in assets; car rental companies are $75.23 million average annual gross receipts; pay telephones is 1,500 employees; and automobile dealers is 350 employees.
30. *Id.*
31. *Id.*
32. *Id.* § 23.35.

and inclusion, pursuant to 49 C.F.R. § 26.39.[33] To be eligible for the program, a business must (1) be a small business under the Small Business Administration size standards; (2) not exceed any additional program size standards that may be adjusted periodically for inflation; (3) be for-profit; (4) have a place of business in the United States; (5) be independently owned and operated; and (6) not be dominant in its field of operation.[34]

Procurement Laws Intersecting with Business Inclusion

Procurement laws for the state of Georgia may largely be found in section 50-5 of the Official Code of Georgia, Annotated.[35] State laws and regulations pertaining to small businesses and minority businesses, as they relate to state purchasing, may primarily be found in sections 50-5-120 to 50-5-124 (Small Business Assistance) and sections 50-5-130 to 50-5-133 (Minority Business Enterprise Development).

- *Tied Bids Preference for Small Businesses*: The Georgia Procurement Manual notes that in resolving a tied bid, the State of Georgia has a preference for the following: (1) "products manufactured or produced . . . in Georgia"; (2) "products sold by local suppliers . . ."; and (3) "products manufactured or sold by small businesses."[36]
- *Price Match and Five Percent Points*: Businesses that are small businesses, Georgia Resident Businesses, and Georgia Resident Small Businesses may qualify for a price match or 5 percent of the available points when competing for bids or submitting a response to a Request for Proposals (RFP) or Request for Qualified Contractors (RFQC).
- *Language in Solicitations*: If the issuing officer (person responsible for all aspects of the solicitation process)[37] determines it is appropriate, based on relevant market data, they may include a statement in the solicitation pertaining to encouraging

33. *Georgia Unified Certification Program Disadvantage Business Enterprise 2019 Program Plan*, Ga. Dep't of Transp. 87 (2019), https://www.dot.ga.gov/PartnerSmart/Business/Documents/Plan/Disadvantaged%20Business%20Enterprise%202019%20Program%20Plan-Signed.pdf.

34. *Id.*

35. *Purchasing Law, Administrative Rules, and Policies*, Dep't of Admin. Servs., https://doas.ga.gov/state-purchasing/law-administrative-rules-and-policies (last visited Feb. 15, 2023).

36. *Georgia Procurement Manual*, *supra* note 11, at 141.

37. *Id.* at 98.

participation of small businesses, Georgia Resident Businesses, and Georgia Resident Small Businesses.[38]

- *Inclusion Goals*: Under Georgia law, there are no contracting goals set for MBE participation.[39] There is, however, a tax deduction available for contractors subcontracting to minority businesses. Additional details pertaining to the tax deduction follow.
- *Tax Deduction*: Under the Official Code of Georgia, Annotated, section 48-7-38, it states that "[i]n computing Georgia taxable net income of a corporation, partnership, or individual, there shall be subtracted from federal taxable income or federal adjusted gross income 10 percent of the amount of qualified payments to minority subcontractors." The minority subcontractor must be certified with DOAS.[40]
- *Reporting Requirements*: Under the Official Code of Georgia, Annotated, section 50-5-122, "Every state agency, office, board, bureau, commission, public corporation, institution, authority, or other entity of this state, including but not limited to the Department of Labor and the Department of Revenue, is authorized to provide data related to Georgia resident businesses and small businesses to the [Department of Administrative Services]. . . ."

Contracting opportunities where the GDOT DBE program applies have several requirements that intersect directly with procurement, contracting, and business inclusion.

- *Goals*: Contract opportunities may not use quotas or set-asides for DBEs.[41] The only exception for using a set-aside is in a limited or extreme circumstance, "when no other method could be reasonably expected to redress egregious instances of discrimination."[42] Instead, an overall goal must be set.[43] The goal must be based on evidence of available "ready, willing and able" DBEs in the market.[44] Once the assessment of "ready, willing and able" DBEs is completed, an overall goal may be established as a percentage of the total amount of contracts receiving U.S. Department

38. *Id.* at 80.
39. *Small Business and Supplier Diversity Initiative Report*, Dep't of Admin. Servs. 21 (Oct. 2022), https://doas.ga.gov/assets/State%20Purchasing/SMALL%20BUSINESS%20RESOURCES/Georgia%20DOAS%20SBSD%20Initiative%20Report%20103122.pdf.
40. Ga. Code Ann. § 48-7-38(d) (2022).
41. 49 C.F.R. § 26.43 (2022).
42. *Id.* § 26.43.
43. *Id.* § 26.45(a)(1).
44. *Id.* § 26.45(b).

of Transportation (U.S. DOT) funds.[45] Participation goals must be set for all certified DBEs and not divided into subcategories.[46] Race- and gender-neutral means must be used to "meet the maximum feasible portion of your overall goal."[47] GDOT, as a recipient of U.S. DOT funds, will not be penalized for failing to meet the overall goal set, if it can establish good faith efforts to meet the goal.[48] When there is a DBE goal on a specific contract opportunity, only the bidder meeting the goal, or establishing good faith efforts to meet the goal, may be awarded the contract.[49]

- *Prompt Payment*: Under 49 C.F.R. part 26, contractors must pay subcontractors within 30 days of receipt of payment from the state DOT for satisfactory performance.[50]
- *Payment of Retainage*: Contractors must pay amounts withheld for retainage to subcontractors within 30 days of their work being satisfactorily completed.[51]

Additional Related Laws, Policies, and Programs

- *Prompt Payment to Small Businesses*: Under the Georgia Prompt Payment Act, owners, which is inclusive of state, local, or municipal government entities, must pay contractors within 15 days of a request for payment, when work has been performed in accordance to the contract.[52] In addition, contractors must pay subcontractors who have performed satisfactorily within 15 days from the request for payment.[53] Although there is no specific language related to prompt payment for small and diverse businesses, this does impact such businesses when contracting in the State of Georgia.
- *Access to Capital*: The Georgia Department of Economic Development lists resources pertaining to loans and grants available to small and diverse businesses from various resources on the following sites on their website: https://www.georgia.org/small-business/grow and https://www.georgia.org/small-business/finance/federal-grants-and-loans.

---

45. *Id.* § 26.45(e).
46. *Id.* § 26.45(h).
47. *Id.* § 26.51.
48. *Id.* § 26.47.
49. *Id.* § 26.53.
50. 49 C.F.R. § 26.29(a) (2023).
51. *Id.* § 26.29(b).
52. Ga. Code Ann. § 13-11-4(a) (2022).
53. *Id.* § 13-11-4(b).

- *Technical Assistance*: One example of technical assistance provided at the state level includes GDOT's Supportive Services program, which is available to assist DBEs through one-to-one assistance, training, and resources.[54]
- *Finding Contract Opportunities*: Information on bids and contract opportunities may be found on DOAS's website: https://doas.ga.gov/state-purchasing/supplier-services/bids-and-contracts. In addition, the Team Georgia Marketplace, the electronic procurement system, may be found here: https://fscm.teamworks.georgia.gov/psc/supp/SUPPLIER/ERP/c/NUI_FRAMEWORK.PT_LANDINGPAGE.GBL?&.

Major City Snapshot: Atlanta

The City of Atlanta has a business inclusion program and offers the following types of certifications:[55] (1) African American Business Enterprise (AABE), Asian (Pacific Islander) American Business Enterprise (APABE), Female Business Enterprise (FBE), Hispanic American Business Enterprise (HABE), Native American Business Enterprise (NABE), and Small Business Enterprise (SBE). All ordinances pertaining to the city's business inclusion programs may be found in the Equal Business Opportunity Program (chapter 2, article X, division 12 of the code of ordinances) and Small Business Opportunity Program (chapter 2, article X, division 9 of the code of ordinances) divisions of the city's code of ordinances. Following are a few highlights regarding the programs:

- *Participation Goal*: The city does set subcontracting participation goals on a contract-by-contract basis for SBE inclusion.[56] The goal set is up to 35 percent and the goal may be lowered or eliminated.[57]
- *Good Faith Efforts*: In solicitations that have an SBE participation goal, if a bidder fails to demonstrate meeting that goal, then the bidder must provide documentation with evidence of their good faith efforts to meet the goal.[58]

---

54. *DBE Supportive Services*, GA. DEP'T OF TRANSP., https://www.gadbesupport.com/ (last visited Feb. 15, 2023).

55. Equal Business Opportunity Program (chapter 2, article X, division 12 of the code of ordinances) and Small Business Opportunity Program (chapter 2, article X, division 9 of the code of ordinances). ATLANTA, GA., CODE ch. 2, art. X, div. 12 (2023); *id.* at ch. 2, art. X, div. 9.

56. *Id.* at ch. 2, art. X, div. 9; ch. 2, art. X, div. 9 § 2-1362(a).

57. *Id.*

58. *Id.* at ch. 2, art. X, div. 9 § 2-1371.

- *Bidding Documents and Responsiveness*: Under the Equal Business Opportunity Program, section 2-1448, a bidder must submit specific documentation with its bid related to the Equal Business Opportunity Program to be considered a responsive bidder.
- *Sheltered Market*: The sheltered market allows for certain procurements to be designated as a sheltered market procurement opportunity.[59] Depending on the dollar threshold for the procurement opportunity, it may allow for instances where SBEs are only competing with other SBEs for the contracting opportunity.[60]

59. *Id.* at ch. 2, art. X, div. 9; ch. 2, art. X, div. 9 § 2-1362(b).
60. *Id.*

CHAPTER 12

Hawaii

Overview of Business Inclusion Program, Policies, and Practices

Government entities seeking to create business inclusion programs have two primary options in terms of the type of program they may create, in terms of who is eligible for the program: (1) a race- and gender-conscious program or (2) a race- and gender-neutral program. Under the Equal Protection Clause of the Fourteenth Amendment, strict scrutiny is applied by the courts when a government actor is creating policies based on race. Strict scrutiny is the highest level of judicial review that may be applied. It requires the government actor to demonstrate that (1) past discrimination exists such that the entity has a "compelling government interest" in rectifying it, and (2) the policies and programs created to do so are "narrowly tailored".[1] Although intermediate scrutiny is often applied when reviewing programs based on gender, strict scrutiny is applied when reviewing race- and gender-conscious business inclusion programs.[2] Disparity studies have become a standard tool used to assist a government entity in withstanding a challenge to its race- and gender-conscious business inclusion programs. These studies aid in demonstrating whether a government entity has engaged

1. City of Richmond v. J.A. Croson Co., 488 U.S. 469 (1989).

2. Since the 1980s with the Supreme Court decision in *City of Richmond v. J.A. Croson Company*, there have been a number of cases across the county that have assessed race- and gender-conscious business inclusion programs. *See* Adarand Constructors, Inc. v. Pena, 515 U.S. 200 (1995); Virdi v. DeKalb Cnty. Sch. Dist., 135 Fed. App'x 262, 268 (11th Cir. 2005); Sherbrooke Turf, Inc. v. Minn. Dep't of Transp., 345 F.3d 964, 971 (8th Cir. 2003); Mountain West Holding Co., Inc. v. The State of Montana, Montana DOT, et al., 2017 WL 2179120 (9th Cir. May 16, 2017).

in past discrimination in its contracting practices, such that the entity may have a compelling government interest in rectifying it.[3]

Conversely, race- and gender-neutral programs are programs that are not only accessible to minority-owned and women-owned businesses but to all businesses, regardless of race or gender. A small business inclusion program would fall into this category. The level of judicial review applied to such a policy to determine its constitutionality is rational basis, which is the lowest threshold for a government to satisfy. For a government entity to satisfy rational basis, the policy or program created must be "related to a legitimate government purpose."[4] Even when a government entity has a race- and gender-conscious program, oftentimes the program may still require the government actor to seek to meet the goals of their program through race- and gender-neutral means where able, so as to be taking the most narrowly tailored means of accomplishing the program goals.

In the state of Hawaii, at the state level of government, there are two main entities certifying businesses for business inclusion programs or more deeply engaged in efforts related to this: (1) the State Procurement Office and (2) the Hawaii Department of Transportation (HDOT).

Summary of Certification Programs and Requirements

The Small Business Assistance Program was not a certification program, but rather a program that came into play when the Office of Procurement engaged in specific types of purchases. This program existed several years ago but was terminated in more recent years.[5] In 2022, the legislature passed a Small Business Initiative with related efforts to start in 2023.[6]

Additional details on HDOT's business inclusion programs are noted next:

- *Disadvantaged Business Enterprise (DBE) Program*: Pursuant to 49 C.F.R. part 26, HDOT administers the state's DBE certification program. As is required under 49 C.F.R. § 26.81, Hawaii has a Unified Certification Program (UCP). The UCP makes all DBE certification decisions and provides a "one-stop shop" to

3. *Promoting Opportunity and Equality in America: A Guide to Federal Circuit Authority on Permissible Government Actions to Promote Racial and Gender Equality*, Am. Civ. Liberties Union & The Opportunity Agenda (Dec. 2010), https://www.aclu.org/sites/default/files/field_document/Promoting_Opportunity_and_Equality_in_America.pdf.

4. 488 U.S. 469 (1989).

5. This was confirmed through outreach to state agencies.

6. *Id.*

DBE applicants.[7] To qualify as a DBE, a business must (1) be for-profit;[8] (2) be a small business concern—with "small" determined by the Small Business Administration (SBA) small business size standards and does not exceed $30.40 million in gross annual receipts;[9] (3) be at least 51 percent owned by socially and economically disadvantaged individuals—there is a rebuttable presumption that women, Black Americans, Hispanic Americans, Native Americans, Asian-Pacific Americans, Subcontinent Asian Americans, or other minorities are disadvantaged;[10] (4) be controlled by one or more of the socially and economically disadvantaged owners;[11] (5) have the socially and economically disadvantaged owners be U.S. citizens or lawfully admitted permanent residents;[12] and (6) have the personal net worth for any socially and economically disadvantaged owner not exceed $1.32 million.[13] The DBE program is required on contracting opportunities that have received funding from the Federal Highway Administration (FHWA), Federal Aviation Administration (FAA), or Federal Transit Administration (FTA).[14]

- *Airport Concession Disadvantaged Business Enterprise (ACDBE)*: In addition to being certified as a DBE under 49 C.F.R. part 26, businesses may also be certified as an Airport Concession Disadvantaged Business Enterprise (ACDBE) under 49 C.F.R. part 23. To qualify as an ACDBE, a business must (1) be a concession for-profit small business concern;[15] (2) qualify as small by having its prior three-year average gross receipts not exceed the applicable size standard of $56.42 million;[16] (3) be 51 percent owned by one or more socially and economically disadvantaged individuals;[17] (4) have one or more of the socially and economically disadvantaged individuals with control and

7. 49 C.F.R. § 26.81(b)(2) (2022).
8. *Id.* § 26.5.
9. *Id.* §§ 26.5, 26.65(b). It is worth noting that under 49 C.F.R. § 26.65(b), the DBE size standard may be adjusted annually for inflation such that in subsequent years the size standard may no longer be $30.40 million.
10. *Id.* § 26.67.
11. *Id.* § 26.5.
12. *Id.* § 26.67.
13. *Id.*
14. *Id.* § 26.21(a).
15. *Id.* § 23.3.
16. *Id.* § 23.33(a). The size standards for the following are exceptions to this: bank and financial institutions is $1 billion in assets; car rental companies are $75.23 million average annual gross receipts; pay telephones is 1,500 employees; and automobile dealers is 350 employees.
17. *Id.*

managing the daily business operations;[18] and (5) have the personal net worth for any socially and economically disadvantaged owner not exceed $1.32 million.[19]

- *Small Business Participation*: HDOT piloted a small business enterprise (SBE) program as a race- and gender-neutral program that included SBE contract goal setting and an SBE set-aside, pursuant to 49 C.F.R. § 26.39.[20] The program expired in May of 2022.[21] To be eligible for the program a business must (1) be a small business under the Small Business Administration size standards; (2) for purposes of being considered a DBE for the FHWA and FTA, the business must have average annual gross receipts from the prior three fiscal years that do not exceed the average gross receipts cap in 49 C.F.R. § 26.65(b); (3) be for-profit; (4) majority owners must be U.S. citizens or lawful permanent residents and exhibit control over the business; and (5) the majority owner must have a personal net worth that does not exceed $1.32 million.[22]

Procurement Laws Intersecting with Business Inclusion

In the state of Hawaii, procurement laws and rules may primarily be found within the following: Hawaii Revised Statutes, sections 103D and 103F, and Hawaii Administrative Rules, title 3.[23] Following are some laws that pertain to small businesses.

- *Solicitations*: Procurements that are set aside for small businesses must include the set-aside solicitation provisions.[24]
- *Prompt Payment*: Although there is no a specific law related to prompt payment for small businesses or diverse businesses, contractors are required to pay subcontractors within 10 days after receipt of money.[25]

---

18. *Id.*
19. *Id.* § 23.35.
20. *Disadvantaged Business Enterprise 2021 Program Plan*, Haw. Dep't of Transp. 21 (Oct. 2021), https://hidot.hawaii.gov/administration/files/2022/02/DBE-PROG-PLAN-2021-REV-1.28.22-part-1-signed.pdf.
21. *Id.*
22. *Id.* at Attachment E,4.
23. *Introduction to State Procurement Office: Procurement Wizard*, State Procurement Off., https://spo.hawaii.gov/procurement-wizard/manual/introduction/ (last visited Feb. 28, 2023).
24. Haw. Admin. R. § 3-124, Dep't of Acct. & Gen. Servs. (July 2009), https://spo.hawaii.gov/wp-content/uploads/2013/11/Subchapter-9.pdf.
25. Haw. Rev. Stat. § 103-10.5(a) (2022).

- *Contracting Set-Asides*: The Procurement Policy Board must create small business set-asides in appropriate classifications.[26]

Contracting opportunities where the HDOT DBE program applies have several requirements that intersect directly with procurement, contracting, and business inclusion.

- *Goals*: Contract opportunities may not use quotas or set-asides for DBEs.[27] The only exception for using a set-aside is in a limited or extreme circumstance, "when no other method could be reasonably expected to redress egregious instances of discrimination."[28] Instead, an overall goal must be set.[29] The goal must be based on evidence of available "ready, willing and able" DBEs in the market.[30] Once the assessment of "ready, willing and able" DBEs is completed, an overall goal may be established as a percentage of the total amount of contracts receiving U.S. Department of Transportation (U.S. DOT) funds.[31] Participation goals must be set for all certified DBEs and not divided into subcategories.[32] Race- and gender-neutral means must be used to "meet the maximum feasible portion of your overall goal."[33] HDOT, as a recipient of U.S. DOT funds, will not be penalized for failing to meet the overall goal set, if it can establish good faith efforts to meet the goal.[34] When there is a DBE goal on a specific contract opportunity, only the bidder meeting the goal, or establishing good faith efforts to meet the goal, may be awarded the contract.[35]
- *Prompt Payment*: Under 49 C.F.R. part 26, contractors must pay subcontractors within 30 days of receipt of payment from the state DOT for satisfactory performance.[36]
- *Payment of Retainage*: Contractors must pay amounts withheld for retainage to subcontractors within 30 days of their work being satisfactorily completed.[37]

---

26. *Id.* § 103D-906.
27. 49 C.F.R. § 26.43 (2022).
28. *Id.* § 26.43.
29. *Id.* § 26.45(a)(1).
30. *Id.* § 26.45(b).
31. *Id.* § 26.45(e).
32. *Id.* § 26.45(h).
33. *Id.* § 26.51.
34. *Id.* § 26.47.
35. *Id.* § 26.53.
36. 49 C.F.R. § 26.29(a) (2023).
37. *Id.* § 26.29(b).

Additional Related Laws, Policies, and Programs

- *Access to Capital*: Under Hawaii Revised Statutes, section 211D-3, the state has established a Capital Access Program administered by the Department of Business, Economic Development and Tourism to "to assist a participating financial institution in making loans to businesses and nonprofit organizations that face barriers in accessing capital."[38]
- *Technical Assistance*: The Chief Procurement Officer, under the Hawaii Public Procurement Code, is to "[d]evelop and conduct training programs to assist small businesses."[39] In addition, the State Procurement Office must establish a "small business initiative program consistent with this chapter to ensure that small businesses, including businesses owned by veterans, Native Hawaiians, and women, are able to effectively participate in small business contracting opportunities in the State."[40]
- *Finding Contract Opportunities*: The Hawaii State Procurement Office has information on finding bidding opportunities as well as its e-Procurement system (HIePRO) on the following site: https://spo.hawaii.gov/for-vendors/bidding-opportunities/.

Major City Snapshot: City and County of Honolulu

The City and County of Honolulu, as a recipient of federal transportation funds, has implemented a DBE program through its Department of Transportation Services.[41] Like the HDOT DBE program noted earlier, the authority for the City and County of Honolulu's program is found under C.F.R. 49, part 26. Besides the DBE program, the City and County of Honolulu does not have any of the following types of business inclusion programs noted within its ordinance: minority-owned business enterprise program; women-owned business enterprise program; veteran-owned business enterprise program; persons with disabilities business enterprise; and/or LGBT-owned business enterprise program.

38. Haw. Rev. Stat. § 211D-3 (2022).
39. *Id.* § 103D-903.
40. *Id.* § 103D-902.
41. *Non-Discrimination Policies*, City & Cnty. of Honolulu, https://www.honolulu.gov/transportation/non-discrimination-policies.html (last visited Feb. 25, 2023).

CHAPTER 13

Idaho

Overview of Business Inclusion Program, Policies, and Practices

Government entities seeking to create business inclusion programs have two primary options in terms of the type of program they may create, in terms of who is eligible for the program: (1) a race- and gender-conscious program or (2) a race- and gender-neutral program. Under the Equal Protection Clause of the Fourteenth Amendment, strict scrutiny is applied by the courts when a government actor is creating policies based on race. Strict scrutiny is the highest level of judicial review that may be applied. It requires the government actor to demonstrate that (1) past discrimination exists such that the entity has a "compelling government interest" in rectifying it, and (2) the policies and programs created to do so are "narrowly tailored."[1] Although intermediate scrutiny is often applied when reviewing programs based on gender, strict scrutiny is applied when reviewing race- and gender-conscious business inclusion programs.[2] Disparity studies have become a standard tool used to assist a government entity in withstanding a challenge to its race- and gender-conscious business inclusion programs. These studies aid in demonstrating whether a government entity has engaged

1. City of Richmond v. J.A. Croson Co., 488 U.S. 469 (1989).

2. Since the 1980s with the Supreme Court decision in *City of Richmond v. J.A. Croson Company*, there have been a number of cases across the county that have assessed race- and gender-conscious business inclusion programs. *See* Adarand Constructors, Inc. v. Pena, 515 U.S. 200 (1995); Virdi v. DeKalb Cnty. Sch. Dist., 135 Fed. App'x 262, 268 (11th Cir. 2005); Sherbrooke Turf, Inc. v. Minn. Dep't of Transp., 345 F.3d 964, 971 (8th Cir. 2003); Mountain West Holding Co., Inc. v. The State of Montana, Montana DOT, et al., 2017 WL 2179120 (9th Cir. May 16, 2017).

in past discrimination in its contracting practices, such that the entity may have a compelling government interest in rectifying it.[3]

Conversely, race- and gender-neutral programs are programs that are not only accessible to minority-owned and women-owned businesses but to all businesses, regardless of race or gender. A small business inclusion program would fall into this category. The level of judicial review applied to such a policy to determine its constitutionality is rational basis, which is the lowest threshold for a government to satisfy. For a government entity to satisfy rational basis, the policy or program created must be "related to a legitimate government purpose."[4] Even when a government entity has a race- and gender-conscious program, oftentimes the program may still require the government actor to seek to meet the goals of their program through race- and gender-neutral means where able, so as to be taking the most narrowly tailored means of accomplishing the program goals.

At the state level in Idaho, the Idaho Department of Transportation (IDT) Disadvantaged Business Enterprise (DBE) program is the only business inclusion program that consists of a certification program and sets goals for inclusion on applicable contracts.[5]

Summary of Certification Programs and Requirements

Following is a summary of the eligibility requirements for each certification:

- *Disadvantaged Business Enterprise (DBE)*: As is required under 49 C.F.R. § 26.81, Idaho has a Unified Certification Program (IUCP). The IUCP makes all DBE certification decisions and provides a "one-stop shop" to DBE applicants.[6] To qualify as a DBE, a business must (1) be for-profit;[7] (2) be a small business concern—with "small" determined by the Small Business Administration (SBA) small business size standards and does not exceed $30.40 million in gross annual receipts;[8] (3) be at

3. *Promoting Opportunity and Equality in America: A Guide to Federal Circuit Authority on Permissible Government Actions to Promote Racial and Gender Equality*, AM. CIV. LIBERTIES UNION & THE OPPORTUNITY AGENDA (Dec. 2010), https://www.aclu.org/sites/default/files/field_document/Promoting_Opportunity_and_Equality_in_America.pdf.

4. 488 U.S. 469 (1989).

5. *DBE Program*, IDAHO DEP'T OF TRANSP., https://itd.idaho.gov/civilrights/ (last visited Feb. 20, 2023).

6. 49 C.F.R. § 26.81(b)(2) (2022).

7. *Id.* § 26.5.

8. *Id.* §§ 26.5, 26.65(b). It is worth noting that under 49 C.F.R. § 26.65(b), the DBE size standard may be adjusted annually for inflation such that in subsequent years the size standard may no longer be $30.40 million.

least 51 percent owned by socially and economically disadvantaged individuals—there is a rebuttable presumption that women, Black Americans, Hispanic Americans, Native Americans, Asian-Pacific Americans, Subcontinent Asian Americans, or other minorities are disadvantaged;[9] (4) be controlled by one or more of the socially and economically disadvantaged owners;[10] (5) have the socially and economically disadvantaged owners be U.S. citizens or lawfully admitted permanent residents;[11] and (6) have the personal net worth for any socially and economically disadvantaged owner not exceed $1.32 million.[12] The DBE program is required on contracting opportunities that have received funding from the Federal Highway Administration (FHWA), Federal Aviation Administration (FAA), or Federal Transit Administration (FTA).[13]

- *Airport Concession Disadvantaged Business Enterprise (ACDBE)*: In addition to being certified as a DBE under 49 C.F.R. part 26, businesses may also be certified as an Airport Concession Disadvantaged Business Enterprise (ACDBE) under 49 C.F.R. part 23. To qualify as an ACDBE, a business must (1) be a concession for-profit small business concern;[14] (2) qualify as small by having its prior three-year average gross receipts not exceed the applicable size standard of $56.42 million;[15] (3) be 51 percent owned by one or more socially and economically disadvantaged individuals;[16] (4) have one or more of the socially and economically disadvantaged individuals with control and managing the daily business operations;[17] and (5) have the personal net worth for any socially and economically disadvantaged owner not exceed $1.32 million.[18]

9. *Id.* § 26.67.
10. *Id.* § 26.5.
11. *Id.* § 26.67.
12. *Id.*
13. *Id.* § 26.21(a).
14. *Id.* § 23.3.
15. *Id.* § 23.33(a). The size standards for the following are exceptions to this: bank and financial institutions is $1 billion in assets; car rental companies are $75.23 million average annual gross receipts; pay telephones is 1,500 employees; and automobile dealers is 350 employees.
16. *Id.*
17. *Id.*
18. *Id.* § 23.35.

Procurement Laws Intersecting with Business Inclusion

The Idaho Department of Administration Division of Purchasing manages purchasing for the state of Idaho.[19] Idaho procurement laws and rules may be found in the State Procurement Act, Idaho Code title 67, chapter 92, and the Administrative Code, Rules of the Division of Purchasing 38.05.01. There are no bidding preferences, laws, or rules specific to business inclusion and minority-owned, women-owned, disability-owned, veteran-owned, and/or LGBT-owned business enterprises in Idaho, outside of what is required by the IDT's DBE program.

Contracting opportunities where the IDT DBE program applies have several requirements that intersect directly with procurement, contracting, and business inclusion.

- *Fostering Small Business Participation*: Pursuant to 49 C.F.R. § 26.39, IDOT has engaged in efforts to foster small business participation.[20] Although it does not have a formal small business enterprise certification within its DBE program, it does verify small business size through bidders list registrations and class evaluations.[21] To be "small" a business must meet the SBA small business size standards, as well as not exceed $23.98 million in average gross receipts over a three-year period.[22] IDOT also seeks to ensure that a "reasonable number of prime construction and consulting contracts are of a size that small businesses can successfully compete for them."[23]
- *Goals*: Contract opportunities may not use quotas or set-asides for DBEs.[24] The only exception for using a set-aside is in a limited or extreme circumstance, "when no other method could be reasonably expected to redress egregious instances of discrimination."[25] Instead, an overall goal must be set.[26] The goal must be based on evidence of available "ready, willing and able" DBEs in the market.[27] Once the assessment of "ready, willing and able" DBEs is completed, an overall goal may be established as a percentage of the total amount of contracts receiving

19. *Division of Purchasing*, Idaho Dep't of Admin., https://purchasing.idaho.gov/ (last visited Feb. 12, 2023).

20. *Disadvantage Business Enterprise Program Plan*, Idaho Dep't of Transp. 18–21 (2017), https://apps.itd.idaho.gov/apps/ocr/documents/dbeplan.pdf.

21. *Id.*

22. *Id.*

23. *Id.*

24. 49 C.F.R. § 26.43 (2022).

25. *Id.* § 26.43.

26. *Id.* § 26.45(a)(1).

27. *Id.* § 26.45(b).

U.S. Department of Transportation (U.S. DOT) funds.[28] Participation goals must be set for all certified DBEs and not divided into subcategories.[29] Race- and gender-neutral means must be used to "meet the maximum feasible portion of your overall goal."[30] IDT, as a recipient of U.S. DOT funds, will not be penalized for failing to meet the overall goal set, if it can establish good faith efforts to meet the goal.[31] When there is a DBE goal on a specific contract opportunity, only the bidder meeting the goal, or establishing good faith efforts to meet the goal, may be awarded the contract.[32]

- *Prompt Payment*: Under 49 C.F.R. part 26, contractors must pay subcontractors within 30 days of receipt of payment from the state DOT for satisfactory performance.[33]
- *Payment of Retainage*: Contractors must pay amounts withheld for retainage to subcontractors within 30 days of their work being satisfactorily completed.[34]

Additional Related Laws, Policies, and Programs

- *Prompt Payment to Subcontractors*: Under Idaho's prompt payment law, it does not identify a prompt payment to subcontractors.[35]
- *Finding Contract Opportunities*: Information about contract opportunities with the State of Idaho may be found on the following Department of Administration's State Division of Purchasing site: https://purchasing.idaho.gov/.

Major City Snapshot: Boise, Meridian, and Nampa

Across some of the largest cities in Idaho—Boise, Meridian, and Nampa—none of these cities have a city-specific business inclusion program.[36] In contracting opportunities and projects receiving federal funding from the Department of Transportation, cities have noted business inclusion goals in accordance with federal regulations and requirements for federal fund recipients.[37]

28. *Id.* § 26.45(e).
29. *Id.* § 26.45(h).
30. *Id.* § 26.51.
31. *Id.* § 26.47.
32. *Id.* § 26.53.
33. 49 C.F.R. § 26.29(a) (2023).
34. *Id.* § 26.29(b).
35. Idaho Code § 67-2302 (2022).
36. A thorough review of each city ordinance was completed for confirmation.
37. As examples, please see the following: *Disadvantage Business Enterprise Program Plan—Nampa Municipal Airport*, City of Nampa, https://www.cityofnampa.us/DocumentCenter/View/6982/2017-DBE-Part-26-Program (last visited Feb. 20, 2023).

CHAPTER 14

Illinois

Overview of Business Inclusion Program, Policies, and Practices

Government entities seeking to create business inclusion programs have two primary options in terms of the type of program they may create, in terms of who is eligible for the program: (1) a race- and gender-conscious program or (2) a race- and gender-neutral program. Under the Equal Protection Clause of the Fourteenth Amendment, strict scrutiny is applied by the courts when a government actor is creating policies based on race. Strict scrutiny is the highest level of judicial review that may be applied. It requires the government actor to demonstrate that (1) past discrimination exists such that the entity has a "compelling government interest" in rectifying it, and (2) the policies and programs created to do so are "narrowly tailored."[1] Although intermediate scrutiny is often applied when reviewing programs based on gender, strict scrutiny is applied when reviewing race- and gender-conscious business inclusion programs.[2] Disparity studies have become a standard tool used to assist a government entity in withstanding a challenge to its race- and gender-conscious business inclusion programs. These studies aid in demonstrating whether a government entity has engaged

1. City of Richmond v. J.A. Croson Co., 488 U.S. 469 (1989).

2. Since the 1980s with the Supreme Court decision in *City of Richmond v. J.A. Croson Company*, there have been a number of cases across the county that have assessed race- and gender-conscious business inclusion programs. *See* Adarand Constructors, Inc. v. Pena, 515 U.S. 200 (1995); Virdi v. DeKalb Cnty. Sch. Dist., 135 Fed. App'x 262, 268 (11th Cir. 2005); Sherbrooke Turf, Inc. v. Minn. Dep't of Transp., 345 F.3d 964, 971 (8th Cir. 2003); Mountain West Holding Co., Inc. v. The State of Montana, Montana DOT, et al., 2017 WL 2179120 (9th Cir. May 16, 2017).

in past discrimination in its contracting practices, such that the entity may have a compelling government interest in rectifying it.[3]

Conversely, race- and gender-neutral programs are programs that are not only accessible to minority-owned and women-owned businesses but to all businesses, regardless of race or gender. A small business inclusion program would fall into this category. The level of judicial review applied to such a policy to determine its constitutionality is rational basis, which is the lowest threshold for a government to satisfy. For a government entity to satisfy rational basis, the policy or program created must be "related to a legitimate government purpose."[4] Even when a government entity has a race- and gender-conscious program, oftentimes the program may still require the government actor to seek to meet the goals of their program through race- and gender-neutral means where able, so as to be taking the most narrowly tailored means of accomplishing the program goals.

In the state of Illinois, at the state level, the primary business inclusion certifying agencies are (1) the State of Illinois Commission on Equity and Inclusion (CEI) Business Enterprise Program (BEP) and (2) the Illinois Department of Transportation (IDOT).

Summary of Certification Programs and Requirements

CEI administers the following certifications for businesses. In addition, CEI works with the Illinois Department of Veteran Affairs regarding the certification of veteran-owned small businesses (VOSBs) and service-disabled veteran-owned small businesses (SDVOSBs) to ensure that businesses are legitimately veterans or service-disabled veterans.[5]

- *Minority Business Enterprise (MBE)*: For a business to be eligible for the MBE certification the business must (1) be 51 percent owned by one or more minorities (or minorities own 51 percent of stock);[6] (2) have the daily business operations and management be controlled by one or more minorities;[7] (3) have the minorities who are owners representing the 51 percent and controlling the business be U.S. citizens or lawful

3. *Promoting Opportunity and Equality in America: A Guide to Federal Circuit Authority on Permissible Government Actions to Promote Racial and Gender Equality*, Am. Civ. Liberties Union & The Opportunity Agenda (Dec. 2010), https://www.aclu.org/sites/default/files/field_document/Promoting_Opportunity_and_Equality_in_America.pdf.

4. 488 U.S. 469 (1989).

5. 30 Ill. Comp. Stat. 500/ § 45-57(f) (2023).

6. 30 Ill. Comp. Stat. 575/ § 2(A)(3) (2023).

7. *Id.*

permanent residents;[8] and (4) have annual gross sales less than $150 million.[9]

- *Women Business Enterprise (WBE)*: For a business to be eligible for the WBE certification, the business must (1) be 51 percent owned by one or more women (or women own 51 percent of stock);[10] (2) have the daily business operations and management be controlled by one or more women;[11] (3) have the women who are owners representing the 51 percent and controlling the business be U.S. citizens or lawful permanent residents;[12] and (4) have annual gross sales less than $150 million.[13] A business owned and controlled by women who are also minorities shall be certified as both a "women-owned business" and a "minority-owned business."[14]
- *Persons with Disability Business Enterprise (PBE)*: For a business to be eligible for the PBE certification, the business must (1) be 51 percent owned by one or more persons with a disability (or persons with disabilities own 51 percent of stock);[15] (2) have the daily business operations and management be controlled by one or more persons with a disability;[16] (3) have the persons with a disability who are owners representing the 51 percent and controlling the business be U.S. citizens or lawful permanent residents;[17] and (4) have annual gross sales less than $150 million.[18] "A not-for-profit agency for persons with disabilities that is exempt from taxation under section 501 of the Internal Revenue Code of 1986 is also considered a 'business owned by a person with a disability.'"[19]
- *Veteran-Owned Small Business (VOSB)*: To be eligible as a veteran-owned small business (VOSB), a business must satisfy the following criteria: (1) 51 percent owned or 51 percent of the stock of the company owned by "one or more qualified veterans";[20] (2) the 51 percent owners that are qualified

---

8. *Id.* § 2(A)(1).
9. *Id.* § 2(A)(10).
10. *Id.* § 2(A)(4).
11. *Id.*
12. *Id.* § 2(A)(2).
13. *Id.* § 2(A)(10).
14. *Id.* § 2(A)(8).
15. *Id.* § 2(A)(4.1).
16. *Id.*
17. *Id.* § 2(A)(2.05).
18. *Id.* § 2(A)(10).
19. *Id.* § 2(A)(4.1).
20. 30 Ill. Comp. Stat. 500/ § 45-57(e) (2023).

veterans must live in Illinois;[21] (3) the home office must be in Illinois;[22] (4) CEI annually verifies that the qualified veterans live in Illinois and have the home office in Illinois;[23] and (5) that the business's annual gross sales is less than $75 million.[24]

- *Service-Disabled Veteran-Owned Small Business (SDVOSB)*: To be eligible as a service-disabled veteran-owned small business (SDVOSB), a business must satisfy the following criteria: (1) 51 percent owned or 51 percent of the stock of the company owned by "one or more qualified service-disabled veterans";[25] (2) the 51 percent owners that are qualified service-disabled veterans must live in Illinois;[26] (3) the home office must be in Illinois;[27] (4) CEI annually verifies that the qualified service-disabled veterans live in Illinois and have the home office in Illinois;[28] and (5) that the business's annual gross sales is less than $75 million.[29]

IDOT administers the Disadvantaged Business Enterprise (DBE) program and the Airport Concessions Disadvantaged Business Enterprise (ACDBE) program.

- *Disadvantaged Business Enterprise (DBE)*: Pursuant to 49 C.F.R. part 26, IDOT administers the state's DBE certification program. As is required under 49 C.F.R. § 26.81, Illinois has a Unified Certification Program (IL UCP). IL UCP consists of the following entities: IDOT, City of Chicago, CTA, Metra, and Pace.[30] The UCP makes all DBE certification decisions and provides a "one-stop shop" to DBE applicants.[31] To qualify as a DBE, a business must (1) be for-profit;[32] (2) be a small business concern—with "small" determined by the Small Business Administration (SBA) small business size standards and does

21. *Id.*
22. *Id.*
23. *Id.*
24. *Id.*
25. *Id.*
26. *Id.*
27. *Id.*
28. *Id.*
29. *Id.*
30. *DBE Certification*, Ill. Dep't of Transp., https://idot.illinois.gov/doing-business/certifications/disadvantaged-business-enterprise-certification/index (last visited Feb. 15, 2023).
31. 49 C.F.R. § 26.81(b)(2) (2022).
32. *Id.* § 26.5.

not exceed $30.40 million in gross annual receipts;[33] (3) be at least 51 percent owned by socially and economically disadvantaged individuals—there is a rebuttable presumption that women, Black Americans, Hispanic Americans, Native Americans, Asian-Pacific Americans, Subcontinent Asian Americans, or other minorities are disadvantaged;[34] (4) be controlled by one or more of the socially and economically disadvantaged owners;[35] (5) have the socially and economically disadvantaged owners be U.S. citizens or lawfully admitted permanent residents;[36] and (6) have the personal net worth for any socially and economically disadvantaged owner not exceed $1.32 million.[37] The DBE program is required on contracting opportunities that have received funding from the Federal Highway Administration (FHWA), Federal Aviation Administration (FAA), or Federal Transit Administration (FTA).[38]

- *Airport Concession Disadvantaged Business Enterprise (ACDBE)*: In addition to being certified as a DBE under 49 C.F.R. part 26, businesses may also be certified as an Airport Concession Disadvantaged Business Enterprise (ACDBE) under 49 C.F.R. part 23. To qualify as an ACDBE, a business must (1) be a concession for-profit small business concern;[39] (2) qualify as small by having its prior three-year average gross receipts not exceed the applicable size standard of $56.42 million;[40] (3) be 51 percent owned by one or more socially and economically disadvantaged individuals;[41] (4) have one or more of the socially and economically disadvantaged individuals with control and managing the daily business operations;[42] and (5) have the personal net worth for any socially and economically disadvantaged owner not exceed $1.32 million.[43]

33. *Id.* §§ 26.5, 26.65(b). It is worth noting that under 49 C.F.R. § 26.65(b), the DBE size standard may be adjusted annually for inflation such that in subsequent years the size standard may no longer be $30.40 million.

34. *Id.* § 26.67.

35. *Id.* § 26.5.

36. *Id.* § 26.67.

37. *Id.*

38. *Id.* § 26.21(a).

39. *Id.* § 23.3.

40. *Id.* § 23.33(a). The size standards for the following are exceptions to this: bank and financial institutions is $1 billion in assets; car rental companies are $75.23 million average annual gross receipts; pay telephones is 1,500 employees; and automobile dealers is 350 employees.

41. *Id.*

42. *Id.*

43. *Id.* § 23.35.

Procurement Laws Intersecting with Business Inclusion

Procurement laws for the state of Illinois may largely be found in the Illinois Procurement Code. State laws and regulations pertaining to small minority-owned, women-owned, and persons with disability-owned businesses may be found in the Business Enterprise for Minorities, Women, and Persons with Disabilities Act. Laws pertaining to veteran-owned small businesses and service-disabled veteran-owned small businesses may be found in the Illinois Procurement Code, section 45-57.

- *Small Businesses Set-Aside*: The chief procurement officer may set aside specific procurement opportunities for small businesses in Illinois.[44] Once a procurement has been designated as a small business set-aside, then only bids from small businesses must be considered.[45] A small business is one that is "independently owned and operated and that is not dominant in its field of operation."[46] The small business must also have annual gross revenue or total number of employees within what is considered small for its industry.[47] As it relates to construction contracts, state agencies of the executive branch must designate a fair portion, which is between 25 percent and 40 percent of total construction contracts to small business set-aside procurement opportunities.[48]
- *Contracting Participation Goals*: There is a goal to have not less than 3 percent of the state's total contracting dollars spent with VOSBs and SDVOSBs.[49] When a contractor subcontracts to VOSBs and/or SDVOSBs those spends may count toward the 3 percent goal.[50] As it relates to BEP-certified MBEs, WBEs, and PBEs, there is an annual aspirational goal to have 30 percent of the state's total contracting dollars spent with such businesses collectively.[51] Specific to state construction contracts, there is a collective 20 percent MBE/WBE/PBE aspirational participation

---

44. 30 Ill. Comp. Stat. 500/ § 45-45(a) (2023).
45. *Id.*
46. *Id.* § 45-45(b).
47. *Id.*
48. *Id.* § 45-45(c).
49. *Id.* § 45-57(a).
50. *Id.*
51. 30 Ill. Comp. Stat. 575/ § 4(a) (2023); under 30 ILCS 575 § 4(a), the collective goal of 30 percent is broken down into the following: MBEs (16 percent), WBEs (10 percent), and PBEs (4 percent).

goal.[52] All of the goals established are contingent on the results of the most recent disparity study conducted.[53]

- *Language in Solicitations*: All state solicitations must include language pertaining to BEP participation goals.[54] Bidders and offerors are required to submit utilization plans at the time of responding to the solicitation.[55] Failure to submit a utilization plan will deem the submission nonresponsive.[56]
- *Good Faith Efforts*: If a bidder or offeror is unable to meet the goal established for the solicitation, then they must demonstrate good faith efforts to meet the goal when they request a waiver.[57]
- *Sheltered Market*: If the Business Enterprise Council for Minorities, Women, and Persons with Disabilities receives and reviews evidence demonstrating "past or present racial, ethnic or gender based discrimination which directly impacts State contracting with businesses owned by minorities, women, and persons with disabilities" then it has the authority to establish sheltered market contracting opportunities for such businesses where they are able to compete only against other MBE/WBE/PBE businesses.[58]
- *Reporting Requirements*: Annually, small business specialists assigned by the chief procurement officer must submit a written report to the Generally Assembly reporting on the contracts designated for the small business set-asides.[59] This report must also note what portion of those contracts went to MBEs, WBEs, and PBEs.[60] Each year, chief procurement officers must report to CEI on its efforts and spends pertaining to the contracting goals for VOSBs and SDVOSBs.[61] CEI then must report to the governor and General Assembly on an annual basis pertaining to VOSB and SDVOSB certifications and contracts awarded.[62]

Contracting opportunities where the IDOT DBE program applies have several requirements that intersect directly with procurement, contracting, and business inclusion.

---

52. 30 Ill. Comp. Stat. 575/ § 4(b) (2023).
53. *Id.* § 4(c-5).
54. *Id.* § 4(e).
55. *Id.*
56. *Id.*
57. *Id.*
58. *Id.* § 8b.
59. *Id.* § 45-45(f).
60. *Id.*
61. *Id.* § 45-57(b).
62. *Id.* § 45-57(b-5).

- *Fostering Small Business Participation*: Under 49 C.F.R. § 26.39, entities receiving U.S. Department of Transportation (U.S. DOT) funding are to fold into their DBE programs efforts to foster small business participation. As of the 2017 IDOT disparity study, IDOT had not "implement[ed] a comprehensive small business program but [did] use small business set-asides for some state-funded contracts worth less than $100,000."[63]
- *Goals*: Contract opportunities may not use quotas or set-asides for DBEs.[64] The only exception for using a set-aside is in a limited or extreme circumstance, "when no other method could be reasonably expected to redress egregious instances of discrimination."[65] Instead, an overall goal must be set.[66] The goal must be based on evidence of available "ready, willing and able" DBEs in the market.[67] Once the assessment of "ready, willing and able" DBEs is completed, an overall goal may be established as a percentage of the total amount of contracts receiving U.S. DOT funds.[68] Participation goals must be set for all certified DBEs and not divided into subcategories.[69] Race- and gender-neutral means must be used to "meet the maximum feasible portion of your overall goal."[70] IDOT, as a recipient of U.S. DOT funds, will not be penalized for failing to meet the overall goal set, if it can establish good faith efforts to meet the goal.[71] When there is a DBE goal on a specific contract opportunity, only the bidder meeting the goal, or establishing good faith efforts to meet the goal, may be awarded the contract.[72]
- *Prompt Payment*: Under 49 C.F.R. part 26, contractors must pay subcontractors within 30 days of receipt of payment from the state DOT for satisfactory performance.[73]

---

63. *2017 Disparity Study*, BBC Rsch. & Consulting, ch. 10, at 5 (2017), https://idot.illinois.gov/Assets/uploads/files/Doing-Business/Reports/OBWD/DBE/2017%20IDOT%20Disparity%20Study_Final%20Report.pdf.
64. 49 C.F.R. § 26.43 (2022).
65. *Id.* § 26.43.
66. *Id.* § 26.45(a)(1).
67. *Id.* § 26.45(b).
68. *Id.* § 26.45(e).
69. *Id.* § 26.45(h).
70. *Id.* § 26.51.
71. *Id.* § 26.47.
72. *Id.* § 26.53.
73. 49 C.F.R. § 26.29(a) (2023).

- *Payment of Retainage*: Contractors must pay amounts withheld for retainage to subcontractors within 30 days of their work being satisfactorily completed.[74]

Additional Related Laws, Policies, and Programs

- *Technical Assistance*: Illinois Office of Minority Economic Empowerment is available to offer technical assistance to minority-, women-, persons with disabilities-, and veteran-owned small businesses and entrepreneurs (https://dceo.illinois.gov/omee.html).[75]
- *Prompt Payment to Subcontractors*: "When a contractor receives any payment, the contractor shall pay each subcontractor and material supplier electronically within 10 business days or 15 calendar days, whichever occurs earlier, or, if paid by a printed check, the printed check must be postmarked within 10 business days or 15 calendar days, whichever occurs earlier, after receiving payment in proportion to the work completed by each subcontractor and material supplier its application or pay estimate, plus interest received under this Act."[76]
- *Finding Contract Opportunities*: The State of Illinois e-Procurement system, BidBuy, may be found at https://www.bidbuy.illinois.gov/bso/.

Major City Snapshot: Chicago

The City of Chicago's Department of Procurement Services certifies businesses for their business inclusion programs.[77] The following city ordinances are most relevant to the city's business inclusion programs: (1) article IV, chapter 2-92-420 *et seq.* (MBE/WBE ordinance); (2) article

74. *Id.* § 26.29(b).

75. *Illinois Office of Minority Economic Empowerment*, Ill. Dep't of Com. & Econ. Opportunity, https://dceo.illinois.gov/omee.html (last visited Feb. 16, 2023).

76. 30 Ill. Comp. Stat. 540/ § 7(a-5) (2023).

77. *Certification M/WBE Program*, City of Chi. Dep't of Procurement, https://www.chicago.gov/city/en/depts/dps/provdrs/cert/svcs/minority_and_womenownedbusinessenterprisecertificationmbewbe.html (last visited Feb. 16, 2023); *Regulations Governing Certification of Minority- and Women-Owned Business Enterprises, Veteran-Owned Business Enterprises, and Business Enterprises Owned or Operated by People with Disabilities for Non-Construction Contracts*, City of Chi. Dep't of Procurement 1 (2022), https://www.chicago.gov/content/dam/city/depts/dps/Certification/Certification%20Documents/CertificationRulesNon-Construction_032322.pdf; *Regulations Governing Certification of Minority- and Women-Owned Business Enterprises, Veteran-Owned Business Enterprises, and Business Enterprises Owned or Operated by People with Disabilities For Construction Contracts*, City of Chi. Dep't of Procurement 1 (2022), https://www.chicago.gov/content/dam/city/depts/dps/Certification/Certification%20Documents/CertificationRulesConstruction_040422.pdf.

VIII of chapter 2-92-910 *et seq.* (VBE Ordinance); (3) section 2-92-586 (BEPD Ordinance).[78] Following is a high-level summary of the city's business inclusion programs and efforts:

- *Certifications*
  - *Minority-Owned Business Enterprise (MBE)*: To be eligible for this certification a business must be "a local business which is at least 51 percent owned by one or more members of one or more minority groups, or, in the case of a publicly held corporation, at least 51 percent of the stock of which is owned by one or more members of one or more minority groups, whose management and daily business operations are controlled by one or more members of one or more minority groups, and which is not an established business."[79]
  - *Women-Owned Business Enterprise (WBE)*: To be eligible for this certification a business must be "a local business which is at least 51 percent owned by one or more women, or, in the case of a publicly held corporation, 51 percent of the stock of which is owned by one or more women, whose management and daily business operations are controlled by one or more women, and which is not an established business."[80]
  - *Business Enterprises Owned or Operated by People with Disabilities (BEPD)*: To be eligible for this certification a business must meet the following criteria: "(1) a business certified by the State of Illinois as a qualified service-disabled veteran-owned small business pursuant to 30 ILCS 500/45-57; or (2) or an entity, other than an established business, that is: (a) a for-profit corporation, partnership, association, business, trust, estate, or other legal entity that is at least 51 percent owned (directly, indirectly, or beneficially) by one or more individuals with disabilities who manages and controls the daily business operations and management of the entity, (b) a nonprofit corporation that employs individuals with disabilities, pays them an hourly wage that is not less than the federal minimum wage and not on a piece work basis, whose management and daily business operations are controlled by one or more individuals with disabilities,

78. *Regulations Governing Certification of Minority- and Women-Owned Business Enterprises, supra* note 77.

79. City of Chi. Mun. Code art. IV, § 2-92-420(s).

80. *Id.* § 2-92-420(y).

and whose corporate purpose includes providing, directly or indirectly, services to individuals with disabilities, or (c) an individual with a disability who is contracting with the City as a sole proprietorship or individually."[81]

- *Veteran-Owned Business Enterprise (VBE)*: To be eligible for this certification a business must meet the following criteria: "(1) is at least 51 percent owned by one or more veterans, or in the case of a publicly held corporation, at least 51 percent of all classes of the stock of which is owned by one or more veterans, whose management, policies, major decisions and daily business operations are independently managed and controlled by one or more veterans" and (2) has either been certified as a veteran-owned small local business; veteran business enterprise; qualified service-disabled veteran-owned small business, or qualified veteran-owned small business by an accepted certifying entity in Illinois; or verified and approved by the U.S. Department of Veterans Affairs.[82]
- *Disadvantaged Business Enterprise (DBE)*: The eligibility requirements for this certification are the same as noted for IDOT's DBE program noted previously in this chapter and in accordance with 49 C.F.R. part 26.[83] The City of Chicago is a member of the Illinois UCP and certifies businesses.[84]
- *Airport Concessions Disadvantaged Business Enterprise (ACDBE)*: The eligibility requirements for this certification are the same as noted for IDOT's ACDBE program noted previously in this chapter and in accordance with 49 C.F.R. part 23.[85] The City of Chicago is a member of the Illinois UCP and certifies businesses.[86]

• *Bidding Specifications and Good Faith Efforts*: For competitive bidding opportunities over $10,000 bidding specifications will include a requirement for contractors to commit to the MWBE goals or to provide good faith efforts.[87]

---

81. *Id.* § 2-92-586; *Regulations Governing Certification of Minority- and Women-Owned Business Enterprises, supra* note 77.
82. City of Chi. Mun. Code art. VIII, § 2-92-920 (2023).
83. *Disadvantaged Business Enterprise Program Document*, City of Ch. (2020), https://www.chicago.gov/content/dam/city/depts/dps/RulesRegulations/Chicago-DBE-Program-07-02-2020%20Final.pdf.
84. *Id.*
85. *Id.*
86. *Id.*
87. City of Chi. Mun. Code art. IV, § 2-92-440 (2023).

- *Bid Incentive for Utilization of Veteran-Owned Subcontractors*: For advertised construction projects, a contractor may receive a bid incentive for subcontracting a percentage of work to veteran-owned businesses.[88] A bid incentive is defined as "an amount deducted, for bid evaluation purposes only, from the contract base bid in order to calculate the bid price to be used to evaluate the bid on a competitively bid contract."[89] The bid incentive is used when calculating the low bid and would provide the contractor with a percentage incentive to deduct that may range from half a percent to 2 percent.[90]
- *MWBE Goals*: Contracting goals are as follows: (1) in terms of the city's annual goals, no less than 25 percent of the annual total dollar value for all city contracts for MBEs and no less than 5 percent of the annual total dollar value for all city contracts for WBEs,[91] and (2) for competitive bidding over $10,000 there is a contract MWBE goal.[92] On contracts over $10,000, the Chief Procurement Office is authorized to set contract-specific veteran-owned small local business participation goals.[93] The goal amount may not exceed 1 percent of the contracts total value.[94]
- *Reporting*: Mayoral Executive Order 2021-2, which pertains to Business Diversity Programs, requires anticipated contract awardees to submit a Project Utilization Schedule with their Compliance Plan.[95] The Project Utilization Schedule should note the efforts to meet the contract-specific MBE, WBE, and/or DBE goals. In addition, contractors must submit Quarterly Utilization Reports.[96]

---

88. *Id.* § 2-92-940.
89. *Id.* § 2-92-920.
90. *Id.* § 2-92-940.
91. *Id.* § 2-92-430.
92. *Id.* § 2-92-440.
93. *Id.* § 2-92-955.
94. *Id.*
95. *Rules Regarding Reporting of Business Diversity Program and Utilization of Certified Firms Pursuant to Mayoral Executive Order 2021-2*, CHI. DEP'T OF PROCUREMENT SERVS. (2021), https://www.chicago.gov/content/dam/city/depts/dps/Outreach/EO2021-2_Reporting_Rules_FINAL_062521.pdf.
96. *Id.*

CHAPTER 15

Indiana

Overview of Business Inclusion Program, Policies, and Practices

Government entities seeking to create business inclusion programs have two primary options in terms of the type of program they may create, in terms of who is eligible for the program: (1) a race- and gender-conscious program or (2) a race- and gender-neutral program. Under the Equal Protection Clause of the Fourteenth Amendment, strict scrutiny is applied by the courts when a government actor is creating policies based on race. Strict scrutiny is the highest level of judicial review that may be applied. It requires the government actor to demonstrate that (1) past discrimination exists such that the entity has a "compelling government interest" in rectifying it, and (2) the policies and programs created to do so are "narrowly tailored."[1] Although intermediate scrutiny is often applied when reviewing programs based on gender, strict scrutiny is applied when reviewing race- and gender-conscious business inclusion programs.[2] Disparity studies have become a standard tool used to assist a government entity in withstanding a challenge to its race- and gender-conscious business inclusion programs. These studies aid in demonstrating whether a government entity has engaged

1. City of Richmond v. J.A. Croson Co., 488 U.S. 469 (1989).

2. Since the 1980s with the Supreme Court decision in *City of Richmond v. J.A. Croson Company*, there have been a number of cases across the county that have assessed race- and gender-conscious business inclusion programs. *See* Adarand Constructors, Inc. v. Pena, 515 U.S. 200 (1995); Virdi v. DeKalb Cnty. Sch. Dist., 135 Fed. App'x 262, 268 (11th Cir. 2005); Sherbrooke Turf, Inc. v. Minn. Dep't of Transp., 345 F.3d 964, 971 (8th Cir. 2003); Mountain West Holding Co., Inc. v. The State of Montana, Montana DOT, et al., 2017 WL 2179120 (9th Cir. May 16, 2017).

in past discrimination in its contracting practices, such that the entity may have a compelling government interest in rectifying it.[3]

Conversely, race- and gender-neutral programs are programs that are not only accessible to minority-owned and women-owned businesses but to all businesses, regardless of race or gender. A small business inclusion program would fall into this category. The level of judicial review applied to such a policy to determine its constitutionality is rational basis, which is the lowest threshold for a government to satisfy. For a government entity to satisfy rational basis, the policy or program created must be "related to a legitimate government purpose."[4] Even when a government entity has a race- and gender-conscious program, oftentimes the program may still require the government actor to seek to meet the goals of their program through race- and gender-neutral means where able, so as to be taking the most narrowly tailored means of accomplishing the program goals.

In the state of Indiana, there are two main entities that certify businesses for business inclusion programs at the state level of government: (1) the Indiana Department of Administration's (IDOA) Division of Supplier Diversity (DSD) and (2) the Indiana Department of Transportation (INDOT).

Summary of Certification Programs and Requirements

IDOA DSD certifies minority business enterprises, women's business enterprises, and Indiana veteran-owned small businesses.[5] Following are the eligibility requirements for each:

- *Minority Business Enterprise (MBE)*: For a business to qualify as an MBE for the IDOA DSD program, it must (1) be 51 percent owned (or holding 51 percent of the corporate stock) by a minority, which includes Blacks, American Indians, Hispanics, Asian Americans, and other minorities defined under 13 C.F.R. 124.103, who is also a U.S. citizen;[6] (2) have one or more minorities with control of the management and active in the day-to-day operations of the business;[7] and (3) have the qualifying

3. *Promoting Opportunity and Equality in America: A Guide to Federal Circuit Authority on Permissible Government Actions to Promote Racial and Gender Equality*, Am. Civ. Liberties Union & The Opportunity Agenda (Dec. 2010), https://www.aclu.org/sites/default/files/field_document/Promoting_Opportunity_and_Equality_in_America.pdf.

4. 488 U.S. 469 (1989).

5. *Division of Supplier Diversity*, Ind. Dep't of Admin., https://www.in.gov/idoa/mwbe/ (last visited Feb. 8, 2023).

6. Ind. Code § 4-13-16.5-1 (2022); 25 Ind. Admin. Code 5-2-1 (2023).

7. *Id.*

minority owners have "an interest in the capital, assets, and profits and losses of the business proportionate to the percentage of ownership."[8] A nonprofit corporation that has at least 51 percent of its board of directors who are minorities may be eligible for an MBE certification as a "qualified minority nonprofit corporation."[9]

- *Women's Business Enterprise (WBE)*: For a business to qualify as a WBE for the IDOA DSD program, it must (1) be 51 percent owned (or holding 51 percent of the corporate stock) by an individual "whose gender is female" and who is also a U.S. citizen;[10] (2) have one or more women with control of the management and active in the day-to-day operations of the business;[11] and (3) have the qualifying women owners with "an interest in the capital, assets, and profits and losses of the business proportionate to the percentage of ownership."[12] A nonprofit corporation that has at least 51 percent of its board of directors who are women may be eligible for a WBE certification as a "qualified women's nonprofit corporation."[13]
- *Indiana Veteran-Owned Small Business (IVOSB)*: For a business to satisfy the eligibility requirements to become an IVOSB for the IDOA DSD program, it must (1) be a small business, which means that it is (a) "independently owned and operated" and (b) "not dominant in its field of operation";[14] (2) have its principal place of business in Indiana;[15] (3) be 51 percent owned (or holding 51 percent of the corporate stock) by one or more veterans;[16] and (4) have one or more veterans with control of the management and active in the day-to-day operations of the business.[17] Also, in defining an IVOSB, the business must have either of the following: (1) "a verification as a veteran owned small business concern . . ." through the Small Business Administration[18] or (2) "a current certification as a

8. *Id.*
9. *Id.*
10. *Id.*
11. *Id.*
12. *Id.*
13. *Id.*
14. IND. CODE § 5-22-14-1 (2022).
15. *Id.* § 5-22-14-3.5.
16. *Id.*
17. *Id.*
18. *Id.* Effective January 1, 2023, the U.S. Department of Veteran Affairs Office of Small & Disadvantaged Business Utilization no longer provides Center of Veterans Enterprise verification. Instead, the Small Business Administration assumed responsibility for certification.

veteran owned small business by the Indiana department of administration."[19]

INDOT administers the Disadvantaged Business Enterprise (DBE) program and Airport Concessions Disadvantaged Business Enterprise (ACDBE) program. Eligibility requirements for each follows:

- *Disadvantaged Business Enterprise (DBE)*: Pursuant to 49 C.F.R. part 26, INDOT administers the state's DBE certification program. As is required under 49 C.F.R. § 26.81, Indiana has a Unified Certification Program. The UCP makes all DBE certification decisions and provides a "one-stop shop" to DBE applicants.[20] To qualify as a DBE, a business must (1) be for-profit;[21] (2) be a small business concern—with "small" determined by the Small Business Administration (SBA) small business size standards and does not exceed $30.40 million in gross annual receipts;[22] (3) be at least 51 percent owned by socially and economically disadvantaged individuals—there is a rebuttable presumption that women, Black Americans, Hispanic Americans, Native Americans, Asian-Pacific Americans, Subcontinent Asian Americans, or other minorities are disadvantaged;[23] (4) be controlled by one or more of the socially and economically disadvantaged owners;[24] (5) have the socially and economically disadvantaged owners be U.S. citizens or lawfully admitted permanent residents;[25] and (6) have the personal net worth for any socially and economically disadvantaged owner not exceed $1.32 million.[26] The DBE program is required on contracting opportunities that have received funding from the Federal Highway Administration (FHWA), Federal Aviation Administration (FAA), or Federal Transit Administration (FTA).[27]
- *Airport Concession Disadvantaged Business Enterprise (ACDBE)*: In addition to being certified as a DBE under 49 C.F.R. part 26, businesses may also be certified as an Airport Concession

19. *Id.* § 5-22-14-3.5.
20. 49 C.F.R. § 26.81(b)(2) (2022).
21. *Id.* § 26.5.
22. *Id.* §§ 26.5, 26.65(b). It is worth noting that under 49 C.F.R. § 26.65(b), the DBE size standard may be adjusted annually for inflation such that in subsequent years the size standard may no longer be $30.40 million.
23. *Id.* § 26.67.
24. *Id.* § 26.5.
25. *Id.* § 26.67.
26. *Id.*
27. *Id.* § 26.21(a).

Disadvantaged Business Enterprise (ACDBE) under 49 C.F.R. part 23. To qualify as an ACDBE, a business must (1) be a concession for-profit small business concern;[28] (2) qualify as small by having its prior three-year average gross receipts not exceed the applicable size standard of $56.42 million;[29] (3) be 51 percent owned by one or more socially and economically disadvantaged individuals;[30] (4) have one or more of the socially and economically disadvantaged individuals with control and managing the daily business operations;[31] and (5) have the personal net worth for any socially and economically disadvantaged owner not exceed $1.32 million.[32]

Procurement Laws Intersecting with Business Inclusion

Indiana procurement laws may be found in title 5, article 22 of the Indiana Code and title 25, article 1.1 of the Indiana Administrative Code. There are a number of laws and regulations pertaining to the IDOA DSD programs where they intersect with procurement. Following are some of the laws that pertain to MBEs, WBEs, and IVOSBs.

- *Inclusion Goals*: Participation goals are set by the Governor's Commission on Supplier Diversity.[33] The MBE and WBE goals are the result of a statistical analysis of the utilization of MBEs and WBEs on Indiana state contracts.[34] Goals may vary on individual contracts.[35] Under Indiana Code section 4-13-16.5-3.5, a 3 percent IVOSB goal is established. Here are the goals set as of July 2021:[36]
  - *Construction*: 7 percent MBE; 5 percent WBE; 3 percent IVOSB
  - *Goods and Services*: 8 percent MBE; 13 percent WBE; 3 percent IVOSB

28. *Id.* § 23.3.
29. *Id.* § 23.33(a). The size standards for the following are exceptions to this: bank and financial institutions is $1 billion in assets; car rental companies are $75.23 million average annual gross receipts; pay telephones is 1,500 employees; and automobile dealers is 350 employees.
30. *Id.*
31. *Id.*
32. *Id.* § 23.35.
33. Ind. Code § 4-13-16.5-2(f) (2022).
34. *Id.*
35. 25 Ind. Admin. Code 5-7-3 (2023).
36. *Participation Goals,* Ind. Dep't of Admin., https://www.in.gov/idoa/mwbe/minority-and-womens-business-enterprises/participation-goals/ (last visited Feb. 2, 2023).

  - *Professional Services*: 8 percent MBE; 11 percent WBE; 3 percent IVOSB
  - *Weighted Average Goal*: 8 percent MBE; 10 percent WBE; 3 percent IVOSB
- *Subcontractor Plans, Waiver Requests, and Contractor Good Faith Efforts*: Contractors must demonstrate good faith efforts to meet the participation goals.[37] When submitting bids, a bidder must submit a completed MBE/WBE subcontractor plan when they plan to meet the goal or most of the MBE/WBE goal.[38] If a bidder is not going to meet a goal, they must submit an application for program waiver.[39] Failure to submit the subcontractor plan and/or application for program waiver in addition to all other required bidding documents "may be the basis for rejection of the bid."[40] Once awarded a contract, if a contract is $100,000 or more, then the awarded bidder must submit participation reports on at least a monthly basis.[41] As it relates to the IVOSB participation and responding to solicitations, a prime bidder with IVOSB subcontractors must submit a percentage commitment form, along with identifying and contact information for the IVOSBs.[42]
- *Sanctions*: If there is a violation[43] or noncompliance[44] as it relates to rules pertaining to the supplier diversity programs, then a number of sanctions may result that include but are not limited to withholding payment, suspending or terminating the contract, and/or consequential damages.[45]
- *Small Business and Veteran-Owned Small Business Price Preference*: Under Indiana Code section 5-22-15-23, an Indiana small business and a veteran-owned small business shall receive a 15 percent price preference from the governmental body issuing a procurement opportunity. When a preference applies, if a small business or a veteran-owned small business is within the noted percentage of the lowest responsive and responsible bidder, then its bid may be accepted instead, if its adjusted total offer is lower than the other offerors.[46]

---

37. IND. CODE § 4-13-16.5-2(g) (2022).
38. 25 IND. ADMIN. CODE 5-6-4 (2023).
39. *Id.*
40. *Id.*
41. *Id.*
42. *Id.* 9-4-2.
43. *Id.* 5-7-8.
44. *Id.* 9-5-2.
45. *Id.*
46. IND. CODE § 5-22-15-11 (2022).

- *Reporting Requirements*: All state agencies must report MBE and WBE spends to the IDOA quarterly.[47] Annually, the IDOA must submit a report to "the governor, the Indiana department of veterans' affairs, and the interim study committee on public safety and military affairs established by [Indiana Code] § 2-5-1.3-4 and the legislative council" that highlights the goals obtained for the IVOSB program and a summary if there was a failure to meet the goals.[48]

Contracting opportunities where the INDOT DBE program applies have several requirements that intersect directly with procurement, contracting, and business inclusion.

- *Fostering Small Business Participation*: Pursuant to 49 C.F.R. § 26.39, INDOT has engaged in efforts to foster small business participation.[49] INDOT relies upon the SBA verification and certification of small business enterprises (SBEs).[50] INDOT seeks to foster small business participation through efforts such as allowing those that are small businesses to work on contracts even if they are not prequalified (prequalification is required for contractors) and through unbundling prime contracts.[51]
- *Goals*: Contract opportunities may not use quotas or set-asides for DBEs.[52] The only exception for using a set-aside is in a limited or extreme circumstance, "when no other method could be reasonably expected to redress egregious instances of discrimination."[53] Instead, an overall goal must be set.[54] The goal must be based on evidence of available "ready, willing and able" DBEs in the market.[55] Once the assessment of "ready, willing and able" DBEs is completed, an overall goal may be established as a percentage of the total amount of contracts receiving U.S. Department of Transportation (U.S. DOT) funds.[56] Participation goals must be set for all certified DBEs

---

47. 25 Ind. Admin. Code 5-5-6 (2023).
48. Ind. Code § 5-22-14-11 (2022).
49. *Disadvantage Business Enterprise Program Manual*, Ind. Dep't of Transp. 16–18 (2021), https://apps.itd.idaho.gov/apps/ocr/documents/dbeplan.pdf.
50. *Id.*
51. *Id.*
52. 49 C.F.R. § 26.43 (2022).
53. *Id.*
54. *Id.* § 26.45(a)(1).
55. *Id.* § 26.45(b).
56. *Id.* § 26.45(e).

and not divided into subcategories.[57] Race- and gender-neutral means must be used to "meet the maximum feasible portion of your overall goal."[58] INDOT, as a recipient of U.S. DOT funds, will not be penalized for failing to meet the overall goal set, if it can establish good faith efforts to meet the goal.[59] When there is a DBE goal on a specific contract opportunity, only the bidder meeting the goal, or establishing good faith efforts to meet the goal, may be awarded the contract.[60]

- *Prompt Payment*: Under 49 C.F.R. part 26, contractors must pay subcontractors within 30 days of receipt of payment from the state DOT for satisfactory performance.[61]
- *Payment of Retainage*: Contractors must pay amounts withheld for retainage to subcontractors within 30 days of their work being satisfactorily completed.[62]

Additional Related Laws, Policies, and Programs

- *Small Business Set-Aside*: Under Indiana Code section 5-22-14, there is a small business set-aside. This set-aside allows for any solicitation designed as a small business set-aside to only accept offers from small businesses.[63]
- *Additional Related Contracting Preferences*: Under Indiana Code section 5-22-15-20.5, there is an Indiana business price preference where, although it is race and gender neutral, a small business, MBE, WBE, and/or IVOSB may also have opportunities.
- *Access to Capital*: The Capital Access Program (CAP) was established under Indiana Code section 5-28-30-4 and provides businesses with access to capital through loans. For more information, please visit https://iedc.in.gov/program/capital-access-program/overview.
- *Prompt Payment to Subcontractors*: On contracts pertaining to any public building, work, or improvement "[w]ithin ten (10) days of the receipt of any payment by the state agency or escrow agent, the contractor or escrow agent shall pay all subcontractors with whom he has contracted their share of the

57. *Id.* § 26.45(h).
58. *Id.* § 26.51.
59. *Id.* § 26.47.
60. *Id.* § 26.53.
61. 49 C.F.R. § 26.29(a) (2023).
62. *Id.* § 26.29(b).
63. Ind. Code § 5-22-14-2 (2022).

payment the contractor received based upon the service performed by the subcontractor. . . ."[64]

- *Finding Contracting Opportunities*: IDOA lists bidding opportunities over $75,000 on the following site: https://www.in.gov/idoa/procurement/supplier-resource-center/find-current-bidding-opportunities/.

Major City Snapshot: Indianapolis

The City of Indianapolis Office of Minority and Women Business Development (OMWBD) manages efforts related to business inclusion.[65]

- *Certifications*: OMWBD certifies businesses as minority business enterprises (MBEs), woman business enterprises (WBEs), veteran business enterprises (VBEs), or disabled-owned business enterprises (DOBEs).[66]
- *Bidding Specifications and Utilization Plan*: Bid specifications and contracts must include language pertaining to the city's utilization plan.[67] When bidding, bidders must submit the "MBE/WBE/VBE/DOBE Participation Goals For Construction, Goods/Supplies, and Services Form."[68]
- *Inclusion Goals*: Under section 202-402 of the Revised Code of the Consolidated City of Indianapolis/Marion County (Revised Code), there are contracting inclusion goals for MBEs (15 percent), WBEs (8 percent), VBEs (3 percent), and DOBEs (1 percent).
- *Contractor Good Faith Efforts*: Bidders must document and demonstrate good faith efforts to meet the participation goals.[69] In addition, if a bidder will not meet the goals, they must submit an "Application for MBE/WBE/VBE/DOBE Program Waiver"

---

64. Ind. Code § 5-16-5.5-5 (2021).

65. *Office of Minority and Women Business Development*, City of Indianapolis Code, https://www.indy.gov/agency/office-of-minority-and-women-business-development (last visited Feb. 3, 2023).

66. *Id.*

67. City of Indianapolis Code § 202-404 (2023); *Diversity Utilization Reports*, City of Indianapolis, https://www.indy.gov/activity/diversity-utilization-reports (last visited Feb. 3, 2023); *The Consolidated City of Indianapolis and Marion County MBE/WBE/VBE/DOBE Business Utilization Plan in Indianapolis Government*, Off. of Minority & Women Bus. Dev. (2020), https://cit9ybase-cms-prod.s3.amazonaws.com/9e6d20e495134a7db8f96210f249fccb.pdf.

68. *The Consolidated City of Indianapolis and Marion County MBE/WBE/VBE/DOBE Business Utilization Plan in Indianapolis Government*, *supra* note 67, at 31.

69. City of Indianapolis Code § 202-404 (2023); *The Consolidated City of Indianapolis and Marion County MBE/WBE/VBE/DOBE Business Utilization Plan in Indianapolis Government*, *supra* note 67, at 33.

form.[70] The form includes a particular number of points for each item that must be demonstrated in terms of good faith efforts.[71] To demonstrate good faith efforts on the form, a minimum of 70 points is required.[72]

- *Noncompliance, Penalties, and Remedies*: If a vendor fails to comply with the program requirements in the utilization plan, then the vendor is in noncompliance and the OMWBD will provide the vendor time to remedy the noncompliance.[73] If the vendor fails to remedy the noncompliance, penalties will ensue.[74]

70. *The Consolidated City of Indianapolis and Marion County MBE/WBE/VBE/DOBE Business Utilization Plan in Indianapolis Government*, *supra* note 67, at 33.

71. *Application for MBE/WBE/VBE/DOBE Program Waiver*, Off. of Minority & Women Bus. Dev. (2020), https://media.graphassets.com/m61tyHSwyCEjb2kME4ew.

72. *Id.*

73. City Of Indianapolis Code § 202-404(1)(d) (2023).

74. *Id.*

CHAPTER 16

Iowa

Overview of Business Inclusion Program, Policies, and Practices

Government entities seeking to create business inclusion programs have two primary options in terms of the type of program they may create, in terms of who is eligible for the program: (1) a race- and gender-conscious program or (2) a race- and gender-neutral program. Under the Equal Protection Clause of the Fourteenth Amendment, strict scrutiny is applied by the courts when a government actor is creating policies based on race. Strict scrutiny is the highest level of judicial review that may be applied. It requires the government actor to demonstrate that (1) past discrimination exists such that the entity has a "compelling government interest" in rectifying it, and (2) the policies and programs created to do so are "narrowly tailored."[1] Although intermediate scrutiny is often applied when reviewing programs based on gender, strict scrutiny is applied when reviewing race- and gender-conscious business inclusion programs.[2] Disparity studies have become a standard tool used to assist a government entity in withstanding a challenge to its race- and gender-conscious business inclusion programs. These studies aid in demonstrating whether a government entity has engaged

1. City of Richmond v. J.A. Croson Co., 488 U.S. 469 (1989).

2. Since the 1980s with the Supreme Court decision in *City of Richmond v. J.A. Croson Company*, there have been a number of cases across the county that have assessed race- and gender-conscious business inclusion programs. *See* Adarand Constructors, Inc. v. Pena, 515 U.S. 200 (1995); Virdi v. DeKalb Cnty. Sch. Dist., 135 Fed. App'x 262, 268 (11th Cir. 2005); Sherbrooke Turf, Inc. v. Minn. Dep't of Transp., 345 F.3d 964, 971 (8th Cir. 2003); Mountain West Holding Co., Inc. v. The State of Montana, Montana DOT, et al., 2017 WL 2179120 (9th Cir. May 16, 2017).

in past discrimination in its contracting practices, such that the entity may have a compelling government interest in rectifying it.[3]

Conversely, race- and gender-neutral programs are programs that are not only accessible to minority-owned and women-owned businesses but to all businesses, regardless of race or gender. A small business inclusion program would fall into this category. The level of judicial review applied to such a policy to determine its constitutionality is rational basis, which is the lowest threshold for a government to satisfy. For a government entity to satisfy rational basis, the policy or program created must be "related to a legitimate government purpose."[4] Even when a government entity has a race- and gender-conscious program, oftentimes the program may still require the government actor to seek to meet the goals of their program through race- and gender-neutral means where able, so as to be taking the most narrowly tailored means of accomplishing the program goals.

In the state of Iowa, at the state level, there are two main agencies with business inclusion programs: (1) the Iowa Economic Development Authority and (2) the Iowa Department of Transportation (Iowa DOT).

Summary of Certification Programs and Requirements

The Iowa Economic Development Authority's Targeted Small Business (TSB) program certifies businesses eligible for the program.[5]

- *TSB Program*: A business must meet the following eligibility requirements: (1) for-profit business; (2) located in Iowa; (3) has an average annual gross income over prior three years that is less than $4 million; (4) is operated under a single management; (5) at least 51 percent "owned, operated, and actively managed by one or more women, minority persons, service-disabled veterans, or persons with a disability."[6] Certification lasts for two years and at such time a business must recertify.[7]

Following are the certification eligibility requirements for the Iowa DOT certifications:

3. *Promoting Opportunity and Equality in America: A Guide to Federal Circuit Authority on Permissible Government Actions to Promote Racial and Gender Equality*, Am. Civ. Liberties Union & The Opportunity Agenda (Dec. 2010), https://www.aclu.org/sites/default/files/field_document/Promoting_Opportunity_and_Equality_in_America.pdf.

4. 488 U.S. 469 (1989).

5. *Targeted Small Business Program: Small Business Resources*, Iowa Econ. Dev. Auth., https://www.iowaeda.com/small-business/targeted-small-business/ (last visited Mar. 1, 2023).

6. Iowa Code § 15.102 (2023).

7. Iowa Admin. Code r. 261-52.2(15)(2) (2023).

- *Disadvantaged Business Enterprise (DBE)*: Pursuant to 49 C.F.R. part 26, Iowa DOT administers the state's DBE certification program. As is required under 49 C.F.R. § 26.81, Iowa has a Unified Certification Program. The UCP provides a "one-stop shop" to DBE applicants.[8] Iowa DOT makes all certification decisions.[9] To qualify as a DBE a business must: (1) be for-profit;[10] (2) be a small business concern—with "small" determined by the Small Business Administration (SBA) small business size standards and does not exceed $30.40 million in gross annual receipts;[11] (3) be at least 51 percent owned by socially and economically disadvantaged individuals—there is a rebuttable presumption that women, Black Americans, Hispanic Americans, Native Americans, Asian-Pacific Americans, Subcontinent Asian Americans, or other minorities are disadvantaged;[12] (4) be controlled by one or more of the socially and economically disadvantaged owners;[13] (5) have the socially and economically disadvantaged owners be U.S. citizens or lawfully admitted permanent residents;[14] and (6) have the personal net worth for any socially and economically disadvantaged owner not exceed $1.32 million.[15] The DBE program is required on contracting opportunities that have received funding from the Federal Highway Administration (FHWA), Federal Aviation Administration (FAA), or Federal Transit Administration (FTA).[16]
- *Airport Concession Disadvantaged Business Enterprise (ACDBE)*: In addition to being certified as a DBE under 49 C.F.R. part 26, businesses may also be certified as an Airport Concession Disadvantaged Business Enterprise (ACDBE) under 49 C.F.R. part 23. To qualify as an ACDBE, a business must (1) be a concession for-profit small business concern;[17] (2) qualify as small by having its prior three-year average gross receipts not exceed

8. 49 C.F.R. § 26.81(b)(2) (2022).

9. *Disadvantaged Business Enterprise Program Plan*, Iowa Dep't of Transp. 25 (Oct. 2018), https://iowadot.gov/civilrights/documents/DBEProgram.pdf.

10. 49 C.F.R. § 26.5 (2022).

11. *Id.* §§ 26.5, 26.65(b). It is worth noting that under 49 C.F.R. § 26.65(b), the DBE size standard may be adjusted annually for inflation such that in subsequent years the size standard may no longer be $30.40 million.

12. *Id.* § 26.67.

13. *Id.* § 26.5.

14. *Id.* § 26.67.

15. *Id.*

16. *Id.* § 26.21(a)

17. *Id.* § 23.3.

the applicable size standard of $56.42 million;[18] (3) be 51 percent owned by one or more socially and economically disadvantaged individuals;[19] (4) have one or more of the socially and economically disadvantaged individuals with control and managing the daily business operations;[20] and (5) have the personal net worth for any socially and economically disadvantaged owner not exceed $1.32 million.[21]

- *Small Business Participation Program*: Iowa DOT has implemented a small business element within its DBE program pursuant to 49 C.F.R. § 26.39 to foster small business participation.[22] This program is race and gender neutral.[23] To be eligible for the program, a business must be a small business as defined under Iowa Code section 15.102, which states the business must be "located in this state, which is operated for profit and under a single management, and which has either fewer than twenty employees or an annual gross income of less than four million dollars computed as the average of the three preceding fiscal years." Businesses must also submit a self-certification form.[24]

Procurement Laws Intersecting with Business Inclusion

Iowa procurement laws and rules pertaining to business inclusion may be found in the following chapters of the Iowa Code and Iowa Administrative Code: chapter 73 (Preferences) of the Iowa Code; chapter 117 of the Iowa Administrative Code (Procurement of Goods and Services of General Use); Iowa Code chapter 15; the Iowa Administrative Code Economic Development Authority [261]; Iowa Code section 12.44; and Iowa Code section 573.2. The following bullet points outline some relevant laws and rules.

- *Bid Notifications*: Purchasing agencies and state departments must provide the marketing manager for TSBs with bid notices

18. *Id.* § 23.33(a). The size standards for the following are exceptions to this: bank and financial institutions is $1 billion in assets; car rental companies are $75.23 million average annual gross receipts; pay telephones is 1,500 employees; and automobile dealers is 350 employees.
19. *Id.*
20. *Id.*
21. *Id.* § 23.35.
22. *Disadvantaged Business Enterprise Program Plan*, Iowa Dep't of Transp. 11 (Oct. 2018), https://iowadot.gov/civilrights/documents/DBEProgram.pdf.
23. *Id.* at 17.
24. *Id.*

to distribute to TSBs at least 48 hours in advance of the issuances of all bid notices.[25]

- *Purchases under $25,000*: State agencies may purchase from TSBs without competition on opportunities up to $25,000.[26]
- *Bond Waiver*: A TSB may request a bond waiver up to $50,000 for state projects when they are "unable to secure a performance, surety, or bid bond because of lack of experience, lack of net worth, or lack of capital."[27]
- *Inclusion Goals*: Every state agency must procure goods and services from TSBs as well as ensure a "proportionate share" of small businesses and TSBs are given an opportunity to bid on all issued state solicitations.[28] Related to this, at the start of each fiscal year, state agencies and departments with purchasing authority must establish a procurement goal for TSBs.[29] This goal applies to procurement of all goods and services, except for those pertaining to utility services.[30] "A community college, area education agency, or school district shall establish a procurement goal from certified targeted small businesses . . . of at least [10 percent] of the value of anticipated procurements. . . ."[31] "Of the total value of anticipated procurements of goods and services under this subsection, an additional goal shall be established to procure at least [40 percent] from minority-owned businesses and [40 percent] from female-owned businesses and [40 percent] from service-disabled veteran-owned businesses . . . that are targeted small businesses."[32]
- *Contractor Good Faith Efforts*: When a primary contractor is subcontracting out part of their contract, then the primary contractor must make a good faith effort to include TSBs.[33] "In cases where the good faith efforts documentation is submitted as part of the bid documents and after review of the low bidder's good faith efforts, departments, agencies and education

---

25. IOWA ADMIN. CODE r. 11-117.8(2) (2023); IOWA CODE § 73.16(2) (2023).
26. IOWA ADMIN. CODE r. 11-117.5(2)(a) (2023); *Policies and Procedures Manual*, IOWA DEP'T OF ADMIN. SERVS.- CENT. PURCHASING 13 (Feb. 2023), https://das.iowa.gov/sites/default/files/procurement/pdf/DAS%20Procurement%20Manual%20-%2002162023.pdf.
27. IOWA ADMIN. CODE r. 261-52.9(15) (2023); IOWA CODE §§ 12.44, 573.2; *Targeted Small Business Program*, IOWA ECON. DEV. AUTH. (Sept. 2021), https://www.iowaeda.com/userdocs/programs/resources/fs_TSB_082021.pdf.
28. IOWA CODE § 73.16(1) (2023).
29. *Id.* § 73.16(2).
30. *Id.*
31. *Id.*
32. *Id.*
33. IOWA ADMIN. CODE r. 261-54.5(1) (2023).

institutions may reject the bid as nonresponsive due to inadequate documentation of good faith efforts."[34]

- *Reporting Requirements*: On a quarterly basis state agencies and departments that have set a procurement TSB goal must report to the TSB marketing and compliance manager of the Economic Development Authority on the total dollar value of procurements to certified TSBs.[35]

Contracting opportunities where the Iowa DOT DBE program applies have several requirements that intersect directly with procurement, contracting, and business inclusion.

- *Goals*: Contract opportunities may not use quotas or set-asides for DBEs.[36] The only exception for using a set-aside is in a limited or extreme circumstance, "when no other method could be reasonably expected to redress egregious instances of discrimination."[37] Instead, an overall goal must be set.[38] The goal must be based on evidence of available "ready, willing and able" DBEs in the market.[39] Once the assessment of "ready, willing and able" DBEs is completed an overall goal may be established as a percentage of the total amount of contracts receiving U.S. Department of Transportation (U.S. DOT) funds.[40] Participation goals must be set for all certified DBEs and not divided into subcategories.[41] Race- and gender-neutral means must be used to "meet the maximum feasible portion of your overall goal."[42] Iowa DOT, as a recipient of U.S. DOT funds, will not be penalized for failing to meet the overall goal set, if it can establish good faith efforts to meet the goal.[43] When there is a DBE goal on a specific contract opportunity, only the bidder meeting the goal, or establishing good faith efforts to meet the goal, may be awarded the contract.[44]

34. *Id.* r. 261-54.5(2).
35. Iowa Code § 73.16(2)(a) (2023).
36. 49 C.F.R. § 26.43 (2022).
37. *Id.*
38. *Id.* § 26.45(a)(1).
39. *Id.* § 26.45(b).
40. *Id.* § 26.45(e).
41. *Id.* § 26.45(h).
42. *Id.* § 26.51.
43. *Id.* § 26.47.
44. *Id.* § 26.53.

- *Prompt Payment*: Under 49 C.F.R. part 26, contractors must pay subcontractors within 30 days of receipt of payment from the state DOT for satisfactory performance.[45]
- *Payment of Retainage*: Contractors must pay amounts withheld for retainage to subcontractors within 30 days of their work being satisfactorily completed.[46]

Additional Related Laws, Policies, and Programs

- *Iowa-Based Business*: "The [Department of Administrative Services] and state agencies shall make every effort to support Iowa-based businesses when making a purchase. Tied responses to solicitations, regardless of the type of solicitation, shall be decided in favor of the Iowa-based business. Tied bids between Iowa-based businesses shall be decided in accordance with subrule 117.13(4)."[47]
- *Access to Capital*: Iowa offers TSB loans for up to $50,000.[48] A business does not have to be TSB certified but does need to be TSB eligible.[49]
- *Prompt Payment to Subcontractors*: On construction contracts "(1) [a] progress payment or final payment to a subcontractor for satisfactory performance of the subcontractor's work shall be made no later than one of the following, as applicable: (a) Seven days after the contractor receives payment for that subcontractor's work. (b) A reasonable time after the contractor could have received payment for the subcontractor's work, if the reason for nonpayment is not the subcontractor's fault."[50]
- *Finding Contracting Opportunities*: The Iowa Department of Administrative Services lists bid opportunities here: https://bidopportunities.iowa.gov/.

Major City Snapshot: Des Moines

Within the City of Des Moines ordinance, there are two references to disadvantaged business enterprises:

---

45. 49 C.F.R. § 26.29(a) (2023).
46. *Id.* § 26.29(b).
47. Iowa Admin. Code r. 11-117.6(2) (2015).
48. *Id.* r. 261-55.3 (2023); *Targeted Small Business Loans*, Iowa Econ. Dev. Auth., https://www.iowaeda.com/small-business/targeted-small-business/tsb-loans/ (last visited Mar. 1, 2023).
49. *Id.*
50. Iowa Code § 573.12(2)(b)(1) (2023).

- *Section 94-198—Disqualification of bidders*: This section states that "[u]pon the recommendation of the city engineer, the city council may disqualify a contractor or subcontractor from bidding on future public improvement construction or repair contracts or from participating in such as a subcontractor for a period of up to three years." One such factor for disqualification is "[h]abitually failed to comply with the city's program to encourage utilization of disadvantaged business enterprises (DBE) subcontractors on city public improvement projects."
- *Section 2-702—Procurement of goods and services under competitive bidding or request for proposal process*: "In procuring concessions at city facilities, selection of the successful proposal may be based upon criteria in addition to revenue to the city and compliance with specifications, including but not limited to capital investment, experience, financial resources, business plan, and involvement of Disadvantaged Business Enterprises."

CHAPTER 17

Kansas

Overview of Business Inclusion Program, Policies, and Practices

Government entities seeking to create business inclusion programs have two primary options in terms of the type of program they may create, in terms of who is eligible for the program: (1) a race- and gender-conscious program or (2) a race- and gender-neutral program. Under the Equal Protection Clause of the Fourteenth Amendment, strict scrutiny is applied by the courts when a government actor is creating policies based on race. Strict scrutiny is the highest level of judicial review that may be applied. It requires the government actor to demonstrate that (1) past discrimination exists such that the entity has a "compelling government interest" in rectifying it, and (2) the policies and programs created to do so are "narrowly tailored."[1] Although intermediate scrutiny is often applied when reviewing programs based on gender, strict scrutiny is applied when reviewing race- and gender-conscious business inclusion programs.[2] Disparity studies have become a standard tool used to assist a government entity in withstanding a challenge to its race- and gender-conscious business inclusion programs. These studies aid in demonstrating whether a government entity has engaged

1. City of Richmond v. J.A. Croson Co., 488 U.S. 469 (1989).

2. Since the 1980s with the Supreme Court decision in *City of Richmond v. J.A. Croson Company*, there have been a number of cases across the county that have assessed race- and gender-conscious business inclusion programs. *See* Adarand Constructors, Inc. v. Pena, 515 U.S. 200 (1995); Virdi v. DeKalb Cnty. Sch. Dist., 135 Fed. App'x 262, 268 (11th Cir. 2005); Sherbrooke Turf, Inc. v. Minn. Dep't of Transp., 345 F.3d 964, 971 (8th Cir. 2003); Mountain West Holding Co., Inc. v. The State of Montana, Montana DOT, et al., 2017 WL 2179120 (9th Cir. May 16, 2017).

in past discrimination in its contracting practices, such that the entity may have a compelling government interest in rectifying it.[3]

Conversely, race- and gender-neutral programs are programs that are not only accessible to minority-owned and women-owned businesses but to all businesses, regardless of race or gender. A small business inclusion program would fall into this category. The level of judicial review applied to such a policy to determine its constitutionality is rational basis, which is the lowest threshold for a government to satisfy. For a government entity to satisfy rational basis, the policy or program created must be "related to a legitimate government purpose."[4] Even when a government entity has a race- and gender-conscious program, oftentimes the program may still require the government actor to seek to meet the goals of their program through race- and gender-neutral means where able, so as to be taking the most narrowly tailored means of accomplishing the program goals.

In the state of Kansas, at the state level of government, there are two primary business inclusion certifying bodies: (1) the Kansas Statewide Certification Program (KSCP), which is a joint effort between the Kansas Department of Transportation (KDOT), Office of Civil Rights Compliance, and the Department of Commerce, Office of Minority and Women Business Development; and (2) the Kansas Department of Administration, Office of Procurement and Contracts.

Summary of Certification Programs and Requirements

KSCP certifies minority-owned business enterprises (MBEs), women-owned business enterprises (WBEs); disadvantaged business enterprises (DBEs); and airport concessions disadvantaged business enterprises (ACDBEs).[5] Following is a summary of the eligibility requirements for each.

- *Minority-Owned Business Enterprises (MBEs) and Women-Owned Business Enterprises (WBEs)*: For the MBE and WBE program, the Kansas Department of Commerce opted to incorporate the federal DBE program regulations found in 49 C.F.R. part 26,

3. *Promoting Opportunity and Equality in America: A Guide to Federal Circuit Authority on Permissible Government Actions to Promote Racial and Gender Equality*, AM. CIV. LIBERTIES UNION & THE OPPORTUNITY AGENDA (Dec. 2010), https://www.aclu.org/sites/default/files/field_document/Promoting_Opportunity_and_Equality_in_America.pdf.

4. 488 U.S. 469 (1989).

5. *Disadvantaged, Minority- and Women-Owned Business Certification*, KAN. DEP'T OF COM., https://www.kansascommerce.gov/program/business-incentives-and-services/mw-development/dmw-certification/ (last visited Feb. 24, 2023).

subpart D, pertaining to "Certification Standards."[6] As a result, eligibility requirements are as follows: (1) the business must be 51 percent owned and controlled by one or more minorities or women who also control the management and daily operations of the business; (2) qualifying owners are U.S. citizens or lawfully admitted permanent residents; (3) the qualifying owners ownership is "real, substantial and continuing, going beyond pro forma ownership of the firm"; (4) the business is small under the Small Business Administration's (SBA) small business size standards for its NAICS code; and (5) the business is an "independent, viable, and for-profit entity."

- *Disadvantaged Business Enterprises (DBEs)*: Pursuant to 49 C.F.R. part 26, the state of Kansas administers a DBE certification program. As is required under 49 C.F.R. § 26.81, Kansas has a Unified Certification Program. As noted earlier, in Kansas, the Kansas Statewide Certification Program (KSCP) is a joint effort managing the certifications. The UCP makes all DBE certification decisions and provides a "one-stop shop" to DBE applicants.[7] To qualify as a DBE, a business must (1) be for-profit;[8] (2) be a small business concern—with "small" determined by the Small Business Administration (SBA) small business size standards and does not exceed $30.40 million in gross annual receipts;[9] (3) be at least 51 percent owned by socially and economically disadvantaged individuals—there is a rebuttable presumption that women, Black Americans, Hispanic Americans, Native Americans, Asian-Pacific Americans, Subcontinent Asian Americans, or other minorities are disadvantaged;[10] (4) be controlled by one or more of the socially and economically disadvantaged owners;[11] (5) have the socially and economically disadvantaged owners be U.S. citizens or lawfully admitted permanent residents;[12] and (6) have the personal net worth for any socially and economically disadvantaged owner

6. *Minority-Owned Business Enterprises (MBEs) / Women-Owned Business Enterprises (WBEs) Eligibility Criteria*, KAN. DEP'T OF COM., (June 2020), https://www.kansascommerce.gov/wp-content/uploads/2020/08/MBE-WBE_Eligibility.pdf.

7. 49 C.F.R. § 26.81(b)(2) (2022).

8. *Id.* § 26.5.

9. *Id.* §§ 26.5, 26.65(b). It is worth noting that under 49 C.F.R. § 26.65(b) the DBE size standard may be adjusted annually for inflation such that in subsequent years the size standard may no longer be $30.40 million.

10. *Id.* § 26.67.

11. *Id.* § 26.5.

12. *Id.* § 26.67.

not exceed $1.32 million.[13] The DBE program is required on contracting opportunities that have received funding from the Federal Highway Administration (FHWA), Federal Aviation Administration (FAA), or Federal Transit Administration (FTA).[14]

- *Airport Concession Disadvantaged Business Enterprises (ACDBEs)*: In addition to being certified as a DBE under 49 C.F.R. part 26, businesses may also be certified as an Airport Concession Disadvantaged Business Enterprise (ACDBE) under 49 C.F.R. part 23. To qualify as an ACDBE, a business must (1) be a concession for-profit small business concern;[15] (2) qualify as small by having its prior three-year average gross receipts not exceed the applicable size standard of $56.42 million;[16] (3) be 51 percent owned by one or more socially and economically disadvantaged individuals;[17] (4) have one or more of the socially and economically disadvantaged individuals with control and managing the daily business operations;[18] and (5) have the personal net worth for any socially and economically disadvantaged owner not exceed $1.32 million.[19]

The Kansas Department of Administration, Office of Procurement and Contracts, certifies disabled veteran-owned businesses.[20] The certification eligibility requirements are listed here:

- *Disabled Veteran Businesses*: A business must (1) be domiciled in Kansas and (2) have the following verified by the Kansas Commission of Veteran Affairs: (a) be 51 percent owned by one or more veterans or 51 percent of stock owned by one or more veterans; (b) management and daily operations controlled by one or more veterans; and (c) maintain the previously noted requirements for the full contract term.[21]

---

13. *Id.*
14. *Id.* § 26.21(a).
15. *Id.* § 23.3.
16. *Id.* § 23.33(a). The size standards for the following are exceptions to this: bank and financial institutions is $1 billion in assets; car rental companies are $75.23 million average annual gross receipts; pay telephones is 1,500 employees; and automobile dealers is 350 employees.
17. *Id.*
18. *Id.*
19. *Id.* § 23.35.
20. *Certified Business and Disabled Veteran-Owned Business*, Kan. Dep't of Admin., https://admin.ks.gov/offices/procurement-contracts/bidding--contracts/bidder-programs/certified-business-and-disabled-veteran-owned-business (last visited Feb. 24, 2023).
21. Kan. Stat. Ann. § 75-3740(g)(6) (2022).

Procurement Laws Intersecting with Business Inclusion

Kansas procurement laws may primarily be found in chapter 75 of the Kansas Statutes Annotated. Laws and regulations related to procurement and small and diverse businesses are found in several statutes that are cited throughout the following bullet points. Following are some laws that pertain to small, minority-owned, women-owned, and disabled veteran-owned businesses.

- *Contracting Preferences*: There is a contracting preference for veteran businesses that are no more than 10 percent higher than the lowest responsible bidder.[22] In such an instance, the contract must be awarded to the veteran business, provided it is a responsible bidder.[23]
- *Inclusion Goals*: Currently, the Kansas Department of Administration, Division of Purchases, does not set contracting inclusion goals for MBEs, WBEs, and/or DBEs.[24]
- *Contract Award and Negotiations*: Under Kansas Statutes Annotated, section 75-37,102, when a procurement negotiating committee is deciding which party to contract with for services or technical products, the committee must consider several factors.[25] One such factor is whether the party is a disabled veteran business.[26]
- *Reporting Requirements*: Under the Small Business Procurement Act, the Department of Administration shall report to the governor, the legislature and the secretary of economic development prior to each regular legislative session, on the following: (1) total estimated contract dollars to small businesses; (2) total estimated number of contracts to small businesses the prior year; (3) "[t]he total dollar value estimated to have been expended on contracts with small businesses and the estimated number of transactions this represents"; (4) actual total dollar value of contracts spent with minority-owned businesses and women-owned businesses; and (5) the actual number of transactions to minority-owned businesses and women-owned businesses.[27]

---

22. *Id.* § 75-3740(b).
23. *Id.*
24. *Disadvantaged, Minority- and Women-Owned Business Certification*, *supra* note 5.
25. Kan. Stat. Ann. § 75-37,102(d) (2022).
26. *Id.*
27. *Id.* § 75-6011.

Contracting opportunities where the KDOT DBE program applies have several requirements that intersect directly with procurement, contracting, and business inclusion.

- *Fostering Small Business Participation*: Pursuant to 49 C.F.R. § 26.39, KDOT has engaged in efforts to foster small business participation.[28] In KDOT's May 2022 "DBE Program Manual," it notes a timeline and plans to develop a Small Business Enterprise (SBE) program. The program would include tracking SBE projects and utilization.[29] Other efforts include unbundling contracts and "letting small projects . . . for small construction companies."[30]
- *Goals*: Contract opportunities may not use quotas or set-asides for DBEs.[31] The only exception for using a set-aside is in a limited or extreme circumstance, "when no other method could be reasonably expected to redress egregious instances of discrimination."[32] Instead, an overall goal must be set.[33] The goal must be based on evidence of available "ready, willing and able" DBEs in the market.[34] Once the assessment of "ready, willing and able" DBEs is completed, an overall goal may be established as a percentage of the total amount of contracts receiving U.S. Department of Transportation (U.S. DOT) funds.[35] Participation goals must be set for all certified DBEs and not divided into subcategories.[36] Race- and gender-neutral means must be used to "meet the maximum feasible portion of your overall goal."[37] KDOT, as a recipient of U.S. DOT funds, will not be penalized for failing to meet the overall goal set, if it can establish good faith efforts to meet the goal.[38] When there is a DBE goal on a specific contract opportunity, only the bidder meeting the goal, or establishing good faith efforts to meet the goal, may be awarded the contract.[39]

---

28. *DBE Program Manual*, Kan. Dep't of Transp. 15 (2022), https://www.ksdot.gov/Assets/wwwksdotorg/bureaus/divAdmin/Documents/DBEPROGRAMMANUAL.pdf.
29. *Id.*
30. *Id.* at 14.
31. 49 C.F.R. § 26.43 (2022).
32. *Id.* § 26.43.
33. *Id.* § 26.45(a)(1).
34. *Id.* § 26.45(b).
35. *Id.* § 26.45(e).
36. *Id.* § 26.45(h).
37. *Id.* § 26.51.
38. *Id.* § 26.47.
39. *Id.* § 26.53.

- *Prompt Payment*: Under 49 C.F.R. part 26, contractors must pay subcontractors within 30 days of receipt of payment from the state DOT for satisfactory performance.[40]
- *Payment of Retainage*: Contractors must pay amounts withheld for retainage to subcontractors within 30 days of their work being satisfactorily completed.[41]

Additional Related Laws, Policies, and Programs

- *Prompt Payment to Subcontractors on Public Construction Contracts*: Under Kansas Statutes Annotated section 16-1903, "[a] contractor shall pay its subcontractors any amounts due within seven business days of receipt of payment from the owner, including payment of retainage, if retainage is released by the owner, if the subcontractor has provided a timely, properly completed and undisputed request for payment to the contractor."
- *Additional Related Contracting Preferences*: If a business is a "certified business," it shall receive a 10 percent preference over the lowest responsible bidder, provided it is also a responsible bidder.[42] A "certified business" is one that (1) is certified by the Department of Administration; (2) is domiciled in Kansas; (3) primarily does business in Kansas or a substantial amount of its production happens in Kansas; (4) at least 10 percent of its employees reside in Kansas and have a disability; (5) has offered to cover at least 75 percent of the cost of health insurance for each employee; and (6) "does not employ individuals under a certificate issued by the United States secretary of labor under 29 U.S.C. § 214(c)."[43]
- *Kansas Lottery Act Procurements*: Under the Kansas Lottery Act, the Kansas Lottery Commission must "designate certain major procurement contracts or portions thereof to be awarded, in accordance with rules and regulations of the commission, solely to minority business enterprises."[44]
- *Finding Contracting Opportunities*: The Kansas eSupplier Portal that lists bidding events may be found here: https://supplier

---

40. 49 C.F.R. § 26.29(a) (2023).
41. *Id.* § 26.29(b).
42. Kan. Stat. Ann. § 75-3740(b) (2022).
43. *Id.* § 75-3740(g)(1).
44. *Id.* § 74-8705(a).

.sok.ks.gov/psc/sokfsprdsup/SUPPLIER/ERP/c/SCP_PUBLIC_MENU_FL.SCP_PUB_BID_CMP_FL.GBL?&.

Major City Snapshot: Wichita

The City of Wichita has an Emerging and Disadvantaged Business Enterprise Program.[45] Following is a summary of their program.

- *Certifications*: The program accepts the State of Kansas DBE program for federally funded KDOT projects and certifies businesses as Emerging Business Enterprises (EBE).[46] To qualify for an EBE certification, a business must (1) have been in business for at least six months;[47] (2) be a small business under the SBA's size standards;[48] (3) meet the City of Wichita additional industry size standards;[49] (4) be independently owned and operated;[50] and (5) not be dominant in its field.[51] This program is a race and gender neutral program.[52]
- *Good Faith Efforts*: "Responsive low bidders and City Departments, as appropriate, will be required to provide evidence of good faith efforts to reach applicable goals for Emerging and Disadvantaged business participation."[53]
- *Inclusion Goals and RFPs*: The city establishes annual participation goals for EBEs and DBEs.[54] "The participation and utilization goals are be based on the availability of qualified Emerging and Disadvantaged Businesses ready, willing and able to provide the needed goods and services."[55] On RFPs, EBE and DBE participation will account for 5 percent of the scoring on all city RFP scoring criteria.[56]
- *Prompt Payment to EBEs and DBEs*: Although the city has a 30-day payment term for vendors, for EBEs and DBEs, the

45. *Emerging & Disadvantaged Business Enterprise Program*, City of Wichita Fin. Dep't, https://www.wichita.gov/Finance/Purchasing/Pages/EBE.aspx (last visited Feb. 23, 2023).

46. *Emerging and Disadvantaged Business Enterprise Policy and Procedure Manual*, City of Wichita (Aug. 2016), https://www.wichita.gov/Finance/Purchasing/Documents/Emerging%20and%20Disadvantaged%20Business%20Enterprise%20Policy%20and%20Procedure%20Manual.pdf.

47. *EBE Certification Overview*, City of Wichita, https://workwith.wichita.gov/ebe-certification (last visited Feb. 23, 2023).

48. *Emerging and Disadvantaged Business Enterprise Policy and Procedure Manual*, *supra* note 46, at 6.

49. *Id.* at 5–6.

50. *Id.* at 5.

51. *Id.*

52. *EBE Certification Overview*, *supra* note 47.

53. *Emerging and Disadvantaged Business Enterprise Policy and Procedure Manual*, *supra* note 46, at 9.

54. *Id.* at 3.

55. *Id.*

56. *Id.* at 4.

"City staff strive to pay all Emerging and Disadvantaged Businesses within net 10 days on City purchase orders and contracts for goods and services rendered."[57]

- *Reporting Requirements*: Although the EBE program is race and gender neutral, it does report on its spends with EBEs that are minority-owned and women-owned and provides quarterly reports to the City Council.[58]

57. *Id.*
58. *Id.* at 8.

CHAPTER 18

Kentucky

Overview of Business Inclusion Program, Policies, and Practices

Government entities seeking to create business inclusion programs have two primary options in terms of the type of program they may create, in terms of who is eligible for the program: (1) a race- and gender-conscious program or (2) a race- and gender-neutral program. Under the Equal Protection Clause of the Fourteenth Amendment, strict scrutiny is applied by the courts when a government actor is creating policies based on race. Strict scrutiny is the highest level of judicial review that may be applied. It requires the government actor to demonstrate that (1) past discrimination exists such that the entity has a "compelling government interest" in rectifying it, and (2) the policies and programs created to do so are "narrowly tailored."[1] Although intermediate scrutiny is often applied when reviewing programs based on gender, strict scrutiny is applied when reviewing race- and gender-conscious business inclusion programs.[2] Disparity studies have become a standard tool used to assist a government entity in withstanding a challenge to its race- and gender-conscious business inclusion programs. These studies aid in demonstrating whether a government entity has engaged

1. City of Richmond v. J.A. Croson Co., 488 U.S. 469 (1989).

2. Since the 1980s with the Supreme Court decision in *City of Richmond v. J.A. Croson Company*, there have been a number of cases across the county that have assessed race- and gender-conscious business inclusion programs. *See* Adarand Constructors, Inc. v. Pena, 515 U.S. 200 (1995); Virdi v. DeKalb Cnty. Sch. Dist., 135 Fed. App'x 262, 268 (11th Cir. 2005); Sherbrooke Turf, Inc. v. Minn. Dep't of Transp., 345 F.3d 964, 971 (8th Cir. 2003); Mountain West Holding Co., Inc. v. The State of Montana, Montana DOT, et al., 2017 WL 2179120 (9th Cir. May 16, 2017).

in past discrimination in its contracting practices, such that the entity may have a compelling government interest in rectifying it.[3]

Conversely, race- and gender-neutral programs are programs that are not only accessible to minority-owned and women-owned businesses but to all businesses, regardless of race or gender. A small business inclusion program would fall into this category. The level of judicial review applied to such a policy to determine its constitutionality is rational basis, which is the lowest threshold for a government to satisfy. For a government entity to satisfy rational basis, the policy or program created must be "related to a legitimate government purpose."[4] Even when a government entity has a race- and gender-conscious program, oftentimes the program may still require the government actor to seek to meet the goals of their program through race- and gender-neutral means where able, so as to be taking the most narrowly tailored means of accomplishing the program goals.

In the state of Kentucky, at the state level of government, there are two main cabinets with business inclusion programs: (1) the Commonwealth of Kentucky Finance and Administration Cabinet, Office of the Secretary, Office of Equal Employment Opportunity and Contract Compliance and (2) the Commonwealth of Kentucky Transportation Cabinet (KYTC).

Summary of Certification Programs and Requirements

The Commonwealth of Kentucky Finance and Administration Cabinet, Office of the Secretary, Office of Equal Employment Opportunity and Contract Compliance administers the following certifications: Minority-Owned Business Enterprises (MBEs); Women-Owned Business Enterprises (WBEs); and Service-Disabled Veteran-Owned Small Businesses (SDVOSBs). Following is a summary of the eligibility requirements for each:

- *Small Business*: This is not a formal certification; however, it is worth noting. To be considered a small business, a business must be (1) independently owned and operated; (2) not dominant in its field of operation in which it is bidding; and (3) be

---

3. *Promoting Opportunity and Equality in America: A Guide to Federal Circuit Authority on Permissible Government Actions to Promote Racial and Gender Equality*, Am. Civ. Liberties Union & The Opportunity Agenda (Dec. 2010), https://www.aclu.org/sites/default/files/field_document/Promoting_Opportunity_and_Equality_in_America.pdf.

4. 488 U.S. 469 (1989).

a small business under the Small Business Administration (SBA) size standards for its industry.[5]

- *Minority-Owned Business Enterprises (MBEs) and Women-Owned Business Enterprises (WBEs)*: To satisfy the eligibility requirements for certification as an MBE, a business must (1) satisfy the criteria for being a small business noted earlier; (2) be ". . . owned and operated by [51 percent] or more females or persons of African American, Hispanic, Asian, Pacific Islander, American Indian, or Alaskan native heritage";[6] (3) have the minority and/or female owners be U.S. citizens or lawfully admitted permanent residents;[7] (4) be located in the United States;[8] (5) demonstrate that the minority and/or female owners have owned and operated the business for at least one year, as well as the business must have been in operation for at least a year;[9] and (6) demonstrate that the minority and/or women owners filed federal business tax returns for at least one year.[10] Nonprofits can apply for certification as an MWBE; they would need to contact the Finance and Administration, Office of EEO and Contract Compliance.[11]
- *Service-Disabled Veteran-Owned Small Business (SDVOSB)*: The eligibility requirements for certification as a SDVOSB are as follows: (1) the business is independently owned and operated; (2) one or more disabled veterans owns 51 percent of the business and has owned it for at least one calendar year or fiscal year; (3) the business is considered small within the SBA size standards for its industry; and (4) business tax returns have been filed for at least one calendar year or fiscal year by the disabled veteran owner(s).[12] A disabled veteran is defined as: "an individual, domiciled in Kentucky, who has served

5. 200 Ky. Admin. Regs. 5:076 (2021).
6. *Id.*
7. *Am I Eligible?*, Fin. and Admin. Cabinet, https://finance.ky.gov/office-of-the-secretary/office-of-equal-employment-opportunity-contract-compliance/minority-and-women-business-enterprise-certification-program/Pages/am-i-eligible.aspx (last visited Feb. 26, 2023); *Minority and Women Business Enterprise Certification Application*, Fin. and Admin. Cabinet Off. of EEO and Contract Compliance 1 (2021), https://finance.ky.gov/office-of-the-secretary/office-of-equal-employment-opportunity-contract-compliance/minority-and-women-business-enterprise-certification-program/Documents/Final%20MWBE%20Certification%20Application.pdf.
8. *Id.*
9. *Id.*
10. *Id.*
11. *Frequently Asked Questions*, Fin. and Admin. Cabinet, https://finance.ky.gov/office-of-the-secretary/office-of-equal-employment-opportunity-contract-compliance/minority-and-women-business-enterprise-certification-program/Pages/frequently-asked-questions.aspx (last visited Feb. 26, 2023).
12. Ky. Rev. Stat. Ann. § 42.0146(1)(b) (2021).

on active duty in the Armed Forces, has been separated there from under honorable or general conditions, and has established the present existence of a service-connected disability or is receiving compensation, disability retirements benefits, or pension because of a public statute administered by the U.S. Department of Veterans Affairs or Department of Defense, or was terminated from active duty by the Department of Defense because of a disability."[13]

KYTC certifies businesses as Disadvantaged Business Enterprises (DBEs), Airport Concession Disadvantaged Business Enterprises (ACDBEs), and Small Business Enterprises (SBEs). Following are the eligibility requirements for each:

- *Disadvantaged Business Enterprise (DBE)*: Pursuant to 49 C.F.R. part 26, the KYTC administers the state's DBE certification program. As is required under 49 C.F.R. § 26.81, Kentucky has a Unified Certification Program (UCP). The UCP provides a "one-stop shop" to DBE applicants.[14] To qualify as a DBE, a business must (1) be for-profit;[15] (2) be a small business concern—with "small" determined by the Small Business Administration (SBA) small business size standards—and does not exceed $30.40 million in gross annual receipts;[16] (3) be at least 51 percent owned by socially and economically disadvantaged individuals—there is a rebuttable presumption that women, Black Americans, Hispanic Americans, Native Americans, Asian-Pacific Americans, Subcontinent Asian Americans, or other minorities are disadvantaged;[17] (4) be controlled by one or more of the socially and economically disadvantaged owners;[18] (5) have the socially and economically disadvantaged owners be U.S. citizens or lawfully admitted permanent residents;[19] and (6) not have the personal net worth for any socially and economically disadvantaged owner exceed $1.32 million.[20] The DBE program is required on contracting opportunities that have received funding from the Federal

13. *Id.* § 42.0146(1)(a).
14. 49 C.F.R. § 26.81(b)(2) (2022).
15. *Id.* § 26.5.
16. *Id.* §§ 26.5, 26.65(b). It is worth noting that under 49 C.F.R. § 26.65(b), the DBE size standard may be adjusted annually for inflation such that in subsequent years the size standard may no longer be $30.40 million.
17. *Id.* § 26.67.
18. *Id.* § 26.5.
19. *Id.* § 26.67.
20. *Id.*

Highway Administration (FHWA), Federal Aviation Administration (FAA), or Federal Transit Administration (FTA).[21]

- *Airport Concession Disadvantaged Business Enterprise (ACDBE)*: In addition to being certified as a DBE under 49 C.F.R. part 26, businesses may also be certified as an Airport Concession Disadvantaged Business Enterprise (ACDBE) under 49 C.F.R. part 23. To qualify as an ACDBE, a business must (1) be a concession for-profit small business concern;[22] (2) qualify as small by having its prior three-year average gross receipts not exceed the applicable size standard of $56.42 million;[23] (3) be 51 percent owned by one or more socially and economically disadvantaged individuals;[24] (4) have one or more of the socially and economically disadvantaged individuals with control and managing the daily business operations;[25] and (5) have the personal net worth for any socially and economically disadvantaged owner not exceed $1.32 million.[26]
- *Small Business Enterprise (SBE)*: KYTC has implemented a small business element within its DBE program for SBE certification and inclusion, pursuant to 49 C.F.R. § 26.39.[27] To be eligible for the program, a business must (1) be a small business under the Small Business Administration size standards; (2) for purposes of being considered a DBE for the FHA and FTA, the business must have average annual gross receipts from the prior three fiscal years that do not exceed the cap in 49 C.F.R. § 26.65(b);[28] (3) be for-profit; (4) have the majority owners be U.S. citizens or lawful permanent residents and exhibit control over the business; and (5) not have the personal net worth of the owner exceed $1.32 million.[29]

---

21. *Id.* § 26.21(a).
22. *Id.* § 23.3.
23. *Id.* § 23.33(a). The size standards for the following are exceptions to this: bank and financial institutions is $1 billion in assets; car rental companies are $75.23 million average annual gross receipts; pay telephones is 1,500 employees; and automobile dealers is 350 employees.
24. *Id.*
25. *Id.*
26. *Id.* § 23.35.
27. *Disadvantaged Business Enterprise (DBE) Program Plan*, KY. TRANSP. CABINET OFF. FOR CIV. RTS. AND SMALL BUS. DEV. 48–49 (Dec. 2019), https://transportation.ky.gov/Civil-Rights-and-Small-Business-Development/Documents/DBE%20Program%20Plan%20Revised%2012.13.19.pdf.
28. This amount may be adjusted for inflation.
29. *Id.*

Procurement Laws Intersecting with Business Inclusion

The Kentucky Procurement Code may be found in Kentucky Revised Statutes Annotated, chapter 045A.[30] Under the Kentucky Small or Small Minority Business Purchasing Act (Ky. Rev. Stat. Ann. 45A.665 to 45A.685) there are statutes pertaining to the intersection of procurement and business inclusion. Following is a summary of some of the laws that pertain to small, minority-owned, women-owned, and service-disabled veteran-owned small businesses.

- *Contracting Set-Asides*: Under the Kentucky Small or Small Minority Business Purchasing Act, the Finance and Administration Cabinet must "designate as small or small minority business set aside state contracts of goods, equipment, construction, or services requested to be purchased by or for any agency whenever there is a reasonable expectation that bids can be obtained from at least three (3) small or small minority businesses capable of furnishing the desired property or services at a fair and reasonable price."[31] As it relates to Capital Construction Projects, "[h]ighly technical and single source projects shall be exempt from the small business and small minority business set aside designation. Single or limited trade projects estimated to cost $10,000 or less, and multitrade projects estimated to cost $25,000 or less, may be designated as small business and small minority business set asides."[32] Separately, under Kentucky Revised Statutes Annotated § 42.0146, certification as a SDVOSB does not create a ". . . preference in state procurement, nor does it create a point system or set aside. . . ."
- *Bidding Specifications*: When a solicitation has been designated as a small or small minority business set-aside contracting opportunity, then the public notice must designate the invitation as a small and small minority business set-aside and the invitation to bid must only be sent to small and small minority businesses.[33]

---

30. *Procurement Law, Regulations, and Policies*, KY. FIN. AND ADMIN. CABINET, https://finance.ky.gov/eProcurement/Pages/procurement-laws-regulations-and-policies.aspx (last visited Feb. 26, 2023).

31. KY. REV. STAT. ANN. § 45A.675 (2022).

32. 200 KY. ADMIN. REGS. 5:076 (2021).

33. *Id.*

- *Utilization Goals Related to Small Purchases and Reporting on Such Goals*: Under 200 Kentucky Administrative Regulations 5:302, which pertains to small purchase authority, it states that "[a]n agency shall set a minimum goal of five (5) percent utilization of small business and small minority business suppliers" and "[a]n agency shall report its progress toward meeting its utilization goal upon the secretary's request."

Contracting opportunities where the KYTC DBE program applies have several requirements that intersect directly with procurement, contracting, and business inclusion.

- *Goals*: Contract opportunities may not use quotas or set-asides for DBEs.[34] The only exception for using a set-aside is in a limited or extreme circumstance, "when no other method could be reasonably expected to redress egregious instances of discrimination."[35] Instead, an overall goal must be set.[36] The goal must be based on evidence of available "ready, willing and able" DBEs in the market.[37] Once the assessment of "ready, willing and able" DBEs is completed, an overall goal may be established as a percentage of the total amount of contracts receiving U.S. Department of Transportation (U.S. DOT) funds.[38] Participation goals must be set for all certified DBEs and not divided into subcategories.[39] Race- and gender-neutral means must be used to "meet the maximum feasible portion of your overall goal."[40] KYTC, as a recipient of U.S. DOT funds, will not be penalized for failing to meet the overall goal set, if it can establish good faith efforts to meet the goal.[41] When there is a DBE goal on a specific contract opportunity, only the bidder meeting the goal, or establishing good faith efforts to meet the goal, may be awarded the contract.[42] Under the KYTC DBE SBE program, "[t]he Cabinet will set a goal on all FHWA-assisted transportation projects of two million dollars ($2,000,000) or more for participation by small businesses. All small businesses, who otherwise meet the requirements set out herein, may compete for these prime contract and subcontract

34. 49 C.F.R. § 26.43 (2022).
35. *Id.* § 26.43.
36. *Id.* § 26.45(a)(1).
37. *Id.* § 26.45(b).
38. *Id.* § 26.45(e).
39. *Id.* § 26.45(h).
40. *Id.* § 26.51.
41. *Id.* § 26.47.
42. *Id.* § 26.53.

awards, regardless of the owner's gender, race or geographic location. This small business goal is in addition to the DBE contract goals, which may be required pursuant to applicable law or policy."[43]

- *Prompt Payment*: Under 49 C.F.R. part 26, contractors must pay subcontractors within 30 days of receipt of payment from the state DOT for satisfactory performance.[44]
- *Payment of Retainage*: Contractors must pay amounts withheld for retainage to subcontractors within 30 days of their work being satisfactorily completed.[45]

Additional Related Laws, Policies, and Programs

- *Access to Capital*: The Kentucky Economic Development Finance Authority (KEDFA) offers a Small Business Loan program.[46] Authority for this program may be found in Kentucky Revised Statutes Annotated § 154.12-325 and §154.12-330. Loans may range from $15,000 to $100,000.[47] Eligible businesses must (1) have 50 or fewer employees and (2) be in one of the following industries: manufacturing, agribusiness, or services and technology.[48]
- *Veteran-Owned Business Filing Fee Exemptions*: Under Kentucky Revised Statutes Annotated § 14A.2-165, a veteran-owned business is exempt from paying certain filing fees for business-related documents, including, but not limited to, articles of incorporation, amendments of articles of incorporation, and articles of organization.
- *Prompt Payment to Subcontractors*: On construction contracts "[a] contractor shall pay its subcontractors any undisputed amounts due within fifteen (15) business days of receipt of payment from the contracting entity, including payment of retainage if retainage is released by the contracting entity, if the subcontractor has provided a timely, properly completed, and undisputed request for payment to the contractor."[49]

---

43. *Disadvantaged Business Enterprise (DBE) Program Plan*, *supra* note 27, at 48.
44. 49 C.F.R. § 26.29(a) (2023).
45. *Id.* § 26.29(b) (2023).
46. *KEDFA Small Business Loans*, Ky. Cabinet for Econ. Dev., https://ced.ky.gov/Entrepreneurship/KEDFA (last visited Feb. 26, 2023).
47. *Id.*
48. *Id.*
49. Ky. Rev. Stat. Ann. § 371.405(8) (2022).

- *Finding Contract Opportunities*: Information on the Commonwealth of Kentucky's e-Procurement website may be found here: https://finance.ky.gov/eProcurement/Pages/default.aspx.

Major City Snapshot: Lexington

Lexington-Fayette Urban County Government (LFUCG) manages a Minority Business Enterprise Program that works with its Central Purchasing.[50] Following is a high-level summary of the program.

- *Certification*: To be eligible for the MWBE certification, a business must be (1) at least 51 percent owned, operated, controlled, and managed by a minority, veteran, and/or non-minority female and (2) the qualifying owners must be U.S. citizens or lawfully admitted permanent residents.[51] To be eligible for the veteran-owned small business or a service disabled veteran-owned business, a business must (1) be at least 51 percent owned, operated, controlled, and managed by a "veteran or a service-disabled veteran who served on active duty with the U.S. Army, Air Force, Navy, Marines or Coast Guard" and (2) be certified by the Vets First Verification Program through the U.S. Department of Veterans Affairs.[52]
- *Recent Disparity Study*: LFUCG conducted a 2022 disparity study that assessed its utilization of MWBEs. Since LFUCG uses race- and gender-neutral means with its MWBE program, some recommendations included, but are not limited to, considering program components such as aspiration goals and small business set-asides to increase MWBE participation.[53]

50. *Minority Business Enterprise Program*, City of Lexington, https://www.lexingtonky.gov/minority-business-enterprise-program (last visited Feb. 26, 2023).

51. *How to Become a Certified Minority, Veteran and Woman Owned Business*, City of Lexington, https://www.lexingtonky.gov/how-become-certified-minority-veteran-and-woman-owned-business (last visited Feb. 23, 2023).

52. *Id.*

53. *2022 Disparity Study Lexington-Fayette Urban County Government*, BBC Rsch. & Consulting (Sept. 2022), https://www.lexingtonky.gov/sites/default/files/2022-11/LFUCG%202022%20Disparity%20Study%20Report_FINAL.pdf_Oct%202022.pdf.

CHAPTER 19

Louisiana

Overview of Business Inclusion Program, Policies, and Practices

Government entities seeking to create business inclusion programs have two primary options in terms of the type of program they may create, in terms of who is eligible for the program: (1) a race- and gender-conscious program or (2) a race- and gender-neutral program. Under the Equal Protection Clause of the Fourteenth Amendment, strict scrutiny is applied by the courts when a government actor is creating policies based on race. Strict scrutiny is the highest level of judicial review that may be applied. It requires the government actor to demonstrate that (1) past discrimination exists such that the entity has a "compelling government interest" in rectifying it, and (2) the policies and programs created to do so are "narrowly tailored."[1] Although intermediate scrutiny is often applied when reviewing programs based on gender, strict scrutiny is applied when reviewing race- and gender-conscious business inclusion programs.[2] Disparity studies have become a standard tool used to assist a government entity in withstanding a challenge to its race- and gender-conscious business inclusion programs. These studies aid in demonstrating whether a government entity has engaged

1. City of Richmond v. J.A. Croson Co., 488 U.S. 469 (1989).

2. Since the 1980s with the Supreme Court decision in *City of Richmond v. J.A. Croson Company*, there have been a number of cases across the county that have assessed race- and gender-conscious business inclusion programs. *See* Adarand Constructors, Inc. v. Pena, 515 U.S. 200 (1995); Virdi v. DeKalb Cnty. Sch. Dist., 135 Fed. App'x 262, 268 (11th Cir. 2005); Sherbrooke Turf, Inc. v. Minn. Dep't of Transp., 345 F.3d 964, 971 (8th Cir. 2003); Mountain West Holding Co., Inc. v. The State of Montana, Montana DOT, et al., 2017 WL 2179120 (9th Cir. May 16, 2017).

in past discrimination in its contracting practices, such that the entity may have a compelling government interest in rectifying it.[3]

Conversely, race- and gender-neutral programs are programs that are not only accessible to minority-owned and women-owned businesses but to all businesses, regardless of race or gender. A small business inclusion program would fall into this category. The level of judicial review applied to such a policy to determine its constitutionality is rational basis, which is the lowest threshold for a government to satisfy. For a government entity to satisfy rational basis, the policy or program created must be "related to a legitimate government purpose."[4] Even when a government entity has a race- and gender-conscious program, oftentimes the program may still require the government actor to seek to meet the goals of their program through race- and gender-neutral means where able, so as to be taking the most narrowly tailored means of accomplishing the program goals.

In the state of Louisiana, at the state level, there are two state departments that certify businesses for business inclusion programs: (1) the Louisiana Department of Economic Development and (2) the Louisiana Department of Transportation and Development (LADOTD).

Summary of Certification Programs and Requirements

The Louisiana Department of Economic Development certifies businesses through its Louisiana Hudson Initiative[5] and its Louisiana Veterans Initiative (LAVETBIZ).[6] Both programs are race and gender neutral. The eligibility requirements for both follow:

- *Hudson Initiative*: To be eligible for this program, a business must (1) be for-profit; (2) be independently owned and operated; (3) not be dominant in its field of operations; (4) be owned and have officers who are U.S. citizens or legal residents and domiciled in Louisiana; (5) have its principal business office in Louisiana; (6) have fewer than 50 full-time employees; and (7) have average annual gross receipts from the prior three

3. *Promoting Opportunity and Equality in America: A Guide to Federal Circuit Authority on Permissible Government Actions to Promote Racial and Gender Equality*, Am. Civ. Liberties Union & The Opportunity Agenda (Dec. 2010), https://www.aclu.org/sites/default/files/field_document/Promoting_Opportunity_and_Equality_in_America.pdf.

4. 488 U.S. 469 (1989).

5. *Hudson Initiative*, La. Dep't of Econ. Dev., https://www.opportunitylouisiana.gov/small-business/special-programs-for-small-business/hudson-initiative (last visited Apr. 3, 2023).

6. *Veteran Initiative*, La. Dep't of Econ. Dev., https://www.opportunitylouisiana.gov/small-business/special-programs-for-small-business/veteran-initiative (last visited Apr. 3, 2023).

years that do not exceed $10 million dollars per year for construction and $5 million for non-construction.[7]

- *Louisiana Veterans Initiative (LAVETBIZ)*: To satisfy the eligibility requirements for this program, a business must (1) be for-profit; (2) be independently owned and operated; (3) not be dominant in its field of operations; (4) be owned and have officers who are U.S. citizens or legal residents and domiciled in Louisiana; (5) have its principal business office in Louisiana; (6) have fewer than 50 full-time employees; (7) have average annual gross receipts from the prior three years that do not exceed $10 million dollars per year for construction and $5 million for non-construction; and (8) be at least 51 percent owned by a veteran of the U.S. Armed Forces.[8] As a separate effort, in 2019, the governor championed the Louisiana Veterans First Business Initiative. More information on this initiative may be found at https://www.opportunitylouisiana.gov/veterans-first.

LADOTD administers the Disadvantaged Business Enterprise (DBE) program, Airport Concession Disadvantaged Business Enterprise (ACDBE) program, and the Small Business Element (SBE) Program.

- *Disadvantaged Business Enterprise (DBE) Program*: As is required under 49 C.F.R. § 26.81, Louisiana has a Unified Certification Program (LAUCP), of which LADOTD is a member.[9] The LAUCP makes all DBE certification decisions and provides a "one-stop shop" to DBE applicants.[10] To qualify as a DBE, a business must (1) be for-profit;[11] (2) be a small business concern—with "small" determined by the Small Business Administration (SBA) small business size standards—and does not exceed $30.40 million in gross annual receipts;[12] (3) be at least 51 percent owned by socially and economically disadvantaged individuals—there is a rebuttable presumption that women, Black Americans, Hispanic Americans, Native Americans, Asian-Pacific Americans, Subcontinent Asian Americans,

---

7. La. Stat. Ann. § 39:2006 (2022).

8. *Id.* §§ 39:2172, 39:2176.

9. *DOTD DBE Certification*, La. Dep't of Transp. & Dev., http://wwwsp.dotd.la.gov/Inside_LaDOTD/Divisions/Administration/Compliance/Pages/DBE_Certification.aspx (last visited Apr. 3, 2023).

10. 49 C.F.R. § 26.81(b)(2) (2022).

11. *Id.* § 26.5.

12. *Id.* §§ 26.5, 26.65(b). It is worth noting that under 49 C.F.R. § 26.65(b) the DBE size standard may be adjusted annually for inflation such that in subsequent years the size standard may no longer be $30.40 million.

or other minorities are disadvantaged;[13] (4) be controlled by one or more of the socially and economically disadvantaged owners;[14] (5) have the socially and economically disadvantaged owners be U.S. citizens or lawfully admitted permanent residents;[15] and (6) not have the personal net worth for any socially and economically disadvantaged owner exceed $1.32 million.[16] The DBE program is required on contracting opportunities that have received funding from the Federal Highway Administration (FHWA), Federal Aviation Administration (FAA), or Federal Transit Administration (FTA).[17]

- *Airport Concession Disadvantaged Business Enterprise (ACDBE) Program*: In addition to being certified as a DBE under 49 C.F.R. part 26, businesses may also be certified as an Airport Concession Disadvantaged Business Enterprise (ACDBE) under 49 C.F.R. part 23. To qualify as an ACDBE, a business must (1) be a concession for-profit small business concern;[18] (2) qualify as small by having its prior three-year average gross receipts not exceed the applicable size standard of $56.42 million;[19] (3) be 51 percent owned by one or more socially and economically disadvantaged individuals;[20] (4) have one or more of the socially and economically disadvantaged individuals with control and managing the daily business operations;[21] and (5) have the personal net worth for any socially and economically disadvantaged owner not exceed $1.32 million.[22]
- *Small Business Element (SBE) Program*: LADOTD has implemented a race- and gener-neutral small business element within its DBE program called the Small Business Element (SBE) Program, pursuant to 49 C.F.R. § 26.39.[23] To be eligible for the program, a business must (1) be a small business under the SBA size standards—and for the purposes of being

13. *Id.* § 26.67.
14. *Id.* § 26.5.
15. *Id.* § 26.67.
16. *Id.*
17. *Id.* § 26.21(a).
18. *Id.* § 23.3.
19. *Id.* § 23.33(a). The size standards for the following are exceptions to this: bank and financial institutions is $1 billion in assets; car rental companies are $75.23 million average annual gross receipts; pay telephones is 1,500 employees; and automobile dealers is 350 employees.
20. *Id.*
21. *Id.*
22. *Id.* § 23.35.
23. *DBE Program Plan*, La. Dep't of Transp. & Dev. 19 (2023), http://wwwsp.dotd.la.gov/Inside_LaDOTD/Divisions/Administration/Compliance/MiscForms/DBE%20Program%20Plan%20-%202023%20Update.pdf.

considered a DBE for the FHWA and FTA, the business must have average annual gross receipts from the prior three fiscal years that do not exceed $30.4 million;[24] (2) be 51 percent owned and controlled by an economically disadvantaged individual;[25] (3) have the qualifying owner's/owners' personal net worth not exceed $1.32 million;[26] (4) have qualifying owners who are U.S. citizens or lawfully admitted permanent residents of the United States;[27] and (5) be organized for profit.[28]

Procurement Laws Intersecting with Business Inclusion

The most relevant procurement laws intersecting with business inclusion laws and rules in Louisiana may be found in title 39, chapter 17, of the Louisiana Procurement Code and title 19 of the Louisiana Administrative Code. Following are some laws that pertain to businesses certified through the Louisiana Hudson Initiative and Louisiana Veterans Initiative.

- *Subcontracting Plans and Contractor Good Faith Efforts*: When engaged in competitive source selection, agencies must require that bidders and offerors "have a good faith subcontracting plan to utilize a certified small entrepreneurship [or a certified veteran and service-connected disabled veteran-owned small entrepreneurship] as part of a competitive bid or a request for proposal, pursuant to guidelines established by the commissioner of administration."[29]
- *Inclusion Goals*: The commissioner of the Department of Administration must establish annual small entrepreneurship (businesses certified through the Hudson Initiative) and veteran/service-connected disabled veteran-owned small entrepreneurship (Veterans Initiative certified) annual goals for state procurements and public contracts.[30] Each state agency is required

---

24. Prior to 2022, the size standard was $26.29 million. However, since 49 C.F.R. 26.65 notes that this amount may be adjusted for inflation annually, in 2022 it was adjusted to $28.48; then effective March 1, 2023, it was adjusted to $30.4 million. *See* https://www.transportation.gov/DBEsizestandards.

25. *Small Business Element Program Certification Application*, La. Dep't of Transp. & Dev. 1 (2021) http://wwwsp.dotd.la.gov/Inside_LaDOTD/Divisions/Administration/Compliance/SBE%20Documents/SBE%20DOTD%20Certification%20Application%205.28.21.docx.pdf.

26. *Id.*

27. *Id.*

28. *Id.*

29. La. Stat. Ann. §§ 39:2005, 39:2175 (2022).

30. *Id.* §§ 39:2004, 39:2174.

to participate in the requirements of the Hudson Initiative and Veterans Initiative pertaining to procurement and public contracts.[31]

- *Purchases Under $30,000*: For purchases under $30,000, the requirements to receive a specific number of quotes may be waived by state agencies if they receive a reasonably priced quote from a business certified through the Hudson Initiative or the Veterans Initiative.[32]
- *Evaluation Points on Bids and RFPs*: Hudson Initiative certified firms who are offerors in response to a request for a proposal shall be awarded 10 percent of the total evaluation points in a request for proposal.[33] For Veterans Initiative certified firms, "[12 percent] of the total evaluation points in a request for proposal shall be awarded. . . . The mandatory award of evaluation points required by this Paragraph shall be included in all requests for proposals, unless the inclusion jeopardizes funding for the procurement or violates any other provision of law. Any request for an exemption from the requirements of this Paragraph shall be submitted in writing to the commissioner of administration who shall either deny or approve the request. The provisions of this Paragraph shall not apply to design-build or construction manager at risk methods of construction."[34]
- *Prompt Payment to Subcontractors*: Prime contractors or subcontractors that have subcontractors must pay their subcontractors within 14 days of receiving payment from the owner, or a penalty must also be paid.[35]
- *Reporting Requirements*: Annually, the commissioner of the Department of Administration must prepare a report on the progress of the Hudson Initiative and the Veterans Initiative.[36] The report must be provided to the "House Committee on Appropriations and the Senate Committee on Finance."[37] State agencies engaged in procurement and public contracts separate from the Department of Administration must also

31. *Id.* §§ 39:2008, 39:2178.

32. *Id.* § 39:1596; *Small Purchase Procedures*, Executive Order Number JBE 2020–21, at 2–3, (Nov. 9, 2020), https://gov.louisiana.gov/assets/ExecutiveOrders/2020/JBE-2020-21-Small-Purchases-Amending-JBE-2017-18.pdf.

33. La. Stat. Ann. § 39:2005 (2022).

34. *Id.* § 39:2175.

35. *Id.* § 9:2784.

36. *Id.* §§ 39:2007, 39:2177.

37. *Id.*

report to the commissioner so that their data may be included in the report.[38] The report must address, at a minimum, the total number of contracts and dollar value awarded to certified firms; the number of contracts awarded that included a good faith subcontracting plan; and information pertaining to graduation rates of certified firms.[39]

Contracting opportunities where the LADOTD DBE program applies have several requirements that intersect directly with procurement, contracting, and business inclusion.

- *Fostering Small Business Participation*: LADOTD establishes SBE goals on FHWA-assisted contracts between $150,000 and $500,000.[40] In addition, LADOTD engages in monitoring contracts with goals as well as outreach regarding the SBE program as additional efforts to foster small business participation.[41]
- *Goals*: Contract opportunities may not use quotas or set-asides for DBEs.[42] The only exception for using a set-aside is in a limited or extreme circumstance, "when no other method could be reasonably expected to redress egregious instances of discrimination."[43] Instead, an overall goal must be set.[44] The goal must be based on evidence of available "ready, willing and able" DBEs in the market.[45] Once the assessment of "ready, willing and able" DBEs is completed, an overall goal may be established as a percentage of the total amount of contracts receiving U.S. Department of Transportation (U.S. DOT) funds.[46] Participation goals must be set for all certified DBEs and not divided into subcategories.[47] Race- and gender-neutral means must be used to "meet the maximum feasible portion of your overall goal."[48] LADOTD, as a recipient of U.S. DOT funds, will not be penalized for failing to meet the overall goal set, if it can establish good faith efforts to meet the goal.[49] When there is a DBE goal on a specific contract opportunity, only the

38. *Id.*
39. *Id.*
40. *DBE Program*, *supra* note 23.
41. *Id.* at 19–20.
42. 49 C.F.R. § 26.43 (2022).
43. *Id.* § 26.43 (2022).
44. *Id.* § 26.45(a)(1).
45. *Id.* § 26.45(b).
46. *Id.* § 26.45(e).
47. *Id.* § 26.45(h).
48. *Id.* § 26.51.
49. *Id.* § 26.47.

bidder meeting the goal, or establishing good faith efforts to meet the goal, may be awarded the contract.[50]

- *Prompt Payment:* Under 49 C.F.R. part 26, contractors must pay subcontractors within 30 days of receipt of payment from the state DOT for satisfactory performance.[51]
- *Payment of Retainage*: Contractors must pay amounts withheld for retainage to subcontractors within 30 days of their work being satisfactorily completed.[52]

Additional Related Laws, Policies, and Programs

- *Access to Capital*: In terms of access to capital, Louisiana's Department of Economic Development offers programs such as their Bonding Assistance Program[53] and their State Small Business Credit Initiative.[54]
- *Technical Assistance*: Louisiana has a Small and Emerging Business Development Program that provides managerial and technical assistance to small businesses.[55]
- *Finding Contract Opportunities*: The "Quick Links" section of the following Office of State Procurement website provides additional information on contracting opportunities: https://www.doa.la.gov/doa/osp/.

Major City Snapshot: New Orleans

As part of the City of New Orleans' (city) Business Opportunity Program, the city maintains a Disadvantaged Business Enterprise program. Relevant city authority for the program may be found in section 6-308 of the Home Rule Charter of the City of New Orleans and division 2 of Article IV of chapter 70 of the Code of the City of New Orleans.[56]

---

50. *Id.* § 26.53.
51. 49 C.F.R. § 26.29(a) (2023).
52. *Id.* § 26.29(b).
53. *Bonding Assistance Program*, La. Dep't of Econ. Dev., https://www.opportunitylouisiana.gov/small-business/special-programs-for-small-business/bonding-assistance-program (last visited Apr. 3, 2023).
54. *State Small Business Credit Initiative*, La. Dep't of Econ. Dev., https://www.louisianassbci.com/ (last visited Apr. 3, 2023).
55. La. Stat. Ann. §§ 51:941–51:947 (2022); *Small and Emerging Business Development Program*, La. Dep't of Econ. Dev., https://www.opportunitylouisiana.gov/small-business/special-programs-for-small-business/small-and-emerging-business-development-program (last visited Apr. 3, 2023).
56. *Equitable Business Opportunities Program (EBO) Rules and Regulations*, City of New Orleans 2 (2022), https://nola.gov/nola/media/Economic-Development/Supplier%20Diversity/EBO-Rules-and-Regulations_Final-V1-052022.pdf.

- *Certifications*: The city's Office of Supplier Diversity (OSD) certifies businesses for its State and Local Disadvantaged Business Enterprise (SLDBE) program.[57] Firms certified through the LAUCP may receive a provisional certification that does allow them to be considered a valid DBE with the city.[58] This is a race- and gender-neutral program.[59]
- *Inclusion Goals*: The city has set a 35 percent overall equity goal "for all public spending or private projects that utilize public funding or incentives."[60]
- *Utilization Plans and Contractor Good Faith Efforts*: If a goal is not waived for a bidder and the bidder fails to meet the goal, then the bidder must demonstrate good faith efforts to meet the goal or its bid will be rejected.[61]
- *Prompt Payment to Subcontractors*: Prime contractors or subcontractors that have subcontractors must pay their subcontractors within 14 days of receiving payment from the owner, or a penalty must also be paid.[62]
- *Reporting Requirements*: "The [Chief Administrative Officer] shall submit an EBO program report to the city council by October 15th of each year identifying the city's equity goals and attainment rates for the prior two years."[63] In addition, "OSD shall prepare and submit an annual report on all contracts executed by the city pursuant to section 6-308(1) of the Home Rule Charter, sorted by department, to the CAO by October 1st of each year identifying equity goals and attainment rates for the prior two years."[64]
- *Remedies for Noncompliance*: Since compliance with the provisions of the city ordinance pertaining to the Equal Business Opportunity Program and SLDBE program is a material term of contracts, failure to comply will lead to corrective action that may include remedies such as liquidated damages.[65]

---

57. *Id.* at 3; City of New Orleans Ordinances § 70-456 (2023).

58. *Equitable Business Opportunities Program (EBO) Rules and Regulations*, *supra* note 57, at 3; City of New Orleans Ordinances § 70-456 (2023).

59. *Equitable Business Opportunity Program*, City of New Orleans Off. Of Supplier Diversity, https://nola.gov/next/supplier-diversity/programs/equitable-business-opportunities-(ebo)-program/ (last visited Apr. 3, 2023).

60. City of New Orleans Ordinances § 70-459 (2023).

61. *Equitable Business Opportunities Program (EBO) Rules and Regulations*, *supra* note 57, at 7; City of New Orleans Ordinances § 70-461 (2023).

62. *Equitable Business Opportunities Program (EBO) Rules and Regulations*, *supra* note 57, at 9.

63. City of New Orleans Ordinances § 70-462 (2023).

64. *Id.*

65. *Equitable Business Opportunities Program (EBO) Rules and Regulations*, *supra* note 57, at 10; City of New Orleans Ordinances § 70-464 (2023).

CHAPTER 20

Maine

Overview of Business Inclusion Program, Policies, and Practices

Government entities seeking to create business inclusion programs have two primary options in terms of the type of program they may create, in terms of who is eligible for the program: (1) a race- and gender-conscious program or (2) a race- and gender-neutral program. Under the Equal Protection Clause of the Fourteenth Amendment, strict scrutiny is applied by the courts when a government actor is creating policies based on race. Strict scrutiny is the highest level of judicial review that may be applied. It requires the government actor to demonstrate that (1) past discrimination exists such that the entity has a "compelling government interest" in rectifying it, and (2) the policies and programs created to do so are "narrowly tailored."[1] Although intermediate scrutiny is often applied when reviewing programs based on gender, strict scrutiny is applied when reviewing race- and gender-conscious business inclusion programs.[2] Disparity studies have become a standard tool used to assist a government entity in withstanding a challenge to its race- and gender-conscious business inclusion programs. These studies aid in demonstrating whether a government entity has engaged

---

1. City of Richmond v. J.A. Croson Co., 488 U.S. 469 (1989).

2. Since the 1980s with the Supreme Court decision in *City of Richmond v. J.A. Croson Company*, there have been a number of cases across the county that have assessed race- and gender-conscious business inclusion programs. *See* Adarand Constructors, Inc. v. Pena, 515 U.S. 200 (1995); Virdi v. DeKalb Cnty. Sch. Dist., 135 Fed. App'x 262, 268 (11th Cir. 2005); Sherbrooke Turf, Inc. v. Minn. Dep't of Transp., 345 F.3d 964, 971 (8th Cir. 2003); Mountain West Holding Co., Inc. v. The State of Montana, Montana DOT, et al., 2017 WL 2179120 (9th Cir. May 16, 2017).

in past discrimination in its contracting practices, such that the entity may have a compelling government interest in rectifying it.[3]

Conversely, race- and gender-neutral programs are programs that are not only accessible to minority-owned and women-owned businesses but to all businesses, regardless of race or gender. A small business inclusion program would fall into this category. The level of judicial review applied to such a policy to determine its constitutionality is rational basis, which is the lowest threshold for a government to satisfy. For a government entity to satisfy rational basis, the policy or program created must be "related to a legitimate government purpose."[4] Even when a government entity has a race- and gender-conscious program, oftentimes the program may still require the government actor to seek to meet the goals of their program through race- and gender-neutral means where able, so as to be taking the most narrowly tailored means of accomplishing the program goals.

At the state level of government in Maine, the Maine Department of Transportation (MaineDOT) is the main entity that certifies businesses for a business inclusion program.

Summary of Certification Programs and Requirements

MaineDOT administers the Disadvantaged Business Enterprise (DBE) program and the Airport Concession Disadvantaged Business Enterprise (ACDBE) program.[5]

- *Disadvantaged Business Enterprise (DBE) Program*: Pursuant to 49 C.F.R. part 26, the MaineDOT administers the state's DBE certification program. As is required under 49 C.F.R. § 26.81, Maine has a Unified Certification Program (UCP). The UCP makes all DBE certification decisions and provides a "one-stop shop" to DBE applicants.[6] To qualify as a DBE, a business must (1) be for-profit;[7] (2) be a small business concern—with "small" determined by the Small Business Administration (SBA) small business size standards—and does not exceed $30.40 million

3. *Promoting Opportunity and Equality in America: A Guide to Federal Circuit Authority on Permissible Government Actions to Promote Racial and Gender Equality*, Am. Civ. Liberties Union & The Opportunity Agenda (Dec. 2010), https://www.aclu.org/sites/default/files/field_document/Promoting_Opportunity_and_Equality_in_America.pdf.

4. 488 U.S. 469 (1989).

5. *Disadvantaged Business Enterprises*, Me. Dep't of Transp., https://www.maine.gov/mdot/civilrights/dbe/ (last visited Mar. 21, 2023).

6. 49 C.F.R. § 26.81(b)(2) (2022).

7. *Id.* § 26.5.

in gross annual receipts;[8] (3) be at least 51 percent owned by socially and economically disadvantaged individuals—there is a rebuttable presumption that women, Black Americans, Hispanic Americans, Native Americans, Asian-Pacific Americans, Subcontinent Asian Americans, or other minorities are disadvantaged;[9] (4) be controlled by one or more of the socially and economically disadvantaged owners;[10] (5) have the socially and economically disadvantaged owners be U.S. citizens or lawfully admitted permanent residents;[11] and (6) have the personal net worth for any socially and economically disadvantaged owner not exceed $1.32 million.[12] The DBE program is required on contracting opportunities that have received funding from the Federal Highway Administration (FHWA), Federal Aviation Administration (FAA), or Federal Transit Administration (FTA).[13]

- *Airport Concession Disadvantaged Business Enterprise (ACDBE) Program*: In addition to being certified as a DBE under 49 C.F.R. part 26, businesses may also be certified as an Airport Concession Disadvantaged Business Enterprise (ACDBE) under 49 C.F.R. part 23. To qualify as an ACDBE, a business must: (1) be a concession for-profit small business concern;[14] (2) qualify as small by having its prior three-year average gross receipts not exceed the applicable size standard of $56.42 million;[15] (3) be 51 percent owned by one or more socially and economically disadvantaged individuals;[16] (4) have one or more of the socially and economically disadvantaged individuals with control and managing the daily business operations;[17] and (5) have the personal net worth for any socially and economically disadvantaged owner not exceed $1.32 million.[18]

8. *Id.* §§ 26.5, 26.65(b). It is worth noting that under 49 C.F.R. § 26.65(b) the DBE size standard may be adjusted annually for inflation such that in subsequent years the size standard may no longer be $30.40 million.
9. *Id.* § 26.67.
10. *Id.* § 26.5.
11. *Id.* § 26.67.
12. *Id.*
13. *Id.* § 26.21(a).
14. *Id.* § 23.3.
15. *Id.* § 23.33(a). The size standards for the following are exceptions to this: bank and financial institutions is $1 billion in assets; car rental companies are $75.23 million average annual gross receipts; pay telephones is 1,500 employees; and automobile dealers is 350 employees.
16. *Id.*
17. *Id.*
18. *Id.* § 23.35.

Procurement Laws Intersecting with Business Inclusion

Procurement in the state of Maine is managed by the Department of Administrative and Financial Services Division of Procurement Services.[19] The authority for procurement in Maine may be found under title 5, Administrative Procedures and Services, chapter 155, Purchases.[20] In Maine, at the state level, there are no bidding preferences, laws, or rules specific to business inclusion and minority-owned, women-owned, disability-owned, veteran-owned, and/or LGBT-owned business enterprises in Maine, outside of what is required by the MaineDOT DBE program.

Contracting opportunities where the MaineDOT DBE program applies have several requirements that intersect directly with procurement, contracting, and business inclusion.

- *Fostering Small Business Participation*: Pursuant to 49 C.F.R. § 26.39, MaineDOT has engaged in efforts to foster small business participation.[21] For example, MaineDOT does not require businesses to go through the prequalification process prior to bidding on contract opportunities under $300,000; it assesses if projects should be unbundled; and it allows primes and subcontractors to subcontract 70 percent of their bids.[22]
- *Goals*: Contract opportunities may not use quotas or set-asides for DBEs.[23] The only exception for using a set-aside is in a limited or extreme circumstance, "when no other method could be reasonably expected to redress egregious instances of discrimination."[24] Instead, an overall goal must be set.[25] The goal must be based on evidence of available "ready, willing and able" DBEs in the market.[26] Once the assessment of "ready, willing and able" DBEs is completed, an overall goal may be established as a percentage of the total amount of contracts receiving U.S. Department of Transportation (U.S. DOT)

19. *Division of Procurement Services*, ME. DEP'T OF ADMIN. & FIN. SERVS., https://www.maine.gov/dafs/bbm/procurementservices/ (last visited Mar. 20, 2023).

20. *Statutes*, ME. DEP'T OF ADMIN. & FIN. SERVS., https://www.maine.gov/dafs/bbm/procurementservices/policies-procedures/statute (last visited Mar. 20, 2023).

21. *Disadvantage Business Enterprise Program*, ME. DEP'T OF TRANSP. 12–13 (2022), https://www.maine.gov/mdot/civilrights/docs/dbe/2023/MaineDOT%20DBE%20Program%202022.pdf.

22. *Id.*

23. 49 C.F.R. § 26.43 (2022).

24. *Id.* § 26.43.

25. *Id.* § 26.45(a)(1).

26. *Id.* § 26.45(b).

funds.[27] Participation goals must be set for all certified DBEs and not divided into subcategories.[28] Race- and gender-neutral means must be used to "meet the maximum feasible portion of your overall goal."[29] MaineDOT, as a recipient of U.S. DOT funds, will not be penalized for failing to meet the overall goal set, if it can establish good faith efforts to meet the goal.[30] When there is a DBE goal on a specific contract opportunity, only the bidder meeting the goal, or establishing good faith efforts to meet the goal, may be awarded the contract.[31]

- *Prompt Payment*: Under 49 C.F.R. part 26, contractors must pay subcontractors within 30 days of receipt of payment from the state DOT for satisfactory performance.[32]
- *Payment of Retainage*: Contractors must pay amounts withheld for retainage to subcontractors within 30 days of their work being satisfactorily completed.[33]

Additional Related Laws, Policies, and Programs

Under Maine procurement laws, there are bidding preferences. None of these bidding preferences pertain to the inclusion of minority-owned, women-owned, disability-owned, veteran-owned, and/or LGBT-owned business enterprises. However, they may benefit a local business that happens to fall into one of these categories.

- *In-State Bidder Preference*: In instances of a tied bid "[t]he Director of the Bureau of General Services shall award contracts, grants or purchases to in-state bidders or to bidders offering commodities produced or manufactured in the State if the price, quality, availability and other factors are equivalent."[34]
- *Prompt Payment to Subcontractors*: On construction contracts "[n]otwithstanding any contrary agreement, when a subcontractor or material supplier has performed in accordance with the provisions of a contract, a contractor shall pay to the subcontractor or material supplier, and each subcontractor shall in turn pay to its subcontractors or material suppliers, the full or

27. *Id.* § 26.45(e).
28. *Id.* § 26.45(h).
29. *Id.* § 26.51.
30. *Id.* § 26.47.
31. *Id.* § 26.53.
32. 49 C.F.R. § 26.29(a) (2023).
33. *Id.* § 26.29(b).
34. Me. Rev. Stat. Ann. tit. 5, § 1825-B(8) (2022).

proportional amount received for each subcontractor's work and materials based on work completed or service provided under the subcontract, 7 days after receipt of each progress or final payment or 7 days after receipt of the subcontractor's or material supplier's invoice, whichever is later."[35]

- *Finding Contract Opportunities*: Information about contracting opportunities may be found on the Division of Procurement Services website here: https://www.maine.gov/dafs/bbm/procurementservices/vendors

Major City Snapshot

In looking at two of the largest cities in Maine—Portland and Lewiston—neither of these cities have a city-specific business inclusion program.[36] In contracting opportunities and projects receiving federal funding from the Department of Transportation, cities have noted business inclusion goals in accordance with federal regulations and requirements for federal fund recipients.[37]

35. *Id.* tit. 10, § 1114(3).

36. A review of each city ordinance was completed.

37. As examples, please see the following: *Terminal Apron Expansion Northwest End—Phase 2*, City of Portland (2023), https://content.civicplus.com/api/assets/12ef5a86-fc6d-4bb3-8d64-fe855f96745e?cache=1800.

CHAPTER 21

Maryland

Overview of Business Inclusion Program, Policies, and Practices

Government entities seeking to create business inclusion programs have two primary options in terms of the type of program they may create, in terms of who is eligible for the program: (1) a race- and gender-conscious program or (2) a race- and gender-neutral program. Under the Equal Protection Clause of the Fourteenth Amendment, strict scrutiny is applied by the courts when a government actor is creating policies based on race. Strict scrutiny is the highest level of judicial review that may be applied. It requires the government actor to demonstrate that (1) past discrimination exists such that the entity has a "compelling government interest" in rectifying it, and (2) the policies and programs created to do so are "narrowly tailored."[1] Although intermediate scrutiny is often applied when reviewing programs based on gender, strict scrutiny is applied when reviewing race- and gender-conscious business inclusion programs.[2] Disparity studies have become a standard tool used to assist a government entity in withstanding a challenge to its race- and gender-conscious business inclusion programs. These studies aid in demonstrating whether a government entity has engaged

1. City of Richmond v. J.A. Croson Co., 488 U.S. 469 (1989).

2. Since the 1980s with the Supreme Court decision in *City of Richmond v. J.A. Croson Company*, there have been a number of cases across the county that have assessed race- and gender-conscious business inclusion programs. *See* Adarand Constructors, Inc. v. Pena, 515 U.S. 200 (1995); Virdi v. DeKalb Cnty. Sch. Dist., 135 Fed. App'x 262, 268 (11th Cir. 2005); Sherbrooke Turf, Inc. v. Minn. Dep't of Transp., 345 F.3d 964, 971 (8th Cir. 2003); Mountain West Holding Co., Inc. v. The State of Montana, Montana DOT, et al., 2017 WL 2179120 (9th Cir. May 16, 2017).

in past discrimination in its contracting practices, such that the entity may have a compelling government interest in rectifying it.[3]

Conversely, race- and gender-neutral programs are programs that are not only accessible to minority-owned and women-owned businesses but to all businesses, regardless of race or gender. A small business inclusion program would fall into this category. The level of judicial review applied to such a policy to determine its constitutionality is rational basis, which is the lowest threshold for a government to satisfy. For a government entity to satisfy rational basis, the policy or program created must be "related to a legitimate government purpose."[4] Even when a government entity has a race- and gender-conscious program, oftentimes the program may still require the government actor to seek to meet the goals of their program through race- and gender-neutral means where able, so as to be taking the most narrowly tailored means of accomplishing the program goals.

In the state of Maryland, at the state level of government, the following are the main entities that certify businesses for business inclusion programs: (1) Governor's Office of Small, Minority, and Women Business Affairs and (2) the Maryland Department of Transportation (MDOT).

Summary of Certification Programs and Requirements

The Governor's Office of Small, Minority and Women Business Affairs has the following types of certifications available: (1) Small Business Reserve (SBR) Program certification and (2) Veteran-Owned Small Business Enterprise (VSBE) program certification.

- *Small Business Reserve (SBR) Program Certification*: The SBR program is a race- and gender-neutral program.[5] A small business is defined as a business that is (1) for profit other than a broker;[6] (2) independently owned and operated;[7] (3) not a subsidiary of another business;[8] (4) not dominant in its field of operation;[9] and

---

3. *Promoting Opportunity and Equality in America: A Guide to Federal Circuit Authority on Permissible Government Actions to Promote Racial and Gender Equality*, Am. Civ. Liberties Union & The Opportunity Agenda (Dec. 2010), https://www.aclu.org/sites/default/files/field_document/Promoting_Opportunity_and_Equality_in_America.pdf.

4. 488 U.S. 469 (1989).

5. *State of Maryland Procurement Manual*, State of Md. 13, https://procurement.maryland.gov/wp-content/uploads/sites/12/2019/07/MarylandProcurementManual.pdf (last visited Feb. 1, 2023).

6. *Small Business Reserve Program*, Governor's Off. of Small, Minority & Women Bus. Affs. Rsrv. Program, https://gomdsmallbiz.maryland.gov/Pages/sbr-Program.aspx (last visited Feb. 1, 2023).

7. Md. Code Ann., State Finance and Procurement § 14-501(b) (LexisNexis 2023).

8. *Id.*

9. *Id.*

(5) has the number of employees or gross receipts for its industry that meet the small business size outlined under the statute.[10] Certification as a small business is completed online through (1) going to the state's e-Procurement platform, eMaryland Marketplace Advantage (eMMA); (2) registering for an account; (3) completing the small business reserve application; and (4) attesting that they meet the eligibility standards.[11] Once certified, recertification must be completed annually.[12]

- *Veteran-Owned Small Business Enterprise (VSBE) Program Certification*: Administration of the VSBE program is handled by the Governor's Office of Small, Minority and Women Business Affairs.[13] A veteran-owned small business enterprise must (1) be a for-profit business; (2) meet the U.S. Small Business Administration (SBA) small business size standards; (3) be 51 percent owned by one or more veterans; and (4) one or more veterans controls the management and daily operations of the business.[14] To get certified as a VSBE, a business must complete vendor registration on eMMA, just like for the aforementioned SBR program.[15] Once the registration is completed, the business must complete the veteran verification process where they must be verified as a veteran by either the Maryland Department of Veteran Affairs or by the SBA Veteran Small Business Certification (VetCert).[16] Lastly, the business must complete the VSBE certification application found on eMMA.[17]

MDOT certifies businesses as Disadvantaged Business Enterprises (DBEs), Airport Concession Disadvantaged Business Enterprises (ACDBEs), Minority Business Enterprises (MBEs), and Small Business Enterprises (SBEs).

---

10. *Id.* Small in terms of employees can range from the following, depending on the industry: (1) no more than 25–100 employed persons or (2) no more than $2 million to $10 million in gross sales in its most recently completed three fiscal years.

11. *Small Business Reserve Program*, GOVERNOR'S OFF. OF SMALL, MINORITY & WOMEN BUS. AFFS. RSRV. PROGRAM, https://gomdsmallbiz.maryland.gov/Pages/sbr-Program.aspx (last visited Feb. 1, 2023).

12. MD. CODE REGS. 21.11.01.04(A) (2023).

13. *State of Maryland Procurement Manual* 13, https://procurement.maryland.gov/wp-content/uploads/sites/12/2019/07/MarylandProcurementManual.pdf (last visited Feb. 1, 2023).

14. MD. CODE REGS. 21.11.14.02(B) (2023).

15. *Veteran-Owned Small Business Enterprise Program*, GOVERNOR'S OFF. OF SMALL, MINORITY & WOMEN BUS. AFFS. RSRV. PROGRAM, https://gomdsmallbiz.maryland.gov/Pages/VSBE-Program.aspx (last visited Feb. 1, 2023).

16. *Id.*

17. *Id.*

- *Disadvantaged Business Enterprise (DBE) Program*: Pursuant to 49 C.F.R. part 26 MDOT administers the state's DBE certification program. As is required under 49 C.F.R. § 26.81, Maryland has a Unified Certification Program (UCP). The UCP makes all DBE certification decisions and provides a "one-stop shop" to DBE applicants.[18] To qualify as a DBE a business must (1) be for-profit;[19] (2) be a small business concern—with "small" determined by the SBA small business size standards—and does not exceed $30.40 million in gross annual receipts;[20] (3) be at least 51 percent owned by socially and economically disadvantaged individuals—there is a rebuttable presumption that women, Black Americans, Hispanic Americans, Native Americans, Asian-Pacific Americans, Subcontinent Asian Americans, or other minorities are disadvantaged;[21] (4) be controlled by one or more of the socially and economically disadvantaged owners;[22] (5) have the socially and economically disadvantaged owners be U.S. citizens or lawfully admitted permanent residents;[23] and (6) have the personal net worth for any socially and economically disadvantaged owner not exceed $1.32 million.[24] The DBE program is required on contracting opportunities that have received funding from the Federal Highway Administration (FHWA), Federal Aviation Administration (FAA), or Federal Transit Administration (FTA).[25]
- *Airport Concession Disadvantaged Business Enterprise (ACDBE) Program*: In addition to being certified as a DBE under 49 C.F.R. part 26, businesses may also be certified as an Airport Concession Disadvantaged Business Enterprise (ACDBE) under 49 C.F.R. part 23. To qualify as an ACDBE, a business must (1) be a concession for-profit small business concern;[26] (2) qualify as small by having its prior three-year average gross receipts not exceed the applicable size standard

---

18. 49 C.F.R. § 26.81(b)(2) (2022).
19. *Id.* § 26.5.
20. *Id.* §§ 26.5, 26.65(b). It is worth noting that under 49 C.F.R. § 26.65(b) the DBE size standard may be adjusted annually for inflation such that in subsequent years the size standard may no longer be $30.40 million.
21. *Id.* § 26.67.
22. *Id.* § 26.5.
23. *Id.* § 26.67.
24. *Id.*
25. *Id.* § 26.21(a).
26. *Id.* § 23.3.

of $56.42 million;[27] (3) be 51 percent owned by one or more socially and economically disadvantaged individuals;[28] (4) have one or more of the socially and economically disadvantaged individuals with control and managing the daily business operations;[29] and (5) have the personal net worth for any socially and economically disadvantaged owner not exceed $1.32 million.[30]

- *Minority Business Enterprise (MBE) Program Certification*: Although this is a race- and gender-conscious program, race-neutral measures must be used to the "maximum extent feasible."[31] MDOT's Office of Minority Business Enterprise is the certification agency responsible for certifying MBEs,[32] while the administration of the program beyond certification rests with the Governor's Office of Small, Minority and Women Business Affairs.[33] To be eligible for the MBE certification, a business must (1) be 51 percent owned and controlled by one or more socially and economically disadvantaged individuals;[34] (2) be managed by one or more of the socially and economically disadvantaged individuals who own the business;[35] (3) have the daily operations controlled by one or more of the socially and economically disadvantaged individuals who own the business;[36] (4) have the personal net worth of the socially and economically disadvantaged owners not exceed $1,995,008;[37] and (5) have the socially and economically disadvantaged owners be U.S. citizens or lawfully admitted permanent residents.[38] The following individuals are presumed to be socially and economically disadvantaged: women, African Americans, American Indian/Native

27. *Id.* § 23.33(a). The size standards for the following are exceptions to this: bank and financial institutions is $1 billion in assets; car rental companies are $75.23 million average annual gross receipts; pay telephones is 1,500 employees; and automobile dealers is 350 employees.

28. *Id.*

29. *Id.*

30. *Id.* § 23.35.

31. MD. CODE REGS. 21.11.03.01(D) (2023).

32. *Id.* 21.11.03.03(B)(2).

33. *Minority Business Enterprise (MBE) Program*, GOVERNOR'S OFF. OF SMALL, MINORITY & WOMEN BUS. AFFS. RSRV. PROGRAM, https://gomdsmallbiz.maryland.gov/Pages/mbe-Program.aspx (last visited Feb. 1, 2023).

34. MD. CODE REGS. 21.01.02.01(B)(54) (2023).

35. *Id.*

36. *Id.*

37. *Id.* 21.11.03.03(B)(5)(b); *New Year New Cap for Personal Net Worth in Maryland's Minority Business Enterprise Program*, MD. DEP'T OF TRANSP. (Dec, 27, 2022), https://www.mdot.maryland.gov/tso/pages/newsroomdetails.aspx?newsId=683&PageId=38.

38. MD. CODE REGS. 21.11.03.03(B)(15)(a) (2023).

Americans, Asian individuals, Hispanic individuals, and physically or mentally disabled individuals.[39] Once certified, recertification must be completed annually.[40]

- *Small Business Enterprise (SBE) Program*: MDOT also administers a Small Business Enterprise (SBE) program. To qualify for this race- and gender-neutral program,[41] a business must (1) be a small business within the SBA size standards for its industry;[42] (2) have annual gross receipts, even if within the SBA size standard, that do not exceed the size standard identified in 49 C.F.R. § 26.65;[43] (3) have average gross receipts that do not exceed the U.S. Department of Transportation's (U.S. DOT) standard for small of $30.4 million;[44] (4) have 51 percent of the firm's owners meet the personal net worth cap of $1.32 million;[45] (5) be a for-profit business;[46] and (6) have the 51 percent owner(s) be U.S. citizen(s) or permanent resident(s).[47]

Procurement Laws Intersecting with Business Inclusion

Many of the laws pertaining to procurement and business inclusion may be found in the Maryland State Finance and Procurement Code. In addition, title 21 of the Code of Maryland Regulations contains the most relevant rules. Following are some of the relevant business inclusion laws related to procurement.

- *Small Business Reserve Program*: This program requires all state agencies to achieve a minimum of 15 percent of their total procurements with certified small businesses.[48] Small Business Reserve Program procurement opportunities are limited to

---

39. *Id.* 21.11.03.03(B)(15)(b).

40. *State of Maryland Procurement Manual*, *supra* note 13, at 14.

41. *Small Business Enterprise (SBE) Program Certification Application*, MD. DEP'T OF TRANSP. (last visited July 11, 2023), https://www.mdot.maryland.gov/MBE_DOCS/SBE_APPLICATION_2023_March%202023.pdf; *Small Business Enterprise (SBE) Certification Application*, MD. DEP'T OF TRANSP., https://www.mdot.maryland.gov/tso/pages/Index.aspx?PageId=106 (last visited Apr. 28, 2023).

42. *Small Business Enterprise (SBE) Program Certification Application*, *supra* note 41; *Small Business Enterprise (SBE) Certification Application*, *supra* note 41.

43. 49 C.F.R. § 26.65(b) (2022).

44. *Small Business Enterprise (SBE) Program Certification Application*, *supra* note 41; *Small Business Enterprise (SBE) Certification Application*, *supra* note 41.

45. *Small Business Enterprise (SBE) Program Certification Application*, *supra* note 41; *Small Business Enterprise (SBE) Certification Application*, *supra* note 41.

46. *Id.*

47. *Id.*

48. MD. CODE ANN., State Finance and Procurement § 14-502(c) (LexisNexis 2023); MD. CODE REGS. 21.11.01.06 (2023).

certified small businesses and are at the prime contract level.[49] All state agencies also must designate an SBR liaison who "shall be responsible for coordinating the procurement unit's outreach efforts to the small business community, reviewing the unit's contracting procedures to ensure compliance with small business reserve requirements, assisting in the resolution of small business reserve contracting issues, and submitting required small business reserve program reports or information."[50]

- *Small Business Preference Program*: This program applies only to procurements by MDOT, Department of General Services, the University System of Maryland, and Morgan State University.[51] It also applies to the Department of Public Safety and Department of Correctional Services only on construction of a state correctional facility.[52] The preference amounts are as follows: (1) small business—5 percent, (2) veteran-owned business—7 percent, (3) disabled-veteran-owned business—8 percent.[53] When a preference applies, if a small business, veteran-owned business, or disabled-veteran-owned business is within the noted percentage of the lowest responsive and responsible bidder, then its bid may be accepted instead.[54] When a procurement is a Small Business Preference Program opportunity, the procurement must note this in the solicitation.[55] The applicable state agencies must report on the preference program annually.[56]
- *Inclusion Goals*: In addition to the small business inclusion goals noted earlier under the SBR program, there are additional contracting inclusion goals. Each state agency has an overall annual aspirational goal to spend 29 percent of the agency's total procurements with certified MBEs on prime contracts (direct spends) and subcontracts (indirect spends).[57] Each procurement opportunity should be reviewed to set an appropriate goal for that opportunity based on procurement scope and

49. MD. CODE REGS. 21.11.01.06 (2023).

50. *Id.*

51. MD. CODE ANN., State Finance and Procurement § 14-202 (LexisNexis 2023); MD. CODE REGS. 21.11.01.05(A) (2023).

52. MD. CODE ANN., State Finance and Procurement § 14-202 (LexisNexis 2023); *Business Opportunities*, DEP'T OF GEN. SERVS., https://dgs.maryland.gov/Pages/SmallBusiness/Small-Business-FAQ.aspx (last visited Feb. 1, 2023).

53. MD. CODE ANN., State Finance and Procurement § 14-206 (LexisNexis 2023); MD. CODE REGS. 21.11.01.05(B)(2)(a) (2023).

54. MD. CODE REGS. 21.11.01.05(B)(4) (2023).

55. *Id.* 21.11.01.05(B)(2)(b).

56. *Id.* 21.11.01.05(B)(5).

57. *Id.* 21.11.03.01(C)(1).

MBE availability.[58] State agencies are to use "[t]o the maximum extent feasible" race-neutral measures to accomplish these goals.[59] These goals are not quotas, and state agencies may not use quotas.[60] Exceptions to attaining the overall goal include (1) if the procurement is a contraction project estimated at less than $50,000 or (2) the procurement has been designated without an MBE goal.[61] As it relates to the VSBE inclusion goals, each state agency must seek to achieve the goal of 1 percent of each state agency's total dollar amount for procurement to go to VSBEs either through prime contract level (direct spends) and/or subcontract level (indirect spends) participation.[62]

- *Solicitation and Bidding Specifications*: MBE subcontract participation goals may be set on any contract.[63] When it is, the solicitation must note the overall MBE subcontracting participation goal.[64] When such a goal is set, under Code of Maryland Regulations section 21.11.03.09(C)(2), bidders have specific notification and outreach efforts they must engage in regarding MBEs.
- *Utilization Plans, Waivers, and Contractor Good Faith Efforts*: Those responding to a solicitation with an MBE prime and/or subcontracting participation goal must submit the following with their response to the solicitation: (1) "[a] completed MBE utilization and fair solicitation affidavit . . ."[65] and (2) "[a] completed MBE participation schedule."[66] A request for full or partial waiver may be made as it relates to the participation requirements.[67]
- *Prompt Payment to Subcontractors*: "A contractor shall pay a subcontractor an undisputed amount to which the subcontractor is entitled within 10 days of receiving a progress or final payment from the State."[68]
- *Reporting Requirements*: "Within 90 days after the end of the fiscal year, each unit shall report to the Governor's Office of Small, Minority, and Women Business Affairs, the certification agency, and, subject to § 2-1257 of the State Government

58. *Id.* 21.11.03.09.
59. *Id.* § 21.11.03.01(D).
60. *Id.* 21.11.03.09(B)(4).
61. *Id.* 21.11.03.09(A).
62. *Id.* 21.11.14.01(A).
63. *Id.* 21.11.03.09(C)(1).
64. *Id.* 21.05.08.04.
65. *Id.* 21.11.03.09(C)(3)(a).
66. *Id.* 21.11.03.09(C)(3)(b).
67. *Id.* 21.11.03.09(C)(3)(a).
68. Md. Code Ann., State Finance and Procurement § 15-226(c) (LexisNexis 2023).

Article, the Joint Committee on Fair Practices and Personnel Oversight."[69] The report must include, among other items, the total number and dollar value of contracts and contracts to minority businesses.[70]

Contracting opportunities where the MDOT DBE program applies have several requirements that intersect directly with procurement, contracting, and business inclusion.

- *Fostering Small Business Participation*: Pursuant to 49 C.F.R. § 26.39, MDOT has engaged in efforts to foster small business participation.[71] One avenue for this is through MDOT's race- and gender-neutral SBE program.[72] One effort noted within MDOT's "Federal Disadvantaged Business Enterprise Program" manual, revised in 2023, is "set[ting] aside an overall percentage of its annual total dollar value of [U.S. DOT] assisted contracts directly to SBEs."[73]
- *Goals*: Contract opportunities may not use quotas or set-asides for DBEs.[74] The only exception for using a set-aside is in a limited or extreme circumstance, "when no other method could be reasonably expected to redress egregious instances of discrimination."[75] Instead, an overall goal must be set.[76] The goal must be based on evidence of available "ready, willing and able" DBEs in the market.[77] Once the assessment of "ready, willing and able" DBEs is completed, an overall goal may be established as a percentage of the total amount of contracts receiving U.S. DOT funds.[78] Participation goals must be set for all certified DBEs and not divided into subcategories.[79] Race- and gender-neutral means must be used to "meet the maximum feasible portion of your overall goal."[80] MDOT, as a recipient of U.S. DOT funds, will not be penalized for failing to meet the overall goal set, if it can establish good faith efforts

69. *Id.* § 14-305 (LexisNexis 2023).
70. *Id.*
71. *Federal Disadvantaged Business Enterprise Program*, Md. Dep't of Transp. 88 (Mar. 2023), https://www.mdot.maryland.gov/MBE_DOCS/DBE_Manualupdated3.2023.pdf.
72. *Id.*
73. *Id.* at 89.
74. 49 C.F.R. § 26.43 (2022).
75. *Id.* § 26.43.
76. *Id.* § 26.45(a)(1).
77. *Id.* § 26.45(b).
78. *Id.* § 26.45(e).
79. *Id.* § 26.45(h).
80. *Id.* § 26.51.

to meet the goal.[81] When there is a DBE goal on a specific contract opportunity, only the bidder meeting the goal, or establishing good faith efforts to meet the goal, may be awarded the contract.[82]

- *Prompt Payment*: Under 49 C.F.R. part 26, contractors must pay subcontractors within 30 days of receipt of payment from the state DOT for satisfactory performance.[83]
- *Payment of Retainage*: Contractors must pay amounts withheld for retainage to subcontractors within 30 days of their work being satisfactorily completed.[84]

Additional Related Laws, Policies, and Programs

- *Access to Capital*: "The Maryland Capital Access Program (MD CAP) is a financing resource administered by the Department of Commerce to stimulate opportunities for small businesses that may have difficulty in obtaining business financing by establishing a Loan Reserve Program."[85] For more information, please visit https://commerce.maryland.gov/fund/Pages/Maryland-Capital-Access-Program.aspx.
- *Prequalification on Construction and Design Contracts $50,000 or More*: "All construction-related contractors and design consultants bidding to perform services of $50,000 or more must be prequalified by The Office of Boards and Commissions (OBC)."[86]
- *Finding Contract Opportunities*: In Maryland, eMMA, as noted previously in the chapter, is the state's online procurement platform with contracting opportunities located here: https://emma.maryland.gov/page.aspx/en/usr/login?ReturnUrl=%2fpage.aspx%2fen%2fbuy%2fhomepage.

---

81. *Id.* § 26.47.
82. *Id.* § 26.53.
83. 49 C.F.R. § 26.29(a) (2023).
84. *Id.* § 26.29(b).
85. *Maryland Capital Access Program*, MD. DEP'T OF COM., https://commerce.maryland.gov/fund/Pages/Maryland-Capital-Access-Program.aspx (last visited Apr. 28, 2023).
86. *Prequalification for City of Baltimore (OBC)*, BALTIMORE CITY DEP'T OF PUB. WORKS, https://publicworks.baltimorecity.gov/contractor-consultant-prequalification (last visited Apr. 28, 2023).

Major City Snapshot: Baltimore

The City of Baltimore (city) has a Minority and Women's Business Opportunity Office located in the Department of Law.[87] City Code Article 5, subtitle 28, guides the office and program efforts.[88] This office handles, among other things, the certification of Minority Business Enterprises (MBEs) and Women Business Enterprises (WBEs).[89] Following is a high-level summary of the program. In 2022, the city completed a disparity study that may impact the future of some of the following information.[90]

- *Policy*: "It is the policy of the City of Baltimore to promote equal business opportunity in the City's contracting process by encouraging full and equitable participation by minority and women's business enterprises in the provision of goods and services to the City on a contractual basis."[91]
- *Certifications*: Following is a summary of the certification eligibility requirements.
  - *MBE*: "(1) . . . [I]s owned, operated, and controlled by [one] or more minority-group members who have at least 51 percent ownership; (2) in which the minority-group members have day-to-day operational and managerial control, interest in capital, and risks and earnings commensurate with their percentage of ownership; and (3) that is located in the Baltimore City Market Area."[92] Minorities include African Americans, Hispanic Americans, Asian Americans, and Native Americans.[93] Ownership for the qualifying owners must be "real and continuous."[94] The business must also (1) be independent; (2) have been in operation for at least 12 months prior to applying for certification; and (3) in the 12 months preceding the application it needed to be minority owned.[95]

---

87. Baltimore, Md. City Code of Ordinances, art. v., § 28-9(a) (2023); *About Us*, Baltimore Md., https://law.baltimorecity.gov/mwboo/about-us (last visited Apr. 28, 2023).
88. *About Us*, *supra* note 87.
89. Baltimore, Md. City Code of Ordinances, art. v., § 28-10(b) (2023).
90. Baltimore City Law Department, Baltimore Md., https://law.baltimorecity.gov/mwboo (last visited Apr. 28, 2023); City of Baltimore 2022 Disparity Study, MGT Consulting Group (2022), https://law.baltimorecity.gov/sites/default/files/City%20of%20Baltimore%20Disparity%20Study%20Final%20Report%20&%20Appendices%20August%2026,%202022.pdf.
91. Baltimore, Md. City Code of Ordinances, art. v., § 28-3(b) (2023).
92. *Id.* § 28-13(g).
93. *Id.* § 28-13(h).
94. *Id.* § 28-13(j).
95. *Id.* § 28-78(a).

- *WBE*: "(1) . . . [I]s owned, operated, and controlled by [one] or more women who have 51 percent ownership; (2) in which the women have day-to-day operational and managerial control, interest in capital, and risk and earnings commensurate with their percentage of ownership; and (3) that is located in the Baltimore City Market Area."[96] Ownership for the qualifying owners must be "real and continuous."[97] The business must also (1) be independent; (2) have been in operation for at least 12 months prior to applying for certification; and (3) in the 12 months preceding the application it needed to be women owned.[98]
- *Inclusion Goals*: "Annually, the Board of Estimates, with the advice of the Minority and Women's Business Opportunity Office, must review and establish the participation goals for Minority Business Enterprises and for Women's Business Enterprises."[99] The annual goals are not quotas.[100] The Minority and Women's Business Opportunity office may also set contract specific goals through following certain considerations.[101]

- *Utilization Requirements*: On contracts between $1,000 and $4,999, "contracting agency must solicit bids from certified business enterprises that are certified to supply the required materials, equipment, supplies, or services."[102] On contracts between $5,000 and $49,999, contracting agencies must share bid documents with the Minority and Women's Business Opportunity office, and the office may recommend certified businesses that may be directly solicited.[103]
- *Certified Business Enterprise Participation Affidavit*: On contracts $50,000 or more, a bidder must submit a certified business enterprise participation affidavit with its bid.[104] Failure to do so will deem the bid nonresponsive.[105]
- *Contractor Good Faith Efforts*: Contractors must make a good faith effort to meet contract-specific goals before the bid opening or

96. *Id.* § 28-13(k).
97. *Id.* § 28-13(j).
98. *Id.* § 28-78(a).
99. *Id.* § 28-16.
100. *Id.* § 28-17.
101. *Id.* §§ 28-21, 28-22.
102. *Id.* § 28-46(c).
103. *Id.* § 28-47.
104. *Id.* § 28-48.
105. *Id.*

proposal submission.[106] Continuing to make good faith efforts to use MBEs and WBEs continues through the life of their contract.[107] If, at the time of bidding the contractor is unable to make the contract goal, it may request a waiver and the waiver must include their good faith efforts to meet the goal.[108]

- *Prompt Payment to Subcontractors*: Contractors must pay their subcontractors within seven days of receiving payment from the city.[109]
- *Reporting Requirements*: The Minority and Women's Business Opportunity office annually reviews MBE/WBE participation on all contracts and reports to the Board of Estimates.[110] The Minority and Women's Business Opportunity office must also annually submit a report to the City Council on the city's utilization goals.[111] Contractors, when requested, must submit reports and documentation regarding contracts awarded to MBEs and WBEs.[112]

106. *Id.* § 28-53.
107. *Id.* § 28-54.
108. *Id.* § 28-62.
109. *Id.* § 28-55.
110. *Id.* § 28-25.
111. *Id.* § 28-91.
112. *Id.* § 28-56.

CHAPTER 22
Massachusetts

Overview of Business Inclusion Program, Policies, and Practices

Government entities seeking to create business inclusion programs have two primary options in terms of the type of program they may create, in terms of who is eligible for the program: (1) a race- and gender-conscious program or (2) a race- and gender-neutral program. Under the Equal Protection Clause of the Fourteenth Amendment, strict scrutiny is applied by the courts when a government actor is creating policies based on race. Strict scrutiny is the highest level of judicial review that may be applied. It requires the government actor to demonstrate that (1) past discrimination exists such that the entity has a "compelling government interest" in rectifying it, and (2) the policies and programs created to do so are "narrowly tailored."[1] Although intermediate scrutiny is often applied when reviewing programs based on gender, strict scrutiny is applied when reviewing race- and gender-conscious business inclusion programs.[2] Disparity studies have become a standard tool used to assist a government entity in withstanding a challenge to its race- and gender-conscious business inclusion programs. These studies aid in demonstrating whether a government entity has engaged

1. City of Richmond v. J.A. Croson Co., 488 U.S. 469 (1989).

2. Since the 1980s with the Supreme Court decision in *City of Richmond v. J.A. Croson Company*, there have been a number of cases across the county that have assessed race- and gender-conscious business inclusion programs. *See* Adarand Constructors, Inc. v. Pena, 515 U.S. 200 (1995); Virdi v. DeKalb Cnty. Sch. Dist., 135 Fed. App'x 262, 268 (11th Cir. 2005); Sherbrooke Turf, Inc. v. Minn. Dep't of Transp., 345 F.3d 964, 971 (8th Cir. 2003); Mountain West Holding Co., Inc. v. The State of Montana, Montana DOT, et al., 2017 WL 2179120 (9th Cir. May 16, 2017).

in past discrimination in its contracting practices, such that the entity may have a compelling government interest in rectifying it.[3]

Conversely, race- and gender-neutral programs are programs that are not only accessible to minority-owned and women-owned businesses but to all businesses, regardless of race or gender. A small business inclusion program would fall into this category. The level of judicial review applied to such a policy to determine its constitutionality is rational basis, which is the lowest threshold for a government to satisfy. For a government entity to satisfy rational basis, the policy or program created must be "related to a legitimate government purpose."[4] Even when a government entity has a race- and gender-conscious program, oftentimes the program may still require the government actor to seek to meet the goals of their program through race- and gender-neutral means where able, so as to be taking the most narrowly tailored means of accomplishing the program goals.

In the state of Massachusetts, at the state level of government, there are two main business inclusion certifying agencies: (1) the Supplier Diversity Office (SDO) within the Executive Office for Administration and Finance and (2) the Massachusetts Department of Transportation (MassDOT).

Summary of Certification Programs and Requirements

The SDO certifies the following types of businesses: (1) Minority Business Enterprise (MBE); (2) Women Business Enterprise (WBE); (3) Portuguese Business Enterprise (PBE); and (4) Veteran Business Enterprise (VBE).[5] Enterprises eligible for certification may be for-profit entities or nonprofit entities.[6] In addition, it has agreements to accept third-party certifications for Service Disabled Veterans (SDVOBE); Lesbian, Gay, Bisexual, and Transgender (LGBTBE); and Disability-Owned (DOBE)

3. *Promoting Opportunity and Equality in America: A Guide to Federal Circuit Authority on Permissible Government Actions to Promote Racial and Gender Equality*, AM. CIV. LIBERTIES UNION & THE OPPORTUNITY AGENDA (Dec. 2010), https://www.aclu.org/sites/default/files/field_document/Promoting_Opportunity_and_Equality_in_America.pdf.

4. 488 U.S. 469 (1989).

5. *Certification Program for SDO*, SUPPLIER DIVERSITY OFF., https://www.mass.gov/certification-program-for-sdo (last visited Mar. 19, 2023); 425 MASS. CODE REGS. 2.00 (2022); MASS. GEN. LAWS ch. 7, § 58 (2022).

6. *Apply for Certification as a Non-Profit Organization*, SUPPLIER DIVERSITY OFF, https://www.mass.gov/how-to/apply-for-certification-as-a-non-profit-organization (last visited Mar. 19, 2023); 425 MASS. CODE REGS. 2.00 (2022).

businesses.[7] The following bullet points provide additional details on eligibility requirements.

- *Minority Business Enterprise (MBE)*: A business must (1) be 51 percent owned by one or more minorities (defined to include but not limited to Indian or Indigenous Person, Asian, Black, Hispanic, Portuguese,[8] Cape Verdeans, Eskimos, and Aleuts) and the ownership for the eligible owners must be "real, actual, genuine and meaningful"; (2) be controlled by one or more minorities such that they have "dominant control over management and daily operations" as well as the background, credentials, and knowledge for the enterprises finances, policies, and affairs; (3) have eligible owners be permanent residents of the United States; (4) be independent and ongoing; and (5) have the eligible owners "invested in an ongoing business free of conversion rights."[9] For qualification as a Minority Nonprofit Organization (MNPO), an organization must (1) be a 501(c)(3) or 501(c)(4) under the U.S. Internal Revenue Code; (2) be in good standing with the Office of the Attorney General of Massachusetts; (3) have 51 percent or more of the voting members and the board of directors be minorities; (4) be independent, ongoing, and controlled by one or more minorities.[10]
- *Women Business Enterprise (WBE)*: A business must (1) be 51 percent owned by one or more women, and the ownership for the eligible owners must be "real, actual, genuine and meaningful"; (2) be controlled by one or more women such that they have "dominant control over management and daily operations" as well as the background, credentials, and knowledge for the enterprises finances, policies, and affairs; (3) have eligible owners be permanent residents of the United States; (4) be independent and ongoing; and (5) have the eligible owners "invested in an ongoing business free of conversion rights."[11] For qualification as a Women Nonprofit Organization (WNPO), an organization must (1) be a 501(c)(3) or 501(c)(4) under the U.S. Internal Revenue Code; (2) be in good standing with the Office of the Attorney General of Massachusetts;

---

7. *Certification Program for SDO*, *supra* note 5; 425 Mass. Code Regs. 2.00 (2022); Mass. Gen. Laws ch. 7, § 58 (2022).

8. A business that is 51 percent owned by an individual who is Portuguese and meets the other eligibility requirements would be certified as a Portuguese Business Enterprise, separate from an MBE.

9. 425 Mass. Code Regs. 2.02 (2022); Mass. Gen. Laws ch. 7, § 58 (2022).

10. 425 Mass. Code Regs. 2.02 (2022).

11. *Id.* 2.02; Mass. Gen. Laws ch. 7, § 58 (2022).

(3) have 51 percent or more of the voting members and the board of directors be women; (4) be independent, ongoing, and controlled by one or more women.[12]

- *Portuguese Business Enterprise (PBE)*: A business must (1) be 51 percent owned by one or more person(s) of Portuguese origin, and the ownership for the eligible owners must be "real, actual, genuine and meaningful"; (2) be controlled by one or more person(s) of Portuguese origin such that they have "dominant control over management and daily operations" as well as the background, credentials, and knowledge for the enterprises finances, policies, and affairs; (3) have eligible owners be permanent residents of the United States; (4) be independent and ongoing; and (5) have the eligible owners "invested in an ongoing business free of conversion rights."[13]
- *Veteran Business Enterprise (VBE)*: A business must (1) be 51 percent owned by one or more veterans, and the ownership for the eligible owners must be "real, actual, genuine and meaningful"; (2) be controlled by one or more veterans such that they have "dominant control over management and daily operations" as well as the background, credentials, and knowledge for the enterprises finances, policies, and affairs; (3) have eligible owners be permanent residents of the United States; (4) be independent and ongoing; and (5) have the eligible owners "invested in an ongoing business free of conversion rights."[14] For qualification as a Veteran Nonprofit Organization (VNPO), an organization must (1) be a 501(c)(3) or 501(c)(4) under the U.S. Internal Revenue Code; (2) be in good standing with the Office of the Attorney General of Massachusetts; (3) have 51 percent or more of the voting members and the board of directors be veterans; (4) be independent, ongoing, and controlled by one or more veterans.[15]
- *Service-Disabled Veteran-Owned Business Enterprise (SDVOBE)*: "[A] business that is verified by the federal government's Department of Veterans Affairs pursuant to the Veterans Benefits, Health Care, and Information Technology Act of 2006, Pub. L. 109–461, and determined to be a service-disabled

---

12. 425 Mass. Code Regs. 2.02 (2022).
13. *Id.*
14. *Id.*; Mass. Gen. Laws ch. 7, § 58 (2022).
15. 425 Mass. Code Regs. 2.02 (2022).

veteran-owned small business concern in accordance with 38 CFR Part 74 and Pub. L. 111–275."[16]

- *Lesbian, Gay, Bisexual, and Transgender Business Enterprise (LGBTBE)*: A business must (1) be 51 percent owned by one or more LGBT individuals, and the ownership for the eligible owners must be "real, actual, genuine and meaningful"; (2) be controlled by one or more LGBT individuals such that they have "dominant control over management and daily operations" as well as the background, credentials, and knowledge for the enterprises finances, policies, and affairs; (3) have eligible owners be permanent residents of the United States; (4) be independent and ongoing; and (5) have the eligible owners "invested in an ongoing business free of conversion rights."[17]
- *Disability-Owned Business Enterprise (DOBE)*: A business must (1) be 51 percent owned by one or more individuals with a disability, and the ownership for the eligible owners must be "real, actual, genuine and meaningful"; (2) be controlled by one or more individuals with a disability such that they have "dominant control over management and daily operations" as well as the background, credentials, and knowledge for the enterprises finances, policies, and affairs; (3) have eligible owners be permanent residents of the United States; (4) be independent and ongoing; and (5) have the eligible owners "invested in an ongoing business free of conversion rights."[18]

The SDO through the Operational Services Division of the Executive Office for Administration and Finance has a Small Business Purchasing Program (SBPP).[19] This program is not a certification program, but it does allow eligible businesses to register for the program through COMMBUYS, the state's online procurement platform.[20] Following are eligibility requirements for that program.

- *Small Business*: (1) Principal place of business in Massachusetts; (2) in business for at least one year; (3) employs 50 or

16. Mass. Gen. Laws ch. 7, § 58 (2022).
17. 425 Mass. Code Regs. 2.02 (2022); Mass. Gen. Laws ch. 7, § 58 (2022).
18. 425 Mass. Code Regs. 2.02 (2022); Mass. Gen. Laws ch. 7, § 58 (2022).
19. *Executive Order No. 523 Establishing the Massachusetts Small Business Purchasing Program* (June 29, 2010), https://archives.lib.state.ma.us/bitstream/handle/2452/50100/ocn456714827-2010-eo523.pdf (this was later revoked by Executive Order No. 599 in 2022, and Executive Order No. 599 reaffirmed programs to ensure diversity, equity, and inclusion for diverse and small Massachusetts businesses in state procurement and contracting); *Register for the Small Business Purchasing Program (SBPP)*, Supplier Diversity Off., https://www.mass.gov/how-to/register-for-the-small-business-purchasing-program-sbpp (last visited Mar. 19, 2023).
20. *Id.*

fewer employees; and (4) has a three-year average for its annual gross receipts reported on the Massachusetts Department of Revenue tax forms of $15 million or less.[21] Nonprofits may also be eligible and meet the preceding criteria as well as the following: (1) be tax exempt under the Internal Revenue Code 501(c); (2) be registered with the Massachusetts Attorney General's Office as a nonprofit or charitable organization and up-to-date on filings; and (3) must be organized and operated exclusively for exempt purposes under 501(c).[22]

MassDOT certifies businesses as Disadvantaged Business Enterprises (DBEs) and Airport Concession Disadvantaged Business Enterprises (ACDBEs). Following are the eligibility requirements.

- *Disadvantaged Business Enterprise (DBE)*: Pursuant to 49 C.F.R. part 26, MassDOT administers the state's DBE certification program. As is required under 49 C.F.R. § 26.81, Massachusetts has a Unified Certification Program (UCP). The UCP makes all DBE certification decisions and provides a "one-stop shop" to DBE applicants.[23] To qualify as a DBE, a business must (1) be for-profit;[24] (2) be a small business concern—with "small" determined by the Small Business Administration (SBA) small business size standards—and does not exceed $30.40 million in gross annual receipts;[25] (3) be at least 51 percent owned by socially and economically disadvantaged individuals—there is a rebuttable presumption that women, Black Americans, Hispanic Americans, Native Americans, Asian-Pacific Americans, Subcontinent Asian Americans, or other minorities are disadvantaged;[26] (4) be controlled by one or more of the socially and economically disadvantaged owners;[27] (5) have the socially and economically disadvantaged owners be U.S. citizens or lawfully admitted permanent residents;[28] and (6) have the personal net worth for any socially and economically disadvantaged owner not exceed $1.32 million.[29] The DBE

21. *Register for the Small Business Purchasing Program (SBPP)*, *supra* note 19; MASS. GEN. LAWS ch. 7, § 220 (2022).

22. *Register for the Small Business Purchasing Program (SBPP)*, *supra* note 19.

23. 49 C.F.R. § 26.81(b)(2) (2022).

24. *Id.* § 26.5.

25. *Id.* §§ 26.5, 26.65(b). It is worth noting that under 49 C.F.R. § 26.65(b), the DBE size standard may be adjusted annually for inflation such that in subsequent years the size standard may no longer be $30.40 million.

26. *Id.* § 26.67.

27. *Id.* § 26.5.

28. *Id.* § 26.67.

29. *Id.*

program is required on contracting opportunities that have received funding from the Federal Highway Administration (FHWA), Federal Aviation Administration (FAA), or Federal Transit Administration (FTA).[30]

- *Airport Concession Disadvantaged Business Enterprise (ACDBE)*: In addition to being certified as a DBE under 49 C.F.R. part 26, businesses may also be certified as an Airport Concession Disadvantaged Business Enterprise (ACDBE) under 49 C.F.R. part 23. To qualify as an ACDBE, a business must (1) be a concession for-profit small business concern;[31] (2) qualify as small by having its prior three-year average gross receipts not exceed the applicable size standard of $56.42 million;[32] (3) be 51 percent owned by one or more socially and economically disadvantaged individuals;[33] (4) have one or more of the socially and economically disadvantaged individuals with control and managing the daily business operations;[34] and (5) have the personal net worth for any socially and economically disadvantaged owner not exceed $1.32 million.[35]

Procurement Laws Intersecting with Business Inclusion

Massachusetts procurement laws may be found in Massachusetts General Laws, Chapter 30B. State laws and regulations pertaining to the Supplier Diversity Office and the certifications noted earlier may be found in Massachusetts General Laws, chapter 7, sections 58 to 62, and 425 Massachusetts Code Regulations 2.00, respectively. Following are some laws that pertain to the small and diverse businesses just listed.

- *Quotes from Diverse and/or Small Businesses*: "Whenever a contract requires the solicitation of multiple quotes, departments shall, at a minimum, notify at least two diverse and/or small

---

30. *Id.* § 26.21(a).
31. *Id.* § 23.3.
32. *Id.* § 23.33(a). The size standards for the following are exceptions to this: bank and financial institutions is $1 billion in assets; car rental companies are $75.23 million average annual gross receipts; pay telephones is 1,500 employees; and automobile dealers is 350 employees.
33. *Id.*
34. *Id.*
35. *Id.* § 23.35.

businesses capable of providing the product or service of the opportunity, if available."[36]

- *Supplier Diversity Program Plans*: The 2022 Executive Order No. 599 "Reaffirming Programs to Ensure Diversity, Equity, and Inclusion for Diverse and Small Massachusetts Businesses in State Procurement and Contracting" requires entities seeking to contract with any Executive Department agency to include with their proposals to provide goods and services a detailed supplier diversity program plan that notes their financial commitments to contract with diverse businesses, provided the contract opportunity exceeds the required contracting thresholds established by the Operational Services Division.[37]
- *Penalties*: The SDO "may . . . impose penalties on contractors for misreporting spending with diverse businesses."[38]
- *Good Faith Efforts*: "[State Departments] are required to make a good faith effort to meet all diverse and small business spending benchmarks."[39]
- *Goals and Benchmark Percentages*: The Operational Services Division must ensure that no less than 15 percent of state contracts are from businesses that "(i) are independently owned and operated; (ii) have a principal place of business in the commonwealth; (iii) have been in business for at least [one] year; and (iv) are defined as a small business under applicable federal law or are defined by the division as small businesses pursuant to the small business purchasing program."[40] For the Small Business Purchasing Program (SBPP), executive departments are directed to spend 3.3 percent of their discretionary budgets with SBPP participants as a benchmark.[41] Every two years,

---

36. *The Commonwealth of Massachusetts Diverse and Small Business Program Policies for Goods and Services Procurements*, Supplier Diversity Off. 5 (June 28, 2021), https://www.mass.gov/doc/the-commonwealth-of-massachusetts-diverse-and-small-business-program-policies-for-goods-and-services-procurements/download.

37. *Executive Order No. 599: Reaffirming Programs to Ensure Diversity, Equity, and Inclusion for Diverse and Small Massachusetts Businesses in State Procurement and Contracting* (July 8, 2022), https://www.mass.gov/executive-orders/no-599-reaffirming-programs-to-ensure-diversity-equity-and-inclusion-for-diverse-and-small-massachusetts-businesses-in-state-procurement-and-contracting. The contracting threshold established in the 2021 *The Commonwealth of Massachusetts Diverse and Small Business Program Policies for Goods and Services Procurements* notes that the threshold for large procurements is a procurement anticipated to exceed $250,000 in terms of its estimated annual value.

38. *Executive Order No. 599*, *supra* note 37.

39. *The Commonwealth of Massachusetts Diverse and Small Business Program Policies for Goods and Services Procurements*, *supra* note 36.

40. Mass. Gen. Laws ch. 7, § 220 (2022).

41. *Learn about the Small Business Purchasing Program (SBPP)*, Supplier Diversity Off., https://www.mass.gov/service-details/learn-about-the-small-business-purchasing-program-sbpp (last visited Mar. 19, 2023).

the SDO must consult with the Massachusetts Office on Disability to set contracting goals for participation of individuals with disabilities.[42] In terms of annual benchmarks for departments, the following benchmark percentages were established for each state department's discretionary budget as of the last policy update for the supplier diversity program: MBE (8 percent), WBE (14 percent), VBE and SDVOBE (3 percent).[43]

- *Contracts $250,000 or Less*: Executive Departments are directed to give special considerations to SBPP participants on non-construction goods and services procurements estimated to be $250,000 or less per year.[44]
- *Reporting Requirements*: The SDO must issue an annual report that includes reporting on the MassDOT M/WBE program.[45] "SDO shall submit by March 15 of each year an annual report to the governor, lieutenant governor, secretariats, and the general court on the prior year performance of all commonwealth supplier diversity and small business programs, including but not limited to the supplier diversity program, the MassDOT M/WBE program, the small business purchasing program and the affirmative marketing program, the SDO's certification efforts, the diverse businesses which it assists, the type of services which it renders and the difficulties it encounters."[46] Each year, state departments must complete an Annual Procurement/Purchasing Plan.[47]

Contracting opportunities where the MassDOT DBE program applies have several requirements that intersect directly with procurement, contracting, and business inclusion.

- *Goals*: Contract opportunities may not use quotas or set-asides for DBEs.[48] The only exception for using a set-aside is in a limited or extreme circumstance, "when no other method could be reasonably expected to redress egregious instances

42. *Executive Order No. 599: supra* note 37.

43. *The Commonwealth of Massachusetts Diverse and Small Business Program Policies for Goods and Services Procurements, supra* note 36.

44. *Learn about the Small Business Purchasing Program (SBPP), supra* note 41; *Executive Order No. 599, supra* note 37; *The Commonwealth of Massachusetts Diverse and Small Business Program Policies for Goods and Services Procurements, supra* note 36.

45. *Executive Order No. 599, supra* note 37.

46. Mass. Gen. Laws ch. 7, § 61 (2022).

47. *The Commonwealth of Massachusetts Diverse and Small Business Program Policies for Goods and Services Procurements, supra* note 36.

48. 49 C.F.R. § 26.43 (2022).

of discrimination."[49] Instead, an overall goal must be set.[50] The goal must be based on evidence of available "ready, willing and able" DBEs in the market.[51] Once the assessment of "ready, willing and able" DBEs is completed, an overall goal may be established as a percentage of the total amount of contracts receiving U.S. Department of Transportation (U.S. DOT) funds.[52] Participation goals must be set for all certified DBEs and not divided into subcategories.[53] Race- and gender-neutral means must be used to "meet the maximum feasible portion of your overall goal."[54] For federal fiscal year 2022–2024 MassDOT's goals are as follows: Race/Gender-Neutral goal is 5 percent and the Race/Gender-Conscious goal is .4 percent.[55] MassDOT, as a recipient of U.S. DOT funds, will not be penalized for failing to meet the overall goal set, if it can establish good faith efforts to meet the goal.[56] When there is a DBE goal on a specific contract opportunity, only the bidder meeting the goal, or establishing good faith efforts to meet the goal, may be awarded the contract.[57]

- *Prompt Payment*: Under 49 C.F.R. part 26, contractors must pay subcontractors within 30 days of receipt of payment from the state DOT for satisfactory performance.[58]
- *Payment of Retainage*: Contractors must pay amounts withheld for retainage to subcontractors within 30 days of their work being satisfactorily completed.[59]

Additional Related Laws, Policies, and Programs

- *Affirmative Action Marketing Project*: "The affirmative marketing program shall be established for the purpose of ensuring the fair participation of minority-owned and women-owned businesses on capital facility projects and state assisted building projects. . . . Participation goals for minority-owned business

49. *Id.*
50. *Id.* § 26.45(a)(1).
51. *Id.* § 26.45(b).
52. *Id.* § 26.45(e).
53. *Id.* § 26.45(h).
54. *Id.* § 26.51.
55. *The MassDOT Transit Division Proposed Overall DBE Goal for FFY2022–FFY2024*, The Commonwealth of Mass. Dep't of Transp. (2022), https://www.mass.gov/doc/dbe-goal-for-fta-assisted-contracts-ffy2022-2024/download.
56. 49 C.F.R. § 26.47 (2022).
57. *Id.* § 26.53.
58. 49 C.F.R. § 26.29(a) (2023).
59. *Id.* § 26.29(b).

and women-owned business shall be based upon the broadest and most inclusive pool of available minority-owned businesses and women-owned businesses interested in and capable of performing construction work and design services on such capital facility projects and state assisted building projects."[60] "The executive director shall develop a written waiver procedure by which, at any time before the award of a contract, it may be determined that compliance with the participation goals is not feasible and by which the participation goals on a state assisted building project may be reduced or waived. Waiver shall be granted only upon a showing that good faith efforts have been made to comply with the participation goals."[61]

- *Sheltered Market Programs*: Under Massachusetts General Laws, chapter 30B, section 18, it provides authority for the creation of sheltered market programs that would allow for certain contracts to be designated for competition only among disadvantaged businesses.
- *Prompt Payment to Subcontractors*: Laws pertaining to payment, penalties, and demands for payment to subcontractors on construction contracts are found under Massachusetts General Laws, chapter 30, section 39F.
- *Finding Contract Opportunities*: On the "Bidding Opportunities" page of the SDO it includes links and information for state, municipal, and quasi-governmental procurement portals: https://www.mass.gov/info-details/bidding-opportunities.

Major City Snapshot: Boston

The City of Boston's (city) Supplier and Workforce Diversity Department manages the city's Supplier Diversity Program.[62] Following are highlights of its program.

- *Certifications*: The city certifies (1) Small Business Enterprises (SBEs); (2) Small Local Business Enterprises (SLBEs); (3) Minority Business Enterprises (MBEs); (4) Women Business Enterprises (WBEs); and (5) Veteran-Owned Small Businesses (VOSBs).[63] For a complete list of eligibility require-

60. Mass. Gen. Laws ch. 7, § 61 (2022).
61. *Id.*
62. *Supplier and Workforce Diversity*, City of Bos., https://www.boston.gov/departments/supplier-and-workforce-diversity (last visited Mar. 19, 2023).
63. *Guide to Specialized Business Certification Requirements*, City of Bos., https://www.boston.gov/departments/supplier-and-workforce-diversity/guide-specialized-business-certification-requirements (last visited Mar. 19, 2023).

ments and needed documents, please visit https://www.boston.gov/departments/supplier-and-workforce-diversity/guide-specialized-business-certification-requirements.

- *Small Business Enterprises (SBEs)*: The business's three-year average annual gross receipts must be 75 percent or less of the dollar amount established by the Small Business Administration's small business size standards for its industry code.[64]
- *Small Local Business Enterprises (SLBEs)*: Meets the preceding criteria for an SBE and has its principal place of business in the city; a majority of partners or shareholders reside in the city; or a majority of its employees reside in the city.[65]
- *Minority Business Enterprises (MBEs)*: (1) 51 percent owned by minorities; (2) minorities have control over management; and (3) "The firm has not been solely established for the purpose of taking advantage of a special program which has been developed to help minority-owned businesses."[66]
- *Women Business Enterprises (WBEs)*: (1) 51 percent owned by women; (2) women have control over management; and (3) "The firm has not been solely established for the purpose of taking advantage of a special program which has been developed to help women-owned businesses."[67]
- *Veteran-Owned Small Businesses (VOSBs)*: Need a certification letter from the U.S. Department of Veteran Affairs.[68]

- *Inclusion Goals*: After the completion of the 2020 disparity study, the city set an annual aspiration goal of 25 percent for MWBE (15 percent WBE and 10 percent MBE) utilization on discretionary contracts and procurements.[69]
- *Sheltered Market Program*: In 2021, the city created a Sheltered Market Program that allows for a competitive procurement process on opportunities only between MWBEs.[70]

---

64. *Id.*
65. *Id.*
66. *Id.*
67. *Id.*
68. *Id.*
69. *An Executive Order Establishing Equitable Procurement Goals in Support of Minority and Women-Owned Businesses*, City of Bos. (Feb. 18, 2021), https://www.boston.gov/sites/default/files/file/2021/02/An%20Executive%20Order%20Establishing%20Equitable%20Procurement%20Goals%20in%20Support%20of%20Minority%20and%20Woman-Owned%20Businesses.pdf.
70. *Sheltered Market Program*, City of Bos., https://www.boston.gov/departments/economic-opportunity-and-inclusion/sheltered-market-pilot-program (last visited Mar. 19, 2023).

CHAPTER 23

Michigan

Overview of Business Inclusion Program, Policies, and Practices

Government entities seeking to create business inclusion programs have two primary options in terms of the type of program they may create, in terms of who is eligible for the program: (1) a race- and gender-conscious program or (2) a race- and gender-neutral program. Under the Equal Protection Clause of the Fourteenth Amendment, strict scrutiny is applied by the courts when a government actor is creating policies based on race. Strict scrutiny is the highest level of judicial review that may be applied. It requires the government actor to demonstrate that (1) past discrimination exists such that the entity has a "compelling government interest" in rectifying it, and (2) the policies and programs created to do so are "narrowly tailored."[1] Although intermediate scrutiny is often applied when reviewing programs based on gender, strict scrutiny is applied when reviewing race- and gender-conscious business inclusion programs.[2] Disparity studies have become a standard tool used to assist a government entity in withstanding a challenge to its race- and gender-conscious business inclusion programs. These studies aid in demonstrating whether a government entity has engaged

1. City of Richmond v. J.A. Croson Co., 488 U.S. 469 (1989).

2. Since the 1980s with the Supreme Court decision in *City of Richmond v. J.A. Croson Company*, there have been a number of cases across the county that have assessed race- and gender-conscious business inclusion programs. *See* Adarand Constructors, Inc. v. Pena, 515 U.S. 200 (1995); Virdi v. DeKalb Cnty. Sch. Dist., 135 Fed. App'x 262, 268 (11th Cir. 2005); Sherbrooke Turf, Inc. v. Minn. Dep't of Transp., 345 F.3d 964, 971 (8th Cir. 2003); Mountain West Holding Co., Inc. v. The State of Montana, Montana DOT, et al., 2017 WL 2179120 (9th Cir. May 16, 2017).

in past discrimination in its contracting practices, such that the entity may have a compelling government interest in rectifying it.[3]

Conversely, race- and gender-neutral programs are programs that are not only accessible to minority-owned and women-owned businesses but to all businesses, regardless of race or gender. A small business inclusion program would fall into this category. The level of judicial review applied to such a policy to determine its constitutionality is rational basis, which is the lowest threshold for a government to satisfy. For a government entity to satisfy rational basis, the policy or program created must be "related to a legitimate government purpose."[4] Even when a government entity has a race- and gender-conscious program, oftentimes the program may still require the government actor to seek to meet the goals of their program through race- and gender-neutral means where able, so as to be taking the most narrowly tailored means of accomplishing the program goals.

In the state of Michigan, at the state level of government, there are two state agencies that certify businesses for business inclusion programs: (1) the Michigan State Housing Development Authority (MSHDA) and (2) the Michigan Department of Transportation (MDOT).

Summary of Certification Programs and Requirements

MSHDA certifies businesses as Minority Businesses Enterprises (MBEs) and Women Business Enterprises (WBEs). The eligibility requirements for both follow:

- *Minority Business Enterprise (MBE)*: To satisfy the eligibility criteria to be certified as an MBE, a business must (1) have one or more minorities who own at least 51 percent interest in the profits and losses of the business; (2) have the minority owner(s) participate in the daily management and operations of the business; (3) one or more minority owners must have authority and exercise it in making significant business

---

3. *Promoting Opportunity and Equality in America: A Guide to Federal Circuit Authority on Permissible Government Actions to Promote Racial and Gender Equality*, AM. CIV. LIBERTIES UNION & THE OPPORTUNITY AGENDA (Dec. 2010), https://www.aclu.org/sites/default/files/field_document/Promoting_Opportunity_and_Equality_in_America.pdf.

4. 488 U.S. 469 (1989).

decisions; and (4) have a state license if one is required for its trade.[5]

- *Women Business Enterprise (WBE)*: To satisfy the eligibility criteria to be certified as a WBE, a business must (1) have one or more women who own at least 51 percent interest in the profits and losses of the business; (2) have the women owners participate in the daily management and operations of the business; (3) one or more woman/women owners must have authority and exercise it in making significant business decisions; and (4) have a state license if one is required for its trade.[6]

The Michigan Department of Technology, Management and Budget (DTMB) does not certify businesses as Service-Disabled Veteran-Owned Businesses; however, it does have a contracting goals and preference for them noted in the next section.[7] A certification from the National Veterans Business Development Council may be accepted for verification of eligibility. MDOTadministers the Disadvantaged Business Enterprise (DBE) program, Airport Concession Disadvantaged Business Enterprise (ACDBE) program, and the Small Business Participation (SBP) program.

- *Disadvantaged Business Enterprise (DBE) Program*: Pursuant to 49 C.F.R. part 26, MDOT administers the state's DBE certification program. As is required under 49 C.F.R. § 26.81, Michigan has a Unified Certification Program (UCP). The UCP makes all DBE certification decisions and provides a "one-stop shop" to DBE applicants.[8] To qualify as a DBE, a business must (1) be for-profit;[9] (2) be a small business concern—with "small" determined by the Small Business Administration (SBA) small business size standards—and does not exceed $30.40 million in gross annual receipts;[10] (3) be at least 51 percent owned by

5. *Tab F: Interim Preliminary Equal Opportunity Plan*, MICH. STATE HOUS. DEV. AUTH. 5 https://www.michigan.gov/mshda/-/media/Project/Websites/mshda/assets/Folder1/TAB_F__EEO_Plan_Requirements.pdf (last visited Mar. 24, 2023); *MBE/WBE Application*, MICH. STATE HOUS. DEV. AUTH. 3 (May 2019), https://www.michigan.gov/mshda/-/media/Project/Websites/mshda/assets/Folder2/MBE_WBE_Application_Revised_Feb_28_2019.pdf.

6. *Tab F: Interim Preliminary Equal Opportunity Plan*, *supra* note 5; *MBE/WBE Application*, *supra* note 5.

7. *Service-Disabled Veteran-Owned Business Preference*, MICH. DEP'T OF TECH., MGMT. & BUDGET, https://www.michigan.gov/dtmb/procurement/contractconnect/programs-and-policies/preferences/service-disabled-veteran-owned-business-preference (last visited Mar. 24, 2023).

8. 49 C.F.R. § 26.81(b)(2) (2022).

9. *Id.* § 26.5 (2022).

10. *Id.* §§ 26.5, 26.65(b). It is worth noting that under 49 C.F.R. § 26.65(b) the DBE size standard may be adjusted annually for inflation such that in subsequent years the size standard may no longer be $30.40 million.

socially and economically disadvantaged individuals—there is a rebuttable presumption that women, Black Americans, Hispanic Americans, Native Americans, Asian-Pacific Americans, Subcontinent Asian Americans, or other minorities are disadvantaged;[11] (4) be controlled by one or more of the socially and economically disadvantaged owners;[12] (5) have the socially and economically disadvantaged owners be U.S. citizens or lawfully admitted permanent residents;[13] and (6) have the personal net worth for any socially and economically disadvantaged owner not exceed $1.32 million.[14] The DBE program is required on contracting opportunities that have received funding from the Federal Highway Administration (FHWA), Federal Aviation Administration (FAA), or Federal Transit Administration (FTA).[15]

- *Airport Concession Disadvantaged Business Enterprise (ACDBE) Program*: In addition to being certified as a DBE under 49 C.F.R. part 26, businesses may also be certified as an Airport Concession Disadvantaged Business Enterprise (ACDBE) under 49 C.F.R. part 23. To qualify as an ACDBE, a business must (1) be a concession for-profit small business concern;[16] (2) qualify as small by having its prior three-year average gross receipts not exceed the applicable size standard of $56.42 million;[17] (3) be 51 percent owned by one or more socially and economically disadvantaged individuals;[18] (4) have one or more of the socially and economically disadvantaged individuals with control and managing the daily business operations;[19] and (5) have the personal net worth for any socially and economically disadvantaged owner not exceed $1.32 million.[20]
- *Small Business Program (SBP)*: MDOT has implemented a small business element within its DBE program called the

11. *Id.* § 26.67.
12. *Id.* § 26.5.
13. *Id.* § 26.67.
14. *Id.*
15. *Id.* § 26.21(a).
16. *Id.* § 23.3.
17. *Id.* § 23.33(a). The size standards for the following are exceptions to this: bank and financial institutions is $1 billion in assets; car rental companies are $75.23 million average annual gross receipts; pay telephones is 1,500 employees; and automobile dealers is 350 employees.
18. *Id.*
19. *Id.*
20. *Id.* § 23.35.

Small Business Program (SBP), pursuant to 49 C.F.R. § 26.39.[21] This program is race and gender neutral.[22] To be eligible for the program, a business must (1) be a small business under the SBA size standards; (2) for purposes of being considered a DBE for the FHWA and FTA, the business must have average annual gross receipts from the prior three fiscal years that do not exceed $28.48 million or the current DBE size standard adjusted for inflation under 49 C.F.R. § 26.65;[23] (3) have the personal net worth for the owners of the firm not exceed $1.32 million;[24] (4) "[b]e approved to work in the classification required to bid on a respective project when required by MDOT or state policy";[25] and (5) have those bidding on highway construction projects have sufficient bidding capacity.[26]

Procurement Laws Intersecting with Business Inclusion

Following are some laws that pertain to the intersection of procurement and small, minority-owned, women-owned, and service-disabled veteran-owned business inclusion.

- *Public Highways and Private Roads*: "Each county road commission shall take all reasonable steps to ensure minority business enterprises have the equal opportunity to compete and perform contracts or purchases of services, or both, for the county road commission. The county road commission shall issue a plan for implementing this subsection."[27]
- *Inclusion Goals*: MSHDA requires contractors to include a commitment to establish MBE and WBE contracting goals and state such goals in their Equal Employment Opportunity (EEO) Plan along with the dollar amount.[28] The State of Michigan has a goal of awarding 5 percent of total expenditures to

21. *DBE Program Procedures*, Mich. Dep't of Transp. 59 (2022), https://www.michigan.gov/mdot/-/media/Project/Websites/MDOT/Business/Contractors/DBE/Requested/DBE-Program-Procedures.pdf.

22. *Id.*

23. Under 49 C.F.R. § 26.65, the DBE-related size standard may be adjusted annually for inflation. It was previously $26.29 million, then in 2022 adjusted to $28.48 million. Effective March 1, 2023, the DBE-related size standard is set to increase from $28.48 million to $30.40 million.

24. *Id.*

25. *Id.*

26. *Id.*

27. Mich. Comp. Laws § 224.10(4) (2021).

28. *Tab F: Interim Preliminary Equal Opportunity Plan*, *supra* note 5.

qualified service-disabled veteran-owned businesses,[29] and 3 percent to businesses owned by individuals with disabilities.[30] "It is the goal of the State that [three percent] or more of contract payments each state fiscal year will be made to certified Geographically-Disadvantaged Business Enterprises by the 2022–23 fiscal year."[31]

- *Contractor Good Faith Efforts*: MSHDA requires contractors with a normal practice of accepting the lowest bid to contain in their EEO plan a commitment to be flexible with bid proposals submitted by MWBEs and give strong consideration to their proposals even if they are 5 percent higher than other proposals.[32] The contractor must make a good faith effort to work with MWBEs.[33]
- *Prompt Payment*: Although not specific to small or diverse businesses, timely payment is important for small and diverse businesses. Under Michigan Compiled Laws § 125.1562, contractors on construction contracts must be paid on progress payments within the following time periods, whichever one is later: "(a) Thirty days after the architect or professional engineer has certified to the public agency that work is in place in the portion of the facility covered by the applicable request for payment in accordance with the contract documents. (b) Fifteen days after the public agency has received the funds with which to make the progress payment from a department or agency of the federal or state government, if any funds are to come from either of those sources."
- *Contracting Preferences*: The State of Michigan has a 10 percent pricing preference for qualified disabled veterans.[34]
- *Reporting Requirements*: Each year DTMB must report to each house of the legislature on its contracting inclusion efforts related to qualified disabled veterans.[35]

---

29. Mich. Comp. Laws § 18.1261(9) (2021); *Michigan Procurement Policy Manual—Chapter 1 Introduction and Overview of the Michigan Procurement Policy Manual (MPPM)*, Mich. Dep't of Tech., Mgmt. & Budget 3 (2022), https://www.michigan.gov/-/media/Project/Websites/dtmb/Procurement/documents/MPPM/Chapter_1__Introduction_and_Overview_of_the_Michigan_Procurement_Manual.pdf.
30. Mich. Comp. Laws § 450.793(1) (2021).
31. Executive Directive No. 2019-08 (Jan. 4, 2019); *Michigan Procurement Policy Manual, supra* note 29.
32. *Tab F: Interim Preliminary Equal Opportunity Plan, supra* note 5.
33. *Id.*
34. Mich. Comp. Laws § 18.1241(3) (2023).
35. *Id.* § 18.1261(9).

Contracting opportunities where the MDOT DBE program applies have several requirements that intersect directly with procurement, contracting, and business inclusion.

- *SBP Prime Set-Aside*: Projects meeting the following criteria will be designated as SBP set-aside prime projects: (1) project is funded in whole or in part with FAA, FHWA, or FTA funds; (2) there are at least three small businesses qualifying to bid; and (3) project has small business subcontracting opportunities.[36]
- *Additional Efforts to Foster Small Business Participation*: MDOT sub-recipient grantees must be in compliance with the SBP provisions. For the MDOT Office of Aeronautics projects on FAA-assisted projects not issued by MDOT, the office must assign a five percent small business participation goal on projects with small business subcontracting opportunities.[37] "Large projects will be reviewed to determine the feasibility of unbundling project elements to promote competition by small business concerns."[38] MDOT also "[p]ost[s] notices to advise potential bidders about upcoming SBP projects; [h]old[s] public participation meetings as appropriate; [p]rovide[s] personal notification to eligible small businesses using E-mail, fax, or telephone contact to identified small businesses. . . ."[39]
- *Goals*: Contract opportunities may not use quotas or set-asides for DBEs.[40] The only exception for using a set-aside is in a limited or extreme circumstance, "when no other method could be reasonably expected to redress egregious instances of discrimination."[41] Instead, an overall goal must be set.[42] The goal must be based on evidence of available "ready, willing and able" DBEs in the market.[43] Once the assessment of "ready, willing and able" DBEs is completed, an overall goal may be established as a percentage of the total amount of contracts receiving U.S. Department of Transportation (U.S. DOT) funds.[44] Participation goals must be set for all certified DBEs and not divided

36. *DBE Program Procedures*, *supra* note 21, at 60.
37. *Id.*
38. *Id.*
39. *The Michigan Department of Transportation's (MDOT's) Small Business Program Procedures*, Mich. Dep't of Transp. 5, https://www.michigan.gov/mdot/-/media/Project/Websites/MDOT/Business/Contractors/Small-Business/Program-Procedures.pdf (last visited Mar. 24, 2023).
40. 49 C.F.R. § 26.43 (2022).
41. *Id.*
42. *Id.* § 26.45(a)(1).
43. *Id.* § 26.45(b).
44. *Id.* § 26.45(e).

into subcategories.[45] Race- and gender-neutral means must be used to "meet the maximum feasible portion of your overall goal."[46] MDOT, as a recipient of U.S. DOT funds, will not be penalized for failing to meet the overall goal set, if it can establish good faith efforts to meet the goal.[47] When there is a DBE goal on a specific contract opportunity only the bidder meeting the goal, or establishing good faith efforts to meet the goal, may be awarded the contract.[48]

- *Prompt Payment*: Under 49 C.F.R. part 26, contractors must pay subcontractors within 30 days of receipt of payment from the state DOT for satisfactory performance.[49]
- *Payment of Retainage*: Contractors must pay amounts withheld for retainage to subcontractors within 30 days of their work being satisfactorily completed.[50]

Additional Related Laws, Policies, and Programs

- *Access to Capital*: The Department of Environment, Great Lakes, and Energy administers the Small Business Pollution Prevention (P2) Loan Program.[51] This loan program makes available loans up to $400,000 at an interest rate of 5 percent or less to small businesses on projects that "eliminate waste generated, energy used, and/or hazards to public health associated with waste generated at the applicant's place of business."
- *Finding Contracting Opportunities*: The DTMB "Contract Connect" site has information on how to do business with the state: https://www.michigan.gov/dtmb/procurement/contractconnect.

45. *Id.* § 26.45(h).
46. *Id.* § 26.51.
47. *Id.* § 26.47.
48. *Id.* § 26.53.
49. 49 C.F.R. § 26.29(a) (2023).
50. *Id.* § 26.29(b).
51. Mich. Admin. Code r. §§ 324.14501 through 324.14508; *Pollution Prevention Small Business Loan Program*, Mich. Dep't of Env't, Great Lakes, & Energy, https://www.michigan.gov/egle/about/organization/materials-management/pollution-prevention/pollution-prevention-small-business-loan (last visited Mar. 24, 2023); *P2 Lenders Loan Brochure*, Mich. Dep't of Env't, Great Lakes, & Energy, https://www.michigan.gov/egle/-/media/Project/Websites/egle/Documents/Programs/MMD/Pollution-Prevention/P2Loan/P2-Lenders-Loan-Brochure.pdf (last visited Mar. 24, 2023).

Major City Snapshot: Detroit

The City of Detroit Civil Rights, Inclusion and Opportunity Department manages the Detroit Business Opportunity Program.[52]

- *Certifications*: The city certifies the following types of businesses: (1) Detroit-Based Business (DBB); (2) Detroit-Based Small Business (DSB); (3) Detroit-Headquartered Business (DHB); (4) Detroit-Resident Business (DRB); (5) Minority-Owned Business Enterprise (MBE); and (6) Women-Owned Business Enterprise (WBE).[53] The city also certifies Detroit-Based Micro Businesses (DBMB) and Detroit Start-Ups (DSU).[54]
- *Equalization Credits*: Under Detroit City Ordinance §§ 17-5-12 through 17-5-13, it notes equalization credits that may be applied during the procurement of competitive bids. It notes that "[a]s the first step in comparing bids, the bid of any Detroit-based business or small Detroit-resident business shall be deemed a better bid than the bid of any competing firm which is not a Detroit-based business or Detroit-resident business whenever the bid of such competing firm shall be equal to or higher than the bid of the Detroit-based business or Detroit-resident business. . . ."[55] Equalization credits of varying percentages are available for the following types of businesses: DBB, DRB, DHB, DSB, DBMB, Joint Venture, and Mentor Venture.[56]
- *Prompt Payment to Detroit-Based Businesses or Small Businesses*: Under the city ordinance the city must pay vendors within 45 business days of receiving a properly executed and submitted invoice.[57] For overdue invoices, the city must pay the vendor interest.[58] Vendors contracting with the city must include terms in their contracts with Detroit-Based Businesses and Small Businesses, noting requirements for prompt payment and any interest for late payments.[59]

---

52. *Detroit Business Opportunity Program*, City of Detroit, https://detroitmi.gov/departments/civil-rights-inclusion-opportunity-department/detroit-business-opportunity-program (last visited Mar. 24, 2023)
53. Detroit City Ordinance § 23-2-32(a) (2022).
54. *Detroit Business Opportunity Program*, *supra* note 52.
55. Detroit City Ordinance § 17-5-12(b)(1) (2022).
56. *Id.* §§ 17-5-12 through 17-5-13 (2022); *Detroit Business Opportunity Program*, *supra* note 52.
57. Detroit City Ordinance § 17-5-284 (2022).
58. *Id.* § 17-5-286.
59. *Id.* § 17-5-288.

CHAPTER 24

Minnesota

Overview of Business Inclusion Program, Policies, and Practices

Government entities seeking to create business inclusion programs have two primary options in terms of the type of program they may create, in terms of who is eligible for the program: (1) a race- and gender-conscious program or (2) a race- and gender-neutral program. Under the Equal Protection Clause of the Fourteenth Amendment, strict scrutiny is applied by the courts when a government actor is creating policies based on race. Strict scrutiny is the highest level of judicial review that may be applied. It requires the government actor to demonstrate that (1) past discrimination exists such that the entity has a "compelling government interest" in rectifying it, and (2) the policies and programs created to do so are "narrowly tailored."[1] Although intermediate scrutiny is often applied when reviewing programs based on gender, strict scrutiny is applied when reviewing race- and gender-conscious business inclusion programs.[2] Disparity studies have become a standard tool used to assist a government entity in withstanding a challenge to its race- and gender-conscious business inclusion programs. These studies aid in demonstrating whether a government entity has engaged

1. City of Richmond v. J.A. Croson Co., 488 U.S. 469 (1989).

2. Since the 1980s with the Supreme Court decision in *City of Richmond v. J.A. Croson Company*, there have been a number of cases across the county that have assessed race- and gender-conscious business inclusion programs. *See* Adarand Constructors, Inc. v. Pena, 515 U.S. 200 (1995); Virdi v. DeKalb Cnty. Sch. Dist., 135 Fed. App'x 262, 268 (11th Cir. 2005); Sherbrooke Turf, Inc. v. Minn. Dep't of Transp., 345 F.3d 964, 971 (8th Cir. 2003); Mountain West Holding Co., Inc. v. The State of Montana, Montana DOT, et al., 2017 WL 2179120 (9th Cir. May 16, 2017).

in past discrimination in its contracting practices, such that the entity may have a compelling government interest in rectifying it.[3]

Conversely, race- and gender-neutral programs are programs that are not only accessible to minority-owned and women-owned businesses but to all businesses, regardless of race or gender. A small business inclusion program would fall into this category. The level of judicial review applied to such a policy to determine its constitutionality is rational basis, which is the lowest threshold for a government to satisfy. For a government entity to satisfy rational basis, the policy or program created must be "related to a legitimate government purpose."[4] Even when a government entity has a race- and gender-conscious program, oftentimes the program may still require the government actor to seek to meet the goals of their program through race- and gender-neutral means where able, so as to be taking the most narrowly tailored means of accomplishing the program goals.

In the state of Minnesota, at the state level of government, there are two main state departments certifying businesses for business inclusion programs: (1) the Department of Administrative Office of Equity in Procurement (OEP) and (2) the Minnesota Department of Transportation (MNDOT).[5]

Summary of Certification Programs and Requirements

The OEP certifies the following types of businesses: (1) Targeted Group Businesses (TG), (2) Economically Disadvantaged Small Business (ED), and (3) Veteran-Owned Business (VO).[6] The eligibility requirements for all follow. For each of the programs listed, the following types of businesses are ineligible: "brokers, third-party lessors, and franchises."[7] In addition, with all certification types, part of the small business procurement program all must be (1) Minnesota-based businesses[8] and

---

3. *Promoting Opportunity and Equality in America: A Guide to Federal Circuit Authority on Permissible Government Actions to Promote Racial and Gender Equality*, Am. Civ. Liberties Union & The Opportunity Agenda (Dec. 2010), https://www.aclu.org/sites/default/files/field_document/Promoting_Opportunity_and_Equality_in_America.pdf.

4. 488 U.S. 469 (1989).

5. Although not state departments, the Metropolitan Council and the Metropolitan Airports Commission, as members of the Minnesota Unified Certification Program, are involved with the certifications of disadvantaged business enterprises (DBEs).

6. *Small Business Procurement Program*, Minn. Dep't of Admin., https://mn.gov/admin/business/vendor-info/oep/sbcp/ (last visited Mar. 25, 2023).

7. Minn. R. 1230.1600 (2022); Minn. Stat. Ann. § 16C.19 (2015).

8. *Small Business Procurement Program*, Minn. Dep't of Admin., https://mn.gov/admin/business/vendor-info/oep/sbcp/ (last visited Mar. 25, 2023).

(2) small businesses, which means they are considered small provided they meet the size standard noted in 49 C.F.R. § 26.65.[9]

- *Targeted Group Business (TG)*: To qualify for this program, a business must be for-profit,[10] an independent business,[11] and ". . . at least 51 percent owned by a woman, racial minority, or person with a substantial physical disability. In addition, the business must be operated and controlled on a day-to-day as well as long-term basis by the qualifying owner. In other words, ownership is not enough; operational control is also required."[12] Qualifying owners' ownership must also be "real, substantial, and continuing, going beyond pro forma ownership of the business as reflected in ownership documents."[13] Owners must be citizens of the United States or lawfully admitted permanent residents.[14] Racial minorities: "Native Americans, Black Americans, Hispanic Americans, Asian-Pacific Americans, subcontinent Asian Americans, or other minorities found to be disadvantaged by the SBA are deemed to be socially and economically disadvantaged individuals."[15] Each qualifying owner must have a personal net worth that does not exceed the limit noted under C.F.R. 49 part 26.[16]
- *Economically Disadvantaged Small Business (ED)*: "To be certified as an Economically Disadvantaged small business, the business must be located (or the owner must reside) in an Economically Disadvantaged Area in Minnesota. These areas include labor surplus areas, as designated by the federal government, and low-income counties in Minnesota. Economically Disadvantaged small businesses must be certified as such by MMD in order to participate in the program."[17] In addition, the business must be 51 percent owned and controlled on a daily basis by persons who are economically disadvantaged U.S. citizens or lawfully admitted permanent residents who reside in

9. MINN. STAT. ANN. § 16C.16, subpt. 2 (2022).

10. MINN. R. 1230.1606(C) (2022). The only exceptions to the requirement to be for-profit is in the case of rehabilitation facilities and extended employment providers.

11. MINN. R. 1230.1605(B) (2022).

12. *Targeted Group Small Business Program*, MINN. DEP'T OF ADMIN., https://mn.gov/admin/business/vendor-info/oep/sbcp/tg/ (last visited Mar. 25, 2023); MINN. R. 1230.0150, subpt. 23 (2022).

13. MINN. R. 1230.1604, subpt. 3 (2022).

14. *Id*. 1230.1603.

15. *Id*.

16. *Id*.

17. *Economically Disadvantaged Small Business Procurement Program*, MINN. DEP'T OF ADMIN., https://mn.gov/admin/business/vendor-info/oep/sbcp/ed/ (last visited Mar. 25, 2023).

an economically disadvantaged area.[18] Each qualifying owner must have a personal net worth that does not exceed the limit noted under C.F.R. 49 part 26.[19] Qualifying owners' ownership must also be "real, substantial, and continuing, going beyond pro forma ownership of the business as reflected in ownership documents."[20] The business must be for-profit[21] and an independent business.[22]

- *Veteran-Owned Business (VO)*: "To be certified as a Veteran-Owned small business, the business must be at least 51 percent owned by a veteran or service-disabled veteran as determined by the Minnesota Department of Veterans Affairs. In addition, the business must be operated and controlled on a day-to-day as well as long-term basis by the qualifying owner. In other words, ownership is not enough; operational control is also required."[23] Qualifying owners' ownership must also be "real, substantial, and continuing, going beyond pro forma ownership of the business as reflected in ownership documents."[24] The business must be for-profit[25] and an independent business.[26] The principal place of business for the business must be in Minnesota.[27]

MNDOT, along with fellow members of the Minnesota Unified Certification Program, administer the Disadvantaged Business Enterprise (DBE) program and the Airport Concession Disadvantaged Business Enterprise (ACDBE) program.

- *Disadvantaged Business Enterprise (DBE) Program*: As is required under 49 C.F.R. § 26.81, Minnesota has a Unified Certification Program (MNUCP). The MNUCP makes all DBE certification decisions and provides a "one-stop shop" to DBE applicants.[28] The MNUCP consists of the following entities: the Minnesota

18. MINN. R. 1230.0150, subpt. 26 (2022); MINN. R. § 1230.1604, subpt. 2 (2022).
19. *Id.* 1230.1603, subpt. (1)(B)(1).
20. *Id.* 1230.1604, subpt. 3.
21. *Id.* 1230.1606(C). The only exceptions to the requirement to be for-profit is in the case of rehabilitation facilities and extended employment providers.
22. *Id.* 1230.1605(B).
23. *Veteran-Owned Small Business Procurement Program*, MINN. DEP'T OF ADMIN., https://mn.gov/admin/business/vendor-info/oep/sbcp/vo/ (last visited Mar. 25, 2023); MINN. STAT. ANN. § 16C.19 (2015); MINN. R. 1230.0150, subpt. 28 (2022).
24. MINN. R. 1230.1604, subpt. 3 (2022).
25. *Id.* 1230.1606(C). The only exceptions to the requirement to be for-profit is in the case of rehabilitation facilities and extended employment providers.
26. *Id.* 1230.1605(B).
27. *Id.*
28. 49 C.F.R. § 26.81(b)(2) (2022).

Department of Transportation, the Metropolitan Council, the Metropolitan Airports Commission, and the City of Minneapolis.[29] To qualify as a DBE, a business must (1) be for-profit;[30] (2) be a small business concern—with "small" determined by the Small Business Administration (SBA) small business size standards—and does not exceed $30.40 million in gross annual receipts;[31] (3) be at least 51 percent owned by socially and economically disadvantaged individuals—there is a rebuttable presumption that women, Black Americans, Hispanic Americans, Native Americans, Asian-Pacific Americans, Subcontinent Asian Americans, or other minorities are disadvantaged;[32] (4) be controlled by one or more of the socially and economically disadvantaged owners;[33] (5) have the socially and economically disadvantaged owners be U.S. citizens or lawfully admitted permanent residents;[34] and (6) not have the personal net worth for any socially and economically disadvantaged owner exceed $1.32 million.[35] The DBE program is required on contracting opportunities that have received funding from the Federal Highway Administration (FHWA), Federal Aviation Administration (FAA), or Federal Transit Administration (FTA).[36]

- *Airport Concession Disadvantaged Business Enterprise (ACDBE) Program*: In addition to being certified as a DBE under 49 C.F.R. part 26, businesses may also be certified as an Airport Concession Disadvantaged Business Enterprise (ACDBE) under 49 C.F.R. part 23. To qualify as an ACDBE, a business must (1) be a concession for-profit small business concern;[37] (2) qualify as small by having its prior three-year average gross receipts not exceed the applicable size standard of $56.42 million;[38] (3) be 51 percent owned by one or more socially

29. *About Us*, MINN. UNITED CERTIFICATION PROGRAM, https://mnucp.org/About/About-the-MNUCP.aspx (last visited Mar. 25, 2023).

30. 49 C.F.R. § 26.5 (2022).

31. *Id.* §§ 26.5, 26.65(b). It is worth noting that under 49 C.F.R. § 26.65(b) the DBE size standard may be adjusted annually for inflation such that in subsequent years the size standard may no longer be $30.40 million.

32. *Id.* § 26.67.

33. *Id.* § 26.5.

34. *Id.* § 26.67.

35. *Id.*

36. *Id.* § 26.21(a).

37. *Id.* § 23.3.

38. *Id.* § 23.33(a). The size standards for the following are exceptions to this: bank and financial institutions is $1 billion in assets; car rental companies are $75.23 million average annual gross receipts; pay telephones is 1,500 employees; and automobile dealers is 350 employees.

and economically disadvantaged individuals;[39] (4) have one or more of the socially and economically disadvantaged individuals with control and managing the daily business operations;[40] and (5) have the personal net worth for any socially and economically disadvantaged owner not exceed $1.32 million.[41]

Procurement Laws Intersecting with Business Inclusion

Relevant Minnesota procurement laws may primarily be found in Minnesota Statute section 16C, whereas the most relevant rules to business inclusion may be found in the Minnesota Rules section 1230. Following are some laws that pertain to small, minority-owned, women-owned, and service-disabled veteran-owned businesses.

- *Equity Select Program*: Equity Select is a procurement method that allows an agency buyer to award directly to a certified TG/ED/VO small business a contract or purchase over $5,000 and at or below $25,000. On contracts of $5,001 to $25,000, the state allows for direct purchases from TG, ED, and VO certified businesses.[42]
- *Purchases Designated for TG, ED, and VO Businesses*: A purchase for goods or services may be designated for award only to certified TG, ED, or VO businesses if it is anticipated that at least three such businesses in ". . . two or more of the disadvantaged business categories are likely to respond . . ." to the solicitation.[43]
- *Contracting Preferences*: Businesses certified as TG, ED, and/or VO qualify for up to 6 percent preference on state contracts and purchases.[44] When a certified TG, ED, and/or VO is within 6 percent of the lowest acceptable response from another vendor, then the award must be made to the lowest certified TG, ED, and/or VO business.[45] This 6 percent preference also exists

39. *Id.*
40. *Id.*
41. *Id.* § 23.35.
42. MINN. STAT. ANN. § 16C.16, subpt. 6(b) (2022); *Equity Select*, MINN. DEP'T OF ADMIN. (2020), https://www.dot.state.mn.us/consult/documents/internal-training/pi-equity-select.docx.
43. MINN. STAT. ANN. § 16C.16 (2022); MINN. R. 1230.1810(A) (2022).
44. MINN. STAT. ANN. § 16C.16 (2022).
45. MINN. R. 1230.1810(B) (2022).

on MNDOT state-funded contract opportunities for TG and VO businesses.[46]

- *Inclusion Goals*: "The commissioner shall for each fiscal year ensure that small businesses receive at least 25 percent of the value of anticipated total state procurement of goods and services, including printing and construction."[47] "Every state agency must for each fiscal year designate for awarding to small businesses at least 25 percent of the value of anticipated procurements of that agency for professional or technical services."[48] The commissioner of the Department of Administration may set contract-specific goals for subcontracting a percentage of a construction contract or a technical and professional services contract to TG, ED, or VO subcontractors.[49] As it relates to subcontractor goals, "[w]hen establishing subcontractor goals . . . , the commissioner may set goals that require the prime contractor to subcontract a portion of the contract to any combination of a small business, small targeted group business, veteran-owned small business, or small business located in an economically disadvantaged area."[50]
- *Waivers for Goals and Contractor Good Faith Efforts*: Waivers for contract-specific subcontracting goals may be requested by a prime contractor and must be accompanied by documentation demonstrating their efforts to include TG, ED, and/or VO businesses.[51]
- *Penalties*: "Prime contractors who have been awarded a contract and fail to meet the project goal for certified targeted group, economically disadvantaged area, or veteran-owned subcontractor use without approved waiver shall be penalized up to six percent of the total project value, not to exceed $60,000."[52]
- *Prompt Payment to Small Businesses*: On building and construction contracts, a prime contractor is required to pay its subcontractors within 10 days of receipt of their payment for "for undisputed services provided" the subcontractor.[53]

---

46. *Small Business Program Information*, MINN. DEP'T OF TRANSP., https://www.dot.state.mn.us/civilrights/small-business-program-information.html (last visited Apr. 19, 2023).
47. MINN. STAT. ANN. § 16C.16 (2022).
48. *Id.*
49. *Id.* § 16C.16 (2022); MINN. R. 1230.1820 (2022).
50. MINN. STAT. ANN. § 16C.16, subpt. 7a(b) (2022).
51. MINN. R. 1230.1820 (2022).
52. *Id.*
53. MINN. STAT. ANN. § 337.10 (2022).

Contracting opportunities where the MNUCP DBE program applies have several requirements that intersect directly with procurement, contracting, and business inclusion.

- *Goals*: Contract opportunities may not use quotas or set-asides for DBEs.[54] The only exception for using a set-aside is in a limited or extreme circumstance, "when no other method could be reasonably expected to redress egregious instances of discrimination."[55] Instead, an overall goal must be set.[56] The goal must be based on evidence of available "ready, willing and able" DBEs in the market.[57] Once the assessment of "ready, willing and able" DBEs is completed, an overall goal may be established as a percentage of the total amount of contracts receiving U.S. Department of Transportation (U.S. DOT) funds.[58] Participation goals must be set for all certified DBEs and not divided into subcategories.[59] Race- and gender-neutral means must be used to "meet the maximum feasible portion of your overall goal."[60] MNDOT, as a recipient of U.S. DOT funds, will not be penalized for failing to meet the overall goal set, if it can establish good faith efforts to meet the goal.[61] When there is a DBE goal on a specific contract opportunity, only the bidder meeting the goal, or establishing good faith efforts to meet the goal, may be awarded the contract.[62]
- *Prompt Payment*: Under 49 C.F.R. part 26, contractors must pay subcontractors within 30 days of receipt of payment from the state DOT for satisfactory performance.[63]
- *Payment of Retainage*: Contractors must pay amounts withheld for retainage to subcontractors within 30 days of their work being satisfactorily completed.[64]

54. 49 C.F.R. § 26.43 (2022).
55. *Id.* § 26.43.
56. *Id.* § 26.45(a)(1).
57. *Id.* § 26.45(b).
58. *Id.* § 26.45(e).
59. *Id.* § 26.45(h).
60. *Id.* § 26.51.
61. *Id.* § 26.47.
62. *Id.* § 26.53.
63. 49 C.F.R. § 26.29(a) (2023).
64. *Id.* § 26.29(b).

Additional Related Laws, Policies, and Programs

- *Technical Assistance*: Through the APEX Accelerator (formerly the Procurement and Technical Assistance program, PTAC) business are able to gain access to a myriad of technical assistance options. For more information, please visit https://mn.gov/admin/business/vendor-info/apexaccelerator/.
- *Finding Contract Opportunities*: The Minnesota Department of Administration has a "Solicitations and Contract Opportunities" page that includes links to various contracting opportunities and the supplier portal: https://mn.gov/admin/osp/vendors/solicitations-and-contract-opportunities/.

Major City Snapshot: City of Saint Paul

The City of Saint Paul is the lead agency for the Central CERT Certification Program, which is the program that certifies business for the city's business inclusion program.[65] Other entities on the CERT board are Hennepin County, Ramsey County, and the City of Minneapolis.[66] Chapter 84 of the city's ordinance pertains to the city's Vendor Outreach Program (VOP), which is the city's primary business inclusion program. Following are additional details on the city's business inclusion efforts.

- *Certifications*: The city, through the CERT program, certifies the following types of businesses: (1) Small Business Enterprises (SBEs), (2) Minority Business Enterprises (MBEs), Women-Owned Business Enterprises (WBEs), and Emerging Small Business Enterprises (ESBEs).[67]
- *Inclusion Goals*: The city sets annual participation goals for certified businesses that may be adjusted throughout the year depending on the availability of certified businesses.[68] In addition, the city sets contract-specific subcontractor participation goals.[69]
- *Contractor Good Faith Efforts*: Before a bid is awarded or 10 days after the bid opening, the apparent low bidder must submit documentation pertaining to its commitment to the VOP

65. *About the CERT Program*, City of Saint Paul, https://www.stpaul.gov/departments/human-rights-equal-economic-opportunity/contract-compliance-business-development-1 (last visited Apr. 22, 2023).
66. *Id.*
67. *Id.*
68. City of Saint Paul, Minn. Ordinance § 84.06 (2023).
69. *Id.*

ordinance or submit good faith efforts.[70] In addition, "[l]evels of certified vendor participation are evaluated throughout the duration of the contract" such that if a contractor fails to meet the contract goals at a point during the contract, then good faith effort documentation must be submitted.[71]

- *Penalty*: Under chapter 84, when a contractor fails to meet a goal and establish good faith efforts, a penalty will result that requires (1) an amount is paid and (2) that the contractor be placed on a list of ineligible bidders.[72]

70. *Id.* § 84.08.
71. *Id.* § 84.11.
72. *Id.* § 84.12.

CHAPTER 25

Mississippi

Overview of Business Inclusion Programs, Policies, and Practices

Government entities seeking to create business inclusion programs have two primary options in terms of the type of program they may create, in terms of who is eligible for the program: (1) a race- and gender-conscious program or (2) a race- and gender-neutral program. Under the Equal Protection Clause of the Fourteenth Amendment, strict scrutiny is applied by the courts when a government actor is creating policies based on race. Strict scrutiny is the highest level of judicial review that may be applied. It requires the government actor to demonstrate that (1) past discrimination exists such that the entity has a "compelling government interest" in rectifying it, and (2) the policies and programs created to do so are "narrowly tailored."[1] Although intermediate scrutiny is often applied when reviewing programs based on gender, strict scrutiny is applied when reviewing race- and gender-conscious business inclusion programs.[2] Disparity studies have become a standard tool used to assist a government entity in withstanding a challenge to its race- and gender-conscious business inclusion programs. These studies aid in demonstrating whether a government entity has engaged

1. City of Richmond v. J.A. Croson Co., 488 U.S. 469 (1989).

2. Since the 1980s with the Supreme Court decision in *City of Richmond v. J.A. Croson Company*, there have been a number of cases across the county that have assessed race- and gender-conscious business inclusion programs. *See* Adarand Constructors, Inc. v. Pena, 515 U.S. 200 (1995); Virdi v. DeKalb Cnty. Sch. Dist., 135 Fed. App'x 262, 268 (11th Cir. 2005); Sherbrooke Turf, Inc. v. Minn. Dep't of Transp., 345 F.3d 964, 971 (8th Cir. 2003); Mountain West Holding Co., Inc. v. The State of Montana, Montana DOT, et al., 2017 WL 2179120 (9th Cir. May 16, 2017).

in past discrimination in its contracting practices, such that the entity may have a compelling government interest in rectifying it.[3]

Conversely, race- and gender-neutral programs are programs that are not only accessible to minority-owned and women-owned businesses but to all businesses, regardless of race or gender. A small business inclusion program would fall into this category. The level of judicial review applied to such a policy to determine its constitutionality is rational basis, which is the lowest threshold for a government to satisfy. For a government entity to satisfy rational basis, the policy or program created must be "related to a legitimate government purpose."[4] Even when a government entity has a race- and gender-conscious program, oftentimes the program may still require the government actor to seek to meet the goals of their program through race- and gender-neutral means where able, so as to be taking the most narrowly tailored means of accomplishing the program goals.

In the state of Mississippi, at the state level of government, there are two main state agencies that certify businesses for business inclusion programs: (1) the Mississippi Development Authority (MDA) and (2) the Mississippi Department of Transportation (MDOT).

Summary of Certification Programs and Requirements

In managing the business inclusion program, MDA has several duties and responsibilities. Under Mississippi Code Annotated section 57-69-5, it notes that MDA is responsible for "[developing] and maintain[ing] a central minority business enterprise certification program" and a list of certified businesses for "all state agencies and educational institutions." Through this program, under Mississippi Code Annotated section 57-69-7, MDA has the authority to certify businesses as a minority business enterprise or minority business enterprise supplier.[5] Following are the criteria articulated under Mississippi Code Annotated section 57-69-3 for a minority business enterprise or minority business enterprise supplier. For the purposes of both certifications that follow, a minority is defined as a person who is a U.S. citizen or lawfully admitted permanent resident who is Black, Hispanic, Asian-American,

3. *Promoting Opportunity and Equality in America: A Guide to Federal Circuit Authority on Permissible Government Actions to Promote Racial and Gender Equality*, Am. Civ. Liberties Union & The Opportunity Agenda (Dec. 2010), https://www.aclu.org/sites/default/files/field_document/Promoting_Opportunity_and_Equality_in_America.pdf.

4. 488 U.S. 469 (1989).

5. Miss. Code Ann. § 57-69-7 (2022); *Minority and Small Businesses*, Miss. Dev. Auth., https://mississippi.org/minority-small-business/ (last visited Oct. 25, 2022).

American Indian or Alaskan Native, or female.[6] If a business is denied certification with MDA, it may appeal the decision. The procedures for doing this may be found in title 6, Code of Mississippi Rules sections 2-2.1 through 2-2.12.

- *Minority Business Enterprise or Minority-Owned Business*: "[A] socially and economically disadvantaged small business concern organized for profit performing a commercially useful function which is owned and controlled by one or more individuals or minority business enterprises certified by the office, at least seventy-five percent (75%) of whom are resident citizens of the State of Mississippi. For purposes of this paragraph, the term 'socially and economically disadvantaged small business concern' shall have the meaning ascribed to such term under the Small Business Act (15 USCS, Section 637(a)). Owned and controlled means a business in which one or more minorities or minority business enterprises certified by the office own at least fifty-one percent (51%) or in the case of a corporation at least fifty-one percent (51%) of the voting stock and control at least fifty-one percent (51%) of the management and daily business operations of the business."[7]
- *Minority Business Enterprise Supplier*: "[A] socially and economically disadvantaged small business concern which is owned and controlled by one or more individuals, at least seventy-five percent (75%) of whom are resident citizens of the State of Mississippi. For purposes of this paragraph, the term 'socially and economically disadvantaged small business concern' shall have the meaning ascribed to such term under the Small Business Act (15 USCS, Section 637(a)) except that the net worth of the business may not be greater than Seven Hundred Fifty Thousand Dollars ($750,000.00). Owned and controlled means a business in which one or more minorities own at least fifty-one percent (51%) or in the case of a corporation at least fifty-one percent (51%) of the voting stock and control at least fifty-one percent (51%) of the management and daily business operations of the business."[8]

MDOT administers the Disadvantaged Business Enterprise (DBE) program and Airport Concession Disadvantaged Business Enterprise (ACDBE) program.

---

6. Miss. Code Ann. §§ 27-104-7(2)(d), 57-69-3.
7. *Id.* § 57-69-3.
8. *Id.*

- *Disadvantaged Business Enterprise (DBE) Program*: Pursuant to 49 C.F.R. part 26, MDOT administers the state's DBE certification program. As is required under 49 C.F.R. § 26.81, Mississippi has a Unified Certification Program (MUCP), and MDOT serves as the lead agency.[9] The MUCP makes all DBE certification decisions and provides a "one-stop shop" to DBE applicants.[10] To qualify as a DBE, a business must (1) be for-profit;[11] (2) be a small business concern—with "small" determined by the Small Business Administration (SBA) small business size standards—and does not exceed $30.40 million in gross annual receipts;[12] (3) be at least 51 percent owned by socially and economically disadvantaged individuals—there is a rebuttable presumption that women, Black Americans, Hispanic Americans, Native Americans, Asian-Pacific Americans, Subcontinent Asian Americans, or other minorities are disadvantaged;[13] (4) be controlled by one or more of the socially and economically disadvantaged owners;[14] (5) have the socially and economically disadvantaged owners be U.S. citizens or lawfully admitted permanent residents;[15] and (6) have the personal net worth for any socially and economically disadvantaged owner not exceed $1.32 million.[16] The DBE program is required on contracting opportunities that have received funding from the Federal Highway Administration (FHWA), Federal Aviation Administration (FAA), or Federal Transit Administration (FTA).[17]
- *Airport Concession Disadvantaged Business Enterprise (ACDBE) Program*: In addition to being certified as a DBE under 49 C.F.R. part 26, businesses may also be certified as an Airport Concession Disadvantaged Business Enterprise (ACDBE) under 49 C.F.R. part 23. To qualify as an ACDBE, a business must (1) be a concession for-profit small business concern;[18] (2) qualify as small by having its prior three-year average gross receipts

9. *Civil Rights*, Miss. Dep't Transp., https://mdot.ms.gov/portal/civil_rights (last visited Oct. 25, 2022).

10. 49 C.F.R. § 26.81(b)(2) (2022).

11. *Id.* § 26.5.

12. *Id.* §§ 26.5, 26.65(b). It is worth noting that under 49 C.F.R. § 26.65(b) the DBE size standard may be adjusted annually for inflation such that in subsequent years the size standard may no longer be $30.40 million.

13. *Id.* § 26.67.

14. *Id.* § 26.5.

15. *Id.* § 26.67.

16. *Id.*

17. *Id.* § 26.21(a).

18. *Id.* § 23.3.

not exceed the applicable size standard of $56.42 million;[19] (3) be 51 percent owned by one or more socially and economically disadvantaged individuals;[20] (4) have one or more of the socially and economically disadvantaged individuals with control and managing the daily business operations;[21] and (5) have the personal net worth for any socially and economically disadvantaged owner not exceed $1.32 million.[22]

Procurement Laws Intersecting with Business Inclusion

Business inclusion in government contracting under Mississippi law may allow for potential preferences, set-asides, and loans for eligible businesses. The most relevant procurement laws intersecting with business inclusion may be found in title 31, chapter 7.[23] The following state statutes exist at the intersection of state procurement and business inclusion laws.

- *Up to 20 Percent Set-Aside*: There is a "minority set-aside authorization" that allows any agency or governing authority to ". . . set aside not more than twenty percent (20%) of its anticipated annual expenditures for the purchase of commodities from minority businesses. . . ."[24] The choice to do this is within the discretion of the agency or governing authority.[25] The presence of the set-aside does not remove the requirement to comply with all Department of Finance and Administration purchasing regulations, and minority business bidders still must satisfy bid requirements.[26] "Set-aside purchases for which competitive bids are required shall be made from the lowest and best minority business bidder."[27]
- *Public Procurement Review Board Set Aside*: The Public Procurement Review Board may "[a]dopt, in its discretion, regulations to set aside at least five percent (5%) of anticipated annual

19. *Id.* § 23.33(a). The size standards for the following are exceptions to this: bank and financial institutions is $1 billion in assets; car rental companies are $75.23 million average annual gross receipts; pay telephones is 1,500 employees; and automobile dealers is 350 employees.
20. *Id.*
21. *Id.*
22. *Id.* § 23.35.
23. Miss. Code Ann. §§ 31-7-1, *et seq.* (2022).
24. *Id.* § 31-7-13(s).
25. *Id.*
26. *Id.*
27. *Id.*

expenditures for the purchase of commodities from minority businesses; however, all such set-aside purchases shall comply with all purchasing regulations promulgated by the department and shall be subject to all bid requirements. Set-aside purchases for which competitive bids are required shall be made from the lowest and best minority business bidder; however, if no minority bid is available or if the minority bid is more than two percent (2%) higher than the lowest bid, then bids shall be accepted and awarded to the lowest and best bidder. However, the provisions in this paragraph shall not be construed to prohibit the rejection of a bid when only one (1) bid is received. Such rejection shall be placed in the minutes."

- *Reporting Requirements*: The Office of Minority Business Enterprises of MDA must report to the governor and the legislature on the economic impact of the efforts pertaining to minority business enterprises.[28] In addition, "[e]ach state agency and educational institution shall report the participation of minority business enterprises in the public works and procurement contracts executed by the agency or institution. The reports shall be made on an annual basis."[29]

Contracting opportunities where the MDOT DBE program applies have several requirements that intersect directly with procurement, contracting, and business inclusion.

- *Fostering Small Business Participation*: Pursuant to 49 C.F.R. § 26.39, MDOT has engaged in efforts to foster small business participation.[30] One effort MDOT explored to advance this was to set aside projects where only small businesses would bid.[31]
- *Goals*: Contract opportunities may not use quotas or set-asides for DBEs.[32] The only exception for using a set-aside is in a limited or extreme circumstance, "when no other method could be reasonably expected to redress egregious instances of discrimination."[33] Instead, an overall goal must be set.[34] The goal must be based on evidence of available "ready,

---

28. *Id.* § 57-69-5(2)(h).
29. *Id.* § 57-69-9.
30. *Disadvantaged Business Enterprise Program Manual*, Miss. Dep't of Transp., Appendix B, at 1 (2022), https://mdot.ms.gov/documents/Civil%20Rights/Manuals/DBE/DBE%20Program%20Manual.pdf.
31. *Id.*
32. 49 C.F.R. § 26.43 (2022).
33. *Id.*
34. *Id.* § 26.45(a)(1).

willing and able" DBEs in the market.[35] Once the assessment of "ready, willing and able" DBEs is completed, an overall goal may be established as a percentage of the total amount of contracts receiving U.S. Department of Transportation (U.S. DOT) funds.[36] Participation goals must be set for all certified DBEs and not divided into subcategories.[37] Race- and gender-neutral means must be used to "meet the maximum feasible portion of your overall goal."[38] MDOT, as a recipient of U.S. DOT funds, will not be penalized for failing to meet the overall goal set, if it can establish good faith efforts to meet the goal.[39] When there is a DBE goal on a specific contract opportunity, only the bidder meeting the goal, or establishing good faith efforts to meet the goal, may be awarded the contract.[40]

- *Prompt Payment*: Under 49 C.F.R. part 26, contractors must pay subcontractors within 30 days of receipt of payment from the state DOT for satisfactory performance.[41]
- *Payment of Retainage*: Contractors must pay amounts withheld for retainage to subcontractors within 30 days of their work being satisfactorily completed.[42]

Additional Related Laws, Policies, and Programs

- *Access to Capital*: For businesses that are certified through MDA under title 6, Code of Mississippi Rules, sections 2-3.1 through 2-4.1 of the Administrative Code, it outlines the parameters for the Minority Business Enterprise Loan (MBE), Micro-Loan (MBEM) programs, and Mississippi Capital Access Contract Loan Program (MS CAP). Following are additional details for each of these programs. There are additional programs for small businesses noted online here: https://mississippi.org/minority-small-business/grants/.
    - *Minority Business Enterprise Loan Program*: This program allows a socially and economically disadvantaged small

35. *Id.* § 26.45(b).
36. *Id.* § 26.45(e).
37. *Id.* § 26.45(h).
38. *Id.* § 26.51.
39. *Id.* § 26.47.
40. *Id.* § 26.53.
41. 49 C.F.R. § 26.29(a) (2023).
42. *Id.* § 26.29(b).

business concern[43] (which is inclusive of minority-owned businesses and women-owned businesses) to apply for a loan. The loans are up to $250,000.

- *Minority Business Enterprise Micro-Loan Program*: This program also allows a socially and economically disadvantaged small business concern[44] (which is inclusive of minority-owned businesses and women-owned businesses) to apply for a loan. The loans are up to $35,000.
- *Mississippi Capital Access Contract Loan Program (MS CAP)*: "The Mississippi Capital Access Program, administered by [MDA], is designed to increase the availability of financing for borrowers who for various reasons might have difficulty in obtaining conventional loans. The essential element of the program is a loan secured by proceeds of a public contract ('Contract Loan'). The loan will be made on the basis of a construction contract with a public entity having been awarded to the borrower."[45]

- *Bidding Preferences*: In addition to considering the size of a business, the race and ethnicity of the owners, and the gender of the owners, there are preferences for businesses that are considered local[46] or "resident contractors."[47] Such preferences would allow, in a competitive bidding situation, for the local business to receive a preference in competing with another business that is not local if all other decision factors are equal.
- *Prompt Payment to Subcontractors*: "When a contractor receives any payment from the owner under a construction contract, other than a public construction contract, the contractor shall, upon receipt of that payment, pay each subcontractor and material supplier in proportion to the percentage of work completed by each such subcontractor and material supplier. . . . If the contractor without reasonable cause fails to make any payment to his subcontractors and material suppliers within fifteen (15) days after the receipt of payment from the owner under the construction contract, the contractor shall pay to his

43. Under the Administrative Code, the definition for a socially and economically disadvantaged small business concern relies on the definition under the Small Business Act (15 U.S.C.S. § 637(A) (2022)). This is defined as any small business concern where it is at least 51 percent unconditionally owned (51 percent of the stock in a publicly owned business) by "one or more socially and economically disadvantaged individuals," Indian tribe, or Native Hawaiian organization.

44. *Id.*

45. 6 Miss. Code. R. § 2-4.1 (2022).

46. Miss. Code Ann. § 31-7-15(1) (2022).

47. *Id.* § 31-7-47.

subcontractors and material suppliers, in addition to the payment due them, a penalty in the amount of one-half of one percent (1/2 of 1%) per day of the delinquency, calculated from the expiration of the fifteen-day period until fully paid. . . ."[48]

- *Finding Contract Opportunities*: A list of procurement opportunities are available on the state's "Buying and Selling to Government in Mississippi" page: https://www.ms.gov/dfa/contract_bid_search/Bid?autoloadGrid=true.

Major City Snapshot: Jackson

The City of Jackson, Mississippi (city) has a minority business enterprise program and a women-owned business enterprise program. Chapter 127 of the city's code of ordinances is the Equal Business Opportunity Ordinance.[49] The program is managed by the Equal Business Opportunity Office. Under the ordinance, the office has the responsibility "for the review, compliance and scoring and approval of equal business opportunity plans that are part of bid submissions by prospective contractors. In addition, the compliance and scoring during the performance of work being performed by contractors."[50]

- *Certifications*: The City of Jackson certifies businesses as Minority Business Enterprises (MBEs) and Female Business Enterprises (FBE).
  - *Minority Business Enterprise (MBE)*: A business must be (1) for profit; (2) performing a commercially useful function; (3) owned and controlled by one or more minorities; and (4) certified by the city.[51]
  - *Female Business Enterprise (FBE)*: A business must be (1) for profit; (2) performing a commercially useful function; (3) owned and controlled by one or more females; and (4) certified by the city.[52]
- *Utilization Plans*: For contracts $50,000 or more, contractors need to submit (1) an Equal Business Opportunity Plan and (2) a sworn affidavit.[53]
- *Modifying Contractors*: Subcontractors cannot be modified unless a letter is sent to the equal business opportunity manager

---

48. *Id.* § 87-7-5.
49. Jackson, Miss., Rev. Ordinances ch. 127, § 1 (2022).
50. *Id.*
51. *Id.* § 52.
52. *Id.*
53. *Id.* § 2(b).

noting probable cause for the change, and the change must be approved or rejected by the office.[54]

- *Prompt Payment to Subcontractors*: Prime contractor must pay all subcontractors within five days of receiving payment from the city.[55]
- *Reporting Requirements*: Monthly reports noting services performed and payments to subcontractors must be submitted.[56]

54. *Id.*
55. *Id.*
56. *Id.*

CHAPTER 26
Missouri

Overview of Business Inclusion Program, Policies, and Practices

Government entities seeking to create business inclusion programs have two primary options in terms of the type of program they may create, in terms of who is eligible for the program: (1) a race- and gender-conscious program or (2) a race- and gender-neutral program. Under the Equal Protection Clause of the Fourteenth Amendment, strict scrutiny is applied by the courts when a government actor is creating policies based on race. Strict scrutiny is the highest level of judicial review that may be applied. It requires the government actor to demonstrate that (1) past discrimination exists such that the entity has a "compelling government interest" in rectifying it, and (2) the policies and programs created to do so are "narrowly tailored."[1] Although intermediate scrutiny is often applied when reviewing programs based on gender, strict scrutiny is applied when reviewing race- and gender-conscious business inclusion programs.[2] Disparity studies have become a standard tool used to assist a government entity in withstanding a challenge to its race- and gender-conscious business inclusion programs. These studies aid in demonstrating whether a government entity has engaged

1. City of Richmond v. J.A. Croson Co., 488 U.S. 469 (1989).

2. Since the 1980s with the Supreme Court decision in *City of Richmond v. J.A. Croson Company*, there have been a number of cases across the county that have assessed race- and gender-conscious business inclusion programs. *See* Adarand Constructors, Inc. v. Pena, 515 U.S. 200 (1995); Virdi v. DeKalb Cnty. Sch. Dist., 135 Fed. App'x 262, 268 (11th Cir. 2005); Sherbrooke Turf, Inc. v. Minn. Dep't of Transp., 345 F.3d 964, 971 (8th Cir. 2003); Mountain West Holding Co., Inc. v. The State of Montana, Montana DOT, et al., 2017 WL 2179120 (9th Cir. May 16, 2017).

in past discrimination in its contracting practices, such that the entity may have a compelling government interest in rectifying it.[3]

Conversely, race- and gender-neutral programs are programs that are not only accessible to minority-owned and women-owned businesses but to all businesses, regardless of race or gender. A small business inclusion program would fall into this category. The level of judicial review applied to such a policy to determine its constitutionality is rational basis, which is the lowest threshold for a government to satisfy. For a government entity to satisfy rational basis, the policy or program created must be "related to a legitimate government purpose."[4] Even when a government entity has a race- and gender-conscious program, oftentimes the program may still require the government actor to seek to meet the goals of their program through race- and gender-neutral means where able, so as to be taking the most narrowly tailored means of accomplishing the program goals.

In the state of Missouri, at the state level of government, there are two main state entities that certify businesses for business inclusion programs: (1) the Office of Administration and (2) the Missouri Department of Transportation (MoDOT).

Summary of Certification Programs and Requirements

The Office of Administration Office of Equal Opportunity Supplier Diversity Program certifies businesses as Minority Businesses Enterprises (MBEs) and Women's Business Enterprises (WBE). The eligibility requirements for both follow:

- *Minority Business Enterprise (MBE)*: To satisfy the eligibility criteria to be certified as an MBE, a business must (1) be 51 percent owned by one or more minorities (defined to include Blacks, American Indians, Hispanics, Asian Americans, and other similar racial minority groups); (2) be 51 percent controlled in terms of the management of the business and day-to-day operations of the business by minorities—and a minority must hold the highest position in the business; (3) have eligible

3. *Promoting Opportunity and Equality in America: A Guide to Federal Circuit Authority on Permissible Government Actions to Promote Racial and Gender Equality*, AM. CIV. LIBERTIES UNION & THE OPPORTUNITY AGENDA (Dec. 2010), https://www.aclu.org/sites/default/files/field_document/Promoting_Opportunity_and_Equality_in_America.pdf.

4. 488 U.S. 469 (1989).

owners who are U.S. citizens or lawfully admitted permanent residents; and (4) be a for-profit business.[5]

- *Women's Business Enterprise (WBE)*: To satisfy the eligibility criteria to be certified as a WBE, a business must (1) be 51 percent owned by one or more women; (2) be 51 percent controlled in terms of the management of the business and day-to-day operations of the business by one or more women—and a woman must hold the highest position in the business; (3) have eligible owners who are U.S. citizens or lawfully admitted permanent residents; and (4) be a for-profit business.[6]

The Office of Administration Division of Purchasing certifies Service-Disabled Veteran Business Enterprises (SDVEs).

- *Service-Disabled Veteran Business Enterprise (SDVE)*: A business must (1) be at least 51 percent owned by one or more service-disabled veterans; (2) have the daily operations of the business managed by one or more service-disabled veterans—and they have the power to make major management decisions; (3) be doing "business as a Missouri firm, corporation, or individual, or maintaining a Missouri office or place of business, not including an office of a registered agent"; and (4) "[have] a copy of the SDV's Certificate of Release or Discharge from Active Duty (DD Form 214), and a copy of the SDV's disability rating letter issued by the Department of Veterans Affairs establishing a service-connected disability rating, or a Department of Defense determination of service-connected disability."[7]

MoDOT, as a member of the Missouri Regional Certification Committee (MRCC), administers the Disadvantaged Business Enterprise (DBE) program, Airport Concession Disadvantaged Business Enterprise (ACDBE) program, and the Small Business Enterprise (SBE) program.

- *Disadvantaged Business Enterprise (DBE) Program*: Pursuant to 49 C.F.R. part 26, MoDOT administers the state's DBE certification program. As is required under 49 C.F.R. § 26.81, Missouri

---

5. Mo. Rev. Stat. §§ 37.020, 37.013 (2022); Mo. Code Regs. Ann. 1 § 10-17.040 (2022); *New Applicants*, Mo. Off. of Equal Opportunity, https://oeo.mo.gov/colibri-wp/new-applicants/ (last visited Apr. 14, 2023).

6. Mo. Rev. Stat. § 37.020 (2022); Mo. Code Regs. Ann. 1 § 10-17.040 (2022); *New Applicants*, *supra* note 5.

7. Mo. Rev. Stat. § 34.074 (2022); *Missouri Service-Disabled Veteran Business Enterprise (SDVE) Application Form*, Off. of Admin. Div. of Purchasing, https://purch.oa.mo.gov/vendor-information/missouri-service-disabled-veteran-business-enterprise-sdve-information/application (last visited Apr. 14, 2023).

has a Unified Certification Program (UCP). The UCP consists of the following entities that make up the MRCC: MoDOT; City of St. Louis, Missouri; Bi-State Development; Kansas City Area Transportation Authority (KCATA); and the City of Kansas City, Missouri.[8] The MRCC through the UCP makes all DBE certification decisions and provides a "one-stop shop" to DBE applicants.[9] To qualify as a DBE, a business must (1) be for-profit;[10] (2) be a small business concern—with "small" determined by the Small Business Administration (SBA) small business size standards—and does not exceed $30.40 million in gross annual receipts;[11] (3) be at least 51 percent owned by socially and economically disadvantaged individuals—there is a rebuttable presumption that women, Black Americans, Hispanic Americans, Native Americans, Asian-Pacific Americans, Subcontinent Asian Americans, or other minorities are disadvantaged;[12] (4) be controlled by one or more of the socially and economically disadvantaged owners;[13] (5) have the socially and economically disadvantaged owners be U.S. citizens or lawfully admitted permanent residents;[14] and (6) have the personal net worth for any socially and economically disadvantaged owner not exceed $1.32 million.[15] The DBE program is required on contracting opportunities that have received funding from the Federal Highway Administration (FHWA), Federal Aviation Administration (FAA), or Federal Transit Administration (FTA).[16]

- *Airport Concession Disadvantaged Business Enterprise (ACDBE) Program:* In addition to being certified as a DBE under 49 C.F.R. part 26, businesses may also be certified as an Airport Concession Disadvantaged Business Enterprise (ACDBE) under 49 C.F.R. part 23. To qualify as an ACDBE, a business must (1) be a concession for-profit small business concern;[17]

8. *Disadvantaged Business Enterprise Program Unified Certification Agreement, Policies & Procedures*, Mo. Dep't of Transp. 4 (Revised 2022), https://www.modot.org/sites/default/files/documents/MRCC%20Policy%20Feb%202022%20-%203.pdf.

9. 49 C.F.R. § 26.81(b)(2) (2022).

10. *Id.* § 26.5.

11. *Id.* §§ 26.5, 26.65(b). It is worth noting that under 49 C.F.R. § 26.65(b) the DBE size standard may be adjusted annually for inflation such that in subsequent years the size standard may no longer be $30.40 million.

12. *Id.* § 26.67.

13. *Id.* § 26.5.

14. *Id.* § 26.67.

15. *Id.*

16. *Id.* § 26.21(a).

17. *Id.* § 23.3.

(2) qualify as small by having its prior three-year average gross receipts not exceed the applicable size standard of $56.42 million;[18] (3) be 51 percent owned by one or more socially and economically disadvantaged individuals;[19] (4) have one or more of the socially and economically disadvantaged individuals with control and managing the daily business operations;[20] and (5) have the personal net worth for any socially and economically disadvantaged owner not exceed $1.32 million.[21]

- *Small Business Enterprise (SBE) Program*: To be eligible for the race- and gender-neutral SBE program, a business must (1) be independently owned and operated; (2) be a for-profit entity; (3) not be dominant in its field of operations; (4) have owners with a personal net worth that does not exceed $1.32 million; and (4) meet the Small Business Administration (SBA) size standard for its industry.[22]

Procurement Laws Intersecting with Business Inclusion

In the state of Missouri, the most relevant laws and administrative rules at the intersection of procurement and business inclusion laws may be found in the Missouri Revisor of Statutes chapter 34; Missouri Revisor of Statutes chapter 37; Missouri Code of State Regulations 40 and 10-17; and Executive Order 15-06.[23] Following is a high-level overview of some of the relevant laws. It is worth noting that in 2022, a "Small Business Impact Study" was completed and may subsequently impact laws, rules, programs, and practices pertaining to business inclusion.[24]

- *Inclusion Goals*: The state of Missouri, pursuant to Executive Order 15-06, has set annual aspirational goals of 10 percent

18. *Id.* § 23.33(a). The size standards for the following are exceptions to this: bank and financial institutions is $1 billion in assets; car rental companies are $75.23 million average annual gross receipts; pay telephones is 1,500 employees; and automobile dealers is 350 employees.

19. *Id.*

20. *Id.*

21. *Id.* § 23.35.

22. *Disadvantaged Business Enterprise Program Unified Certification Agreement, Policies & Procedures*, *supra* note 8, at 31.

23. *Procurement Authority*, Off. of Admin. Div. of Purchasing, https://purch.oa.mo.gov/procurement-authority (last visited Apr. 14, 2023); *Vendor Manual*, State of Mo. Off. of Admin. Div. of Purchasing & Materials Mgmt. 7 (2014), https://oa.mo.gov/sites/default/files/vendormanual.pdf; *Small Business Impact Study 2022*, Mo. Off. of Admin. 89 (2022), https://oeo.mo.gov/wp-content/uploads/2023/01/FINALSmall-Business-Impact-Study.pdf.

24. *Small Business Impact Study 2022*, *supra* note 23.

MBE and 10 percent WBE inclusion on all state procurements by executive branch agencies.[25] These goals are for all state agencies to "make every feasible effort to" increase spends with MWBEs to attain these goals.[26] The Office of Equal Opportunity will collaborate with other state agencies and divisions such as the Division of Purchasing and Division of Facilities Management, Design and Construction on setting contract specific goals across state procurement opportunities.[27] With a lens toward a narrowly tailored program, contract-specific goals are set by evaluating the availability of "ready, willing, and able" MWBEs in the applicable commodity codes and geography.[28] Contract-specific MWBE goals may be higher or lower than the state's annual aspirational goals, based on MWBE availability.[29] There is also a 3 percent inclusion goal for SDVEs on state contracts.[30]

- *SDVE Three-Point Preference*: "In letting contracts for the performance of any job or service, all agencies, departments, institutions, and other entities of this state and of each political subdivision of this state shall give a three-point bonus preference to service-disabled veteran businesses doing business as Missouri firms, corporations, or individuals, or which maintain Missouri offices or places of business."[31]
- *Bidder Responsiveness and Good Faith Efforts*: In considering the award of a bid, MWBE participation will be evaluated when determining responsiveness of the bid.[32] If a contractor is unable to meet the contract-specific MWBE goals established, a waiver is possible for those establishing good faith efforts to meet the goal.[33] Documentation of good faith efforts may be submitted with the bid to be reviewed.[34] Failure to meet the goals and to be deemed to have established good faith efforts will result in the bid being rejected.[35]

---

25. Executive Order No. 15-06 (Oct. 21, 2015), https://www.sos.mo.gov/library/reference/orders/2015/eo6; Mo. Code Regs. Ann. 1 § 40-1.050 (2022); *id.* § 10-17.050.
26. Executive Order No. 15-06 (Oct. 21, 2015), https://www.sos.mo.gov/library/reference/orders/2015/eo6; Mo. Code Regs. Ann. 1 § 10-17.050 (2022).
27. Executive Order No. 15-06 (Oct. 21, 2015), https://www.sos.mo.gov/library/reference/orders/2015/eo6; Mo. Code Regs. Ann. 1 § 10-17.050 (2022).
28. Executive Order No. 15-06 (Oct. 21, 2015), https://www.sos.mo.gov/library/reference/orders/2015/eo6; Mo. Code Regs. Ann. 1 § 40-1.050 (2022); *id.* § 10-17.050.
29. Mo. Code Regs. Ann. 1 § 40-1.050 (2022).
30. Mo. Rev. Stat. § 34.074 (2022); Mo. Code Regs. Ann. 1 § 40-1.050 (2022).
31. Mo. Rev. Stat. § 34.074 (2022); Mo. Code Regs. Ann. 1 § 40-1.050 (2022).
32. Mo. Code Regs. Ann. 1 § 40-1.050 (2022); *id.* § 10-17.050.
33. *Id.* § 40-1.050; *id.* § 10-17.050.
34. *Id.* § 40-1.050.
35. *Id.*

- *Prompt Payment to Subcontractors*: Contractors must pay their subcontractors within 15 days after receipt of payment on a public construction contract unless there is reasonable cause not to. If payment is not made within 15 days, then interest at 1.5 percent will be calculated for payment in addition to the amount due.[36]
- *Remedies and Sanctions*: "If the bidder/offeror's bid/proposal is awarded, the percentage level of the M/WBE vendor participation committed to by the bidder/offeror is a binding contractual requirement."[37] "Contractors that fail to comply with their M/WBE contractual requirements may be considered in breach of contract and may be subject to the remedies in the contract and as otherwise allowable by law."[38]
- *Reporting Requirements*: Throughout the duration of a contract with contract-specific goals, the Office of Equal Opportunity does monitor the contract for compliance with MWBE utilization.[39] The Office of Equal Opportunity must also maintain statistics and issue annual reports to the governor and General Assembly pertaining to the MWBE program and efforts.[40] Lastly, the Office of Administration must report on SDVE participation.[41]

Contracting opportunities where the DBE program applies have several requirements that intersect directly with procurement, contracting, and business inclusion.

- *Fostering Small Business Participation*: Pursuant to 49 C.F.R. § 26.39, MoDOT and the MRCC have engaged in efforts to foster small business participation.[42] To advance this, the SBE program referenced above was created.[43] Although SBE goals are not set, participation is tracked, monitored, and reported on.[44]

---

36. Mo. Rev. Stat. § 8.960 (2022).
37. Mo. Code Regs. Ann. 1 § 40-1.050 (2022).
38. *Id.* § 10-17.050.
39. *Id.*
40. Executive Order No. 15-06 (Oct. 21, 2015), https://www.sos.mo.gov/library/reference/orders/2015/eo6; Mo. Code Regs. Ann. 1 § 10-17.050 (2022).
41. *Id.* § 40-1.050.
42. *Disadvantaged Business Enterprise Program Submittal*, Mo. Dep't of Transp. 67 (2020), https://www.modot.org/sites/default/files/documents/DBE%20Program%20Submittal%20FFY20.pdf; *Disadvantaged Business Enterprise Program Unified Certification Agreement, Policies & Procedures*, *supra* note 8, at 31.
43. *Disadvantaged Business Enterprise Program Submittal*, *supra* note 42; *Disadvantaged Business Enterprise Program Unified Certification Agreement, Policies & Procedures*, *supra* note 8.
44. *Disadvantaged Business Enterprise Program Submittal*, *supra* note 42.

- *Goals*: Contract opportunities may not use quotas or set-asides for DBEs.[45] The only exception for using a set-aside is in a limited or extreme circumstance, "when no other method could be reasonably expected to redress egregious instances of discrimination."[46] Instead, an overall goal must be set.[47] The goal must be based on evidence of available "ready, willing and able" DBEs in the market.[48] Once the assessment of "ready, willing and able" DBEs is completed an overall goal may be established as a percentage of the total amount of contracts receiving U.S. Department of Transportation (U.S. DOT) funds.[49] Participation goals must be set for all certified DBEs and not divided into subcategories.[50] Race- and gender-neutral means must be used to "meet the maximum feasible portion of your overall goal."[51] MoDOT, as a recipient of U.S. DOT funds, will not be penalized for failing to meet the overall goal set, if it can establish good faith efforts to meet the goal.[52] When there is a DBE goal on a specific contract opportunity, only the bidder meeting the goal, or establishing good faith efforts to meet the goal, may be awarded the contract.[53]
- *Prompt Payment*: Under 49 C.F.R. part 26, contractors must pay subcontractors within 30 days of receipt of payment from the state DOT for satisfactory performance.[54]
- *Payment of Retainage*: Contractors must pay amounts withheld for retainage to subcontractors within 30 days of their work being satisfactorily completed.[55]

Additional Related Laws, Policies, and Programs

- *Access to Capital*: The Missouri Department of Economic Development has a Small Business Loan Program. More information may be found online at https://ded.mo.gov/programs/business/small-business-loan-program.

45. 49 C.F.R. § 26.43 (2022).
46. *Id.*
47. *Id.* § 26.45(a)(1).
48. *Id.* § 26.45(b).
49. *Id.* § 26.45(e).
50. *Id.* § 26.45(h).
51. *Id.* § 26.51.
52. *Id.* § 26.47.
53. *Id.* § 26.53.
54. 49 C.F.R. § 26.29(a) (2023).
55. *Id.* § 26.29(b).

- *Finding Contracting Opportunities*: Contracting opportunities with the state of Missouri may be found on the state's e-Procurement system, MissouriBUYS: https://missouribuys.mo.gov/bidboard.

Major City Snapshot: St. Louis

The City of St. Louis Minority and Women's Business Enterprise Program exists pursuant to its City Ordinance #70767.

- *Certifications*: The program certifies the following types of businesses:
  - *Minority Business Enterprise (MBE)*: An MBE is defined as "[a] for-profit sole proprietorship, partnership, limited liability company, or corporation owned, operated and controlled by Minority Group Members who (a) have at least 51 percent ownership of the business entity; (b) maintain day-to-day operational and managerial control of the business entity; and (c) have interest in capital and earnings commensurate with the Minority Group Member(s)' percentage of ownership. For purposes of these Rules, the MBE firm must be a Local Firm, certified as an MBE by the Program Review Committee."[56]
  - *Women's Business Enterprise (WBE)*: A WBE is defined as "a for-profit sole proprietorship, partnership, limited liability company, or corporation owned, operated and controlled by one or more Women who (a) have at least 51 percent ownership of the business entity; (b) maintain day-to-day operational and managerial control of the business entity; and (c) have an interest in capital and earnings commensurate with Women's percentage of ownership. For purposes of these Rules, the WBE firm must be a Local Firm, certified as a WBE by the Program Review Committee."[57]
- *Construction Inclusion Goals*: "Based on availability, the construction project goal shall be 21 [percent] for African American-owned business enterprises, [two percent] for Hispanic American-owned business enterprises, 11.50 [percent] for Asian American-owned business enterprises, [half a percent] for Native

56. *Certification and Compliance Rules*, City of Saint Louis Minority & Women's Bus. Enter. Program 5 (2020), https://www.stlouis-mo.gov/government/departments/sldc/documents/upload/Final-M-WBE-Cert-Compliance-Rules-1.pdf.

57. *Id.* at 6.

American-owned business enterprises and 11 [percent] for Women-owned business enterprises."[58]

- *Utilization Plans and Contractor Good Faith Efforts*: An MWBE Utilization Plan must be submitted at the time of bid opening.[59] Failure to meet the construction project's goals or demonstrate good faith efforts will deem the bid to be nonresponsive and ineligible for award.[60]
- *MWBE Prime Contractor Bid Discount*: A 5 percent MWBE contractor bid discount must be applied on construction, goods, and other services prime contracts of $300,000 or less that "lower[s] the eligible M/WBE's bid but shall not reduce the contract award amount."[61]
- *Incentive Credits*: On professional services prime contracts, a 15 percent incentive credit will be applied as part of the total points evaluated for MWBEs.[62]
- *Reporting Requirements*: Compliance reports must be submitted annually by the Minority Business Development and compliance officer to the mayor and board of aldermen on the MWBE program.[63]

58. City of Saint Louis Ord. 70767 (2018).
59. *Id.*
60. *Id.*
61. *Id.*
62. *Id.*
63. *Id.*

CHAPTER 27

Montana

Overview of Business Inclusion Program, Policies, and Practices

Government entities seeking to create business inclusion programs have two primary options in terms of the type of program they may create, in terms of who is eligible for the program: (1) a race- and gender-conscious program or (2) a race- and gender-neutral program. Under the Equal Protection Clause of the Fourteenth Amendment, strict scrutiny is applied by the courts when a government actor is creating policies based on race. Strict scrutiny is the highest level of judicial review that may be applied. It requires the government actor to demonstrate that (1) past discrimination exists such that the entity has a "compelling government interest" in rectifying it, and (2) the policies and programs created to do so are "narrowly tailored."[1] Although intermediate scrutiny is often applied when reviewing programs based on gender, strict scrutiny is applied when reviewing race- and gender-conscious business inclusion programs.[2] Disparity studies have become a standard tool used to assist a government entity in withstanding a challenge to its race- and gender-conscious business inclusion programs. These studies aid in demonstrating whether a government entity has engaged

1. City of Richmond v. J.A. Croson Co., 488 U.S. 469 (1989).

2. Since the 1980s with the Supreme Court decision in *City of Richmond v. J.A. Croson Company*, there have been a number of cases across the county that have assessed race- and gender-conscious business inclusion programs. *See* Adarand Constructors, Inc. v. Pena, 515 U.S. 200 (1995); Virdi v. DeKalb Cnty. Sch. Dist., 135 Fed. App'x 262, 268 (11th Cir. 2005); Sherbrooke Turf, Inc. v. Minn. Dep't of Transp., 345 F.3d 964, 971 (8th Cir. 2003); Mountain West Holding Co., Inc. v. The State of Montana, Montana DOT, et al., 2017 WL 2179120 (9th Cir. May 16, 2017).

in past discrimination in its contracting practices, such that the entity may have a compelling government interest in rectifying it.[3]

Conversely, race- and gender-neutral programs are programs that are not only accessible to minority-owned and women-owned businesses but to all businesses, regardless of race or gender. A small business inclusion program would fall into this category. The level of judicial review applied to such a policy to determine its constitutionality is rational basis, which is the lowest threshold for a government to satisfy. For a government entity to satisfy rational basis, the policy or program created must be "related to a legitimate government purpose."[4] Even when a government entity has a race- and gender-conscious program, oftentimes the program may still require the government actor to seek to meet the goals of their program through race- and gender-neutral means where able, so as to be taking the most narrowly tailored means of accomplishing the program goals.

At the state level of government in Montana, the Montana Department of Transportation (MDT) is the primary state department that certifies businesses for a business inclusion program.[5]

Summary of Certification Programs and Requirements

MDT administers the Disadvantaged Business Enterprise (DBE) program, Airport Concession Disadvantaged Business Enterprise (ACDBE) program, and the Small Business Enterprise (SBE) program.

- *Disadvantaged Business Enterprise (DBE) Program*: Pursuant to 49 C.F.R. part 26, MDT administers the state's DBE certification program. As is required under 49 C.F.R. § 26.81, Montana has a Unified Certification Program (UCP). The UCP makes all DBE certification decisions and provides a "one-stop shop" to DBE applicants.[6] MDT serves as the lead agency responsible for the certification of DBEs.[7] To qualify as a DBE, a business must (1) be for-profit;[8] (2) be a small business concern—with

3. *Promoting Opportunity and Equality in America: A Guide to Federal Circuit Authority on Permissible Government Actions to Promote Racial and Gender Equality*, Am. Civ. Liberties Union & The Opportunity Agenda (Dec. 2010), https://www.aclu.org/sites/default/files/field_document/Promoting_Opportunity_and_Equality_in_America.pdf.

4. 488 U.S. 469 (1989).

5. *Disadvantaged Business Enterprise*, Mont. Dep't of Transp., https://www.mdt.mt.gov/business/contracting/civil/dbe.aspx (last visited Jan. 20, 2023).

6. 49 C.F.R. § 26.81(b)(2) (2022).

7. *Montana Department of Transportation*, Mont. Dep't of Transp., https://www.mdt.mt.gov/ (last visited July 5, 2023).

8. 49 C.F.R. § 26.5 (2022).

"small" determined by the Small Business Administration (SBA) small business size standards—and does not exceed $30.40 million in gross annual receipts;[9] (3) be at least 51 percent owned by socially and economically disadvantaged individuals—there is a rebuttable presumption that women, Black Americans, Hispanic Americans, Native Americans, Asian-Pacific Americans, Subcontinent Asian Americans, or other minorities are disadvantaged;[10] (4) be controlled by one or more of the socially and economically disadvantaged owners;[11] (5) have the socially and economically disadvantaged owners be U.S. citizens or lawfully admitted permanent residents;[12] and (6) have the personal net worth for any socially and economically disadvantaged owner not exceed $1.32 million.[13] The DBE program is required on contracting opportunities that have received funding from the Federal Highway Administration (FHWA), Federal Aviation Administration (FAA), or Federal Transit Administration (FTA).[14]

- *Airport Concession Disadvantaged Business Enterprise (ACDBE) Program*: In addition to being certified as a DBE under 49 C.F.R. part 26, businesses may also be certified as an Airport Concession Disadvantaged Business Enterprise (ACDBE) under 49 C.F.R. part 23. To qualify as an ACDBE, a business must (1) be a concession for-profit small business concern;[15] (2) qualify as small by having its prior three-year average gross receipts not exceed the applicable size standard of $56.42 million;[16] (3) be 51 percent owned by one or more socially and economically disadvantaged individuals;[17] (4) have one or more of the socially and economically disadvantaged individuals with control and managing the daily business operations;[18] and (5) have

9. *Id.* §§ 26.5, 26.65(b). It is worth noting that under 49 C.F.R. § 26.65(b) the DBE size standard may be adjusted annually for inflation such that in subsequent years the size standard may no longer be $30.40 million.

10. *Id.* § 26.67.

11. *Id.* § 26.5.

12. *Id.* § 26.67.

13. *Id.*

14. *Id.* § 26.21(a).

15. *Id.* § 23.3.

16. *Id.* § 23.33(a). The size standards for the following are exceptions to this: bank and financial institutions is $1 billion in assets; car rental companies are $75.23 million average annual gross receipts; pay telephones is 1,500 employees; and automobile dealers is 350 employees.

17. *Id.*

18. *Id.*

the personal net worth for any socially and economically disadvantaged owner not exceed $1.32 million.[19]

- *Small Business Enterprise (SBE) Program*: MDT also manages a small business inclusion program (SBE).[20] To be eligible for the SBE certification, a business must (1) be for-profit; (2) be majority owned and controlled (51 percent) by someone with a personal net worth less than $1.32 million; (3) have owners who are U.S. citizens or lawfully admitted permanent residents of the United States; and (4) meet the Small Business Administration, DBE, and ACDBE applicable size standards.[21]

Procurement Laws Intersecting with Business Inclusion

Procurement in Montana is managed by the State Procurement Bureau, which is located within the State Financial Services Division of the Department of Administration.[22] The authority for procurement in Montana may be found in the following:[23]

- Montana Code Annotated title 18, Public Contracts
- Montana Code Annotated title 28, Contracts and Other Obligations
- Administrative Rules of Montana title 2, chapter 5, State Procurement

There are no bidding preferences, laws, or rules specific to business inclusion and minority-owned, women-owned, disability-owned, veteran-owned, and/or LGBT-owned business enterprises in Montana, outside of what is required by the MDT DBE program.

Contracting opportunities where the MDT DBE program applies have several requirements that intersect directly with procurement, contracting, and business inclusion.

---

19. *Id.* § 23.35.

20. *Small Business Enterprise*, Mont. Dep't of Transp., https://www.mdt.mt.gov/business/contracting/civil/sbe.aspx (last visited Jan. 20, 2023).

21. *Certification Application—Small Business Enterprise (SBE)*, Mont. Dep't of Transp., https://www.mdt.mt.gov/other/webdata/external/civilrights/forms/MDT-CIV-029_SBE_Application.pdf (last visited Jan. 20, 2023).

22. *State of Montana Procurement Manual*, Mont. Dep't of Admin. 3, https://spb.mt.gov/_docs/A-PROCUREMENT-FORMS-GUIDE/SPBM_A_Chapters_8_22_Update.pdf (last visited Jan. 20, 2023); *Welcome to the State Procurement Bureau*, State Procurement Bureau, https://spb.mt.gov/index (last visited Jan. 20, 2023).

23. *State of Montana Procurement Manual*, *supra* note 22, at 4.

- *Fostering Small Business Participation*: Pursuant to 49 C.F.R. § 26.39, MDT has engaged in efforts to foster small business participation.[24] MDT advances this through efforts like the following: (1) ensuring there are prime contracts of a size small businesses can perform; (2) ensuring prime contractors provide subcontracting opportunities small businesses can perform rather than self-performing; (3) providing training; and (4) working to ensure prompt payment to subcontractors.[25]
- *Goals*: Contract opportunities may not use quotas or set-asides for DBEs.[26] The only exception for using a set-aside is in a limited or extreme circumstance, "when no other method could be reasonably expected to redress egregious instances of discrimination."[27] Instead, an overall goal must be set.[28] The goal must be based on evidence of available "ready, willing and able" DBEs in the market.[29] Once the assessment of "ready, willing and able" DBEs is completed, an overall goal may be established as a percentage of the total amount of contracts receiving U.S. Department of Transportation (U.S. DOT) funds.[30] Participation goals must be set for all certified DBEs and not divided into subcategories.[31] Race- and gender-neutral means must be used to "meet the maximum feasible portion of your overall goal."[32] MDT, as a recipient of U.S. DOT funds, will not be penalized for failing to meet the overall goal set, if it can establish good faith efforts to meet the goal.[33] When there is a DBE goal on a contract opportunity only the bidder meeting the goal, or establishing good faith efforts to meet the goal, may be awarded the contract.[34]
- *Prompt Payment*: Under 49 C.F.R. part 26, contractors must pay subcontractors within 30 days of receipt of payment from the state DOT for satisfactory performance.[35]

---

24. *DBE Program Plan*, Mont. Dep't of Transp. 12–13 (2023), https://www.mdt.mt.gov/other/webdata/external/civilrights/dbe/program-guide.pdf.
25. *Id.*
26. 49 C.F.R. § 26.43 (2022).
27. *Id.*
28. *Id.* § 26.45(a)(1).
29. *Id.* § 26.45(b).
30. *Id.* § 26.45(e).
31. *Id.* § 26.45(h).
32. *Id.* § 26.51.
33. *Id.* § 26.47.
34. *Id.* § 26.53.
35. 49 C.F.R. § 26.29(a) (2023).

- *Payment of Retainage*: Contractors must pay amounts withheld for retainage to subcontractors within 30 days of their work being satisfactorily completed.[36]

Additional Related Laws, Policies, and Programs

- *Contracting Preference*: Although not specific to a minority-, women-, veteran-, disabled-, or LGBT-owned enterprise, the state does, however, provide a preference to blind persons under Montana Code Annotated section18-5-502. It states that, "(1) Whenever state property is proposed to be made available to private persons for use as a vending facility, if two or more substantially equal proposals submitted by responsible bidders are determined to most closely meet the purchasing agency's specifications and if one of the proposals has been submitted by a blind person, the contract must be awarded to the blind person. (2) For purposes of this section, proposals are substantially equal if their overall ratings, as determined by the purchasing agency in accordance with the request for proposal, do not differ by more than [three percent]. (3) Any contract awarded pursuant to this section to a blind person must prohibit transfer of the contract by sublease, assignment, or any other method."
- *Prompt Payment to Subcontractors*: On construction contracts, "[w]ithin [seven] days after a contractor receives a periodic or final payment from an owner or a state agency, the contractor shall pay the subcontractor, if any, the full amount due the subcontractor in accordance with the subcontract for work performed or materials provided in accordance with that subcontract."[37]
- *Finding Contract Opportunities*: Contracting opportunities may be found on the Montana Acquisition and Contracting System (eMACS), located here: https://bids.sciquest.com/apps/Router/PublicEvent?CustomerOrg=StateOfMontana.

---

36. *Id.* § 26.29(b).
37. Mont. Code Ann. § 28-2-2103(2)(a) (2021).

Major City Snapshot

Across some of the largest cities in Montana—Billings, Helena, Bozeman, Great Falls, and Missoula—none have a city-specific business inclusion program.[38] In contracting opportunities and projects receiving federal funding from the U.S. DOT or U.S. Environmental Protection Agency, cities have noted business inclusion goals in accordance with federal regulations and requirements for federal fund recipients.[39]

38. A thorough review of each city ordinance was completed.

39. As examples, please see the following: *City of Missoula Brownfield Revitalization Project Request for Qualifications*, City Of Missoula, http://www.ci.missoula.mt.us/DocumentCenter/View/48327/2019-Brownfields-QEP-RFQ-Final?bidId (last visited July 5, 2023); City of Billings, Mont. Res. 05-18295 (2005).

CHAPTER 28

Nebraska

Overview of Business Inclusion Program, Policies, and Practices

Government entities seeking to create business inclusion programs have two primary options in terms of the type of program they may create, in terms of who is eligible for the program: (1) a race- and gender-conscious program or (2) a race- and gender-neutral program. Under the Equal Protection Clause of the Fourteenth Amendment, strict scrutiny is applied by the courts when a government actor is creating policies based on race. Strict scrutiny is the highest level of judicial review that may be applied. It requires the government actor to demonstrate that (1) past discrimination exists such that the entity has a "compelling government interest" in rectifying it, and (2) the policies and programs created to do so are "narrowly tailored."[1] Although intermediate scrutiny is often applied when reviewing programs based on gender, strict scrutiny is applied when reviewing race- and gender-conscious business inclusion programs.[2] Disparity studies have become a standard tool used to assist a government entity in withstanding a challenge to its race- and gender-conscious business inclusion programs. These studies aid in demonstrating whether a government entity has engaged

1. City of Richmond v. J.A. Croson Co., 488 U.S. 469 (1989).

2. Since the 1980s with the Supreme Court decision in *City of Richmond v. J.A. Croson Company*, there have been a number of cases across the county that have assessed race- and gender-conscious business inclusion programs. *See* Adarand Constructors, Inc. v. Pena, 515 U.S. 200 (1995); Virdi v. DeKalb Cnty. Sch. Dist., 135 Fed. App'x 262, 268 (11th Cir. 2005); Sherbrooke Turf, Inc. v. Minn. Dep't of Transp., 345 F.3d 964, 971 (8th Cir. 2003); Mountain West Holding Co., Inc. v. The State of Montana, Montana DOT, et al., 2017 WL 2179120 (9th Cir. May 16, 2017).

in past discrimination in its contracting practices, such that the entity may have a compelling government interest in rectifying it.[3]

Conversely, race- and gender-neutral programs are programs that are not only accessible to minority-owned and women-owned businesses but to all businesses, regardless of race or gender. A small business inclusion program would fall into this category. The level of judicial review applied to such a policy to determine its constitutionality is rational basis, which is the lowest threshold for a government to satisfy. For a government entity to satisfy rational basis, the policy or program created must be "related to a legitimate government purpose."[4] Even when a government entity has a race- and gender-conscious program, oftentimes the program may still require the government actor to seek to meet the goals of their program through race- and gender-neutral means where able, so as to be taking the most narrowly tailored means of accomplishing the program goals.

In the state of Nebraska, at the state level of government, the Nebraska Department of Transportation (NDOT) is the only state department that certifies businesses for business inclusion programs.

Summary of Certification Programs and Requirements

NDOT administers the Disadvantaged Business Enterprise (DBE) program and Airport Concession Disadvantaged Business Enterprise (ACDBE) program.

- *Disadvantaged Business Enterprise (DBE) Program*: Pursuant to 49 C.F.R. part 26, NDOT administers the state's DBE certification program. As is required under 49 C.F.R. § 26.81, Nebraska has a Unified Certification Program (NUCP).[5] The NUCP has NDOT as the sole certifying agency for NUCP making all DBE certification decisions and provides a "one-stop shop" to DBE applicants.[6] To qualify as a DBE, a business must (1) be for-profit;[7] (2) be a small business concern—with "small" determined by the Small Business Administration (SBA) small

3. *Promoting Opportunity and Equality in America: A Guide to Federal Circuit Authority on Permissible Government Actions to Promote Racial and Gender Equality*, Am. Civ. Liberties Union & The Opportunity Agenda (Dec. 2010), https://www.aclu.org/sites/default/files/field_document/Promoting_Opportunity_and_Equality_in_America.pdf.

4. 488 U.S. 469 (1989).

5. *Nebraska Unified Certification Program for Disadvantaged Business Enterprises*, Neb. Dep't of Transp. 1 (2018), https://dot.nebraska.gov/media/113234/nebraska_ucp.pdf.

6. 49 C.F.R. § 26.81(b)(2) (2022); *Nebraska Unified Certification Program for Disadvantaged Business Enterprises*, *supra* note 5.

7. 49 C.F.R. § 26.5 (2022).

business size standards—and does not exceed $30.40 million in gross annual receipts;[8] (3) be at least 51 percent owned by socially and economically disadvantaged individuals—there is a rebuttable presumption that women, Black Americans, Hispanic Americans, Native Americans, Asian-Pacific Americans, Subcontinent Asian Americans, or other minorities are disadvantaged;[9] (4) be controlled by one or more of the socially and economically disadvantaged owners;[10] (5) have the socially and economically disadvantaged owners be U.S. citizens or lawfully admitted permanent residents;[11] and (6) have the personal net worth for any socially and economically disadvantaged owner not exceed $1.32 million.[12] The DBE program is required on contracting opportunities that have received funding from the Federal Highway Administration (FHWA), Federal Aviation Administration (FAA), or Federal Transit Administration (FTA).[13]

- *Airport Concession Disadvantaged Business Enterprise (ACDBE) Program*: In addition to being certified as a DBE under 49 C.F.R. part 26, businesses may also be certified as an Airport Concession Disadvantaged Business Enterprise (ACDBE) under 49 C.F.R. part 23. To qualify as an ACDBE, a business must (1) be a concession for-profit small business concern;[14] (2) qualify as small by having its prior three-year average gross receipts not exceed the applicable size standard of $56.42 million;[15] (3) be 51 percent owned by one or more socially and economically disadvantaged individuals;[16] (4) have one or more of the socially and economically disadvantaged individuals with control and managing the daily business operations;[17] and (5) have the personal net worth for any socially and economically disadvantaged owner not exceed $1.32 million.[18]

---

8. *Id.* §§ 26.5, 26.65(b). It is worth noting that under 49 C.F.R. § 26.65(b) the DBE size standard may be adjusted annually for inflation such that in subsequent years the size standard may no longer be $30.40 million.
9. *Id.* § 26.67.
10. *Id.* § 26.5.
11. *Id.* § 26.67.
12. *Id.*
13. *Id.* § 26.21(a).
14. *Id.* § 23.3.
15. *Id.* § 23.33(a). The size standards for the following are exceptions to this: bank and financial institutions is $1 billion in assets; car rental companies are $75.23 million average annual gross receipts; pay telephones is 1,500 employees; and automobile dealers is 350 employees.
16. *Id.*
17. *Id.*
18. *Id.* § 23.35.

Procurement Laws Intersecting with Business Inclusion

In the state of Nebraska, purchasing is managed by the Nebraska Department of Administrative Services State Purchasing Bureau. Currently, the contracting preference noted next is the most relevant law at the intersection of procurement and business inclusion for small and diverse businesses.

- *Contracting Preferences*: "When a state contract is to be awarded to the lowest responsible bidder, a resident disabled veteran or a business located in a designated enterprise zone under the Enterprise Zone Act shall be allowed a preference over any other resident or nonresident bidder if all other factors are equal."[19]

Contracting opportunities where the NDOT DBE program applies have several requirements that intersect directly with procurement, contracting, and business inclusion.

- *Fostering Small Business Participation*: Pursuant to 49 C.F.R. § 26.39, NDOT has engaged in efforts to foster small business participation.[20] Although it does not have a formal small business enterprise certification within its DBE program, it does define small business as is noted under 49 C.F.R. part 26.5, which notes that "pursuant to section 3 of the Small Business Act and Small Business Administration regulations implementing it (13 CFR part 121) that [the small business] also does not exceed the cap on average annual gross receipts specified in §26.65(b)."[21] NDOT also seeks to ensure it is unbundling contracts and that 25 percent of contracts are for $1 million or less.[22]
- *Goals*: Contract opportunities may not use quotas or set-asides for DBEs.[23] The only exception for using a set-aside is in a limited or extreme circumstance, "when no other method could be reasonably expected to redress egregious instances of discrimination."[24] Instead, an overall goal must be set.[25]

---

19. Neb. Rev. Stat. § 73-107 (2022).
20. *Disadvantaged Business Enterprise Program Plan*, Neb. Dep't of Transp. 62 (2017), https://dot.nebraska.gov/media/10735/ndot-dbe-program-plan.pdf.
21. *Id.*
22. *Id.* at 62–63.
23. 49 C.F.R. § 26.43 (2022).
24. *Id.*
25. *Id.* § 26.45(a)(1).

The goal must be based on evidence of available "ready, willing and able" DBEs in the market.[26] Once the assessment of "ready, willing and able" DBEs is completed, an overall goal may be established as a percentage of the total amount of contracts receiving U.S. Department of Transportation (U.S. DOT) funds.[27] Participation goals must be set for all certified DBEs and not divided into subcategories.[28] Race- and gender-neutral means must be used to "meet the maximum feasible portion of your overall goal."[29] NDOT, as a recipient of U.S. DOT funds, will not be penalized for failing to meet the overall goal set, if it can establish good faith efforts to meet the goal.[30] When there is a DBE goal on a specific contract opportunity, only the bidder meeting the goal, or establishing good faith efforts to meet the goal, may be awarded the contract.[31]

- *Prompt Payment*: Under 49 C.F.R. part 26, contractors must pay subcontractors within 30 days of receipt of payment from the state DOT for satisfactory performance.[32]
- *Payment of Retainage*: Contractors must pay amounts withheld for retainage to subcontractors within 30 days of their work being satisfactorily completed.[33]

Additional Related Laws, Policies, and Programs

- *Lottery*: Under 370 Nebraska Administrative Code section 301.04, the Lottery Division of the Nebraska Department of Revenue has a policy to ". . . contribute to the establishment, preservation, and strengthening of businesses owned by women and minorities to encourage their participation in state procurement activities. . . ."
- *Prompt Payment to Subcontractors*: "When a subcontractor has performed work in accordance with the provisions of a subcontract and all conditions precedent to payment contained in the subcontract have been satisfied, the contractor shall pay the subcontractor and the subcontractor shall pay his, her, or its subcontractor, within ten days after receipt by the contractor

26. *Id.* § 26.45(b).
27. *Id.* § 26.45(e).
28. *Id.* § 26.45(h).
29. *Id.* § 26.51.
30. *Id.* § 26.47.
31. *Id.* § 26.53.
32. 49 C.F.R. § 26.29(a) (2023).
33. *Id.* § 26.29(b).

or subcontractor of each periodic or final payment, the full amount received for the subcontractor's work and materials based on work completed or service provided under the subcontract for which the subcontractor has properly requested payment, if the subcontractor provides or has provided satisfactory and reasonable assurances of continued performance and financial responsibility to complete the work."[34]

- *Finding Contract Opportunities*: Contracting opportunities may be found on the Nebraska Department of Administrative Services' "Current Bid Opportunities" page: https://das.nebraska.gov/materiel/bidopps.html.

Major City Snapshot: Omaha

The City of Omaha's (city) Human Rights and Relations Department manages the city's Small and Emerging Small Business Program.[35] This program is governed by chapter 10, Article V, division 5 of the City Code of Ordinances. Following is a high-level overview of the program.

- *Certifications*: The city certifies Small Businesses (SBs) and Emerging Small Businesses (ESBs).[36]
- *Inclusion Goals*: Annually, the mayor establishes an overall goal and sub-goals for SB and ESB utilization on all city contracts.[37] Each city department must also set department-specific goals to attain the overall goal.[38]
- *Priority for SBs and ESEBs*: On solicitations for supplies, materials, technical, professional, or other services, if ". . . an adequate number of authorized [SBs or ESBs] are available, the solicitation or request for proposal will give priority to certified Tier I and/or Tier II small businesses and/or emerging small businesses. . . ."[39] It is possible that, prior to soliciting bids or proposals, the Human Rights and Relations Department and the department soliciting the bid may determine that SBs and ESBs are not utilized on a contract opportunity if there are not sufficient SBs and ESBs or no subcontracting opportunities.[40]

---

34. Neb. Rev. Stat. § 45-1203(2) (2022).
35. *Small and Emerging Small Business*, City of Omaha Hum. Rts. & Rels, https://humanrights.cityofomaha.org/small-and-emerging-small-business-seb (last visited Apr. 14, 2023).
36. *Id.*
37. Omaha City Code of Ordinances ch. 10, art. V, div. 5, § 10-200.3 (2023).
38. *Id.*
39. *Id.*
40. *Id.*

- *Penalties*: If a contractor does not comply with the city ordinance, then the contractor may be subject to penalties such as (1) withholding payment until the contractor is in compliance or (2) excluding the contractor from bidding on city contracts until the contactor demonstrates it can carry out the policies of the program.[41]

41. *Id.*

CHAPTER 29

Nevada

Overview of Business Inclusion Program, Policies, and Practices

Government entities seeking to create business inclusion programs have two primary options in terms of the type of program they may create, in terms of who is eligible for the program: (1) a race- and gender-conscious program or (2) a race- and gender-neutral program. Under the Equal Protection Clause of the Fourteenth Amendment, strict scrutiny is applied by the courts when a government actor is creating policies based on race. Strict scrutiny is the highest level of judicial review that may be applied. It requires the government actor to demonstrate that (1) past discrimination exists such that the entity has a "compelling government interest" in rectifying it, and (2) the policies and programs created to do so are "narrowly tailored."[1] Although intermediate scrutiny is often applied when reviewing programs based on gender, strict scrutiny is applied when reviewing race- and gender-conscious business inclusion programs.[2] Disparity studies have become a standard tool used to assist a government entity in withstanding a challenge to its race- and gender-conscious business inclusion programs. These studies aid in demonstrating whether a government entity has engaged

1. City of Richmond v. J.A. Croson Co., 488 U.S. 469 (1989).

2. Since the 1980s with the Supreme Court decision in *City of Richmond v. J.A. Croson Company*, there have been a number of cases across the county that have assessed race- and gender-conscious business inclusion programs. *See* Adarand Constructors, Inc. v. Pena, 515 U.S. 200 (1995); Virdi v. DeKalb Cnty. Sch. Dist., 135 Fed. App'x 262, 268 (11th Cir. 2005); Sherbrooke Turf, Inc. v. Minn. Dep't of Transp., 345 F.3d 964, 971 (8th Cir. 2003); Mountain West Holding Co., Inc. v. The State of Montana, Montana DOT, et al., 2017 WL 2179120 (9th Cir. May 16, 2017).

in past discrimination in its contracting practices, such that the entity may have a compelling government interest in rectifying it.[3]

Conversely, race- and gender-neutral programs are programs that are not only accessible to minority-owned and women-owned businesses but to all businesses, regardless of race or gender. A small business inclusion program would fall into this category. The level of judicial review applied to such a policy to determine its constitutionality is rational basis, which is the lowest threshold for a government to satisfy. For a government entity to satisfy rational basis, the policy or program created must be "related to a legitimate government purpose."[4] Even when a government entity has a race- and gender-conscious program, oftentimes the program may still require the government actor to seek to meet the goals of their program through race- and gender-neutral means where able, so as to be taking the most narrowly tailored means of accomplishing the program goals.

In the state of Nevada, at the state level of government, there are two state agencies certifying businesses for business inclusion programs: (1) the Governor's Office of Economic Development (GOED) and (2) the Nevada Department of Transportation (NDOT).

Summary of Certification Programs and Requirements

GOED certifies Local Emerging Small Businesses (ESBs).[5] This is a race- and gender-neutral program. Following are the eligibility requirements for certification.

- *Local Emerging Small Businesses (ESBs)*: A business must (1) be for-profit; (2) maintain a principal place of business in Nevada; (3) be in existence and operational; (4) "[b]e in compliance with all applicable licensing and registration requirements" in Nevada; (5) qualify as either a Tier 1 or Tier 2 firm, which requires (a) as a Tier 1 firm the firm must have 20 or fewer full-time employees and the immediately preceding three-year averaged annual gross receipts must not exceed $1.7 million for construction services and $700,000 for nonconstruction goods or services (b) as a Tier 2 firm the firm must have 30 or fewer

3. *Promoting Opportunity and Equality in America: A Guide to Federal Circuit Authority on Permissible Government Actions to Promote Racial and Gender Equality*, Am. Civ. Liberties Union & The Opportunity Agenda (Dec. 2010), https://www.aclu.org/sites/default/files/field_document/Promoting_Opportunity_and_Equality_in_America.pdf.

4. 488 U.S. 469 (1989).

5. *NV Local Emerging Small Business*, Nev. Governor's Off. of Econ. Dev., https://goed.nv.gov/programs-incentives/emerging-small-business/ (last visited Mar. 24, 2023).

full-time employees and the immediately preceding three-year averaged annual gross receipts must not exceed $3.5 million for construction services and $1.3 million for nonconstruction goods or services—for both Tier 1 and Tier 2 owners are not included in the employee count; and (6) not be a subsidiary or parent company such that the group of firms would make the business ineligible to meet the employee threshold to be considered a Tier 1 or Tier 2 firm under these eligibility requirements.[6] Certification lasts for two years prior to needing to renew.[7]

NDOT administers the Disadvantaged Business Enterprise (DBE) program, Airport Concession Disadvantaged Business Enterprise (ACDBE) program, and the Small Business Enterprise (SBE) program.

- *Disadvantaged Business Enterprise (DBE) Program*: Pursuant to 49 C.F.R. part 26, NDOT administers the state's DBE certification program. As is required under 49 C.F.R. § 26.81, Nevada has a Unified Certification Program (UCP). The UCP makes all DBE certification decisions and provides a "one-stop shop" to DBE applicants.[8] To qualify as a DBE, a business must (1) be for-profit;[9] (2) be a small business concern—with "small" determined by the Small Business Administration (SBA) small business size standards—and does not exceed $30.40 million in gross annual receipts;[10] (3) be at least 51 percent owned by socially and economically disadvantaged individuals—there is a rebuttable presumption that women, Black Americans, Hispanic Americans, Native Americans, Asian-Pacific Americans, Subcontinent Asian Americans, or other minorities are disadvantaged;[11] (4) be controlled by one or more of the socially and economically disadvantaged owners;[12] (5) have the socially and economically disadvantaged owners be U.S. citizens or lawfully admitted permanent residents;[13] and (6) have the personal net worth for any socially and economically

---

6. Nev. Rev. Stat. § 231.1405 (2022).
7. Nev. Admin. Code § 231.215 (2023).
8. 49 C.F.R. § 26.81(b)(2) (2022).
9. *Id.* § 26.5 (2022).
10. *Id.* §§ 26.5, 26.65(b). It is worth noting that under 49 C.F.R. § 26.65(b) the DBE size standard may be adjusted annually for inflation such that in subsequent years the size standard may no longer be $30.40 million.
11. *Id.* § 26.67.
12. *Id.* § 26.5.
13. *Id.* § 26.67.

disadvantaged owner not exceed $1.32 million.[14] The DBE program is required on contracting opportunities that have received funding from the Federal Highway Administration (FHWA), Federal Aviation Administration (FAA), or Federal Transit Administration (FTA).[15]

- *Airport Concession Disadvantaged Business Enterprise (ACDBE) Program*: In addition to being certified as a DBE under 49 C.F.R. part 26, businesses may also be certified as an Airport Concession Disadvantaged Business Enterprise (ACDBE) under 49 C.F.R. part 23. To qualify as an ACDBE, a business must (1) be a concession for-profit small business concern;[16] (2) qualify as small by having its prior three-year average gross receipts not exceed the applicable size standard of $56.42 million;[17] (3) be 51 percent owned by one or more socially and economically disadvantaged individuals;[18] (4) have one or more of the socially and economically disadvantaged individuals with control and managing the daily business operations;[19] and (5) have the personal net worth for any socially and economically disadvantaged owner not exceed $1.32 million.[20]
- *Small Business Enterprise (SBE) Program*: NDOT has implemented a small business element within its DBE program pursuant to 49 C.F.R. § 26.39.[21] This program is race and gender neutral.[22] To be eligible for the program, a business must (1) be a small business under the SBA size standards; (2) for purposes of being considered a DBE for the FHWA and FTA, the business must have average annual gross receipts from the prior three fiscal years that do not exceed $28.48 million or the current DBE size standard adjusted for inflation under 49 C.F.R.

---

14. *Id.*
15. *Id.* § 26.21(a).
16. *Id.* § 23.3.
17. *Id.* § 23.33(a). The size standards for the following are exceptions to this: bank and financial institutions is $1 billion in assets; car rental companies are $75.23 million average annual gross receipts; pay telephones is 1,500 employees; and automobile dealers is 350 employees.
18. *Id.*
19. *Id.*
20. *Id.* § 23.35.
21. *Disadvantaged Business Enterprise Program*, NEV. DEP'T OF TRANSP. 14 (Aug. 2017), https://www.dot.nv.gov/home/showpublisheddocument/13980/636560078838630000.
22. *Id.*

§ 26.65;[23] and (3) the personal net worth for the owners of the firm must not exceed $1.32 million.[24]

Procurement Laws Intersecting with Business Inclusion

Following is a high-level summary of regulations and laws pertaining to small and diverse businesses at the intersection of business inclusion and procurement.

- *Inclusion Goals*: GOED must establish goals for ESBs as follows: (1) submission of bids or proposals, as well as the awarding of contracts for ESBs for state contracts; (2) submission of bids or proposals, as well as the awarding of contracts for ESBs for Nevada public works contracts estimated to be less than $100,000; and (3) for local governments to establish goals and award contracts to ESBs.[25] Under Nevada Revised Statutes section 408.38724 on nonfederally funded projects, NDOT sets goals for awarding contracts to "[s]mall business enterprises, local emerging small businesses and LGBTQ-owned businesses for (1) Highway construction, reconstruction, improvements and maintenance on projects estimated to cost $250,000 or more that do not receive federal funding; and (2) Architectural, engineering and planning services for projects that do not receive federal funding."
- *Contracting Preferences*: There is a 5 percent preference for bids or proposals submitted by local business owned and operated by veterans with service-connected disability under Nevada Revised Statutes section 333.3366.
- *Reporting Requirements*: Every six months, counties with a population over 100,000 and local government entities within counties in Nevada with a population less than 100,000 must report on the number of solicitations to ESBs; the number of ESBs responding to those solicitations; and the number of contracts and dollar value awarded to ESBs.[26] Each year, GOED must submit a report to "the Governor and to the Director of the Legislative Counsel Bureau for transmittal to the

23. Under 49 C.F.R. § 26.65, the DBE-related size standard may be adjusted annually for inflation. It was previously $26.29 million, then in 2022 adjusted to $28.49 million. Effective March 1, 2023, it is set to increase from $28.48 million to $30.40 million.

24. *Disadvantaged Business Enterprise Program*, *supra* note 21, at 15.

25. Nev. Rev. Stat. § 231.1407 (2022).

26. *Id.* § 332.201.

Interim Finance Committee" regarding ESB contracting and certifications.[27]

Contracting opportunities where the NDOT DBE program applies have several requirements that intersect directly with procurement, contracting, and business inclusion.

- *Fostering Small Business Participation*: Pursuant to 49 C.F.R. § 26.39, NDOT has engaged in efforts to foster small business participation.[28] One way NDOT has done this is ". . . set[ting] a SBE program goal requiring prime contractors to identify elements of the contract or specific subcontracts that are of a size that small businesses, including DBEs, can reasonably perform."[29] In addition, "NDOT will track the total dollar amount and number of SBE contracts awarded each year and will monitor to help ensure to meet or exceed the race neutral portion of our three-year overall DBE goal. When practical, the SBE contracts will be prime contracts."[30]
- *Goals*: Contract opportunities may not use quotas or set-asides for DBEs.[31] The only exception for using a set-aside is in a limited or extreme circumstance, "when no other method could be reasonably expected to redress egregious instances of discrimination."[32] Instead, an overall goal must be set.[33] The goal must be based on evidence of available "ready, willing and able" DBEs in the market.[34] Once the assessment of "ready, willing and able" DBEs is completed, an overall goal may be established as a percentage of the total amount of contracts receiving U.S. Department of Transportation (U.S. DOT) funds.[35] Participation goals must be set for all certified DBEs and not divided into subcategories.[36] Race- and gender-neutral means must be used to "meet the maximum feasible portion of your overall goal."[37] NDOT, as a recipient of U.S. DOT funds, will not be penalized for failing to meet the overall goal set,

27. *Id.* § 231.14075.
28. *Disadvantaged Business Enterprise Program*, *supra* note 21, at 14–17 (2017).
29. *Id.* at 16.
30. *Id.*
31. 49 C.F.R. § 26.43 (2022).
32. *Id.*
33. *Id.* § 26.45(a)(1).
34. *Id.* § 26.45(b).
35. *Id.* § 26.45(e).
36. *Id.* § 26.45(h).
37. *Id.* § 26.51.

if it can establish good faith efforts to meet the goal.[38] When there is a DBE goal on a specific contract opportunity, only the bidder meeting the goal, or establishing good faith efforts to meet the goal, may be awarded the contract.[39]

- *Prompt Payment*: Under 49 C.F.R. part 26, contractors must pay subcontractors within 30 days of receipt of payment from the state DOT for satisfactory performance.[40]
- *Payment of Retainage*: Contractors must pay amounts withheld for retainage to subcontractors within 30 days of their work being satisfactorily completed.[41]

Additional Related Laws, Policies, and Programs

- *Access to Capital*: Pursuant to Nevada Revised Statutes section 231.14055, when a business is certified as an ESB, GOED must provide the business with "information concerning public and private programs to provide financing for small businesses and the criteria for obtaining financing through such programs."[42]
- *Secretary of State Providing Information*: "(1) The Secretary of State shall ensure that the state business portal enables a person who applies through the state business portal for the issuance or renewal of a state business license . . . to indicate whether the applicant is a minority-owned business, a woman-owned business, a veteran-owned business or an LGBTQ-owned business. (2) If a person who applies through the state business portal for the issuance or renewal of a state business license . . . indicates that the business is a minority-owned business, a woman-owned business, a veteran-owned business or an LGBTQ-owned business, the Secretary of State shall provide . . . (a) Information concerning programs to provide financing for small businesses . . . and (b) Information concerning the process by which the business may become certified as a disadvantaged business enterprise for the purposes of 49 C.F.R. § 26.5 or a program to provide financing for disadvantaged business enterprises."[43]

38. *Id.* § 26.47.
39. *Id.* § 26.53.
40. 49 C.F.R. § 26.29(a) (2023).
41. *Id.* § 26.29(b).
42. Nev. Rev. Stat. § 231.14055(2) (2022).
43. *Id.* §75A.350.

- *Prompt Payment*: Although not specific to small and diverse businesses, under Nevada Revised Statutes section 624.624, if a higher tiered contractor enters into an agreement with a lower tiered contractor and there is a schedule for payment, then payment is due to that contract on or before the payment due date or within 10 days after the higher tiered contractor receives payment.[44]
- *Finding Contract Opportunities*: Contracting opportunities may be found on the state's electronic procurement system, NevadaE-Pro: https://nevadaepro.com/bso/.

Major City Snapshot: Las Vegas

The City of Las Vegas (city) engages in supplier diversity efforts.[45] Following is a summary.

- *Certifications*: The city allows businesses to self-certify at the time they register for online bidding through the Nevada Government eMarketplace (NGEM).[46]
- *Technical Assistance*: City staff meet with local emerging small businesses to provide 1:1 technical assistance related to identifying bidding opportunities, as well as facilitate meetings between businesses and other city staff.[47]

---

44. *Id.* § 624.624.
45. *Purchasing & Contracts-Certification*, City of Las Vegas, https://www.lasvegasnevada.gov/Business/Purchasing/Purchasing-Resources/tab/3 (last visited Mar. 24, 2023).
46. *Id.*
47. *Id.*

CHAPTER 30

New Hampshire

Overview of Business Inclusion Program, Policies, and Practices

Government entities seeking to create business inclusion programs have two primary options in terms of the type of program they may create, in terms of who is eligible for the program: (1) a race- and gender-conscious program or (2) a race- and gender-neutral program. Under the Equal Protection Clause of the Fourteenth Amendment, strict scrutiny is applied by the courts when a government actor is creating policies based on race. Strict scrutiny is the highest level of judicial review that may be applied. It requires the government actor to demonstrate that (1) past discrimination exists such that the entity has a "compelling government interest" in rectifying it, and (2) the policies and programs created to do so are "narrowly tailored."[1] Although intermediate scrutiny is often applied when reviewing programs based on gender, strict scrutiny is applied when reviewing race- and gender-conscious business inclusion programs.[2] Disparity studies have become a standard tool used to assist a government entity in withstanding a challenge to its race- and gender-conscious business inclusion programs. These studies aid in demonstrating whether a government entity has engaged

1. City of Richmond v. J.A. Croson Co., 488 U.S. 469 (1989).

2. Since the 1980s with the Supreme Court decision in *City of Richmond v. J.A. Croson Company*, there have been a number of cases across the county that have assessed race- and gender-conscious business inclusion programs. *See* Adarand Constructors, Inc. v. Pena, 515 U.S. 200 (1995); Virdi v. DeKalb Cnty. Sch. Dist., 135 Fed. App'x 262, 268 (11th Cir. 2005); Sherbrooke Turf, Inc. v. Minn. Dep't of Transp., 345 F.3d 964, 971 (8th Cir. 2003); Mountain West Holding Co., Inc. v. The State of Montana, Montana DOT, et al., 2017 WL 2179120 (9th Cir. May 16, 2017).

in past discrimination in its contracting practices, such that the entity may have a compelling government interest in rectifying it.[3]

Conversely, race- and gender-neutral programs are programs that are not only accessible to minority-owned and women-owned businesses but to all businesses, regardless of race or gender. A small business inclusion program would fall into this category. The level of judicial review applied to such a policy to determine its constitutionality is rational basis, which is the lowest threshold for a government to satisfy. For a government entity to satisfy rational basis, the policy or program created must be "related to a legitimate government purpose."[4] Even when a government entity has a race- and gender-conscious program, often times the program may still require the government actor to seek to meet the goals of their program through race- and gender-neutral means where able, so as to be taking the most narrowly tailored means of accomplishing the program goals.

In the state of New Hampshire, at the state level of government, the New Hampshire Department of Transportation (NHDOT) is the main state department that certifies businesses for business inclusion programs.[5]

Summary of Certification Programs and Requirements

NHDOT administers the Disadvantaged Business Enterprise (DBE) program and the Airport Concessions Disadvantaged Business Enterprise (ACDBE) program.

- *Disadvantaged Business Enterprise (DBE) Program*: Pursuant to 49 C.F.R. part 26, the NHDOT administers the state's DBE certification program. As is required under 49 C.F.R. § 26.81, New Hampshire has a Unified Certification Program (UCP). The UCP makes all DBE certification decisions and provides a "one-stop shop" to DBE applicants.[6] NHDOT has the sole authority to make certification decisions on behalf of the UCP.[7]

3. *Promoting Opportunity and Equality in America: A Guide to Federal Circuit Authority on Permissible Government Actions to Promote Racial and Gender Equality*, AM. CIV. LIBERTIES UNION & THE OPPORTUNITY AGENDA (Dec. 2010), https://www.aclu.org/sites/default/files/field_document/Promoting_Opportunity_and_Equality_in_America.pdf.

4. 488 U.S. 469 (1989).

5. *DBE*, N.H. DEP'T OF TRANSP., https://www.nh.gov/dot/org/administration/ofc/dbe.htm (last visited Apr. 14, 2023).

6. 49 C.F.R. § 26.81(b)(2) (2022).

7. *Disadvantaged Business Enterprise (DBE) Program Manual*, N.H. DEP'T OF TRANSP. 29 (2018), https://www.nh.gov/dot/org/administration/ofc/documents/dbe-program-manual.pdf (last visited Apr. 14, 2023).

To qualify as a DBE, a business must (1) be for-profit;[8] (2) be a small business concern—with "small" determined by the Small Business Administration (SBA) small business size standards—and does not exceed $30.40 million in gross annual receipts;[9] (3) be at least 51 percent owned by socially and economically disadvantaged individuals—there is a rebuttable presumption that women, Black Americans, Hispanic Americans, Native Americans, Asian-Pacific Americans, Subcontinent Asian Americans, or other minorities are disadvantaged;[10] (4) be controlled by one or more of the socially and economically disadvantaged owners;[11] (5) have the socially and economically disadvantaged owners be U.S. citizens or lawfully admitted permanent residents;[12] and (6) not have the personal net worth for any socially and economically disadvantaged owner exceed $1.32 million.[13] The DBE program is required on contracting opportunities that have received funding from the Federal Highway Administration (FHWA), Federal Aviation Administration (FAA), or Federal Transit Administration (FTA).[14]

- *Airport Concession Disadvantaged Business Enterprise (ACDBE) Program*: In addition to being certified as a DBE under 49 C.F.R. part 26, businesses may also be certified as an Airport Concession Disadvantaged Business Enterprise (ACDBE) under 49 C.F.R. part 23. To qualify as an ACDBE, a business must (1) be a concession for-profit small business concern;[15] (2) qualify as small by having its prior three-year average gross receipts not exceed the applicable size standard of $56.42 million;[16] (3) be 51 percent owned by one or more socially and economically disadvantaged individuals;[17] (4) have one or more of the socially and economically disadvantaged individuals with

8. 49 C.F.R. § 26.5 (2022).

9. *Id.* §§ 26.5, 26.65(b). It is worth noting that under 49 C.F.R. § 26.65(b) the DBE size standard may be adjusted annually for inflation such that in subsequent years the size standard may no longer be $30.40 million.

10. *Id.* § 26.67.

11. *Id.* § 26.5.

12. *Id.* § 26.67.

13. *Id.*

14. *Id.* § 26.21(a).

15. *Id.* § 23.3.

16. *Id.* § 23.33(a). The size standards for the following are exceptions to this: bank and financial institutions is $1 billion in assets; car rental companies are $75.23 million average annual gross receipts; pay telephones is 1,500 employees; and automobile dealers is 350 employees.

17. *Id.*

control and managing the daily business operations;[18] and (5) have the personal net worth for any socially and economically disadvantaged owner not exceed $1.32 million.[19]

Procurement Laws Intersecting with Business Inclusion

Contracting opportunities where the NHDOT DBE program applies have several requirements that intersect directly with procurement, contracting, and business inclusion.

- *Fostering Small Business Participation*: Pursuant to 49 C.F.R. § 26.39, NHDOT has engaged in efforts to foster small business participation.[20] For example, NHDOT has provided training and technical assistance as well as made resources available for small businesses.[21]
- *Goals*: Contract opportunities may not use quotas or set-asides for DBEs.[22] The only exception for using a set-aside is in a limited or extreme circumstance, "when no other method could be reasonably expected to redress egregious instances of discrimination."[23] Instead, an overall goal must be set.[24] The goal must be based on evidence of available "ready, willing and able" DBEs in the market.[25] Once the assessment of "ready, willing and able" DBEs is completed, an overall goal may be established as a percentage of the total amount of contracts receiving U.S. Department of Transportation (U.S. DOT) funds.[26] Participation goals must be set for all certified DBEs and not divided into subcategories.[27] Race- and gender-neutral means must be used to "meet the maximum feasible portion of your overall goal."[28] NHDOT, as a recipient of U.S. DOT funds, will not be penalized for failing to meet the overall goal set,

18. *Id.*
19. *Id.* § 23.35.
20. *Disadvantaged Business Enterprise (DBE) Program Manual*, *supra* note 7, at 11.
21. *Id.* Through contacting NHDOT it was learned that updates were being made to the DBE plan such that goals in the 2018 plan may be different; as a result, this book has not addressed the goals pertaining to NHDOT's current efforts to foster small business participation.
22. 49 C.F.R. § 26.43 (2022).
23. *Id.*
24. *Id.* § 26.45(a)(1).
25. *Id.* § 26.45(b).
26. *Id.* § 26.45(e).
27. *Id.* § 26.45(h).
28. *Id.* § 26.51.

if it can establish good faith efforts to meet the goal.[29] When there is a DBE goal on a specific contract opportunity only the bidder meeting the goal, or establishing good faith efforts to meet the goal, may be awarded the contract.[30]

- *Prompt Payment*: Under 49 C.F.R. part 26, contractors must pay subcontractors within 30 days of receipt of payment from the state DOT for satisfactory performance.[31]
- *Payment of Retainage*: Contractors must pay amounts withheld for retainage to subcontractors within 30 days of their work being satisfactorily completed.[32]

Additional Related Laws, Policies, and Programs

Under New Hampshire state statute, there are bidding preferences. None of these bidding preferences pertain to the inclusion of minority-owned, women-owned, disability-owned, veteran-owned, and/or LGBT-owned business enterprises. However, they may benefit a local business that happens to fall into one of these categories.

- *Bidding Preference for New Hampshire Vendors*: Under New Hampshire Revised Statutes Annotated section 21-I:11-b, ". . . when qualified lowest bids, proposals, or quotations are received by the division of procurement and support services at the same price, the division's selection or recommendation for selection shall, if the process is not cancelled by the state, be made by drawing lots, provided, however, that if only one of the vendors offering that price has a principal place of business in New Hampshire, that vendor shall, if the process is not cancelled by the state, be selected or recommended for selection."
- *Finding Contracting Opportunities*: The Department of Administrative Services Procurement and Supportive Services "Statewide Bids and Proposals" site lists contracting opportunities: https://apps.das.nh.gov/bidscontracts/bids.aspx.

---

29. *Id.* § 26.47.
30. *Id.* § 26.53.
31. 49 C.F.R. § 26.29(a) (2023).
32. *Id.* § 26.29(b).

Major City Snapshot

Through review of city ordinances for the two largest cities in New Hampshire—Manchester and Nashua—neither have a formal business inclusion program outside of when federal DOT funds are issued.[33]

33. *See FAA Airport Improvement Program (AIP) Disadvantaged Business Enterprise (DBE) Plan in Accordance with 49 CFR 26 for Manchester-Boston Regional Airport*, MANCHESTER, N.H. (Nov. 2020), https://www.flymanchester.com/wp-content/uploads/2021/01/MHT-DBE-Plan-FFY2021-23-DRAFT.pdf.

CHAPTER 31

New Jersey

Overview of Business Inclusion Program, Policies, and Practices

Government entities seeking to create business inclusion programs have two primary options in terms of the type of program they may create, in terms of who is eligible for the program: (1) a race- and gender-conscious program or (2) a race- and gender-neutral program. Under the Equal Protection Clause of the Fourteenth Amendment, strict scrutiny is applied by the courts when a government actor is creating policies based on race. Strict scrutiny is the highest level of judicial review that may be applied. It requires the government actor to demonstrate that (1) past discrimination exists such that the entity has a "compelling government interest" in rectifying it, and (2) the policies and programs created to do so are "narrowly tailored."[1] Although intermediate scrutiny is often applied when reviewing programs based on gender, strict scrutiny is applied when reviewing race- and gender-conscious business inclusion programs.[2] Disparity studies have become a standard tool used to assist a government entity in withstanding a challenge to its race- and gender-conscious business inclusion programs. These studies aid in demonstrating whether a government entity has engaged

1. City of Richmond v. J.A. Croson Co., 488 U.S. 469 (1989).

2. Since the 1980s with the Supreme Court decision in *City of Richmond v. J.A. Croson Company*, there have been a number of cases across the county that have assessed race- and gender-conscious business inclusion programs. *See* Adarand Constructors, Inc. v. Pena, 515 U.S. 200 (1995); Virdi v. DeKalb Cnty. Sch. Dist., 135 Fed. App'x 262, 268 (11th Cir. 2005); Sherbrooke Turf, Inc. v. Minn. Dep't of Transp., 345 F.3d 964, 971 (8th Cir. 2003); Mountain West Holding Co., Inc. v. The State of Montana, Montana DOT, et al., 2017 WL 2179120 (9th Cir. May 16, 2017).

in past discrimination in its contracting practices, such that the entity may have a compelling government interest in rectifying it.[3]

Conversely, race- and gender-neutral programs are programs that are not only accessible to minority-owned and women-owned businesses but to all businesses, regardless of race or gender. A small business inclusion program would fall into this category. The level of judicial review applied to such a policy to determine its constitutionality is rational basis, which is the lowest threshold for a government to satisfy. For a government entity to satisfy rational basis the policy or program created must be "related to a legitimate government purpose."[4] Even when a government entity has a race- and gender-conscious program, oftentimes the program may still require the government actor to seek to meet the goals of their program through race- and gender-neutral means where able, so as to be taking the most narrowly tailored means of accomplishing the program goals.

In the state of New Jersey, at the state level, there are two main state agencies certifying businesses for business inclusion programs: (1) Department of the Treasury Division of Revenue and Enterprise Services[5] and (2) the New Jersey Department of Transportation (NJDOT).[6]

Summary of Certification Programs and Requirements

The Department of the Treasury Division of Revenue and Enterprise Services certifies businesses as (1) Small Business Enterprises (SBEs); (2) Minority Business Enterprises (MBEs); (3) Women Business Enterprises (WBEs); (4) Veteran-Owned Businesses (VOB); (5) Disabled Veteran-Owned Businesses (DVOB); and (6) LGBTQ+ Owned Businesses.[7] An overview of the eligibility requirements for all follow. Detailed eligibility requirements may be found under title 17 of the New Jersey Administrative Code.

- *Small Business Enterprise (SBE)*: A business must (1) be independently owned and operated; (2) have its principal place of business in New Jersey and be incorporated or registered

3. *Promoting Opportunity and Equality in America: A Guide to Federal Circuit Authority on Permissible Government Actions to Promote Racial and Gender Equality*, Am. Civ. Liberties Union & The Opportunity Agenda (Dec. 2010), https://www.aclu.org/sites/default/files/field_document/Promoting_Opportunity_and_Equality_in_America.pdf.

4. 488 U.S. 469 (1989).

5. *Division of Revenue and Enterprise Services*, N.J. Dep't of The Treasury, https://www.state.nj.us/treasury/revenue/business-cert-program.shtml (last visited Mar. 20, 2023).

6. *Disadvantaged and Small Business Programs Unit*, N.J. Dep't of Transp., https://www.state.nj.us/transportation/business/civilrights/dbe.shtm#contracting (last visited Mar. 20, 2023).

7. *Division of Revenue and Enterprise Services*, *supra* note 5.

to do business in New Jersey; (3) be a for-profit business (sole proprietorship, partnership, limited liability company, or corporation) with 100 or fewer full-time employees; and (4) have gross revenues that do not exceed (a) $12 million or the Small Business Administration (SBA) size standards for its industry, whichever is higher, or (b) $3 million for state construction contracts or the SBA size standards for its industry, whichever is higher—for both (a) and (b), the process for calculating the gross revenues varies depending on how long the business has been in operation.[8] There are three categories that goods and services small businesses will be registered into based on their gross receipts: (1) $500,000 or less; (2) $5 million or less; or (3) $12 million or the SBA size standards for its industry, whichever is higher.[9] Similarly, there are three categories that small businesses for state construction contracts will be registered into based on their gross receipts: (1) $3 million or less; (2) does not exceed 50 percent of the revenues for its relevant SBA size standard; or (3) gross revenues do not exceed the applicable SBA size standards for its industry.[10]

- *Minority Business Enterprise (MBE)*: A business must (1) be a sole proprietorship, partnership, joint venture, or corporation at least 51 percent owned by a minority (includes Black, Hispanic, Asian American, American Indian, or Alaskan native) and (2) have one or more minorities who own the business controlling the daily business operations and management.[11]
- *Women Business Enterprise (WBE)*: A business must (1) be a sole proprietorship, partnership, joint venture, or corporation at least 51 percent owned by a woman/women (defined as "an individual, regardless of race, who self-identifies her gender as a woman, without regard to the individual's designated sex at birth") and (2) have one woman or more women who own the business controlling the daily business operations and management.[12]
- *Veteran-Owned Businesses (VOB)*: A business must be (1) independently owned and operated by at least 51 percent persons who are veterans and (2) controlled by one or more persons who are veterans.[13]

8. N.J. Admin. Code § 17:13-2.1 (2023); *id.* § 17:13-1.2.
9. N.J. Admin. Code § 17:13-2.1 (2023); *id.* § 17:13-1.2.
10. N.J. Admin. Code § 17:13-2.1 (2023); *id.* § 17:13-1.2.
11. N.J. Admin. Code § 17:46-1.2 (2023); *id.* § 17:46-1.3; N.J. Rev. Stat. § 52:27H-21.18 (2022).
12. N.J. Admin. Code § 17:46-1.2 (2023); *id.* § 17:46-1.3; N.J. Rev. Stat. § 52:27H-21.18 (2022).
13. N.J. Stat. Ann. § 52:32-50 (2022).

- *Disabled Veteran-Owned Business (DVOB)*: A business must (1) have its principal place of business in New Jersey; (2) be incorporated or registered to do business in New Jersey; (3) be independently owned by at least 51 percent of the owners being disabled veteran(s); (4) have a disabled veteran who is an owner controlling its management, daily, and long-term operations; and (5) have a certification noting a service-connected disability from the U.S. Department of Veteran Affairs for the disabled veteran owner.[14]
- *LGBTQ+ Owned Business*: A business must (1) be a sole proprietorship, partnership, joint venture, or corporation at least 51 percent owned by a person who identifies as LGBTQ+ (defined as "a person who identifies as lesbian, gay, bisexual, transgender, queer, questioning +, or who otherwise does not identify as heterosexual or cisgender") and (2) have one or more LGBTQ+ individuals who own the business controlling the daily business operations and management.[15]

NJDOT certifies Disadvantaged Business Enterprises (DBEs), Airport Concession Disadvantaged Business Enterprises (ACDBEs), and Emerging Small Business Enterprises (ESBEs).

- *Disadvantaged Business Enterprise (DBE) Program*: Pursuant to 49 C.F.R. part 26, the NJDOT administers the state's DBE certification program. As is required under 49 C.F.R. § 26.81, New Jersey has a Unified Certification Program (NJUCP). The NJUCP makes all DBE certification decisions and provides a "one-stop shop" to DBE applicants.[16] To qualify as a DBE, a business must (1) be for-profit;[17] (2) be a small business concern—with "small" determined by the SBA small business size standards—and does not exceed $30.40 million in gross annual receipts;[18] (3) be at least 51 percent owned by socially and economically disadvantaged individuals—there is a rebuttable presumption that women, Black Americans, Hispanic Americans, Native Americans, Asian-Pacific Americans, Subcontinent Asian Americans, or other minorities are disadvantaged;[19]

14. N.J. Admin. Code § 17:14-2.1 (2023).
15. *Id.* § 17:47-1.2.
16. 49 C.F.R. § 26.81(b)(2) (2022).
17. *Id.* § 26.5.
18. *Id.* §§ 26.5, 26.65(b). It is worth noting that under 49 C.F.R. § 26.65(b) the DBE size standard may be adjusted annually for inflation such that in subsequent years the size standard may no longer be $30.40 million.
19. *Id.* § 26.67.

(4) be controlled by one or more of the socially and economically disadvantaged owners;[20] (5) have the socially and economically disadvantaged owners be U.S. citizens or lawfully admitted permanent residents;[21] and (6) not have the personal net worth for any socially and economically disadvantaged owner exceed $1.32 million.[22] The DBE program is required on contracting opportunities that have received funding from the Federal Highway Administration (FHWA), Federal Aviation Administration (FAA), or Federal Transit Administration (FTA).[23]

- *Airport Concession Disadvantaged Business Enterprise (ACDBE) Program*: In addition to being certified as a DBE under 49 C.F.R. part 26, businesses may also be certified as an Airport Concession Disadvantaged Business Enterprise (ACDBE) under 49 C.F.R. part 23. To qualify as an ACDBE, a business must (1) be a concession for-profit small business concern;[24] (2) qualify as small by having its prior three-year average gross receipts not exceed the applicable size standard of $56.42 million;[25] (3) be 51 percent owned by one or more socially and economically disadvantaged individuals;[26] (4) have one or more of the socially and economically disadvantaged individuals with control and managing the daily business operations;[27] and (5) have the personal net worth for any socially and economically disadvantaged owner not exceed $1.32 million.[28]
- *Emerging Small Business Enterprises (ESBEs)*: NJDOT has implemented a small business element within its DBE program called the Emerging Small Business Enterprises certification, pursuant to 49 C.F.R. § 26.39.[29] This program is race and gender neutral.[30] To be eligible for the program, a business must (1) be a small business under the SBA size standards and (2) be 51 percent owned and controlled by one or more economically

20. *Id.* § 26.5.
21. *Id.* § 26.67.
22. *Id.*
23. *Id.* § 26.21(a).
24. *Id.* § 23.3.
25. *Id.* § 23.33(a). The size standards for the following are exceptions to this: bank and financial institutions is $1 billion in assets; car rental companies are $75.23 million average annual gross receipts; pay telephones is 1,500 employees; and automobile dealers is 350 employees.
26. *Id.*
27. *Id.*
28. *Id.* § 23.35.
29. *Disadvantaged and Small Business Programs Unit*, *supra* note 6.
30. *Id.*

disadvantaged individuals who have a personal net worth not exceeding $1.32 million.[31]

Procurement Laws Intersecting with Business Inclusion

Procurement in the state of New Jersey is managed by the Department of the Treasury Division of Purchase and Property.[32] Following are some laws that pertain to small, minority-owned, women-owned, and service-disabled veteran-owned businesses.

- *Contracting Set-Asides and Goals*: Pursuant to Executive Order 71, the state of New Jersey no longer sets goals nor has set-asides for minority-owned businesses or female-owned businesses.[33] Now, in New Jersey there are two relevant set-aside programs. There is a goal for state agencies to set aside 25 percent of the value of state goods, services, design, and construction contracts for small businesses and a 3 percent goal for service-disabled veteran-owned businesses.[34] Participation in the small business set-aside may be limited to businesses satisfying the eligibility criteria for an SBE noted earlier as well as that the personal net worth for its individual owners does not exceed $750,000.[35]
- *Bidding Specifications*: A designation as a small business set-aside must be made prior to the public advertising for the bid.[36] Such a designation may be made provided the contracting agency reasonably expects to receive bids from at least three "qualified eligible businesses capable of furnishing the specified products or services."[37] Bidding specifications must note whether there is a small business or veteran-owned business set-aside goal on the project or the project is designated for a set-aside.[38]

31. *Id.*
32. *Division of Purchase and Property*, N.J. Dep't of the Treasury, https://www.nj.gov/treasury/purchase/ (last visited Mar. 20, 2023).
33. Executive Order No. 71 (Oct. 2, 2003), https://nj.gov/infobank/circular/eom71.htm.
34. N.J. Admin. Code § 17:13-4.1 (2023); *id.* § 17:14-4.1.
35. *Id.* § 17:13-2.1(b).
36. *Id* § 17:13-4.1; *id.* § 17:14-4.1.
37. *Id* § 17:13-4.1; *id.* § 17:14-4.1.
38. *Id.* § 17:13-4.1; *id.* § 17:14-4.1.

Contracting opportunities where the NJDOT DBE program applies have several requirements that intersect directly with procurement, contracting, and business inclusion.

- *Fostering Small Business Participation*: Pursuant to 49 C.F.R. § 26.39, NJDOT's ESBE certification seeks to foster small business participation. "NJDOT will establish ESBE participation goals on its federally funded contracts. Prime contractors may use DBE and/or ESBE firms in order to satisfy these ESBE goals."[39]
- *Goals*: Contract opportunities may not use quotas or set-asides for DBEs.[40] The only exception for using a set-aside is in a limited or extreme circumstance, "when no other method could be reasonably expected to redress egregious instances of discrimination."[41] Instead, an overall goal must be set.[42] The goal must be based on evidence of available "ready, willing and able" DBEs in the market.[43] Once the assessment of "ready, willing and able" DBEs is completed, an overall goal may be established as a percentage of the total amount of contracts receiving U.S. Department of Transportation (U.S. DOT) funds.[44] Participation goals must be set for all certified DBEs and not divided into subcategories.[45] Race- and gender-neutral means must be used to "meet the maximum feasible portion of your overall goal."[46] NJDOT, as a recipient of U.S. DOT funds, will not be penalized for failing to meet the overall goal set, if it can establish good faith efforts to meet the goal.[47] When there is a DBE goal on a specific contract opportunity, only the bidder meeting the goal, or establishing good faith efforts to meet the goal, may be awarded the contract.[48]
- *Prompt Payment*: Under 49 C.F.R. part 26, contractors must pay subcontractors within 30 days of receipt of payment from the state DOT for satisfactory performance.[49]

---

39. *Emerging Small Business Enterprise Policy Statement*, N.J. Dep't of Transp. 1 (2011), https://www.state.nj.us/transportation/business/civilrights/pdf/esbepolicystatement.pdf.
40. 49 C.F.R. § 26.43 (2022).
41. *Id.*
42. *Id.* § 26.45(a)(1).
43. *Id.* § 26.45(b).
44. *Id.* § 26.45(e).
45. *Id.* § 26.45(h).
46. *Id.* § 26.51.
47. *Id.* § 26.47.
48. *Id.* § 26.53.
49. 49 C.F.R. § 26.29(a) (2023).

- *Payment of Retainage*: Contractors must pay amounts withheld for retainage to subcontractors within 30 days of their work being satisfactorily completed.[50]

Additional Related Laws, Policies, and Programs

- *Access to Capital*: The New Jersey Economic Development Authority has a "Small Business Fund" that is available to New Jersey-based small businesses.[51] To be eligible, a business must be "[a] creditworthy small, minority-owned or women-owned business in New Jersey in operation for at least one full year or [nonprofit] corporation in operation for at least three full years."[52]
- *Prompt Payment to Subcontractors*: "If a subcontractor or sub-subcontractor has performed in accordance with the provisions of its contract with the prime contractor or subcontractor and the work has been accepted by the owner, the owner's authorized approving agent, or the prime contractor, as applicable, and the parties have not otherwise agreed in writing, the prime contractor shall pay to its subcontractor and the subcontractor shall pay to its subsubcontractor within 10 calendar days of the receipt of each periodic payment, final payment or receipt of retainage monies, the full amount received for the work of the subcontractor or subsubcontractor based on the work completed or the services rendered under the applicable contract."[53]
- *Finding Contract Opportunities*: Goods and services contract opportunities may be found on NJSTART, the Division of Purchase and Property's eProcurement system: https://www.njstart.gov/bso/. To see where other agencies may share opportunities, please visit https://business.nj.gov/pages/government-contracting?locale=en.

50. *Id.* § 26.29(b).

51. *Small Business Fund*, N.J. ECON. DEV. AUTH., https://www.njeda.com/smallbusinessfund/ (last visited Mar. 20, 2023).

52. *Small Business Fund*, N.J. ECON. DEV. AUTH. (2020), https://www.njeda.com/wp-content/uploads/2022/01/2020-Product-Pages-Small-Business-Fund.pdf.

53. N.J. REV. STAT. § 2A:30A-2 (2022).

Major City Snapshot: Jersey City

The City of Jersey City (city) Office of Diversity and Inclusion maintains a Supplier Diversity Directory and manages the city's supplier diversity program.[54] Following is a high-level summary of the program.

- *Certifications*: The certifications maintained by the city and listed within its directory include the following: (1) Minority-Owned Business Enterprise (MBE); (2) Women-Owned Business Enterprise (WBE); (3) Veteran Owned Business (VOB); (4) Disabled Veteran Owned Business (DVOB); (5) Disadvantaged Business Enterprise (DBE); (6) LGBT Owned Business Enterprise (LGBTE); and Small Business Enterprise (SBE).[55]
- *Contracting Set-Asides*: Under the authority of New Jersey Statutes Annotated sections 40A:11-41 through 40A:11-49, the city has established a set-aside program.[56]
- *Reporting Requirements*: The director of the Office of Diversity and Inclusion must submit quarterly reports, as well as an annual report, to the business administrator pertaining to the city's business inclusion efforts set forth under the city ordinance.[57]

---

54. *Office of Diversity & Inclusion*, City of Jersey City, https://www.jerseycitynj.gov/resident resources/inclusion (last visited Mar. 21, 2023).
55. *Id.*; City of Jersey City Code of Ordinance, Ord. § 3-54.3 (2022).
56. City of Jersey City Code of Ordinance, Ord. 21-039 (2022).
57. *Id.* § 3-54.3.

CHAPTER 32

New Mexico

Overview of Business Inclusion Program, Policies, and Practices

Government entities seeking to create business inclusion programs have two primary options in terms of the type of program they may create, in terms of who is eligible for the program: (1) a race- and gender-conscious program or (2) a race- and gender-neutral program. Under the Equal Protection Clause of the Fourteenth Amendment, strict scrutiny is applied by the courts when a government actor is creating policies based on race. Strict scrutiny is the highest level of judicial review that may be applied. It requires the government actor to demonstrate that (1) past discrimination exists such that the entity has a "compelling government interest" in rectifying it, and (2) the policies and programs created to do so are "narrowly tailored."[1] Although intermediate scrutiny is often applied when reviewing programs based on gender, strict scrutiny is applied when reviewing race- and gender-conscious business inclusion programs.[2] Disparity studies have become a standard tool used to assist a government entity in withstanding a challenge to its race- and gender-conscious business inclusion programs. These studies aid in demonstrating whether a government entity has engaged

1. City of Richmond v. J.A. Croson Co., 488 U.S. 469 (1989).

2. Since the 1980s with the Supreme Court decision in *City of Richmond v. J.A. Croson Company*, there have been a number of cases across the county that have assessed race- and gender-conscious business inclusion programs. *See* Adarand Constructors, Inc. v. Pena, 515 U.S. 200 (1995); Virdi v. DeKalb Cnty. Sch. Dist., 135 Fed. App'x 262, 268 (11th Cir. 2005); Sherbrooke Turf, Inc. v. Minn. Dep't of Transp., 345 F.3d 964, 971 (8th Cir. 2003); Mountain West Holding Co., Inc. v. The State of Montana, Montana DOT, et al., 2017 WL 2179120 (9th Cir. May 16, 2017).

in past discrimination in its contracting practices, such that the entity may have a compelling government interest in rectifying it.[3]

Conversely, race- and gender-neutral programs are programs that are not only accessible to minority-owned and women-owned businesses but to all businesses, regardless of race or gender. A small business inclusion program would fall into this category. The level of judicial review applied to such a policy to determine its constitutionality is rational basis, which is the lowest threshold for a government to satisfy. For a government entity to satisfy rational basis, the policy or program created must be "related to a legitimate government purpose."[4] Even when a government entity has a race- and gender-conscious program, oftentimes the program may still require the government actor to seek to meet the goals of their program through race- and gender-neutral means where able, so as to be taking the most narrowly tailored means of accomplishing the program goals.

At the state level of government in New Mexico, the New Mexico Department of Transportation (NMDOT) is the primary state agency that certifies businesses for a business inclusion program.

Summary of Certification Programs and Requirements

NMDOT administers the Disadvantaged Business Enterprise (DBE) program and Airport Concession Disadvantaged Business Enterprise (ACDBE) program.

- *Disadvantaged Business Enterprise (DBE) Program*: As is required under 49 C.F.R. § 26.81, New Mexico has a Unified Certification Program (NMUCP). The NMUCP makes all DBE certification decisions and provides a "one-stop shop" to DBE applicants.[5] To qualify as a DBE, a business must (1) be for-profit;[6] (2) be a small business concern—with "small" determined by the Small Business Administration (SBA) small business size standards—and does not exceed $30.40 million in gross annual receipts;[7] (3) be at least 51 percent owned by

3. *Promoting Opportunity and Equality in America: A Guide to Federal Circuit Authority on Permissible Government Actions to Promote Racial and Gender Equality*, Am. Civ. Liberties Union & The Opportunity Agenda (Dec. 2010), https://www.aclu.org/sites/default/files/field_document/Promoting_Opportunity_and_Equality_in_America.pdf.

4. 488 U.S. 469 (1989).

5. 49 C.F.R. § 26.81(b)(2) (2022).

6. *Id.* § 26.5.

7. *Id.* §§ 26.5, 26.65(b). It is worth noting that under 49 C.F.R. § 26.65(b) the DBE size standard may be adjusted annually for inflation such that in subsequent years the size standard may no longer be $30.40 million.

socially and economically disadvantaged individuals—there is a rebuttable presumption that women, Black Americans, Hispanic Americans, Native Americans, Asian-Pacific Americans, Subcontinent Asian Americans, or other minorities are disadvantaged;[8] (4) be controlled by one or more of the socially and economically disadvantaged owners;[9] (5) have the socially and economically disadvantaged owners be U.S. citizens or lawfully admitted permanent residents;[10] and (6) have the personal net worth for any socially and economically disadvantaged owner not exceed $1.32 million.[11] The DBE program is required on contracting opportunities that have received funding from the Federal Highway Administration (FHWA), Federal Aviation Administration (FAA), or Federal Transit Administration (FTA).[12]

- *Airport Concession Disadvantaged Business Enterprise (ACDBE) Program*: In addition to being certified as a DBE under 49 C.F.R. part 26, businesses may also be certified as an Airport Concession Disadvantaged Business Enterprise (ACDBE) under 49 C.F.R. part 23. To qualify as an ACDBE, a business must (1) be a concession for-profit small business concern;[13] (2) qualify as small by having its prior three-year average gross receipts not exceed the applicable size standard of $56.42 million;[14] (3) be 51 percent owned by one or more socially and economically disadvantaged individuals;[15] (4) have one or more of the socially and economically disadvantaged individuals with control and managing the daily business operations;[16] and (5) not have the personal net worth for any socially and economically disadvantaged owner exceed $1.32 million.[17]

8. *Id.* § 26.67.
9. *Id.* § 26.5.
10. *Id.* § 26.67.
11. *Id.*
12. *Id.* § 26.21(a).
13. *Id.* § 23.3.
14. *Id.* § 23.33(a). The size standards for the following are exceptions to this: bank and financial institutions is $1 billion in assets; car rental companies are $75.23 million average annual gross receipts; pay telephones is 1,500 employees; and automobile dealers is 350 employees.
15. *Id.*
16. *Id.*
17. *Id.* § 23.35.

Procurement Laws Intersecting with Business Inclusion

In the state of New Mexico, the General Services Department State Purchasing Division handles procurement.[18] The Procurement Code is found in chapter 13, Article 1, of the New Mexico Statues Annotated. Although the state of New Mexico does not certify businesses as minority-owned, women-owned, disability-owned, veteran-owned, and/or LGBT-owned business enterprises, it does have contracting preferences for veteran businesses.[19] In addition, it does have a policy pertaining to small businesses. The bullet points that follow provide additional context.

- *Assistance to Small Business Policy*: The policy states that "[i]t shall be the policy of this state to encourage small businesses to do business with state agencies and local public bodies."[20]
- *Contracting Preferences*: "When a public body makes a purchase using a formal request for proposals process, not including contracts awarded on a point-based system, the public body shall award an additional: (1) eight percent of the total weight of all the factors used in evaluating the proposals to a resident business or Native American resident business; and (2) ten percent of the total weight of all the factors used in evaluating the proposals to a resident veteran business or Native American resident veteran business that has annual gross revenues of up to six million dollars ($6,000,000) in the preceding tax year."[21] In addition, "[w]hen a public body makes a purchase using a formal request for proposals process, and the contract is awarded based on a point-based system, the public body shall award additional points equivalent to: (1) eight percent of the total possible points to a resident business or Native American resident business; or (2) ten percent of the total possible points to a resident veteran business or Native American resident veteran business that has annual gross revenues of up to six million dollars ($6,000,000) in the preceding tax year."[22] In a formal bid process, a resident business or Native American resident business receives an 8 percent bid preference, and a resident veteran business or Native American resident veteran business

18. *State Purchasing Division*, GEN. SERVS. DEP'T, https://www.generalservices.state.nm.us/state-purchasing/ (last visited Apr. 24, 2023).

19. *How to Do Business with NMDWS*, N.M. DEP'T OF WORKFORCE SOLS., https://www.dws.state.nm.us/en-us/Business/Procurement/How-To-Do-Business-With-NMDWS (last visited Apr. 25, 2023).

20. N.M. STAT. ANN. § 13-1-184 (2023).

21. *Id.* § 13-1-21 (2023).

22. *Id.*

receives a 10 percent preference.[23] In instances where bids for both recycled content goods and nonrecycled content goods are received in a formal bid process, recycled content goods bids will receive an 8 percent preference, with the exception of resident veteran businesses and Native American resident veteran businesses, which receive a 10 percent preference.[24] As it relates to being designated as a Native American resident business, resident veteran business, or Native American resident veteran business, the business must have a "valid . . . certificate issued by the taxation and revenue department pursuant to Section 13-1-22 NMSA 1978."[25]

Contracting opportunities where the NMDOT DBE program applies have several requirements that intersect directly with procurement, contracting, and business inclusion.

- *Fostering Small Business Participation*: Pursuant to 49 C.F.R. § 26.39, NMDOT has engaged in efforts to foster small business participation.[26] Although it does not have a formal small business enterprise certification within its DBE program, it does include the following on invitations to bid on federally funded projects "regardless of whether a DBE goal is set on a contract, and in accordance with NMSA 1978 Section 13-1-184, 'Assistance to Small Business Policy,' NMDOT encourages Contractors to use small businesses, including DBEs, on its projects."[27] It also reviews annually "as appropriate, its DBE Program should participation of small businesses fall below 50 percent for subcontracts or 20 percent for prime contracts in any operating administration area."[28]
- *Goals*: Contract opportunities may not use quotas or set-asides for DBEs.[29] The only exception for using a set-aside is in a limited or extreme circumstance, "when no other method could be reasonably expected to redress egregious instances

23. *Id.*
24. *Id.*
25. *Id.*
26. *Disadvantage Business Enterprise Program Manual*, N.M. Dep't of Transp. 16–17 (2021), https://realfilef260a66b364d453e91ff9b3fedd494dc.s3.amazonaws.com/71ad094a-6bdd-4b8d-86ab-535f75ac6de8?AWSAccessKeyId=AKIAJBKPT2UF7EZ6B7YA&Expires=1694707367&Signature=gTSMK0pA7%2B0JWuaLG7wPLvjnRvA%3D&response-content-disposition=inline%3B%20filename%3D%22DBE%20Program%20Manual.pdf%22&response-content-type=application%2Fpdf.
27. *Id.*
28. *Id.*
29. 49 C.F.R. § 26.43 (2022).

of discrimination."[30] Instead, an overall goal must be set.[31] The goal must be based on evidence of available "ready, willing and able" DBEs in the market.[32] Once the assessment of "ready, willing and able" DBEs is completed, an overall goal may be established as a percentage of the total amount of contracts receiving U.S. Department of Transportation (U.S. DOT) funds.[33] Participation goals must be set for all certified DBEs and not divided into subcategories.[34] Race- and gender-neutral means must be used to "meet the maximum feasible portion of your overall goal."[35] NMDOT, as a recipient of U.S. DOT funds, will not be penalized for failing to meet the overall goal set, if it can establish good faith efforts to meet the goal.[36] When there is a DBE goal on a specific contract opportunity only the bidder meeting the goal, or establishing good faith efforts to meet the goal, may be awarded the contract.[37]

- *Prompt Payment*: Under 49 C.F.R. part 26, contractors must pay subcontractors within 30 days of receipt of payment from the state DOT for satisfactory performance.[38]
- *Payment of Retainage*: Contractors must pay amounts withheld for retainage to subcontractors within 30 days of their work being satisfactorily completed.[39]

Additional Related Laws, Policies, and Programs

- *Technical Assistance*: The State Purchasing Agent has duties as it relates to providing assistance to small businesses.[40] Some of these include (1) issuing publications to assist small businesses learn how to do business with the state; (2) make small business listings available to state agencies to encourage procurement; (3) ensure small business are solicited for contract opportunities; and (4) develop training programs for small businesses.[41]

30. *Id.*
31. *Id.* § 26.45(a)(1).
32. *Id.* § 26.45(b).
33. *Id.* § 26.45(e).
34. *Id.* § 26.45(h).
35. *Id.* § 26.51.
36. *Id.* § 26.47.
37. *Id.* § 26.53.
38. 49 C.F.R. § 26.29(a) (2023).
39. *Id.* § 26.29(b).
40. N.M. Stat. Ann. § 13-1-185 (2023).
41. *Id.*

- *Prompt Payment to Subcontractors*: "All construction contracts shall provide that contractors and subcontractors make prompt payment to their subcontractors and suppliers for amounts owed for work performed on the construction project within seven days after receipt of payment from the owner, contractor or subcontractor."[42]
- *Finding Contract Opportunities*: New Mexico's electronic procurement website, eProNM, is available here: https://bids.sciquest.com/apps/Router/PublicEvent?CustomerOrg=StateOfNewMexico&tab=PHX_NAV_SourcingOpenForBid&tmstmp=1467214109161.

Major City Snapshot: Albuquerque

The City of Albuquerque allows for a self-certification of local businesses, Minority-Owned Businesses (MBEs), and Women-Owned Businesses (WBEs).[43]

- *Certifications*: Following are the requirements to qualify for each type of self-certification.
  - *Local Business*: "A local business is one that maintains its principal office and place of business within the Greater Albuquerque Metropolitan Area (City of Albuquerque or Bernalillo County) and ownership resides 51 percent in the Greater Albuquerque Metropolitan Area."[44]
  - *Minority-Owned Business (MBE)*: A business must (1) be 51 percent owned and controlled by one or more minorities (for public companies 51 percent of the stock owned) and (2) one or more minorities control the management and daily operations.[45]
  - *Women-Owned Business (WBE)*: A business must (1) be 51 percent owned and controlled by one or more women (for public companies, 51 percent of the stock owned) and (2) one or more women control the management and daily operations.[46]
- *Active Solicitation of MBEs*: "In addition to following normal processes, the City shall directly solicit bids and offers of goods

42. *Id.* § 57-28-5(C).
43. *ABQ Buys Local*, City of Albuquerque, https://www.cabq.gov/abq-buys-local (last visited Apr. 25, 2023).
44. *Id.*; Albuquerque, N.M. Code of Ordinance § 13-14-3 (2023).
45. *ABQ Buys Local*, *supra* note 43; Albuquerque, N.M. Code of Ordinance § 5-6-2 (2023).
46. *ABQ Buys Local*, *supra* note 43; Albuquerque, N.M. Code of Ordinance § 5-6-2 (2023).

and services for the city from MBEs to the extent necessary to ensure that MBEs are aware of the opportunities for such business and of the city policy as set out in this article."[47]

- *Reporting Requirements*: "The Mayor shall submit quarterly reports to the Council regarding steps taken and progress made in the implementation of [Article 6: Minority and Women's Business Enterprises]."[48]

---

47. Albuquerque, N.M. Code of Ordinance § 5-6-6 (2023).
48. *Id.* § 5-6-11.

CHAPTER 33

New York

Overview of Business Inclusion Program, Policies, and Practices

Government entities seeking to create business inclusion programs have two primary options in terms of the type of program they may create, in terms of who is eligible for the program: (1) a race- and gender-conscious program or (2) a race- and gender-neutral program. Under the Equal Protection Clause of the Fourteenth Amendment, strict scrutiny is applied by the courts when a government actor is creating policies based on race. Strict scrutiny is the highest level of judicial review that may be applied. It requires the government actor to demonstrate that (1) past discrimination exists such that the entity has a "compelling government interest" in rectifying it, and (2) the policies and programs created to do so are "narrowly tailored."[1] Although intermediate scrutiny is often applied when reviewing programs based on gender, strict scrutiny is applied when reviewing race- and gender-conscious business inclusion programs.[2] Disparity studies have become a standard tool used to assist a government entity in withstanding a challenge to its race- and gender-conscious business inclusion programs. These studies aid in demonstrating whether a government entity has engaged

1. City of Richmond v. J.A. Croson Co., 488 U.S. 469 (1989).

2. Since the 1980s with the Supreme Court decision in *City of Richmond v. J.A. Croson Company*, there have been a number of cases across the county that have assessed race- and gender-conscious business inclusion programs. *See* Adarand Constructors, Inc. v. Pena, 515 U.S. 200 (1995); Virdi v. DeKalb Cnty. Sch. Dist., 135 Fed. App'x 262, 268 (11th Cir. 2005); Sherbrooke Turf, Inc. v. Minn. Dep't of Transp., 345 F.3d 964, 971 (8th Cir. 2003); Mountain West Holding Co., Inc. v. The State of Montana, Montana DOT, et al., 2017 WL 2179120 (9th Cir. May 16, 2017)

in past discrimination in its contracting practices, such that the entity may have a compelling government interest in rectifying it.[3]

Conversely, race- and gender-neutral programs are programs that are not only accessible to minority-owned and women-owned businesses but to all businesses, regardless of race or gender. A small business inclusion program would fall into this category. The level of judicial review applied to such a policy to determine its constitutionality is rational basis, which is the lowest threshold for a government to satisfy. For a government entity to satisfy rational basis, the policy or program created must be "related to a legitimate government purpose."[4] Even when a government entity has a race- and gender-conscious program, oftentimes the program may still require the government actor to seek to meet the goals of their program through race- and gender-neutral means where able, so as to be taking the most narrowly tailored means of accomplishing the program goals.

In the state of New York, at the state level of government, there are three main entities certifying businesses for business inclusion programs: (1) the Empire State Development Agency's (ESD) Division of Minority and Women's Business Development (DMWBD); (2) the New York State Office of General Services Division of Service-Disabled Veterans' Business Development; and (3) the New York State Department of Transportation (NYSDOT).

Summary of Certification Programs and Requirements

DMWBD certifies businesses as Minority-Owned (MBE) and Women-Owned Business Enterprises (WBE).[5] Details on the eligibility requirements for each follow:

- *Minority-Owned Business Enterprise (MBE)*: To be eligible for the DMWBD MBE certification, a business must (1) be for-profit and independently owned and operated; (2) be at least 51 percent owned by one or more minority and the ownership is "real, substantial, and continuing"—minorities include the following groups of persons: Black, Hispanic/Latino, Native American or Alaskan native, and Asian and Pacific Islander;

3. *Promoting Opportunity and Equality in America: A Guide to Federal Circuit Authority on Permissible Government Actions to Promote Racial and Gender Equality*, Am. Civ. Liberties Union & The Opportunity Agenda (Dec. 2010), https://www.aclu.org/sites/default/files/field_document/Promoting_Opportunity_and_Equality_in_America.pdf.

4. 488 U.S. 469 (1989).

5. *Division of Minority and Women's Business Development (DMWBD)*, https://esd.ny.gov/doing-business-ny/mwbe, (last visited Jan. 20, 2023).

(3) have day-to-day control resting with the minority/minorities who own the company; (4) be authorized to do business in New York; (5) have a personal net worth not exceeding $15 million for the minority/minorities owning the company; (6) have qualifying owners who are U.S. citizens or permanent residents; and (7) be a small business.[6] To be considered a small business, a business must (1) have a "significant presence" in New York, which means that a business is authorized to do business in New York and makes a contribution to the New York economy;[7] (2) not be "dominant in its field of operation"; (3) be independently owned and operated; (4) have the total number of employees not exceed 300; and (5) be small within the Small Business Administration (SBA) size standards.[8]

- *Women-Owned Business Enterprise (WBE)*: Eligibility for the WBE certification through DMWBD is the same as the MBE certification with the exception that the company must be owned by one or more women instead of minorities.[9] A woman who is also a minority may be certified as both an MBE and WBE but would only be able to count toward contracting inclusion goals for one of the certifications.[10]

Following are the eligibility requirements for the New York State Office of General Services Division of Service-Disabled Veterans' Business Development service-disabled veteran-owned business enterprise (SDVBE) certification.[11]

- *Service-Disabled Veteran-Owned Business Enterprise (SDVBE)*: A business must (1) be 51 percent owned by a service-disabled veteran and the ownership is "real, substantial, and continuing"; (2) have the service-disabled veteran with day-to-day control of the business; (3) be independently owned and operated; (4) be authorized to do business in New York; (5) be a small business meeting the same requirements as just defined for MWBEs; and (6) be certified by the Office of General Services.[12]

---

6. N.Y. Exec. L. § 310(7) (2022); *id.* § 310(8); N.Y. Comp. Codes R. & Regs. tit. 5 § 144.2 (2022).
7. N.Y. Comp. Codes R. & Regs. tit. 5 § 140.1(ag) (2022).
8. N.Y. Exec. L. § 310(20) (2022).
9. *Id.* § 310(15).
10. *Id.*
11. *Become a Certified Service-Disabled Veteran-Owned Small Business*, https://www.ny.gov/services/become-certified-service-disabled-veteran-owned-small-business (last visited Jan. 20, 2023).
12. N.Y. Exec. L. § 369-H(1) (2022).

NYSDOT administers the Disadvantaged Business Enterprise (DBE) program and the Airport Concession Disadvantaged Business Enterprise (ACDBE) program.[13]

- *Disadvantage Business Enterprise (DBE)*: Pursuant to 49 C.F.R. part 26, NYSDOT administers the state's DBE certification program. As is required under 49 C.F.R. § 26.81, New York has a Unified Certification Program (NYSUCP). The NYSUCP makes all DBE certification decisions and provides a "one-stop shop" to DBE applicants.[14] To qualify as a DBE, a business must (1) be for-profit;[15] (2) be a small business concern—with "small" determined by the Small Business Administration (SBA) small business size standards—and does not exceed $30.40 million in gross annual receipts;[16] (3) be at least 51 percent owned by socially and economically disadvantaged individuals—there is a rebuttable presumption that women, Black Americans, Hispanic Americans, Native Americans, Asian-Pacific Americans, Subcontinent Asian Americans, or other minorities are disadvantaged;[17] (4) be controlled by one or more of the socially and economically disadvantaged owners;[18] (5) have the socially and economically disadvantaged owners be U.S. citizens or lawfully admitted permanent residents;[19] and (6) have the personal net worth for any socially and economically disadvantaged owner not exceed $1.32 million.[20] The DBE program is required on contracting opportunities that have received funding from the Federal Highway Administration (FHWA), Federal Aviation Administration (FAA), or Federal Transit Administration (FTA).[21]
- *Airport Concession Disadvantaged Business Enterprise (ACDBE)*: In addition to being certified as a DBE under 49 C.F.R. part 26, businesses may also be certified as an Airport Concession Disadvantaged Business Enterprise (ACDBE) under 49 C.F.R. part 23. To qualify as an ACDBE, a business must (1) be a

13. *DBE Certification Program*, https://www.dot.ny.gov/main/business-center/audit/dbe-certification (last visited Jan. 20, 2023).
14. 49 C.F.R. § 26.81(b)(2) (2022).
15. *Id.* § 26.5.
16. *Id.* §§ 26.5, 26.65(b). It is worth noting that under 49 C.F.R. § 26.65(b) the DBE size standard may be adjusted annually for inflation such that in subsequent years the size standard may no longer be $30.40 million.
17. *Id.* § 26.67.
18. *Id.* § 26.5.
19. *Id.* § 26.67.
20. *Id.*
21. *Id.* § 26.21(a)

concession for-profit small business concern;[22] (2) qualify as small by having its prior three-year average gross receipts not exceed the applicable size standard of $56.42 million;[23] (3) be 51 percent owned by one or more socially and economically disadvantaged individuals;[24] (4) have one or more of the socially and economically disadvantaged individuals with control and managing the daily business operations;[25] and (5) not have the personal net worth for any socially and economically disadvantaged owner exceed $1.32 million.[26]

Procurement Laws Intersecting with Business Inclusion

New York procurement laws may be found in Article 11 of the New York State Finance Law.[27] State laws and regulations pertaining to the DMWBD program may primarily be found in New York State Executive Law Article 15-A and title 5 of the New York Code, Rules, and Regulations (CRR), chapter XIV, sections 140–147. Laws and regulations related to the SDVBE program may be found in New York State Executive Law Article 17-B and title 9, section 252 of the Official Compilation of Codes, Rules and Regulations of the State of New York. Following are some laws that pertain to small, minority-owned, women-owned, and service-disabled veteran-owned businesses.

- *Discretionary Buying Threshold*: Under State Finance Article 11 section 163, state agencies may purchase the following from small businesses, MBEs, WBEs,[28] and SDVBEs[29] without a formal competitive process: (1) commodities, services, or "commodities or technology that are recycled or remanufacturing" if the amount does not exceed $500,000; and (2) "commodities that are food, including milk and milk products, or animal or plant fiber products, grown, produced, harvested, or processed in New York state or textile products manufactured

22. *Id.* § 23.3.
23. *Id.* § 23.33(a). The size standards for the following are exceptions to this: bank and financial institutions is $1 billion in assets; car rental companies are $75.23 million average annual gross receipts; pay telephones is 1,500 employees; and automobile dealers is 350 employees.
24. *Id.*
25. *Id.*
26. *Id.* § 23.35.
27. *New York State Procurement Guidelines* 1 (May 2014), https://ogs.ny.gov/system/files/documents/2018/08/psnys-procurement-guidelines.pdf.
28. N.Y. Exec. L. § 310 (2022).
29. *Id.* § 369-H.

from animal or plant fiber grown or produced predominantly in New York state" if the amount does not exceed $200,000.[30]

- *Prompt Payment to Small Businesses*: Small businesses that have submitted an invoice conforming to required policies and procedures must receive payment within 15 calendar days.[31]
- *Inclusion Goals*: State agencies must adopt agency-specific MWBE and SDVBE goals as well as a master goal plan.[32] State agencies must "make a good faith effort to achieve the maximum feasible portion" of their MWBE goals.[33] Similarly, state agencies must make a good faith effort to achieve their SDVBE goals.[34] In addition, contracting state agencies must evaluate each contract to determine the appropriate MWBE participation goal to set for that contract.[35] The contract-specific goal should be based on recent disparity study MWBE availability noted, disparities found in contracting, and utilization findings per industry.[36] As it relates to the SDVBE goals, state agencies should establish a 6 percent goal on state contracts where "practical, feasible, and appropriate."[37]
- *SDVBE Set-Asides*: State agencies may set aside procurement opportunities for SDVBEs so as to achieve participation goals.[38]
- *Bidding Specifications and Contracts*: Contracting state agencies must include provisions requiring contractors to make good faith efforts to solicit participation of certified MWBEs as well as agree to be bound to provisions pertaining to enforcement of Article 15-A.[39] These terms must also be included in every subcontract so that subcontractors are also bound to these terms on state contracts.[40]
- *Utilization Plans and Contractor Good Faith Efforts*: After bids are open and prior to award, contractors are required to submit utilization plans.[41] If the state agency sees any deficiencies in the plan, the contractor may have time to remedy the

30. N.Y. State Fin. L. § 163(6) (2022).

31. *Id.* § 179-F(2); *15-Day Prompt Payments for Small Businesses*, Off. of the N.Y. State Comptroller 9, https://www.osc.state.ny.us/state-vendors/portal/15-day-prompt-payments-small-businesses (last visited Jan. 20, 2023).

32. N.Y. Exec. L. § 313 (2022); N.Y. Comp. Codes R. & Regs. tit. 5, § 141.2 (2022); *id.* tit. 9, § 252.2.

33. N.Y. Comp. Codes R. & Regs. tit. 5, § 141.7 (2022).

34. *Id.* tit. 9, § 252.2.

35. N.Y. Exec. L. § 313(4) (2022).

36. *Id.*

37. N.Y. Comp. Codes R. & Regs. tit. 9, § 252.2(h) (2022).

38. *Id.* tit. 9, § 252.2(j).

39. N.Y. Exec. L. § 313(3) (2022).

40. *Id.*

41. *Id.* § 313(5).

deficiencies or ask for a waiver of the MWBE participation requirements.[42] Utilization plans may include the contractor's good faith efforts to include MWBE participation.[43] If a contractor fails to remedy a deficiency in their utilization plan within the time required, it may be deemed nonresponsible and disqualified on those grounds.[44] A disqualified contractor is entitled to an administrative hearing.[45] In such instances where a contractor has made a good faith effort, but still will not meet the MWBE participation requirements of a contract, the contractor may file a written application with the contracting agency for a total or partial waiver from the participation requirements.[46]

- *Certification of Work Completed by Certified MWBEs*: Prior to receiving payment, prime contractors are required to certify that the MWBE subcontractors identified on their project did perform the service and/or provide the materials noted.[47] MWBE subcontractors also must certify that they performed the services and/or provided the materials.[48]
- *Liquidated Damages*: Every state contract must include the following: "any contractor who willfully and intentionally fails to comply with the minority and women-owned participation requirements of this article as set forth in such state contract shall be liable to the contracting agency for liquidated or other appropriate damages and shall provide for other appropriate remedies on account of such breach."[49]
- *Reporting Requirements*: Each contracting state agency must submit an annual report to the DMWBD regarding its efforts to promote increased participation of MWBEs as well as quarterly compliance reports.[50] The DMWBD must report each year the MWBE participation of each state agencies' contracts to the governor and chairpersons of the Senate Finance and Assembly Ways and Means Committees.[51] All contracting state agencies must develop a four-year growth plan related

42. *Id.*
43. *Id.*
44. *Id.*
45. *Id.*
46. *Id.* § 313(6).
47. *Id.* § 314-A.
48. *Id.*
49. *Id.* § 316-A; N.Y. Comp. Codes R. & Regs. tit. 5, § 142.13(a) (2022).
50. N.Y. Exec. L. § 315(3) (2022); N.Y. Comp. Codes R. & Regs. tit. 5, § 141.6 (2022).
51. N.Y. Exec. L. § 311(3) (2022).

to their efforts to increase MWBE participation.[52] The Office of General Services also must submit an annual report to the "governor, the temporary president of the senate, the speaker of the assembly and the chairpersons of the senate finance and assembly ways and means committees" regarding SDVBE participation and efforts.[53]

Contracting opportunities where the NYSDOT DBE program applies have several requirements that intersect directly with procurement, contracting, and business inclusion.

- *Fostering Small Business Participation*: Pursuant to 49 C.F.R. § 26.39, NYSDOT has engaged in efforts to foster small business participation.[54] Per the 2019 DBE Program Plan, "NYSDOT developed a Small Business Development Initiative as an element of the DBE Program. The Initiative is designed to increase competition, provide more opportunities for small businesses, and increase the support to meet NYSDOT's contracting needs. Key aspects of this initiative are to reserve certain contracts for small consultant engineering firms which include both DBE and non-DBE firms."[55]
- *Goals*: Contract opportunities may not use quotas or set-asides for DBEs.[56] The only exception for using a set-aside is in a limited or extreme circumstance, "when no other method could be reasonably expected to redress egregious instances of discrimination."[57] Instead, an overall goal must be set.[58] The goal must be based on evidence of available "ready, willing and able" DBEs in the market.[59] Once the assessment of "ready, willing and able" DBEs is completed, an overall goal may be established as a percentage of the total amount of contracts receiving U.S. Department of Transportation (U.S. DOT) funds.[60] Participation goals must be set for all certified DBEs and not divided into subcategories.[61] Race- and gender-neutral

52. *Id.*

53. *Id.* § 369-I(4)(f).

54. *Disadvantaged Business Enterprise (DBE) Program*, N.Y. Dep't of Transp. 25 (2019), https://www.dot.ny.gov/main/business-center/civil-rights2/civil-rights-repository/Tab/DBE%20Program%20Plan%202019%20Final%20%20121719.pdf.

55. *Id.*

56. 49 C.F.R. § 26.43 (2022).

57. *Id.*

58. *Id.* § 26.45(a)(1).

59. *Id.* § 26.45(b).

60. *Id.* § 26.45(e).

61. *Id.* § 26.45(h).

means must be used to "meet the maximum feasible portion of your overall goal."[62] NYSDOT, as a recipient of U.S. DOT funds, will not be penalized for failing to meet the overall goal set, if it can establish good faith efforts to meet the goal.[63] When there is a DBE goal on a specific contract opportunity, only the bidder meeting the goal, or establishing good faith efforts to meet the goal, may be awarded the contract.[64]

- *Prompt Payment*: Under 49 C.F.R. part 26, contractors must pay subcontractors within 30 days of receipt of payment from the state DOT for satisfactory performance.[65]
- *Payment of Retainage*: Contractors must pay amounts withheld for retainage to subcontractors within 30 days of their work being satisfactorily completed.[66]

Additional Related Laws, Policies, and Programs

- *Access to Capital*:[67] Under New York law, there are a number of loan programs available for small businesses and MWBEs. These include but are not limited to the following: Small Business Revolving Loan Fund;[68] Regional Revolving Loan Trust Fund;[69] Minority and Women Business Development and Revolving Loan Fund;[70] Minority and Women Revolving Loan Trust Fund;[71] Commercial Revitalization Revolving Loan Trust Fund;[72] Minority and Women-Owned Business Development and Lending Program;[73] Small, Minority Business and Women-Owned Business Enterprises Transportation Capital Assistance and Guaranteed Loan Program;[74] Upstate Regional Blueprint Fund Program;[75] Downstate Revitalization Fund Program;[76]

62. *Id.* § 26.51.
63. *Id.* § 26.47.
64. *Id.* § 26.53.
65. 49 C.F.R. § 26.29(a) (2023).
66. *Id.* § 26.29(b).
67. The Empire State Development Agency lists a number of opportunities to assist with access to capital on its State Small Business Credit Initiative page: https://esd.ny.gov/ssbci (last visited Feb. 1, 2023).
68. https://esd.ny.gov/nys-small-business-revolving-loan-fund-round-2.
69. N.Y. Comp. Codes R. & Regs. tit. 21, § 4209.2 (2022).
70. *Id.* § 4213.
71. *Id.* § 4215.
72. *Id.* § 4216.
73. *Id.* § 4230.
74. *Id.* § 4240.
75. *Id.* § 4247.
76. *Id.* § 4249.

Capital Access Program;[77] and Bonding Guarantee Assistance Program.[78]

- *Technical Assistance*: Under Article 15-A, it notes that the DMWB shall provide technical assistance to certified MWBEs.[79] Similarly, under Article 17-B, the Office of General Services must provide technical assistance to SDVBEs.[80]
- *Finding Business Opportunities*: The Office of the New York State Comptroller has a list of online resources related to state bidding opportunities on its "Find Opportunities to Do Business with New York State" page: https://www.osc.state.ny.us/state-vendors/resources/find-opportunities-do-business-new-york-state.

Major City Snapshot: New York City

In terms of New York City's business inclusion efforts, there is collaboration among the Mayor's Office of Contract Services (MOCS); Mayor's Office of Minority and Women-Owned Business Enterprises (OM/WBE); and the Department of Small Business Services (SBS).[81] SBS handles the certification of Minority-Owned Business Enterprises (MBEs), Women-Owned Business Enterprises (WBEs), Emerging Business Enterprises (EBEs), and Locally Based Enterprises (LBEs).[82]

- *Certifications*: Businesses may get certified faster if they are already certified with one of the city's partners.[83] This list of partners now also includes LGBT-owned Business Enterprises (LGBTBEs) certified with the National Gay & Lesbian Chamber of Commerce.[84] Following is a summary of the eligibility requirements for each certification.
  - *Minority-Owned Business Enterprises (MBEs)*: A business must (1) be for-profit; (2) be legally authorized to transact business in New York state; (3) provide documentation of one year's business activity; (4) have a proper "nexus" with the city such that it has "a real and substantial business

77. *Id.* §§ 4249, 4251.
78. *Id.* §§ 4249, 4253.
79. N.Y. Exec. L. § 311 (2022).
80. *Id.* § 369-I(4).
81. *Minority and Women-Owned Business Enterprise (M/WBE) Program First and Second Quarter of Fiscal Year 2023*, City of New York 15 (2022), https://www.nyc.gov/assets/mocs/downloads/Opportunities/m-wbe-reports/MWBEComplianceReport_FY23Q1Q2.pdf.
82. *Certify with the City*, City of New York, https://www.nyc.gov/site/sbs/businesses/certify-with-the-city.page (last visited Apr. 29, 2023).
83. *Id.*
84. *Id.*

presence in the geographic market for the city of New York," which can be demonstrated through several ways outlined in the city ordinance; (5) be at least 51 percent owned, operated, and controlled by a minority (includes people who are Black, Hispanic, Asian and Pacific Islander, Asian-Indian, and Native American); and (6) have minority owners who are U.S. citizens or U.S. permanent residents.[85]

- *Women-Owned Business Enterprises (WBEs)*: A business must (1) be for-profit; (2) be legally authorized to transact business in New York state; (3) provide documentation of one year's business activity; (4) have a proper "nexus" with the city such that it has "a real and substantial business presence in the geographic market for the city of New York," which can be demonstrated through several ways outlined in the city ordinance; (5) be at least 51 percent owned, operated, and controlled by one or more women; and (6) have women owners who are U.S. citizens or U.S. permanent residents.[86]
- *Emerging Business Enterprises (EBEs)*: A business must (1) be for-profit; (2) be legally authorized to transact business in New York state; (3) provide documentation of one year's business activity; (4) have a proper "nexus" with the city such that it has "a real and substantial business presence in the geographic market for the city of New York," which can be demonstrated through several ways outlined in the city rules; (5) be at least 51 percent owned, operated, and controlled by one or more socially and economically disadvantaged individuals; and (6) have the net worth of qualifying owners be less than $1 million.[87]
- *Locally Based Enterprises (LBEs)*: A business must (1) be for-profit; (2) be legally authorized to transact business in New York state; (3) provide documentation of one year's business activity; (4) have average annual gross receipts over the prior three years of less than $2 million for all construction and construction-related work; (5) be independent; and (6) have in the tax year before applying for certification

---

85. The Rules of the City of New York § 11-22 (2023); *Minority and Women-Owned Business Enterprise (M/WBE) Certification Program*, *supra* note 81.

86. 66 RCNY § 11-22 (2023); *Minority and Women-Owned Business Enterprise (M/WBE) Certification Program*, *supra* note 81.

87. 66 RCNY § 11-82 (2023); *Emerging Business Enterprise (EBE) Certification Program*, City Of New York, https://nyc-business.nyc.gov/nycbusiness/description/emerging-business-enterprise-ebe-program (last visited Apr. 29, 2023).

either "(i) earned at least 25 percent of its gross receipts from work performed on construction projects located in economic development areas; or (ii) employed a work force of which at least 25 percent were economically disadvantaged persons."[88]

- *Inclusion Goals*: The city sets citywide contracting participation goals for MBEs, WBEs, and EBEs that may be met through prime contractors or subcontractors.[89] Each agency must develop its own utilization plan and set goals that may be higher, lower, or the same as the citywide goals.[90] Goals are also set for LBEs on construction projects during the fiscal year.[91]
- *Solicitations*: "All agency solicitations for bids or proposals must include information referring potential bidders or proposers to the directories of MBEs, WBEs and EBEs prepared by the division."[92]
- *Utilization Plans, Waivers, and Good Faith Efforts*: For each contract with MBE, WBE, and/or EBE goals set contractors must submit utilization plans with their bids.[93] Contracting agencies may grant a full or partial waiver of participation goals to bidders or proposers.[94] In assessing whether or not to grant the waiver, one thing the contracting agency may assess is the bidder or proposer's good faith efforts to identify contracting opportunities for certified businesses.[95]
- *Reporting Requirements*: The mayor must submit an annual report to the council on the administration of the LBE program.[96] The chief procurement officer must submit quarterly reports to the speaker of the council on the MWBE program efforts that include, among other things, the total amount of contracts and dollar value of contracts and the total amount of each awarded to MBE, WBEs, and EBEs.[97]

---

88. N.Y.C. Admin. Code § 6-108.1; 66 RCNY § 11-02 (2023); *id.* § 11-03(b)(11); *Locally Based Enterprise (LBE) Certification Program*, City of New York, https://nyc-business.nyc.gov/nycbusiness/description/locally-based-enterprise-lbe-program (last visited Apr. 29, 2023).
89. 66 RCNY § 11-61(1) (2023).
90. *Id.* § 11-61(2)(b).
91. *Id.* § 11-04(a).
92. *Id.* § 11-65(2)(c).
93. *Id.* § 11-66(5).
94. *Id.* § 11-66(11)(c).
95. *Id.*
96. N.Y.C. Admin. Code § 6-108.1(h) (2023).
97. 66 RCNY § 11-69(1) (2023).

CHAPTER 34

North Carolina

Overview of Business Inclusion Program, Policies, and Practices

Government entities seeking to create business inclusion programs have two primary options in terms of the type of program they may create, in terms of who is eligible for the program: (1) a race- and gender-conscious program or (2) a race- and gender-neutral program. Under the Equal Protection Clause of the Fourteenth Amendment, strict scrutiny is applied by the courts when a government actor is creating policies based on race. Strict scrutiny is the highest level of judicial review that may be applied. It requires the government actor to demonstrate that (1) past discrimination exists such that the entity has a "compelling government interest" in rectifying it, and (2) the policies and programs created to do so are "narrowly tailored."[1] Although intermediate scrutiny is often applied when reviewing programs based on gender, strict scrutiny is applied when reviewing race- and gender-conscious business inclusion programs.[2] Disparity studies have become a standard tool used to assist a government entity in withstanding a challenge to its race- and gender-conscious business inclusion programs. These studies aid in demonstrating whether a government entity has engaged

1. City of Richmond v. J.A. Croson Co., 488 U.S. 469 (1989).

2. Since the 1980s with the Supreme Court decision in *City of Richmond v. J.A. Croson Company*, there have been a number of cases across the county that have assessed race- and gender-conscious business inclusion programs. *See* Adarand Constructors, Inc. v. Pena, 515 U.S. 200 (1995); Virdi v. DeKalb Cnty. Sch. Dist., 135 Fed. App'x 262, 268 (11th Cir. 2005); Sherbrooke Turf, Inc. v. Minn. Dep't of Transp., 345 F.3d 964, 971 (8th Cir. 2003); Mountain West Holding Co., Inc. v. The State of Montana, Montana DOT, et al., 2017 WL 2179120 (9th Cir. May 16, 2017).

in past discrimination in its contracting practices, such that the entity may have a compelling government interest in rectifying it.[3]

Conversely, race- and gender-neutral programs are programs that are not only accessible to minority-owned and women-owned businesses but to all businesses, regardless of race or gender. A small business inclusion program would fall into this category. The level of judicial review applied to such a policy to determine its constitutionality is rational basis, which is the lowest threshold for a government to satisfy. For a government entity to satisfy rational basis, the policy or program created must be "related to a legitimate government purpose."[4] Even when a government entity has a race- and gender-conscious program, oftentimes the program may still require the government actor to seek to meet the goals of their program through race- and gender-neutral means where able, so as to be taking the most narrowly tailored means of accomplishing the program goals.

In the state of North Carolina, at the state level of government, there are two main state agencies certifying businesses for business inclusion programs: (1) the North Carolina Department of Administration Office for Historically Underutilized Businesses and (2) the North Carolina Department of Transportation (NCDOT).

Summary of Certification Programs and Requirements

The North Carolina Department of Administration Office for Historically Underutilized Businesses certifies businesses as Historically Underutilized Businesses (HUB) and North Carolina Small Business Enterprises (SBE). The eligibility requirements for both follow:

- *Historically Underutilized Businesses (HUB)*: To satisfy the eligibility requirements to be certified as an HUB, a business must (1) be at least 51 percent owned, or 51 percent of stock owned, by one or more minorities (Black, Hispanic, Asian American, American India), females, persons with a disability, or disadvantaged person(s) who are socially and economically disadvantaged as defined in 15 U.S.C. § 637 who are also U.S. citizens or lawful permanent residents; (2) have management and daily business operations controlled by one or more of the

3. *Promoting Opportunity and Equality in America: A Guide to Federal Circuit Authority on Permissible Government Actions to Promote Racial and Gender Equality*, Am. Civ. Liberties Union & The Opportunity Agenda (Dec. 2010), https://www.aclu.org/sites/default/files/field_document/Promoting_Opportunity_and_Equality_in_America.pdf.

4. 488 U.S. 469 (1989).

qualifying owners noted in (1).[5] "[T]he term 'minority business' means a historically underutilized business."[6]

- *North Carolina Small Business Enterprise (NCSBE)*: To be eligible for the NCSBE program a business must (1) be headquartered in North Carolina; (2) be for-profit; (3) have fewer than 100 employees; and (4) have annual income after the Cost of Goods Sold is deducted that does not exceed $1,500,000.[7]

NCDOT administers the Disadvantaged Business Enterprise (DBE) program, Airport Concession Disadvantaged Business Enterprise (ACDBE) program; the Small Business Enterprise (SBE) program, and the Small Professional Services Firm (SPSF). Eligibility requirements for each are noted next.

- *Disadvantaged Business Enterprise (DBE) Program*: Pursuant to 49 C.F.R. part 26, the NCDOT administers the state's DBE certification program. As is required under 49 C.F.R. § 26.81, North Carolina has a Unified Certification Program (UCP). The UCP makes all DBE certification decisions and provides a "one-stop shop" to DBE applicants.[8] To qualify as a DBE, a business must (1) be for-profit;[9] (2) be a small business concern—with "small" determined by the Small Business Administration (SBA) small business size standards—and does not exceed $30.40 million in gross annual receipts;[10] (3) be at least 51 percent owned by socially and economically disadvantaged individuals—there is a rebuttable presumption that women, Black Americans, Hispanic Americans, Native Americans, Asian-Pacific Americans, Subcontinent Asian Americans, or other minorities are disadvantaged;[11] (4) be controlled by one or more of the socially and economically disadvantaged owners;[12] (5) have the socially and economically disadvantaged owners be U.S. citizens or lawfully admitted permanent residents;[13] and (6) have the personal net worth for any socially

5. N.C. Gen. Stat. § 143-128.4 (2020).

6. *Id.*

7. *NCSBE Certification*, N.C. Dep't of Admin., https://ncadmin.nc.gov/businesses/historically-underutilized-businesses-hub/hub-certification/ncsbe-certification#NCSBERulesandGeneralStatutes-6876 (last visited Mar. 24, 2023).

8. 49 C.F.R. § 26.81(b)(2) (2022).

9. *Id.* § 26.5.

10. *Id.* §§ 26.5, 26.65(b). It is worth noting that under 49 C.F.R. § 26.65(b) the DBE size standard may be adjusted annually for inflation such that in subsequent years the size standard may no longer be $30.40 million.

11. *Id.* § 26.67.

12. *Id.* § 26.5.

13. *Id.* § 26.67.

and economically disadvantaged owner not exceed $1.32 million.[14] The DBE program is required on contracting opportunities that have received funding from the Federal Highway Administration (FHWA), Federal Aviation Administration (FAA), or Federal Transit Administration (FTA).[15]

- *Airport Concession Disadvantaged Business Enterprise (ACDBE) Program*: In addition to being certified as a DBE under 49 C.F.R. part 26, businesses may also be certified as an Airport Concession Disadvantaged Business Enterprise (ACDBE) under 49 C.F.R. part 23. To qualify as an ACDBE, a business must (1) be a concession for-profit small business concern;[16] (2) qualify as small by having its prior three-year average gross receipts not exceed the applicable size standard of $56.42 million;[17] (3) be 51 percent owned by one or more socially and economically disadvantaged individuals;[18] (4) have one or more of the socially and economically disadvantaged individuals with control and managing the daily business operations;[19] and (5) not have the personal net worth for any socially and economically disadvantaged owner exceed $1.32 million.[20]
- *Small Business Enterprise (SBE) Program*: NCDOT has implemented a small business element within its DBE program called the Small Business Enterprise (SBE) Program, pursuant to 49 C.F.R. § 26.39.[21] This program is race and gender neutral.[22] To be eligible for the program, a business must (1) be for-profit; (2) have "annual net income of not more than $1,500,000, after 'Cost of Goods Sold' is deducted"; (3) be independent (". . . absence of control or influence of a non-qualifying firm . . ."); (4) be a business of integrity; and (5) cooperate with NCDOT in terms of requests for information throughout the certification process.[23]

---

14. *Id.*
15. *Id.* § 26.21(a).
16. *Id.* § 23.3.
17. *Id.* § 23.33(a). The size standards for the following are exceptions to this: bank and financial institutions is $1 billion in assets; car rental companies are $75.23 million average annual gross receipts; pay telephones is 1,500 employees; and automobile dealers is 350 employees.
18. *Id.*
19. *Id.*
20. *Id.* § 23.35.
21. *Small Business Enterprise Program Guidelines—For New Applicants and Renewals*, N.C. Dep't of Transp. 4–5 (2017), https://connect.ncdot.gov/business/SmallBusiness/Documents/SBE%20Program%20Guidelines.pdf.
22. *Id.*
23. *Id.* at 8.

- *Small Professional Services Firm (SPSF)*: SPSF is a race- and gender-neutral program.[24] To be eligible for the program, a business must (1) be for-profit; (2) be small under the SBA size standard for NAICS sector 54; (3) be independent (". . . absence of control or influence of a non-qualifying firm . . ."); (4) be a business of integrity; and (5) cooperate with NCDOT in terms of requests for information throughout the certification process.[25]

Procurement Laws Intersecting with Business Inclusion

Relevant laws at the intersection of procurement and business inclusion noted next may primarily be found in North Carolina General Statutes sections 143-128.2 and 143-128.3.

- *Inclusion Goals*: Under North Carolina General Statutes section 143-128.2, there is a verifiable 10 percent participation goal for minority businesses on the total value of state building projects.[26] Inclusion goals and requirement set forth under North Carolina General Statutes section 143-128.2 only apply to building projects costing $300,000 or more, unless a different standard is noted in the section.[27] On local government unit, or public or private building projects with state appropriations, on projects that are $100,000 or more, there is also a 10 percent minority business participation goal on the total value of the work.[28] In setting participation goals it is not intended to require awarding contracts to minority businesses who are not the lowest responsible and responsive bidders.[29]
- *Contractor Good Faith Efforts*: As it relates to state building projects, "[e]ach entity required to have verifiable percentage goals . . . shall make a good faith effort to recruit minority participation. . . ."[30] Bidders must identify in their bid the minority businesses it will use on its project as well as an affidavit

---

24. *Small Professional Services Firm Program Guidelines—For New Applicants and Renewals*, N.C. Dep't of Transp. 2 (2016), https://connect.ncdot.gov/business/SmallBusiness/Documents/SPSF%20 Guidelines.pdf.
25. *Id.* at 4 5.
26. N.C. Gen. Stat. § 143-128.2(a) (2020). The goal is to be based on adequate data.
27. *Id.* § 143-128.2(j).
28. *Id.* However, the local government unit may apply to use a different goal.
29. *Id.* § 143-128.2(h).
30. *Id.* § 143-128.2(a).

identifying its good faith efforts.[31] Failure to appropriately submit this information is grounds for rejection of the bid.[32] When reviewing for good faith efforts, the secretary of the Department of Administration uses a point system that awards points for each good faith effort action taken up to 50 points.[33]

- *Prompt Payment to Subcontractors*: Contractors must pay their subcontractors within seven days of receipt of their payment.[34]
- *Reporting Requirements*: "All public entities subject to [N.C. GEN. STAT.] 143-128.2 shall report to the Department of Administration, Office of Historically Underutilized Business . . ." on the following related to minority businesses: verifiable participation percentage goal, type of projects, total dollar value, contracts awarded, good faith effort guidelines and rules, good faith effort documentation, and minority business utilization under different construction methods.[35] The Secretary of the Department of Administration must also report annually to the Joint Legislative Committee on Governmental Operations and the Joint Legislative Oversight Committee on General Government.[36]

Contracting opportunities for NCDOT programs have several requirements that intersect directly with procurement, contracting, and business inclusion.

- *Contracts for SPSFs*: "General Assembly House Bill 200, Session Law 2011-145, states that NCDOT will identify 'Professional Services Contracts of $250,000 or less that are likely to attract increased participation by Small Professional Services Firms and then direct the solicitation of applicable contracts to those firms.'"[37]
- *SBE Contracts*: ". . . [F]or Highway Fund or Highway Trust Fund construction and repair projects of one million dollars ($1,000,000) or less, and maintenance projects of one million dollars ($1,000,000) or less per year, the Board of Transportation may, after soliciting and receiving at least three informal bids in writing from Small Business Enterprises, award

31. *Id.* § 143-128.2(c).
32. *Id.*
33. *Id.* § 143-128.2(f).
34. *Id.* § 22C-3.
35. *Id.* § 143-128.3(a).
36. *Id.* § 143-128.3(g).
37. *Small Professional Services Firm Program Guidelines—For New Applicants and Renewals, supra* note 24, at 2.

contracts to the lowest responsible bidder. The Department of Transportation may identify projects likely to attract increased participation by Small Business Enterprises, and restrict the solicitation and award to those bidders."[38]

- *Waived Bonding and Licensing Requirements for SBEs*: "The [NCDOT] may waive the bonding requirements of Chapter 44A of the General Statutes and the licensing requirements of Chapter 87 for contracts awarded under this section."[39]
- *Goals*: Contract opportunities may not use quotas or set-asides for DBEs.[40] The only exception for using a set-aside is in a limited or extreme circumstance, "when no other method could be reasonably expected to redress egregious instances of discrimination."[41] Instead, an overall goal must be set.[42] The goal must be based on evidence of available "ready, willing and able" DBEs in the market.[43] Once the assessment of "ready, willing and able" DBEs is completed, an overall goal may be established as a percentage of the total amount of contracts receiving U.S. Department of Transportation (U.S. DOT) funds.[44] Participation goals must be set for all certified DBEs and not divided into subcategories.[45] Race- and gender-neutral means must be used to "meet the maximum feasible portion of your overall goal."[46] NCDOT, as a recipient of U.S. DOT funds, will not be penalized for failing to meet the overall goal set, if it can establish good faith efforts to meet the goal.[47] When there is a DBE goal on a specific contract opportunity, only the bidder meeting the goal, or establishing good faith efforts to meet the goal, may be awarded the contract.[48]
- *Prompt Payment*: Under 49 C.F.R. part 26, contractors must pay subcontractors within 30 days of receipt of payment from the state DOT for satisfactory performance.[49]

---

38. N.C. Gen. Stat. § 136-28.10(a) (2020).
39. *Id.* § 136-28.10(b).
40. 49 C.F.R. § 26.43 (2022).
41. *Id.*
42. *Id.* § 26.45(a)(1).
43. *Id.* § 26.45(b).
44. *Id.* § 26.45(e).
45. *Id.* § 26.45(h).
46. *Id.* § 26.51.
47. *Id.* § 26.47.
48. *Id.* § 26.53.
49. 49 C.F.R. § 26.29(a) (2023).

- *Payment of Retainage*: Contractors must pay amounts withheld for retainage to subcontractors within 30 days of their work being satisfactorily completed.[50]

Additional Related Laws, Policies, and Programs

- *Technical Assistance*: The North Carolina Minority Business Development Agency Business Center offers services and technical assistance to MBEs.[51]
- *Finding Contract Opportunities*: The North Carolina Interactive Purchasing System may be found here: https://www.ips.state.nc.us/IPS/Default.aspx. Additional information related to the system may also be found here: https://ncadmin.nc.gov/nc-bids-vendors.

Major City Snapshot: Charlotte

The City of Charlotte (city) is engaged in business inclusion efforts for minority-owned businesses and women-owned business enterprises (MWBEs) as well as small business enterprises (SBEs) through the Charlotte Business INClusion (CBI) program.[52]

- *Certifications*: The city does not certify MWBEs; instead they must be certified through the State of North Carolina Historically Underutilized Business Office.[53] The city does certify Charlotte Small Business Enterprises (SBEs), which is a race- and gender-neutral program.[54]
- *Access to Capital*: The city offers a Small Business Mobilization Loan.[55] This loan intends to ". . . assist owners of certified Small Business Enterprises (SBEs) acquire short-term, low-rate financing to support their temporary working capital needs as they participate in City projects."[56]

---

50. *Id.* § 26.29(b).

51. *NC Minority Business Development Agency Business Center*, N.C. Dep't of Admin., https://ncadmin.nc.gov/businesses/historically-underutilized-businesses-hub/ncmbda (last visited Mar. 24, 2023).

52. *Charlotte Business Inclusion*, City of Charlotte, https://charlottenc.gov/gs/procurement/cbi/Pages/default.aspx (last visited Mar. 24, 2023).

53. *Id.*

54. *Id.*

55. *Small Business Mobilization Loan*, City of Charlotte, https://www.charlottenc.gov/Growth-and-Development/Doing-Business/CBI/Mobilization-Loan (last visited May 11, 2023).

56. *Id.*; Charlotte City Ordinance ch. 8, § 8.88.

- *Bidding Specifications, Goals, and Good Faith Efforts*: Section 8.82 of the city ordinance states, "The Council may establish minimum Minority and/or Women's Business Enterprise participation (M/WBE) requirements and in that event shall include such requirements in the specifications for City contracts. In addition, in construction and repair contracts under which subcontracts are customarily awarded by that primary contractor, the Council may establish specifications requiring bidders to subcontract a certain designated percentage of the construction and repair work amount; provided, that nothing in the specifications or requirements developed shall be construed to require that the award of subcontracts be made to subcontractors who do not submit the lowest responsible sub-bid and do not meet the bonding requirements otherwise required by law. Notwithstanding the provisions of G.S. 143-129 and G.S. 143-131, the Council may consider a bidder's compliance with specifications containing M/WBE or subcontracting requirements in its award of contracts, and may, in its discretion, refuse to award a contract to a bidder if it determines that the bidder has failed to make a good faith effort to comply with said requirements."

CHAPTER 35

North Dakota

Overview of Business Inclusion Program, Policies, and Practices

Government entities seeking to create business inclusion programs have two primary options in terms of the type of program they may create, in terms of who is eligible for the program: (1) a race- and gender-conscious program or (2) a race- and gender-neutral program. Under the Equal Protection Clause of the Fourteenth Amendment, strict scrutiny is applied by the courts when a government actor is creating policies based on race. Strict scrutiny is the highest level of judicial review that may be applied. It requires the government actor to demonstrate that (1) past discrimination exists such that the entity has a "compelling government interest" in rectifying it, and (2) the policies and programs created to do so are "narrowly tailored."[1] Although intermediate scrutiny is often applied when reviewing programs based on gender, strict scrutiny is applied when reviewing race- and gender-conscious business inclusion programs.[2] Disparity studies have become a standard tool used to assist a government entity in withstanding a challenge to its race- and gender-conscious business inclusion programs. These studies aid in demonstrating whether a government entity has engaged

1. City of Richmond v. J.A. Croson Co., 488 U.S. 469 (1989).

2. Since the 1980s with the Supreme Court decision in *City of Richmond v. J.A. Croson Company*, there have been a number of cases across the county that have assessed race- and gender-conscious business inclusion programs. *See* Adarand Constructors, Inc. v. Pena, 515 U.S. 200 (1995); Virdi v. DeKalb Cnty. Sch. Dist., 135 Fed. App'x 262, 268 (11th Cir. 2005); Sherbrooke Turf, Inc. v. Minn. Dep't of Transp., 345 F.3d 964, 971 (8th Cir. 2003); Mountain West Holding Co., Inc. v. The State of Montana, Montana DOT, et al., 2017 WL 2179120 (9th Cir. May 16, 2017).

in past discrimination in its contracting practices, such that the entity may have a compelling government interest in rectifying it.[3]

Conversely, race- and gender-neutral programs are programs that are not only accessible to minority-owned and women-owned businesses but to all businesses, regardless of race or gender. A small business inclusion program would fall into this category. The level of judicial review applied to such a policy to determine its constitutionality is rational basis, which is the lowest threshold for a government to satisfy. For a government entity to satisfy rational basis, the policy or program created must be "related to a legitimate government purpose."[4] Even when a government entity has a race- and gender-conscious program, oftentimes the program may still require the government actor to seek to meet the goals of their program through race- and gender-neutral means where able, so as to be taking the most narrowly tailored means of accomplishing the program goals.

At the state level of government in North Dakota, the North Dakota Department of Transportation (NDDOT) is the only entity that certifies businesses for a business inclusion program.[5]

Summary of Certification Programs and Requirements

NDDOT administers the Disadvantaged Business Enterprise (DBE) program and the Airport Concession Disadvantaged Business Enterprise (ACDBE) program.

- *Disadvantaged Business Enterprise (DBE)*: Pursuant to 49 C.F.R. part 26, NDDOT administers the state's DBE certification program. As is required under 49 C.F.R. § 26.81, North Dakota has a Unified Certification Program (UCP). The UCP makes all DBE certification decisions and provides a "one-stop shop" to DBE applicants.[6] To qualify as a DBE, a business must (1) be for-profit;[7] (2) be a small business concern—with "small" determined by the Small Business Administration (SBA) small business size standards—and does not exceed $30.40 million

3. *Promoting Opportunity and Equality in America: A Guide to Federal Circuit Authority on Permissible Government Actions to Promote Racial and Gender Equality*, Am. Civ. Liberties Union & The Opportunity Agenda (Dec. 2010), https://www.aclu.org/sites/default/files/field_document/Promoting_Opportunity_and_Equality_in_America.pdf.

4. 488 U.S. 469 (1989).

5. *Disadvantaged Business Enterprise Program*, N.D. Dep't of Transp., https://www.dot.nd.gov/divisions/civilrights/dbeprogram.htm (last visited Jan. 20, 2023).

6. 49 C.F.R. § 26.81(b)(2).

7. *Id.* § 26.5.

in gross annual receipts;[8] (3) be at least 51 percent owned by socially and economically disadvantaged individuals—there is a rebuttable presumption that women, Black Americans, Hispanic Americans, Native Americans, Asian-Pacific Americans, Subcontinent Asian Americans, or other minorities are disadvantaged;[9] (4) be controlled by one or more of the socially and economically disadvantaged owners;[10] (5) have the socially and economically disadvantaged owners be U.S. citizens or lawfully admitted permanent residents;[11] and (6) not have the personal net worth for any socially and economically disadvantaged owner exceed $1.32 million.[12] The DBE program is required on contracting opportunities that have received funding from the Federal Highway Administration (FHWA), Federal Aviation Administration (FAA), or Federal Transit Administration (FTA).[13]

- *Airport Concession Disadvantaged Business Enterprise (ACDBE)*: In addition to being certified as a DBE under 49 C.F.R. part 26, businesses may also be certified as an Airport Concession Disadvantaged Business Enterprise (ACDBE) under 49 C.F.R. part 23. To qualify as an ACDBE, a business must (1) be a concession for-profit small business concern;[14] (2) qualify as small by having its prior three-year average gross receipts not exceed the applicable size standard of $56.42 million;[15] (3) be 51 percent owned by one or more socially and economically disadvantaged individuals;[16] (4) have one or more of the socially and economically disadvantaged individuals with control and managing the daily business operations;[17] and (5) have the personal net worth for any socially and economically disadvantaged owner not exceed $1.32 million.[18]

8. *Id.* §§ 26.5, 26.65(b). It is worth noting that under 49 C.F.R. § 26.65(b), the DBE size standard may be adjusted annually for inflation such that in subsequent years the size standard may no longer be $30.40 million.
9. *Id.* § 26.67.
10. *Id.* § 26.5.
11. *Id.* § 26.67.
12. *Id.*
13. *Id.* § 26.21(a).
14. *Id.* § 23.3.
15. *Id.* § 23.33(a). The size standards for the following are exceptions to this: bank and financial institutions is $1 billion in assets; car rental companies are $75.23 million average annual gross receipts; pay telephones is 1,500 employees; and automobile dealers is 350 employees.
16. *Id.*
17. *Id.*
18. *Id.* § 23.35.

Procurement Laws Intersecting with Business Inclusion

Procurement in the state of North Dakota is managed by the State Procurement Office, a division within the Office of Management and Budget.[19] The authority for procurement in North Dakota may be found in the following:[20]

- North Dakota Century Code 54-44.4: State Purchasing Practices
- North Dakota Century Code 54-44.7: State Government, Office of Management and Budget—Architect, Engineer and Land Surveying Services
- North Dakota Century Code 46-01: Printing Laws, Supervision of State Printing
- North Dakota Century Code 46-02: Printing Laws, Printing and Binding General Provisions
- North Dakota Century Code 46-05: Printing Laws, Newspapers
- North Dakota Administrative Code Article 4-12: State Procurement Practices

There are no bidding preferences, laws, or rules specific to business inclusion and minority-owned, women-owned, disability-owned, veteran-owned, and/or LGBT-owned business enterprises in North Dakota, outside of what is required by the NDDOT DBE program.

Contracting opportunities where the NDDOT DBE program applies have several requirements that intersect directly with procurement, contracting, and business inclusion.

- *Fostering Small Business Participation*: Pursuant to 49 C.F.R. § 26.39, NDDOT has engaged in efforts to foster small business participation.[21] NDDOT seeks to foster small business participation through efforts including but not limited to unbundling contracts, access to pre-bid reports, and training.[22]
- *Goals*: Contract opportunities may not use quotas or set-asides for DBEs.[23] The only exception for using a set-aside is in a limited or extreme circumstance, "when no other method could be reasonably expected to redress egregious instances

---

19. *State of North Dakota State Procurement Manual*, Office of Mgmt. & Budget 6 (July 2021), https://www.omb.nd.gov/sites/www/files/documents/doing-business-with-the-state/procurement/omb-procurement-manual-level1.pdf.

20. *Id.* at 4.

21. *Disadvantage Business Enterprise Program, Program Administration Manual*, N.D. Dep't of Transp. 23–24 (Jan. 1, 2022), https://www.dot.nd.gov/manuals/civilrights/dbe-program-manual.pdf.

22. *Id.*

23. 49 C.F.R. § 26.43 (2022).

of discrimination."[24] Instead, an overall goal must be set.[25] The goal must be based on evidence of available "ready, willing and able" DBEs in the market.[26] Once the assessment of "ready, willing and able" DBEs is completed, an overall goal may be established as a percentage of the total amount of contracts receiving U.S. Department of Transportation (U.S. DOT) funds.[27] Participation goals must be set for all certified DBEs and not divided into subcategories.[28] Race- and gender-neutral means must be used to "meet the maximum feasible portion of your overall goal."[29] NDDOT, as a recipient of U.S. DOT funds, will not be penalized for failing to meet the overall goal set, if it can establish good faith efforts to meet the goal.[30] When there is a DBE goal on a specific contract opportunity, only the bidder meeting the goal, or establishing good faith efforts to meet the goal, may be awarded the contract.[31]

- *Prompt Payment*: Under 49 C.F.R. part 26, contractors must pay subcontractors within 30 days of receipt of payment from the state DOT for satisfactory performance.[32]
- *Payment of Retainage*: Contractors must pay amounts withheld for retainage to subcontractors within 30 days of their work being satisfactorily completed.[33]

Additional Related Laws, Policies, and Programs

Under North Dakota procurement laws, there are a number of bidding preferences. The North Dakota "Guidelines to North Dakota Purchasing Preference Laws" defines a preference as "an advantage in consideration for award of a contract given to particular types of products or vendors."[34] None of North Dakota's bidding preferences pertain to the inclusion of minority-owned, women-owned, disability-owned, veteran-owned, and/or LGBT-owned business enterprises. However,

24. *Id.*
25. *Id.* § 26.45(a)(1).
26. *Id.* § 26.45(b).
27. *Id.* § 26.45(e).
28. *Id.* § 26.45(h).
29. *Id.* § 26.51.
30. *Id.* § 26.47.
31. *Id.* § 26.53.
32. 49 C.F.R. § 26.29(a) (2023).
33. *Id.* § 26.29(b).
34. *Guidelines to North Dakota Purchasing Preference Laws*, Office of Mgmt. & Budget 2 (July 2019), https://www.omb.nd.gov/sites/www/files/documents/doing-business-with-the-state/procurement/guidelines-to-nd-purchasing-preference-laws.pdf.

they may benefit a local business that happens to fall into one of these categories.

- *In-State Preference*: In North Dakota, there are preferences for purchasing from resident North Dakota bidders or for materials from North Dakota when purchasing the following goods and services: printing,[35] coal,[36] and certain types of food.[37]
- *Tied Bid Preference*: If there is a tied bid between a nonresident bidder and a North Dakota bidder, then preference must be given to the North Dakota bidder.[38]
- *Prompt Payment to Subcontractors*: "Upon payment by a state agency, political subdivision, school district, or agency of the United States, a business which has acquired under contract, property or services in connection with its contract with such agency, political subdivision, or school district, from a subcontractor or supplier, shall pay such subcontractor or supplier within forty-five days after payment from such agency."[39]
- *Finding Contract Opportunities*: Information about finding bidding opportunities may be found on the North Dakota Management and Budget page "Bidding Opportunities": https://www.omb.nd.gov/doing-business-state/procurement/bidding-opportunities.

Major City Snapshot: Grand Forks

The City of Grand Forks does not have a city-specific business inclusion program focused on minority-owned, women-owned, disability-owned, veteran-owned, and/or LGBT-owned business enterprises. It does, however, establish DBE goals on DOT-assisted projects. In its 2022–2024 Disadvantaged Business Enterprise Goals document posted on its website, it does note that it will be using race- and gender-neutral means to accomplish its goals that are based on availability in the marketplace.[40]

35. N.D. Cent. Code § 46-02-15 (2022).

36. *Id.* § 48-05-02.1.

37. S. Con. Res. 4018, 62d Sess. (N.D. 2011), https://www.ndlegis.gov/assembly/68-2023/regular/documents/23-3086-01000.pdf.

38. N.D. Cent. Code § 44-08-01.1 (2022).

39. *Id.* § 13-01.1-06.

40. *Accessibility*, City of Grand Forks, https://www.grandforksgov.com/government/city-departments/cities-area-transit-cat/accessibility (last visited Jan. 8, 2022).

CHAPTER 36

Ohio

Overview of Business Inclusion Program, Policies, and Practices

Government entities seeking to create business inclusion programs have two primary options in terms of the type of program they may create, in terms of who is eligible for the program: (1) a race- and gender-conscious program or (2) a race- and gender-neutral program. Under the Equal Protection Clause of the Fourteenth Amendment, strict scrutiny is applied by the courts when a government actor is creating policies based on race. Strict scrutiny is the highest level of judicial review that may be applied. It requires the government actor to demonstrate that (1) past discrimination exists such that the entity has a "compelling government interest" in rectifying it, and (2) the policies and programs created to do so are "narrowly tailored."[1] Although intermediate scrutiny is often applied when reviewing programs based on gender, strict scrutiny is applied when reviewing race- and gender-conscious business inclusion programs.[2] Disparity studies have become a standard tool used to assist a government entity in withstanding a challenge to its race- and gender-conscious business inclusion programs. These studies aid in demonstrating whether a government entity has engaged

1. City of Richmond v. J.A. Croson Co., 488 U.S. 469 (1989).

2. Since the 1980s with the Supreme Court decision in *City of Richmond v. J.A. Croson Company*, there have been a number of cases across the county that have assessed race- and gender-conscious business inclusion programs. *See* Adarand Constructors, Inc. v. Pena, 515 U.S. 200 (1995); Virdi v. DeKalb Cnty. Sch. Dist., 135 Fed. App'x 262, 268 (11th Cir. 2005); Sherbrooke Turf, Inc. v. Minn. Dep't of Transp., 345 F.3d 964, 971 (8th Cir. 2003); Mountain West Holding Co., Inc. v. The State of Montana, Montana DOT, et al., 2017 WL 2179120 (9th Cir. May 16, 2017).

in past discrimination in its contracting practices, such that the entity may have a compelling government interest in rectifying it.[3]

Conversely, race- and gender-neutral programs are programs that are not only accessible to minority-owned and women-owned businesses but to all businesses, regardless of race or gender. A small business inclusion program would fall into this category. The level of judicial review applied to such a policy to determine its constitutionality is rational basis, which is the lowest threshold for a government to satisfy. For a government entity to satisfy rational basis, the policy or program created must be "related to a legitimate government purpose."[4] Even when a government entity has a race- and gender-conscious program, oftentimes the program may still require the government actor to seek to meet the goals of their program through race- and gender-neutral means where able, so as to be taking the most narrowly tailored means of accomplishing the program goals.

In the state of Ohio, at the state level of government, there are two state agencies that certify businesses for business inclusion programs: (1) the Ohio Department of Development and (2) the Ohio Department of Transportation (ODOT).

Summary of Certification Programs and Requirements

The Ohio Department of Development Minority Business Development Division has the following types of certification programs: (1) Minority Business Enterprises (MBE) Program; (2) Women-Owned Business Enterprises (WBE) Program; (3) Veteran-Friendly Business Enterprises (VBE) Program; and (4) Encouraging Diversity, Growth and Equity (EDGE) Program. The following bullet points have additional details on eligibility requirements.

- *Minority Business Enterprise (MBE)*: To satisfy the eligibility criteria to be certified as an MBE, the business owner(s) must (1) be a U.S. citizen; (2) be a resident of Ohio; (3) "[be] members of one of the following economically disadvantaged groups: Blacks or African Americans, American Indians, Hispanics or Latinos, and Asians"; (4) own 51 percent of the business; (5) "have control over the management and day-to-day operations of the business and an interest in the capital, assets, and

3. *Promoting Opportunity and Equality in America: A Guide to Federal Circuit Authority on Permissible Government Actions to Promote Racial and Gender Equality*, AM. CIV. LIBERTIES UNION & THE OPPORTUNITY AGENDA (Dec. 2010), https://www.aclu.org/sites/default/files/field_document/Promoting_Opportunity_and_Equality_in_America.pdf.

4. 488 U.S. 469 (1989).

profits and losses of the business proportionate to their percentage of ownership"; and (6) own the business and control it for a minimum of one year prior to being awarded any contract opportunities under the MBE program.[5] The business must also (1) be a for-profit business;[6] (2) have eligible owner's ownership be "real and substantial";[7] and (3) have eligible owners with the ". . . experience, expertise, and knowledge to operate the particular type of business requesting certification."[8]

- *Women-Owned Business Enterprise (WBE)*: To satisfy the eligibility criteria to be certified as a WBE, the business owner(s) must (1) be a U.S. citizen; (2) be a resident of Ohio or a reciprocal state; (3) be a woman or women; (4) have women owners who own 51 percent of the business; (5) "have control over the management and day-to-day operations of the business and an interest in the capital, assets, and profits and losses of the business proportionate to their percentage of ownership"; and (6) own the business and control it for a minimum of one year.[9] The business must also (1) be a for-profit business;[10] (2) have eligible owner's ownership be "real and substantial";[11] and (3) have eligible owners with the ". . . experience, expertise, and knowledge to operate the particular type of business requesting certification."[12] The director of the Department of Development may enter into agreements with other states to allow for certified WBEs in Ohio to have a reciprocal process such that their WBE certification may apply in that state and WBEs in the reciprocal state may be certified in Ohio.[13]
- *Veteran-Friendly Business Enterprise (VFBE)*: To be eligible for the VFBE program, a business must (1) be "a sole proprietorship, association, partnership, corporation, limited liability company, or joint venture" and (2) "meets veteran employment standards established by the director of development and the director of transportation under this section."[14]
- *Encouraging Diversity, Growth and Equity (EDGE)*: To be eligible for this program, a business must (1) be for-profit; (2) exist

5. Ohio Rev. Code Ann. § 122.71 (2022).
6. Ohio Admin. Code 123:2-14-02(L) (2020).
7. *Id.* 123:2-14-02(P).
8. *Id.*
9. Ohio Rev. Code Ann. § 122.924 (2022).
10. Ohio Admin. Code 123:2-14-02(L) (2020).
11. *Id.* 123:2-14-02(P).
12. *Id.*
13. Ohio Rev. Code Ann. § 122.924 (2022).
14. *Id.* § 122.925.

for a minimum of one year; (3) have eligible owners who are Ohio residents or reside in a reciprocal state and are U.S. citizens; (4) have eligible owners control the business; (5) be small within the U.S. Small Business Administration (SBA) small business size standards; (6) have eligible business owner(s) whose net worth does not exceed the established threshold for the program.[15] The business must be 51 percent owned by socially and economically disadvantaged individuals whose ownership is real and substantial, and they have the "experience, expertise, and knowledge to operate the particular type of business requesting certification."[16] There is a rebuttable presumption of being socially disadvantaged if you are in one of the following groups: Black or African Americans; American Indian; Hispanic or Latino; Asian; female; with chronic physical or mental disability that has led to discrimination; "[a] business owner's long-term residence in an environment isolated from the mainstream of American society"; business owner can demonstrate chronic and substantial disadvantage; "[e]vidence of difficulty on entering or succeeding in the business world because of disadvantages"; or a primary office in a HUBZone.[17]

ODOT administers the Disadvantaged Business Enterprise (DBE) program, Airport Concession Disadvantaged Business Enterprise (ACDBE) program, and the Small Business Enterprise (SBE) program.

- *Disadvantaged Business Enterprise (DBE) Program*: Pursuant to 49 C.F.R. part 26, ODOT administers the state's DBE certification program. As is required under 49 C.F.R. § 26.81, Ohio has a Unified Certification Program (UCP). The UCP makes all DBE certification decisions and provides a "one-stop shop" to DBE applicants.[18] To qualify as a DBE, a business must (1) be for-profit;[19] (2) be a small business concern—with "small" determined by the SBA small business size standards—and does not exceed $30.40 million in gross annual receipts;[20] (3) be

15. Ohio Admin. Code § 123:2-14-02 (2020); *id.* § 123:2-14-01; Ohio Rev. Code Ann. § 122.922 (2021).

16. Ohio Admin. Code § 123:2-14-02 (2020); *id.* § 123:2-14-01; Ohio Rev. Code Ann. § 122.922 (2021).

17. Ohio Admin. Code 123:2-14-01(J) (2020).

18. 49 C.F.R. § 26.81(b)(2) (2022).

19. *Id.* § 26.5.

20. *Id.* §§ 26.5, 26.65(b). It is worth noting that under 49 C.F.R. § 26.65(b), the DBE size standard may be adjusted annually for inflation such that in subsequent years the size standard may no longer be $30.40 million.

at least 51 percent owned by socially and economically disadvantaged individuals—there is a rebuttable presumption that women, Black Americans, Hispanic Americans, Native Americans, Asian-Pacific Americans, Subcontinent Asian Americans, or other minorities are disadvantaged;[21] (4) be controlled by one or more of the socially and economically disadvantaged owners;[22] (5) have the socially and economically disadvantaged owners be U.S. citizens or lawfully admitted permanent residents;[23] and (6) not have the personal net worth for any socially and economically disadvantaged owner exceed $1.32 million.[24] The DBE program is required on contracting opportunities that have received funding from the Federal Highway Administration (FHWA), Federal Aviation Administration (FAA), or Federal Transit Administration (FTA).[25]

- *Airport Concession Disadvantaged Business Enterprise (ACDBE) Program*: In addition to being certified as a DBE under 49 C.F.R. part 26, businesses may also be certified as an Airport Concession Disadvantaged Business Enterprise (ACDBE) under 49 C.F.R. part 23. To qualify as an ACDBE, a business must (1) be a concession for-profit small business concern;[26] (2) qualify as small by having its prior three-year average gross receipts not exceed the applicable size standard of $56.42 million;[27] (3) be 51 percent owned by one or more socially and economically disadvantaged individuals;[28] (4) have one or more of the socially and economically disadvantaged individuals with control and managing the daily business operations;[29] and (5) have the personal net worth for any socially and economically disadvantaged owner not exceed $1.32 million.[30]
- *Small Business Enterprise (SBE)*: ODOT has implemented a race- and gender-neutral small business element within its DBE program called the Small Business Enterprise (SBE) certification,

21. *Id.* § 26.67.
22. *Id.* § 26.5.
23. *Id.* § 26.67.
24. *Id.*
25. *Id.* § 26.21(a).
26. *Id.* § 23.3.
27. *Id.* § 23.33(a). The size standards for the following are exceptions to this: bank and financial institutions is $1 billion in assets; car rental companies are $75.23 million average annual gross receipts; pay telephones is 1,500 employees; and automobile dealers is 350 employees.
28. *Id.*
29. *Id.*
30. *Id.* § 23.35.

pursuant to 49 C.F.R. § 26.39.[31] To be eligible for the program, a business must (1) be a small business under the SBA size standards; (2) have owners with a personal net worth that does not exceed $1.32 million and their adjusted gross income is $350,000 or less; (3) the business must be in construction or a construction-related consulting service; (4) intend to participate in ODOT contracting opportunities as a prime and can perform on 30 percent of the total construction or construction services costs; (5) have annual average gross receipts over the prior three fiscal years of $15 million or less as a construction firm or $7 million or less as a construction-related consultant services firm.[32]

Procurement Laws Intersecting with Business Inclusion

Generally, State of Ohio procurement is governed by Ohio Revised Code section 125 and Ohio Administrative Code section 123:5-1.[33] Following are some of the laws and administrative rules pertaining to MBEs, EDGE-certified businesses, and VFBEs.

- *Contracting Set-Asides*: Under Ohio Revised Code Annotated section 125.081, set-asides exist for MBEs. The Department of Administrative Services and state agencies are required to set aside contracting opportunities that in the aggregate equal 15 percent of the estimated total value of all purchases in a given fiscal year.[34] The individual contracting opportunities included within the 15 percent are to be set aside for competition only among MBEs.[35] If no MBEs respond, to the contract-

31. *Disadvantaged Business Enterprise Program Plan*, Ohio Dep't of Transp. 25 (May 2021), https://www.transportation.ohio.gov/wps/wcm/connect/gov/c7a29250-3bb9-4209-a041-01b9392df8ea/Ohio+DBE+Program+Plan+-+Revised+May+2021+-+Effective+July+2021.pdf?MOD=AJPERES&CONVERT_TO=url&CACHEID=ROOTWORKSPACE.Z18_M1HGGIK0N0JO00QO9DDDDM3000-c7a29250-3bb9-4209-a041-01b9392df8ea-nIXluxf.

32. *SBE Certification*, Ohio Dep't of Transp., https://www.transportation.ohio.gov/programs/business-economic-opportunity/sbe/sbe-certification (last visited Mar. 25, 2023).

33. *State of Ohio Procurement Manual*, Ohio Dep't of Admin. Serv. 1 (2023), https://das.ohio.gov/wps/wcm/connect/gov/ee83d462-3cac-46f0-965b-05c2940df454/State+of+Ohio+Procurement+Manual.pdf?MOD=AJPERES&CONVERT_TO=url&CACHEID=ROOTWORKSPACE.Z18_K9I401S01H7F40QBNJU3SO1F56-ee83d462-3cac-46f0-965b-05c2940df454-o0JNeWK.

34. Ohio Rev. Code Ann. § 125.081 (2023). Some state agencies set goals that are higher than the 15 percent goal noted, such as the Department of Transportation, which sets a 20 percent goal on state-funded purchases of goods and service (see https://www.transportation.ohio.gov/programs/business-economic-opportunity/mbe).

35. *Id.*

ing opportunity then the purchase must be "made according to usual procedures."[36] Prior to bidding on or being awarded a set-aside contract, a certified MBE must have been issued the appropriate classification code for their industry, goods, and services.[37]

- *Inclusion Goals and Good Faith Efforts*: The Department of Administration establishes annual EDGE procurement percentage goals based on availability of program participants in the following procurement categories: Goods, Information Technology Services, Construction, Architecture and Engineering, and Professional Services.[38] On contract opportunities with EDGE subcontracting goals, a bidder or proposer may request a waiver from the goals and provide good faith efforts documentation.[39] Procurement goals are not set for WBEs or VFBEs.[40]
- *Contracting Preferences*: There is a 5 percent VFBE preference such that if there is an apparent low bidder who is not a VFBE and the VFBE is within 5 percent of the lowest bid, the VFBE may still be awarded the contract.[41] Similarly, when analyzing proposals that are submitted, "[i]f the apparent most advantageous proposal is one other than a veteran-friendly business enterprise proposal, subtract five percent of the available points from the proposal's score."[42] "In order to qualify for this preference, a bidder or offer must have an active veteran-friendly business enterprise certification at the due date and time of bid or offer."[43] For ODOT, on construction of transportation facilities projects when considering a VFBE preference in a low bid situation, 2.5 percentage above the low bid rather than 5 percent is considered an excessive price, such that the department will not proceed with the preference.[44]
- *Prompt Payment to Small Businesses*: Contractors submitting a subcontractor's pay request with the contractor's request for payment from the owner must pay the subcontractor within ten calendar days of being paid by the owner.[45]

---

36. *Id.*
37. Ohio Admin. Code 123:2-14-02(V) (2020).
38. *Id.* 123:2-14-09.
39. *Id.* 123:2-14-10.
40. *State of Ohio Procurement Manual, supra* note 3, at 16.
41. Ohio Admin. Code 123:5-1-16(B)(3) (2017).
42. *Id.* 123:5-1-16(B)(4).
43. Ohio Admin. Code 123:5-1-06(A)(3) (2022).
44. *Id.* 5501:2-12-03.
45. Ohio Rev. Code Ann. § 4113.61 (2023).

- *Reporting Requirements*: Every state agency and port authority authorized to enter contracts must report to the Department of Development every 90 days on their MBE contracts and spends for the prior 90 days.[46] If a state agency fails to comply with the reporting requirements, then the director of the Department of Development will notify the agency and provide a 30-day period to comply.[47] If after that period the agency has failed to comply, the director of Development will certify to the director of Budget and Management and "[t]hereafter, no funds of the state agency shall be expended during the fiscal year for construction or purchases of equipment, materials, supplies, contracts of insurance, or services until the director of development certifies to the director of budget and management that the state agency has complied with the reporting requirements of this division for the prior fiscal year."[48] If any port authority fails to comply with the reporting requirements, then the director of the Department of Development notifies and certifies to the speaker of the house of representatives and the president of the senate and they in turn make recommendations to the members of the general assembly in terms of corrective action.[49]

Contracting opportunities where the ODOT DBE program applies have several requirements that intersect directly with procurement, contracting, and business inclusion.

- *Fostering Small Business Participation*: Pursuant to 49 C.F.R. § 26.39, ODOT has engaged in efforts to foster small business participation.[50] ODOT has engaged in the following: (1) setting aside bid opportunities anticipated not to exceed $2 million for SBEs to compete for prime contracts on federally funded highway construction and construction design contracts; (2) evaluating contracts for bundling and assessing if it is unjustifiable; (3) "examine[s] the possibility of facilitating joint ventures among SBEs to bid on contracts"; and (4) exploring and sharing best practices with SBEs.[51]

---

46. Ohio Rev. Code Ann. § 122.921(C) (2022).
47. *Id.*
48. *Id.*
49. *Id.*
50. *Disadvantaged Business Enterprise Program Plan, supra* note 31.
51. *Exhibit H-Small Business Enterprise Program Participation Plan*, Ohio Dep't of Transp. 5 (2015), https://www.dot.state.oh.us/Divisions/ODI/CRC/SOPDocuments/Exhibit%20F%20SBE%20Program%20Participation%20Plan%20v5%2012%202015%20and%20FINAL%20-%20Copy.pdf; *SBE Certification, supra* note 32.

- *Goals*: Contract opportunities may not use quotas or set-asides for DBEs.[52] The only exception for using a set-aside is in a limited or extreme circumstance, "when no other method could be reasonably expected to redress egregious instances of discrimination."[53] Instead, an overall goal must be set.[54] The goal must be based on evidence of available "ready, willing and able" DBEs in the market.[55] Once the assessment of "ready, willing and able" DBEs is completed, an overall goal may be established as a percentage of the total amount of contracts receiving U.S. Department of Transportation (U.S. DOT) funds.[56] Participation goals must be set for all certified DBEs and not divided into subcategories.[57] Race- and gender-neutral means must be used to "meet the maximum feasible portion of your overall goal."[58] ODOT, as a recipient of U.S. DOT funds, will not be penalized for failing to meet the overall goal set, if it can establish good faith efforts to meet the goal.[59] When there is a DBE goal on a specific contract opportunity only the bidder meeting the goal, or establishing good faith efforts to meet the goal, may be awarded the contract.[60]
- *Prompt Payment*: Under 49 C.F.R. part 26, contractors must pay subcontractors within 30 days of receipt of payment from the state DOT for satisfactory performance.[61]
- *Payment of Retainage*: Contractors must pay amounts withheld for retainage to subcontractors within 30 days of their work being satisfactorily completed.[62]

Additional Related Laws, Policies, and Programs

- *Access to Capital*: The State of Ohio offers a number of programs to advance access to capital for small and diverse businesses. Such programs include the following: Ohio Capital

52. 49 C.F.R. § 26.43 (2022).
53. *Id.*
54. *Id.* § 26.45(a)(1).
55. *Id.* § 26.45(b).
56. *Id.* § 26.45(e).
57. *Id.* § 26.45(h).
58. *Id.* § 26.51.
59. *Id.* § 26.47.
60. *Id.* § 26.53.
61. 49 C.F.R. § 26.29(a) (2023).
62. *Id.* § 26.29(b).

Access Program (OCAP),[63] Ohio Micro-Loan Program,[64] Ohio Minority Business Bonding,[65] Ohio Minority Business Direct Loan,[66] and Women's Business Enterprise Loan.[67]

- *Technical Assistance*: The Department of Development's Minority Business Development Division provides an array of technical assistance, including but not limited to managerial and consulting services, procurement and bid packaging assistance, and bonding technical assistance.[68]
- *Finding Contract Opportunities*: Public solicitations may be viewed on OhioBuys: https://ohiobuys.ohio.gov/page.aspx/en/rfp/request_browse_public.

Major City Snapshot: Cleveland

The City of Cleveland's (city) Mayor's Office of Equal Opportunity manages the city's business inclusion programs.

- *Certifications*: The city certifies the following types of businesses: Cleveland Area Small Business (CSB), Minority Owned Business Enterprise (MBE), Female Business Enterprise (FBE), a local producer also including local food producer (LPE), and a sustainable business enterprise (SUBE).[69]
- *Bidding Specifications and Good Faith Efforts*: Bid invitations require bidders to submit documentation noting their efforts to utilize CSBs, MBEs, and FBEs.[70] If a bidder cannot meet the goal, then an exception may be requested and the department may waive or reduce the goal.[71] "Each Bidder for a Contract shall make a good-faith effort to utilize certified CSBs, MBEs,

---

63. *Ohio Capital Access Program (OCAP)*, Ohio Dep't of Dev., https://development.ohio.gov/business/minority-business/ohio-capital-access-program (last visited Mar. 25, 2023).

64. *Ohio Micro-Loan Program*, Ohio Dep't of Dev., https://development.ohio.gov/business/minority-business/ohio-micro-loan-program (last visited Mar. 25, 2023).

65. *Ohio Minority Business Bonding Program*, Ohio Dep't of Dev., https://development.ohio.gov/business/minority-business/ohio-minority-business-bonding-program (last visited Mar. 25, 2023).

66. *Ohio Minority Business Direct Loan Program* Ohio Dep't of Dev., https://development.ohio.gov/business/minority-business/ohio-minority-business-direct-loan-program (last visited Mar. 25, 2023).

67. *Women's Business Enterprise Loan Program* Ohio Dep't of Dev., https://development.ohio.gov/business/minority-business/womens-business-enterprise-loan-program (last visited Mar. 25, 2023).

68. Ohio Rev. Code Ann. § 122.92 (2021).

69. Cleveland, Ohio, Code ch. 187 (2023); *Office of Equal Opportunity FAQ's*, City of Cleveland Mayor's Off. of Equal Opportunity, https://www.clevelandohio.gov/CityofCleveland/Home/Government/CityAgencies/OfficeofEqualOpportunity/OEOFAQ (last visited Mar. 25, 2023).

70. Cleveland, Ohio, Code § 187.08 (2023).

71. *Id.* §§ 187.08, 187.13.

and FBEs in a percentage that equals or exceeds the applicable goal."[72]

- *Inclusion Goals*: On city contracts over $50,000, each City Contracting Department must use its best efforts to utilize CSBs, MBEs, and FBEs as contractors and subcontractors.[73] "The annual City-wide goal for CSB participation in Public Improvement Contracts shall be thirty percent (30%), in Professional Services Contracts shall be ten percent (10%), and in all other Contracts shall be twenty percent (20%) or such other goal fixed by the Director for a particular Contract."[74] "The Director may determine the appropriate annual City-wide goals for MBE and FBE participation for each type of Contract, including, but not limited to, Construction, nonprofessional and professional services, supplies, and concessions, and for each type of work to be performed under a particular Contract, based on the availability of certified MBEs and FBEs as to which past or present discrimination has been demonstrated. . . ."[75]

72. *Id.* §§ 187.08, 187.13.
73. *Id.* §§ 187.04, 187.06.
74. *Id.* § 187.04.
75. *Id.* § 187.06.

CHAPTER 37

Oklahoma

Overview of Business Inclusion Program, Policies, and Practices

Government entities seeking to create business inclusion programs have two primary options in terms of the type of program they may create, in terms of who is eligible for the program: (1) a race- and gender-conscious program or (2) a race- and gender-neutral program. Under the Equal Protection Clause of the Fourteenth Amendment, strict scrutiny is applied by the courts when a government actor is creating policies based on race. Strict scrutiny is the highest level of judicial review that may be applied. It requires the government actor to demonstrate that (1) past discrimination exists such that the entity has a "compelling government interest" in rectifying it, and (2) the policies and programs created to do so are "narrowly tailored."[1] Although intermediate scrutiny is often applied when reviewing programs based on gender, strict scrutiny is applied when reviewing race- and gender-conscious business inclusion programs.[2] Disparity studies have become a standard tool used to assist a government entity in withstanding a challenge to its race- and gender-conscious business inclusion programs. These studies aid in demonstrating whether a government entity has engaged

1. City of Richmond v. J.A. Croson Co., 488 U.S. 469 (1989).

2. Since the 1980s with the Supreme Court decision in *City of Richmond v. J.A. Croson Company*, there have been a number of cases across the county that have assessed race- and gender-conscious business inclusion programs. *See* Adarand Constructors, Inc. v. Pena, 515 U.S. 200 (1995); Virdi v. DeKalb Cnty. Sch. Dist., 135 Fed. App'x 262, 268 (11th Cir. 2005); Sherbrooke Turf, Inc. v. Minn. Dep't of Transp., 345 F.3d 964, 971 (8th Cir. 2003); Mountain West Holding Co., Inc. v. The State of Montana, Montana DOT, et al., 2017 WL 2179120 (9th Cir. May 16, 2017).

in past discrimination in its contracting practices, such that the entity may have a compelling government interest in rectifying it.[3]

Conversely, race- and gender-neutral programs are programs that are not only accessible to minority-owned and women-owned businesses but to all businesses, regardless of race or gender. A small business inclusion program would fall into this category. The level of judicial review applied to such a policy to determine its constitutionality is rational basis, which is the lowest threshold for a government to satisfy. For a government entity to satisfy rational basis, the policy or program created must be "related to a legitimate government purpose."[4] Even when a government entity has a race- and gender-conscious program, oftentimes the program may still require the government actor to seek to meet the goals of their program through race- and gender-neutral means where able, so as to be taking the most narrowly tailored means of accomplishing the program goals.

In the state of Oklahoma, at the state level of government, there are three state departments that certify businesses for business inclusion programs: (1) the Oklahoma Department of Commerce, (2) the Office of Management and Enterprise Services, and (3) the Oklahoma Department of Transportation (ODOT).

Summary of Certification Programs and Requirements

The Department of Commerce certifies businesses as Women-Owned Businesses (WBEs) and Diverse Business Enterprise. The eligibility requirements for both follow:

- *Women-Owned Business (WBE)*: To satisfy the eligibility requirements for a WBE certification, a business must (1) be a small business concern, as defined in 15 U.S.C. § 632; (2) be 51 percent owned by one or more women (or 51 percent of stock owned by one or more women); and (3) have one or more women control management and daily business operations.[5] Certification lasts five years prior to needing to recertify, unless something changes earlier than five years in the eligibility of the business.[6]

---

3. *Promoting Opportunity and Equality in America: A Guide to Federal Circuit Authority on Permissible Government Actions to Promote Racial and Gender Equality*, Am. Civ. Liberties Union & The Opportunity Agenda (Dec. 2010), https://www.aclu.org/sites/default/files/field_document/Promoting_Opportunity_and_Equality_in_America.pdf.
4. 488 U.S. 469 (1989).
5. Okla. Admin. Code § 150:60-1-2 (2022); Okla. Stat. tit. 74, § 5010.5 (2022).
6. Okla. Admin. Code § 150:60-1-6 (2022).

- *Diverse Business Enterprise*: To satisfy the eligibility criteria to be certified as a Diverse Business Enterprise, a business must (1) have fewer than 500 employees; (2) have annual revenue of $25 million or less; (3) be Oklahoma owned, meaning that 51 percent of the owners reside in Oklahoma as their primary residence and have filed income taxes there for the prior two years; (4) be Oklahoma operated; (5) be registered to do business with the Oklahoma Secretary of State (if applicable); (6) not be publicly traded; and (7) meet one or more of the following criteria: (a) be certified by the Small Business Administration (SBA) as a Women-Owned Small Business, Minority-Business Enterprise, Small Disadvantaged Business, Service-Disabled Veteran-Owned Small Business, HUBZone Small Business Concern, or Business Development Program member; (b) be 51 percent or more owned and controlled by Native Americans, United States Military Veterans, Women, or Racial Minorities; or (c) be an ODOT Disadvantaged Business Enterprise.[7] Certification lasts five years prior to needing to recertify, unless something changes earlier than five years in the eligibility of the business.[8]

The Office of Management and Enterprise Services manages the implementation of the Disabled Veterans Enterprise Act.[9]

- *Service-Disabled Veteran Business*: Under the act, a Service-Disabled Veteran Business is defined as a business that (1) is at least 51 percent owned by one or more service-disabled veterans (or 51 percent of stock owned by one or more service-disabled veterans) and (2) has one or more service-disabled veterans controlling the management and daily business operations.[10]

ODOT administers the Disadvantaged Business Enterprise (DBE) program and Airport Concession Disadvantaged Business Enterprise (ACDBE) program.

- *Disadvantaged Business Enterprise (DBE) Program*: Pursuant to 49 C.F.R. part 26, ODOT administers the state's DBE certification program. As is required under 49 C.F.R. § 26.81, Oklahoma

7. *Id.* § 150: 155-1-3; Okla. Stat. tit. 74, § 85.45j.11 (2023).
8. Okla. Admin. Code § 150: 155-1-5 (2022).
9. *74 O.S. § 85.44E. Disabled Veterans Enterprise Act*, Okla. Off. of Mgmt. & Enter. Serv., https://oklahoma.gov/omes/legal/statutes/74/85-44e.html (last visited Apr. 14, 2023).
10. Okla. Stat. tit. 74, § 85.44E (2023).

has a Unified Certification Program (UCP). The UCP makes all DBE certification decisions and provides a "one-stop shop" to DBE applicants.[11] To qualify as a DBE, a business must (1) be for-profit;[12] (2) be a small business concern—with "small" determined by the Small Business Administration (SBA) small business size standards—and does not exceed $30.40 million in gross annual receipts;[13] (3) be at least 51 percent owned by socially and economically disadvantaged individuals—there is a rebuttable presumption that women, Black Americans, Hispanic Americans, Native Americans, Asian-Pacific Americans, Subcontinent Asian Americans, or other minorities are disadvantaged;[14] (4) be controlled by one or more of the socially and economically disadvantaged owners;[15] (5) have the socially and economically disadvantaged owners be U.S. citizens or lawfully admitted permanent residents;[16] and (6) have the personal net worth for any socially and economically disadvantaged owner not exceed $1.32 million.[17] The DBE program is required on contracting opportunities that have received funding from the Federal Highway Administration (FHWA), Federal Aviation Administration (FAA), or Federal Transit Administration (FTA).[18]

- *Airport Concession Disadvantaged Business Enterprise (ACDBE) Program*: In addition to being certified as a DBE under 49 C.F.R. part 26, businesses may also be certified as an Airport Concession Disadvantaged Business Enterprise (ACDBE) under 49 C.F.R. part 23. To qualify as an ACDBE, a business must (1) be a concession for-profit small business concern;[19] (2) qualify as small by having its prior three-year average gross receipts not exceed the applicable size standard of $56.42 million;[20] (3) be 51 percent owned by one or more socially and economically

11. 49 C.F.R. § 26.81(b)(2) (2022).
12. *Id.* § 26.5 (2022).
13. *Id.* §§ 26.5, 26.65(b). It is worth noting that under 49 C.F.R. § 26.65(b), the DBE size standard may be adjusted annually for inflation such that in subsequent years the size standard may no longer be $30.40 million.
14. *Id.* § 26.67.
15. *Id.* § 26.5.
16. *Id.* § 26.67.
17. *Id.*
18. *Id.* § 26.21(a).
19. *Id.* § 23.3.
20. *Id.* § 23.33(a). The size standards for the following are exceptions to this: bank and financial institutions is $1 billion in assets; car rental companies are $75.23 million average annual gross receipts; pay telephones is 1,500 employees; and automobile dealers is 350 employees.

disadvantaged individuals;[21] (4) have one or more of the socially and economically disadvantaged individuals with control and managing the daily business operations;[22] and (5) have the personal net worth for any socially and economically disadvantaged owner not exceed $1.32 million.[23]

Procurement Laws Intersecting with Business Inclusion

In Oklahoma, contracting goals, preferences, or set-asides are not established for WBEs or diverse business enterprises. However, following are some laws and rules pertaining to service-disabled veteran businesses and businesses who are subcontractors.

- *Three-Point Bonus Preference*: "In awarding contracts for the performance of any job or service, all agencies, departments, institutions and other entities of this state and of each political subdivision of this state shall give a three-point bonus preference to service-disabled veteran businesses doing business as Oklahoma firms, corporations or individuals, or which maintain Oklahoma offices or places of business."[24]
- *Inclusion Goals*: There is a goal that 3 percent of contract opportunities from all agencies, departments, institutions, and other entities of the state are awarded to service-disabled veteran businesses.[25]
- *Prompt Payment to Subcontractors*: On construction contracts, a prime contractor must ". . . make payment to the subcontractor or material supplier no later than ten (10) calendar days after the prime contractor receives its corresponding payment for the work performed."[26]
- *Reporting Requirements*: "On or before September 1 of each year, each state entity shall submit an electronic report to the State Purchasing Director documenting all solicitations awarded by the state entity in the previous fiscal year. The State Purchasing Director will define the report format and content required to collect the service-disabled veteran business data."[27]

---

21. *Id.*
22. *Id.*
23. *Id.* § 23.35.
24. Okla. Stat. tit. 74, § 85.44E(C) (2023).
25. *Id.* § 85.44E(D)(1).
26. *Id.* § 61-224.
27. Okla. Admin. Code § 260:115-13-1(3) (2023).

Contracting opportunities where the ODOT DBE program applies have several requirements that intersect directly with procurement, contracting, and business inclusion.

- *Fostering Small Business Participation*: Pursuant to 49 C.F.R. § 26.39, ODOT has engaged in efforts to foster small business participation.[28] ODOT does not have a formal small business enterprise certification within its DBE program.[29] It did, however, launch a Small Enterprise Training (SET) program in 2021 "to facilitate increased participation in construction contracting opportunities by Oklahoma's small businesses."[30] In working to foster small business participation, ODOT does provide a waiver for prequalification of bidders seeking to perform as primes, when possible.[31] It also provides for bids on sections of road construction on specific scopes of work for surface treatment on roads in eight-mile or 20-mile segments if a particular contract opportunity is longer than either eight or 20 miles.[32]
- *Goals*: Contract opportunities may not use quotas or set-asides for DBEs.[33] The only exception for using a set-aside is in a limited or extreme circumstance, "when no other method could be reasonably expected to redress egregious instances of discrimination."[34] Instead, an overall goal must be set.[35] The goal must be based on evidence of available "ready, willing and able" DBEs in the market.[36] Once the assessment of "ready, willing and able" DBEs is completed, an overall goal may be established as a percentage of the total amount of contracts receiving U.S. Department of Transportation (U.S. DOT) funds.[37] Participation goals must be set for all certified DBEs and not divided into subcategories.[38] Race- and gender-neutral means must be used to "meet the maximum feasible portion of your overall goal."[39] ODOT, as a recipient of U.S. DOT funds, will not be penalized for failing to meet the overall goal set,

28. *DBE Program Manual*, OKLA. DEP'T OF TRANSP. 18 (2021), https://oklahoma.gov/content/dam/ok/en/odot/civil-rights/2021_DBE_Program_Manual.pdf.
29. *Id.*
30. *Id.* at 17.
31. *Id.*
32. *Id.*
33. 49 C.F.R. § 26.43 (2022).
34. *Id.*
35. *Id.* § 26.45(a)(1).
36. *Id.* § 26.45(b).
37. *Id.* § 26.45(e).
38. *Id.* § 26.45(h).
39. *Id.* § 26.51.

if it can establish good faith efforts to meet the goal.[40] When there is a DBE goal on a specific contract opportunity only the bidder meeting the goal, or establishing good faith efforts to meet the goal, may be awarded the contract.[41]

- *Prompt Payment*: Under 49 C.F.R. part 26, contractors must pay subcontractors within 30 days of receipt of payment from the state DOT for satisfactory performance.[42]
- *Payment of Retainage*: Contractors must pay amounts withheld for retainage to subcontractors within 30 days of their work being satisfactorily completed.[43]

Additional Related Laws, Policies, and Programs

- *Access to Capital*: Under § 74-5060.21, a Seed Capital Revolving Loan Fund was created to make investments in businesses in technology and involved in innovation. It is managed by an outside nonprofit partner, i2E, Inc. For more information, please visit https://oklahoma.gov/ocast/services/capital.html.
- *Technical Assistance*: The Oklahoma Department of Veteran Affairs has a Veteran Entrepreneur Program that provides veterans with resources and training opportunities. For additional information, please visit https://oklahoma.gov/veterans/veterans-services/okvetworks.html.
- *Finding Contracting Opportunities*: Contracting opportunities may be found on the Oklahoma Supplier Portal: https://oklahoma.gov/omes/services/purchasing/supplier-portal.html

Major City Snapshot: Tulsa

The City of Tulsa has a race- and gender-neutral Small Business Enterprise program. The authority for the program exists in title 5, section 100 of the Tulsa Revised Ordinances and Executive Order Number 2018-01 "Establishing the City of Tulsa Small Business Enterprise (SBE) Program and Establishing the SBE Oversight Committee." The Tulsa Authority for Economic Opportunity (TAEO) handles the administration of the SBE program.[44]

---

40. *Id.* § 26.47.
41. *Id.* § 26.53.
42. 49 C.F.R. § 26.29(a) (2023).
43. *Id.* § 26.29(b).
44. *Annual Report: Small Business Enterprise Program*, City of Tulsa 8 (2022), https://www.cityoftulsa.org/media/19934/2021-sbe-annual-report-final.pdf.

- *Certifications*: To satisfy the eligibility requirements for the SBE program a business must (1) be located in the Tulsa Metropolitan Statistical Area (Tulsa, Osage, Rogers, Pawnee, Wagoner, Creek, and Okmulgee Counties); (2) have adequate workforce to meet the contract performance requirements; (3) have the average annual gross receipts from the prior three years less than $5 million for construction industries and less than $3 million for all other industries; (4) not be dominant in its field of operation; (5) have owners and employees with the adequate training, expertise, and ability to perform the work required; (6) have owners and employees have the necessary licenses and certificates in their names; (7) be independently owned, operated, and controlled at a physical address in the Tulsa Metropolitan Statistical Area.[45]
- *Inclusion Goals*: The city has an overall SBE utilization goal of ". . . ten percent (10%) of all contracts and agreements for services, goods, supplies, and construction activities."[46]

45. Executive Order No. 2018-01 § 3 (Jan. 18, 2018), https://www.sos.ok.gov/documents/executive/1798.pdf.

46. *Id.* § 4.

CHAPTER 38

Oregon

Overview of Business Inclusion Program, Policies, and Practices

Government entities seeking to create business inclusion programs have two primary options in terms of the type of program they may create, in terms of who is eligible for the program: (1) a race- and gender-conscious program or (2) a race- and gender-neutral program. Under the Equal Protection Clause of the Fourteenth Amendment, strict scrutiny is applied by the courts when a government actor is creating policies based on race. Strict scrutiny is the highest level of judicial review that may be applied. It requires the government actor to demonstrate that (1) past discrimination exists such that the entity has a "compelling government interest" in rectifying it, and (2) the policies and programs created to do so are "narrowly tailored."[1] Although intermediate scrutiny is often applied when reviewing programs based on gender, strict scrutiny is applied when reviewing race- and gender-conscious business inclusion programs.[2] Disparity studies have become a standard tool used to assist a government entity in withstanding a challenge to its race- and gender-conscious business inclusion programs. These studies aid in demonstrating whether a government entity has engaged

1. City of Richmond v. J.A. Croson Co., 488 U.S. 469 (1989).

2. Since the 1980s with the Supreme Court decision in *City of Richmond v. J.A. Croson Company*, there have been a number of cases across the county that have assessed race- and gender-conscious business inclusion programs. *See* Adarand Constructors, Inc. v. Pena, 515 U.S. 200 (1995); Virdi v. DeKalb Cnty. Sch. Dist., 135 Fed. App'x 262, 268 (11th Cir. 2005); Sherbrooke Turf, Inc. v. Minn. Dep't of Transp., 345 F.3d 964, 971 (8th Cir. 2003); Mountain West Holding Co., Inc. v. The State of Montana, Montana DOT, et al., 2017 WL 2179120 (9th Cir. May 16, 2017).

in past discrimination in its contracting practices, such that the entity may have a compelling government interest in rectifying it.[3]

Conversely, race- and gender-neutral programs are programs that are not only accessible to minority-owned and women-owned businesses but to all businesses, regardless of race or gender. A small business inclusion program would fall into this category. The level of judicial review applied to such a policy to determine its constitutionality is rational basis, which is the lowest threshold for a government to satisfy. For a government entity to satisfy rational basis, the policy or program created must be "related to a legitimate government purpose."[4] Even when a government entity has a race- and gender-conscious program, oftentimes the program may still require the government actor to seek to meet the goals of their program through race- and gender-neutral means where able, so as to be taking the most narrowly tailored means of accomplishing the program goals.

In the state of Oregon, at the state level of government, there is one state agency that certifies businesses for business inclusion programs: the Oregon Certification Office for Business Inclusion and Diversity (COBID).

Summary of Certification Programs and Requirements

COBID certifies the following type of businesses: (1) state programs include Minority Business Enterprise (MBE), Women Business Enterprise (WBE), Service-Disabled Business Enterprise (SDVBE), Emerging Small Business (ESB); and (2) federal programs include Disadvantaged Business Enterprises (DBEs) and Airport Concession Disadvantaged Business Enterprises (ACDBEs).[5] Although the DBE and ACDBE programs are managed by the Oregon Department of Transportation (ODOT), the certification is managed by COBID. The eligibility requirements for all certifications follow:

- *Minority Business Enterprise (MBE)*: A business must (1) be a small business concern as defined by the U.S. Small Business Administration (SBA) under 13 C.F.R. part 121;[6] (2) be at least

---

3. *Promoting Opportunity and Equality in America: A Guide to Federal Circuit Authority on Permissible Government Actions to Promote Racial and Gender Equality*, Am. Civ. Liberties Union & The Opportunity Agenda (Dec. 2010), https://www.aclu.org/sites/default/files/field_document/Promoting_Opportunity_and_Equality_in_America.pdf.

4. 488 U.S. 469 (1989).

5. *Certification Office for Business Inclusion and Diversity (COBID)*, State of Or., https://www.oregon.gov/biz/programs/COBID/Pages/default.aspx (last visited Apr. 17, 2023).

6. Or. Rev. Stat. § 200.005(10) (2022).

51 percent owned and controlled by one or more minorities (or they own 51 percent of the stock in the case of a corporation), which includes Black Americans, Hispanic Americans, Native Americans, Asian-Pacific Americans, Subcontinent Asian Americans, other groups designated as socially disadvantaged by the SBA; or "[o]ther minority group membership as established by the applicant . . . based on evidence provided by the applicant . . .";[7] (3) have qualifying owners who are U.S citizens or lawful permanent residents;[8] (4) have owners who have made a capital contribution;[9] (5) be for-profit;[10] and (6) be registered with the Oregon Secretary of State.[11] Owners "must possess sufficient knowledge, managerial and technical competence, and experience . . . ," which may be evidence by such factors including but not limited to holding a current license essential to their field.[12] In terms of the control of the business by qualifying owners, it must also include management of the day-to-day operations of the business.[13]

- *Women Business Enterprise (WBE)*: A business must (1) be a small business concern as defined by the SBA under 13 C.F.R. part 121;[14] (2) be at least 51 percent owned and controlled by one or more women (or they own 51 percent of the stock in the case of a corporation);[15] (3) have qualifying owners who are U.S. citizens or lawful permanent residents;[16] (4) have owners who have made a capital contribution;[17] (5) be for-profit;[18] and (6) be registered with the Oregon Secretary of State.[19] Owners "must possess sufficient knowledge, managerial and technical competence, and experience. . . ," which may be evidence

7. *Id.* § 200.005(7); Or. Admin. R. 123-200-1100(10) (2022).
8. Or. Admin. R. 123-200-1100(10) (2022).
9. *Id.* 123-200-1220(6).
10. *Id.* 123-200-1600(3)(a); *Qualifications by Certification Program*, Certification Off. for Bus. Inclusion & Diversity, https://www.oregon.gov/biz/programs/COBID/Pages/program-qualifications.aspx (last visited Apr. 17, 2023); *Minority/Women Business Enterprise (MBE/WBE) Certification*, Certification Off. for Bus. Inclusion & Diversity, https://www.oregon.gov/biz/programs/COBID/MBE-WBE/Pages/default.aspx (last visited Apr. 17, 2023).
11. Or. Admin. R. 123-200-1600(3)(a) (2022); *Qualifications by Certification Program*, *supra* note 10; *Minority/Women Business Enterprise (MBE/WBE) Certification*, *supra* note 10.
12. Or. Admin. R. 123-200-1240 (2022).
13. *Id.* 123-200-1240.
14. Or. Rev. Stat. § 200.005(10) (2022).
15. *Id.* § 200.005(7); Or. Admin. R. 123-200-1100(19) (2022).
16. Or. Rev. Stat. § 200.005(16) (2022).
17. Or. Admin. R. 123-200-1220(6) (2022).
18. *Id.* 123-200-1600(3)(a); *Qualifications by Certification Program*, *supra* note 10; *Minority/Women Business Enterprise (MBE/WBE) Certification*, *supra* note 10.
19. Or. Admin. R. 123-200-1600(3)(a) (2022); *Qualifications by Certification Program*, *supra* note 10; *Minority/Women Business Enterprise (MBE/WBE) Certification*, *supra* note 10.

by such factors including but not limited to holding a current license essential to their field.[20] In terms of the control of the business by qualifying owners, it must also include management of the day-to-day operations of the business.[21]

- *Service-Disabled Veteran Business Enterprise (SDVBE)*: A business must (1) be a small business concern as defined by the SBA under 13 C.F.R. part 121;[22] (2) be at least 51 percent owned and controlled by one or more service-disabled veterans (or they own 51 percent of the stock in the case of a corporation);[23] (3) have qualifying owners who are U.S. citizens or lawful permanent residents;[24] (4) have owners who have made a capital contribution;[25] (5) be for-profit;[26] and (6) be registered with the Oregon Secretary of State.[27] Owners "must possess sufficient knowledge, managerial and technical competence, and experience. . . ," which may be evidence by such factors including but not limited to holding a current license essential to their field.[28] In terms of the control of the business by qualifying owners, it must also include management of the day-to-day operations of the business.[29]
- *Emerging Small Business (ESB)*: To be eligible for this race- and gender-neutral program, a business must (1) be for-profit;[30] (2) be registered with the Oregon Secretary of State;[31] (3) have a principal place of business located in Oregon;[32] (4) not be a subsidiary or parent company where collectively the business would not qualify;[33] (5) have annual gross receipts averaged over three years that do not exceed the size limits set by

---

20. Or. Admin. R. 123-200-1240 (2022).
21. *Id.*
22. Or. Rev. Stat. § 200.005(10) (2022).
23. *Id.* § 200.005(7).
24. *Service Disabled Veteran (SDV) Certification*, Certification Off. for Bus. Inclusion & Diversity, https://www.oregon.gov/biz/programs/COBID/SDV/Pages/default.aspx (last visited Apr. 17, 2023).
25. Or. Admin. R. 123-200-1220(6) (2022).
26. *Id.* 123-200-1600(3)(a); *Qualifications by Certification Program, supra* note 10; *Service Disabled Veteran (SDV) Certification, supra* note 24.
27. Or. Admin. R. 123-200-1600(3)(a) (2022); *Qualifications by Certification Program, supra* note 10; *Service Disabled Veteran (SDV) Certification, supra* note 24.
28. Or. Admin. R. 123-200-1240 (2022).
29. *Id.*
30. *Id.* 123-200-1600(3)(a); *Qualifications by Certification Program, supra* note 10; *Emerging Small Business (ESB) Certification*, Certification Off. for Bus. Inclusion & Diversity, https://www.oregon.gov/biz/programs/COBID/ESB/Pages/default.aspx (last visited Apr. 17, 2023).
31. Or. Admin. R. 123-200-1600(3)(a) (2022); *Qualifications by Certification Program, supra* note 10; *Emerging Small Business (ESB) Certification, supra* note 30.
32. Or. Admin. R. 123-200-1600(3)(b) (2022).
33. *Id.* 123-200-1600(3)(d).

COBID;[34] (6) have owners who possess any particular licenses or credential to own or control their business, if it is needed;[35] (7) have owner/owners working at least 20 hours per week for the business;[36] have the required number of employees to qualify for either tier 1 (19 or fewer full-time employees) or tier 2 (29 or fewer full-time employees).[37]

- *Disadvantaged Business Enterprise (DBE)*: To qualify as a DBE, a business must (1) be for-profit;[38] (2) be a small business concern—with "small" determined by the Small Business Administration (SBA) small business size standards—and does not exceed $30.40 million in gross annual receipts;[39] (3) be at least 51 percent owned by socially and economically disadvantaged individuals—there is a rebuttable presumption that women, Black Americans, Hispanic Americans, Native Americans, Asian-Pacific Americans, Subcontinent Asian Americans, or other minorities are disadvantaged;[40] (4) be controlled by one or more of the socially and economically disadvantaged owners;[41] (5) have the socially and economically disadvantaged owners be U.S. citizens or lawfully admitted permanent residents;[42] and (6) have the personal net worth for any socially and economically disadvantaged owner not exceed $1.32 million.[43] The DBE program is required on contracting opportunities that have received funding from the Federal Highway Administration (FHWA), Federal Aviation Administration (FAA), or Federal Transit Administration (FTA).[44]
- *Airport Concession Disadvantaged Business Enterprise (ACDBE)*: In addition to being certified as a DBE under 49 C.F.R. part 26, businesses may also be certified as an Airport Concession Disadvantaged Business Enterprise (ACDBE) under 49 C.F.R. part 23. To qualify as an ACDBE, a business must (1) be a concession for-profit small business concern;[45] (2) qualify as small by

34. *Id.* 123-200-1600(3)(e).
35. *Id.* 123-200-1600(3)(f).
36. *Id.* 123-200-1600(3)(g).
37. *Id.* 123-200-1600(3)(h).
38. 49 C.F.R. § 26.5 (2022).
39. *Id.* §§ 26.5, 26.65(b). It is worth noting that under 49 C.F.R. § 26.65(b), the DBE size standard may be adjusted annually for inflation such that in subsequent years the size standard may no longer be $30.40 million.
40. *Id.* § 26.67.
41. *Id.* § 26.5.
42. *Id.* § 26.67.
43. *Id.*
44. *Id.* § 26.21(a).
45. *Id.* § 23.3.

having its prior three-year average gross receipts not exceed the applicable size standard of $56.42 million;[46] (3) be 51 percent owned by one or more socially and economically disadvantaged individuals;[47] (4) have one or more of the socially and economically disadvantaged individuals with control and managing the daily business operations;[48] and (5) have the personal net worth for any socially and economically disadvantaged owner not exceed $1.32 million.[49]

Procurement Laws Intersecting with Business Inclusion

In the state of Oregon, the Department of Administrative Services (DAS) handles all contracting for the state.[50] Following are some of the relevant laws at the intersection of procurement and business inclusion programs. It is worth noting that the State of Oregon's Department of Administrative Services has started conducting a disparity study, set to end late 2023, that may impact programs, policies, rules, and laws.[51]

- *Contractor Good Faith Efforts*: "If a public contract requires participation from a required participant [disadvantaged business enterprise, minority-owned business, a woman-owned business or a business that a service-disabled veteran owns, or an emerging small business] and a bidder or proposer for the public contract is not a required participant, a contracting agency may award the public contract to the bidder or proposer only if the bidder or proposer: (a) Demonstrates that the bidder or proposer is responsible; and (b) Has made good faith efforts to encourage required participants to participate in the public contract."[52]
- *Subcontracting to ESBs or SDVBE*: "A contracting agency may require a contractor to subcontract some part of a contract to, or to obtain materials for use in performing the contract from,

46. *Id.* § 23.33(a). The size standards for the following are exceptions to this: bank and financial institutions is $1 billion in assets; car rental companies are $75.23 million average annual gross receipts; pay telephones is 1,500 employees; and automobile dealers is 350 employees.

47. *Id.*

48. *Id.*

49. *Id.* § 23.35.

50. *Determine Authority*, Or. Dep't of Admin. Servs., https://www.oregon.gov/das/OPM/Pages/authority.aspx (last visited Apr. 17, 2023).

51. *Disparity Study*, Or. Dep't of Admin. Servs., https://www.oregon.gov/das/pages/disparity-study.aspx (last visited Apr. 17, 2023).

52. Or. Rev. Stat. § 200.045 (2022).

a business that is certified under ORS 200.055 as an emerging small business or as a business that a service-disabled veteran owns."[53]

- *Limited Competition*: Although a specific contracting goal is not specified under statute for MBEs, WBEs, ESBs, or SDVBEs, under state statute it does note that "[t]he provisions of the Public Contracting Code may not be construed to prohibit a contracting agency from engaging in public contracting practices designed to promote affirmative action goals, policies or programs for disadvantaged or minority groups or to give a preference in awarding public contracts to disabled veterans. . . . In carrying out an affirmative action goal, policy or program, a contracting agency by appropriate ordinance, resolution or rule may limit competition for a public contract for goods and services, or for any other public contract estimated to cost $50,000 or less, to contracting entities owned or controlled by persons described in subsection (1) of this section."[54]
- *Payment to Subcontractors*: State law requires contractors to pay their subcontractors on construction contracts within ten days after receiving the request.[55] Although not specific to only MBEs, WBEs, ESBs, and/or SDVBEs, these smaller businesses may be in subcontracting roles, and prompt payment can be critical to the cash flow for a small business.
- *Reporting Requirements*: Twice a year, a committee appointed by the Oregon Transportation Committee must report on its efforts pertaining to emerging small businesses.[56]

Contracting opportunities where the ODOT DBE program applies have several requirements that intersect directly with procurement, contracting, and business inclusion.

- *Fostering Small Business Participation*: Pursuant to 49 C.F.R. § 26.39, ODOT has engaged in efforts to foster small business participation.[57] Such efforts include but are not limited to the following: "(1) ODOT Small Contracting Program, (2) Small

53. *Id.* § 279A.105.
54. *Id.* § 279A.100.
55. *Id.* § 279C.570.
56. *Id.* § 200.160.
57. *Disadvantaged Business Enterprise (DBE) Program Plan*, Or. Dep't of Transp. 4-14 (Sept. 2012), https://www.oregon.gov/ODOT/Business/OCR/Documents/DBE_Program_Plan_2012_09_17.pdf.

Business Supportive Services, and (3) [Nonbundling] Contract Practices."[58]

- *Goals*: Contract opportunities may not use quotas or set-asides for DBEs.[59] The only exception for using a set-aside is in a limited or extreme circumstance, "when no other method could be reasonably expected to redress egregious instances of discrimination."[60] Instead, an overall goal must be set.[61] The goal must be based on evidence of available "ready, willing and able" DBEs in the market.[62] Once the assessment of "ready, willing and able" DBEs is completed, an overall goal may be established as a percentage of the total amount of contracts receiving U.S. Department of Transportation (U.S. DOT) funds.[63] Participation goals must be set for all certified DBEs and not divided into subcategories.[64] Race- and gender-neutral means must be used to "meet the maximum feasible portion of your overall goal."[65] ODOT, as a recipient of U.S. DOT funds, will not be penalized for failing to meet the overall goal set, if it can establish good faith efforts to meet the goal.[66] When there is a DBE goal on a specific contract opportunity, only the bidder meeting the goal, or establishing good faith efforts to meet the goal, may be awarded the contract.[67]
- *Prompt Payment*: Under 49 C.F.R. part 26, contractors must pay subcontractors within 30 days of receipt of payment from the state DOT for satisfactory performance.[68]
- *Payment of Retainage*: Contractors must pay amounts withheld for retainage to subcontractors within 30 days of their work being satisfactorily completed.[69]

Additional Related Laws, Policies, and Programs

- *Access to Capital*: Under the Oregon Revised Statues 285B.740 to 285B.758, it provides the authority for the creation of the

58. *Id.*
59. 49 C.F.R. § 26.43 (2022).
60. *Id.*
61. *Id.* § 26.45(a)(1).
62. *Id.* § 26.45(b).
63. *Id.* § 26.45(e).
64. *Id.* § 26.45(h).
65. *Id.* § 26.51.
66. *Id.* § 26.47.
67. *Id.* § 26.53.
68. 49 C.F.R. § 26.29(a) (2023).
69. *Id.* § 26.29(b).

Entrepreneurial Development Loan Fund. "The intent of the Entrepreneurial Development Loan Fund is to provide direct loans to help start-ups, micro-enterprises and small businesses expand, become established, and/or retain operations in Oregon."[70] For more information, please visit https://www.oregon.gov/biz/programs/EDLF/Pages/default.aspx.

- *Finding Contracting Opportunities*: Contracting opportunities may be found on the state's e-Procurement system, OregonBuys: https://oregonbuys.gov/bso/.

Major City Snapshot: Portland

The City of Portland (city) has a Subcontractor Equity Program (Program) that applies to all city-owned and all city-sponsored projects $150,000 or more.[71]

- *Certifications*: For the program, the city looks to provide opportunities for businesses certified as DBEs, MBEs, WBEs, ESBs, and SDVBEs by COBID.[72]
- *Inclusion Goals*: There is a 20 percent of hard construction costs aspiration goal for the program.[73] There is a desired 14 percent goal for utilization of D/M/WBEs.[74]
- *Utilization Plans*: A utilization plan must be submitted within the time specified for the bid to be considered responsive.[75]
- *Reporting Requirements*: The prime contractor and subcontractors must engage in compliance reporting under this program.[76]
- *Penalties*: "A Contractor's failure to comply with the Subcontractor Equity Program may result in a breach of contract, possible disqualification of the Contractor's ability to bid on or receive future contracts . . . and/or the assessment of penalties."[77]

---

70. Or. Admin. R. 123-019-0000 (2023).
71. *Subcontractor Equity Program*, City of Portland 1 (2020), https://www.portland.gov/sites/default/files/2021/sep-subcontractor-equity-program-rev-aug-2020.pdf.
72. *Id.*
73. *Id.*
74. *Id.*
75. *Id.* at 2.
76. *Id.* at 1.
77. *Id.* at 4.

CHAPTER 39

Pennsylvania

Overview of Business Inclusion Program, Policies, and Practices

Government entities seeking to create business inclusion programs have two primary options in terms of the type of program they may create, in terms of who is eligible for the program: (1) a race- and gender-conscious program or (2) a race- and gender-neutral program. Under the Equal Protection Clause of the Fourteenth Amendment, strict scrutiny is applied by the courts when a government actor is creating policies based on race. Strict scrutiny is the highest level of judicial review that may be applied. It requires the government actor to demonstrate that (1) past discrimination exists such that the entity has a "compelling government interest" in rectifying it, and (2) the policies and programs created to do so are "narrowly tailored."[1] Although intermediate scrutiny is often applied when reviewing programs based on gender, strict scrutiny is applied when reviewing race- and gender-conscious business inclusion programs.[2] Disparity studies have become a standard tool used to assist a government entity in withstanding a challenge to its race- and gender-conscious business inclusion programs. These studies aid in demonstrating whether a government entity has engaged

1. City of Richmond v. J.A. Croson Co., 488 U.S. 469 (1989).

2. Since the 1980s with the Supreme Court decision in *City of Richmond v. J.A. Croson Company*, there have been a number of cases across the county that have assessed race- and gender-conscious business inclusion programs. *See* Adarand Constructors, Inc. v. Pena, 515 U.S. 200 (1995); Virdi v. DeKalb Cnty. Sch. Dist., 135 Fed. App'x 262, 268 (11th Cir. 2005); Sherbrooke Turf, Inc. v. Minn. Dep't of Transp., 345 F.3d 964, 971 (8th Cir. 2003); Mountain West Holding Co., Inc. v. The State of Montana, Montana DOT, et al., 2017 WL 2179120 (9th Cir. May 16, 2017).

in past discrimination in its contracting practices, such that the entity may have a compelling government interest in rectifying it.[3]

Conversely, race- and gender-neutral programs are programs that are not only accessible to minority-owned and women-owned businesses but to all businesses, regardless of race or gender. A small business inclusion program would fall into this category. The level of judicial review applied to such a policy to determine its constitutionality is rational basis, which is the lowest threshold for a government to satisfy. For a government entity to satisfy rational basis, the policy or program created must be "related to a legitimate government purpose."[4] Even when a government entity has a race- and gender-conscious program, oftentimes the program may still require the government actor to seek to meet the goals of their program through race- and gender-neutral means where able, so as to be taking the most narrowly tailored means of accomplishing the program goals.

In the state of Pennsylvania, at the state level of government, there are two state agencies certifying businesses for business inclusion programs: (1) Department of General Services, Bureau of Diversity, Inclusion and Small Business Opportunities (BDISBO)[5] and (2) the Pennsylvania Department of Transportation, Bureau of Equal Opportunity (PennDOT).[6]

Summary of Certification Programs and Requirements

BDISBO provides for self-certification and engages in a Small Diverse Business verification process through the verification of third-party certifications for the following types of business certifications for its Small Business Contracting Program for Small Diverse Business Status: (1) Minority Business Enterprise (MBE), (2) Woman Business Enterprise (WBE), (3) Veteran-Owned Small Business Enterprise (VBE), (4) Service-Disabled Veteran-Owned Small Business Enterprise (SDVBE), (5) Disability-Owned Business Enterprise (DOBE), and (6) LGBT Business

3. *Promoting Opportunity and Equality in America: A Guide to Federal Circuit Authority on Permissible Government Actions to Promote Racial and Gender Equality*, Am. Civ. Liberties Union & The Opportunity Agenda (Dec. 2010), https://www.aclu.org/sites/default/files/field_document/Promoting_Opportunity_and_Equality_in_America.pdf.

4. 488 U.S. 469 (1989).

5. *Bureau of Diversity, Inclusion, and Small Business Opportunities*, Pa. Dep't of Gen. Servs., https://www.dgs.pa.gov/Small%20Diverse%20Business%20Program/Pages/default.aspx (last visited Mar. 23, 2023).

6. *Disadvantaged Business Enterprise (DBE)*, Pa. Dep't of Transp., https://www.penndot.pa.gov/about-us/EqualEmployment/Pages/Disadvantaged-Business-Enterprise.aspx (last visited Mar. 24, 2023).

Enterprise (LGBTBE).[7] All businesses must first meet the definition for a "small business," defined as (1) a for-profit business in the United States; (2) independently owned; (3) not dominant in its field of operation; (4) employs no more than 100 employees; (5) has annual gross revenues less than $20 million "($25 million in gross annual revenues for those businesses in the information technology sales or information technology service business and $7 million in gross annual revenues for those businesses performing building design services)."[8] The remaining eligibility requirements for all follow:

- *Minority Business Enterprise (MBE)*: To satisfy the eligibility criteria to be certified as an MBE, a business must be (1) a small business; (2) at least 51 percent owned by one or more minorities (African Americans, Hispanic Americans, Native Americans, Asian Americans, Alaskans or Pacific Islanders) or at least 51 percent of the stock of a corporation owned by one or more minorities; and (3) controlled by one or more minorities.[9]
- *Woman Business Enterprise (WBE)*: To satisfy the eligibility criteria to be certified as a WBE, a business must be (1) a small business; (2) at least 51 percent owned by one or more women or at least 51 percent of the stock of a corporation owned by one or more women; and (3) controlled by one or more women.[10]
- *Veteran-Owned Small Business Enterprise (VBE)*: To satisfy the eligibility criteria to be certified as a VBE, a business must be (1) a small business; (2) at least 51 percent owned by one or more veterans or at least 51 percent of the stock of a corporation owned by one or more veterans; and (3) controlled by one or more veterans.[11] A veteran is defined as "[o]ne of the following: (i) A person who served on active duty in the United States Armed Forces, including the Reserve and National Guard, who was discharged or released from service under honorable conditions. (ii) A Reservist or member of the National Guard who completed an initial term of enlistment or qualifying period of service. (iii) A Reservist or member of the National Guard who was disabled in the line of duty during training."[12]

---

7. *Small Diverse Businesses*, Dep't of Gen. Servs., https://www.dgs.pa.gov/Small%20Diverse%20Business%20Program/Small-Diverse-Business-Verification/Pages/default.aspx (last visited Mar. 23, 2023).
8. Pa. Code § 58.302 (2023).
9. 62 Pa. Cons. Stat. § 2201 (2023); 4 Pa. Code § 58.302 (2023).
10. 62 Pa. Cons. Stat. § 2201 (2023); 4 Pa. Code § 58.302 (2023).
11. 62 Pa. Cons. Stat. § 2201 (2023); 4 Pa. Code § 58.302 (2023).
12. 4 Pa. Code § 58.302 (2023).

- *Service-Disabled Veteran-Owned Small Business Enterprise (SDVBE)*: To satisfy the eligibility criteria to be certified as an SDVBE, a business must be (1) a small business; (2) at least 51 percent owned by one or more service-disabled veterans; and (3) controlled by one or more service-disabled veterans.[13] When the service-disabled veteran has a permanent or severe disability, the spouse or permanent caregiver of the service-disabled veteran may control the business.[14] A service-disabled veteran is defined as "[a] veteran who possesses either a disability rating letter issued by the United States Department of Veterans Affairs or a disability determination from the United States Department of Defense."[15]
- *Disability-Owned Business Enterprise (DOBE)*: To satisfy the eligibility criteria to be certified as a DOBE, a business must be (1) a small business; (2) at least 51 percent owned by one or more persons with disabilities or at least 51 percent of the stock of a corporation owned by one or more persons with disabilities; and (3) controlled by one or more persons with disabilities.[16]
- *LGBT Business Enterprise (LGBTBE)*: To satisfy the eligibility criteria to be certified as an LGBTBE, a business must be (1) a small business; (2) at least 51 percent owned by one or more lesbian, gay, bisexual, or transgender (LGBT) persons or at least 51 percent of the stock of a corporation owned by one or more LGBT persons; and (3) controlled by one or more LGBT persons.[17]

PennDOT administers the Disadvantaged Business Enterprise (DBE) program, Airport Concession Disadvantaged Business Enterprise (ACDBE) program, and the Small Business Participation (SBP) program.

- *Disadvantaged Business Enterprise (DBE) Program*: Pursuant to 49 C.F.R. part 26, PennDOT administers the state's DBE certification program. As is required under 49 C.F.R. § 26.81, Pennsylvania has a Unified Certification Program (PA UCP). The PA UCP makes all DBE certification decisions and provides a "one-stop shop" to DBE applicants.[18] To qualify as a DBE, a business must (1) be for-profit;[19] (2) be a small busi-

13. *Id.*
14. *Id.*
15. *Id.*
16. *Id.*
17. *Id.*
18. 49 C.F.R. § 26.81(b)(2) (2022).
19. *Id.* § 26.5.

ness concern—with "small" determined by the Small Business Administration (SBA) small business size standards—and does not exceed $30.40 million in gross annual receipts;[20] (3) be at least 51 percent owned by socially and economically disadvantaged individuals—there is a rebuttable presumption that women, Black Americans, Hispanic Americans, Native Americans, Asian-Pacific Americans, Subcontinent Asian Americans, or other minorities are disadvantaged;[21] (4) be controlled by one or more of the socially and economically disadvantaged owners;[22] (5) have the socially and economically disadvantaged owners be U.S. citizens or lawfully admitted permanent residents;[23] and (6) have the personal net worth for any socially and economically disadvantaged owner not exceed $1.32 million.[24] The DBE program is required on contracting opportunities that have received funding from the Federal Highway Administration (FHWA), Federal Aviation Administration (FAA), or Federal Transit Administration (FTA).[25]

- *Airport Concession Disadvantaged Business Enterprise (ACDBE) Program*: In addition to being certified as a DBE under 49 C.F.R. part 26, businesses may also be certified as an Airport Concession Disadvantaged Business Enterprise (ACDBE) under 49 C.F.R. part 23. To qualify as an ACDBE, a business must (1) be a concession for-profit small business concern;[26] (2) qualify as small by having its prior three-year average gross receipts not exceed the applicable size standard of $56.42 million;[27] (3) be 51 percent owned by one or more socially and economically disadvantaged individuals;[28] (4) have one or more of the socially and economically disadvantaged individuals with control and managing the daily business operations;[29] and (5) have

20. *Id.* §§ 26.5, 26.65(b). It is worth noting that under 49 C.F.R. § 26.65(b), the DBE size standard may be adjusted annually for inflation such that in subsequent years the size standard may no longer be $30.40 million.

21. *Id.* § 26.67.

22. *Id.* § 26.5.

23. *Id.* § 26.67.

24. *Id.*

25. *Id.* § 26.21(a).

26. *Id.* § 23.3.

27. *Id.* § 23.33(a). The size standards for the following are exceptions to this: bank and financial institutions is $1 billion in assets; car rental companies are $75.23 million average annual gross receipts; pay telephones is 1,500 employees; and automobile dealers is 350 employees.

28. *Id.*

29. *Id.*

the personal net worth for any socially and economically disadvantaged owner not exceed $1.32 million.[30]

- *Small Business Enterprise (SBE)Program*: PennDOT has implemented a small business element within its DBE program pursuant to 49 C.F.R. § 26.39.[31] To be eligible for the program, a business must be "(1) A for-profit business, owned by a [United States] citizen or lawfully admitted permanent resident of the [United States]; (2) A firm that does not exceed the [SBA's] size standards; (3) A firm whose average annual gross receipts for the three previous fiscal years does not exceed $28.48 million [or the current size standard set under 49 C.F.R. §26.65 that may be adjusted annually for inflation]; and (4) A [United States] citizen or lawfully admitted permanent resident with a personal net worth that does not exceed $1.32 million."[32]

Procurement Laws Intersecting with Business Inclusion

In Pennsylvania, procurement laws may be found in title 62. Business inclusion-related laws may also be found in title 62 as well as regulations in the Pennsylvania Code title 4, chapter 58. In 2022, "Bureau of Procurement Policy Directive 2020-1" was revised and a memorandum issued that included language to revise the Procurement Code, Procurement Handbook, and relevant business-inclusion laws and policies to align with and/or advance recommendations in Pennsylvania's most recent statewide disparity study.[33] Advancement of such recommendations may alter laws and policies over time. Following are some laws that pertain to small, diverse, and veteran-owned businesses.

- *Bidding Specifications*: In the 2022 revised "Bureau of Procurement Policy Directive 2020-1" it notes that each solicitation that has a contract-specific goal should note this in the solicitation, along with any terms, conditions, or related forms required.[34]

---

30. *Id.* § 23.35.

31. *Disadvantaged Business Enterprise Program Plan*, PA. DEP'T OF TRANSP. 23, https://www.dot.state.pa.us/public/PubsForms/Publications/PUB%20404.pdf (last visited Mar. 23, 2023).

32. *Small Business Enterprise (SBE)*, PA. DEP'T OF TRANSP., https://www.penndot.pa.gov/about-us/EqualEmployment/Pages/Small-Business-Enterprise-(SBE).aspx (last visited Mar. 23, 2023).

33. *Bureau of Procurement Policy Directive 2020-1* (Apr. 20, 2022), https://www.dgs.pa.gov/Documents/Procurement%20Forms/BOP%20Policy%20Directive/BOP%20Revised%20Policy%20Directive%202020-1%204.20.2022.pdf.

34. *Id.* at 17.

- *Utilization Plans and Contractor Good Faith Efforts*: In the 2022 revised "Bureau of Procurement Policy Directive 2020-1" it notes that when there is a contract-specific goal, a bidder must submit an SDB Participation Submittal where they identify (1) their agreement to meet the goal; (2) their agreement to meet part of the goal and a request for a partial waiver and submit good faith efforts regarding the unmet portion of the goal; or (3) a full waiver from the goals and good faith efforts documentation.[35] Failure to submit the appropriate documentation may result in the bid or proposal being nonresponsive.[36]
- *Inclusion Goals*: There is an overall aspirational target of 26.3 percent for Small Diverse Businesses and 4.6 percent for Veteran Business Enterprises.[37] In addition, there are contract-specific narrowly tailored goals that are set based on factors such as "scope of work, geographic location for the work, the availability of SDB or VBE firms, and SDB and VBE utilization on prior similar contracts."[38]
- *Reducing Bonding Level*: "[A] purchasing agency may reduce the level or change the types of bonding normally required or accept alternative forms of security to the extent reasonably necessary to encourage procurement from small and disadvantaged businesses."[39]
- *Progress Payments*: "[A] purchasing agency may make special provisions for progress payments as it deems reasonably necessary to encourage procurement from small and disadvantaged businesses."[40]
- *Liquidated Damages*: "[A] prime contractor's failure to meet the SDB commitments may result in the imposition of sanctions as set forth in Section XVIII(d) of this policy, Section 531 of the Commonwealth Procurement Code, (62 Pa. C.S. § 531), and any additional sanctions available under the contract."[41]
- *Small Business Set-Asides*: As a race- and gender-neutral method, through the Small Business Reserve Program state agencies may set aside procurements for award only to small

---

35. *Id.*
36. *Id.*
37. *Id.* at 1.
38. *Id.*
39. 62 Pa. Cons. Stat. § 2105 (2023).
40. *Id.*
41. *Bureau of Procurement Policy Directive 2020-1*, *supra* note 33, at 18.

businesses.[42] In addition, there is a goal for the state in achieving a 15 percent spend with Pennsylvania certified small businesses.[43]

- *Reporting Requirements*: Annually, the Department of General Services must report to the General Assembly regarding contract awards to small and disadvantaged businesses.[44]

Contracting opportunities through PennDOT have several requirements that intersect directly with procurement, contracting, and business inclusion.

- *Diverse Business Program*: On public transportation projects that are 100 percent state funded, 74 Pennsylvania Consolidated Statutes section 303 (which focuses on diverse business participation) applies for certain contracting entities. They must "seek to maximize participation by diverse businesses."[45] Solicitations for competitive contracting opportunities for which this statute applies must provide notice to bidders that they must document and provide good faith efforts to solicit bids from diverse businesses and within seven days of being declared the low bidder or successful offeror they must provide the name(s) and address/addresses of each subcontractor that is a diverse business.[46] Failure to comply with this statute may result in sanctions or debarment of a business.[47]
- *Fostering Small Business Participation*: As noted earlier, PennDOT has an SBE program, pursuant to 49 C.F.R. § 26.39 to foster small business participation. To accomplish this, PennDOT engages in a number of activates, including but not limited to the following: (1) collect data and produce reports on SBE participation; (2) encourage prime contractors to use SBEs as subcontractors; and (3) maintain a list of prime contractors that are certified SBEs.[48] In addition, in 2018, PennDOT

42. *Bureau of Procurement Policy Directive 2020-1*, *supra* note 33; *Small Business Reserve Program*, DEP'T OF GEN. SERVS. (Dec. 26, 2019), https://www.dgs.pa.gov/Small%20Diverse%20Business%20Program/Documents/SBR%20FAQs.pdf.
43. *Id.*
44. 62 PA. CONS. STAT. § 2107 (2023).
45. 74 PA. CONS. STAT. § 303 (2023).
46. *Id.*
47. *Id.*
48. *Disadvantaged Business Enterprise Program Plan*, *supra* note 31.

introduced a Small Business Set-Aside pilot program for SBEs to increase contract participation for SBEs.[49]

- *Goals*: Contract opportunities may not use quotas or set-asides for DBEs.[50] The only exception for using a set-aside is in a limited or extreme circumstance, "when no other method could be reasonably expected to redress egregious instances of discrimination."[51] Instead, an overall goal must be set.[52] The goal must be based on evidence of available "ready, willing and able" DBEs in the market.[53] Once the assessment of "ready, willing and able" DBEs is completed, an overall goal may be established as a percentage of the total amount of contracts receiving U.S. Department of Transportation (U.S. DOT) funds.[54] Participation goals must be set for all certified DBEs and not divided into subcategories.[55] Race- and gender-neutral means must be used to "meet the maximum feasible portion of your overall goal."[56] PennDOT, as a recipient of U.S. DOT funds, will not be penalized for failing to meet the overall goal set, if it can establish good faith efforts to meet the goal.[57] When there is a DBE goal on a specific contract opportunity only the bidder meeting the goal, or establishing good faith efforts to meet the goal, may be awarded the contract.[58]
- *Prompt Payment*: Under 49 C.F.R. part 26, contractors must pay subcontractors within 30 days of receipt of payment from the state DOT for satisfactory performance.[59]
- *Payment of Retainage*: Contractors must pay amounts withheld for retainage to subcontractors within 30 days of their work being satisfactorily completed.[60]

---

49. *Small Business Set-Aside Pilot Program*, Pa. Dep't of Transp., https://www.penndot.pa.gov/about-us/EqualEmployment/Pages/Small-Business-Set-Aside-Pilot-Program.aspx (last visited Mar. 23, 2023).

50. 49 C.F.R. § 26.43 (2022).

51. *Id.*

52. *Id.* § 26.45(a)(1).

53. *Id.* § 26.45(b).

54. *Id.* § 26.45(e).

55. *Id.* § 26.45(h).

56. *Id.* § 26.51.

57. *Id.* § 26.47.

58. *Id.* § 26.53.

59. 49 C.F.R. § 26.29(a) (2023).

60. *Id.* § 26.29(b).

Additional Related Laws, Policies, and Programs

- *Access to Capital*: The Pennsylvania Industrial Development Authority (PIDA) administers the Small Diverse Business Capital Access Program (SDBCA).[61] This program "provides low-interest loans and lines of credit to small diverse businesses that commit to creating and retaining full-time jobs within the Commonwealth."[62]
- *Technical Assistance*: The Department of General Services has a responsibility to "[w]here feasible, provide appropriate staff who shall be responsible to the department and who shall serve within designated Commonwealth agencies to assist small and disadvantaged businesses in this Commonwealth in learning how to do business with Commonwealth agencies."[63]
- *Prompt Payment to Subcontractors*: "When a subcontractor has performed in accordance with the provisions of the contract, a contractor shall pay to the subcontractor, and each subcontractor shall in turn pay to its subcontractors, the full or proportional amount received for each such subcontractor's work and material, based on work completed or services provided under the subcontract, 14 days after receipt of a progress payment. . . ."[64]
- *Finding Contract Opportunities*: Contracting opportunities may be found on the Pennsylvania eMarketplace portal: http://www.emarketplace.state.pa.us/.

Major City Snapshot: Philadelphia

The City of Philadelphia (city) Office of Economic Opportunity processes applications to join the city's registry of small and diverse businesses.[65] In addition, under title 17, chapter 17-500 of the Philadelphia Code it provides guidance on "goals for participation of disadvantaged owned business enterprises in City contracts."

61. *Small Diverse Business Capital Access Program*, Pa. Dep't of Comm. & Econ. Dev., https://dced.pa.gov/programs/small-diverse-business-capital-access-program-sdbca/ (last visited Mar. 23, 2023).
62. *Id.*
63. 2 Pa. Cons. Stat. § 2104 (2023).
64. 62 Pa. Cons. Stat. § 3933(c) (2023).
65. *Register as a Minority, Woman, or Disabled-Owned Business*, City of Phila., https://www.phila.gov/services/business-self-employment/bidding-on-a-city-contract/register-as-a-minority-woman-or-disabled-owned-business/ (last visited Mar. 23, 2023).

- *Certifications*: A business must first get certified through a certification agency.[66] Once that is completed, the business may then sign up for the Office of Economic Opportunity's registry by submitting an application.[67] The following types of businesses may apply: Minority-Owned Enterprises, Women-Owned Enterprises, and Disability-Owned Enterprises (M/W/DSBEs).[68]
- *Bidding Specifications*: Under City Ordinance 17-504 "Participation Goals," it notes that when there is a contract goal, bidders must "make every effort before the opening of bids to meet the contract goal." In addition, the contract incorporates by reference chapter 17-500.
- *Contractor Good Faith Efforts*: When a contract specific goal is set under 17-504, a contractor may request a waiver from the goal requirements and in doing so must present good faith efforts to meet the goal.[69]
- *Inclusion Goals*: The city sets an annual goal to have 35 percent of all contracts through M/W/DSBEs.[70]
- *Payments to Subcontractors*: Under 17-507, contractors must pay subcontractors "no later than 7 days after the contractor receives payment from the City."
- *Penalties*: Under 17-511 of the City Ordinance, if a contractor fails to comply with any provision of chapter 17-500, then it may be subject to penalties.
- *Reporting Requirements*: Under article VI, 6-109 of the Preamble of the Philadelphia Home Rule Charter it states that "[a]t least thirty (30) days before the start of each fiscal year, the Finance Director shall file with the Mayor a written report. . ." that includes information on the city's efforts related to disadvantaged business enterprises participation in contracts.

---

66. *Id.*
67. *Id.*
68. *Id.*
69. City of Phila. Ordinance § 17-509(2) (2021).
70. *Register as a Minority, Woman, or Disabled-Owned Business*, *supra* note 65.

CHAPTER 40

Rhode Island

Overview of Business Inclusion Program, Policies, and Practices

Government entities seeking to create business inclusion programs have two primary options in terms of the type of program they may create, in terms of who is eligible for the program: (1) a race- and gender-conscious program or (2) a race- and gender-neutral program. Under the Equal Protection Clause of the Fourteenth Amendment, strict scrutiny is applied by the courts when a government actor is creating policies based on race. Strict scrutiny is the highest level of judicial review that may be applied. It requires the government actor to demonstrate that (1) past discrimination exists such that the entity has a "compelling government interest" in rectifying it, and (2) the policies and programs created to do so are "narrowly tailored."[1] Although intermediate scrutiny is often applied when reviewing programs based on gender, strict scrutiny is applied when reviewing race- and gender-conscious business inclusion programs.[2] Disparity studies have become a standard tool used to assist a government entity in withstanding a challenge to its race- and gender-conscious business inclusion programs. These studies aid in demonstrating whether a government entity has engaged

1. City of Richmond v. J.A. Croson Co., 488 U.S. 469 (1989).

2. Since the 1980s with the Supreme Court decision in *City of Richmond v. J.A. Croson Company*, there have been a number of cases across the county that have assessed race- and gender-conscious business inclusion programs. *See* Adarand Constructors, Inc. v. Pena, 515 U.S. 200 (1995); Virdi v. DeKalb Cnty. Sch. Dist., 135 Fed. App'x 262, 268 (11th Cir. 2005); Sherbrooke Turf, Inc. v. Minn. Dep't of Transp., 345 F.3d 964, 971 (8th Cir. 2003); Mountain West Holding Co., Inc. v. The State of Montana, Montana DOT, et al., 2017 WL 2179120 (9th Cir. May 16, 2017).

in past discrimination in its contracting practices, such that the entity may have a compelling government interest in rectifying it.[3]

Conversely, race- and gender-neutral programs are programs that are not only accessible to minority-owned and women-owned businesses but to all businesses, regardless of race or gender. A small business inclusion program would fall into this category. The level of judicial review applied to such a policy to determine its constitutionality is rational basis, which is the lowest threshold for a government to satisfy. For a government entity to satisfy rational basis, the policy or program created must be "related to a legitimate government purpose."[4] Even when a government entity has a race- and gender-conscious program, oftentimes the program may still require the government actor to seek to meet the goals of their program through race- and gender-neutral means where able, so as to be taking the most narrowly tailored means of accomplishing the program goals.

In the state of Rhode Island, at the state level of government, there are two state agencies that certify businesses for business inclusion programs: (1) State of Rhode Island Department of Administration, Division of Equity, Diversity and Inclusion and (2) the Governor's Commission on Disabilities.

Summary of Certification Programs and Requirements

The Department of Administration, Division of Equity, Diversity and Inclusion certifies (1) state programs, including Minority Business Enterprise (MBE), Women Business Enterprise (WBE), and Veteran Business Enterprise (VBE); and (2) federal programs that include Disadvantaged Business Enterprises (DBEs) and Airport Concession Disadvantaged Business Enterprises (ACDBEs). Although the Rhode Island Department of Administration handles the certifications for the federal programs previously noted, the Rhode Island Department of Transportation (RIDOT) administers the programs outside of certification. The eligibility requirements for all certifications follow:

- *Minority Business Enterprise and Women Business Enterprise (MBE/WBE)*: A business must (1) be for-profit; (2) be a small business concern as defined under section 3 of the federal Small Business Act, 15 U.S.C. § 632; (3) be at least 51 percent

3. *Promoting Opportunity and Equality in America: A Guide to Federal Circuit Authority on Permissible Government Actions to Promote Racial and Gender Equality*, Am. Civ. Liberties Union & The Opportunity Agenda (Dec. 2010), https://www.aclu.org/sites/default/files/field_document/Promoting_Opportunity_and_Equality_in_America.pdf.

4. 488 U.S. 469 (1989).

owned and controlled by one or more socially and economically disadvantaged individuals (or they own 51 percent of the stock in the case of a corporation)—the following are presumed to be socially and economically disadvantaged: Black, Hispanic, Portuguese, Asian American, American Indian or Alaskan Native, Asian-Pacific Americans, women, and other groups designated as socially disadvantaged by the Small Business Administration (SBA) under 8(a) of the Small Business Act; (4) as it relates to control, have the management and daily business operations controlled by one or more eligible owners; (5) have U.S. citizens or lawfully admitted permanent residents as the eligible owners; (6) have eligible owners demonstrate a substantial personal investment in the business; and (7) have the ownership of the eligible owners be real, substantial, and continuing.[5]

- *Veteran Business Enterprise (VBE)*: A business must (1) be a small business concern as defined under the SBA criteria and size standards; (2) be at least 51 percent owned and controlled by one or more socially and economically disadvantaged veterans (or they own 51 percent of the stock in the case of a corporation); (3) as it relates to control, have the management and daily business operations controlled by one or more eligible owners; and (4) have the ownership of the eligible owners be real, substantial, and continuing.[6] Eligible owners of this certification may include the "surviving spouse or permanent caregiver of a veteran."[7]
- *Disadvantaged Business Enterprise (DBE)*: To qualify as a DBE, a business must (1) be for-profit;[8] (2) be a small business concern—with "small" determined by the SBA small business size standards—and does not exceed $30.40 million in gross annual receipts;[9] (3) be at least 51 percent owned by socially and economically disadvantaged individuals—there is a rebuttable

5. 37 R.I. Gen. Laws § 37-14.1-3 (2023); 220-80 R.I. Code R. § 10-1 (2022); *Minority Business Enterprise (MBE) & Women Business Enterprise (WBE) Program*, R.I. Dep't of Admin. Div. of Equity, Diversity & Inclusion, https://dedi.ri.gov/divisions-units/minority-business-enterprise-compliance-office/minority-business-enterprise-mbe-0 (last visited Apr. 19, 2023).

6. 37 R.I. Gen. Laws § 37-14.3-3 (2023); 220-80 R.I. Code R. § 15-1 (2022); *Veteran Business Enterprise (VBE) Program*, R.I. Dep't of Admin. Div. of Equity, Diversity & Inclusion, https://dedi.ri.gov/divisions-units/minority-business-enterprise-compliance-office/veteran-business-enterprise-vbe-0 (last visited Apr. 19, 2023).

7. 220-80 R.I. Code R. § 15-1 (2022).

8. 49 C.F.R.§ 26.5 (2022).

9. *Id.* §§ 26.5, 26.65(b). It is worth noting that under 49 C.F.R. § 26.65(b), the DBE size standard may be adjusted annually for inflation such that in subsequent years the size standard may no longer be $30.40 million.

presumption that women, Black Americans, Hispanic Americans, Native Americans, Asian-Pacific Americans, Subcontinent Asian Americans, or other minorities are disadvantaged;[10] (4) be controlled by one or more of the socially and economically disadvantaged owners;[11] (5) have the socially and economically disadvantaged owners be U.S. citizens or lawfully admitted permanent residents;[12] and (6) have the personal net worth for any socially and economically disadvantaged owner not exceed $1.32 million.[13] The DBE program is required on contracting opportunities that have received funding from the Federal Highway Administration (FHWA), Federal Aviation Administration (FAA), or Federal Transit Administration (FTA).[14]

- *Airport Concession Disadvantaged Business Enterprise (ACDBE):* In addition to being certified as a DBE under 49 C.F.R. part 26, businesses may also be certified as an Airport Concession Disadvantaged Business Enterprise (ACDBE) under 49 C.F.R. part 23. To qualify as an ACDBE, a business must (1) be a concession for-profit small business concern;[15] (2) qualify as small by having its prior three-year average gross receipts not exceed the applicable size standard of $56.42 million;[16] (3) be 51 percent owned by one or more socially and economically disadvantaged individuals;[17] (4) have one or more of the socially and economically disadvantaged individuals with control and managing the daily business operations;[18] and (5) have the personal net worth for any socially and economically disadvantaged owner not exceed $1.32 million.[19]

The Disability Business Enterprise Committee of the Governor's Commission on Disabilities certifies businesses as Disability Business Enterprises. The eligibility requirements for this certification follow.

---

10. *Id.* § 26.67.
11. *Id.* § 26.5.
12. *Id.* § 26.67.
13. *Id.*
14. *Id.* § 26.21(a).
15. *Id.* § 23.3.
16. *Id.* § 23.33(a). The size standards for the following are exceptions to this: bank and financial institutions is $1 billion in assets; car rental companies are $75.23 million average annual gross receipts; pay telephones is 1,500 employees; and automobile dealers is 350 employees.
17. *Id.*
18. *Id.*
19. *Id.* § 23.35.

- *Disability Business Enterprise (DBE)*: A business must (1) be a small business concern; (2) be at least 51 percent owned by one or more persons with disabilities (or they own 51 percent of the stock in the case of a corporation); (3) have the management and daily operations managed by one or more of the eligible owners; and (4) have 50 or fewer employees.[20] The following may also deem a business eligible: "[1] Manufacturers of any goods or merchandise if not less than sixty percent (60%) of the work hours or direct labor required for the products are performed by persons with disabilities; [2] Service Providers if not less than sixty percent (60%) of the work hours or direct labor required for the services are performed by persons with disabilities; [or][3] Nonprofit rehabilitation facilities."[21]

Procurement Laws Intersecting with Business Inclusion

In the state of Rhode Island, in terms of procurement-related laws and rules relevant to business inclusion those highlighted next may be found in title 37 and title 42 of the Rhode Island General Laws, as well as 220-80 of the Code of Rhode Island Rules. A few relevant laws and rules follow.

- *Solicitations*: "All RFP solicitations for goods, services, and/or public works projects must include a criterion for [MBE, WBE, and/or Disability Business Enterprise] participation."[22] It is worth noting that the state laws pertaining to Disability Business Enterprises do state that, "[n]otwithstanding anything to the contrary, the provisions of this chapter shall not apply to any business whose primary business is road or highway construction."[23]
- *Weighted Points on RFPs*: "The standard weight for the [MBE, WBE, and/or Disability Business Enterprise] participation criteria shall be 6 points out of a total of 106 evaluation points available to the Proposers."[24]
- *Participation Rate on Contracts in Response to an RFP*: A contract-specific participation rate in the form of a percentage is

20. 37 R.I. Gen. Laws § 37-2.2-2 (2023).
21. *Disability Business Enterprise*, Governor's Comm'n on Disabilities, https://gcd.ri.gov/title-i-employment/disability-business-enterprise (last visited Apr. 19, 2023).
22. 220-80 R.I. Code R. § 10-2.7 (2022).
23. 37 R.I. Gen. Laws § 37-2.2-5 (2023).
24. 220-80 R.I. Code R. § 10-2.7 (2022).

set based on the total contract price of work subcontracted to MBEs, WBEs, and/or Disability Business Enterprises divided by the total contract price to the Proposal.[25]

- *Inclusion Goals*: "Minority business enterprises shall be included in all procurements and construction projects under this chapter and shall be awarded a minimum of ten percent (10%) of the dollar value of the entire procurement or project."[26] As noted earlier, under the state law, the definition for a minority business enterprise includes both minorities and women.[27] On a Request for Quote (RFQ) an aggregate utilization rate of 10 percent is set in alignment with the state law.[28] If sub-goals are set on an RFQ, then they must be "consistent with underutilization data received through a disparity study and/or pertinent analytic data derived from the recordkeeping of State Agencies."[29]
- *MBE/WBE Compliance Plan and Contractor Good Faith Efforts*: Bidders in response to an RFQ are required to submit an MBE/WBE Compliance Plan within five days of receipt of a tentative award.[30] If compliance with the aggregated utilization rate is impossible for the bidder, then the bidder must demonstrate good faith efforts.[31]
- *Prompt Payment to Subcontractors*: Contractors must pay their subcontractors within ten days of receiving payment from the state.[32]
- *Sanctions*: Contractors failing to comply with contract-specific participation rates set in contracts in response to a proposal or failure to meet the requirements of an approved MBE/WBE compliance plan will be in noncompliance with state law and subject to sanctions.[33]
- *Reporting Requirements*: State agencies must complete standard forms and report on their efforts to effectuate the regulations governing participation of small businesses, inclusive of MBEs, WBEs, and Disability Business Enterprise on an annual basis

---

25. *Id.*
26. 37 R.I. Gen. Laws § 37-14.1-6 (2023).
27. *Id.* § 37-14.1-3.
28. 220-80 R.I. Code R. § 10-2.8 (2022).
29. *Id.*
30. *Id.*
31. *Id.*
32. 42 R.I. Gen. Laws § 42-11.1-3 (2023).
33. 220-80 R.I. Code R. § 10-2.7 (2022); *id.* § 10-2.8; 37 R.I. Gen. Laws § 37-14.1-8 (2023).

or as requested by the Office of Diversity, Equity and Opportunity or the Governor's Commission on Disabilities.[34]

Contracting opportunities where the RIDOT DBE program applies have several requirements that intersect directly with procurement, contracting, and business inclusion.

- *Fostering Small Business Participation*: Pursuant to 49 C.F.R. § 26.39, RIDOT has engaged in efforts to foster small business participation.[35] As part of this plan, RIDOT created a Very Small Business Program (VSBP).[36] To be eligible for the program, a business must (1) be for-profit; (2) be a DBE or non-DBE; (3) have a principal place of business in the United States; (4) pay taxes in the United States or use American products, materials, or services; (5) not have more than 15 employees and no more than $1.5 million in annual revenue.[37] RIDOT engages in efforts to allow for referrals that may benefit VSBPs as well as identifies potential projects to tag for VSBPs.[38]
- *Goals*: Contract opportunities may not use quotas or set-asides for DBEs.[39] The only exception for using a set-aside is in a limited or extreme circumstance, "when no other method could be reasonably expected to redress egregious instances of discrimination."[40] Instead, an overall goal must be set.[41] The goal must be based on evidence of available "ready, willing and able" DBEs in the market.[42] Once the assessment of "ready, willing and able" DBEs is completed, an overall goal may be established as a percentage of the total amount of contracts receiving U.S. Department of Transportation (U.S. DOT) funds.[43] Participation goals must be set for all certified DBEs and not divided into subcategories.[44] Race- and gender-neutral means must be used to "meet the maximum feasible portion of your overall goal."[45] RIDOT, as a recipient of U.S. DOT funds, will not be penalized for failing to meet the overall goal set,

34. 220-80 R.I. Code R. § 10-2.11 (2022).
35. *Disadvantage Business Enterprise (DBE) Program*, R.I. Dep't of Transp. 19 (2019), https://www.dot.ri.gov/documents/doingbusiness/DBE_Program.pdf.
36. *Id.*
37. *Id.*
38. *Id.*
39. 49 C.F.R. § 26.43 (2022).
40. *Id.*
41. *Id.* § 26.45(a)(1).
42. *Id.* § 26.45(b).
43. *Id.* § 26.45(e).
44. *Id.* § 26.45(h).
45. *Id.* § 26.51.

if it can establish good faith efforts to meet the goal.[46] When there is a DBE goal on a specific contract opportunity, only the bidder meeting the goal, or establishing good faith efforts to meet the goal, may be awarded the contract.[47]

- *Prompt Payment*: Under 49 C.F.R. part 26, contractors must pay subcontractors within 30 days of receipt of payment from the state DOT for satisfactory performance.[48]
- *Payment of Retainage*: Contractors must pay amounts withheld for retainage to subcontractors within 30 days of their work being satisfactorily completed.[49]

Additional Related Laws, Policies, and Programs

- *Technical Assistance*: The Supplier Diversity Office provides training sessions and workshops for MBEs, WBEs, and Disability Business Enterprises. For more information, please visit https://dedi.ri.gov/divisions-units/minority-business-enterprise-compliance-office/supplier-diversity-office.
- *Finding Contracting Opportunities*: Bidding opportunities may be found on the Department of Administration Division of Purchases' Bidding Opportunities page: https://ridop.ri.gov/vendors/bidding-opportunities.

Major City Snapshot: Providence

The City of Providence has a Minority and Women-Owned Business Enterprise Program.

- *City Policy*: "It is the policy of the City of Providence that minority business enterprises (MBEs) and women business enterprises (WBEs) shall have the maximum opportunity to participate in the performance of procurements and projects as prime contractors and vendors as outlined in subsection (d), below. In addition, prime contractors shall utilize MBEs and WBEs so as to enable the city, its purchasing department, and all its contracting departments to meet or exceed the goals set forth in this section. The utilization of MBEs and WBEs as subcontractors and/or suppliers to the prime contractor, and/or

46. *Id.* § 26.47.
47. *Id.* § 26.53.
48. 49 C.F.R. § 26.29(a) (2023).
49. *Id.* § 26.29(b).

the use of minority and women laborers, will be considered in determining the lowest possible bidder."[50]

- *Certifications*: Business must be certified with the state of Rhode Island Department of Administration, Division of Equity, Diversity and Inclusion.[51]
- *Inclusion Goals*: The city sets a 10 percent MBE and 10 percent WBE participation goal, for a combined MBE/WBE participation goal of 20 percent.[52]
- *Contractor Good Faith Efforts*: If a contractor that is using subcontractors fails to meet the MBE/WBE goal, then they may request an MBE/WBE Waiver Request Form and demonstrate good faith efforts.[53]

---

50. Code of Ordinances Providence, R.I. § 21-52(c) (2023).

51. *Minority and Women-owned Business (M/WBE) Procurement Program*, City of Providence, https://www.providenceri.gov/purchasing/minority-women-owned-business-mbewbe-procurement-program/ (last visited Apr. 19, 2023).

52. *MBE/WBE Participation Affidavit*, City of Providence, https://www.providenceri.gov/wp-content/uploads/2017/08/mwbe-bid-submission-packet.pdf (last visited Apr. 19, 2023).

53. *Id.*

CHAPTER 41

South Carolina

Overview of Business Inclusion Program, Policies, and Practices

Government entities seeking to create business inclusion programs have two primary options in terms of the type of program they may create, in terms of who is eligible for the program: (1) a race- and gender-conscious program or (2) a race- and gender-neutral program. Under the Equal Protection Clause of the Fourteenth Amendment, strict scrutiny is applied by the courts when a government actor is creating policies based on race. Strict scrutiny is the highest level of judicial review that may be applied. It requires the government actor to demonstrate that (1) past discrimination exists such that the entity has a "compelling government interest" in rectifying it, and (2) the policies and programs created to do so are "narrowly tailored."[1] Although intermediate scrutiny is often applied when reviewing programs based on gender, strict scrutiny is applied when reviewing race- and gender-conscious business inclusion programs.[2] Disparity studies have become a standard tool used to assist a government entity in withstanding a challenge to its race- and gender-conscious business inclusion programs. These studies aid in demonstrating whether a government entity has engaged

1. City of Richmond v. J.A. Croson Co., 488 U.S. 469 (1989).

2. Since the 1980s with the Supreme Court decision in *City of Richmond v. J.A. Croson Company*, there have been a number of cases across the county that have assessed race- and gender-conscious business inclusion programs. *See* Adarand Constructors, Inc. v. Pena, 515 U.S. 200 (1995); Virdi v. DeKalb Cnty. Sch. Dist., 135 Fed. App'x 262, 268 (11th Cir. 2005); Sherbrooke Turf, Inc. v. Minn. Dep't of Transp., 345 F.3d 964, 971 (8th Cir. 2003); Mountain West Holding Co., Inc. v. The State of Montana, Montana DOT, et al., 2017 WL 2179120 (9th Cir. May 16, 2017).

in past discrimination in its contracting practices, such that the entity may have a compelling government interest in rectifying it.[3]

Conversely, race- and gender-neutral programs are programs that are not only accessible to minority-owned and women-owned businesses but to all businesses, regardless of race or gender. A small business inclusion program would fall into this category. The level of judicial review applied to such a policy to determine its constitutionality is rational basis, which is the lowest threshold for a government to satisfy. For a government entity to satisfy rational basis, the policy or program created must be "related to a legitimate government purpose."[4] Even when a government entity has a race- and gender-conscious program, oftentimes the program may still require the government actor to seek to meet the goals of their program through race- and gender-neutral means where able, so as to be taking the most narrowly tailored means of accomplishing the program goals.

In the state of South Carolina, at the state level of government, there are two state agencies that certify businesses for business inclusion programs: (1) the South Carolina Division of Small and Minority Business Contracting and Certification (SMBCC) and (2) the South Carolina Department of Transportation (SCDOT).

Summary of Certification Programs and Requirements

SMBCC certifies businesses as minority business enterprises (MBEs). The MBE eligibility requirements follow:

- *Minority Business Enterprise (MBE)*: To satisfy the eligibility criteria to be certified as an MBE, a business must (1) be for-profit; (2) be independently owned and operated; (3) not be dominant in its field of operation; (4) qualify as a small business under the U.S. Small Business Administration's (SBA) size standards (see 13 C.F.R. § 121); (5) be at least 51 percent owned by one or more U.S. citizens who are socially and economically disadvantaged; (6) have the qualifying owners exercise control over the business; (7) have the qualifying owners ownership be "real, substantial, and continuing"; (8) have an office in South Carolina; (9) be registered and licensed as a South Carolina business; (10) have the personal net worth of the eligible

3. *Promoting Opportunity and Equality in America: A Guide to Federal Circuit Authority on Permissible Government Actions to Promote Racial and Gender Equality*, Am. Civ. Liberties Union & The Opportunity Agenda (Dec. 2010), https://www.aclu.org/sites/default/files/field_document/Promoting_Opportunity_and_Equality_in_America.pdf.

4. 488 U.S. 469 (1989).

owner(s) not exceed $1.32 million; and (11) be in business for at least one year.[5]

SCDOT administers the Disadvantaged Business Enterprise (DBE) program, Airport Concession Disadvantaged Business Enterprise (ACDBE) program, and the Small Business Enterprise (SBE) program.

- *Disadvantaged Business Enterprise (DBE) Program*: Pursuant to 49 C.F.R. part 26, the SCDOT administers the state's DBE certification program. As is required under 49 C.F.R. § 26.81, South Carolina has a Unified Certification Program (UCP). The UCP makes all DBE certification decisions and provides a "one-stop shop" to DBE applicants.[6] To qualify as a DBE, a business must (1) be for-profit;[7] (2) be a small business concern—with "small" determined by the SBA small business size standards—and does not exceed $30.40 million in gross annual receipts;[8] (3) be at least 51 percent owned by socially and economically disadvantaged individuals—there is a rebuttable presumption that women, Black Americans, Hispanic Americans, Native Americans, Asian-Pacific Americans, Subcontinent Asian Americans, or other minorities are disadvantaged;[9] (4) be controlled by one or more of the socially and economically disadvantaged owners;[10] (5) have the socially and economically disadvantaged owners be U.S. citizens or lawfully admitted permanent residents;[11] and (6) have the personal net worth for any socially and economically disadvantaged owner not exceed $1.32 million.[12] The DBE program is required on contracting opportunities that have received funding from the Federal Highway Administration (FHWA), Federal Aviation Administration (FAA), or Federal Transit Administration (FTA).[13]
- *Airport Concession Disadvantaged Business Enterprise (ACDBE) Program*: In addition to being certified as a DBE under 49 C.F.R. part 26, businesses may also be certified as an Airport Concession Disadvantaged Business Enterprise (ACDBE) under

5. S.C. Code Ann. Regs.19-445.2160 (2007); *Applications*, S.C. Div. of Small & Minority Bus. Contracting & Certification, https://smbcc.sc.gov/applications.html (last visited Apr. 19, 2023).
6. 49 C.F.R. § 26.81(b)(2) (2022).
7. *Id.* § 26.5.
8. *Id.* §§ 26.5, 26.65(b). It is worth noting that under 49 C.F.R. § 26.65(b), the DBE size standard may be adjusted annually for inflation such that in subsequent years the size standard may no longer be $30.40 million.
9. *Id.* § 26.67.
10. *Id.* § 26.5.
11. *Id.* § 26.67.
12. *Id.*
13. *Id.* § 26.21(a).

49 C.F.R. part 23. To qualify as an ACDBE, a business must (1) be a concession for-profit small business concern;[14] (2) qualify as small by having its prior three-year average gross receipts not exceed the applicable size standard of $56.42 million;[15] (3) be 51 percent owned by one or more socially and economically disadvantaged individuals;[16] (4) have one or more of the socially and economically disadvantaged individuals with control and managing the daily business operations;[17] and (5) not have the personal net worth for any socially and economically disadvantaged owner exceed $1.32 million.[18]

- *Small Business Enterprise (SBE) Program*: SCDOT has implemented a small business element within its DBE program called the Small Business Enterprise (SBE) program, pursuant to 49 C.F.R. § 26.39.[19] To be eligible for the program, a business must (1) be a for-profit business; (2) meet the SBA small business size standard and have an average gross receipt over the prior five years that does not exceed $7.5 million; (3) have owners whose personal net worth does not exceed $1.32 million; (4) have eligible owners involved in the management and day-to-day control of the business; and (5) be an independent business.[20]

Procurement Laws Intersecting with Business Inclusion

In the state of South Carolina, in terms of procurement-related laws and rules relevant to business inclusion those highlighted here may be found in the South Carolina Procurement Code located in (1) title 11, chapter 35, sections 11-35-5210 to 11-35-5270, as well as section

14. *Id.* § 23.3.

15. *Id.* § 23.33(a). The size standards for the following are exceptions to this: bank and financial institutions is $1 billion in assets; car rental companies are $75.23 million average annual gross receipts; pay telephones is 1,500 employees; and automobile dealers is 350 employees.

16. *Id.*

17. *Id.*

18. *Id.* § 23.35.

19. *Disadvantaged Business Enterprise 2022 Program Document*, S.C. DEP'T OF TRANSP. 25 (2022), https://www.scdot.org/business/pdf/businessDevelop/1-2022%20SCDOT%20DBE%20Program%20Plan%20FINAL%20WEBSITE.pdf?v=2.

20. *South Carolina Small Business Enterprise Program Uniform Certification Application*, S.C. DEP'T OF TRANSP. 5 (2012), https://www.scdot.org/business/pdf/businessDevelop/SBEApplication.pdf?v=2; *Small Business Enterprise (SBE) Program*, S.C. DEP'T OF TRANSP., https://www.scdot.org/business/bus-development-sbe.aspx (last visited Apr. 17, 2023).

11-35-1520 and (2) the South Carolina Code of Regulations 19-445.2160. A few relevant laws and rules follow.

- *Inclusion Goals*: There is a goal for state agencies to expend 10 percent of their total amount of funds to expend with certified MBEs.[21] "Upon petition by the governmental body, SMBAO may authorize an MBE utilization plan that establishes a goal of less than ten percent of the governmental body's total dollar amount of funds expended."[22]
- *Utilization Plans*: Each state agency director must develop a Minority Business Enterprise Utilization Plan that, among other requirements, includes the 10 percent goal just noted.[23]
- *Reporting Requirements*: State agencies must submit quarterly progress reports containing the following information: "(a) number of minority firms solicited; (b) number of minority bids received; (c) total dollar amount of funds expended on contracts awarded to minority firms certified pursuant to Section 11-35-5230; and (d) total dollar amount of funds expended."[24] In addition, "[t]he Small and Minority Business Assistance Office shall report annually in writing to the Governor concerning the number and dollar value of contracts awarded for each governmental body to a firm certified as a minority firm pursuant to Section 11-35-5230 during the preceding fiscal year. These records must be maintained to evaluate the progress of this program."[25]
- *Tied Bids*: If there are two bids tied in price and both meet all other required conditions, there is an order of priority in terms of how to determine the tie, which is as follows: "(a) If there is a South Carolina firm tied with an out-of-state firm, the award must be made automatically to the South Carolina firm. (b) Tie bids involving South Carolina produced or manufactured products, when known, and items produced or manufactured out of the State must be resolved in favor of the South Carolina commodity. (c) Tie bids involving a business certified by the South Carolina Office of Small and Minority Business Assistance as a Minority Business Enterprise must be resolved in favor of the Minority Business Enterprise. (d) Tie bids involving South Carolina firms must be resolved in favor of the

21. S.C. Code Ann. § 11-35-5240(1) (2022).
22. *Id.* § 11-35-5240(2).
23. *Id.* § 11-35-5240(1).
24. *Id.* § 11-35-5240(2).
25. *Id.* § 11-35- 5260.

South Carolina firm located in the same taxing jurisdiction as the governmental body's consuming location. (e) In all other situations in which bids are tied, the award must be made to the tied bidder offering the quickest delivery time, or if the tied bidders have offered the same delivery time, the tie must be resolved by the flip of a coin witnessed by the procurement officer. All responding vendors must be invited to attend."[26]

Contracting opportunities where the SCDOT DBE program applies have several requirements that intersect directly with procurement, contracting, and business inclusion.

- *Goals*: Contract opportunities may not use quotas or set-asides for DBEs.[27] The only exception for using a set-aside is in a limited or extreme circumstance, "when no other method could be reasonably expected to redress egregious instances of discrimination."[28] Instead, an overall goal must be set.[29] The goal must be based on evidence of available "ready, willing and able" DBEs in the market.[30] Once the assessment of "ready, willing and able" DBEs is completed, an overall goal may be established as a percentage of the total amount of contracts receiving U.S. Department of Transportation (U.S. DOT) funds.[31] Participation goals must be set for all certified DBEs and not divided into subcategories.[32] Race- and gender-neutral means must be used to "meet the maximum feasible portion of your overall goal."[33] SCDOT, as a recipient of U.S. DOT funds, will not be penalized for failing to meet the overall goal set, if it can establish good faith efforts to meet the goal.[34] When there is a DBE goal on a specific contract opportunity, only the bidder meeting the goal, or establishing good faith efforts to meet the goal, may be awarded the contract.[35]
- *Prompt Payment*: Under 49 C.F.R. part 26, contractors must pay subcontractors within 30 days of receipt of payment from the state DOT for satisfactory performance.[36]

---

26. *Id.* § 11-35-1520(9).
27. 49 C.F.R. § 26.43 (2022).
28. *Id.*
29. *Id.* § 26.45(a)(1).
30. *Id.* § 26.45(b).
31. *Id.* § 26.45(e).
32. *Id.* § 26.45(h).
33. *Id.* § 26.51.
34. *Id.* § 26.47.
35. *Id.* § 26.53.
36. 49 C.F.R. § 26.29(a) (2023).

- *Payment of Retainage*: Contractors must pay amounts withheld for retainage to subcontractors within 30 days of their work being satisfactorily completed.[37]

Additional Related Laws, Policies, and Programs

- *Additional Related Procurement Preferences*: South Carolina has the following procurement preferences found under South Carolina Code Annotated section 11-35-1524: (1) Commodity Contract Preferences: (a) United States End Product Preference, (b) South Carolina End Product Preference, (c) Resident Vendor Preference; (2) Service Contract Preferences: (a) Resident Contractor Preference, (b) Resident Subcontractor Preference, 2 percent, (c) Resident Subcontractor Preference, 4 percent.[38] Although not limited to small and diverse businesses, these bidder preference may be beneficial for the small and diverse businesses certified by SMBCC since a requirement of certification is being a South Carolina business.
- *Prompt Payment to Subcontractors*: "When a contractor or a subcontractor has performed in accordance with the provisions of his contract, the owner shall pay the contractor by mailing via first class mail or delivering the undisputed amount of any pay request within twenty-one days of receipt by the owner of any pay request based upon work completed or service provided under the contract, and the contractor shall pay to his subcontractor and each subcontractor shall pay to his subcontractor, within seven days of receipt by the contractor or subcontractor of each periodic or final payment, by mailing via first class mail or delivering the full amount received for that subcontractor's work and materials based on work completed or service provided under the subcontract."[39]
- *Tax Credit*: "A taxpayer having a contract with this State who subcontracts with a socially and economically disadvantaged small business is eligible for an income tax credit equal to four percent of the payments to that subcontractor for work pursuant to the contract. The subcontractor must be certified as a socially and economically disadvantaged small business as

37. *Id.* § 26.29(b).

38. *Procurement Preferences: Vendor Preferences: Frequently Asked Questions from the Vendor's Perspective*, Div. of Procurement Servs., https://procurement.sc.gov/osp/preferences/faqs#ditem-15583 (last visited Apr. 18, 2023).

39. S.C. Code Ann. § 29-6-30 (2022).

defined in Section 11-35-5010 and regulations pursuant to it."[40] "Firms claiming the income tax credit shall maintain evidence of work performed for a state contract by minority subcontractors and shall present such evidence on a form and in a manner prescribed by the Department of Revenue at the time of filing its state income tax return and claim such credit at the time of filing. All records shall be available for audit by the Department of Revenue in accordance with prevailing tax statutes."[41]

- *Access to Capital*: "When a minority business firm certified by the Department of Revenue receives a contract with the State, the appropriate chief procurement officer shall furnish a letter, upon request, stating the dollar value and duration of, and other information about the contract, which may be used by the minority firm in negotiating lines of credit with lending institutions."[42]
- *Technical Assistance*: The state chief procurement officers are charged with "work[ing] with appropriate state offices and minority groups in conducting seminars to assist minority business owners in learning how to do business with the State."[43]
- *Finding Contracting Opportunities*: The Division of Procurement Services "Doing Business with Us" page includes links for where to find bidding opportunities: https://procurement.sc.gov/doing-biz/bid-ops.

Major City Snapshot: Charleston

The City of Charleston's Minority and Women-Owned Business Enterprise Office certifies businesses as MBEs and WBEs.

- *Certifications*: Eligibility requirements are:
  - *MBE*: (1) applicants are U.S. citizens; (2) business has been owned for at least one full year; (3) gross revenue does not exceed $7.5 million; (4) personal net worth of the applicant does not exceed $1.32 million; (5) the business is at least 51 percent "owned and managed by an individual who is Black or African American, Hispanic or Latino, Native American, Asian American, or Native Hawaiian/Pacific

40. *Id.* § 12-6-3350(A); *see also id.* § 11-35-5230(B).
41. *Id.* § 11-35-5230(B).
42. *Id.* § 11-35- 5250.
43. *Id.* § 11-35-5220(5).

Islander"; and (6) the eligible owner actively oversees the daily business operations.[44]

- *WBE*: (1) applicants are U.S. citizens; (2) business has been owned for at least one full year; (3) gross revenue does not exceed $7.5 million; (4) personal net worth of the applicant does not exceed $1.32 million; (5) the business is at least 51 percent "owned and managed by a woman"; and (6) the eligible owner actively oversees the daily business operations.[45]

- *Inclusion Goals*: The combined MWBE minimum contracting goals are as follows: (1) Construction, 20 percent; (2) Services, 20 percent; and (3) Supplies, 12 percent.[46] Annually, the mayor must recommend to City Council program goals for their approval.[47] The city does have a methodology in place for determining the goals.[48]
- *Bidding Specifications*: If a goal is set, it must be noted in the bid specifications.
- *Reporting Requirements*: On a quarterly basis, the procurement director must submit a report to the manager of minority business enterprises on the following: "(a) The total number of procurements awarded; (b) The total monetary value of procurements awarded; (c) The type of procurements awarded; (d) The total monetary amount of the procurements awarded to MBEs and WBEs; (e) The percentage of total combined city procurements awarded to MBEs and WBEs."[49] Also on a quarterly basis, the manager of minority business enterprises must report to city council on "the percentage of total combined city procurements awarded to MBEs and WBEs and a description of the procurement categories represented. . . ."[50]

---

44. *Minority & Women-Owned Business Enterprise Office*, City of Charleston, https://www.charleston-sc.gov/127/Minority-Women-Owned-Business-Enterprise (last visited Apr. 17, 2023).

45. *Id.*

46. City of Charleston Ordinance § 2-268 (2022).

47. *Id.*

48. *Id.*

49. *Id.*

50. *Id.*

CHAPTER 42

South Dakota

Overview of Business Inclusion Program, Policies, and Practices

Government entities seeking to create business inclusion programs have two primary options in terms of the type of program they may create, in terms of who is eligible for the program: (1) a race- and gender-conscious program or (2) a race- and gender-neutral program. Under the Equal Protection Clause of the Fourteenth Amendment, strict scrutiny is applied by the courts when a government actor is creating policies based on race. Strict scrutiny is the highest level of judicial review that may be applied. It requires the government actor to demonstrate that (1) past discrimination exists such that the entity has a "compelling government interest" in rectifying it, and (2) the policies and programs created to do so are "narrowly tailored."[1] Although intermediate scrutiny is often applied when reviewing programs based on gender, strict scrutiny is applied when reviewing race- and gender-conscious business inclusion programs.[2] Disparity studies have become a standard tool used to assist a government entity in withstanding a challenge to its race- and gender-conscious business inclusion programs. These studies aid in demonstrating whether a government entity has engaged

1. City of Richmond v. J.A. Croson Co., 488 U.S. 469 (1989).

2. Since the 1980s with the Supreme Court decision in *City of Richmond v. J.A. Croson Company*, there have been a number of cases across the county that have assessed race- and gender-conscious business inclusion programs. *See* Adarand Constructors, Inc. v. Pena, 515 U.S. 200 (1995); Virdi v. DeKalb Cnty. Sch. Dist., 135 Fed. App'x 262, 268 (11th Cir. 2005); Sherbrooke Turf, Inc. v. Minn. Dep't of Transp., 345 F.3d 964, 971 (8th Cir. 2003); Mountain West Holding Co., Inc. v. The State of Montana, Montana DOT, et al., 2017 WL 2179120 (9th Cir. May 16, 2017).

in past discrimination in its contracting practices, such that the entity may have a compelling government interest in rectifying it.[3]

Conversely, race- and gender-neutral programs are programs that are not only accessible to minority-owned and women-owned businesses but to all businesses, regardless of race or gender. A small business inclusion program would fall into this category. The level of judicial review applied to such a policy to determine its constitutionality is rational basis, which is the lowest threshold for a government to satisfy. For a government entity to satisfy rational basis, the policy or program created must be "related to a legitimate government purpose."[4] Even when a government entity has a race- and gender-conscious program, oftentimes the program may still require the government actor to seek to meet the goals of their program through race- and gender-neutral means where able, so as to be taking the most narrowly tailored means of accomplishing the program goals.

At the state level of government in South Dakota, the South Dakota Department of Transportation (SDDOT) is the only entity that certifies businesses for a business inclusion program.[5]

Summary of Certification Programs and Requirements

SDDOT administers the Disadvantaged Business Enterprise (DBE) program and the Airport Concession Disadvantaged Business Enterprise (ACDBE) program. Following is a summary of the eligibility requirements for each certification:

- *Disadvantaged Business Enterprise (DBE)*: Pursuant to 49 C.F.R. part 26, SDDOT administers the state's DBE certification program. As is required under 49 C.F.R. § 26.81, South Dakota has a Unified Certification Program (UCP). The UCP makes all DBE certification decisions and provides a "one-stop shop" to DBE applicants.[6] To qualify as a DBE, a business must (1) be for-profit;[7] (2) be a small business concern—with "small" determined by the Small Business Administration (SBA) small business size standards—and does not exceed $30.40 million

3. *Promoting Opportunity and Equality in America: A Guide to Federal Circuit Authority on Permissible Government Actions to Promote Racial and Gender Equality*, Am. Civ. Liberties Union & The Opportunity Agenda (Dec. 2010), https://www.aclu.org/sites/default/files/field_document/Promoting_Opportunity_and_Equality_in_America.pdf.

4. 488 U.S. 469 (1989).

5. *Disadvantaged Business Enterprise*, S.D. Dep't of Transp., https://dot.sd.gov/doing-business/contractors/dbe#listItemLink_1269 (last visited Jan. 20, 2023).

6. 49 C.F.R. § 26.81(b)(2) (2022).

7. *Id.* § 26.5.

in gross annual receipts;[8] (3) be at least 51 percent owned by socially and economically disadvantaged individuals—there is a rebuttable presumption that women, Black Americans, Hispanic Americans, Native Americans, Asian-Pacific Americans, Subcontinent Asian Americans, or other minorities are disadvantaged;[9] (4) be controlled by one or more of the socially and economically disadvantaged owners;[10] (5) have the socially and economically disadvantaged owners be U.S. citizens or lawfully admitted permanent residents;[11] and (6) have the personal net worth for any socially and economically disadvantaged owner not exceed $1.32 million.[12] The DBE program is required on contracting opportunities that have received funding from the Federal Highway Administration (FHWA), Federal Aviation Administration (FAA), or Federal Transit Administration (FTA).[13]

- *Airport Concession Disadvantaged Business Enterprise (ACDBE)*: In addition to being certified as a DBE under 49 C.F.R. part 26, businesses may also be certified as an Airport Concession Disadvantaged Business Enterprise (ACDBE) under 49 C.F.R. part 23. To qualify as an ACDBE, a business must (1) be a concession for-profit small business concern;[14] (2) qualify as small by having its prior three-year average gross receipts not exceed the applicable size standard of $56.42 million;[15] (3) be 51 percent owned by one or more socially and economically disadvantaged individuals;[16] (4) have one or more of the socially and economically disadvantaged individuals with control and managing the daily business operations;[17] and (5) have the personal net worth for any socially and economically disadvantaged owner not exceed $1.32 million.[18]

8. *Id.* §§ 26.5, 26.65(b). It is worth noting that under 49 C.F.R. § 26.65(b), the DBE size standard may be adjusted annually for inflation such that in subsequent years the size standard may no longer be $30.40 million.
9. *Id.* § 26.67.
10. *Id.* § 26.5.
11. *Id.* § 26.67.
12. *Id.*
13. *Id.* § 26.21(a).
14. *Id.* § 23.3.
15. *Id.* § 23.33(a). The size standards for the following are exceptions to this: bank and financial institutions is $1 billion in assets; car rental companies are $75.23 million average annual gross receipts; pay telephones is 1,500 employees; and automobile dealers is 350 employees.
16. *Id.*
17. *Id.*
18. *Id.* § 23.35.

Procurement Laws Intersecting with Business Inclusion

Procurement in the state of South Dakota is managed by the Bureau of Administration's Office of Procurement Management.[19] The authority for procurement in South Dakota may be found in South Dakota Codified Laws 5-18A. Under 5-18A, there are no bidding preferences, laws, or rules specific to business inclusion and minority-owned, women-owned, disability-owned, veteran-owned, and/or LGBT-owned business enterprises in South Dakota, outside of what is required by the SDDOT DBE program. However, the state Vendor Manual does note that if a contract is to exceed $5,000 then, "It is the policy of the Government that minority business enterprises shall have the maximum practicable opportunity to participate in the performance of Government contracts."[20]

Contracting opportunities where the SDDOT DBE program applies have several requirements that intersect directly with procurement, contracting, and business inclusion.

- *Fostering Small Business Participation*: Pursuant to 49 C.F.R. § 26.39, SDDOT has engaged in efforts to foster small business participation.[21] SDDOT seeks to foster small business participation through efforts such as unbundling contracts.[22]
- *Goals*: Contract opportunities may not use quotas or set-asides for DBEs.[23] The only exception for using a set-aside is in a limited or extreme circumstance, "when no other method could be reasonably expected to redress egregious instances of discrimination."[24] Instead, an overall goal must be set.[25] The goal must be based on evidence of available "ready, willing and able" DBEs in the market.[26] Once the assessment of "ready, willing and able" DBEs is completed, an overall goal may be established as a percentage of the total amount of contracts receiving U.S. Department of Transportation (U.S. DOT)

19. *Procurement Management*, S.D. Bureau of Admin., https://boa.sd.gov/central-services/procurement-management/default.aspx (last visited Jan. 20, 2023).

20. *Doing Business with the State of South Dakota*, Bureau of Admin. Off. of Procurement Mgmt. 15 (2021), https://boa.sd.gov/central-services/procurement-management/docs/SDVendorManual_12-21-2021.pdf.

21. *Disadvantage Business Enterprise Program Plan*, S.D. Dep't of Transp. 17–20 (Feb. 2023), https://dot.sd.gov/media/documents/DBEProgramPlan.pdf.

22. *Id.*

23. 49 C.F.R. § 26.43 (2022).

24. *Id.*

25. *Id.* § 26.45(a)(1).

26. *Id.* § 26.45(b).

funds.[27] Participation goals must be set for all certified DBEs and not divided into subcategories.[28] Race- and gender-neutral means must be used to "meet the maximum feasible portion of your overall goal."[29] SDDOT, as a recipient of U.S. DOT funds, will not be penalized for failing to meet the overall goal set, if it can establish good faith efforts to meet the goal.[30] When there is a DBE goal on a specific contract opportunity only the bidder meeting the goal, or establishing good faith efforts to meet the goal, may be awarded the contract.[31]

- *Prompt Payment*: Under 49 C.F.R. part 26, contractors must pay subcontractors within 30 days of receipt of payment from the state DOT for satisfactory performance.[32]
- *Payment of Retainage*: Contractors must pay amounts withheld for retainage to subcontractors within 30 days of their work being satisfactorily completed.[33]

Additional Related Laws, Policies, and Programs

Under South Dakota procurement laws, there are bidding preferences. None of these bidding preferences pertain to the inclusion of minority-owned, women-owned, disability-owned, veteran-owned, and/or LGBT-owned business enterprises. However, they may benefit a local business that happens to fall into one of these categories.

- *Resident Bidder Preference*: Preference shall be given to "a resident business if the other equal low bid or proposal was submitted by a nonresident business."[34]
- *Prompt Payment to Subcontractors*: "Upon payment by an agency, a business that has acquired under contract, property or services in connection with the business's contract with the agency from a subcontractor or supplier, shall pay the subcontractor or supplier within thirty days after receiving payment from the agency. . . ."[35]
- *Finding Contract Opportunities*: The Bureau of Administration's "Eprocurement Login" page links to login to view and bid

27. *Id.* § 26.45(e).
28. *Id.* § 26.45(h).
29. *Id.* § 26.51.
30. *Id.* § 26.47.
31. *Id.* § 26.53.
32. 49 C.F.R. § 26.29(a) (2023).
33. *Id.* § 26.29(b).
34. S.D. Codified Laws § 5-18A-25 (2023).
35. *Id.* § 5-26-6.

on current invitations to bid: https://boa.sd.gov/central-services/procurement-management/procurement-management-eprocurement.aspx.

Major City Snapshot: Aberdeen

The City of Aberdeen does not have a city-specific business inclusion program focused on minority-owned, women-owned, disability-owned, veteran-owned, and/or LGBT-owned business enterprises under its city ordinances. It does, however, establish DBE goals on DOT-assisted projects.[36]

36. As an example of DBE terms included within a DOT-assisted project, please see the following: *Specifications for High Speed Rotary Snow Blower*, City of Aberdeen, S.D. (Aug. 2020), https://www.aberdeen.sd.us/DocumentCenter/View/9855/20200805-Aberdeen-Regional-Airport-SRE-Procurement-Contract-Documents-a.

CHAPTER 43

Tennessee

Overview of Business Inclusion Program, Policies, and Practices

Government entities seeking to create business inclusion programs have two primary options in terms of the type of program they may create, in terms of who is eligible for the program: (1) a race- and gender-conscious program or (2) a race- and gender-neutral program. Under the Equal Protection Clause of the Fourteenth Amendment, strict scrutiny is applied by the courts when a government actor is creating policies based on race. Strict scrutiny is the highest level of judicial review that may be applied. It requires the government actor to demonstrate that (1) past discrimination exists such that the entity has a "compelling government interest" in rectifying it, and (2) the policies and programs created to do so are "narrowly tailored."[1] Although intermediate scrutiny is often applied when reviewing programs based on gender, strict scrutiny is applied when reviewing race- and gender-conscious business inclusion programs.[2] Disparity studies have become a standard tool used to assist a government entity in withstanding a challenge to its race- and gender-conscious business inclusion programs. These studies aid in demonstrating whether a government entity has engaged

1. City of Richmond v. J.A. Croson Co., 488 U.S. 469 (1989).

2. Since the 1980s with the Supreme Court decision in *City of Richmond v. J.A. Croson Company*, there have been a number of cases across the county that have assessed race- and gender-conscious business inclusion programs. *See* Adarand Constructors, Inc. v. Pena, 515 U.S. 200 (1995); Virdi v. DeKalb Cnty. Sch. Dist., 135 Fed. App'x 262, 268 (11th Cir. 2005); Sherbrooke Turf, Inc. v. Minn. Dep't of Transp., 345 F.3d 964, 971 (8th Cir. 2003); Mountain West Holding Co., Inc. v. The State of Montana, Montana DOT, et al., 2017 WL 2179120 (9th Cir. May 16, 2017).

in past discrimination in its contracting practices, such that the entity may have a compelling government interest in rectifying it.[3]

Conversely, race- and gender-neutral programs are programs that are not only accessible to minority-owned and women-owned businesses but to all businesses, regardless of race or gender. A small business inclusion program would fall into this category. The level of judicial review applied to such a policy to determine its constitutionality is rational basis, which is the lowest threshold for a government to satisfy. For a government entity to satisfy rational basis, the policy or program created must be "related to a legitimate government purpose."[4] Even when a government entity has a race- and gender-conscious program, oftentimes the program may still require the government actor to seek to meet the goals of their program through race- and gender-neutral means where able, so as to be taking the most narrowly tailored means of accomplishing the program goals.

In the state of Tennessee, at the state level of government, there are two state agencies that certify businesses for business inclusion programs: (1) the Governor's Office of Diversity Business Enterprise (Go-DBE) and (2) the Tennessee Department of Transportation (TDOT).

Summary of Certification Programs and Requirements

Go-DBE certifies businesses for Tennessee's Diversity Business Enterprise program as Minority Business Enterprise (MBE), Woman Business Enterprise (WBE), Persons with Disabilities (DSBE), Service-Disabled Veteran (SDVBE), and Small Business Enterprise (SBE).[5] For each, certification is valid for three years before the business would need to renew.[6] The eligibility requirements for all follow:

- *Minority Business Enterprise (MBE)*: To satisfy the eligibility criteria to be certified as an MBE, a business must (1) be for-profit; (2) perform a commercially useful function; (3) be continuing and independent; and (4) be ". . . at least fifty-one percent (51%) owned and controlled by one (1) or more

3. *Promoting Opportunity and Equality in America: A Guide to Federal Circuit Authority on Permissible Government Actions to Promote Racial and Gender Equality*, Am. Civ. Liberties Union & The Opportunity Agenda (Dec. 2010), https://www.aclu.org/sites/default/files/field_document/Promoting_Opportunity_and_Equality_in_America.pdf.

4. 488 U.S. 469 (1989).

5. *Certification Overview*, Tenn. Dep't of Gen. Servs., https://www.tn.gov/generalservices/procurement/central-procurement-office--cpo-/go-dbe/certification-overview.html (last visited Apr. 19, 2023).

6. *Frequently Asked Questions*, Tenn. Dep't of Gen. Servs. 5 (2019), https://www.tn.gov/content/dam/tn/generalservices/documents/cpo/godbe/godbe-home-page/Website_FAQ_January_2019.pdf.

minority individuals who are impeded from normal entry into the economic mainstream because of past practices of discrimination based on race or ethnic background."[7] A minority is defined as someone who is (1) African American, Hispanic, Asian American, or Native American and (2) a U.S. citizen or lawful permanent resident.[8]

- *Woman Business Enterprise (WBE)*: To satisfy the eligibility criteria to be certified as a WBE, a business must (1) be for-profit; (2) perform a commercially useful function; (3) be continuing and independent; (4) be at least 51 percent owned by one or more women (51 percent of the stock in a publicly owned business); and (5) be controlled by one or more women, including control of the management and daily business operations.[9]
- *Persons with Disabilities, Disabled Business Enterprise (DSBE)*: To satisfy the eligibility criteria to be certified as a DSBE, a business must (1) be for-profit; (2) perform a commercially useful function; (3) be continuing and independent; (4) be at least 51 percent owned by one or more persons with a disability (51 percent of the stock in a publicly owned business); and (5) be controlled by one or more persons with a disability, including control of the management and daily business operations.[10]
- *Service-Disabled Veteran Business Enterprise (SDVBE)*: To satisfy the eligibility criteria to be certified as a SDVBE, a business must (1) be located in the state of Tennessee; (2) be for-profit; (3) perform a commercially useful function; (4) be continuing and independent; (5) be at least 51 percent owned by one or more service-disabled veterans (51 percent of the stock in a publicly owned business) or 50 percent owned by a service-disabled veteran if the other 50 percent owner is the spouse of the service-disabled veteran; and (6) be controlled by one or more service-disabled veterans including control of the management and daily business operations.[11]
- *Small Business Enterprise (SBE)*: To satisfy the eligibility criteria to be certified as an SBE, a business must (1) reside in the state of Tennessee; (2) be for-profit; (3) perform a commercially useful function; (4) be continuing and independent; and (5) have

---

7. Tenn. Code Ann. § 12-3-1102(4) (2022).
8. *Id.* § 12-3-1102(3).
9. *Id.* § 12-3-1102(4).
10. *Id.* § 12-3-1102(1).
11. *Id.* § 12-3-1102(8).

annual gross receipts averaged over three years not to exceed $10 million or have no more than 99 full-time employees.[12]

TDOT administers the Disadvantaged Business Enterprise (DBE) program, Airport Concession Disadvantaged Business Enterprise (ACDBE) program, and the Small Business Enterprise (SBE) program.

- *Disadvantaged Business Enterprise (DBE) Program*: Pursuant to 49 C.F.R. part 26, TDOT administers the state's DBE certification program. As is required under 49 C.F.R. § 26.81, Tennessee has a Unified Certification Program (UCP). The UCP makes all DBE certification decisions and provides a "one-stop shop" to DBE applicants.[13] To qualify as a DBE, a business must (1) be for-profit;[14] (2) be a small business concern—with "small" determined by the Small Business Administration (SBA) small business size standards—and does not exceed $30.40 million in gross annual receipts;[15] (3) be at least 51 percent owned by socially and economically disadvantaged individuals—there is a rebuttable presumption that women, Black Americans, Hispanic Americans, Native Americans, Asian-Pacific Americans, Subcontinent Asian Americans, or other minorities are disadvantaged;[16] (4) be controlled by one or more of the socially and economically disadvantaged owners;[17] (5) have the socially and economically disadvantaged owners be U.S. citizens or lawfully admitted permanent residents;[18] and (6) have the personal net worth for any socially and economically disadvantaged owner not exceed $1.32 million.[19] The DBE program is required on contracting opportunities that have received funding from the Federal Highway Administration (FHWA), Federal Aviation Administration (FAA), or Federal Transit Administration (FTA).[20]
- *Airport Concession Disadvantaged Business Enterprise (ACDBE) Program*: In addition to being certified as a DBE under 49 C.F.R. part 26, businesses may also be certified as an Airport Concession

12. *Id.* § 12-3-1102(9).
13. 49 C.F.R. § 26.81(b)(2) (2022).
14. *Id.* § 26.5.
15. *Id.* §§ 26.5, 26.65(b). It is worth noting that under 49 C.F.R. § 26.65(b), the DBE size standard may be adjusted annually for inflation such that in subsequent years the size standard may no longer be $30.40 million.
16. *Id.* § 26.67.
17. *Id.* § 26.5.
18. *Id.* § 26.67.
19. *Id.*
20. *Id.* § 26.21(a).

Disadvantaged Business Enterprise (ACDBE) under 49 C.F.R. part 23. To qualify as an ACDBE, a business must (1) be a concession for-profit small business concern;[21] (2) qualify as small by having its prior three-year average gross receipts not exceed the applicable size standard of $56.42 million;[22] (3) be 51 percent owned by one or more socially and economically disadvantaged individuals;[23] (4) have one or more of the socially and economically disadvantaged individuals with control and managing the daily business operations;[24] and (5) have the personal net worth for any socially and economically disadvantaged owner not exceed $1.32 million.[25]

- *Small Business Enterprise (SBE) Program*: TDOT implemented a small business element within its DBE program called the Small Business Enterprise (SBE) program, pursuant to 49 C.F.R. § 26.39.[26] This program is race and gender neutral.[27] To be eligible for the program, a business must (1) be for-profit; (2) perform a commercially useful function; (3) be independently owned and operated and not under the control or influence of a non-SBE firm; (4) have owner demonstrate "real and substantial" control of daily business operations; and (5) have annual gross receipts averaged over three years not to exceed $10 million or have no more than 30 full-time employees.[28] Certification for the SBE program is handled by Go-DBE.[29] Per TDOT's Small Business Development Program website the SBE program is currently under review.[30]

21. *Id.* § 23.3.
22. *Id.* § 23.33(a). The size standards for the following are exceptions to this: bank and financial institutions is $1 billion in assets; car rental companies are $75.23 million average annual gross receipts; pay telephones is 1,500 employees; and automobile dealers is 350 employees.
23. *Id.*
24. *Id.*
25. *Id.* § 23.35.
26. *Disadvantaged Business Enterprise Plan*, Tenn. Dep't of Transp. 17 (2019), https://www.tn.gov/content/dam/tn/tdot/civilrights/small-business/2019.04.10%20TDOT-DBE-Plan.pdf.
27. *Id.*
28. *Id.*
29. *Id.*
30. *Small Business Development Program*, Tenn. Dep't of Transp., https://www.tn.gov/tdot/civil-rights/small-business-development-program.html (last visited Apr. 19, 2023).

Procurement Laws Intersecting with Business Inclusion

In the state of Tennessee, relevant rules and laws pertaining to the intersection of procurement and business inclusion may primarily be found in the "Tennessee Minority-Owned, Woman-Owned, Service-Disabled Veteran-Owned, Business Owned by Persons with Disabilities, and Small Business Procurement and Contracting Act." Following is a summary of some of the relevant laws.

- *Active Bid Solicitation*: "All state agencies are required to actively solicit bids and proposals for equipment, supplies, personal services, professional services, consulting services, construction contracts, and architectural and engineering services from a minority-owned business, woman-owned business, service-disabled veteran-owned business, business owned by persons with disabilities, or small business in order to strive to obtain a fair proportion of procurements from any minority-owned business, woman-owned business, service-disabled veteran-owned business, business owned by persons with disabilities, or small business."[31] The "fair portion" is not intended to be a mandatory goal or quota and what is considered a "fair portion" is to be recommended annually by Go-DBE to the procurement commission.[32]
- *Annual Goals*: "All state agencies shall fully cooperate with the governor's office of diversity business enterprises and shall provide staff support and any other assistance upon request of the chief procurement officer. This cooperation specifically includes, but is not limited to, establishing and striving to achieve annual state agency level internal goals for minority-owned business, woman-owned business, service-disabled veteran-owned business, business owned by persons with disabilities, or small business contracting. In establishing and striving to achieve these annual goals, each agency shall work closely with the governor's office of diversity business enterprises."[33]
- *Reporting Requirements*: "Each agency shall provide as requested to the governor's office of diversity business enterprises periodic reports on upcoming procurement and contract

31. Tenn. Code Ann. § 12-3-1104(a) (2022).
32. *Id.*
33. *Id.* § 12-3-1106(b).

> opportunities and on the level of participation by minority-owned business, woman-owned business, service-disabled veteran-owned business, business owned by persons with disabilities, or small business in that agency's procurements and contracts."[34] In addition, "[t]he chief procurement officer shall annually report, on or before each December 31, to the governor and to each member of the general assembly concerning the awarding of purchases to minority-owned business, woman-owned business, service-disabled veteran-owned business, business owned by persons with disabilities, or small business and the total value of awards made during the preceding fiscal year. . . ."[35] Lastly, "[t]he office of diversity business enterprises shall publish an annual report listing each state department's aspirational goals and achievements for businesses owned by minorities, women, persons with disabilities, and service-disabled veterans, as well as other small businesses. The report must be published on the office's website."[36]

Contracting opportunities where the TDOT DBE program applies have several requirements that intersect directly with procurement, contracting, and business inclusion.

- *Fostering Small Business Participation*: Pursuant to 49 C.F.R. § 26.39, TDOT has engaged in efforts to foster small business participation through its SBE program.[37] Currently the SBE program is under review.[38] However, its efforts to foster small business participation, as noted in its 2019 "Disadvantaged Business Enterprise Plan," have included efforts such as unbundling projects and project set-asides.[39]
- *Goals*: Contract opportunities may not use quotas or set-asides for DBEs.[40] The only exception for using a set-aside is in a limited or extreme circumstance, "when no other method could be reasonably expected to redress egregious instances of discrimination."[41] Instead, an overall goal must be set.[42] The goal must be based on evidence of available "ready, willing and

34. *Id.* § 12-3-1106(b).
35. *Id.* § 12-3-1107.
36. *Id.* § 12-3-1112(f).
37. *Disadvantaged Business Enterprise Plan*, *supra* note 26.
38. *Small Business Development Program*, *supra* note 30.
39. *Disadvantaged Business Enterprise Plan*, *supra* note 26, at 19.
40. 49 C.F.R. § 26.43 (2022).
41. *Id.*
42. *Id.* § 26.45(a)(1).

able" DBEs in the market.[43] Once the assessment of "ready, willing and able" DBEs is completed, an overall goal may be established as a percentage of the total amount of contracts receiving U.S. Department of Transportation (U.S. DOT) funds.[44] Participation goals must be set for all certified DBEs and not divided into subcategories.[45] Race- and gender-neutral means must be used to "meet the maximum feasible portion of your overall goal."[46] TDOT, as a recipient of U.S. DOT funds, will not be penalized for failing to meet the overall goal set, if it can establish good faith efforts to meet the goal.[47] When there is a DBE goal on a specific contract opportunity, only the bidder meeting the goal, or establishing good faith efforts to meet the goal, may be awarded the contract.[48]

- *Prompt Payment*: Under 49 C.F.R. part 26, contractors must pay subcontractors within 30 days of receipt of payment from the state DOT for satisfactory performance.[49]
- *Payment of Retainage*: Contractors must pay amounts withheld for retainage to subcontractors within 30 days of their work being satisfactorily completed.[50]

Additional Related Laws, Policies, and Programs

- *Waiver for Protest Bond Requirement*: "At the time of filing a notice of a protest of a solicitation, award, or proposed award of a contract in which the estimated maximum liability, estimated maximum revenue, or lowest evaluated cost proposal is less than one million dollars ($1,000,000), a minority-owned business, woman-owned business, Tennessee service-disabled veteran-owned business, business owned by persons with disabilities, or small business, as those terms are defined in § 12-3-1102, may submit a written petition for exemption from the protest bond requirement. . . ."[51]
- *Prompt Payment to Subcontractors*: "If a remote contractor has performed in accordance with the remote contractor's written

43. *Id.* § 26.45(b).
44. *Id.* § 26.45(e).
45. *Id.* § 26.45(h).
46. *Id.* § 26.51.
47. *Id.* § 26.47.
48. *Id.* § 26.53.
49. 49 C.F.R. § 26.29(a) (2023).
50. *Id.* § 26.29(b).
51. TENN. CODE ANN. § 12-3-514(g) (2022).

contract with the prime contractor, then the prime contractor shall pay to the remote contractor the full amount earned by the remote contractor, subject only to any condition precedent for payment clause in the contract, and less only those amounts withheld in accordance with § 66-34-303. The payment must be made in accordance with the schedule for payments established within the contract and within thirty (30) days after application for payment is timely submitted by the remote contractor to the prime contractor, in accordance with the schedule."[52]

- *Finding Contracting Opportunities*: The Department of General Services "Current Procurement Opportunities" page includes information pertaining to contracting opportunities: https://www.tn.gov/generalservices/procurement/central-procurement-office--cpo-/go-dbe/current-procurement-opportunities.html.

Major City Snapshot: Memphis

The City of Memphis' (city) Office of Business Diversity and Compliance manages the in-house certifications for the city.[53] In addition, the city's certification does accept reciprocal applications from other entities that certify businesses.[54] Following are a few program highlights.

- *Certifications*: The city certifies businesses as Minority-owned Business Enterprises (MBEs), Woman-owned Business Enterprises (WBEs), or Small Business Enterprises (SBEs).[55]
  - *Minority-owned Business Enterprises (MBEs)*: To be eligible for the MBE certification, a business must (1) be at least 51 percent owned (in a publicly held business 51 percent of the stock) by one or more minorities, which includes U.S. citizens and lawfully admitted resident aliens who are African American, Hispanic, Asian, or Native American; (2) have one or more minorities who independently control the "management, policies, major decisions and daily business operations" of the business; (3) perform a commercially useful function; (4) "be properly licensed and/or otherwise authorized to do business in the State of Tennessee"

52. *Id.* § 66-34-302(a).
53. *Certification*, City of Memphis, https://www.memphistn.gov/business/certification/ (last visited Apr. 20, 2023).
54. *Id.*
55. *Id.*

as well as a Shelby County business license; (5) be "located within the Memphis MSA (Crittenden County in Arkansas (AR), Desoto, Marshall, Tate, and Tunica Counties in Mississippi (MS), and Fayette, Shelby and Tipton Counties in Tennessee)"; and (6) have "[p]roof of Shelby County Personal Property Taxes and all other necessary local business operational taxes inherit to business in Shelby County are appropriately paid."[56]

- *Woman-owned Business Enterprises (WBEs)*: To be eligible for the WBE certification, a business must (1) be at least 51 percent owned (in a publicly held business 51 percent of the stock) by one or more women, which includes U.S. citizens and lawfully admitted resident aliens who are "of the female gender, and not otherwise included in one of the specific ethnic minority groups"; (2) have one or more women who independently control the "management, policies, major decisions and daily business operations" of the business; (3) perform a commercially useful function; (4) "be properly licensed and/or otherwise authorized to do business in the State of Tennessee" as well as a Shelby County business license; (5) be "located within the Memphis MSA (Crittenden County in Arkansas (AR), Desoto, Marshall, Tate, and Tunica Counties in Mississippi (MS), and Fayette, Shelby and Tipton Counties in Tennessee)"; and (6) have "[p]roof of Shelby County Personal Property Taxes and all other necessary local business operational taxes inherit to business in Shelby County are appropriately paid."[57]
- *Small Business Enterprises (SBEs)*: To be eligible for the SBE certification, a business must (1) have its headquarters and/or principal office in Memphis; (2) be for-profit; (3) be an independent and continuing enterprise; (4) perform a commercially useful function; (5) be owned and controlled by one or more economically disadvantaged individuals; (6) not exceed the SBA size standard; (7) have owners whose net worth does not exceed $1.32 million and they maintain a residence in the Memphis MSA (Crittenden County in Arkansas (AR), Desoto, Marshall, Tate, and Tunica Counties in Mississippi (MS), and Fayette, Shelby and Tipton Counties in Tennessee); (8) have a Shelby County and State

56. MEMPHIS, TENN., ORDINANCES § 6-92-1 (2022); *Certification*, *supra* note 53.
57. MEMPHIS, TENN., ORDINANCES § 6-92-1 (2022); *Certification*, *supra* note 53.

of Tennessee business license; and (9) have "[p]roof of Shelby County Personal Property Taxes and all other necessary local business operational taxes inherit to business in Shelby County are appropriately paid."[58]

- *Bidding Specifications and Contract Language*: On projects with participation goals, contracts must incorporate by reference the City Ordinance Chapter 6-92 "Equal Business Opportunity Program" and note that any breach of that ordinance will subject the contractor to penalties.[59] In addition, all city solicitations will note the city's SBE goal.[60]
- *Inclusion Goals*: For contracts with subcontracting or supplier possibilities, there is a 25 percent SBE goal, which may be reduced or removed on a contract-by-contract basis.[61] As it relates to the MWBE goals, the city does have a methodology in place for determining goals that does include factors such as the availability of such businesses in their relevant market.[62] The annual MWBE goals are as follows, per the city ordinance:[63]
  (1) Subcontracting for Construction: (a) Minority/Diverse, 20 percent, (b) Women, 5 percent, and (c) Total, 25 percent
  (2) Goals for Prime Construction: (a) Minority/Diverse, 15 percent, (b) Women, 3 percent, and (c) Total, 18 percent
  (3) Goals for Architecture and Engineering: (a) Minority/Diverse, 22 percent, (b) Women, 7 percent, and (c) Total, 29 percent
  (4) Goals for Subcontracting on Architecture and Engineering: (a) Minority/Diverse, 15 percent, (b) Women, 5 percent, and (c) Total, 20 percent
  (5) Goals for Goods and Supplies: (a) Minority/Diverse, 12 percent, (b) Women, 1 percent, and (c) Total, 13 percent
  (6) Goals for Other Nonprofessional Services: (a) Minority/Diverse, 23 percent, (b) Women, 2 percent, and (c) Total, 25 percent
  (7) Goals for Other Professional Services: (a) Minority/Diverse, 13 percent, (b) Women, 2 percent, and (c) Total, 15 percent
- *Subcontractor Project Plans and Contractor Good Faith Efforts*: Successful bidders must submit a Subcontractor Project Plan that

58. Memphis, Tenn., Ordinances § 6-94-8 (2022); *Certification*, *supra* note 53.
59. Memphis, Tenn., Ordinances § 6-92-2 (2022).
60. *Id.* § 6-94-15.
61. *Id.* § 6-94-7.
62. *Id.* § 6-92-3.
63. *Id.*

identifies "the name, address, telephone number and contact person of each subcontractor or other business to be used in the contract, the NAICS Code and the type of work or service each business will perform, the dollar value of the work and the scope of work, the ownership of each business by race and gender, if applicable the AABE, HBE, ABE, NABE, or WBE certification number of each business" with their executed contract.[64] Similarly on contracts with SBE contract goals, bidders must submit SBE participation information.[65] If the SBE goal is not met, then good faith efforts must be submitted.[66]

64. *Id.* § 6-92-2.
65. *Id.* § 6-94-16.
66. *Id.*

CHAPTER 44

Texas

Overview of Business Inclusion Program, Policies, and Practices

Government entities seeking to create business inclusion programs have two primary options in terms of the type of program they may create, in terms of who is eligible for the program: (1) a race- and gender-conscious program or (2) a race- and gender-neutral program. Under the Equal Protection Clause of the Fourteenth Amendment, strict scrutiny is applied by the courts when a government actor is creating policies based on race. Strict scrutiny is the highest level of judicial review that may be applied. It requires the government actor to demonstrate that (1) past discrimination exists such that the entity has a "compelling government interest" in rectifying it, and (2) the policies and programs created to do so are "narrowly tailored."[1] Although intermediate scrutiny is often applied when reviewing programs based on gender, strict scrutiny is applied when reviewing race- and gender-conscious business inclusion programs.[2] Disparity studies have become a standard tool used to assist a government entity in withstanding a challenge to its race- and gender-conscious business inclusion programs. These studies aid in demonstrating whether a government entity has engaged

1. City of Richmond v. J.A. Croson Co., 488 U.S. 469 (1989).

2. Since the 1980s with the Supreme Court decision in *City of Richmond v. J.A. Croson Company*, there have been a number of cases across the county that have assessed race- and gender-conscious business inclusion programs. *See* Adarand Constructors, Inc. v. Pena, 515 U.S. 200 (1995); Virdi v. DeKalb Cnty. Sch. Dist., 135 Fed. App'x 262, 268 (11th Cir. 2005); Sherbrooke Turf, Inc. v. Minn. Dep't of Transp., 345 F.3d 964, 971 (8th Cir. 2003); Mountain West Holding Co., Inc. v. The State of Montana, Montana DOT, et al., 2017 WL 2179120 (9th Cir. May 16, 2017).

in past discrimination in its contracting practices, such that the entity may have a compelling government interest in rectifying it.[3]

Conversely, race- and gender-neutral programs are programs that are not only accessible to minority-owned and women-owned businesses but to all businesses, regardless of race or gender. A small business inclusion program would fall into this category. The level of judicial review applied to such a policy to determine its constitutionality is rational basis, which is the lowest threshold for a government to satisfy. For a government entity to satisfy rational basis, the policy or program created must be "related to a legitimate government purpose."[4] Even when a government entity has a race- and gender-conscious program, oftentimes the program may still require the government actor to seek to meet the goals of their program through race- and gender-neutral means where able, so as to be taking the most narrowly tailored means of accomplishing the program goals.

In the state of Texas, at the state level of government, there are two state agencies certifying businesses for business inclusion programs: (1) the Statewide Procurement Division of the Comptroller of Public Accounts[5] and (2) the Texas Department of Transportation (TxDOT).[6]

Summary of Certification Programs and Requirements

The Statewide Procurement Division of the Comptroller of Public Accounts certifies businesses as Historically Underutilized Businesses (HUBs).[7] The Statewide Procurement Division of the Comptroller of Public Accounts may enter into Memorandums of Agreements with other small business certifying entities to increase the number of HUBs certified.[8] The eligibility requirements follow:

- *Historically Underutilized Businesses (HUBs)*: To satisfy the eligibility criteria to be certified as a HUB, a business must (1) have its principal place of business in Texas; (2) have formed for the purpose of making a profit; (3) as a corporation have

3. *Promoting Opportunity and Equality in America: A Guide to Federal Circuit Authority on Permissible Government Actions to Promote Racial and Gender Equality*, Am. Civ. Liberties Union & The Opportunity Agenda (Dec. 2010), https://www.aclu.org/sites/default/files/field_document/Promoting_Opportunity_and_Equality_in_America.pdf.

4. 488 U.S. 469 (1989).

5. *Historically Underutilized Business Program*, Tex. Comptroller of Pub. Accounts, https://comptroller.texas.gov/purchasing/vendor/hub/ (last visited Mar. 22, 2023).

6. *Disadvantaged and Small Business Enterprise Programs*, Tex. Dep't of Transp., https://www.txdot.gov/business/disadvantaged-small-business-enterprise.html (last visited Mar. 22, 2023).

7. *Historically Underutilized Business Program*, *supra* note 5.

8. *HUB Resources*, Tex. Comptroller of Pub. Accounts, https://comptroller.texas.gov/purchasing/vendor/hub/resources.php (last visited Mar. 22, 2023).

51 percent or more of all shares of stock or other equitable securities owned by one or more economically disadvantaged persons; as a sole proprietor must completely be owned by an economically disadvantaged person; as a partnership have 51 percent or more of its assets and interests owned by one or more economically disadvantaged persons; and as a joint venture have each entity as a HUB; (4) be controlled, operated, and managed by one or more economically disadvantaged persons; (5) not exceed the comptroller's graduation size standards; and (6) have the qualifying owner be a U.S. citizen, born or naturalized.[9] An economically disadvantaged person is defined as including Black Americans, Hispanic Americans, Asian Pacific Americans, Native Americans, women, and veterans with at least a 20 percent service-connected disability who have "suffered the effects of discriminatory practices or other similar insidious circumstances over which the person has no control."[10] Certification lasts four years and at such time of expiration of that period a HUB may recertify.[11]

TxDOT administers the Disadvantaged Business Enterprise (DBE) program, Airport Concession Disadvantaged Business Enterprise (ACDBE) program, and the Small Business Enterprise program (SBE).

- *Disadvantaged Business Enterprise (DBE) Program*: Pursuant to 49 C.F.R. part 26, TxDOT administers the state's DBE certification program. As is required under 49 C.F.R. § 26.81, Texas has a Unified Certification Program (TUCP). The TUCP makes all DBE certification decisions and provides a "one-stop shop" to DBE applicants.[12] To qualify as a DBE, a business must (1) be for-profit;[13] (2) be a small business concern—with "small" determined by the Small Business Administration (SBA) small business size standards—and does not exceed $30.40 million in gross annual receipts;[14] (3) be at least 51 percent owned by socially and economically disadvantaged individuals—there is a rebuttable presumption that women, Black Americans, Hispanic Americans, Native Americans, Asian-Pacific

9. Tex. Gov't. Code Ann. § 2161.001 (2021); 34 Tex. Admin. Code § 20.282 (2022).
10. *Id.*
11. 34 Tex. Admin. Code § 20.290 (2022).
12. 49 C.F.R. § 26.81(b)(2) (2022).
13. *Id.* § 26.5.
14. *Id.* §§ 26.5, 26.65(b). It is worth noting that under 49 C.F.R. § 26.65(b), the DBE size standard may be adjusted annually for inflation such that in subsequent years the size standard may no longer be $30.40 million.

Americans, Subcontinent Asian Americans, or other minorities are disadvantaged;[15] (4) be controlled by one or more of the socially and economically disadvantaged owners;[16] (5) have the socially and economically disadvantaged owners be U.S. citizens or lawfully admitted permanent residents;[17] and (6) have the personal net worth for any socially and economically disadvantaged owner not exceed $1.32 million.[18] The DBE program is required on contracting opportunities that have received funding from the Federal Highway Administration (FHWA), Federal Aviation Administration (FAA), or Federal Transit Administration (FTA).[19]

- *Airport Concession Disadvantaged Business Enterprise (ACDBE) Program*: In addition to being certified as a DBE under 49 C.F.R. part 26, businesses may also be certified as an Airport Concession Disadvantaged Business Enterprise (ACDBE) under 49 C.F.R. part 23. To qualify as an ACDBE, a business must (1) be a concession for-profit small business concern;[20] (2) qualify as small by having its prior three-year average gross receipts not exceed the applicable size standard of $56.42 million;[21] (3) be 51 percent owned by one or more socially and economically disadvantaged individuals;[22] (4) have one or more of the socially and economically disadvantaged individuals with control and managing the daily business operations;[23] and (5) have the personal net worth for any socially and economically disadvantaged owner not exceed $1.32 million.[24]
- *Small Business Enterprise (SBE)*: TxDOT has implemented a small business element within its DBE program called the Small Business Enterprise (SBE) Program, pursuant to 49 C.F.R. § 26.39.[25] This program applies on contracts where there is not a DBE goal or a state HUB goal and the project

15. *Id.* § 26.67.
16. *Id.* § 26.5.
17. *Id.* § 26.67.
18. *Id.*
19. *Id.* § 26.21(a).
20. *Id.* § 23.3.
21. *Id.* § 23.33(a). The size standards for the following are exceptions to this: bank and financial institutions is $1 billion in assets; car rental companies are $75.23 million average annual gross receipts; pay telephones is 1,500 employees; and automobile dealers is 350 employees.
22. *Id.*
23. *Id.*
24. 49 C.F.R. § 23.35 (2022).
25. 43 TEX. ADMIN. CODE § 9.300 (2022).

is funded by state or local funds only.[26] To be eligible for the program, a business must (1) be a small business under the SBA size standards evidenced by its three-year average of its annual gross receipts and (2) have one or more U.S. citizens or lawfully admitted permanent residents own at least 51 percent of the firm's assets, interest, and/or classes of stock and equitable securities.[27]

Procurement Laws Intersecting with Business Inclusion

There are two relevant places where Texas procurement laws may be found: title 10, subtitle D of the Texas Government Code, and chapters 2261 and 2262.[28] Following are some laws that pertain to HUBs.

- *Subcontracting Plans*: On contracts expected to be $100,000 or more, a state agency must determine prior to solicitation for the contract opportunity whether subcontracting opportunities are probable on the contract, and, if so, then the agency must require each bid, proposal, offer, or other applicable expression of interest for the contract includes a HUB subcontracting plan.[29] Failure to include a plan would render the response to the solicitation as nonresponsive.[30]
- *Good Faith Efforts*: For both construction contracts and purchases for goods and services, state agencies must make a good faith effort to increase contract awards to HUBs.[31] When a contracting opportunity requires a subcontracting plan, the awarded contractor must make a good faith effort to implement the subcontracting plan.[32] A determination of failure to demonstrate good faith efforts may result in the contractor being barred from further contracting opportunities with the agency.[33]

---

26. *Id.* § 9.301; *Small Business Enterprise Program*, Tex. Dep't of Transp., https://www.txdot.gov/business/disadvantaged-small-business-enterprise/sbe.html (last visited Mar. 22, 2023).
27. 43 Tex. Admin. Code § 9.304 (2022).
28. *State of Texas Procurement and Contract Management Guide*, Statewide Procurement Div., https://comptroller.texas.gov/purchasing/publications/procurement-contract.php (last visited Mar. 22, 2023).
29. Tex. Gov't. Code Ann. § 2161.252 (2021); Tex. Admin. Code § 20.285 (2022).
30. Tex. Gov't. Code Ann. § 2161.252 (2021); Tex. Admin. Code § 20.285 (2022).
31. Tex. Gov't. Code Ann. § 2161.181 (2021); Tex. Gov't. Code Ann. § 2161.182 (2021).
32. Tex. Gov't. Code Ann. § 2161.253 (2021).
33. *Id.*

- *Purchasing Goals*: Pursuant to Texas Administrative Code section 20.284(b), statewide HUB goals are as follows: (1) 11.2 percent for heavy construction other than building contracts; (2) 21.1 percent for all building construction, including general contractors and operative builders contracts; (3) 32.9 percent for all special trade construction contracts; (4) 23.7 percent for professional services contracts; (5) 26.0 percent for all other services contracts; and (6) 21.1 percent for commodities contracts. State agencies must establish their own goals, and those goals may be higher or lower than the statewide goal.[34]
- *Mentor Protégé Program*: The comptroller must "design a mentor-protégé program to foster long-term relationships between prime contractors and historically underutilized businesses and to increase the ability of historically underutilized businesses to contract with the state or to receive subcontracts under a state contract. Each state agency with a biennial appropriation that exceeds $10 million shall implement the program designed by the comptroller. . . . Participation in the program must be voluntary for both the contractor and the historically underutilized business subcontractor."[35]
- *Purchases Over $10,000 and Not More Than $25,000*: "The Contract Developer must solicit bids from a minimum of three active vendors on the [Centralized Master Bidders List], two of which must be current Texas-certified HUBs; the last vendor who was awarded a contract for the same goods or services may be provided the request for bid, if applicable."[36]
- *Prompt Payment to Contractors and Subcontractors on Construction Services Projects*: Owners (here defined as the state) receiving a request for payment on properly performed work must pay the contractor within 35 days.[37] Contractors who have been paid must pay their subcontractors who had a portion of the payment the contractor received from the owner within seven days of receiving payment from the owner.[38]
- *Penalties*: If a person intentionally applies as HUB for a contract award and knows the person is not a HUB, it is a third-degree felony.[39]

---

34. 43 Tex. Admin. Code § 20.284(c) (2022).
35. Tex. Gov't. Code Ann. § 2161.065 (2021).
36. *State of Texas Procurement and Contract Management Guide, supra* note 28.
37. Tex. Gov't. Code Ann. § 28.002 (2021).
38. *Id.*
39. *Id.* § 2161.231.

- *Contracting Preferences*: If the cost to the state and quality are equal on bid between a service-disabled veteran and a Texas bidder, the service-disabled veteran must be given first preference and the Texas bidder second preference.[40]
- *Reporting Requirements*: The comptroller will report twice a year to the "presiding officer of each house of the legislature" on spends, number of contracts awarded, graduation rates, and reports from state agencies.[41] State agencies must maintain monthly information related to its efforts pertaining to historically underutilized businesses and report to the comptroller.[42]

Contracting opportunities where the TxDOT DBE program applies have several requirements that intersect directly with procurement, contracting, and business inclusion.

- *SBE Inclusion*: An overall annual SBE goal will be set by the executive director of TxDOT, and TxDOT "will make a good faith effort to meet or exceed the annual goal."[43] In addition, annually, TxDOT will report on its SBE participation and certifications.[44] "The department may assign individual contract goals for SBE participation contracts as necessary to cumulatively meet the overall annual SBE goals."[45]
- *Goals*: Contract opportunities may not use quotas or set-asides for DBEs.[46] The only exception for using a set-aside is in a limited or extreme circumstance, "when no other method could be reasonably expected to redress egregious instances of discrimination."[47] Instead, an overall goal must be set.[48] The goal must be based on evidence of available "ready, willing and able" DBEs in the market.[49] Once the assessment of "ready, willing and able" DBEs is completed, an overall goal may be established as a percentage of the total amount of contracts receiving U.S. Department of Transportation (U.S. DOT) funds.[50] Participation goals must be set for all certified DBEs

40. *Id.* § 2155.444.
41. *Id.* § 2161.121.
42. *Id.* § 2161.122.
43. 43 Tex. Admin. Code § 9.314 (2022).
44. *Id.*
45. *Id.* § 9.315.
46. 49 C.F.R. § 26.43 (2022).
47. *Id.*
48. *Id.* § 26.45(a)(1).
49. *Id.* § 26.45(b).
50. *Id.* § 26.45(e).

and not divided into subcategories.[51] Race- and gender-neutral means must be used to "meet the maximum feasible portion of your overall goal."[52] TxDOT, as a recipient of U.S. DOT funds, will not be penalized for failing to meet the overall goal set, if it can establish good faith efforts to meet the goal.[53] When there is a DBE goal on a specific contract opportunity, only the bidder meeting the goal, or establishing good faith efforts to meet the goal, may be awarded the contract.[54]

- *Prompt Payment*: Under 49 C.F.R. part 26, contractors must pay subcontractors within 30 days of receipt of payment from the state DOT for satisfactory performance.[55]
- *Payment of Retainage*: Contractors must pay amounts withheld for retainage to subcontractors within 30 days of their work being satisfactorily completed.[56]

Additional Related Laws, Policies, and Programs

- *Formation Fee Waiver for Veterans Forming a Business*: For businesses 100 percent veteran-owned where the owners were honorably discharged from active duty that were/will be formed between January 1, 2022 and December 31, 2025, the business formation fee is waived.[57] In addition, such businesses are also relieved from paying the Texas franchise tax for the initial five-year period.
- *Technical Assistance*: Under state law, the comptroller "shall offer historically underutilized businesses assistance and training regarding state procurement procedures"[58] as well as "design a program of forums in which historically underutilized businesses are invited by state agencies to deliver technical and business presentations that demonstrate their capability to do business with the agency."[59] In addition, state agencies

51. *Id.* § 26.45(h).
52. *Id.* § 26.51.
53. *Id.* § 26.47.
54. *Id.* § 26.53.
55. 49 C.F.R. § 26.29(a) (2023).
56. *Id.* § 26.29(b).
57. *Veteran Entrepreneur Resources*, TEX. VETERANS COMM'N, https://www.tvc.texas.gov/entrepreneurs/entrepreneur-resources/ (last visited Mar. 22, 2023); *New Veteran-Owned Business Pre-Qualification Process Business Entity Formation Fee and Franchise Tax Waiver*, TEX. VETERANS COMM'N (2021), https://www.tvc.texas.gov/wp-content/uploads/2021/10/New-Veteran-Owned-Business-Pre-Qualification-Process_final_2022.pdf.
58. TEX. GOV'T. CODE ANN. § 2161.062(b) (2021).
59. *Id.* § 2161.066(a) (2021); 34 TEX. ADMIN. CODE § 20.297 (2022).

with a biennial budget over $10 million must designate a staff person to serve as the historically underutilized business coordinator who must ". . . (1) coordinate training programs for the recruitment and retention of historically underutilized businesses; (2) report required information to the comptroller; and (3) match historically underutilized businesses with key staff within the agency."[60]

- *Finding Contracting Opportunities*: Contracting opportunities may be viewed on the Texas Comptroller of Public Accounts "Electronic State Business Daily Search" site: https://www.txsmartbuy.com/esbd.

Major City Snapshot: Austin

The City of Austin's (city) Small and Minority Business Resources Department manages the certification for the city's business inclusion program.[61] The goals and program components that follow reflect what is currently in the city ordinance from the prior disparity study. However, the city recently completed a disparity study in 2022 and the goals and program components that follow, as well as the city ordinance, may be updated as a result of the recent study.

- *Authority*: City of Austin Ordinance Chapter(s) 2-9 (A)(B)(C) and (D).[62]
- *Certifications*: The city certifies the following type of businesses: Minority-Owned Business Enterprises (MBE), Women-Owned Business Enterprises (WBE), Disadvantaged Business Enterprises (DBE), Airport Concession Disadvantaged Business Enterprise (ACDBE), and Small Business Enterprises (SBE).[63] For additional details on certification eligibility requirements visit https://www.austintexas.gov/department/certification-overview.
- *Bidding Specifications*: On all contracting opportunities where a goal or sub-goal has been established the solicitation must note the goals and/sub-goals.[64]

---

60. Tex. Gov't. Code Ann. § 2161.062(e) (2021).

61. *Certification Overview*, City of Austin, https://www.austintexas.gov/department/certification-overview (last visited Mar. 22, 2023).

62. *Id.*

63. *Id.*

64. City of Austin Code of Ordinances §§ 2-9A-21, 2-9B-21, 2-9C-21, 2-9D-21.

- *Good Faith Efforts*: For solicitations that have noted a goal or sub-goal, if a bidder/proposer does not achieve the goal, they must demonstrate good faith efforts.[65]
- *Inclusion Goals*:
  - *Construction*: African-American Owned Business Enterprises (1.7 percent); Hispanic-Owned Business Enterprises (9.7 percent); Asian-American and Native American Owned Business Enterprises (2.3 percent); Minority-Owned Business Enterprises (13.7 percent); and Women-Owned Business Enterprises (13.8 percent).[66]
  - *Professional Services*: African-American Owned Business Enterprises (1.9 percent); Hispanic-Owned Business Enterprises (9.0 percent); Asian-American and Native American Owned Business Enterprises (4.9 percent); Minority-Owned Business Enterprises (15.8 percent); and Women-Owned Business Enterprises (15.8 percent).[67]
  - *Nonprofessional Services*: African-American Owned Business Enterprises (2.5 percent); Hispanic-Owned Business Enterprises (9.9 percent); Asian-American and Native American Owned Business Enterprises (1.7 percent); Minority-Owned Business Enterprises (14.1 percent); and Women-Owned Business Enterprises (15.0 percent).[68]
  - *Commodities*: African-American Owned Business Enterprises (0.3 percent); Hispanic Owned Business Enterprises (2.5 percent); Asian-American and Native American Owned Business Enterprises (0.7 percent); Minority-Owned Business Enterprises (3.5 percent); and Women-Owned Business Enterprises (6.2 percent).[69]

---

65. *Id.*
66. *Id.* § 2-9A-3.
67. *Id.* § 2-9B-3.
68. *Id.* § 2-9C-3.
69. *Id.* § 2-9D-3.

CHAPTER 45

Utah

Overview of Business Inclusion Program, Policies, and Practices

Government entities seeking to create business inclusion programs have two primary options in terms of the type of program they may create, in terms of who is eligible for the program: (1) a race- and gender-conscious program or (2) a race- and gender-neutral program. Under the Equal Protection Clause of the Fourteenth Amendment, strict scrutiny is applied by the courts when a government actor is creating policies based on race. Strict scrutiny is the highest level of judicial review that may be applied. It requires the government actor to demonstrate that (1) past discrimination exists such that the entity has a "compelling government interest" in rectifying it, and (2) the policies and programs created to do so are "narrowly tailored."[1] Although intermediate scrutiny is often applied when reviewing programs based on gender, strict scrutiny is applied when reviewing race- and gender-conscious business inclusion programs.[2] Disparity studies have become a standard tool used to assist a government entity in withstanding a challenge to its race- and gender-conscious business inclusion programs. These studies aid in demonstrating whether a government entity has engaged

1. City of Richmond v. J.A. Croson Co., 488 U.S. 469 (1989).

2. Since the 1980s with the Supreme Court decision in *City of Richmond v. J.A. Croson Company*, there have been a number of cases across the county that have assessed race- and gender-conscious business inclusion programs. *See* Adarand Constructors, Inc. v. Pena, 515 U.S. 200 (1995); Virdi v. DeKalb Cnty. Sch. Dist., 135 Fed. App'x 262, 268 (11th Cir. 2005); Sherbrooke Turf, Inc. v. Minn. Dep't of Transp., 345 F.3d 964, 971 (8th Cir. 2003); Mountain West Holding Co., Inc. v. The State of Montana, Montana DOT, et al., 2017 WL 2179120 (9th Cir. May 16, 2017).

in past discrimination in its contracting practices, such that the entity may have a compelling government interest in rectifying it.[3]

Conversely, race- and gender-neutral programs are programs that are not only accessible to minority-owned and women-owned businesses but to all businesses, regardless of race or gender. A small business inclusion program would fall into this category. The level of judicial review applied to such a policy to determine its constitutionality is rational basis, which is the lowest threshold for a government to satisfy. For a government entity to satisfy rational basis, the policy or program created must be "related to a legitimate government purpose."[4] Even when a government entity has a race- and gender-conscious program, oftentimes the program may still require the government actor to seek to meet the goals of their program through race- and gender-neutral means where able, so as to be taking the most narrowly tailored means of accomplishing the program goals.

At the state level of government in Utah, the Utah Department of Transportation (UDOT) and Utah Transit Authority (UTA) Disadvantaged Business Enterprise (DBE) programs are the only business inclusion programs that consist of a certification program and set goals for inclusion on applicable contracts.

Summary of Certification Programs and Requirements

UDOT, along with UTA and the Salt Lake City Airport administer the Disadvantaged Business Enterprise (DBE) program and Airport Concession Disadvantaged Business Enterprise (ACDBE) program. Following are the eligibility requirements.[5]

- *Disadvantaged Business Enterprise (DBE)*: As is required under 49 C.F.R. § 26.81, Utah has a Unified Certification Program (UCP). The UCP makes all DBE certification decisions and provides a "one-stop shop" to DBE applicants.[6] To qualify as a DBE, a business must (1) be for-profit;[7] (2) be a small business

3. *Promoting Opportunity and Equality in America: A Guide to Federal Circuit Authority on Permissible Government Actions to Promote Racial and Gender Equality*, Am. Civ. Liberties Union & The Opportunity Agenda (Dec. 2010), https://www.aclu.org/sites/default/files/field_document/Promoting_Opportunity_and_Equality_in_America.pdf.

4. 488 U.S. 469 (1989).

5. *Civil Rights*, Utah Dep't of Transp., https://udot.utah.gov/connect/business/civil-rights/ (last visited Mar. 19, 2023); *Disadvantaged Enterprises*, Utah Transit Auth., https://www.rideuta.com/doing-business/disadvantaged-enterprises (last visited Mar. 19, 2023); *Disadvantaged Business Enterprise (DBE)*, Salt Lake City Dep't of Airports, https://slcairport.com/business-services/disadvantaged-business-enterprise/ (last visited Mar. 19, 2023).

6. 49 C.F.R. § 26.81(b)(2) (2022).

7. *Id.* § 26.5.

concern—with "small" determined by the Small Business Administration (SBA) small business size standards—and does not exceed $30.40 million in gross annual receipts;[8] (3) be at least 51 percent owned by socially and economically disadvantaged individuals—there is a rebuttable presumption that women, Black Americans, Hispanic Americans, Native Americans, Asian-Pacific Americans, Subcontinent Asian Americans, or other minorities are disadvantaged;[9] (4) be controlled by one or more of the socially and economically disadvantaged owners;[10] (5) have the socially and economically disadvantaged owners be U.S. citizens or lawfully admitted permanent residents;[11] and (6) have the personal net worth for any socially and economically disadvantaged owner not exceed $1.32 million.[12] The DBE program is required on contracting opportunities that have received funding from the Federal Highway Administration (FHWA), Federal Aviation Administration (FAA), or Federal Transit Administration (FTA).[13]

- *Airport Concession Disadvantaged Business Enterprise (ACDBE)*: In addition to being certified as a DBE under 49 C.F.R. part 26, businesses may also be certified as an Airport Concession Disadvantaged Business Enterprise (ACDBE) under 49 C.F.R. part 23. To qualify as an ACDBE, a business must (1) be a concession for-profit small business concern;[14] (2) qualify as small by having its prior three-year average gross receipts not exceed the applicable size standard of $56.42 million;[15] (3) be 51 percent owned by one or more socially and economically disadvantaged individuals;[16] (4) have one or more of the socially and economically disadvantaged individuals with control and managing the daily business operations;[17] and (5) have the

8. *Id.* §§ 26.5, 26.65(b). It is worth noting that under 49 C.F.R. § 26.65(b), the DBE size standard may be adjusted annually for inflation such that in subsequent years the size standard may no longer be $30.40 million.

9. *Id.* § 26.67.

10. *Id.* § 26.5.

11. *Id.* § 26.67.

12. *Id.*

13. *Id.* § 26.21(a).

14. *Id.* § 23.3.

15. *Id.* § 23.33(a). The size standards for the following are exceptions to this: bank and financial institutions is $1 billion in assets; car rental companies are $75.23 million average annual gross receipts; pay telephones is 1,500 employees; and automobile dealers is 350 employees.

16. *Id.*

17. *Id.*

personal net worth for any socially and economically disadvantaged owner not exceed $1.32 million.[18]

Procurement Laws Intersecting with Business Inclusion

Procurement in the state of Utah is managed by the Division of Purchasing and General Services.[19] The authority for procurement in Utah may be found in the Utah Procurement Code (title 63G, chapter 6A). Under the Utah Procurement Code, there are no bidding preferences, laws, or rules specific to business inclusion and small, minority-owned, women-owned, disability-owned, veteran-owned, and/or LGBT-owned business enterprises in Utah, outside of what is required by the UDOT DBE program. There is a Quote Local search engine on the Division of Purchasing and General Services website that "can be used by public entities in Utah to find local vendors to provide quotes for procurement."[20]

Contracting opportunities where the UDOT/UTA/Salt Lake City Airport DBE program applies have several requirements that intersect directly with procurement, contracting, and business inclusion.

- *Goals*: Contract opportunities may not use quotas or set-asides for DBEs.[21] The only exception for using a set-aside is in a limited or extreme circumstance, "when no other method could be reasonably expected to redress egregious instances of discrimination."[22] Instead, an overall goal must be set.[23] The goal must be based on evidence of available "ready, willing and able" DBEs in the market.[24] Once the assessment of "ready, willing and able" DBEs is completed, an overall goal may be established as a percentage of the total amount of contracts receiving Department of Transportation (U.S. DOT) funds.[25] Participation goals must be set for all certified DBEs and not divided into subcategories.[26] Race- and gender-neutral means must be used to "meet the maximum feasible portion of your

18. *Id.* § 23.35.
19. *The Division of Purchasing and General Services*, State of Utah, https://purchasing.utah.gov/about-us/ (last visited Mar. 19, 2023).
20. *Think Utah Quote Local*, Utah Div. of Purchasing & Gen. Servs., https://purchasing.utah.gov/quote-local/ (last visited May 13, 2023).
21. 49 C.F.R. § 26.43 (2022).
22. *Id.*
23. *Id.* § 26.45(a)(1).
24. *Id.* § 26.45(b).
25. *Id.* § 26.45(e).
26. *Id.* § 26.45(h).

overall goal."[27] UDOT, as a recipient of U.S. DOT funds, will not be penalized for failing to meet the overall goal set, if it can establish good faith efforts to meet the goal.[28] When there is a DBE goal on a specific contract opportunity, only the bidder meeting the goal, or establishing good faith efforts to meet the goal, may be awarded the contract.[29]

- *Prompt Payment*: Under 49 C.F.R. part 26, contractors must pay subcontractors within 30 days of receipt of payment from the state DOT for satisfactory performance.[30]
- *Payment of Retainage*: Contractors must pay amounts withheld for retainage to subcontractors within 30 days of their work being satisfactorily completed.[31]

Additional Related Laws, Policies, and Programs

- *Additional Related Contracting Preferences*: Under Utah Code Annotated 63G-6a-1003, "Preference for Resident Contractors," a person or entity may receive a reciprocal preference if it (1) has a principal place of business in Utah or employs workers residing in Utah and (2) was transacting business on the date of the solicitation of bids.
- *Access to Capital*: Under the State Small Business Credit Initiative Program Fund it states that "[t]he office shall make loans and loan guarantees from the fund for the Small Business Credit Initiative created under the Small Business Jobs Act of 2010, 12 U.S.C. Sec. 5701 et seq., as amended, to use federal money for programs that leverage private lending to help finance small businesses and manufacturers that are creditworthy but not receiving the loans needed to expand and create jobs."[32]
- *Prompt Payment to Subcontractors*: "Upon payment by an agency of the state of Utah or by an agency of the United States, a business which has acquired under contract, property or services in connection with its contract with such an agency from a subcontractor or supplier, shall pay such subcontractor or supplier within 30 days after payment from such agency. . . ."[33]

27. *Id.* § 26.51.
28. *Id.* § 26.47.
29. *Id.* § 26.53.
30. 49 C.F.R. § 26.29(a) (2023).
31. *Id.* § 26.29(b).
32. Utah Code Ann. § 63N-3-802 (2022).
33. *Id.* § 15-6-5.

- *Finding Contracting Opportunities*: Contracting opportunities may be found on the "Utah Public Procurement Place" website: https://bids.sciquest.com/apps/Router/PublicEvent?CustomerOrg=StateOfUtah.

Major City Snapshot: West Valley City

West Valley City does not have a city-specific business inclusion program focused on minority-owned, women-owned, disability-owned, veteran-owned, and/or LGBT-owned business enterprises under its city ordinance. It does, however, state in its city ordinance that it "may include in any bid a preference for any provider who is a Veteran as defined by Title 71of the Utah Code."[34]

34. W. Valley City Mun. Code § 5-2-109 (2023).

CHAPTER 46

Vermont

Overview of Business Inclusion Program, Policies, and Practices

Government entities seeking to create business inclusion programs have two primary options in terms of the type of program they may create, in terms of who is eligible for the program: (1) a race- and gender-conscious program or (2) a race- and gender-neutral program. Under the Equal Protection Clause of the Fourteenth Amendment, strict scrutiny is applied by the courts when a government actor is creating policies based on race. Strict scrutiny is the highest level of judicial review that may be applied. It requires the government actor to demonstrate that (1) past discrimination exists such that the entity has a "compelling government interest" in rectifying it, and (2) the policies and programs created to do so are "narrowly tailored."[1] Although intermediate scrutiny is often applied when reviewing programs based on gender, strict scrutiny is applied when reviewing race- and gender-conscious business inclusion programs.[2] Disparity studies have become a standard tool used to assist a government entity in withstanding a challenge to its race- and gender-conscious business inclusion programs. These studies aid in demonstrating whether a government entity has engaged

1. City of Richmond v. J.A. Croson Co., 488 U.S. 469 (1989).

2. Since the 1980s with the Supreme Court decision in *City of Richmond v. J.A. Croson Company*, there have been a number of cases across the county that have assessed race- and gender-conscious business inclusion programs. *See* Adarand Constructors, Inc. v. Pena, 515 U.S. 200 (1995); Virdi v. DeKalb Cnty. Sch. Dist., 135 Fed. App'x 262, 268 (11th Cir. 2005); Sherbrooke Turf, Inc. v. Minn. Dep't of Transp., 345 F.3d 964, 971 (8th Cir. 2003); Mountain West Holding Co., Inc. v. The State of Montana, Montana DOT, et al., 2017 WL 2179120 (9th Cir. May 16, 2017).

in past discrimination in its contracting practices, such that the entity may have a compelling government interest in rectifying it.[3]

Conversely, race- and gender-neutral programs are programs that are not only accessible to minority-owned and women-owned businesses but to all businesses, regardless of race or gender. A small business inclusion program would fall into this category. The level of judicial review applied to such a policy to determine its constitutionality is rational basis, which is the lowest threshold for a government to satisfy. For a government entity to satisfy rational basis, the policy or program created must be "related to a legitimate government purpose."[4] Even when a government entity has a race- and gender-conscious program, oftentimes the program may still require the government actor to seek to meet the goals of their program through race- and gender-neutral means where able, so as to be taking the most narrowly tailored means of accomplishing the program goals.

In the state of Vermont, at the state level of government, there are two state agencies that certify businesses for business inclusion programs: (1) the Agency of Administration, Department of Buildings and General Services (BGS) and (2) the Vermont Department of Transportation (VTrans).

Summary of Certification Programs and Requirements

Businesses interested in the state of Vermont's Minority Owned Business Enterprise/Women Owned Busienss Enterprise (MWBE) efforts may complete a Minority/Women Owned Business Enterprise Self Certification Form and submit it to BGS.[5] The form asks for business contact information, owner race and gender, and business categories.[6] Outside of the self-certification form, BGS does not have a rigorous certification process with specific eligibility requirements noted. BGS does maintain a directory of MWBEs that is available for download on their website: https://bgs.vermont.gov/facilities/forms/minority-women.

---

3. *Promoting Opportunity and Equality in America: A Guide to Federal Circuit Authority on Permissible Government Actions to Promote Racial and Gender Equality*, Am. Civ. Liberties Union & The Opportunity Agenda (Dec. 2010), https://www.aclu.org/sites/default/files/field_document/Promoting_Opportunity_and_Equality_in_America.pdf.

4. 488 U.S. 469 (1989).

5. *Minority and Women Owned Business Enterprises*, Agency of Admin. Dep't of Bldgs. & Gen. Servs., https://bgs.vermont.gov/facilities/forms/minority-women (last visited Apr. 22, 2023).

6. *Minority/Women Owned Business Enterprise Self-Certification Form*, Agency of Admin. Dep't of Bldgs. & Gen. Servs., https://bgs.vermont.gov/sites/bgs/files/files/purchasing-contracting/Publications/2018%20BGS-Facilities-MWBE-Self-Certification-Form%20fillable%2011.01.2021.pdf (last visited Apr. 22, 2023).

VTrans administers the Disadvantaged Business Enterprise (DBE) program, Airport Concession Disadvantaged Business Enterprise (ACDBE) program, and the VTrans Small Business Program.

- *Disadvantaged Business Enterprise (DBE) Program*: Pursuant to 49 C.F.R. part 26 VTrans administers the state's DBE certification program. As is required under 49 C.F.R. § 26.81, Vermont has a Unified Certification Program (UCP). The UCP makes all DBE certification decisions and provides a "one-stop shop" to DBE applicants.[7] To qualify as a DBE, a business must (1) be for-profit;[8] (2) be a small business concern—with "small" determined by the Small Business Administration (SBA) small business size standard—and does not exceed $30.40 million in gross annual receipts;[9] (3) be at least 51 percent owned by socially and economically disadvantaged individuals—there is a rebuttable presumption that women, Black Americans, Hispanic Americans, Native Americans, Asian-Pacific Americans, Subcontinent Asian Americans, or other minorities are disadvantaged;[10] (4) be controlled by one or more of the socially and economically disadvantaged owners;[11] (5) have the socially and economically disadvantaged owners be U.S. citizens or lawfully admitted permanent residents;[12] and (6) have the personal net worth for any socially and economically disadvantaged owner not exceed $1.32 million.[13] The DBE program is required on contracting opportunities that have received funding from the Federal Highway Administration (FHWA), Federal Aviation Administration (FAA), or Federal Transit Administration (FTA).[14]
- *Airport Concession Disadvantaged Business Enterprise (ACDBE) Program*: In addition to being certified as a DBE under 49 C.F.R. part 26, businesses may also be certified as an Airport Concession Disadvantaged Business Enterprise (ACDBE) under 49 C.F.R. part 23. To qualify as an ACDBE, a business must (1) be a concession for-profit small business

7. 49 C.F.R. § 26.81(b)(2) (2022).
8. *Id.* § 26.5.
9. *Id.* §§ 26.5, 26.65(b). It is worth noting that under 49 C.F.R. § 26.65(b), the DBE size standard may be adjusted annually for inflation such that in subsequent years the size standard may no longer be $30.40 million.
10. *Id.* § 26.67.
11. *Id.* § 26.5.
12. *Id.* § 26.67.
13. *Id.*
14. *Id.* § 26.21(a).

concern;[15] (2) qualify as small by having its prior three-year average gross receipts not exceed the applicable size standard of $56.42 million;[16] (3) be 51 percent owned by one or more socially and economically disadvantaged individuals;[17] (4) have one or more of the socially and economically disadvantaged individuals with control and managing the daily business operations;[18] and (5) have the personal net worth for any socially and economically disadvantaged owner not exceed $1.32 million.[19]

- *Small Business Program*: VTrans implemented a small business element within its DBE program called the VTrans Small Business Program, pursuant to 49 C.F.R. § 26.39.[20] This program is race- and gender-neutral.[21] To be eligible for the program, a business must have annual gross receipts under the SBA size standards for their industry as well as the DBE size standard noted in 49 C.F.R. § 26.65.[22]

Procurement Laws Intersecting with Business Inclusion

In the state of Vermont, there are not any state statues or rules pertaining to business inclusion. There is an executive order that lays the foundation for the policy of the state related to MWBEs.

- *Policy*: Executive Order #15-91 states that, "[t]he State of Vermont recognizes the important contributions and vital impact which small businesses have on the state's economy. In this regard, the state prescribes to a free and open bidding process that affords all businesses equal access and opportunity to compete for state contracts for goods and services. The state also recognizes the existence of businesses owned by minorities and women and directs all state agencies and departments

15. *Id.* § 23.3.

16. *Id.* § 23.33(a). The size standards for the following are exceptions to this: bank and financial institutions is $1 billion in assets; car rental companies are $75.23 million average annual gross receipts; pay telephones is 1,500 employees; and automobile dealers is 350 employees.

17. *Id.*

18. *Id.*

19. *Id.* § 23.35.

20. *Disadvantaged Business Enterprise Program*, Vt. Agency of Transp. 15 (2017), https://vtrans.vermont.gov/sites/aot/files/civilrights/documents/dbe/VTransDBEProgram.pdf.

21. *Id.* at 53.

22. *Vermont Agency of Transportation (VTrans) Small Business Program*, Vt. Agency of Transp., https://vtrans.vermont.gov/sites/aot/files/civilrights/documents/dbe/SmallBusinessProgram-Handout.pdf (last visited Apr. 20, 2023).

to make a good faith effort to encourage these firms to compete for state contracts."

- *Outreach to MWBEs*: The Executive Order further notes that the Purchasing Department must engage in outreach to MWBEs regarding how to contract with the state.
- *Data*: The Executive Order further notes that "[d]ata on women and minority businesses will be integrated into the state's vendor list and into the list of awarded contracts."

Contracting opportunities where the VTrans DBE program applies have several requirements that intersect directly with procurement, contracting, and business inclusion.

- *Fostering Small Business Participation*: Pursuant to 49 C.F.R. § 26.39, VTrans has engaged in efforts to foster small business participation.[23] Such efforts include but are not limited to the following: unbundling projects, providing technical assistance to help build capacity, and providing business development information.[24]
- *Goals*: Contract opportunities may not use quotas or set-asides for DBEs.[25] The only exception for using a set-aside is in a limited or extreme circumstance, "when no other method could be reasonably expected to redress egregious instances of discrimination."[26] Instead, an overall goal must be set.[27] The goal must be based on evidence of available "ready, willing and able" DBEs in the market.[28] Once the assessment of "ready, willing and able" DBEs is completed, an overall goal may be established as a percentage of the total amount of contracts receiving U.S. Department of Transportation (U.S. DOT) funds.[29] Participation goals must be set for all certified DBEs and not divided into subcategories.[30] Race- and gender-neutral means must be used to "meet the maximum feasible portion of your overall goal."[31] VTrans, as a recipient of U.S. DOT funds, will not be penalized for failing to meet the overall goal set, if it can establish good faith efforts to meet the goal.[32] When

23. *Disadvantaged Business Enterprise Program*, *supra* note 20.
24. *Id.* at 53.
25. 49 C.F.R. § 26.43 (2022).
26. *Id.*
27. *Id.* § 26.45(a)(1).
28. *Id.* § 26.45(b).
29. *Id.* § 26.45(e).
30. *Id.* § 26.45(h).
31. *Id.* § 26.51.
32. *Id.* § 26.47.

there is a DBE goal on a specific contract opportunity, only the bidder meeting the goal, or establishing good faith efforts to meet the goal, may be awarded the contract.[33]

- *Prompt Payment*: Under 49 C.F.R. part 26, contractors must pay subcontractors within 30 days of receipt of payment from the state DOT for satisfactory performance.[34]
- *Payment of Retainage*: Contractors must pay amounts withheld for retainage to subcontractors within 30 days of their work being satisfactorily completed.[35]

Additional Related Laws, Policies, and Programs

- *Technical Assistance*: The Vermont Business Development Program managed by VTrans helps certified DBEs develop business plans and participate on VTrans federally funded projects. For more information, please visit https://vtrans.vermont.gov/civil-rights/doing-business/dbe-center/supportive-services.
- *Payment to Subcontractors*: On construction contracts, "[n]otwithstanding any contrary agreement, when a subcontractor has performed in accordance with the provisions of its contract, a contractor shall pay to the subcontractor, and each subcontractor shall in turn pay to its subcontractors, the full or proportional amount received for each such subcontractor's work and materials based on work completed or service provided under the subcontract, seven days after receipt of each progress or final payment or seven days after receipt of the subcontractor's invoice, whichever is later."[36]
- *Finding Contract Opportunities*: Information about contracting opportunities may be found on BGS's "Bid Information" page: https://bgs.vermont.gov/purchasing/bids.

Major City Snapshot: Burlington

The City of Burlington offers an online registry where minority-owned and women-owned businesses may complete an application

33. *Id.* § 26.53.
34. 49 C.F.R. § 26.29(a) (2023).
35. *Id.* § 26.29(b).
36. Vt. Stat. Ann. tit. 9, § 4003 (2022).

so they may be included in the registry.[37] While completing this self-certification, a business may also complete the application to be certified as a Section 3 business.[38] Under the city ordinance, no contracting goals are noted.

---

37. *Registry, Resources, and Previous Studies*, City of Burlington, https://www.burlingtonvt.gov/CEDO/MWBE-and-Section-3-Registry (last visited Apr. 21, 2023).

38. *Id.*

CHAPTER 47

Virginia

Overview of Business Inclusion Program, Policies, and Practices

Government entities seeking to create business inclusion programs have two primary options in terms of the type of program they may create, in terms of who is eligible for the program: (1) a race- and gender-conscious program or (2) a race- and gender-neutral program. Under the Equal Protection Clause of the Fourteenth Amendment, strict scrutiny is applied by the courts when a government actor is creating policies based on race. Strict scrutiny is the highest level of judicial review that may be applied. It requires the government actor to demonstrate that (1) past discrimination exists such that the entity has a "compelling government interest" in rectifying it, and (2) the policies and programs created to do so are "narrowly tailored."[1] Although intermediate scrutiny is often applied when reviewing programs based on gender, strict scrutiny is applied when reviewing race- and gender-conscious business inclusion programs.[2] Disparity studies have become a standard tool used to assist a government entity in withstanding a challenge to its race- and gender-conscious business inclusion programs. These studies aid in demonstrating whether a government entity has engaged

1. City of Richmond v. J.A. Croson Co., 488 U.S. 469 (1989).

2. Since the 1980s with the Supreme Court decision in *City of Richmond v. J.A. Croson Company*, there have been a number of cases across the county that have assessed race- and gender-conscious business inclusion programs. *See* Adarand Constructors, Inc. v. Pena, 515 U.S. 200 (1995); Virdi v. DeKalb Cnty. Sch. Dist., 135 Fed. App'x 262, 268 (11th Cir. 2005); Sherbrooke Turf, Inc. v. Minn. Dep't of Transp., 345 F.3d 964, 971 (8th Cir. 2003); Mountain West Holding Co., Inc. v. The State of Montana, Montana DOT, et al., 2017 WL 2179120 (9th Cir. May 16, 2017).

in past discrimination in its contracting practices, such that the entity may have a compelling government interest in rectifying it.[3]

Conversely, race- and gender-neutral programs are programs that are not only accessible to minority-owned and women-owned businesses but to all businesses, regardless of race or gender. A small business inclusion program would fall into this category. The level of judicial review applied to such a policy to determine its constitutionality is rational basis, which is the lowest threshold for a government to satisfy. For a government entity to satisfy rational basis, the policy or program created must be "related to a legitimate government purpose."[4] Even when a government entity has a race- and gender-conscious program, oftentimes the program may still require the government actor to seek to meet the goals of their program through race- and gender-neutral means where able, so as to be taking the most narrowly tailored means of accomplishing the program goals.

In the state of Virginia, the primary business inclusion certifying body is the Virginia Department of Small Business and Supplier Diversity (SBSD).

Summary of Certification Programs and Requirements

SBSD has the following types of certifications available specific to the Commonwealth of Virginia: (1) Micro Business, (2) Small Business, (3) Women-Owned Business, and (4) Minority-Owned Business (collectively SWaM).[5] Service-Disabled Veteran-owned Business status is also available as a designation through SBSD (not a certification).[6] Lastly, a business may acquire Disadvantaged Business Enterprises (DBE) and Airport Concession Disadvantaged Business Enterprise (ACDBE) certification through SBSD. The following bullet points provide an overview of the eligibility requirements for each certification or designation.

- *Micro Business*: A business is eligible for a Micro Business certification if the business (1) has been certified as a small business and (2) has no more than 25 employees and $3 million or less in annual revenues averaged over the prior three years.[7]

---

3. *Promoting Opportunity and Equality in America: A Guide to Federal Circuit Authority on Permissible Government Actions to Promote Racial and Gender Equality*, AM. CIV. LIBERTIES UNION & THE OPPORTUNITY AGENDA (Dec. 2010), https://www.aclu.org/sites/default/files/field_document/Promoting_Opportunity_and_Equality_in_America.pdf.

4. 488 U.S. 469 (1989).

5. *Small, Women-owned, and Minority-owned Business (SWaM)*, VA. DEP'T OF SMALL BUS. & SUPPLIER DIVERSITY, https://www.sbsd.virginia.gov/certification-division/swam/ (last visited Feb. 8, 2023).

6. *Id.*

7. 7 VA. ADMIN. CODE § 13-20-40 (2022).

- *Small Business*: To be eligible for a Small Business certification a business must (1) be "independently owned and controlled by one or more individuals. . ." who also control the management and daily operations of the business; (2) have owners who are U.S. citizens or legal resident aliens; (3) have 250 or fewer employees (this includes the small business's affiliates, if any) or have average (over prior three years) annual gross receipts of $10 million or less (this includes the small business's affiliates, if any).[8]
- *Women-Owned Business*: A business must meet the following eligibility requirements to be certified as a women-owned business: (1) 51 percent owned, or 51 percent of the equity ownership interest in the case of a corporation, partnership, or limited liability corporation, by one or more women; (2) the women owning the company are U.S. citizens or legal resident aliens; and (3) the daily business operations are managed by one or more women.[9]
- *Minority-Owned Business*: A business must meet the following eligibility requirements to be certified as a minority-owned business: (1) 51 percent owned, or 51 percent of the equity ownership interest in the case of a corporation, partnership, or limited liability corporation, by one or more minorities (includes African American, Asian American, Hispanic American, and Native American); (2) the minorities owning the company are U.S. citizens or legal resident aliens; and (3) the daily business operations are managed by one or more minorities (or a historically black college or university).[10] In defining who is a minority, the person claiming to be a minority must also be "regarded as such by the community of which this person claims to be a part."[11]
- *Service-Disabled Veteran-Owned Business*: This is not an SBSD certification, but rather a "status" in the vendor database.[12] A business must be "at least 51 percent owned by one or more service disabled veterans or, in the case of a corporation, partnership, or limited liability company or other entity, at least 51 percent of the equity ownership interest in the corporation, partnership, or limited liability company or other entity

8. Va. Code Ann. § 2.2-1604 (2022).
9. *Id.*
10. *Id.*
11. *Id.*
12. *Small, Women-owned, and Minority-Owned*, *supra* note 5.

is owned by one or more individuals who are service disabled veterans and both the management and daily business operations are controlled by one or more individuals who are service disabled veterans."[13] Veterans claiming a service-disabled veteran status must be certified as such by the Virginia Department of Veteran Services.[14]

- *Disadvantaged Business Enterprise (DBE)*: Pursuant to 49 C.F.R. part 26, the Commonwealth of Virginia administers a DBE/ACDBE certification program. As is required under 49 C.F.R. § 26.81, Virginia has a Unified Certification Program (UCP). SBSD and the Metropolitan Washington Airports Authority (MWAA) are the two certifying agencies for the UCP.[15] The Virginia UCP makes all DBE certification decisions and provides a "one-stop shop" to DBE applicants.[16] To qualify as a DBE, a business must (1) be for-profit;[17] (2) be a small business concern—with "small" determined by the Small Business Administration (SBA) small business size standards—and does not exceed $30.40 million in gross annual receipts;[18] (3) be at least 51 percent owned by socially and economically disadvantaged individuals—there is a rebuttable presumption that women, Black Americans, Hispanic Americans, Native Americans, Asian-Pacific Americans, Subcontinent Asian Americans, or other minorities are disadvantaged;[19] (4) be controlled by one or more of the socially and economically disadvantaged owners;[20] (5) have the socially and economically disadvantaged owners be U.S. citizens or lawfully admitted permanent residents;[21] and (6) have the personal net worth for any socially and economically disadvantaged owner not exceed $1.32 million.[22] The DBE program is required on contracting opportunities that have received funding from the Federal Highway

---

13. VA. CODE ANN. § 2.2-4310(F) (2022).
14. *Small, Women-owned, and Minority-Owned*, *supra* note 5.
15. *Disadvantaged Business Enterprise*, VA. DEP'T OF SMALL BUS. & SUPPLIER DIVERSITY, https://www.sbsd.virginia.gov/certification-division/dbe/ (last visited Feb. 8, 2023).
16. 49 C.F.R. § 26.81(b)(2) (2022).
17. *Id.* § 26.5.
18. *Id.* §§ 26.5, 26.65(b). It is worth noting that under 49 C.F.R. § 26.65(b), the DBE size standard may be adjusted annually for inflation such that in subsequent years the size standard may no longer be $30.40 million.
19. *Id.* § 26.67.
20. *Id.* § 26.5.
21. *Id.* § 26.67.
22. *Id.*

Administration (FHWA), Federal Aviation Administration (FAA), or Federal Transit Administration (FTA).[23]

- *Airport Concession Disadvantaged Business Enterprise (ACDBE)*: In addition to being certified as a DBE under 49 C.F.R. part 26, businesses may also be certified as an Airport Concession Disadvantaged Business Enterprise (ACDBE) under 49 C.F.R. part 23. To qualify as an ACDBE, a business must (1) be a concession for-profit small business concern;[24] (2) qualify as small by having its prior three-year average gross receipts not exceed the applicable size standard of $56.42 million;[25] (3) be 51 percent owned by one or more socially and economically disadvantaged individuals;[26] (4) have one or more of the socially and economically disadvantaged individuals with control and managing the daily business operations;[27] and (5) have the personal net worth for any socially and economically disadvantaged owner not exceed $1.32 million.[28]

Procurement Laws Intersecting with Business Inclusion

In the state of Virginia, many laws pertaining to the intersection of procurement and small and diverse businesses may be found in the Virginia Code Annotated title 2.2, chapter 43 (Virginia Public Procurement Act) and title 2.2, chapter 16.1 (Department of Small Business and Supplier Diversity). Following is a summary of some of the relevant laws.

- *Price Preference*: If an enhancement or remedial measure has been authorized by the governor pursuant to section 2.2-4310(C), it may allow for a price preference for businesses certified by SBSD over noncertified businesses.[29] Two considerations that lead to this authorization are if the following exists "(i) a rational basis for small business or employment services organization enhancement or (ii) a persuasive analysis that documents a statistically significant disparity between

23. *Id.* § 26.21(a).
24. *Id.* § 23.3.
25. *Id.* § 23.33(a). The size standards for the following are exceptions to this: bank and financial institutions is $1 billion in assets; car rental companies are $75.23 million average annual gross receipts; pay telephones is 1,500 employees; and automobile dealers is 350 employees.
26. *Id.*
27. *Id.*
28. *Id.* § 23.35.
29. Va. Code Ann. § 2.2-4310(C) (2022).

the availability and utilization of women-owned and minority-owned businesses."[30] In such an instance, when a bid is submitted by a certified business on a designated procurement and the bid does not exceed the low bid by more than 5 percent the certified business will have a price preference.[31]

- *Contract Terms*: For service contracts over $10,000 awarded to SBSD-certified businesses or service-disabled veteran-owned businesses through the price preference noted earlier, the contract must include the following language: "If the contractor intends to subcontract work as part of its performance under this contract, the contractor shall include in the proposal a plan to subcontract to small, women-owned, minority-owned, and service-disabled veteran-owned businesses."[32]
- *Set-Aside Award Priority*: On contract opportunities up to and including $10,000, there is an award priority to first award to an SBSD-certified micro business responsive and responsible in the case of bids or the fully qualified or most suitable in terms of proposal, provided the price is fair and reasonable (within 5 percent of the lowest responsive and responsible noncertified bidder).[33] Second priority on opportunities up to and including $10,000 is to an SBSD certified small business.[34] If neither an SBSD-certified micro business or small business meets the criteria, then the procurement may be cancelled and re-solicited without the set-aside award priority. For contract opportunities over $10,000 and up to and including $100,000, first priority would go to SBSD-certified small businesses (including micro businesses) before opening the procurement opportunity up to all, if no SBSD-certified small businesses meet the criteria.[35]
- *Inclusion Goals*: The Commonwealth of Virginia has a goal that "more than 42 percent of its purchases are made from small businesses."[36] When contracting for goods and services and a state executive agency has established participation goals for

30. *Id.*
31. *Id.*
32. *Id.* § 2.2-4310(D).
33. *Vendor's Manual,* VA. DEP'T OF GEN. SERVS. DIV. OF PURCHASES & SUPPLY 18 (2022), https://dgs.virginia.gov/globalassets/business-units/dps/documents/vendorsmanual/vendorsmanual_2022_final.pdf.
34. *Id.*
35. *Id.*
36. *Agency Procurement and Surplus Property Manual,* VA. DEP'T OF GEN. SERVS. DIV. OF PURCHASES & SUPPLY 45 (2022), https://dgs.virginia.gov/globalassets/business-units/dps/documents/apspm/apspm-2022.pdf; *Vendor's Manual, supra* note 33.

small businesses, the agency must also include a minimum goal of 3 percent for participation by service-disabled veteran-owned businesses.[37]

- *Small Business Subcontracting Plan*: On all procurements in excess of $100,000, it is required as part of the evaluation criteria that a Small Business Subcontracting Plan be submitted to ensure participation at the prime and subcontracting levels for SBSD-certified businesses in an effort to assist in achieving the 42 percent discretionary spending goal for the Commonwealth.[38]
- *Prompt Payment*: Contractors must pay subcontractors within seven days of receiving payment for work performed by the subcontractors.[39]
- *Reporting Requirements*: All public bodies are required to create a program to "facilitate the participation of small businesses, businesses owned by women, minorities, and service disabled veterans, and employment services organizations in procurement transactions."[40] State agencies must submit annual progress reports to SBSD.[41] These reports must include progress on the following: "(i) small, women-owned, and minority-owned business procurement, (ii) service disabled veteran-owned business procurement, and (iii) employment services organization procurement."[42] In addition, "[t]he [SBSD] shall make information on service disabled veteran-owned procurement available to the Department of Veterans Services upon request."[43] Lastly, "[t]he Department of General Services shall make available a dashboard of purchase order reports from the Commonwealth's statewide electronic procurement system known as eVA. The dashboard shall include aggregated data showing (i) current fiscal year purchase orders, (ii) purchase orders from the previous fiscal year, and (iii) other relevant data derived from any enhancement or remedial measure implemented by the Governor pursuant to subsection C of § 2.2-4310."[44]

37. Va. Code Ann. § 2.2-4310.2 (2022).
38. *Vendor's Manual*, *supra* note 33, at 17–18.
39. Va. Code Ann. § 2.2-4354 (2022); *Vendor's Manual*, *supra* note 33, at 63.
40. Va. Code Ann. § 2.2-4310(B) (2022).
41. *Id.*
42. *Id.*
43. *Id.*
44. *Id.* § 2.2-4310.3 (2022).

Contracting opportunities where the DBE program applies have several requirements that intersect directly with procurement, contracting, and business inclusion.

- *Goals*: Contract opportunities may not use quotas or set-asides for DBEs.[45] The only exception for using a set-aside is in a limited or extreme circumstance, "when no other method could be reasonably expected to redress egregious instances of discrimination."[46] Instead, an overall goal must be set.[47] The goal must be based on evidence of available "ready, willing and able" DBEs in the market.[48] Once the assessment of "ready, willing and able" DBEs is completed, an overall goal may be established as a percentage of the total amount of contracts receiving U.S. Department of Transportation (U.S. DOT) funds.[49] Participation goals must be set for all certified DBEs and not divided into subcategories.[50] Race- and gender-neutral means must be used to "meet the maximum feasible portion of your overall goal."[51] Virginia, as a recipient of U.S. DOT funds, will not be penalized for failing to meet the overall goal set, if it can establish good faith efforts to meet the goal.[52] When there is a DBE goal on a specific contract opportunity, only the bidder meeting the goal, or establishing good faith efforts to meet the goal, may be awarded the contract.[53]
- *Prompt Payment*: Under 49 C.F.R. part 26, contractors must pay subcontractors within 30 days of receipt of payment from the state DOT for satisfactory performance.[54]
- *Payment of Retainage*: Contractors must pay amounts withheld for retainage to subcontractors within 30 days of their work being satisfactorily completed.[55]

45. 49 C.F.R. § 26.43 (2022).
46. *Id.*
47. *Id.* § 26.45(a)(1).
48. *Id.* § 26.45(b).
49. *Id.* § 26.45(e).
50. *Id.* § 26.45(h).
51. *Id.* § 26.51.
52. *Id.* § 26.47.
53. *Id.* § 26.53.
54. 49 C.F.R. § 26.29(a) (2023).
55. *Id.* § 26.29(b).

Additional Related Laws, Policies, and Programs

- *Access to Capital*: "The Small Business Investment Grant Fund (SBIG), as directed by the Code of Virginia §2.2-1616, incentivizes Investors to inject capital into Virginia's small businesses by offering them an opportunity to receive a cash return on their investment of up to $50,000. The Virginia Small Business Financing Authority (VSBFA), under the auspices of the Department of Small Business and Supplier Diversity, administers the SBIG program."[56]
- *Finding Contracting Opportunities*: Contracting opportunities may be found on eVA, Virginia's eProcurement Marketplace: https://eva.virginia.gov/.

Major City Snapshot: Alexandria

The City of Alexandria (city) allows for businesses certified through the Commonwealth of Virginia SBSD as a SWaM to register as such on its online portal to do business with the city.[57] Under the city ordinance, the city seeks to facilitate participation of SWaMs in their procurement opportunities in accordance with state statutes pertaining to any enhancements or remedial measures.[58]

---

56. *Id.* § 2.2-1616; *Small Business Investment Grant Fund*, VA. DEP'T OF SMALL BUS. & SUPPLIER DIVERSITY, (2022), https://www.sbsd.virginia.gov/wp-content/uploads/2022/06/SBIG_Info-Sheet_2022-0614-hp-final.pdf; *Virginia Small Business Financing Authority*, VA. DEP'T OF SMALL BUS. & SUPPLIER DIVERSITY, https://www.sbsd.virginia.gov/virginia-small-business-financing-authority/ (last visited Apr. 28, 2023).

57. *Small, Women, and Minority-Owned (SWaM) Businesses*, CITY OF ALEXANDRIA, https://www.alexandriava.gov/finance/small-women-and-minority-owned-swam-businesses (last visited Apr. 28, 2023).

58. ALEXANDRIA, VA. CODE OF ORDINANCES § 3-3-111 (2023).

CHAPTER 48
Washington

Overview of Business Inclusion Program, Policies, and Practices

Government entities seeking to create business inclusion programs have two primary options in terms of the type of program they may create, in terms of who is eligible for the program: (1) a race- and gender-conscious program or (2) a race- and gender-neutral program. Under the Equal Protection Clause of the Fourteenth Amendment, strict scrutiny is applied by the courts when a government actor is creating policies based on race. Strict scrutiny is the highest level of judicial review that may be applied. It requires the government actor to demonstrate that (1) past discrimination exists such that the entity has a "compelling government interest" in rectifying it, and (2) the policies and programs created to do so are "narrowly tailored."[1] Although intermediate scrutiny is often applied when reviewing programs based on gender, strict scrutiny is applied when reviewing race- and gender-conscious business inclusion programs.[2] Disparity studies have become a standard tool used to assist a government entity in withstanding a challenge to its race- and gender-conscious business inclusion programs. These studies aid in demonstrating whether a government entity has engaged

1. City of Richmond v. J.A. Croson Co., 488 U.S. 469 (1989).

2. Since the 1980s with the Supreme Court decision in *City of Richmond v. J.A. Croson Company*, there have been a number of cases across the county that have assessed race- and gender-conscious business inclusion programs. *See* Adarand Constructors, Inc. v. Pena, 515 U.S. 200 (1995); Virdi v. DeKalb Cnty. Sch. Dist., 135 Fed. App'x 262, 268 (11th Cir. 2005); Sherbrooke Turf, Inc. v. Minn. Dep't of Transp., 345 F.3d 964, 971 (8th Cir. 2003); Mountain West Holding Co., Inc. v. The State of Montana, Montana DOT, et al., 2017 WL 2179120 (9th Cir. May 16, 2017)

in past discrimination in its contracting practices, such that the entity may have a compelling government interest in rectifying it.[3]

Conversely, race- and gender-neutral programs are programs that are not only accessible to minority-owned and women-owned businesses but to all businesses, regardless of race or gender. A small business inclusion program would fall into this category. The level of judicial review applied to such a policy to determine its constitutionality is rational basis, which is the lowest threshold for a government to satisfy. For a government entity to satisfy rational basis, the policy or program created must be "related to a legitimate government purpose."[4] Even when a government entity has a race- and gender-conscious program, oftentimes the program may still require the government actor to seek to meet the goals of their program through race- and gender-neutral means where able, so as to be taking the most narrowly tailored means of accomplishing the program goals.

In the state of Washington, at the state level of government, the following three state agencies certify businesses for business inclusion programs: (1) Washington State Office of Minority and Women's Business Enterprises (OMWBE), (2) the Washington Department of Veterans Affairs, and (3) the Washington Department of Enterprise Services (DES).

Summary of Certification Programs and Requirements

OMWBE certifies businesses for both state and federal business inclusion programs. In terms of the state programs, it certifies the following types of businesses: (1) Minority-Owned Business Enterprises (MBEs), (2) Women-Owned Business Enterprises (WBEs), (3) Minority Women Business Enterprise (MWBEs)—owned by minority women; (4) Combination Business Enterprise (CBEs)—owned by women and minorities; and (5) Socially and Economically Disadvantaged Business Enterprise (SEDBEs)—owned by nonminority men who are found to be socially and economically disadvantaged on a case-by-case basis.[5] "A firm owned by a Native American tribe, native Hawaiian organization, or

---

3. *Promoting Opportunity and Equality in America: A Guide to Federal Circuit Authority on Permissible Government Actions to Promote Racial and Gender Equality*, Am. Civ. Liberties Union & The Opportunity Agenda (Dec. 2010), https://www.aclu.org/sites/default/files/field_document/Promoting_Opportunity_and_Equality_in_America.pdf.

4. 488 U.S. 469 (1989).

5. *State Certification*, Wash. State Off. of Minority & Women's Bus. Enters., https://omwbe.wa.gov/certification/state-certification (last visited Mar. 18, 2023); *Federal Certification*, Wash. State Off. of Minority & Women's Bus. Enters., https://omwbe.wa.gov/certification/federal-certification (last visited Mar. 18, 2023).

Alaska native corporation, rather than by individuals, may be eligible for certification."[6] In terms of federal programs, OMWBE certifies businesses as (1) Disadvantaged Business Enterprises (DBEs), (2) Airport Concession Disadvantaged Business Enterprise (ACDBE), and (3) Small Business Enterprises (SBEs). Although OMWBE manages the certification for the federal programs, the Washington Department of Transportation (WSDOT) administers the programs. Following are the eligibility requirements for each.

- *Minority-Owned Business Enterprises (MBEs) (State)*: A business must (1) be for-profit;[7] (2) registered with the Washington Secretary of State;[8] (3) qualify as a small business concern in terms of meeting the size standard limit "in the current table of North American Industrial Classification System (NAICS) codes or corresponding industry size standards as set forth in 49 C.F.R. Part 26 . . .";[9] (4) be at least 51 percent owned and controlled by a socially and economically disadvantaged individual(s)[10]—the following are presumed to be socially disadvantaged: "[w]omen; persons who are black/African American, Hispanic/Latino, Native American, Asian, Pacific Islander, native Hawaiian, and Alaska native; and other minorities found disadvantaged by the small business association";[11] (5) have eligible owners whose personal net worth does not exceed $1.32 million;[12] (6) one or more of the qualifying owners control and manage day-to-day operations;[13] (7) have qualifying owners who made capital contribution to the business;[14] (8) have "obtained all licenses necessary to lawfully conduct business in the state of Washington";[15] (9) have the eligible owners' ownership ". . . be real, substantial, and continuing, going beyond pro forma ownership of the firm. . .";[16] (10) not be dominant in its field of operations;[17] and (11) be ". . . an independent business [which] . . . is one the viability of which

6. Wash. Admin. Code § 326-20-086 (2023).
7. *Id.* § 326-02-030.
8. *Certification*, Wash. State Off. of Minority & Women's Bus. Enters., https://omwbe.wa.gov/certification (last visited Apr. 23, 2023).
9. Wash. Admin. Code § 326-20-099 (2023).
10. *Id.* § 326-20-050.
11. *Id.* § 326-20-048.
12. *Id.* § 326-20-048.
13. *Id.* § 326-20-080.
14. *Id.* § 326-20-050.
15. *Id.* § 326-20-010.
16. *Id.* § 326-20-050.
17. *Id.* § 326-20-099.

does not depend on its relationship with another business or businesses."[18]

- *Women-Owned Business Enterprises (WBEs) (State)*: The preceding requirements for an MBE are the same for WBEs.
- *Minority Women Business Enterprise (MWBE)(State)*: The preceding requirements for an MBE are the same for MWBEs.
- *Combination Business Enterprise (CBE) (State)*: The preceding requirements for an MBE are the same for CBEs.
- *Socially and Economically Disadvantaged Business Enterprise (SEDBE) (State)*: The preceding requirements for an MBE are the same for SEDBEs.
- *Disadvantaged Business Enterprise (DBE) (Federal)*: To qualify as a DBE, a business must (1) be for-profit;[19] (2) be a small business concern—with "small" determined by the Small Business Administration (SBA) small business size standards—and does not exceed $30.40 million in gross annual receipts;[20] (3) be at least 51 percent owned by socially and economically disadvantaged individuals—there is a rebuttable presumption that women, Black Americans, Hispanic Americans, Native Americans, Asian-Pacific Americans, Subcontinent Asian Americans, or other minorities are disadvantaged;[21] (4) be controlled by one or more of the socially and economically disadvantaged owners;[22] (5) have the socially and economically disadvantaged owners be U.S. citizens or lawfully admitted permanent residents;[23] and (6) have the personal net worth for any socially and economically disadvantaged owner not exceed $1.32 million.[24] The DBE program is required on contracting opportunities that have received funding from the Federal Highway Administration (FHWA), Federal Aviation Administration (FAA), or Federal Transit Administration (FTA).[25]
- *Airport Concession Disadvantaged Business Enterprise (DBE) (Federal)*: In addition to being certified as a DBE under 49 C.F.R. part 26, businesses may also be certified as an Airport Concession Disadvantaged Business Enterprise (ACDBE) under 49 C.F.R.

18. *Id.* § 326-20-081.
19. 49 C.F.R. § 26.5 (2022).
20. *Id.* §§ 26.5, 26.65(b). It is worth noting that under 49 C.F.R. § 26.65(b), the DBE size standard may be adjusted annually for inflation such that in subsequent years the size standard may no longer be $30.40 million.
21. *Id.* § 26.67.
22. *Id.* § 26.5.
23. *Id.* § 26.67.
24. *Id.*
25. *Id.* § 26.21(a).

part 23. To qualify as an ACDBE, a business must (1) be a concession for-profit small business concern;[26] (2) qualify as small by having its prior three-year average gross receipts not exceed the applicable size standard of $56.42 million;[27] (3) be 51 percent owned by one or more socially and economically disadvantaged individuals;[28] (4) have one or more of the socially and economically disadvantaged individuals with control and managing the daily business operations;[29] and (5) have the personal net worth for any socially and economically disadvantaged owner not exceed $1.32 million.[30]

- *Small Business Enterprise (SBE) (Federal)*: The business must (1) be at least 51 percent owned and controlled (including managing day-to-day management) by an economically disadvantaged individual who is a U.S. citizen; (2) have eligible owners whose personal net worth does not exceed $1.32 million; (3) meet the size standard to be considered small under 49 C.F.R. § 26.65; (4) be registered with the Washington Secretary of State; (5) be a Washington business; (6) be for-profit; (7) have eligible owners who made capital contributions; and (8) have proper professional licenses.[31]

The Department of Veteran Affairs certifies veteran-owned businesses.[32] Following are the certification eligibility requirements:

- *Veteran-Owned Business*: (1) Must be at least 51 percent owned and controlled by a veteran, someone receiving disability compensation from the department of veteran affairs, or an active or reserve member of the U.S. armed forces; and (2) the business enterprise is either incorporated in the state of Washington or has its principal place of business there.[33] The business may also be eligible for certification if the business is owned by the following: (1) a married couple or domestic partner where at least one individual meets the criteria just noted; (2) is

26. *Id.* § 23.3.

27. *Id.* § 23.33(a). The size standards for the following are exceptions to this: bank and financial institutions is $1 billion in assets; car rental companies are $75.23 million average annual gross receipts; pay telephones is 1,500 employees; and automobile dealers is 350 employees.

28. *Id.*

29. *Id.*

30. *Id.* § 23.35.

31. *Certification*, *supra* note 8; *Small Business Enterprise Participation Plan*, Wash. Dep't of Transp. 4 (2021), https://wsdot.wa.gov/sites/default/files/2021-10/SBE-Participation-Plan.pdf.

32. *Veteran Owned Businesses*, Wash. State Dep't of Veteran Affs., https://www.dva.wa.gov/veterans-service-members-and-their-families/veteran-owned-businesses (last visited Mar. 18, 2023).

33. Wash. Admin. Code § 484-60-010 (2023).

owned by a nonveteran widower; (3) a franchise owned by a veteran; (4) a nonprofit veteran service organization department; or (5) the business has been certified by the Vets First Verification Program or VetBiz.[34]

DES allows for small businesses to self-certify.

- *Small Business*: A small business is defined as (1) a Washington business; (2) a business that certifies that it is independently owned and operated and has either 50 or fewer employees or annual gross receipts less than $7 million reported on its federal income taxes over the prior three years.[35] A small business may also include businesses certified through OMWBE.[36]

Procurement Laws Intersecting with Business Inclusion

Within chapter 39 of the Washington Revised Code there are laws related to business inclusion that pertain to the award of contracts to veteran-owned businesses as well as minority-owned and women-owned businesses. Additional laws pertaining to business inclusion may be found in chapter 43.19 (laws pertaining to veteran-owned businesses and small businesses), chapter 43.60A (laws pertaining to veteran owned businesses), and chapter 39.19 (laws pertaining to minority-owned and women-owned businesses). In terms of administrative rules, the following are most relevant: title 326 of Washington Administrative Code (rules pertaining to minority-owned and women-owned businesses) and title 484, chapter 60 (rules pertaining to veteran owned businesses). Following is a high-level summary of several laws and rules related to business inclusion.

- *Contracts under $150,000*: One way state agencies will achieve supplier diversity goals is by "[a]ward[ing] competitively procured contracts with an initial value less than $150,000 to the highest-ranked responsive and responsible small or veteran-owned business, unless there was no responsive and responsible bid from a small or veteran-owned business."[37]

---

34. *Id.*; Wash. Rev. Code § 43.60A.190 (2023).
35. Wash. Rev. Code § 39.26.010(22) (2023).
36. *Id.*
37. *Enterprise Services Policy No. POL-DES-090-06 Supplier Diversity*, Wash Dep't of Enter. Servs. (2022), https://www.des.wa.gov/sites/default/files/policy-documents/POL-DES-090-06SupplierDiversity.pdf.

- *Direct Buy Purchases*: Direct buy purchases are purchases that do not require a competitive process.[38] The Direct Buy Level 2 is "$40,000 if the purchase is being made from a small business as defined by RCW 39.26.010(22); or from a certified veteran-owned business."[39]
- *Inclusion Goals*: "State agencies are encouraged to award [three percent] of all procurement contracts that are exempt from competitive bidding requirements . . . to veteran-owned businesses certified by the [Department of Veterans Affairs]."[40] Under the Washington Revised Code 39.19.030, OMWBE is responsible for "[e]stablish[ing] annual overall goals for participation by qualified minority and women-owned and controlled businesses for each state agency and educational institution to be administered on a contract by-contract basis or on a class-of-contracts basis." It is worth noting that under the Washington Revised Code section 49.60.400 that "The state shall not discriminate against, or grant preferential treatment to, any individual or group on the basis of race, sex, color, ethnicity, or national origin in the operation of public employment, public education, or public contracting." As a result, solicitations currently may note an agency goal, however it would also include language along the lines of ". . . no minimum level of minority- and women-owned business enterprise (MWBE), Washington Small Business, or Washington State certified Veteran Business participation is required as a condition for receiving an award."[41]
- *Penalties*: If a contractor does not comply with the provisions of chapter 39.19 of the Washington Revised Code, the state may impose penalties.[42]
- *Unbundling Contracts*: One of the strategies to advance business inclusion that is noted under Washington Revised Code section 39.26.090 is for the director of DES to "[d]evelop procurement policies and procedures, such as unbundled contracting and subcontracting, that encourage and facilitate the purchase of goods and services from Washington small businesses,

38. *Enterprise Services Policy No. POL-DES-125-03 Direct Buy Purchases*, Wash Dep't of Enter. Servs. 1 (2020), https://des.wa.gov/sites/default/files/policy-documents/POL-DES-125-03DirectBuy.pdf.
39. *Id.* at 2.
40. Wash. Rev. Code § 43.60A.200 (2023).
41. RFP NO. PPCEP-3152023 (Apr. 24, 2023), https://deptofcommerce.app.box.com/s/ucndlnwggzq6d0ps8rueoaikoxq47m13.
42. *Id.* § 39.19.090.

microbusinesses, and minibusinesses, and minority- and women-owned businesses."

- *Waiver of Performance Bond*: "State agencies shall not require a performance bond for any public works project that does not exceed twenty-five thousand dollars awarded to a prequalified and certified minority or woman-owned business that has been prequalified as provided under subsection (2) of this section."[43]
- *Prompt Payment to Subcontractors*: "When payment is received by a contractor or subcontractor for work performed on a public work, the contractor or subcontractor shall pay to any subcontractor not later than ten days after the receipt of the payment, amounts allowed the contractor on account of the work performed by the subcontractor, to the extent of each subcontractor's interest therein."[44]
- *Reporting Requirements*: OMWBE must submit an annual report to the governor and the legislature regarding progress in implementing chapter 39.19 of the Washington Revised Code.[45] State agencies and educational institutions must also report data on the participation of MBEs and WBEs on their contracts.[46]

Contracting opportunities where the DBE program applies have several requirements that intersect directly with procurement, contracting, and business inclusion.

- *Fostering Small Business Participation*: Pursuant to 49 C.F.R. § 26.39, WSDOT has engaged in efforts to foster small business participation.[47] Some of its efforts to foster small business participation include "Unbundling Contracts Analysis; Small Business Set-Asides; Developmental Goals—Consulting; Small Business Goals; Small Business Certification; and Alternative Acquisition Strategies Evaluation."[48]
- *Goals*: Contract opportunities may not use quotas or set-asides for DBEs.[49] The only exception for using a set-aside is in a limited or extreme circumstance, "when no other method could be reasonably expected to redress egregious instances

43. Wash. Rev. Code § 39.19.170 (2023).
44. *Id.* § 39.04.250.
45. *Id.* § 39.19.030.
46. *Id.* § 39.19.250.
47. *Disadvantaged Business Enterprise Program Participation Plan*, Wash. Dep't of Transp. 43 (2021), https://wsdot.wa.gov/sites/default/files/2022-05/DBE-Participation-Plan.pdf.
48. *Small Business Enterprise Participation Plan*, Wash. Dep't of Transp. 1 (2021), https://wsdot.wa.gov/sites/default/files/2021-10/SBE-Participation-Plan.pdf.
49. 49 C.F.R. § 26.43 (2022).

of discrimination."[50] Instead, an overall goal must be set.[51] The goal must be based on evidence of available "ready, willing and able" DBEs in the market.[52] Once the assessment of "ready, willing and able" DBEs is completed, an overall goal may be established as a percentage of the total amount of contracts receiving U.S. Department of Transportation (U.S. DOT) funds.[53] Participation goals must be set for all certified DBEs and not divided into subcategories.[54] Race- and gender-neutral means must be used to "meet the maximum feasible portion of your overall goal."[55] WSDOT, as a recipient of U.S. DOT funds, will not be penalized for failing to meet the overall goal set, if it can establish good faith efforts to meet the goal.[56] When there is a DBE goal on a specific contract opportunity only the bidder meeting the goal, or establishing good faith efforts to meet the goal, may be awarded the contract.[57]

- *Prompt Payment*: Under 49 C.F.R. part 26, contractors must pay subcontractors within 30 days of receipt of payment from the state DOT for satisfactory performance.[58]
- *Payment of Retainage*: Contractors must pay amounts withheld for retainage to subcontractors within 30 days of their work being satisfactorily completed.[59]

Additional Related Laws, Policies, and Programs

- *Access to Capital*: Through the 1993 Minority and Women Owned Business Assistance Act the "Linked Deposit Program" was created.[60] A few program highlights include (1) businesses eligible for the program must be certified; (2) the total principal amount of a single loan must be not exceed $1 million; (3) there is a $5 million lifetime limit per individual in terms of

50. *Id.*
51. *Id.* § 26.45(a)(1).
52. *Id.* § 26.45(b).
53. *Id.* § 26.45(e).
54. *Id.* § 26.45(h).
55. *Id.* § 26.51.
56. *Id.* § 26.47.
57. *Id.* § 26.53.
58. 49 C.F.R. § 26.29(a) (2023).
59. *Id.* § 26.29(b).
60. *Linked Deposit Loan Program*, Wash. State Off. of Minority & Women's Bus. Enters., https://omwbe.wa.gov/small-business-assistance/linked-deposit-loan-program (last visited Mar. 18, 2023).

the loans; and (4) businesses may be eligible for an interest rate reduction up to 2 percent.[61]

- *Technical Assistance*: Under Washington Revised Code section 43.19.725 (Department of Enterprise Services), ". . . the director, under the powers granted under this chapter, and the department, the department of transportation, and institutions of higher education as defined in RCW 28B.10.016 . . ." must provide technical assistance to small businesses related to navigating state bidding.
- *Finding Contracting Opportunities*: On DES's "Bid Opportunities" page, information and links are available for finding contracting opportunities: https://des.wa.gov/sell/bid-opportunities.

Major City Snapshot: Seattle

The City of Seattle (city) supports MWBE utilization.[62] In addition, as a recipient of federal FTA funds, it also has a DBE program.[63] Currently, the city is in the midst of a disparity study.[64] Results of the study may impact the current city programs, practices, policies, and ordinances.

- *Certifications*: The city "defines WMBE firms as state-certified or self-identified firms at least 51 percent owned by women and/or minorities."[65] The city notes that a business may be recognized as a WMBE through self-identification on their Online Business Directory or through getting certified through OMWBE.[66] In addition, for the city's DBE program, a business may also pursue certification through OMWBE.[67]
- *Plans and Voluntary Goals*: "Each Contract awarding authority shall adopt a plan, developed in consultation with the Director, to afford Women and Minority Businesses the maximum practicable opportunity to directly and meaningfully participate on City Contracts. The plan shall include specific measures the Contract awarding authority will undertake to increase the

61. *Id.*; WASH. ADMIN. CODE § 326-70 (2023).

62. *Women- and Minority-Owned Businesses*, CITY OF SEATTLE, https://www.seattle.gov/purchasing-and-contracting/social-equity/wmbe (last visited Apr. 23, 2023).

63. *Federal Transit Administration—Disadvantaged Business Enterprise Program*, CITY OF SEATTLE, https://www.seattle.gov/purchasing-and-contracting/social-equity/fta/dbe-program (last visited Apr. 23, 2023).

64. *Women- and Minority-Owned Businesses*, *supra* note 64.

65. *Id.*; SEATTLE, WASH. ORDINANCE § 20.42.020 (2023).

66. *Women- and Minority-Owned Businesses*, *supra* note 64.

67. *Federal Transit Administration—Disadvantaged Business Enterprise Program*, *supra* note 65.

participation of Women and Minority Businesses. Each Contract awarding authority shall make efforts to comply with any goals established in the plan for that Contract awarding authority under these provisions for public works, consultant services and procuring goods or services. The Contract awarding authority may also establish aspirational goals for the participation of Women and Minority Businesses in a particular City Contract on a case-by-case basis."[68]

68. SEATTLE, WASH. ORDINANCE § 20.42.060 (2023).

CHAPTER 49

West Virginia

Overview of Business Inclusion Program, Policies, and Practices

Government entities seeking to create business inclusion programs have two primary options in terms of the type of program they may create, in terms of who is eligible for the program: (1) a race- and gender-conscious program or (2) a race- and gender-neutral program. Under the Equal Protection Clause of the Fourteenth Amendment, strict scrutiny is applied by the courts when a government actor is creating policies based on race. Strict scrutiny is the highest level of judicial review that may be applied. It requires the government actor to demonstrate that (1) past discrimination exists such that the entity has a "compelling government interest" in rectifying it, and (2) the policies and programs created to do so are "narrowly tailored."[1] Although intermediate scrutiny is often applied when reviewing programs based on gender, strict scrutiny is applied when reviewing race- and gender-conscious business inclusion programs.[2] Disparity studies have become a standard tool used to assist a government entity in withstanding a challenge to its race- and gender-conscious business inclusion programs. These studies aid in demonstrating whether a government entity has engaged

1. City of Richmond v. J.A. Croson Co., 488 U.S. 469 (1989).

2. Since the 1980s with the Supreme Court decision in *City of Richmond v. J.A. Croson Company*, there have been a number of cases across the county that have assessed race- and gender-conscious business inclusion programs. *See* Adarand Constructors, Inc. v. Pena, 515 U.S. 200 (1995); Virdi v. DeKalb Cnty. Sch. Dist., 135 Fed. App'x 262, 268 (11th Cir. 2005); Sherbrooke Turf, Inc. v. Minn. Dep't of Transp., 345 F.3d 964, 971 (8th Cir. 2003); Mountain West Holding Co., Inc. v. The State of Montana, Montana DOT, et al., 2017 WL 2179120 (9th Cir. May 16, 2017).

in past discrimination in its contracting practices, such that the entity may have a compelling government interest in rectifying it.[3]

Conversely, race- and gender-neutral programs are programs that are not only accessible to minority-owned and women-owned businesses but to all businesses, regardless of race or gender. A small business inclusion program would fall into this category. The level of judicial review applied to such a policy to determine its constitutionality is rational basis, which is the lowest threshold for a government to satisfy. For a government entity to satisfy rational basis, the policy or program created must be "related to a legitimate government purpose."[4] Even when a government entity has a race- and gender-conscious program, oftentimes the program may still require the government actor to seek to meet the goals of their program through race- and gender-neutral means where able, so as to be taking the most narrowly tailored means of accomplishing the program goals.

In the state of West Virginia, at the state level of government, there are two state agencies that certify businesses for business inclusion programs: (1) the West Virginia Department of Administration Purchasing Division and (2) the West Virginia Department of Transportation (WVDOT).

Summary of Certification Programs and Requirements

The Department of Administration Purchasing Division manages the Small, Women-, and Minority-Owned Businesses (SWaM) Certification Program.[5] Certifications last for two years prior to expiring, unless renewed.[6] The eligibility requirements for each follow:

- *Small Business*: A business must (1) be independently owned and operated;[7] (2) have owners where one or more are "citizens of the United States or a noncitizen who is in full compliance with United States immigration law";[8] (3) have 250 or fewer employees or annual gross receipts averaged over the

3. *Promoting Opportunity and Equality in America: A Guide to Federal Circuit Authority on Permissible Government Actions to Promote Racial and Gender Equality*, Am. Civ. Liberties Union & The Opportunity Agenda (Dec. 2010), https://www.aclu.org/sites/default/files/field_document/Promoting_Opportunity_and_Equality_in_America.pdf.

4. 488 U.S. 469 (1989).

5. *Purchasing Division Procedures Handbook*, Dep't of Admin. Purchasing Div. 55 (2022), http://www.state.wv.us/admin/purchase/handbook/.

6. W. Va. Code R. § 148-22-8.1 (2022).

7. W. Va. Code § 5A-3-59(a)(3) (2022).

8. *Id.*

prior three years of $10 million or less;[9] (4) "certify that is not intertwined with a noncertified business";[10] and (5) "obtain all licenses, certifications, and authorizations necessary to lawfully conduct business in the State of West Virginia."[11]

- *Women-Owned Business (WBE)*: A business must (1) be at least 51 percent owned—for corporations, partnerships, or limited liability companies at least a 51 percent equity ownership interest—by one or more women;[12] (2) have owners who are "citizens of the United States or a noncitizen who is in full compliance with United States immigration law";[13] (3) have the management and daily operations controlled by one or more women;[14] (4) "certify that is not intertwined with a noncertified business";[15] and (5) "obtain all licenses, certifications, and authorizations necessary to lawfully conduct business in the State of West Virginia."[16]
- *Minority Business Enterprise (MBE)*: A business must (1) be at least 51 percent owned—for corporations, partnerships, or limited liability companies at least a 51 percent equity ownership interest—by one or more minority individuals (minorities include African Americans, Asian Americans, Hispanic Americans, and Native Americans);[17] (2) have owners who are "citizens of the United States or a noncitizen who is in full compliance with United States immigration law";[18] (3) have the management and daily operations controlled by one or more minorities;[19] (4) "certify that is not intertwined with a noncertified business";[20] and (5) "obtain all licenses, certifications, and authorizations necessary to lawfully conduct business in the State of West Virginia."[21]

WVDOT administers the Disadvantaged Business Enterprise (DBE) program and the Airport Concession Disadvantaged Business Enterprise (ACDBE) program.

---

9. *Id.*
10. W. Va. Code R. § 148-22-5.2 (2022).
11. *Id.* § 148-22-6.
12. W. Va. Code § 5A-3-59(a)(5) (2022).
13. *Id.*
14. *Id.*
15. W. Va. Code R. § 148-22-5.2 (2022).
16. *Id.* § 148-22-6.
17. W. Va. Code § 5A-3-59(a)(2) (2022).
18. *Id.* § 5A-3-59(a)(1).
19. *Id.* § 5A-3-59(a)(2).
20. W. Va. Code R. § 148-22-5.2 (2022).
21. *Id.* § 148-22-6.

- *Disadvantaged Business Enterprise (DBE) Program*: Pursuant to 49 C.F.R. part 26, WVDOT administers the state's DBE certification program. As is required under 49 C.F.R. § 26.81, West Virginia has a Unified Certification Program (UCP). The UCP makes all DBE certification decisions and provides a "one-stop shop" to DBE applicants.[22] To qualify as a DBE, a business must (1) be for-profit;[23] (2) be a small business concern—with "small" determined by the Small Business Administration (SBA) small business size standards—and does not exceed $30.40 million in gross annual receipts;[24] (3) be at least 51 percent owned by socially and economically disadvantaged individuals—there is a rebuttable presumption that women, Black Americans, Hispanic Americans, Native Americans, Asian-Pacific Americans, Subcontinent Asian Americans, or other minorities are disadvantaged;[25] (4) be controlled by one or more of the socially and economically disadvantaged owners;[26] (5) have the socially and economically disadvantaged owners be U.S. citizens or lawfully admitted permanent residents;[27] and (6) have the personal net worth for any socially and economically disadvantaged owner not exceed $1.32 million.[28] The DBE program is required on contracting opportunities that have received funding from the Federal Highway Administration (FHWA), Federal Aviation Administration (FAA), or Federal Transit Administration (FTA).[29]
- *Airport Concession Disadvantaged Business Enterprise (ACDBE) Program*: In addition to being certified as a DBE under 49 C.F.R. part 26, businesses may also be certified as an Airport Concession Disadvantaged Business Enterprise (ACDBE) under 49 C.F.R. part 23. To qualify as an ACDBE, a business must (1) be a concession for-profit small business concern;[30] (2) qualify as small by having its prior three-year average gross receipts

22. 49 C.F.R. § 26.81(b)(2) (2022).
23. *Id.* § 26.5.
24. *Id.* §§ 26.5, 26.65(b). It is worth noting that under 49 C.F.R. § 26.65(b), the DBE size standard may be adjusted annually for inflation such that in subsequent years the size standard may no longer be $30.40 million.
25. *Id.* § 26.67.
26. *Id.* § 26.5.
27. *Id.* § 26.67.
28. . *Id.*
29. *Id.* § 26.21(a).
30. *Id.* § 23.3.

not exceed the applicable size standard of $56.42 million;[31] (3) be 51 percent owned by one or more socially and economically disadvantaged individuals;[32] (4) have one or more of the socially and economically disadvantaged individuals with control and managing the daily business operations;[33] and (5) have the personal net worth for any socially and economically disadvantaged owner not exceed $1.32 million.[34]

Procurement Laws Intersecting with Business Inclusion

West Virginia purchasing laws and rules relevant to business inclusion may be found in West Virginia Code section 5A-3-59 and the West Virginia Code of State Rules section 148-22. Following are some relevant laws at the intersection of procurement and business inclusion.

- *Contracting Preferences*: "A [nonresident] vendor certified as [SWaM] business, pursuant to W. Va. Code § 5A-3-59, must be provided the same preference made available to any resident vendor when requested. The [SWaM] rules found in W. Va. § 148 C.S.R. 22-9 further explain that a [nonresident SWaM] business will receive the highest preference made available to a resident vendor in the solicitation for which the [SWaM] business has submitted a bid. In order to obtain this preference, however, a [nonresident SWaM] business must identify itself as such in writing with the bid and must be properly certified under the rules governing certification pursuant in W. Va. § 148 C.S.R. 22-1 et seq. The Vendor Preference Request form can be accessed online at www.state.wv.us/admin/purchase/forms.html."[35] Resident vendors who are veterans may also receive 3.5 percent preference.[36]
- *Reporting Requirements*: State agencies must report procurement transactions from the prior fiscal year related to certified SWaMs to the Department of Administration.[37] When

31. *Id.* § 23.33(a). The size standards for the following are exceptions to this: bank and financial institutions is $1 billion in assets; car rental companies are $75.23 million average annual gross receipts; pay telephones is 1,500 employees; and automobile dealers is 350 employees.
32. *Id.*
33. *Id.*
34. *Id.* § 23.35.
35. *Purchasing Division Procedures Handbook*, *supra* note 5, at 49.
36. W. Va. Code § 5A-3-37(c)(2)(E) (2022); *id.* § 5A-3-37(c)(2)(F).
37. W. Va. Code § 5A-3-59(b) (2022); W. Va. Code R. § 148-22-7.2 (2022).

applicable, this reporting is done through the following two reports: (1) a report generated in *wv*OASIS Business Intelligence (WV-FIN-PROC-039) that reports on transactions with non-purchasing card vendors and (2) a report generated in *wv*OASIS Business Intelligence (WV-FIN-AP-061) that reports on purchasing card transactions with SWaM vendors.[38]

Contracting opportunities where the WVDOT DBE program applies have several requirements that intersect directly with procurement, contracting, and business inclusion.

- *Goals*: Contract opportunities may not use quotas or set-asides for DBEs.[39] The only exception for using a set-aside is in a limited or extreme circumstance, "when no other method could be reasonably expected to redress egregious instances of discrimination."[40] Instead, an overall goal must be set.[41] The goal must be based on evidence of available "ready, willing and able" DBEs in the market.[42] Once the assessment of "ready, willing and able" DBEs is completed, an overall goal may be established as a percentage of the total amount of contracts receiving U.S. Department of Transportation (U.S. DOT) funds.[43] Participation goals must be set for all certified DBEs and not divided into subcategories.[44] Race- and gender-neutral means must be used to "meet the maximum feasible portion of your overall goal."[45] WVDOT, as a recipient of U.S. DOT funds, will not be penalized for failing to meet the overall goal set, if it can establish good faith efforts to meet the goal.[46] When there is a DBE goal on a specific contract opportunity, only the bidder meeting the goal, or establishing good faith efforts to meet the goal, may be awarded the contract.[47]
- *Prompt Payment*: Under 49 C.F.R. part 26, contractors must pay subcontractors within 30 days of receipt of payment from the state DOT for satisfactory performance.[48]

38. *Purchasing Division Procedures Handbook*, *supra* note 5, at 56.
39. 49 C.F.R. § 26.43 (2022).
40. *Id.*
41. *Id.* § 26.45(a)(1).
42. *Id.* § 26.45(b).
43. *Id.* § 26.45(e).
44. *Id.* § 26.45(h).
45. *Id.* § 26.51.
46. *Id.* § 26.47.
47. *Id.* § 26.53.
48. 49 C.F.R. § 26.29(a) (2023).

- *Payment of Retainage*: Contractors must pay amounts withheld for retainage to subcontractors within 30 days of their work being satisfactorily completed.[49]

Additional Related Laws, Policies, and Programs

- *Veteran Business Waiver*: The secretary of state manages the Veteran Owned Business Boots to Business Waiver.[50] This program ". . . waives both the initial fee to register [a] business as well as the fee to file . . . annual reports for the first four years through the Secretary of State's office. In 2021, the West Virginia legislature extended the reach of the Boots to Business waiver from service members to also include the spouses of veterans or military members."[51] To qualify for the program, a business must be (1) "at least 51 percent unconditionally owned by one or more veterans, active-duty members of any branch of the United States military or their respective spouses" or (2) "at least 51 percent of the stock is unconditionally owned by one or more veterans, active-duty members of any branch of the United States military or their respective spouses."[52]
- *Finding Contracting Opportunities*: The West Virginia Purchasing Division's "Vendor Resources Center" page has information on bid opportunities: http://www.state.wv.us/admin/purchase/vrc/default.html#VendorOpportunities.

Major City Snapshot: Huntington

Through reviewing the ordinances for the three largest cities in West Virginia—Charleston, Huntington, and Morgantown—Huntington was the only city with reference to assist small and disadvantaged businesses. It's ordinance states that "[a]ssistance to small and disadvantaged businesses shall be by solicitation. The director of purchasing shall maintain a bidders list of small and disadvantaged businesses, and shall solicit those firms on such list for each procurement for which they are qualified."[53]

---

49. *Id.* § 26.29(b).
50. *Veteran Owned Business Waiver*, Sec'y of State, https://sos.wv.gov/business/Pages/VetOwnBusWaiver.aspx (last visited Apr. 27, 2023).
51. *Id.*
52. W. Va. Code § 59-1-2a (2022).
53. Huntington, W. Va. Ordinance § 107.03 (2023).

CHAPTER 50

Wisconsin

Overview of Business Inclusion Program, Policies, and Practices

Government entities seeking to create business inclusion programs have two primary options in terms of the type of program they may create, in terms of who is eligible for the program: (1) a race- and gender-conscious program or (2) a race- and gender-neutral program. Under the Equal Protection Clause of the Fourteenth Amendment, strict scrutiny is applied by the courts when a government actor is creating policies based on race. Strict scrutiny is the highest level of judicial review that may be applied. It requires the government actor to demonstrate that (1) past discrimination exists such that the entity has a "compelling government interest" in rectifying it, and (2) the policies and programs created to do so are "narrowly tailored."[1] Although intermediate scrutiny is often applied when reviewing programs based on gender, strict scrutiny is applied when reviewing race- and gender-conscious business inclusion programs.[2] Disparity studies have become a standard tool used to assist a government entity in withstanding a challenge to its race- and gender-conscious business inclusion programs. These studies aid in demonstrating whether a government entity has engaged

1. City of Richmond v. J.A. Croson Co., 488 U.S. 469 (1989).

2. Since the 1980s with the Supreme Court decision in *City of Richmond v. J.A. Croson Company*, there have been a number of cases across the county that have assessed race- and gender-conscious business inclusion programs. *See* Adarand Constructors, Inc. v. Pena, 515 U.S. 200 (1995); Virdi v. DeKalb Cnty. Sch. Dist., 135 Fed. App'x 262, 268 (11th Cir. 2005); Sherbrooke Turf, Inc. v. Minn. Dep't of Transp., 345 F.3d 964, 971 (8th Cir. 2003); Mountain West Holding Co., Inc. v. The State of Montana, Montana DOT, et al., 2017 WL 2179120 (9th Cir. May 16, 2017).

in past discrimination in its contracting practices, such that the entity may have a compelling government interest in rectifying it.[3]

Conversely, race- and gender-neutral programs are programs that are not only accessible to minority-owned and women-owned businesses but to all businesses, regardless of race or gender. A small business inclusion program would fall into this category. The level of judicial review applied to such a policy to determine its constitutionality is rational basis, which is the lowest threshold for a government to satisfy. For a government entity to satisfy rational basis, the policy or program created must be "related to a legitimate government purpose."[4] Even when a government entity has a race- and gender-conscious program, oftentimes the program may still require the government actor to seek to meet the goals of their program through race- and gender-neutral means where able, so as to be taking the most narrowly tailored means of accomplishing the program goals.

In the state of Wisconsin, at the state level of government, there are three state agencies that certify businesses for business inclusion programs: (1) the Department of Administration WI Supplier Diversity Program (SDP); (2) the Wisconsin Department of Veteran Affairs (WDVA); and (3) the Wisconsin Department of Transportation (WisDOT).

Summary of Certification Programs and Requirements

The SDP certifies businesses as Minority Businesses Enterprises (MBEs), Women Business Enterprises (WBEs), and Disabled Veteran Businesses (DVBs).[5] The eligibility requirements for each follow:

- *Minority Business Enterprise (MBE)*: To satisfy the eligibility criteria to be certified as an MBE, a business must (1) be a for-profit business as a "sole proprietorship, partnership, limited liability company, joint venture or corporation";[6] (2) be at least 51 percent owned, controlled, and managed by one or more minorities (this includes persons who are Black, Hispanic, American Indian, Eskimo, Aleut, Native Hawaiian, Asian-Indian, of Asian-Pacific origin);[7] (3) have eligible owners

3. *Promoting Opportunity and Equality in America: A Guide to Federal Circuit Authority on Permissible Government Actions to Promote Racial and Gender Equality*, Am. Civ. Liberties Union & The Opportunity Agenda (Dec. 2010), https://www.aclu.org/sites/default/files/field_document/Promoting_Opportunity_and_Equality_in_America.pdf.

4. 488 U.S. 469 (1989).

5. *WI Supplier Diversity Program*, Wis. Dep't of Admin., https://supplierdiversity.wi.gov/Pages/Home.aspx (last visited Apr. 24, 2023).

6. Wis. Stat. § 16.287(1)(e) (2023).

7. *Id.*

be U.S. citizens or lawfully admitted permanent residents;[8] (4) have eligible owners' ownership be "real, substantial and continuing";[9] and (5) be performing a useful business function.[10] "Firms formed within one year prior to an application for certification or whose ownership or control has changed within one year prior to an application for certification are not considered eligible for certification."[11]

- *Women Business Enterprise (WBE)*: To satisfy the eligibility criteria to be certified as a WBE, a business must (1) be a for-profit business as a "sole proprietorship, partnership, limited liability company, joint venture or corporation";[12] (2) be at least 51 percent owned, controlled, and managed by one or more women;[13] (3) have eligible owners be U.S. citizens or lawfully admitted permanent residents;[14] (4) have eligible owners' ownership be "real, substantial and continuing";[15] and (5) be performing a useful business function.[16] "Firms formed within one year prior to an application for certification or whose ownership or control has changed within one year prior to an application for certification are not considered eligible for WBE certification."[17]
- *Disabled Veteran Business (DVB)*: To satisfy the eligibility criteria to be certified as a DVB, a business must (1) be a for-profit business as a "sole proprietorship, partnership, limited liability company, joint venture or corporation";[18] (2) have a principal place of business in Wisconsin;[19] (3) be at least 51 percent owned, controlled, and managed by one or more disabled veterans who have a certificate of release or discharge from active duty and a disability rating "under 38 USC 1114 or 1134";[20] (4) have eligible owners be U.S. citizens or lawfully admitted permanent residents;[21] (5) have eligible owners' ownership be

8. *Id.*
9. Wis. Admin. Code Adm. § 84.05 (2021).
10. Wis. Stat. § 16.287(1)(e) (2023).
11. *MBE Eligibility Criteria*, Wis. Dep't of Admin., https://supplierdiversity.wi.gov/Pages/MBE/EligibilityCriteria.aspx (last visited Apr. 24, 2023).
12. Wis. Stat. § 16.285(1) (2023).
13. *Id.*
14. Wis. Admin. Code Adm. § 83.12(53) (2021).
15. *Id.* § 83.24(1)(a)(1).
16. Wis. Stat. § 16.285(1) (2023).
17. *WBE Eligibility Criteria*, *supra* note 11.
18. Wis. Admin. Code Adm. § 82.12(17) (2021).
19. *Id.*
20. Wis. Stat. § 16.283(1) (2023); *id.* § 16.283(3); Wis. Admin. Code Adm. § 82.12(17) (2021).
21. Wis. Admin. Code Adm. § 82.12(17) (2021).

"real, substantial and continuing";[22] and (6) be performing a useful business function.[23] "Firms formed within one year prior to an application for certification or whose ownership or control has changed within one year prior to an application for certification are not considered eligible for DVB certification."[24]

WDVA certifies businesses Veteran Owned Businesses.[25]

- *Veteran Owned Business*: To satisfy the eligibility requirements, a business must be (1) a small business, which means it has less than $1.5 million in gross annual sales in the prior fiscal year and (2) 51 percent owned by one or more veterans.[26]

WisDOT administers the Disadvantaged Business Enterprise (DBE) program and Airport Concession Disadvantaged Business Enterprise (ACDBE) program.

- *Disadvantaged Business Enterprise (DBE) Program*: As is required under 49 C.F.R. § 26.81, Wisconsin has a Unified Certification Program (UCP). The UCP makes all DBE certification decisions and provides a "one-stop shop" to DBE applicants.[27] To qualify as a DBE, a business must (1) be for-profit;[28] (2) be a small business concern—with "small" determined by the Small Business Administration (SBA) small business size standards—and does not exceed $30.40 million in gross annual receipts;[29] (3) be at least 51 percent owned by socially and economically disadvantaged individuals—there is a rebuttable presumption that women, Black Americans, Hispanic Americans, Native Americans, Asian-Pacific Americans, Subcontinent Asian Americans, or other minorities are disadvantaged;[30] (4) be controlled by one or more of the socially and economically disadvantaged owners;[31] (5) have the socially and economically disadvantaged owners be U.S. citizens or lawfully

22. *Id.* § 82.24(1)(a)1.
23. *Id.* § 82.12(17).
24. *DVB Eligibility Criteria*, Wis. Dep't of Admin., https://supplierdiversity.wi.gov/Pages/DVB/EligibilityCriteria.aspx (last visited Apr. 24, 2023).
25. *Veteran Owned Business*, Wis. Dep't of Vet. Affs., https://dva.wi.gov/Pages/benefitsClaims/VeteranOwnedBusiness.aspx (last visited Apr. 24, 2023).
26. Wis. Stat. § 16.75(4)(d) (2023).
27. 49 C.F.R. § 26.81(b)(2) (2022).
28. *Id.* § 26.5.
29. *Id.* §§ 26.5, 26.65(b). It is worth noting that under 49 C.F.R. § 26.65(b), the DBE size standard may be adjusted annually for inflation such that in subsequent years the size standard may no longer be $30.40 million.
30. *Id.* § 26.67.
31. *Id.* § 26.5.

admitted permanent residents;[32] and (6) not have the personal net worth for any socially and economically disadvantaged owner exceed $1.32 million.[33] The DBE program is required on contracting opportunities that have received funding from the Federal Highway Administration (FHWA), Federal Aviation Administration (FAA), or Federal Transit Administration (FTA).[34]

- *Airport Concession Disadvantaged Business Enterprise (ACDBE) Program*: In addition to being certified as a DBE under 49 C.F.R. part 26, businesses may also be certified as an Airport Concession Disadvantaged Business Enterprise (ACDBE) under 49 C.F.R. part 23. To qualify as an ACDBE, a business must (1) be a concession for-profit small business concern;[35] (2) qualify as small by having its prior three-year average gross receipts not exceed the applicable size standard of $56.42 million;[36] (3) be 51 percent owned by one or more socially and economically disadvantaged individuals;[37] (4) have one or more of the socially and economically disadvantaged individuals with control and managing the daily business operations;[38] and (5) have the personal net worth for any socially and economically disadvantaged owner not exceed $1.32 million.[39]

Procurement Laws Intersecting with Business Inclusion

In the state of Wisconsin, relevant procurement laws that intersect with business inclusion may be found in Wisconsin Statutes section 16.75. Following are some laws that pertain to small, minority-owned, women-owned, and service-disabled veteran-owned businesses.

- *Contracting Preferences*: There is a 5 percent bid preference for certified MBEs and DVBs such that if they are within 5 percent

32. *Id.* § 26.67.
33. *Id.*
34. *Id.* § 26.21(a).
35. *Id.* § 23.3.
36. *Id.* § 23.33(a). The size standards for the following are exceptions to this: bank and financial institutions is $1 billion in assets; car rental companies are $75.23 million average annual gross receipts; pay telephones is 1,500 employees; and automobile dealers is 350 employees.
37. *Id.*
38. *Id.*
39. *Id.* § 23.35.

of the lowest bid or most advantageous competitive proposal that the contracting agency may award to the MBE or DVB.[40]

- *Inclusion Goals*: The University of Wisconsin and any state agency with purchasing authority or making a purchase must "attempt to ensure that [five] percent of the total amount expended . . ." on goods and services is paid to MBEs.[41] There is a 1 percent participation goal for spends with DVBs.[42] "Currently there are no diverse spend goals or permissive bid allowances for WBEs."[43]
- *Prompt Payment to Subcontractors*: "[P]rincipal contractors that engage subcontractors to perform part of the work on an order or contract from an agency shall pay subcontractors for satisfactory work in a timely fashion. A payment is timely if it is mailed, delivered or transferred to the subcontractor no later than [seven] days after the principal contractor's receipt of any payment from the agency."[44] "If a subcontractor is not paid in a timely fashion, the principal contractor shall pay interest on the balance due from the [eighth] day after the principal contractor's receipt of any payment from the agency. . . ."[45]
- *Reporting Requirements*: Each year the Department of Administration must "submit a report to the council on small business, veteran-owned business and minority business opportunities which evaluates the performance of small businesses located in this state in submitting bids or proposals to the state and makes recommendations for increased involvement of such businesses in submitting competitive bids and proposals. . . ."[46]

Contracting opportunities where the WisDOT DBE program applies have several requirements that intersect directly with procurement, contracting, and business inclusion.

- *Fostering Small Business Participation*: Pursuant to 49 C.F.R. § 26.39, WisDOT has engaged in efforts to foster small business participation.[47] WisDOT has a small business initiative that, among other things, facilitates competition among small

40. Wis. Stat. § 16.75(3m)(b)(3) (2023).
41. *Id.* § 16.75(3m)(b)(1).
42. *Id.* § 16.75(3m)(b)(2).
43. *WBE Program Description*, Wis. Dep't of Admin., https://supplierdiversity.wi.gov/Pages/WBE/ProgramDescription.aspx (last visited Apr. 24, 2023).
44. Wis. Stat. § 16.528(2m) (2023).
45. *Id.*
46. *Id.* § 16.75(4)(a)(5).
47. *2021 DBE Program Plan*, Wis. Dep't of Transp. 15 (2021), https://wisconsindot.gov/Documents/doing-bus/civil-rights/dbe/2021dbeprgmplan.pdf.

businesses and unbundling contracts.[48] To be eligible for participation, a business must (1) be a small business by meeting the SBA size standard for industries purchased by WisDOT; (2) have owners with a personal net worth that does not exceed $1.32 million; and (3) have owners submit a Statement of Non-Collusion.[49] WisDOT does not handle a robust certification for this program, but instead accepts SBA HUBZone certification or DBE certifications.[50]

- *Goals*: Contract opportunities may not use quotas or set-asides for DBEs.[51] The only exception for using a set-aside is in a limited or extreme circumstance, "when no other method could be reasonably expected to redress egregious instances of discrimination."[52] Instead, an overall goal must be set.[53] The goal must be based on evidence of available "ready, willing and able" DBEs in the market.[54] Once the assessment of "ready, willing and able" DBEs is completed, an overall goal may be established as a percentage of the total amount of contracts receiving U.S. Department of Transportation (U.S. DOT) funds.[55] Participation goals must be set for all certified DBEs and not divided into subcategories.[56] Race- and gender-neutral means must be used to "meet the maximum feasible portion of your overall goal."[57] WisDOT, as a recipient of U.S. DOT funds, will not be penalized for failing to meet the overall goal set, if it can establish good faith efforts to meet the goal.[58] When there is a DBE goal on a specific contract opportunity, only the bidder meeting the goal, or establishing good faith efforts to meet the goal, may be awarded the contract.[59]
- *Prompt Payment*: Under 49 C.F.R. part 26, contractors must pay subcontractors within 30 days of receipt of payment from the state DOT for satisfactory performance.[60]

---

48. *Id.*
49. *Id.* at 16.
50. *Id.*
51. 49 C.F.R. § 26.43 (2022).
52. *Id.*
53. *Id.* § 26.45(a)(1).
54. *Id.* § 26.45(b).
55. *Id.* § 26.45(e).
56. *Id.* § 26.45(h).
57. *Id.* § 26.51.
58. *Id.* § 26.47.
59. *Id.* § 26.53.
60. 49 C.F.R. § 26.29(a) (2023).

- *Payment of Retainage*: Contractors must pay amounts withheld for retainage to subcontractors within 30 days of their work being satisfactorily completed.[61]

Additional Related Laws, Policies, and Programs

- *Technical Assistance*: Through the Wisconsin Procurement Institute (WPI), which serves as Wisconsin's APEX Accelerator, businesses are able to gain access to a myriad of technical assistance options. For more information, please visit https://www.wispro.org/about-wpi-2/.
- *Finding Contracting Opportunities*: The Department of Administration's "Solicitations & Contracts" page includes information and links on searching for contract opportunities: https://doa.wi.gov/Pages/DoingBusiness/BidsProposals.aspx. This includes information on the eSupplier Portal, which allows bidders to search for and respond to solicitations: https://esupplier.wi.gov/psp/esupplier/SUPPLIER/ERP/h/?tab=WI_BIDDER.

Major City Snapshot: Madison

The City of Madison (city) has a Targeted Business Enterprise Program.[62]

- *Certifications*: The city's Targeted Business Enterprise Program allows for Small Business Enterprises (SBEs), Minority Business Enterprises (MBEs), Women Business Enterprises (WBEs), and Disadvantaged Business Enterprises (DBEs) to be certified through their application process.[63] They also accept DBE certifications from other UCP partners.
  - *SBE*: "[A]n independent and bona fide business concern, in good standing with the State of Wisconsin if such registration is required for the business concern, that has averaged no more than four million dollars ($4.0 million) in annual gross receipts over the prior three- (3) year period, and the principal owner(s) of which does not have a personal net

61. *Id.* § 26.29(b).
62. *Targeted Business Enterprise Programs*, CITY OF MADISON, https://www.cityofmadison.com/civil-rights/contract-compliance/targeted-business-enterprise-programs (last visited Apr. 24, 2023).
63. MADISON, WIS. ORDINANCE § 39.02 (2023); *Targeted Business Enterprise Programs*, *supra* note 62.

worth in excess of one million three hundred twenty thousand dollars ($1.32 million)."[64]

- *MBE*: "An independent and valid business concern that is owned and controlled by minority person(s). A minority person or persons must own fifty-one percent (51%) of the business and control the management and daily operations of the business."[65]
- *WBE*: "An independent and valid business concern that is owned and controlled by women. A woman or women must own fifty-one percent (51%) of the business and must control the management and daily operations of the business."[66]
- *DBE*: "A small business concern: (a.) Which is at least fifty-one percent (51%) owned by one or more socially and economically disadvantaged individuals, or, in the case of any publicly owned business, at least fifty-one percent (51%) of the stock of which is owned by one or more socially and economically disadvantaged individuals; and (b.) Whose management and daily business operations are controlled by one or more of the socially and economically disadvantaged individuals who own it."[67]

- *Contract Language*: All city contracts contain the following language to ensure compliance with the ordinance "[t]he contractor shall allow the maximum feasible opportunity to small business enterprises to compete for any subcontracts entered into pursuant to this contract and shall document all good faith efforts. (In federally funded contracts the terms 'DBE, MBE, and WBE' shall be substituted for the term 'small business' in this article.)"[68]
- *Inclusion Goals*: The city has an overall goal to spend 10 percent of its public works funds with certified small business enterprises.[69] "Public Works contracts estimated to cost $100,000 or more that are funded solely with City dollars will have an SBE goal attached."[70] Goals for MBEs, WBEs, and/or DBEs are set on contracts with federal funding.[71]

64. Madison, Wis. Ordinance § 39.02 (2023).
65. *Id.*
66. *Id.*
67. *Id.*
68. *Id.*
69. *Id.*
70. *Targeted Business Enterprise Programs*, *supra* note 62.
71. *Id.*

CHAPTER 51

Wyoming

Overview of Business Inclusion Program, Policies, and Practices

Government entities seeking to create business inclusion programs have two primary options in terms of the type of program they may create, in terms of who is eligible for the program: (1) a race- and gender-conscious program or (2) a race- and gender-neutral program. Under the Equal Protection Clause of the Fourteenth Amendment, strict scrutiny is applied by the courts when a government actor is creating policies based on race. Strict scrutiny is the highest level of judicial review that may be applied. It requires the government actor to demonstrate that (1) past discrimination exists such that the entity has a "compelling government interest" in rectifying it, and (2) the policies and programs created to do so are "narrowly tailored."[1] Although intermediate scrutiny is often applied when reviewing programs based on gender, strict scrutiny is applied when reviewing race- and gender-conscious business inclusion programs.[2] Disparity studies have become a standard tool used to assist a government entity in withstanding a challenge to its race- and gender-conscious business inclusion programs. These studies aid in demonstrating whether a government entity has engaged

1. City of Richmond v. J.A. Croson Co., 488 U.S. 469 (1989).

2. Since the 1980s with the Supreme Court decision in *City of Richmond v. J.A. Croson Company*, there have been a number of cases across the county that have assessed race- and gender-conscious business inclusion programs. *See* Adarand Constructors, Inc. v. Pena, 515 U.S. 200 (1995); Virdi v. DeKalb Cnty. Sch. Dist., 135 Fed. App'x 262, 268 (11th Cir. 2005); Sherbrooke Turf, Inc. v. Minn. Dep't of Transp., 345 F.3d 964, 971 (8th Cir. 2003); Mountain West Holding Co., Inc. v. The State of Montana, Montana DOT, et al., 2017 WL 2179120 (9th Cir. May 16, 2017).

in past discrimination in its contracting practices, such that the entity may have a compelling government interest in rectifying it.[3]

Conversely, race- and gender-neutral programs are programs that are not only accessible to minority-owned and women-owned businesses but to all businesses, regardless of race or gender. A small business inclusion program would fall into this category. The level of judicial review applied to such a policy to determine its constitutionality is rational basis, which is the lowest threshold for a government to satisfy. For a government entity to satisfy rational basis the policy or program created must be "related to a legitimate government purpose."[4] Even when a government entity has a race- and gender-conscious program, oftentimes the program may still require the government actor to seek to meet the goals of their program through race- and gender-neutral means where able, so as to be taking the most narrowly tailored means of accomplishing the program goals.

At the state level in Wyoming, the Wyoming Department of Transportation (WYDOT) Disadvantaged Business Enterprise (DBE) program is the only business inclusion program that consists of a certification program and sets goals for inclusion on applicable contracts.[5]

Summary of Certification Programs and Requirements

WYDOT administers the Disadvantaged Business Enterprise (DBE) program and the Airport Concession Disadvantaged Business Enterprise (ACDBE) program.

- *Disadvantaged Business Enterprise (DBE) Program*: Pursuant to 49 C.F.R. part 26 the WYDOT administers the state's DBE certification program. As is required under 49 C.F.R. § 26.81, Wyoming has a Unified Certification Program (UCP). The UCP makes all DBE certification decisions and provides a "one-stop shop" to DBE applicants.[6] WYDOT is the lead agency of the

3. *Promoting Opportunity and Equality in America: A Guide to Federal Circuit Authority on Permissible Government Actions to Promote Racial and Gender Equality*, Am. Civ. Liberties Union & The Opportunity Agenda (Dec. 2010), https://www.aclu.org/sites/default/files/field_document/Promoting_Opportunity_and_Equality_in_America.pdf.

4. 488 U.S. 469 (1989).

5. *Disadvantaged Business Enterprise*, Wyo. Dep't of Transp., https://www.dot.state.wy.us/home/business_with_wydot/contractors/Disadvantaged_Business_Enterprise.html (last visited Mar. 22, 2023).

6. 49 C.F.R. § 26.81(b)(2) (2022).

UCP.[7] To qualify as a DBE a business must (1) be for-profit;[8] (2) be a small business concern—with "small" determined by the Small Business Administration (SBA) small business size standards—and does not exceed $30.40 million in gross annual receipts;[9] (3) be at least 51 percent owned by socially and economically disadvantaged individuals—there is a rebuttable presumption that women, Black Americans, Hispanic Americans, Native Americans, Asian-Pacific Americans, Subcontinent Asian Americans, or other minorities are disadvantaged;[10] (4) be controlled by one or more of the socially and economically disadvantaged owners;[11] (5) have the socially and economically disadvantaged owners be U.S. citizens or lawfully admitted permanent residents;[12] and (6) have the personal net worth for any socially and economically disadvantaged owner not exceed $1.32 million.[13] The DBE program is required on contracting opportunities that have received funding from the Federal Highway Administration (FHWA), Federal Aviation Administration (FAA), or Federal Transit Administration (FTA).[14]

- *Airport Concession Disadvantaged Business Enterprise (ACDBE) Program*: In addition to being certified as a DBE under 49 C.F.R. part 26, businesses may also be certified as an Airport Concession Disadvantaged Business Enterprise (ACDBE) under 49 C.F.R. part 23. To qualify as an ACDBE, a business must (1) be a concession for-profit small business concern;[15] (2) qualify as small by having its prior three-year average gross receipts not exceed the applicable size standard of $56.42 million;[16] (3) be 51 percent owned by one or more socially and economically disadvantaged individuals;[17] (4) have one or more of the

7. *Disadvantaged Business Enterprise Program Plan*, Wyo. Dep't of Transp. 56, https://www.dot.state.wy.us/files/live/sites/wydot/files/shared/Civil_Rights_Coordinator/DBE/Program%20Plan%20FY19%20Revision%2001-12-21.pdf (last visited Mar. 22, 2023).

8. 49 C.F.R. § 26.5 (2022).

9. *Id.* §§ 26.5, 26.65(b). It is worth noting that under 49 C.F.R. § 26.65(b), the DBE size standard may be adjusted annually for inflation such that in subsequent years the size standard may no longer be $30.40 million.

10. *Id.* § 26.67.

11. *Id.* § 26.5.

12. *Id.* § 26.67.

13. *Id.*

14. *Id.* § 26.21(a).

15. *Id.* § 23.3.

16. *Id.* § 23.33(a). The size standards for the following are exceptions to this: bank and financial institutions is $1 billion in assets; car rental companies are $75.23 million average annual gross receipts; pay telephones is 1,500 employees; and automobile dealers is 350 employees.

17. *Id.*

socially and economically disadvantaged individuals with control and managing the daily business operations;[18] and (5) have the personal net worth for any socially and economically disadvantaged owner not exceed $1.32 million.[19]

Procurement Laws Intersecting with Business Inclusion

Procurement in the state of Wyoming is managed by the Department of Administrative and Information.[20] In Wyoming, at the state level, there are no bidding preferences, laws, or rules specific to business inclusion and minority-owned, women-owned, disability-owned, veteran-owned, and/or LGBT-owned business enterprises outside of what is required by the WYDOT DBE program.

Contracting opportunities where the WYDOT DBE program applies have several requirements that intersect directly with procurement, contracting, and business inclusion.

- *Fostering Small Business Participation*: Pursuant to 49 C.F.R. § 26.39, WYDOT has engaged in efforts to foster small business participation.[21] For example, WYDOT provides numerous contracting opportunities under $1 million and maintains reports showing small business participation.[22]
- *Goals*: Contract opportunities may not use quotas or set-asides for DBEs.[23] The only exception for using a set-aside is in a limited or extreme circumstance, "when no other method could be reasonably expected to redress egregious instances of discrimination."[24] Instead, an overall goal must be set.[25] The goal must be based on evidence of available "ready, willing and able" DBEs in the market.[26] Once the assessment of "ready, willing and able" DBEs is completed, an overall goal may be established as a percentage of the total amount of contracts receiving U.S. Department of Transportation (U.S. DOT)

18. *Id.*
19. *Id.* § 23.35.
20. *Purchasing and Bid Information*, Wyo. Dep't of Admin. & Info., https://ai.wyo.gov/divisions/general-services/purchasing (last visited Mar. 22, 2023).
21. *Disadvantaged Business Enterprise Program Plan*, *supra* note 7, at 22.
22. *Id.*
23. 49 C.F.R. § 26.43 (2022).
24. *Id.*
25. *Id.* § 26.45(a)(1).
26. *Id.* § 26.45(b).

funds.[27] Participation goals must be set for all certified DBEs and not divided into subcategories.[28] Race- and gender-neutral means must be used to "meet the maximum feasible portion of your overall goal."[29] WYDOT, as a recipient of U.S. DOT funds, will not be penalized for failing to meet the overall goal set, if it can establish good faith efforts to meet the goal.[30] When there is a DBE goal on a specific contract opportunity, only the bidder meeting the goal, or establishing good faith efforts to meet the goal, may be awarded the contract.[31]

- *Prompt Payment*: Under 49 C.F.R. part 26, contractors must pay subcontractors within 30 days of receipt of payment from the state DOT for satisfactory performance.[32]
- *Payment of Retainage*: Contractors must pay amounts withheld for retainage to subcontractors within 30 days of their work being satisfactorily completed.[33]

Additional Related Laws, Policies, and Programs

Under Wyoming state statute, there are bidding preferences. None of these bidding preferences pertain to the inclusion of minority-owned, women-owned, disability-owned, veteran-owned, and/or LGBT-owned business enterprises. However, they may benefit a local business that happens to fall into one of these categories.

- *Wyoming Resident Contractor Preference*: Under Wyoming Statutes Annotated section 16-6-102, "[i]f advertisement for bids is required, the contract shall be let to the responsible certified resident making the lowest bid if the certified resident's bid is not more than five percent (5%) higher than that of the lowest responsible nonresident bidder."
- *Finding Contracting Opportunities*: The Wyoming Department Administration and Information "Current Bid Opportunities & Recaps" page has information and links for finding contracting opportunities: https://ai.wyo.gov/divisions/general-services/purchasing/bid-opportunities.

27. *Id.* § 26.45(e).
28. *Id.* § 26.45(h).
29. *Id.* § 26.51.
30. *Id.* § 26.47.
31. *Id.* § 26.53.
32. 49 C.F.R. § 26.29(a) (2023).
33. *Id.* § 26.29(b).

Major City Snapshot

Through review of city ordinances for the two largest cities in Wyoming—Cheyenne and Casper—neither have a formal business inclusion program outside of when federal DOT funds are issued.[34]

34. *See DBE Goal*, City of Cheyenne, https://www.cheyennecity.org/Your-Government/Departments/Public-Works/Transit/DBE-Goal (last visited Mar. 22, 2023); *MPO Governing Documents*, City of Casper, https://www.casperwy.gov/residents/roads_and_parking/metropolitan_planning_organization/governing_documents (last visited Mar. 22, 2023).